DECISIONS BY THE NUMBERS

An Introduction to
Quantitative Techniques for
Public Policy Analysis and
Management

Dipak K. Gupta

School of Public Administration and Urban Studies
San Diego State University

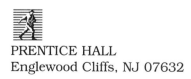
PRENTICE HALL
Englewood Cliffs, NJ 07632

Library of Congress Cataloging-in-Publication Data

Gupta, Dipak K.
    Decisions by the numbers : an introduction to quantitative
techniques for public policy analysis / Dipak K. Gupta.
        p.   cm.
    Includes index.
        ISBN 0-13-474438-1
    1. Policy sciences—Statistical methods. 2. Policy sciences—
Mathematical models.   I. Title.
H97.G87   1994
320'.6'01151—dc20   93-3898
                                                          CIP

Acquisitions Editor: Julie Berrisford
Production Editor: Fred Dahl
Copy Editor: Fred Dahl
Designer: Fred Dahl
Prepress Buyer: Kelly Behr
Manufacturing Buyer: Mary Ann Gloriande

© 1994 by Prentice-Hall, Inc.
A Simon & Schuster Company
Englewood Cliffs, New Jersey 07632

Printed in the United States of America

10   9   8   7   6   5   4   3   2   1

ISBN 0-13-474438-1 {IBM 3-1/2}
ISBN 0-13-492240-9 {IBM 5-1/4}
ISBN 0-13-475641-X {MAC 3-1/2}
ISBN 0-13-492265-4 {NO DISK}

PRENTICE-HALL INTERNATIONAL (UK) LIMITED, *London*
PRENTICE-HALL OF AUSTRALIA PTY. LIMITED, *Sydney*
PRENTICE-HALL CANADA INC., *Toronto*
PRENTICE-HALL HISPANOAMERICANA, S.A. *Mexico*
PRENTICE-HALL OF INDIA PRIVATE LIMITED, *New Delhi*
PRENTICE-HALL OF JAPAN, INC., *Tokyo*
PRENTICE-HALL OF SOUTHEAST ASIA PTE. LTD., *Singapore*
EDITORA PRENTICE-HALL DO BRASIL, LTDA., *Rio de Janeiro*

To
Munia

Contents

Preface, xiii

Chapter 1
QUESTIONS, QUESTIONS! 1

A Framework for Objective Analysis, 2
Problem Solving in Context, 7
The Plan of This Book, 9
A Few Words about the Computers, 10
    Personal Computers, 13
Computers in Public Organizations, 14
Computer Software for This Book, 15

PART I
THE BASIC TOOLBOX, 17

Chapter 2
Descriptive Statistics and Probability Theory, 18

Numbers as Storytellers, 19
The Building Blocks of Quantitative Analysis, 19
Methods of Descriptive Statistics, 20
    Measures of Central Tendency, 20
    Measures of Dispersion, 27
    Skewness and Symmetry of Distribution, 31
    Which Measure of Central Tendency to Use, 34
    A Quick Glance at the Distribution: The Stem-Leaf Method, 35
Introduction to Probability Theory, 36
Objective Probability, 37
    Probability Distribution, 39
    Hypothesis Testing and Confidence Intervals, 43
Subjective Probability, 60
    Sources of Personal Biases, 61

Chapter 3
Source of Data, 71

Where Do We Find the Numbers? 72
What Are We Measuring? 72
    Types of Measurement, 72

How Valid Are the Measuring Scales? 74

The Primary Data: Doing a Survey, 75
The Sources of Systematic Errors in Sampling, 77
Random Sampling Errors, 79

Survey Design, 80
Choosing the Sample Population, 80
Choosing the Size of the Sample, 83
Choosing the Survey Instruments, 86
Choosing the Method of Polling, 90

Quantification of Survey Data, 92
Pretesting Questionnaire, 92

Analysis of Survey Data, 92

Reporting of Survey Results, 94

Survey Design: A Step-by-Step Approach, 94
When the Polls Are Suspect, 95

The Secondary Data, 97
Library Search, 98
Traditional Library Search, 98
When Data Are Not Available, 100

Chapter 4
Making Sense of Numbers, 102

Managing Those Numbing Numbers, 103
Techniques of Statistical Assessment, 103
Tabular Presentation of Data, 104

The Worth of a Picture: The Graphical Methods of Analysis, 105
Use of the Current Dollar Figure, 105
Percentage Change, 108
In the Perspective of a Base: Creating an Index, 109
Choosing the Type of Graph to Use, 110
Graphical Methods in Decision Making, 110

To Tell the Truth and Nothing But the Truth, 111
Interpretation and Deception, 113
Those Not So Innocent Numbers, 119
Structure above a Swamp, 120

PART II

CAN WE FORECAST THE FUTURE? 125

Chapter 5
Projection Techniques: When History Is Inadequate, 126

Projection Versus Causal Prediction, 127
Inadequacy of History, 128

Single-Factor Projection, 128
Problems of Single-Factor Analysis, 131

Judgmental Methods of Projection, 133
The Delphi Technique, 133
The Feasibility Assessment Technique, 138
The Expected Utility Model, 142

Shortcomings of the Judgmental Methods, 144

Chapter 6
Projection Techniques: Analysis of Historical Data, 148

The Problem, 149
Patterns of Trend, 152

Methods of Seasonal and Trend Adjustment, 155
Seasonal Adjustment, 156
Trend Adjustment, 158

Smoothing Out the Fluctuations, 159
Projecting the Immediate Past: Naive Projection, 161
Projecting by the Mean, 161
Moving Average, 162

Markov's Chain, 164
The Problem, 164
Markov's Chain, 164
A Lesson in Matrix Operation, 166
Projection by Markov's Chain, 167
The Absorbing State, 170
Policy Analysis with Markov's Chain, 171
When Is It Appropriate to Use Markov's Chain? 171

Chapter 7
Projection Techniques: The Method of Least Squares, 177

The Problem, 178
Building a Least Squares Model, 178
Straight Line Trend, 182
Projection into the Future, 186

How Good Are the Results? 186
How Much Is Being Explained? 187
What Is a High R^2? 189
How Relevant Are the Estimated Coefficients? 189
The Significance of Individual Coefficients, 191
The Significance of Coefficients Taken Together, 194
Presentation of Estimation Results, 195

What Happens If the Trend Changes? 196
Abrupt Changes in Trend, 196
Abrupt Change in Slope, 200

Best Linear Unbiased Estimator (BLUE), 204

Gradual Changes in Trend: Estimation of Nonlinear Trends, 205

Polynomial Forms, 207
Higher-Order Polynomials, 210
Log Transformed Forms, 212
Inverse Forms, 214
Other Nonlinear Forms, 215
How Do I Choose the Correct Functional Form? 216

Forecasting and Its Problems, 216

Point Forecast, 216
Interval Forecast, 217

Explaining the Present with the Past: Lagged Dependent Variables, 220

Chapter 8
Models of Causal Prediction: Multiple Regression, 225

The Problem, 226

Building a Causal Model, 226

Causality, Co-occurrence, and Acts of Trivial Pursuit, 227

Estimation of the Model, 229

Interpretation of the Estimated Results, 230

How Significant Are the Estimated Results? 230
The Uses of the Estimated Results, 230

How Good Is the Model? 231

What Happens When We Leave Out Important Explanatory Variables? 231
What Happens When We Include Irrelevant Independent Variables? 233
How to Search for the Proper List of Independent Variables, 235

When Regression Results Are Suspect: The Errors of Estimation, 240

When the Independent Variables Are Highly Correlated, 240
Serial Correlation: When the Successive Error Terms Are Correlated, 246
Heteroskedasticity: The Problem of Scaling of Variables, 248
When the Data Are Imperfect, 253

PART III
THE LOGIC OF EFFICIENT MANAGEMENT, 259

Chapter 9
How to Plan a Large Project:
Gantt, PERT, and the Critical Path Method, 260

The Problem, 261

Gantt Chart, 261

PERT Network, 262
  Estimation of Time, 265
  Calculation of Critical Path, 267
  Slack Time and Critical Path, 268
  Can We Finish This Project Before a Certain Time? The Use of Variance, 269
  Things to Avoid in Preparing PERT and Critical Path, 271
Survey of the Homeless Population: An Example, 273
  Crashing Time on the Critical Path, 275
  When to Use PERT, 277
Words of Caution, 278

Chapter 10
Inventory and Cash Management, 282

The Problem, 283
Inventory Management, 283
  The Concept of Average Inventory, 283
  Posing the Problem of Inventory Management, 284
  The Problems of Reordering, 285
  The Safety Stock Model, 287
  The Economic Ordering Quantity Model, 289
  Variable Ordering Costs, 293
  Quantity Discounts, 294
  When Usage and Supply Are Uncertain, 295
  Inventory Classification: The Place of Maximum Saving, 298
  How Useful Is the EOQ Model? 299
Cash Management, 299
  The Elements of Cash Management, 302
  Determining the Optimal Number of Withdrawals, 302
  The Trade-Off between Investments and Withdrawals, 304
  The Miller-Orr Method, 306
  Practical Steps toward Efficient Cash Management, 307

PART IV
HOW TO CHOOSE THE BEST ALTERNATIVE, 311

Chapter 11
Elements of Social Choice, 312

What Is Best for Society? 313
Choosing the Best Alternative, 314
  Problems of Multiple Attributes, 314
  Problems of Inconsistency in Choice, 316

Laying Down the Rules of a Logically Consistent Social Preference, 318
The Problem of More than Two Attributes, 322

Chapter 12
Choosing the Best Alternative: Benefit-Cost Analysis, 325

The Problem, 326
The Theory of Social Benefit-Cost Analysis, 326
  External Effects on Costs and Benefits, 331
Steps toward Conducting a Benefit-Cost Analysis, 333
  Defining the Goals, 334
  Identifying the Alternatives, 334
  Listing the Costs and Benefits of the Alternatives, 335
  Estimating and Valuating Benefits and Costs, 336
  Choosing the Best Alternative, 343
Introduction of Time: Present Value Analysis, 344
  Choice of Time Horizon, 349
  Choice of Discount Rate, 350
The Internal Rate of Return, 352
Some Additional Considerations, 354
  Redistribution of Income, 354
  Uncertainty, 354
  Benefit-Cost Ratio, 354
Cost-Effectiveness Analysis, 355
  The Problem of an Ill-Defined Objective Function, 355

Chapter 13
Linear Programming: Choosing the Optimal Mix of Alternatives, 360

Introduction, 361
Facilities Planning: An Example, 361
Expressing Linear Programming in Algebraic Form, 368
Accommodation of Policy Considerations, 369
When Social Preferences Change, 369
Mathematical Solution for Linear Programming Problems, 371
Logical Inconsistency and an Empty Feasibility Zone, 372
The Consideration of Shadow Price, 372
The Logic of Minimization Problems, 374
Example of Another Application of Linear Programming, 375
  Prison Planning, 375
Sensitivity Analysis, 379
The Limitations of Linear Programming, 379
Integer Programming, 380

PART V
HOW TO DEAL WITH UNCERTAINTY, 387

Chapter 14
The Elements of Strategic Thinking:
Decision Tree and Game Theory, 388
The Problem, 389
Uncertainty and Expected Payoff, 390
The Decision Tree, 390
  To Tell or Not to Tell Your Boss, 391
  Playing the Dominant Strategy, 394
  Two Active Players: The Game Theory, 396
  The Golden Rules of Decision Making under Uncertainty, 398
The Pitfalls of Dominant Strategy: The Prisoner's Dilemma, 399
  Strategies to Overcome the Prisoner's Dilemma, 400

Chapter 15
Queuing Theory and Simulations, 405

Queuing Theory, 406
  The Problem, 406
  The Elements of Rational Queuing Model, 406
  The Diverse Structure of Queues, 407
  A Deterministic Solution, 408
  Queuing Theory in an Uncertain World, 410
  The Use of Theoretical Distributions in a Queuing Model, 414
The Use of Simulations, 416
  System Simulation, 417
  Heuristic Simulation, 418
  Game Simulation, 418
  Monte Carlo Method, 418

Chapter 16
Decisions by the Numbers:
Problems and Solutions, 423

The Princes, The High Priests, and Public Policy, 424
The Methodological Question, 426
  Designing Research, 427
  Choosing the Right Model: How Much Abstraction? 431
  Whose Goals to Maximize? 433
  The Test of Pudding: Suggestions for Framing an Analysis, 440

Decisions Within an Organization: How Objective Is the Analysis? 445
The Individual Biases, 446
The Organization and the Question of Objective Rationality, 446
Avoiding the Psychological Impediments to Objective Analysis, 456
In Analysts Do We Trust? 457
Whose Ball Is It, Anyway? Playing the Political Game, 457
Say It with Numbers, 459
When Time Is of the Essence: Researched Analysis Versus Quick Decision
   Making, 461
Using Quantitative Techniques: Some Parting Suggestions, 463

**Appendix A Areas of the Standard Normal Distribution
(the Z Table), 467**

Appendix B Critical Values of the t Distribution, 468

**Appendix C Critical Values of the F Statistic: 5 Percent Level of
Significance, 470**

**Appendix D Critical Values of the F Statistic: 1 Percent Level of
Significance, 471**

Appendix E The Chi-Square Distribution, 472

Appendix F Mystat Instruction Manuals, 473
Macintosh Version, 473
IBM Version, 503

Subject Index, 531

Author Index, 534

Preface

Books do not dream, but their authors do. I have aspired to accomplish a daunting task—to make some of the most difficult concepts in the fields of statistics and operations research accessible to students with no particular background in mathematics. This book is aimed at the students of the 1990s. Today's students, especially the ones enrolled in professional degree programs, are different from their predecessors. They are older, often working, with less time, and with a motivation which is eminently practical. Yet these students are not satisfied with a mere how-to-do approach; they also want to know *why*. Therefore, the challenge for a textbook is to be practical, informative, readable, and relevant.

The present generation of students is also different from previous generations in its increasing levels of computer literacy. Advances in technology and the consequent decline in prices have made personal computers accessible to ordinary students. With the proliferation of computers, their use in the pedagogic process has become imperative. Since books on quantitative techniques for public sector management do not generally stress the use of computers, I have tried to fill this void by integrating the use of computers in solving analytical problems.

My motivation in writing this book is not to provide an exercise in erudition. Rather, my challenge has been to present the material in a way which the average student in the fields of public administration and public policy analysis can understand. In my years of teaching, I have found students to be excited about the material, but they are often frustrated by their lack of mathematical preparation or their fear of numbers. This book is specifically designed for these students.

This book aims to provide readers with a variety of tools for problem solving which can be used in government, business, or even in private lives. This book does not guarantee that the decisions made on the basis of these techniques will be beyond reproach. Instead, the attempted application of these techniques will provide a systematic approach to problem solving. Most importantly, the analytical exercise will help illuminate zones of ignorance, bias, and presupposition on the part of the individual doing the analysis.

In the field of quantitative decision making, one must use a number of different techniques, ranging from statistics and econometrics on the one hand, to operations research on the other. I have attempted to bring these techniques together. In my quest for brevity, some might find that I have not delved sufficiently deep into theoretical discussion of some of the difficult topics. There is a branch of Indian philosophy which states that any serious proposition, if asked for every conceivable question, ends up in a vacuous nothingness, promoting more confusion than the original proposition had suggested. I am not implying that scholarly discourses necessarily end up in an exercise in futility, but given the practical aim of this book, I hope that readers will find that I have done my best within the practical limitations of time, space, and the level of mathematical sophistication.

Finally, this is a book of quantitative techniques with an "attitude." The chasm between the theorists and the practitioners is nowhere deeper than in the use of objective tools for the prescription of policies in a subjective world. I have not knelt down in the fabled Oxonian (Oxford Univ.) prayer, "O God, save our theories from practice." I have attacked the problem headlong by borrowing some of the recent developments in the social psychology of decision making, which are traditionally omitted in books of similar aspirations. In choosing the techniques for discussion, my criterion has been their actual use in the world of management and analysis. Therefore, based on their usage, I have discussed a wide range of tools, from simple to highly sophisticated. In keeping with this goal, the layout of this book is driven more by the needs of individuals working in the field than the set standards of traditional pedagogy. For instance, since a vast majority of policy decisions are made on the basis of simple decision rules, presented in the most easily accessible manner to legislatures, council meetings, or corporate boardrooms, I have discussed the methods of graphical presentation, simple descriptive statistics, and single-factor projection techniques at length. However, the arsenals of a policy analyst should not be confined to the ranges of these relatively simple tools. I have devoted a good deal of effort to presenting highly complex techniques. Throughout the text, I discuss these techniques in response to the relevant questions frequently raised during actual applications within a public organization.

Since this book contains a mix of simple and sophisticated tools of analysis, it can be adopted in a wide variety of courses. Across the United States, quantitative methods for public policy analysis are taught at various levels. Hence, I had to be inclusive in this book. Those courses which are designed primarily for the undergraduate or first-year graduate students can profitably use chapters 1 through 7 (leaving out the discussion of Markov's Chain in chapter 6). Such courses can also include the discussion of cost-benefit analysis. The broader methodological questions have been presented in the concluding chapter. Students and faculty will find it useful. The remaining chapters are better suited for more advanced students and especially those who are enrolled in courses on public sector management or public policy analysis.

As the saying goes, "The most creative person is the most indebted person." If the degree of intellectual indebtedness is the sole determinant of creativity, I believe that I would qualify as a creative person. Many teachers, friends, colleagues, and students of the present, past, and distant past have contributed to my present effort. Authors are particularly privileged in that they can thank these individuals in writing. During my years as a student, I was fortunate to have many teachers who have inspired me to look beyond the obvious. My debt to my teacher Professor Ashok Rudra, one of the best-known Indian statisticians and a noted humanitarian, runs particularly deep. I am also grateful to Professor Robert Waste and Edward J. Miller for reading the entire manuscript and significantly improving it. I thank Dr. Shona Chatterjee for his help in drawing the many diagrams in this book. I also wish to gratefully acknowledge George Carvalho, Eunice Ferris, Sukehendu Deb, Eve Goldman, Mrinmoy Roy, Joy Maitra, Lou Rea, Hari Singh, Elaine Wansowicz,

Leland Wilkinson, Daniel Wolfe, and especially to Marco Walshok for their intellectual contributions.

Writing a book is not easy. This book is no exception, and it reflects the shared agony of my family. My children, Shalini and Rohan, learned the art of patience; the experience of single motherhood was often foisted upon my wife, Munia. This book is dedicated to her; without her help, encouragement, and love this book would not have been possible.

Quantitative techniques, however complicated and esoteric, are extensions of generally agreed upon logical thinking. If they are explained properly, there is no reason for anyone without much formal training in mathematics beyond high school algebra to feel that these techniques are beyond their comprehension. Therefore, in explaining the mathematical models I have depended more on intuitive explanations and graphical presentation of the concepts at hand rather than algebraic derivations. Further, along with discussing knowledge that is new to the students and the applicators of these techniques, I have taken a great deal of pain to throw light on old ignorances, prejudices, and biases. Drawing from recent work in social and organizational psychology, I have attempted to provide a road map for pitfalls of scientific reasonings, which can seriously undermine an otherwise carefully designed study. My dream will be fulfilled if readers, in their final analysis, feel that this book offers more than it demands.

Chapter 1

Questions, Questions!

During the course of a day, decision makers in public organizations are bombarded with questions: What are the present and future needs of our clientele? Should we invest in that project? Of the three possible projects, which one is the best? When can we expect to finish this project? How many people will be on welfare five years from now? How much, how many, when, which one? As the questions pile up, the decision makers make up their minds on the basis of personal experiences or on pure hunch. Or, if they are really desperate, they may call on their policy analysts or go outside the organization and hire a consultant to provide them with the answers. If these bold individuals want to make some sense out of a jumble of seemingly meaningless numbers, or if they want to make use of a report submitted by a consultant or an in-house analyst, they will need a deep appreciation of the capabilities and limitations of the various tools of statistics and operations research.

The purpose of this book is twofold: First, it intends to offer these bewildered decision makers a helping hand by introducing them to a set of tools that will enable them to judge an analysis intelligently (or, if they so choose, allow them to analyze the problem on their own). Second, this book aims to provide prospective policy analysts with a framework for an objective analysis of public policy based on numerical data. However, remember that despite explanations of relevant theoretical issues, the primary purpose of this book is eminently practical. Further, note that public policy is not made in a vacuum. Even the most objective analysis based on widely accepted data is constrained by questions of political feasibility, as well as social and cultural acceptability; the mere demonstration of maximization of economic objective is not sufficient cause for its adoption as a public policy. The broad framework within which public policies are actually adopted is beyond the scope of this book on policy analysis. Therefore, the emphasis of this book is not to provide an evaluation of public policy formulation; rather it is to establish a framework for how a policy should be analyzed by using various tools developed in the areas of statistics, economics, mathematics, and operations research. Our normative claim relates solely to the process of analysis and does not extend to the actual policies adopted through the political-bureaucratic process of a public organization.

A Framework for Objective Analysis

The strength of modern social science has been its ability to transcend from vague philosophical discourse to more rigorous objective analysis. The *New Webster Dictionary* defines *objectivism* as a "doctrine which postulates that reality exists independent of mind," an outlook that views the world without prejudice, feeling, or subjective judgment. The twentieth-century development of Western social science, in general, and policy analysis, in particular, has been shaped by this notion of "objective professionalism."[1] At the root of this objectivism is the inductive logic of empirical verification of inferences. In contrast, medieval reasoning was to a large extent dependent on deductive logic, where conclusions were reached based on given premises whose validity was considered beyond reproach. Thus, Galileo's discovery of the earth's motion around the sun, despite empirical evidence, could not have been taken as truth, because the accepted church principle held a contrary view based purely on faith. Similarly, when Mundinus Vessalius presented the accurate human anatomical structure, the scientific community, holding the ancient Roman physician Galen's view as infallible, refused to consider the obvious evidence.

The birth of scientific reasoning saw the gradual acceptance of empirical verification. In fact, by today's accepted standards the hallmark of objective, scientific reasoning is based on the premise of empirical verification.[2] However, this notion of empirical verification and objective reasoning runs headlong into the problem of the subjective nature of human cognition. The cognitive scientists tell us that we gain information through observation, which is processed in the brain and filtered through a number of vignettes of culture, upbringing, knowledge, values, tastes, and personal interests. If the perception is subjective, how can we claim objectivity in our analysis? And if we cannot, then are we not destined to flounder around forever without the firm anchor of objective reasoning?

Upon further reflection, however, it may seem reasonable to assume that although our perceptions are slanted by subjective perceptions, there exists at the core a steady thread of commonality of reasoning. This thread of objective reasoning is shaped by our communal existence in a shared scientific society. Based on that very thin but resolute structure of reasoning, we can develop a framework of objective reasoning.[3] In the subsequent chapters of this book we will discuss the various methods of objective analysis in light of subjective reality.

For an objective analysis of a public policy, we can identify five steps:

1. Since, without prejudice and without any pejorative connotation, we acknowledge that "truth" in the realm of social science is relative, an objective analysis must begin with a clear definition of the context of investigation and its goals. In other words, before we begin our analysis, we must make sure *what the fundamental issue at hand is*, and *what we want to accomplish by this analysis*. Let us suppose we are conducting a search for an alternate site for our city's airport.

---

[1] William N. Dunn, *Public Policy Analysis* (Englewood Cliffs, NJ: Prentice-Hall, 1981).

[2] Karl R. Popper, *The Poverty of Historicism* (Boston: Beacon Press, 1960).

[3] Thomas Kuhn, *The Structure of Scientific Reasoning* (Chicago: University of Chicago Press, 1970).

While conducting an analysis, we would first have to establish the nature of the problem at hand. We would find out why the need exists and the extent of it. Thus, in our example, we must identify the size of the city we are looking at, the present adequacy of air traffic and the future needs, as well as the desirable qualities of the alternate site. Also, we would want to establish what this analysis should accomplish. The aim of an analysis may be restricted to pointing out the feasible alternatives or may be broad enough to include a specific recommendation for the best site for the airport.

We may clarify this point further with a personal example, buying a new car. Since there are so many kinds of cars available—new and used—before I start my search for the ideal choice, I must establish my objective: For whom am I buying this car, and what will this car be expected to achieve? If my primary motivation for the purchase is commuting from home to my place of work, my field of choice will be narrowed to exclude those automobiles that I would like to have for either taking my family of four for a vacation, or for projecting a certain image of myself as a successful individual. As you can see, defining my goals for my project makes the subsequent task easier by narrowing the virtually infinite number of possible options.

2. Having defined our objective, we need to *identify the alternate courses of action.* The choice of alternatives should be guided by two factors: *consistency* and *feasibility.* The consistency criterion tells us that the alternatives should be consistent with our goal. Thus, if our goal is to find the site for a new airport to accommodate a specific amount of air traffic, our considering sites that are not sufficiently large will negate the stated purpose. Further, if we include in our consideration sites outside the realm of economic, political, or social feasibility, we will unnecessarily waste valuable time and ultimately weaken our analysis.

Going back to the example of buying a car, if my goal is to acquire a car for family outings, the inclusion of a small two-seater sports car will be inconsistent with the goal. Also, if it is outside my economic feasibility, the inclusion of a Rolls Royce as an alternative will serve no purpose.

3. The third step for an objective public policy analysis is *forecasting the consequences of the chosen alternatives.* Projection of alternatives may be based on relative certainty (e.g., the revenues from landing airplanes in an airport) or be clouded by a good deal of *uncertainty* (the social and economic impact on the community for the relocation of an airport). When there is uncertainty of outcome, we need to consider the appropriate model to deal with the problem. Uncertainty about the future forces an analyst to rely on past experiences with the implementation of similar policies. However, the task of forecasting the consequences of a public policy is especially difficult when very little history is available. Also, often the extreme complexity of the social and political environment makes predictions of consequences of public policy impossible to foretell. For example, during the 1960s, the Indian province of Punjab became a showcase of successful government policy that introduced high-yielding varieties of

wheat and rice to its farmers. What could be less controversial than attempting to increase food production in an overpopulated nation perennially in need of expensive imported food? As it turned out, there were plenty of problems that no planner, short of having clairvoyance, could have foreseen in the implementation of the so-called green revolution. For starters, this improved variety of seeds needed a higher level of irrigation and a willingness on the part of the farmers to experiment with something new. Both of these prerequisites were restricted to the relatively affluent farmers.[4] Therefore, this sudden increase in grain production caused two unintended consequences for the most innocuous of government policies. First, the bumper crop gave the affluent farmers of Punjab surplus money, which they promptly invested to mechanize their production process, causing an increase in rural unemployment. Second, without any farm subsidy program, the increased supply caused a sudden drop in food prices, which delivered a fatal blow to a large number of subsistence farmers, pushing them off their farms into the streets. This apparent "unmixed blessing" soon caused bloody conflicts, turning the green revolution red. Similar examples of unintended consequences of public policy abound in every country. For example, many urban renewal projects in the United States, while "revitalizing" urban centers, have thrown out the least able—the poor and the elderly—often to swell the ranks of the homeless. Similarly, it has been alleged that the social welfare system has created a permanent underclass by taking away their incentive to better their economic lot.[5]

The dilemma of not knowing the full consequences of a policy is beautifully illustrated by a story narrated by philosopher Thomas Nagel:[6]

> One summer more than ten years ago, when I taught at Princeton, a large spider appeared in the urinal of the men's room in 1879 Hall, a building that houses the Philosophy department. When the urinal wasn't in use, he would perch on the metal drain at its base, and when it was, he would try to scramble out of the way, sometimes managing to climb an inch or two up the porcelain wall at a point that wasn't too wet. But sometimes he was caught, tumbled and drenched by the flushing torrent. He didn't seem to like it, and always got out of it if he could. But it was a floor length urinal with a sunken base and a smooth overhanging lip: he was below the floor level and couldn't get out.
>
> Somehow he survived, presumably feeding on tiny insects attracted to the site, and was still there when the Fall term began. The urinal must have been used more than a hundred times a day, and always it was the same desperate scramble to get out of the way. His life seemed miserable and exhausting.
>
> Gradually our encounters began to oppress me. Of course it might be his natural

---

[4] The poor are always less willing to experiment. Their economic position allows them to afford little risk, especially in the area of agriculture, since crop failure in one season will certainly push them to starvation.

[5] Charles Murrey, *Losing Grounds* (New York: Basic Books, 1982).

[6] Thomas Nagel, *The View from Nowhere* (Oxford: Oxford University Press, 1986), pp. 208–9.

habitat, but because he was trapped by the smooth porcelain overhang, there was no way for him to get out even if he wanted to, and no way to tell whether he wanted to. None of the other regulars did anything to alter the situation, but as the months wore on and fall turned to winter I arrived with much uncertainty and hesitation at the decision to liberate him. I reflected that if he didn't like it on the outside, or didn't find enough to eat, he could easily go back. So one day toward the end of the term I took a paper towel and extended it to him. His legs grasped the end of the towel and I lifted him out and deposited him on the tile floor.

He just sat there, not moving a muscle. I nudged him slightly with the towel, but nothing happened. I pushed him an inch or two along the tiles, right next to the urinal, but he still didn't respond. He seem to be paralyzed. I felt uneasy but thought that if he didn't want to stay on the tiles when he came to, a few steps would put him back. Meanwhile he was close to the wall and not in danger of being trodded on. I left, but when I came back two hours later he hadn't moved.

The next day I found him in the same place, his legs shrivelled in that way characteristic of dead spiders. His corpse stayed there for a week, until they finally swept the floor.

4. The fourth step toward an objective analysis is systematically to *valuate all the possible outcomes*. Having recognized the complexity of analysis, an analyst compares the alternatives under consideration with regard to the stated criteria of evaluation. Thus, if a policy goal is defined in terms of maximizing the number of air travelers per dollar, then an analyst would take into account all the possible costs of placing an airport in the alternate sites and place a valuation on each option.

5. Finally, after conducting a thorough analysis and by drawing on all its aspects, we will *choose the most preferred alternative*, in light of the stated goal of the project, based on some *decision criteria*. These decision criteria can take several forms. Where the costs are the same, the decision criterion should be to maximize the total benefits. On the other hand, where costs of the alternatives are the same, we should choose the one that costs the least. Where both costs and benefits vary, we try to maximize the net benefit (the difference between benefits and costs).

In real life, these criteria can take on a more complex character when one includes uncertainty. Facing an uncertainty, decision makers may not go for the alternative that has the highest expected net benefit; their choice of the best alternative can be influenced by their ability or willingness to take risk. Thus, if I am a cautious person (in technical terms, a **risk averter**), I may choose certainty of earnings over the lure of more attractive but uncertain returns. On the other hand, if I am a **risk taker**, I may go for higher returns.

One does not go through this elaborate process each time a problem crops up. However, this does provide the confounded decision maker a frame of reference with which to view an otherwise confusing problem.

However, we should note that in a real-life situation—especially in a democratic, pluralistic society—many of these steps may not provide us with an unambiguous direction. Establishing an objective itself can be confusing; also, there may be a multitude of mutually exclusive goals. Often, important public policies are made without sufficiently defining their goals, which puts us at risk of willy-nilly attempting to shoot a moving target. For example, in 1986 President Reagan deployed a contingent of U.S. marines in Beirut, Lebanon, without specifying what this force was to accomplish by their presence in that troubled land. The lack of specification of a goal led to their confinement within the poorly defended perimeters of a military barrack. Consequently, the U.S. marine contingent proved to be an easy mark for a devastating terrorist attack, which caused widespread death and injury. In contrast, President Reagan's economic policies, based on supply side philosophy, had a much clearer set of goals.

In the area of public policy, we often find goals to be contradictory. In our private discourse, or in political rhetoric, we frequently hear of "national interest," "will of the nation," or "best course for the United States." Economic theorists such as Kenneth Arrow and Amartya K. Sen have pointed out the impossibility of defining one single goal for an entire society.[7] Consider, for instance, the problem of formulating a national energy policy. Facing recurrent threats to our oil supply and our need to embark on risky adventures in the volatile Middle East, we frequently hear the cry for a coherent national energy policy. Yet despite a broad agreement that there should be a national policy to reduce dependence on imported oil, a deeper look into the problem will convince anybody that it is impossible to develop a policy of energy self-sufficiency that will be universally acceptable. This is because within the United States there are groups whose interests are diametrically opposed. For instance, the formulation of a national energy policy must contend with the conflicting goals of the energy producers (who want more production) and the environmentalists (who want to preserve environmental quality), or the consumers (who want lower prices) and the producers (who want higher prices), or the importers of oil (who want cheap foreign oil) and the domestic producers of oil (who want more expensive foreign oil).

Problem Solving in Context

The primary purpose of this book is to offer students who are working in a public organization, or are planning to do so, a collection of extremely useful tools that will aid in their effort at making better public policy analysis. Among the diverse techniques discussed, several underlying tones resonate throughout the book.

---

[7] Kenneth J. Arrow, *Social Choice and Individual Values* (New York: John Wiley and Sons, 1951) and Amartya K. Sen, *Collective Choice and Social Welfare* (San Francisco: Holden-Day, 1970).

In the heady days of the 1960s, when America was flushed with spectacular achievements in space and computer technology, many social problems seemed to have physical solutions. It was widely held that for all of these problems, there exist unique optimum solutions that can be derived by the application of rational analysis. Much of the impetus to use the techniques of operations research (and their subsequent development) can be traced to this sense of can-do optimism. However, the glory of operations research and the so-called rational approach to public policy have been short lived. While dealing with earthly problems the universal law of gravitation could not be averted: What went up, came down. The rigor of mathematical analysis was no match for the complexities of real life. Yet, through this failure, we have gained a better understanding of the strength of these elegant techniques; we now know what they can do for us, but more importantly we know what they cannot. I have attempted to present these techniques with a seed of circumspection, a ubiquitous doubt in the existence of a universal truth when dealing with social issues. One of the reasons for the asymmetry between theory and practice is that as individuals we view the world through a series of vignettes. Recent developments in decision theory have uncovered some of the most significant systematic biases in our cognitive scheme of information processing. Similarly, studies have shown that some of the major problems of psychological barriers to objective analysis are due to organizational mind-set or groupthink. I have attempted to present these techniques in the context of some of these anomalies of rational decision making. Finally, I have attempted to impart some sensitivity to the conflict between economic and political rationality in the area of public policy analysis. In our quest for government efficiency, we are frequently misled by analogies to the private sector. In contrast to the private sector, the primary motivation for public policy does not have singularity of purpose, a well-defined maxim. In fact, the goals of public policies reflect the push and pull of various interest groups, which, often in disdain, we call politics. Therefore, there is always the tendency to hold what one derives through analysis as the truth, which in practice gets polluted by politics. Yet to deny politics a pivotal role in determining policy is to go against the very democratic principles on which the United States and many other countries are founded. Professor Aron Wildavsky, a conservative political scientist, correctly reminded us that to run the government as business (by considering only economic rationality and abandoning political rationality) is "undemocratic and un-American."[8] In sum, this book promotes the idea that as analysts, we should approach our craft with professional pride mixed with a good deal of caution and humility.

[8] Aron Wildavsky, *The Politics of Budgetary Process* (Boston: Little Brown, 1964).

The Plan of This Book

This book is divided into five sections. The first section is concerned with presenting a basic toolbox of analysis. The building blocks of quantitative analysis are the measures of descriptive statistics, the theory of probability, and the gathering and presentation of numerical data. These topics are covered in chapters 2 through 4. As mentioned earlier, the emphasis in the first section and in the rest of this book is the caveat that at the core of even the most sophisticated and objective method of quantitative evaluation are the kernel of subjective judgment and the self-serving objective of the person conducting the investigation. Further, the objectiveness of the study is often compromised by biases in the available data. Therefore, in the fluid world of relative truth and biased perceptions, the integrity of an analysis is preserved by the scrupulous disclosure of all hidden assumptions as well as the sources of possible biases and shortcomings.

The gathering of sample data, the use of descriptive statistics, the testing of hypotheses, and the presentation of data help an organization assess its past and present position. On the basis of its experience, the organization often takes the next step—planning for the future. To plan for the future, we need to forecast. Chapters 5 through 8 are concerned with the task of forecasting. In our effort at predicting the future, we start with the most simple methods of single-factor projection. Then through more sophisticated analysis of time trends, we introduce the reader to regression models, which are used both for projection based on past trends and prediction based on causal analysis. For ease of explanation, we differentiate between the methods of projection and prediction. We call those methods that rely on projecting the trend into the future without attempting to know the causes behind the incidence the methods of *projection*. Single-factor trend analysis, Time Series Analysis, and Markov's chain are classified as projection techniques. In contrast, those analyses that intend to discover the causal relationship between the dependent and a set of independent variables are classified as methods of *prediction*. Under this category we discuss simple and multiple regression models.

The third part of this book focuses on the logic of efficient management. Often a decision maker must plan for an intricate project. The use of PERT (Planning Evaluation Review Technique) network and critical path analysis provides some extremely useful answers to the thorny questions of management of resources and effective control of complex interconnected events, which we discuss in chapter 9. In the pursuit of efficiency, a policy maker needs to manage inventory and look into the problems of cash management. Chapter 10 introduces the techniques used for choosing the most efficient use of space and liquid cash. Although it may appear that the two problems are not similar, they both are concerned with a basic trade-off. In inventory management, the problem is that apart from the cost of storage, if we order now we will have to pay for the goods immediately, and therefore we will forgo the possible returns of money that could have been invested. On the other hand, if we do not order now, we risk running out of goods. Similarly, in cash management the conflicting concerns are that on the one hand, we want to keep all our liquid (and therefore non-interest-bearing) cash invested to earn returns; at the same time if we are unable to meet our immediate cash obligations, we are in trouble.

Part Four, consisting of chapters 11 through 13, deals with the important question of choosing among competing alternatives. The first step toward the best course of action is to define what is the best. The complexity of this issue is presented in chapter 11. Having defined *social goal*, we proceed to chapter 12, which discusses benefit-cost analysis. While the technique of benefit-cost analysis points us to the best alternative, frequently the problem is not to choose the single best alternative, but to find the optimal mix among competing alternatives. The solution to this problem is given by linear and integer programming, discussed in chapter 13.

The outcomes of policies are often uncertain. Therefore, the fifth and final section concentrates on uncertainty. We look at the techniques of the decision tree (chapter 14) and the queuing theory (chapter 15).

The role of quantitative techniques in the formulation of public policy raises some interesting points. The failed experiments with the Planning, Programming, and Budgeting System (PPBS) and other so-called rational or scientific methods of decision making brought public policy making with the aid of quantitative techniques under sharp focus. In the concluding section, we discuss in detail the role of quantitative methods in public policy debate.

A Few Words about the Computers

Looking at the world today, it is almost impossible to imagine a time without computers. Indeed, there is hardly an area of life that is not affected by computer technology. If you start thinking about all the things you do, eat, touch, or ride in your everyday life, how many of them can you identify as not having any direct or indirect impact by the ubiquitous computer? *Revolution* is perhaps the most grossly overused word in the modern English vocabulary; yet when it comes to computers, there is no other word that is more appropriate in describing the change. Every year more people become computer literate. Therefore, in this book I will assume some familiarity with computers and software. Students have the option of purchasing some of the software that comes with this book. But before introducing specific software, let me familiarize readers with basic computer technology and terms.

In the development of computer technology, as in history, the precise turning points are open to question. However, generally speaking, the course of the computer's development can be divided into four segments. Although the spirit of computers dates back at least 5,000 years to the Chinese use of the abacus, the modern computer age began with the development of the **first generation** of computers in the early 1950s. The first installation of a commercial computer took place in 1951 in the U.S. Bureau of the Census. Occupying a large room, this behemoth, made of innumerable vacuum tubes, was called the Universal Automatic Computer, or UNIVAC I, and was built by the Remington-Rand Corporation. With its initial success, other companies joined the commercial computer market, including Burroughs, Honeywell, International Business Machines (IBM), and Radio Corporation of America (RCA). With increased competition and advancement in technology, the costs of computing started to come down dramatically.

The **second generation** of computers started with the invention of the transistor toward the end of the decade. With this development, the cumbersome and expensive vacuum tubes were no longer necessary. Yet the infant technology remained diffused, suffering from lack of standardization across companies and machines.

The **third generation** of computers dawned with the announcement of IBM's 360 series (the name taken from 360°, signifying an all-around application) on April 7, 1964. The revolutionary feature of this series of computers was the introduction of integrated circuits, or densely packed electrical circuitry on a silicon chip. The silicon chip helped bring down the already shrinking cost of computing to an astonishing level. Equally importantly, it reduced the size of the computer itself. The large **mainframe** computers, which were prohibitively expensive, could now be shrunk in size and sold to smaller government organizations and computer firms at a much lower price. As a result, companies such as the Digital Equipment Corporation (DEC) and Data General Corporation started marketing the **minicomputer**. Now a small organization could afford to buy a minicomputer for a fraction of the price of a mainframe. Also, the new technology allowed a large number of users to access the computer from their interactive terminals (which, not having "brains" of their own, were called **dumb terminals**) or from card reading machines (often called the **remote job entry stations**).

With further development in chip manufacturing technology, computers became even faster and increasingly compact. This process of miniaturization of computers saw the birth and eventual proliferation of **personal computers**, beginning in the late 1970s. Personal computers are the replicas of the large mainframes, in the sense that they are not connected to any one large machine and can function on their own. This development of personal computers reduced dependence on the large centralized machines; the shutdown of these machines due to a breakdown, or for routine maintenance, can paralyze the computing capabilities of the entire organization.

After the third generation, many computer companies and writers for

Figure 1.1 The Computer and Its User

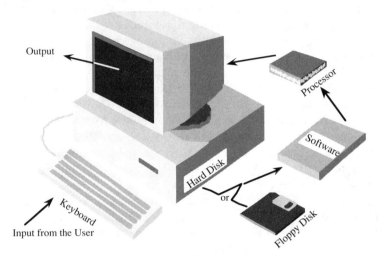

computer magazines have attempted to identify the fourth or fifth generation of machines. However, for the most part such labels have turned out to be gimmicks and not based on any significant departure from existing technology, as we saw in the development of vacuum tubes, transistors, and integrated circuits.

So far we have talked about computers without explaining some of the basic terminology. Figure 1.1 shows the computer and its process as well as the most important aspects of computer use. For instance, when you, the user, ask a computer to perform a certain task, you enter the information on the keyboard. The computer understands the question or the string of instructions through **software**, which is analogous to our verbal language. If we hear something, the information is registered in our brain through language. Language translates the happenings of the outside world so the brain can process the information. Similarly, software translates the instructions of users so the computer can process them. Software is specialized. For example, the word processing software I used to write this manuscript translated the string of letters in a particular form or **format** for the computer to process.

The software and the data inserted into the computer can be stored in a **hard disk** or in a **floppy disk**. Hard disks generally have a much larger storage capacity than floppies. Hard disks can be externally located or can be built inside the computer.

The part of the computer "brain" that processes the information is called a **processor**. The capability of a computer to perform a task depends both on the software and the processor. If the software is not sophisticated enough for your needs, even the most powerful computer will not be able to perform the task you want done. If you are telling a genius to perform a simple task but you are not using a common language, the task will not be performed. On the other hand, if the processor is not fully capable of handling a sophisticated software, you will be in trouble. The result will be the same as asking a child to do something beyond his or her capability. Even the use of a common language will not solve the problem. Frequently, first-time or occasional users of computers become frustrated because they do not realize that to get the desired result, they must have a match between the software and the **hardware** (the physical machine or, in this case, the processor).

The capacity of a computer to process information also depends on its memory or the capacity to store information. The computer can store in several places, but it will be sufficient for the capacity of a computer to process information on the random access memory or **RAM**. Computer memory is measured in terms of the number of **bytes**, which are roughly equal to one single character (such as A, 5, etc.). The memory capacity is expressed in terms of 1,000 bytes or **K** (derived from the Greek word *kilo*, meening a thousand), or **megabytes**, a million bytes. Therefore, if you hear that a particular computer has "2 megabytes of memory," it can process 2 million words. This is an extremely important concept since every software that you will be buying will specify the amount of computer memory it would require. For instance, if you have a MacIntosh, a MYSTAT program would require at least 1 megabyte of RAM, and for DOS machines at least 512K of RAM.

Personal Computers

There are many ways of looking at the world. The present world of personal computers is divided into those who use **DOS-based** computers and those who use **Apple** products. This division reflects the market reality for personal computers. IBM was primarily responsible for developing processors that operate on a system called MS-DOS, or simply DOS (Disk Operating System). IBM personal computers and their "clones" are based on this operating system. On the other hand, Apple developed its own operating system and refused to join the DOS crowd. As a result, the two systems became incompatible, and software meant for one cannot be used in the other.[9]

Although generalizations about computer technology are extremely hazardous due to the fluidity of the market and the rate of technological change, we may point out some of the relative advantages and disadvantages of machines that operate on these two systems exclusively. After developing its processing technology, IBM chose an "open shop" policy, which allowed other manufacturers to develop both hardware and softwares for machines that use the DOS operating system. In contrast, for business reasons, Apple chose to follow a "closed shop"

[9] DOS and Apple-based processors by no means exhaust the spectrum of processors. There have been a number of other processors including the CP/M and UNIX. However, the market selection process has largely pushed them away from the personal computer field.

policy, which restricted the Apple processor exclusively for its own brands of machines. The result of this development has been that the DOS-based machines and their software are more numerous (and therefore often less expensive) than the Apples. Also, IBM, because of its long-standing line of mainframes, has been able to adopt its machines for greater computational flexibility. Despite these positive aspects of DOS-based machines, the Apple-based processors are often judged as simpler to use (**user-friendly**) and carry a superior graphics capability.

Therefore, if you are a DOS user, you should be happy to know that you will be able to find a lot more software for your machines. At the same time, you may find that the operating instructions are more complicated and your capability to draw graphs, charts, and pictures is somewhat restricted. You should note, however, that these are not categorical statements, since anything that can be said about computers will become obsolete even before the ink is dry. Recent advancements in the **windows** technology allow the best features of Apple computers to be used in DOS-based machines. Therefore, to be safe, if you are not already familiar with computers, you should try out the various systems and find out for yourself which one you like the best.

Computers in Public Organizations

Computer literacy has skyrocketed. It is increasingly impossible to live, work, and otherwise function in a technological society without knowledge of computers. Further, if we look into the history of computer use in government and other commercial and non-profit organizations, we can see that in the first phase the use of computers was restricted to data processing (as in the case of UNIVAC I). With time, computers have taken over more routine operations, such as functioning as a

Figure 1.2 The Development of Computer Use in Public Organizations

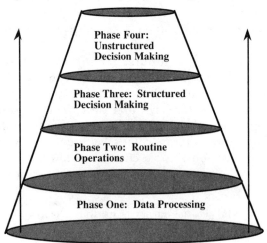

bank teller or a checkout clerk. Similarly, we receive computer-generated letters reminding us to pay our property taxes or our bills (see Figure 1.2).

Computer software programmers are coming up with programmed tools for decision making in some of the more structured areas of decision making. For example, computers routinely check for inventories and flag decision makers when inventory levels fall below a certain predetermined mark decided by the appropriate decision maker. Perhaps the best-known example of computers making structured decisions is preprogrammed computer selling in the stock market. To save time and money, computers are instructed to initiate selling if the price of a holding dips below a certain percentage point predetermined by the stock analyst. The airlines often use computerized scheduling programs that without the help of an on-the-spot analyst, chalk out the optimal network of stops if there is an unforeseen delay in taking off or a diversion of traffic from one scheduled airport. Such uses in the government sector are still relatively rare. However, new innovations are being made in computer use every day. As a result, soon the government sector may walk in locked step with the private sector in this area.

Finally, in the fourth phase computers act as aids to the unstructured decision-making process (that is, where the decisions are not routine and must be made with the help of a host of different criteria). The techniques discussed in this book are designed for this level of computer use. You may notice that at the present level of technology, unless a truly "smart" computer with independent logic is devised, computers cannot make decisions at this level and must work as aids to human decision makers.

Computer Software for This Book

Most of the analytical techniques mentioned in this book can be performed by hand in their simplest forms. However, a more realistic application would require calculation of numbers to an extent that is not possible without the help of a computer. These problems can be solved on a computer by using a number of software programs available for mainframe/minicomputers or personal computers.

The software programs in the larger computers (such as a mini or mainframe) are able to handle a more complicated set of operations with a much larger amount of data. Even for personal computers there is a wide range of softwares. They vary from simple (and consequently relatively inexpensive) ones with limited capabilities to highly complex ones costing hundreds of dollars. Also, while choosing a software you must understand the computing capabilities of your machine. If the software you want to use requires more memory space than your computer can provide, you will not be able to use it.

Facing such a wide range of choices, which software should you get? An ancient Greek philosopher, noting the nature of the changing world, observed that it is impossible to dip in the same stream twice. When it comes to software, the stream is a torrent; if you set out to conduct a comparative study of the statistical softwares available, your list will require significant revision, or will be obsolete, even before the ink from your printer has dried. My task of choosing a particular software for use with this book was difficult because this book presents a number of techniques spanning a wide variety of disciplines. Specifically, the entire range of techniques discussed in this book requires three broad categories of software able to perform (1) statistical operations, including procedures of time series and econometric analyses; (2) graphics; and (3) techniques of operations research. There is no single software that can perform all of these diverse tasks.

However, having researched the market, I decided to include with the book two software packages: the *business version* of MYSTAT, and OPTIZE. The business MYSTAT program is a multipurpose statistical package and is a subset of a much larger package called SYSTAT. MYSTAT is able to do a large number of statistical operations and data transformations required for several techniques mentioned in this book. It also has a good graphing capability. OPTIZE, on the other hand, is designed for the application of linear and integer programming. The OPTIZE disk also contains a program called MATRIX which can perform matrix operations needed for Markov's chain. Since it is important that you use a computer, I will show you how to get a computer solution at the end of the discusion of each technique. My demonstration will involve MYSTAT wherever it is applicable. Where MYSTAT does not provide application or is limited in its capabilities, I will suggest other softwares that are readily available in the United States. In general, I will recommend, along with MYSTAT, a good graphics program such as HARVARD GRAPHICS (for DOS users) or CRICKET GRAPH (for MacIntosh users). For other techniques of operations research, I highly recommend the use of *QS (QUANTITATIVE SYSTEMS)* by Yih-Long Chang and Robert S. Sullivan (Prentice-Hall). QS is available in both DOS and Mac versions. If you are a DOS user, you may also look into the following softwares: LOTUS, QUATRO, EXECUSTAT for students, MINITAB for students, SPSS/PC+ STUDENT WARE, and SYSTAT. For Apples, look into DATA DESK student version, JMP-IN student, EXCELL, and SYSTAT.

Key Words

Bytes	Megabytes
DOS (Disk Operating System)	Minicomputers
Dumb terminal	Operating system
First, second, and third generation computers	Personal computers
Floppy disk	Processor
Format	RAM
Hard disk	Remote job entry (RJE)
Hardware	Software
K	Terminals
Mainframe computers	Windows

PART I

THE BASIC TOOLBOX

Chapter 2

Descriptive Statistics and Probability Theory

Numbers as Storytellers

The footprints of history are preserved in recorded information. By looking at the numbers and interpreting their implications, we can understand a great deal about the past. We readily understand that data collected from autopsies of Egyptian mummies give us indications about their physical well-being, which we can extend to the general population of the time. But what about their feelings? Properly collected and analyzed numbers can shed light even on this seemingly non-numerical aspect of human lives.

One of the most skillful uses of archival data to learn about thoughts and feelings can be found in the work of historian Lawrence Stone.[1] By piecing together data from previous years, he draws conclusions about feelings of love, romance, and social mores, which otherwise would not have been evident. For example, attitudes toward love and romance started changing rapidly in eighteenth-century England. Reflecting the traditional views of the day, in 1723 Jonathan Swift called romantic love "a ridiculous passion which hath no being but in plays and romances."[2] In those days, the notion of romantic love was often rejected, since it was considered to be either impractical or too closely linked to bodily passion. Instead, unrequited love was glorified in the literature; marriages were arranged for financial and other "practical" reasons. However, although the most influential men and women were still opposed to the idea of romantic love in the middle of the 18th century, they were fighting a losing battle. Since literature is often shaped by popular demand, Professor Stone infers a changing attitude toward love and romance by showing a steady surge in the number of romantic novels written by female authors during the decades of that century. Figure 2.1 redraws the evidence.[3]

The Building Blocks of Quantitative Analysis

The present age is aptly called the Information Age. The amount of information collected every day is phenomenal. However, the problem of dealing with a large amount of statistical information is that the story behind the numbers is often hidden. The task of quantitative analysis is to make sense out of this torrent of information, like a sculptor, an analyst, or a researcher chisels out the unnecessary and arranges and rearranges the relevant information to create something new—a logically coherent set of arguments.

There are many ways of looking at the world of information. We may look at the world as *ex post facto* and *ex ante facto*—that is, what has already taken place (ex

---

[1] Lawrence Stone, *The Family, Sex, and Marriage in England 1500–1800.* (New York: Harper & Row, 1978).

[2] Quoted in Lawrence Stone, ibid., p. 283.

Figure 2.1 The Number of Romantic Novels Published by Women Authors in England, 1740–1800

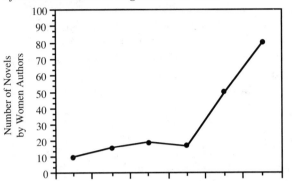

post) and what will take place (ex ante). The basic tools for analyzing ex post data are the measure of central tendency and dispersion; and the tool for analyzing ex ante data is probability theory. Certainty is what has already taken place, uncertainty is what may follow. Analysis of data expressed in numbers starts with the measures of central tendency and dispersion. Together these two are called *descriptive statistics*. The term *descriptive* obviously implies description— yet, from description one starts analysis; from the understanding of the past one looks for clues to forecast the future. Therefore, in this chapter we will start with the methods of descriptive statistics and then introduce the theories of probability.

Methods of Descriptive Statistics

Measures of Central Tendency

The aim of descriptive statistics is to describe a situation or assess the prevailing condition with numbers. In our daily communications, we can describe a situation verbally without the use of numbers. Anthropologists tell of primitive tribes whose

---

[3] As a result of this flood of romantic novels, in 1799 a (fictitious) mother complained to *The Lady's Monthly Museum* that her daughter

reads nothing in the world but novels—nothing but novels, Madam, from morning to night. . . . The maid is generally dispatched to the library two or three times in the day, to change books. One week she will read in the following order: *Excessive Sensibility, Refined Delicacy, Disinterested Love, Sentimental Beauty,* etc. In the next come *Horrid Mysteries, Haunted Caverns, Black Towers, Direful Incantations* and an endless list of similar title. [From Lawrence Stone, ibid., p. 283]

abilities to express quantities with numbers are limited.[4] However, the power of description increases with the proper quantification of the situation. Thus, one may describe the day's temperature as "unusually hot," or one can express the temperature in Fahrenheit or in measures of Celsius. The use of a recognizable index for measuring temperature immediately facilitates its understanding at the absolute level ("it is really hot today") as well as its comparative evaluation ("the highest recorded temperature in twenty years" or "it was hotter here today than it was in Phoenix").

Since a series of numbers do not readily convey a coherent picture, the purpose of descriptive statistics is to look for the number around which a series has a tendency to cluster, so that it can be seen as the *representative* of that series. The tendency of a numerical series to cluster around a number is called the *central tendency*. By this measure, we offer the number that best represents the series. For instance, consider Table 2.1, which presents the prices of five houses in a neighborhood. To convey a quick impression about this neighborhood, we can either reproduce the entire table, which is rather cumbersome, or we may try to describe it by using a single number. There are many measures of central tendency, three of which are most commonly used in the area of social sciences: the *mean, median*, and *mode*.

The **mean** is the arithmetic average of a series and is expressed as

$$\mu = \frac{\sum_{i=1}^{n}(x_i)}{n}$$

where x_i is a series of n numbers, and μ is the mean.

This is the formula for arithmetic average. Those of you who have forgotten how to look at a mathematical expression may recall that the Greek capital sigma (Σ) is used as a sign for summation. The term x with subscript i denotes that it is a **variable** (thus, in Table 2.1, it is the price of the houses, which varies with each house). The i refers to the specific observation, or in this case individual homes.

Table 2.1 Distribution of Housing Prices

Houses	Price
I	$ 65,000
II	$ 65,000
III	$150,000
IV	$230,000
V	$390,000

[4] The people of the Nambiquara tribe of the Matto Grosso forest in Brazil, for example, lack any system of numbers. The closest they come to expressing equality between two sets of items is by using a verb that means "they are alike." (Guiness Book of Records, 1992, p. 269).

Thus when $i = 2$, then x_2 refers to the second observation in the series, which in this case is the price of the second house, $65,000. The term n is a **constant** and measures the number of observations, which in this case is 5. The subscripts below and superscripts above the summation sign Σ read as, "the sum of variable x, with observation varying from 1 though 5." Therefore, in this case, we add up the values of our five observations to arrive at $900,000. Dividing it by 5, we get the average value of a neighborhood house as $180,000.

You may notice that I have expressed the mean with the Greek letter μ (pronounced as *meu*). However, sometimes you will find the mean being written as $\overline{X}$. It is important to note that it is a common tradition in statistics to denote the mean of a **population** (the entire group in question) as μ, and the mean of a **sample** (a small fraction of the population chosen by a researcher to observe) as $\overline{X}$. Unless I note otherwise, I am assuming that we are talking in terms of a population.

The arithmetic mean is the most commonly used measure of central tendency. You may notice that most of the quantitative techniques (many of which are discussed in this book) are built around the analytical anchor provided by the mean. This is because the implication of the mean is rather intuitive. Also, in mathematical statistics, mean as the measure of central tendency has the highly desirable property of *asymptotic convergence*. That is, suppose I have an unbiased coin, which I flip, and every time I get a head, I note it. If the coin is not flawed, as I continue to repeat my experiment over a number of times, the ratio of the number of heads over the total number of tosses will become closer and closer to .5 as the number of tosses increases. This number (.5) is the same as the theoretically derived ratio of *relative frequency*—that is, the number of desired alternatives divided by the total number of alternatives. Thus, in this case, we have just one desired alternative, head, and two possible alternatives, a head and a tail. Therefore, by using this rule we can calculate that the odds of getting a head are $1 : 2 = .5$. Or the possibility of getting either a 1 or a 6 in the toss of dice is $2 : 6 = .333$. This neat mathematical property allows the mean to be used in statistical theorems.

However, the problem with the mean is that it becomes influenced by the extreme values in the series, especially when the sample size is small. Thus, in our example of the small number but unequal prices of houses in a neighborhood, the mean price of housing is $180,000, which is higher than two thirds of the houses in our sample. This is because the mean is being influenced by the existence of an extremely high-priced house valued at $390,000.

The **median** is the middle number in a series. In our example, the median price of a house in the neighborhood is $150,000. Since it is the middle number, it is impervious to the extremes in the series. However, the problem with the median is that it is not as easily calculable as the mean and requires the physical inspection of the series to determine the midpoint. Also, it does not have the asymptotic property of consistency that makes the mean such an attractive measure of central tendency in statistics and mathematics.

Finally, the **mode** is the most frequent number in a series. In this simple example, it happens to be $65,000, since it occurs more frequently than any other number in the series.

Since the mean price of housing is $180,000, the median is $150,000, and the mode is $65,000, we may ask you to judge which number should represent the average price of houses in the neighborhood. Let us elaborate.

Consider for example, Figure 2.2. By looking at the distribution, you can tell that it is a symmetric distribution. In this case, the choice of a measure of central tendency is not going to be controversial since, for this distribution, the mean, median, and mode will coincide.

Controversy will soon ensue if the distribution is not symmetric. Consider, for instance, Figure 2.3. In this case, we have a situation in which all the numbers cluster close to each other, except for one, which is an extreme value. If we calculate the mean, the derived number will be unduly influenced by the existence of an unusually large number. Therefore, in this situation either the median or mode can be used to represent the series.

In Figure 2.4 we can see that while there are other values in the series, there is a preponderance of one observation with a particular value. Therefore, the series will be best represented using the modal value. Since there is an extreme value, the mean will be inappropriate. Similarly, due to the prevalence of one value, even the use of the median may be considered to be less than appropriate.

The use of a measure of central tendency is for ease of description of a series of numbers with a single representative number. However, easy comprehension breaks down as the situation to be described becomes more complex. Consider the example of presenting the day's temperature in your city on a local television

Figure 2.2 A Symmetric Distribution

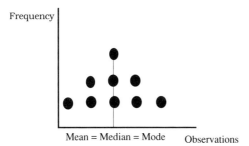

Frequency

Mean = Median = Mode   Observations

In this figure, the distribution of observations show a clear tendency to cluster around the middle number. Therefore, since this series of numbers is evenly distributed, we may accept either of the three measures of central tendency as appropriate. However, at the same time, we recommend that unless there is a special reason when reporting the central tendency, one should always calculate the mean.

Figure 2.3 Distribution with an Extreme Value

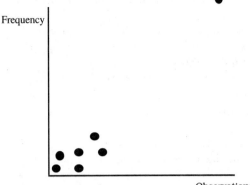

When there is an extreme value, the total picture of a distribution becomes complex. In these cases, the use of any one measure of central tendency would be controversial since one can always question the "representativeness" of the number.

station's weather map. At the outset it looks like a simple enough task. However, controversy would arise if the city recorded a high temperature at noon, but the temperature fell precipitously as a cold weather front moved in. The question then would be to decide which measure to choose as representative of the day's temperature. This problem is further complicated if the city has varied geographical areas with several mini climate zones. In this case, the weather station located in the coastal area may record a significantly different temperature from the one located inland.

Figure 2.4 Distribution when the Modal Value
Is Best Representative

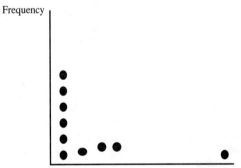

This figure shows a hypothetical situation in which the use of the mode would be appropriate. Since there is an extreme value, the mean would be unduly influenced by it.

The fundamental question is, Why do such problems arise? These kinds of controversies arise anytime we try to describe a complex, multidimensional phenomenon with a one-dimensional measure. The more complex a situation is, the more problematic is its representation with just one set of numbers. Therefore, the alternative is to describe a multidimensional phenomenon with several different sets of numbers. However, more than one number tends to numb one's senses. Representing a complex situation with just one number may have its disadvantages, but the alternative does not seem all that attractive either. Therefore, choice of the best measure of central tendency often calls for subjective judgment.

When There Are Weights or Data Are "Grouped"

If I ask you, "How long would it take you to go to the airport?" You might say, "If the traffic is *exceptionally* heavy, it can take 55 minutes, if it is *unusually* light, 15 minutes, but in general, it should take you about 20 minutes." Not knowing the traffic condition, we may estimate the travel time to the airport by averaging the three numbers. If we do that we come up with an estimate of 30 minutes. Notice that this time is far too pessimistic, since it is one and a half times the time it usually takes to drive to the airport. This average reflects the extreme nature of the most pessimistic assessment of the situation. In such cases, when you do not want to be influenced by the presence of extreme values, yet you do not want to disregard them, you may derive your estimate by giving **weights** to the observation. That is, you may give a weight of 4 to the average time. We can write the series as shown in Table 2.2.

From this data, we can calculate the weighted average as $(15 \times 1) + (20 \times 4) + (55 \times 1)/6 = 25$. Notice that now we are not dividing the sum by the number of observations; instead, we are dividing the sum by the total of the weights. Also notice that this number (25) is a lot closer to the "most likely" number (20) than the unweighted average (30). Therefore, by attributing weights, we have made the estimate a lot more realistic. In mathematical symbols, the calculation of weighted average is written as

$$\mu = \frac{\sum (f_i \times X_i)}{\sum f_i}$$

(2.1a)

where f_i are the respective weights for the observations.

Table 2.2

	Time (in minutes)	Weight
Optimistic assessment	15	1
Most likely assessment	20	4
Pessimistic assessment	55	1

Similar logic is applicable when data are available in **groups**. The range of a group is called the **interval**. For instance, the data on housing prices for a neighborhood may be available only in groups. I have written the housing price data given in Table 2.1 in group form in Table 2.3.

By using the formula given by equation (2.1a), we can calculate the weighted mean as

$$\frac{\$850,000}{5} = \$170,000$$

You may note that the weighted average of $170,000 is $10,000 lower than the true (unweighted) average. This is because weighted averages are less precise than unweighted averages. By calculating the midpoints of an interval, we are only estimating the actual values of the observations. Therefore, if actual data are available, I would recommend their use over weighted data. However, when we are presented with a large set of numbers, it is often more convenient to present it in terms of a small number of groups.

The median for interval data is calculated somewhat differently. To calculate the median, first inspect the data to locate the middle observation. Then assume that all the observations are evenly spaced within an interval. Thus, if there is only one observation, assume that it is located in the middle of the interval. That is, for the present example, the median price is $150,000. If there are more than one observation within an interval, we have to divide the range by the number of observations and then estimate the distance of the median number from the boundaries of the range. Suppose there were not one but 17 observations that fall within the interval containing the median in our example. Also assume that the median number is the tenth observation. In such a case, we would divide the interval by the number of observations within it: $100,000/17 = 5,882.4. Then we can estimate the location of the tenth observation by multiplying it by 10 (58,824). By adding this number to the lower limit of the interval ($100,000), we get $158,824, which is our estimate of the median price. Therefore,

weighted averages are only approximations of the actual ungrouped data. So, whenever possible, use ungrouped data for the calculation of central tendency.

Table 2.3 Grouped Data

Price Range	Number of Houses (f_i)	Midpoint of intervals (X_i)	Midpoint X Number of Houses
$0–$99,999	2	$50,000	100,000
$100,000–199,999	1	$150,000	150,000
$200,000–400,000	2	$300,000	600,000
	$\Sigma f_i = 5$		$\Sigma f_i X_i = 850,000$

Measures of Dispersion

A series is characterized not only by its central tendency, but also by how strong this central tendency is. That is, how closely does the series cluster around the measure of central tendency? In Figure 2.5, both of the series have the same mean, but obviously the first series (Figure 2.5a) is more bunched together than the second (Figure 2.5b).

The closer this clustering is, the more confident we can be of the representativeness of our measure of central tendency. To understand the measures of dispersion, let us compare our first neighborhood with a second neighborhood. Consider Table 2.4. We can measure the relative dispersion or the "scatteredness" of a series by using **range**, **mean absolute deviation**, **variance**, or **standard deviation**.

The range simply measures the difference between the highest and the lowest values in a series. From Table 2.4, we can see that the houses located in neighborhood A have a range of $325,000, while the range for neighborhood B is $50,000.

The concept of range is also associated with what are known as the hinge and the midspread. The **lower hinge** is the observation, below which lies one quarter of the observations in the series. The **upper hinge** points to the observation above which lies a quarter of the distribution. The distance between the two hinges, containing half the observations around the median, is called the **midspread**. For example, consider the series of numbers: 3, 17, 69, 85, 97, 117, 198, 211, 217, 300, 301. Since this arrangement does not tell us very much about the nature of its distribution, we may express it with the help of the range, the median and hinges, as shown in Figure 2.6. This dipiction sheds more light on the characteristic of the

Figure 2.5 The Effects of Different Dispersion

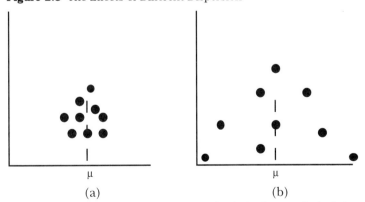

If the observations are closely bunched together, the distribution has a smaller level of dispersion (a) compared to the one in which the observations are widely scattered (b).

Table 2.4 Relative Distribution of Housing Prices between Two Neighborhoods

Houses	Neighborhood A	Neighborhood B
I	$65,000	$150,000
II	$65,000	$180,000
III	$150,000	$180,000
IV	$230,000	$190,000
V	$390,000	$200,000

series. As you can see, in this series, 117 is the median value of the series of 11 numbers, the third and the ninth observations are the two hinges, and the difference between them is the midspread.

To measure how scattered or dispersed a distribution is, we need to find out how far, on the average, the individual observation within the series is from the mean. However, if we add up the differences from the mean, the positive numbers cancel out the negative numbers. Thus, if we subtract $180,000 (the mean value of the series) from the various values of the housing prices of the two neighborhoods, we get the results shown in Table 2.5. From this table, it should be apparent that if we try to compare the deviation from the mean for the two series, the addition of columns 3 and 5 will give us 0. Therefore, it is important for you to note that

the sum of deviations from the mean is always equal to 0.

It is an axiomatic truth that the sum of the deviations from the mean is always equal to 0. One can avoid this problem by either disregarding the signs of the deviations or by squaring them (since the square of a negative number is positive). The first method of calculating the average dispersion of a series is called the **mean absolute deviation**. The mean absolute deviation is written as

$$\text{Mean absolute deviation} = \frac{\Sigma |x_i - \mu|}{n}.$$

(2.2)

By using this formula, we can see in Table 2.6 that the mean absolute deviation for the first neighborhood is $104,000 = ($520,000/5), while for the second, $12,000 = ($60,000/5). According to the mean absolute deviation measure, the second neighborhood is nearly 8.7 times more homogeneous (less dispersed) in its distribution of housing prices than the first neighborhood.

Figure 2.6

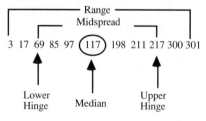

Table 2.5 Relative Distribution of Housing Prices: Deviation from the Mean

Houses	Neighborhood A (X)	$X_i - \mu$	Neighborhood B (X)	$X_j - \mu$
I	$ 65,000	-$115,000	$150,000	-$30,000
II	$ 65,000	-$115,000	$180,000	0
III	$150,000	-$ 30,000	$180,000	0
IV	$230,000	$ 50,000	$190,000	$10,000
V	$390,000	$210,000	$200,000	$20,000
Total		**0.0**		**0.0**

However, there are several problems with the mean absolute deviation. First, computationally it is cumbersome; second, it does not possess some of the most desirable mathematical properties. Therefore, we may try another way to eliminate the negative signs in the deviation from the mean—that is, by squaring the deviations. This process can be written as

$$\sigma^2 = \frac{\sum_{i=0}^{n}(x_i - \mu)^2}{n}.$$

(2.3)

This is the measure of **variance**, which is expressed as σ^2. To calculate the variance of the two neighborhoods, we need to square the deviations from the mean (the third and the fifth columns in Table 2.3), add them up, and divide by 5. The calculated variances for the two neighborhoods are 14,790,000,000 and 240,000,000. The problem with variance is that the numbers are often extremely large. Therefore, we can reduce the size of the variance by taking its square root. The resulting number is called the **standard deviation** of the series. Owing to several highly desirable mathematical properties, standard deviation (expressed by σ) is by far the best used measure of dispersion. Standard deviation of a series is calculated by the following formula:

$$\sigma = \sqrt{\frac{\sum_{i=0}^{n}(x_i - \mu)^2}{n}}.$$

(2.4)

Table 2.6 Calculation of Mean Absolute Deviation and Variance

Houses	Neighborhood A (Mean Absolute Deviation) $|X_i - \mu|$	Neighborhood A (Squared Deviation from the Mean) $(X_i - \mu)^2$	Neighborhood B (Mean Absolute Deviation) $|X_j - \mu|$	Neighborhood B (Squared Deviation from the Mean) $(X_j - \mu)^2$
I	$115,000	13,225,000,000	$30,000	900,000,000
II	$115,000	13,225,000,000	0	0
III	$ 30,000	900,000,000	0	0
IV	$ 50,000	2,500,000,000	$10,000	100,000,000
V	$210,000	44,100,000,000	$20,000	200,000,000
Total	$520,000	73,950,000,000	$60,000	1,200,000,000

Therefore, by deriving the square root of the variances of the two ser calculated the standard deviations, which turned out to be 121,614.14 and 15,491.92. Obviously, these numbers are much more manageable than the variances. Thus, from these measures, we can see that the dispersion for the first neighborhood is more than seven times the dispersion for the second neighborhood.

When we are speaking in terms of population variance or standard deviation, we use the Greek alphabet σ^2 and σ (sigma). When we consider sample variance and sample standard deviation, we use the Roman (English) alphabet S and S^2. Therefore, you should note a rather important convention in statistical terminology:

> *When denoting population mean, variance, and standard deviations, we use the Greek alphabets μ, σ^2, σ. However, sample mean, variance, and standard deviations are written as $\overline{X}$, S^2, and S.*

At this point, you should note another significant difference between the formula for calculating the population standard deviation (σ) and sample standard deviation (S). Since the sample standard deviation is only an estimate of the population standard deviation, it has to be corrected for bias by dividing the sum of squares by $n-1$, instead of n. This implies that as the size of the sample (n) increases, the subtraction of 1 will have less and less impact on the calculated value of standard deviation. The formula for calculating **sample standard deviation** is given by

$$S = \sqrt{\frac{\sum_{i=0}^{n}\left(x_i - \mu\right)^2}{n-1}}.$$

(2.4a)

Which Distribution is More Dispersed?

Suppose we have two distributions and we want to know which one has more variations within it. Unfortunately, unlike the mean, standard deviations cannot be readily used to compare the relative dispersion of distributions. The problem with standard deviation is that it is an absolute measure. That is, it is influenced by the unit of measurement. Consider two sample distributions, I and II. You will notice that B is A X 5.

Table 2.7

Series I	Series II
0	0
1	5
2	10
3	15
4	20

The sample standard deviation (*S*) is calculated to be 1.58 for series I and 7.91 for II. Thus, since series II is five times the values of series I, so is the value of the resepective standard deviation. This can sometimes pose a practical problem. Suppose we want to compare the dispersion of housing prices of two diverse cities, Tijuana, Mexico, and San Diego, California. We will face a problem in our attempt: Since housing prices in San Diego are much higher than those in Tijuana, the dispersion in the San Diego real estate price will be magnified by the absolute difference in the price level. However, it is entirely possible that the disparity in housing prices is greater in Tijuana than in San Diego. To compare the relative dispersion between the two cities, we have to divide the standard deviation by the mean. This measure, known as the **coefficient of variation**, is then written as

$$\text{Coefficient of variation} = \frac{\sigma}{\mu}. \tag{2.5}$$

Thus, looking at the two neighborhoods in our previous example (Table 2.4), we can calculate the coefficient of variation for them as

$$\text{Neighborhood A} = \frac{135,968.7}{165,000} = .824; \quad \text{Neighborhood B} = \frac{18,708.3}{120,000} = .156.$$

The calculated coefficients of variation show that the variance for the first neighborhood is over five times (5.28, to be precise) that of the second one. Incidentally, you may also notice that by using this measure, we come to the conclusion that despite the difference in scale, the distribution of values for series I and II have the same relative dispersion.

Skewness and Symmetry of Distribution

When looking at a series of numbers, often the question is, Where are the mean, median, and mode of the distribution? The positions of these three measures of central tendency can give decision makers extremely valuable clues about the distribution of the series. Take, for example, a series of numbers shown in Table 2.8.

Table 2.8

Observation	Frequency
1	5
2	8
3	12
4	15
5	21
6	35
7	21
8	15
9	12
10	8
11	5

Figure 2.7 Example of a Symmetric Distribution

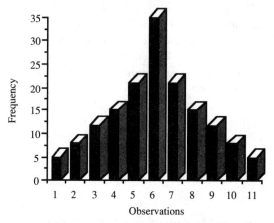

The data from Table 2.8 have been plotted in Figure 2.7. The distribution shown in this figure is called symmetric, as it depicts a perfect bell shape. For distributions like these, all three measures of central tendency—the mean, median, and mode—fall on the same point. If you calculate the mean for the distribution shown in Table 2.3, you can see that it is approximately (with the appropriate rounding off for the decimal points) equal to 6. Also, since there are five numbers above and five numbers below, the median for the distribution is also 6. Finally, since the observation 6 has the highest frequency, it is also the modal point for the distribution.

However, this happy situation changes if the distribution is tilted to the right or to the left of the perfect bell shape. A tilted distribution is called a **skewed distribution**. If a distribution is tilted to the right, it is called a **positively skewed distribution**, and if it tilts to the left, it is called a **negatively skewed distribution** (see Figure 2.8). Consider, for example, two new series along with the one given in Table 2.8. Table 2.9 presents data for three different series. The symmetric series is being called frequency (A), and the two subsequent series are labeled as frequencies (B) and (C).

The plotting of these three series will result in the curves shown in Figure 2.8.

Table 2.9 Examples of Symmetric and Asymmetric Distributions

Observation	Frequency (A)	Frequency (B)	Frequency (C)
1	5	25	5
2	8	35	6
3	12	20	7
4	15	18	8
5	21	15	10
6	35	12	12
7	21	10	15
8	15	8	18
9	12	7	20
10	8	6	35
11	5	5	20

Figure 2.8 Comparison of Symmetric and Asymmetric Series

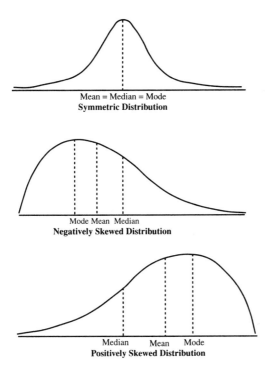

Mean = Median = Mode
Symmetric Distribution

Mode Mean Median
Negatively Skewed Distribution

Median   Mean   Mode
Positively Skewed Distribution

Notice that the median for the three distributions remains the same, as we have 11 observations. Therefore, the sixth observation is the middle point for each of these distributions. The means for the two series are 4.3 and 6.8, respectively. The mode for series B is 2, and for series C it is 10. Table 2.10 summarizes this information.

For a policy maker who needs to make a quick judgment about a data series, it is extremely important to remember that

for a negatively skewed distribution the mean is less than the median;
and for a positively skewed distribution, the mean is greater than the median.

These are important facts to remember because these two figures can give a rough picture for the distribution. In fact, you may notice that the greater the difference between the two, the greater the extent of skewness of distribution.

Table 2.10

	Mean	Median	Mode
Symmetric Distribution (A)	6.0	6.0	6.0
Negatively Skewed Distribution	4.3	6.0	2
Positively Skewed Distribution	6.8	6.0	10

■ **Using the Computer to Calculate Measures of Central Tendency** ▬▬▬▬
and Dispersion

Business MYSTAT allows you to calculate a number of measures of central tendency and dispersion. If you have a DOS-based computer, the following commands give you these options:

MEAN	= mean of a series
SD	= sample standard deviation
MAX	= the maximum value of the series
MIN	= the minimum value of the series
RANGE	= the range of the series
SUM	= the sum of the series
SKEWNESS	= the measure of skewness

To compute these statistics, choose the option **STATS**, identify the variables for which you want to have these statistics calculated, and then specify the statistics. Thus, to calculate the mean, standard deviation, and the range of variables 1 and 2, type in the following:

STATS <var 1> <var 2>..../ MEAN SD RANGE

If you have a MacIntosh, choose **STATS**. This will show you a box. Select the variables by clicking on their names on the variable box. *Do not simply type in their names.* Then click on the appropriate boxes next to their names. Thus to get the above statistics, click on the boxes for **MEAN**, **SD**, and **RANGE**. Then click on **OK**.

Which Measure of Central Tendency to Use

In our previous discussion, I have argued that the choice of a measure of central tendency depends on the subjective assessment of the person making a statement. However, there are a few rules of thumb.

1. If a distribution is symmetric, all three measures would be the same. Therefore, choosing any one would be fine.
2. If a distribution is highly skewed, we may find the median to be the most useful measure of central tendency.
3. If there is an overwhelming preponderance of one number, we may use mode.
4. Unless there is a special need, while calculating average, arithmetic mean should be used.
5. If, for any reason median or mode is used, this should be made clear to the reader.

A Quick Glance at the Distribution: The Stem-Leaf Method

A series of numbers often do not convey a coherent picture. Consider, for example, that we are given arrest totals of individuals on drug-related charges over a 15-week period:

[15, 23, 8, 31, 9, 45, 41, 18, 11, 3, 13, 25, 33, 40, 10, 102].

Clearly, one cannot draw too many conclusions from these numbers. However, a policy analyst must frequently elicit quick conclusions about a distribution, such as housing prices in a neighborhood, age of children in a detention center, or the time taken by various employees to complete a task. In such cases, the stem-leaf method offers a helping hand.

A stem-leaf method arranges a series of numbers by *stems* and *leafs*. For example, in the preceding series of numbers, the first digit is the stem, and the second digit is the leaf. Thus, for the number 15, 1 is the stem and 5 is the leaf. For a single-digit number, such as 3, the stem is 0 and the leaf is 3. Business MYSTAT gives you a stem-leaf analysis as shown in Table 2.11.

You may notice that you can get a histogram or a bar chart simply by rotating the stem-leaf diagram.

The advantage of a stem-leaf method, as presented by MYSTAT, over a histogram is that it contains a lot more information regarding the distribution. For instance, we can tell from Table 2.11 that although there is a good deal of variation in the data, the median value 25 is much closer to the minimum (3) than the maximum (102). Therefore, it is clearly a negatively skewed distribution. The

Table 2.11 Stem-Leaf Analysis

Stem and Leaf Plot of Variable: Drug Arrests, $N = 16$

Minimum is: 3.000
Lower hinge is: 10.500
Median is: 20.500
Upper hinge is: 36.500
Maximum is: 102.000

```
    0 3
    0 89
    1 H 013
    1 58
    2 M 3
    2 5
    3 13
    3 H
    4 01
    4 5
***Outside values***
   10 2
```

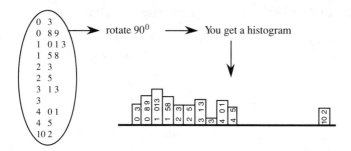

output also indicates that the maximum value is an outlier, or a real exception to the rest of the values in the series. In many decision-making instances these methods can provide some rather important insights.

Introduction to Probability Theory

As the old adage goes, there is no certainty except for taxes and death. Even then we cannot foretell the changes in tax law; neither can we predict the exact time of our demise with any kind of accuracy. Therefore, we need to venture into the world of uncertainty. Uncertainty means that decisions must be made *before* we

---

■ Computer Application ■

All of the statistical packages would allow you to calculate the mean and the median of a series of data. In MYSTAT, the stem-leaf method falls under the graphing menu. If you have an Apple computer, you may access it by dragging down the icon. For stem leaf, (1) you need to select the variable on which you want the procedure done, and (2) you may also specify the number of lines (or stems). If you do not specify the number, the program will automatically determine the number of lines. In computer terms, this process of automatic choosing by the computer is called a **default**. If you have a DOS-based machine, you will have to type the following instructions:

STEM [<Var1>,<Var2,<...>/LINES=<#>]

Where the command STEM tells the computer to do stem-leaf analysis, Var1, Var2, etc. are the variables on which you want this analysis. By filling in the # sign, you can specify the number of lines or stems.

MYSTAT also calculates the measures of descriptive statistics. For Apple computers, drag down the STATS icon, select the variable, and then click on the items, such as the minimum, maximum, mean, range, standard deviation, etc. For DOS, simply type in STATS. The computer will calculate default statistics MIN, MAX, MEAN, and SD for all the variables. If you do not want these statistics for all the variables, or want different ones, you can specify them in your command statement.

know which one from a set of possible outcomes will come to pass. While deciding on a possible outcome, we assign probability values. We have become accustomed to using probability measures in our everyday conversations. We attach probability values to the odds of winning the jackpot in a lottery, the chances of a rain storm, point spreads in football game, or the behavior of the stock market. Yet probability cannot be easily defined any more than we can easily define time or space. Nevertheless, we use measures of probability in our everyday conversation with as much ease as the measures of time and space.

If we stop to think about where these numbers originate, it will be apparent that the sources of probability measures are either objective (based on actual facts) or subjective (based on personal judgment). Let us discuss these two sources of probability.

Objective Probability

An objective measure defines probability as the relative frequency of occurrence of a given event over an infinite number of tries. Therefore, objective probability is also known as **relative frequency**. However, it is obvious that we cannot keep on tossing a coin to see that the probability of getting a head is $1/2$. Hence, you must recognize that calculated probability in actual practice is only an approximation of the "true" probability. The fact that it is an approximation does not pose a serious problem if the number of experiments becomes larger and larger. This is an extremely important concept. Therefore, let us take a moment to explain this notion properly.

Despite its everyday use, the concept of probability remains shrouded in misinterpretation and misperception. For example, if the weather report tells us that there is a 50% chance of rain, can we take it to mean that it would rain on half the day, or that we can expect rain every half hour? Or, if it rains, does it mean that we will not see the sun at all? Or, if it has rained quite a bit already this season, can we expect a clear day with such a forecast? These questions raised here are rooted in the concept of probability and, therefore, merit a closer look.

First, it is obvious that a forecast of a 50% chance of rain does not imply that it would rain half the day or that it would rain every half hour. In fact, it will either rain or it will not (even drizzle should count as rain). Therefore, the only way to interpret the result is the same as interpreting the outcome of a coin toss. Since by tossing a coin you will either win (get a head) or lose (get a tail), you should interpret the probability measure as if you were to toss the coin umpteen number of times. You will see that as the number of tosses increases, the ratio of heads over the total number of attempts approaches .5. This has been shown in Figure 2.8. Suppose we are tossing a coin in groups of four. After each set of tosses we record the number and average it over the previous ones. Thus, suppose in the first try, we got one head and three tails. This gives us a ratio $1/3$. Suppose in the next try, we get two heads and two tails. By averaging the total number of tosses, we get the ratio of heads over tails to be 3/4. If we continue to do this, we will see a curve similar to the one presented in Figure 2.9, where in the beginning, when the number of tries were small, we may see wide fluctuations. However, as the number of tries increased, the average approached the "true" probability figure of .5.

This is the basis of objective probability. Imbedded in this simple example are some of the most important assumptions and axioms that form the basic building blocks of statistical reasoning. A proper understanding must begin with the examination of these properties of objective probability. First, the events in a probability experiment (in this case, each toss) must be **independent**. Perhaps the most common cause for misinterpreting probability is the question of independence. Suppose you have placed a bet on a toss of a coin. You are calling for a head, and you have called it correctly the last four times. On the fifth try, what should you do? Should you call for a head and see your luck run out, or should you try to be smart by calling for a tail? You should know that the tosses are independent and, therefore, what you received last time or the time before has no bearing whatsoever on what may happen this time. As a result, unless the coin is biased, it should not matter whether you call for a head or a tail even after you have received four heads in a row.

The second assumption of objective probability is that the events are **mutually exclusive**. Two outcomes are mutually exclusive if they cannot take place simultaneously. For example, we cannot get both a head and tail in a single try. But it is entirely possible to have both rain and sunshine within a single day. Therefore, while the outcomes of a coin toss or a roll of a die are mutually exclusive, rain and sunshine are not.

Finally, the probability measures are **asymptotic**. That is, the probability of getting a head with an unbiased coin is .5. However, that does not imply that we are going to get exactly two heads and two tails in four tries. It simply means that if we repeat the experiment over a large number of times, as the number of tosses increases we will see that the ratio will approach .5. Similarly, going back to our

Figure 2.9 Probability and the Number of Tries

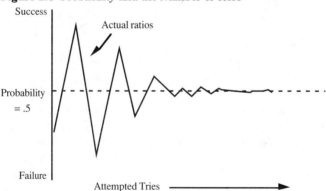

previous example, we must interpret the meteorological prediction as follows: If the weather conditions (temperature, barometric pressure, wind condition, humidity, etc.) become the same as the condition we are having at this time over a long period of time this combination of conditions would produce rain half of the time.

While discussing the asymptotic property of probability, I specified the coin as unbiased. This is an extremely important concept. Suppose the coin we are tossing is biased in favor of heads. In such a case, tossing the infinite number of times will not give us the probability (.5) of getting a head. We can show the effect of this bias with the help of the diagram shown in Figure 2.10.

We will refer to the concept of bias many times during our discussion of regression analysis. You should remember that among all the measures of central tendency and dispersion, only the mean is unbiased. That is, if we keep on taking the average, as the number of samples increases the sample average will tend to coincide with the true or population average. This important property sets the mean apart from all other measures and is why it is the most widely used measure in statistics and mathematics.

Figure 2.10 Bias in Probability

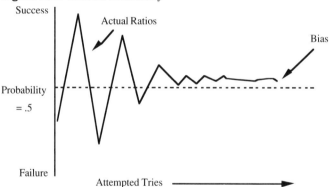

In statistics, a sample number is said to be biased when the average of repeated trials does not converge to its population number. Thus, tossing a biased coin (heavier on one side) will cause the average to diverge from its true expected value determined by relative frequency (.5).

Probability Distribution

When we assign probability to a series of independent and mutually exclusive events, we get a **probability distribution**. Let us suppose we are looking at the probability of case loads coming to a social worker on a given day. The workers were observed over a period of 100 days, and then by dividing each day's frequency by the total number of arrivals, the probability column of the arrival of the case

Table 2.12 Probability and Cumulative Probability Distributions for a Social Worker on a Given Day

Number of Cases (x)	Observed Frequencies	Probability Distribution	Cumulative Probability Distribution
1	5	.05	.05
2	10	.10	.15
3	15	.15	.30
4	17	.17	.47
5	20	.20	.67
6	15	.15	.82
7	8	.08	.90
8	7	.07	.97
9	3	.03	1.00
Total	100		

loads was constructed. This hypothetical data has been presented in Table 2.12 and in Figure 2.11. By looking at the table, you can tell that the probability that the social worker would handle just one case is 5%, two cases is 10%, etc. The third column of the table shows the cumulative probability totals. This is called a **cumulative probability distribution**, and is interpreted as the probability of having a value less than or equal to a specific value of x. Thus, by looking at the cumulative probability distribution data, one can conclude that the social worker having a case load of four or less on a given day is 47%.

Knowledge of the mean and standard deviation of a probability distribution provides us with a good deal of information about the nature of the distribution. Most importantly, this information gives us some of the most powerful analytical tools in the field of applied statistics. Probability distributions can take on an infinite number of shapes. However, for analytical purposes, a perfectly symmetric distribution, known as the **normal distribution**, serves as the fundamental building block. Again, a symmetric distribution can also take on various shapes. As you can see in Figure 2.12, I have drawn three normal distributions with different means.

Symmetric distributions can also have the same mean and yet be different. In

Figure 2.11 Plot of Probability Distribution

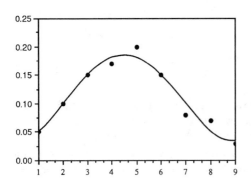

Figure 2.12 Normal Distributions with Different Means

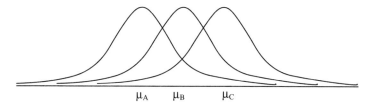

Figure 2.13, you can see that despite having the same mean, the three distributions have their relative levels of dispersion, measured in terms of standard deviation, σ. Clearly, of the three normal distributions, the tall and skinny one has the lowest standard deviation, while the short and fat one has the largest dispersion. Because of these variations, a **standard normal distribution** is defined as the one whose mean is equal to 0 and standard deviation is equal to 1. This standard normal distribution serves as the "ideal type" or the beacon against which the probabilities of an uncertain world are measured.

The beauty of a standard normal distribution is that since the distribution is standardized, we are able to measure any segment of it with utmost precision. Since for a standard normal distribution the standard deviation is 1, any distance from the mean can therefore be measured in terms of the standard deviation. For example, from Figure 2.14, you can see that 68.26% of all the observations in the distribution will fall within $\pm 1\sigma$ distance from the mean. Similarly, the area within the boundaries of $\pm 2\sigma$ will capture 95.46% of the observations. Based on the formula of the normal distribution, statisticians are able to calculate any defined area under the curve.

Standard normal distribution is, of course, a theoretical concept. The bridge between the theory and its practical use has been accomplished by perhaps the most remarkable theorem in the field of mathematics and statistics, known as the **central limits theorem**. The compelling nature of this theorem can be understood with the help of an example. We all know that human beings come in all shapes and sizes. Therefore, if we plot the percentages of males in the United States falling in various groups of heights, we will see a distribution with a strong central

Figure 2.13 Normal Distributions with Various Levels of Dispersion

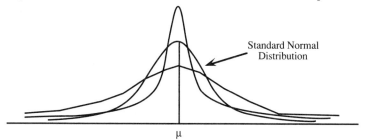

Figure 2.14 Area under Normal Distribution

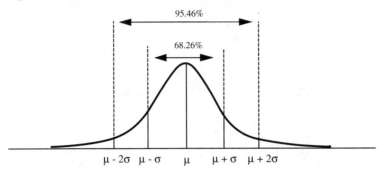

$$\mu - 2\sigma \quad \mu - \sigma \quad \mu \quad \mu + \sigma \quad \mu + 2\sigma$$

tendency and relatively few observations on the extreme ends of the spectrum (extremely tall and extremely short). But this plot will not show a perfectly symmetric distribution. However, we can get a standard normal distribution if we follow a simple procedure. Suppose we already know the mean (μ) and the standard deviation (σ) for the height of the U.S. male population. We collect 10 males at random, note their average (mean) height, and let them go. Again we collect another group of men, note their average height, and let them go. If we perform this operation a number of times, we will get a series of numbers showing sample means, which we may call $\overline{X}_i$.

The central limits theorem tells us that if we subtract the sample means from the population mean and then divide by the standard deviation, as we repeat the experiment we will obtain a standard normal distribution. We can write this with the help of mathematical symbols as follows:

$$\frac{\overline{X}_i - \mu}{\sigma} \sim (0,\ 1) \ \text{ as } i \to \infty. \tag{2.6}$$

The foregoing expression is read as, *the series derived by subtracting the population mean from sample means, and divided by the population standard deviation, is distributed with mean = 0 and standard deviation = 1.* The enormous practical implication of this property will be apparent with the help of an example.

Several years ago, the skeletal remains of a group of prehistoric settlers were found in an area that was being claimed by two neighboring countries in a border dispute. The discovery of these remains caused excitement in some quarters, as they could "prove" the antiquity of claims on the land by determining the racial origin of the original inhabitants. To determine the racial identity of the ancient inhabitants, researchers took the average cranial measurement of the newly discovered skeletons. Thanks to previous anthropological studies, the average cranial measurement and the standard deviation of the present stock of occupiers of the land are known. It was decided to test the hypothesis that the people whose skeletons were discovered came from the same group of people as today's inhabitants.

However, the problem in mathematics is that it is often impossible to prove the *existence* of a relationship. For instance, if we state that all As are B, it would be impossible to go check every A to prove the relationship. Instead, it is often simpler to nullify an opposite hypothesis in its negative form, such as "there are some As that are not B." If we do not find any example where any A is B in our sample, then we become more and more confident in our assertion that there is no A that is B as the size of the sample increases. In statistical terminology, this alternate hypothesis is called a **null hypothesis**. We call it "null" (defined by the *Webster Dictionary* as "none," "invalid," or "void") because while testing, the analyst is usually interested in its falsification.

The idea behind this test can be explained with the help of Figure 2.13. If the cranial average of the skeletal remains is very close to that of the present group, it is then possible to assume that they both belong to the same racial stock. However, if the average falls outside the 2σ measurement from the mean, then by looking at the probability distribution, we can say that, since nearly 98% of all the observations (in this case, people of this particular race) will fall within this range, there is only about a 2% chance that these people belonged to the same racial group. The process that we just described is known as **hypothesis testing**. Since hypothesis testing is part of the fundamental construct of analytical reasoning, let us discuss it in more detail.

Hypothesis Testing and Confidence Intervals

In real life truth is often elusive, especially if we are dealing with an uncertain world of probability. The theoretical framework derived by the *central limits theorem* can be used for testing the probability of a hypothesis or estimating a band within which we can reasonably expect to find the "true" value. Let us consider another example. Suppose the average dropout rate in a school district is 15.5%, with a standard deviation of 1.05. Within the school district, one particular school is being touted as exceptional in its achievement of a lower dropout rate. Last year, this school showed only a 15.3% dropout rate in a graduating class of 100. The question is, is this truly exceptional, or is it possible to see such a performance merely as a result of chance factors? The basis of this question forms the core of hypothesis testing.

Hypothesis testing starts with a question. In the preceding example, the question is whether the dropout rate of the school in question is significantly smaller than the average for the district. The second step toward hypothesis testing is the formulation of a specific null hypothesis. Statistical convention generally expresses the research hypothesis as H_1 and the null hypothesis as H_0.

These two hypotheses can then be written as follows:

H_1: *The school's record is significantly smaller than the district average.*

H_0: *The school is not exceptional, and the difference between its mean and the average of the school district can be explained by chance.*

In social science research, we can think of numerous examples of research and null hypothesis. Since it is extremely important to construct a null hypothesis correctly, I offer another example of setting up a research and a null hypotheses. Society is deeply concerned about what to do with juvenile delinquents, since these youngsters have to be punished for their offenses; yet sending them to prison might transform them into more hardened criminals. Therefore, suppose we are attempting to find out if setting up military-style boot camps for first-time juvenile offenders has any bearing on their future criminal activities. We have collected data by tracking two groups of recently paroled offenders: those who were sent to the boot camps and those who were sent through the usual criminal justice system. We can form the two hypotheses as follows:

H_1: Boot camps do reduce the probability of a juvenile's future conviction rate.

H_0: The future conviction rates have no bearing on an individual's enrollment in a boot camp.

In the third step, we must determine the **level of significance** for rejecting the null hypothesis. That is, by using the standard normal distribution, we must determine the level of certainty we must seek for its rejection. This level can be set at 90%, 95%, or even 99%. The level of significance in statistical jargon is often denoted as α. Let us suppose, for testing our hypothesis, that we have set the α level at 90%. If we want to include 90% of the observations in a symmetric distribution, the remaining 10% must be divided equally between the two tails of the distribution. Therefore, in this case, when we want to know if the sample mean (the average for the particular school) is significantly *less* than the population average (the district average), we set the α value at half of .10, or at .05. This is called a **one-tailed test** and is shown in Figure 2.15. The probability value corresponding to the predetermined level of α is also called the **critical value**, since it determines the threshold of rejecting the null hypothesis. If we set the critical value at the 95% level of probability, we want to be 95% certain that what we see in our sample result has only a 5% chance of being caused by chance alone. If the sample value falls below the critical value, we will not be able to reject the null hypothesis.

Z test

Since we know the mean and standard deviation for the district, it is a simple matter to calculate how far the individual school's record is from the district average, measured by units of the district's standard deviation. This number can

Figure 2.15 One-Tailed Test

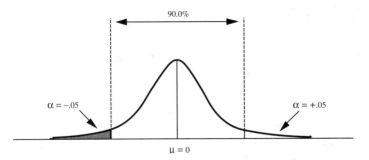

then be compared to a theoretical distribution for rejecting or not rejecting a null hypothesis. If the number of samples is large and we know the population mean and standard deviation, we can derive the value for a **Z distribution**, which is given by the formula

$$Z = \frac{\overline{X} - \mu}{\sigma / \sqrt{n}}$$

(2.7)

where n is the number of observations in the sample, which, in this case is 100 (the number of graduating seniors).

$$Z = \frac{15.2 - 15.5}{1.05 / \sqrt{100}}$$

$$= \frac{-.3}{.105}$$

$$= -2.86$$

Our calculated **Z score** is 2.86, which means that the sample mean (mean of the school in question) is 2.86 times the standard deviation away from the population mean. The corresponding critical value of the Z-distribution is given in Appendix A. This Table in Appendix A gives the area under the right hand side of the standard normal distribution, corresponding to the various calculated Z values. From this table, you can determine the area of the normal distribution below our calculated Z value of 2.86. To do this, go down the first column and find 2.8. Then move to the right across the row to locate the number corresponding to column .06. The number corresponding to the row 2.8 and the column .06 is .4979, which is the area under the normal distribution below $Z = 2.86$.

■ **Using a Computer to Generate a Z Table** ▬▬▬▬▬▬▬▬▬▬▬▬

These are wonderful times for computer users! If you do not want to take the trouble to consult a Z table, or if you look up the wrong number, you may generate the table with your MYSTAT program using the **ZIF** and **ZCF** functions:
If you have a DOS-based machine,

1. At the MYSTAT prompt in the main command screen, type **EDIT** and then press **[ENTER]**. This will take you into the Editor.
2. Type '**ALPHA** and press **[ENTER]**.
3. Now type '**CRIT_Z** and press **[ENTER]**. This will create a column of critical Z values.
4. Press the **[HOME]** key and place the cursor in the first cell under ALPHA.
5. Now you can type in your alpha values. For instance, you can specify your ALPHA levels at **.001, .010, .025, .050**, and **.10**.
6. Press **[Esc]** and move to the command line.

7. Now when you type **LET CRIT_Z = ZIF(ALPHA)**, and press **[ENTER]**, the MYSTAT will give you a column of critical Z values.

If you have an Apple computer,

1. Create a variable with **.001**, **.010**, **.025**, **.050**, and **.10** in the data file. You may name the variable **ALPHA**.
2. Drag down **Editor** and select **MATH**.
3. Type **CRITZ** in the box to the left of Set.
4. Click on **Select** to choose **ZIF( )** in the **to** box.
5. Place your cursor within the brackets of **ZIF( )** and click on **Select** to choose **ALPHA**. This will now look like

	Variable		Variable or Expression
Set	**CRITZ**	to	**ZIF(ALPHA)**

6. Click on **OK** and MYSTAT will calculate the column of critical Z values.

Your screen should show:

ALPHA	*CRIT Z*
.001	-3.090
.010	-2.326
.025	-1.960
.050	-1.645
.100	-1.282

Remember to use the [Select] box to choose the variables and functions. Do not simply type their names in the box.
   You may also calculate the Z value for a given critical value using the **ZIF** function by following the foregoing procedure but reversing the variable names (for your own convenience, because the computer does not really mind what you call these variables) and using **ZCF** instead of **ZIF**. Thus, by using the critical value of 2.86, we find the probability to be .998.
   Remember to use the cumulative function (ZCF) to calculate the probability associated with a particular sample value. For determining the critical value and confidence intervals, use the inverse function (ZIF).
   You may also note that you can use use MYSTAT to calculate the Z score or, for that matter, any numerical calculation. For instance, if you want the computer to calculate the Z value given in the expression

$$Z = \frac{15.2 - 15.5}{1.05 / \sqrt{100}}$$

you can do so by going into the **Editor** and then to **Math** and specifying your equation as Set Z = (15.2-15.5)/(1.05/SQR(100)). Make sure that the equation is correctly expressed. An open bracket or a mistake in the logic will give you incorrect results.

Notice that this number relates only to the right hand side of the distribution. Since it is a symmetric distribution, the other half contains 50% of the distribution. Therefore, by adding .5 to .4979, we get .9979, the cummulative value of the toal area below the area of the Z value of 2.86. This implies that we can be 99.79% certain that the difference between the average district dropout rate and the experience of the model school is not due to chance; this school is justified in its claim to have significantly reduced the dropout rate.

You may also notice that our calculated Z values has a negative sign. Since the Z distribution is symmetric, this sign is of no consequence. It simply points to the direction of the difference from the mean.

You can use the Z table in two different ways. You can find the corresponding probability value, and if it is less than your set standard, reject the null hypothesis. Or, you can find a critical value of Z score corresponding to your standard, which in the case of an α value of .05 is approximately 1.6 (go down the column of α = .05 until you come as close as possible to the .05 without going over, which in this case is .0495. Now look up the corresponding Z score).

Confidence interval

The results of the Z tables can also be used to develop what is commonly known as the **confidence interval**. You can readily see that the "true" values of a population distribution are unknowable. For instance, if we want to know the average height of American females, we have to measure every female in the United States, which is an impossible task. Since the actual height is not available, it will have to be inferred from sample results. Sample results converge with the actual value when the sample size becomes extremely large. Therefore, unless we want to continue taking larger and larger samples, we would be safer to express the population value with a band or an interval. Thus, without saying that the average is 5'6", we will say that the average will lie between, say, 5'3" and 5'8". If we express this band in terms of a probability figure (e.g., "We are 95% certain that the average height falls within this range"), then it is called a confidence interval.

A confidence interval tells us the range within which we can expect the population mean to fall with a certain level of confidence or probability. Thus, when radio or television newscasters tell us poll results, they almost always include corresponding confidence intervals. We are told that "67% of people support the proposed legislation, which has an error margin of plus or minus three percentage points." In other words, we are being asked to hold with a high degree of confidence (usually at a 95% or 99% level) that the actual ratio of people in the general population who support this legislation will fall within 70 and 64%. To derive a confidence interval, we need to use a *two-tailed test* since we are not sure of the direction of the deviation from the sample value. Therefore, consider the logic of a critical value for rejecting the null hypothesis on the basis of the Z score once again: Reject null hypothesis if

$$Z = \frac{\overline{X} - \mu}{\sigma / \sqrt{n}} > Z_{.05}$$

Figure 2.16 Two-Tailed Test and Confidence Interval

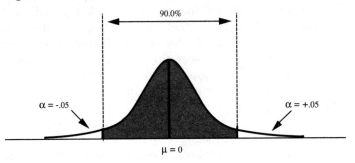

or

$$Z = \frac{\overline{X} - \mu}{\sigma / \sqrt{n}} < -Z_{.05}.$$

These two expressions tell us to reject the null hypothesis if the Z scores are greater than the stipulated value. Diagramatically this means that if the Z scores fall outside the shaded area in Figure 2.16, reject the null hypothesis.

The two algebraic forms can be rewritten as: Reject null hypothesis if:

$$-Z_{.05} > \frac{\overline{X} - \mu}{\sigma / \sqrt{n}} > Z_{.05}.$$

(2.8)

When we want to construct a confidence interval, we choose not to know a specific estimate for the population value μ. Instead, by manipulating equation (2.8), we can write

$$-Z_{.05} \times \frac{\sigma}{\sqrt{n}} > \overline{X} - \mu > +Z_{.05} \times \frac{\sigma}{\sqrt{n}},$$

(2.9)

which is rewritten as

$$\mu - Z_{.05} \times \frac{\sigma}{\sqrt{n}} > \overline{X} > \mu + Z_{.05} \times \frac{\sigma}{\sqrt{n}}.$$

(2.10)

Equation (2.9) gives us the confidence interval for our population (μ). In this equation, we set the value for the desired level of confidence, which in this case is 10%, or 5% on either side of the curve. By looking at the Z table, we can see that the value of $Z_{.05}$ is approximately 1.65. We know that the population standard deviation (σ) = 1.05, $N = 100$, and the population mean (μ) = 15.5. Therefore, the confidence interval for our population mean is calculated by inserting these numbers in equation 2.10:

$$15.5 - 1.65 \times \frac{1.05}{\sqrt{100}} > \overline{X} > 15.5 + 1.65 \times \frac{1.05}{\sqrt{100}}$$

$15.33 > \mu > 15.67.$

In plain English, the results mean that we can expect 90% of all the schools in the district to exhibit a dropout pattern that will vary between 15.33 and 15.67%. This information can be of great help to administrators evaluating the performances of individual schools in the district. Those that exceed 15.67% are doing significantly poorly. Those that have dropout rates less than 15.33% are doing significantly better than the district at large.

t Test

The *Z* test assumes that we know the population standard deviation and that the number of observations in the sample is large. However, both of these assumptions are frequently violated while hypothesis testing because we do not know the population standard deviation and the sample size is often small (usually less than 30). In such a case, the *Z* table, which is calculated with the assumption of a large number of samples, becomes inappropriate. W. S. Gossett, writing under the pseudonym *Student*, devised another test for these kinds of problems, which has since been called the *t* **distribution**. The results of this distribution are presented in a *t* table (Appendix B). The formula for the use of *t* statistics is similar to that of *Z*, and when there is a large enough sample, the two will coincide. The formula for *t* distribution is given as

$$t = \frac{\overline{X} - \mu}{s / \sqrt{n-1}}.$$

(2.11)

Notice that this new statistic (*t*) differs from *Z* in that its denominator contains the sample standard deviation (*s*) instead of the population standard deviation (σ), and we take the square root of the number of observations in the sample (*n*) *minus* 1. The subtraction of 1 from *N* gives us the **degrees of freedom**. The concept of degrees of freedom can be explained easily; however, its use in this statistic is not intuitive, and therefore I will not attempt to explain it. It is important, however, to remember to subtract 1 from the number of observations to calculate the *t* value and to look up the correct critical value from the *t* table.

Let us go back to the example of the discovered remains of inhabitants of the disputed land in antiquity. Suppose we have found skulls of 17 adults, with an average circumference of 21.5 inches and a sample standard deviation of 1.4. The average for the present population is 23 inches. Therefore, to test the null hypothesis that these ancient people belonged to the same race, we set up the *t* score as

$$t = \frac{21.5 - 23.0}{1.4 / \sqrt{17 - 1}}$$

$$= \frac{1.5}{1.4 / \sqrt{16}}$$

$$= \frac{1.5}{1.4 / 4} = 4.29.$$

Let us suppose that we want to evaluate the null hypothesis at the .01 (alternatively, 99th percentile level) level, which as a one-tailed test is $\alpha = .005$. Now we can look up the t table. By going across the column, pick out the .005 level. Then come down along the rows until this level is matched with 16 degrees of freedom (17 observations minus 1). This will give you the critical t value of 2.921. Since our calculated t value is larger than the critical value, we can reject the null hypothesis and conclude that it is highly unlikely that they belong to the same race of people.

Comparing Two Different Series of Numbers

In the previous examples, we tested the hypothesis that *a particular sample was different from the population.* However, we may frequently need to test whether two samples are *significantly different from each other.* In the previous example, we discussed whether the remains of the ancient settlers belonged to the racial stock of the present population. In contrast, suppose we have found two sets of remains from two different time periods. We want to know whether these two groups of people came from the same stock. In such a case, we will test the null hypothesis that

$$\overline{X}_1 \neq \overline{X}_2$$

where $\overline{X}_1$ is the mean of the first series, and
$\overline{X}_2$ is the mean of the second series.

Since we are not making any assumption regarding the relative size of the difference between the two means (that is, if $\overline{X}_1 > \overline{X}_2$ or $\overline{X}_1 < \overline{X}_2$), we have to use a two-tailed test. If the number of samples (n_1 and n_2) is more than 30 for each series, we can use a Z statistic; otherwise we need to use a t statistic. To test the hypothesis that the two means are equal, the difference between the two means is converted to a standard score by dividing it by the standard deviation. That is,

$$t = \frac{\overline{X}_1 - \overline{X}_2}{\sigma_{x_1 x_2}}$$

$$(2.12)$$

Using a Computer to Calculate *t* Values

Like *Z* values, you can calculate *t* values by using MYSTAT. However, you may note that unlike the *Z* table, *t* requires specification of the alpha value as well as the degrees of freedom. Therefore, you need to create two variables, one on the desired (**ALPHA**) and the other on the degrees of freedom (**DF**).
For DOS-based machines,

1. At the MYSTAT prompt in the main command screen, type **EDIT** and then press [**Enter**].
2. Type '**ALPHA** and then press [**Enter**].
3. Type '**CRIT_T** and then press [**Enter**].
4. Press [**Home**] and place the cursor in the first cell under **ALPHA**.
5. Type in the desired levels of **ALPHA**.
6. Type '**DF** and then press [**Enter**].
7. Type in the degrees of freedom.
8. Press [**Esc**] to move to the command line.
9. Type **LET CRIT_T = TIF(ALPHA,DF)** and then press [**Enter**].

For Apples,

1. Create two variables **ALPHA** and **DF** in the data file.
2. Drag down **Editor** and select **MATH**.
3. Type **CRITT** in the box to the left of **Set**.
4. Click on **Select** to choose **TIF()** in the **to** box.
5. Place your cursor within the brackets of **TIF()** and click on **Select** to choose **ALPHA**. Type in a comma (**,**) and then select **DF**. This will now look like

	Variable		Variable or Expression
Set	CRITT	to	TIF(ALPHA,DIF)

6. Click on **OK** and MYSTAT will calculate the column of critical *t* values.

where $\overline{X}_1 - \overline{X}_2$ is the difference between the two means, and

$\sigma x_1 x_2$ is the standard deviation of the sampling distribution of the difference between two means.

If the *t* statistic is applicable, its degree of freedom is given by $(n_1 + n_2 - 2)$, where n_1 is the number of sample observations in series 1 and n_2 is the number of sample observations in series 2.

Comparing a Sample with the Population

Suppose the public schools in your district are experimenting with a special education program designed to lower absenteeism among students. The school officials show a 12% decrease in the average percentage of students absent per day in the district's 10 schools. However, the critics doubt that the program has much effectiveness in lowering absenteeism. We have to settle the issue. Therefore, we form the null hypothesis that

$$\overline{X} \neq \mu.$$

That is, the sample average $(\overline{X})$ is no different than the overall average (μ) of all the schools in the region. We know that the average absenteeism among students is 5% for the schools in the region. The averages for the sample of 10 schools are as follows:

School	Rate of Absenteeism
1	4
2	3
3	4
4	5
5	3
6	9
7	2
8	3
9	3
10	8

To solve the problem with the help of MYSTAT, you must first enter the data on school absenteeism. Since MYSTAT, while conducting a t test, compares two independent variables, you will have to create a column consisting solely of the population average. This, in effect, will create the following table:

School	Rate of Absenteeism	Regional Average
1	4	5.0
2	3	5.0
3	4	5.0
4	5	5.0
5	3	5.0
6	9	5.0
7	2	5.0
8	3	5.0
9	3	5.0
10	8	5.0

When we do a pair-wise t test between the rate of absenteeism and the regional average, MYSTAT gives us the following output:

Paired samples t test on **ABSENTEE** vs. **AVERAGE** with 10 cases
Mean difference = -0.600
SD difference = 2.319

T = .818
DF = 9
Prob = .434

The results indicate that the *t* ratio is .818, which at 9 degrees of freedom shows a probability factor far less than the required 95% level of confidence. Therefore, we cannot reject the null hypothesis and agree with the critics that the innovators in the sample schools still cannot lay claim to a significant decrease in absenteeism among students.

Once the data have been inserted in the program, the DOS-based machines test the hypothesis with the command

TTEST [<VAR1>,<VAR2>,<....>]

where, in our example, **VAR1** is **ABSENTEE** and **VAR2** is the **AVERAGE**.
For MacIntosh, drag down **Analyze** and click on the **Ttest** icon. Then **Select** the two variables, which will now show in the **Variables** box. Click on **OK**.

Since we have the observations of the two series, we know their means. However, the question arises, What is the standard deviation of the distribution of the means? If there are reasons to believe that the standard deviations of the two sample series are, in fact, equal, the standard deviation of the combined series is calculated as

$$\sigma_{x_1 x_2} = \sqrt{\frac{n_1 S_1^2 + n_2 S_2^2}{n_1 + n_2 - 2}} \sqrt{\frac{n_1 + n_2}{n_1 n_2}}. \tag{2.13}$$

If, on the other hand, there is no reason to believe that the two standard deviations are the same, then we should use the following formula:

$$\sigma_{x_1 x_2} = \sqrt{\frac{s_1^2}{n_1 - 1} + \frac{s_2^2}{n_2 - 1}}. \tag{2.14}$$

Let us consider a numerical example. Suppose we have two series with the following characteristics:

	Series A	Series B
Mean	25.0 ($\overline{X}_1$)	20.6 ($\overline{X}_2$)
Standard deviations	5.75 (s_1)	6.05 (s_2)
Number of observations	28 (n_1)	16 (n_2)

If we believe that the two standard deviations are equal, then by using equation (2.13), we can estimate the pooled standard deviation as

$$\sigma_{x_1 x_2} = \sqrt{\frac{28(5.75)^2 + 16(6.05)^2}{28 + 16 - 2}} \quad \sqrt{\frac{28 + 16}{28 \times 16}} = .589.$$

By substituting this estimated number in equation (2.12), we get

$$t = \frac{25.0 - 20.6}{.589} = \frac{4.4}{.589} = -5.77.$$

Since t has 42 degrees of freedom $(28 + 16 - 2)$, the corresponding probability value for alpha = .025 is approximately equal to 2.02. Since our calculated t score, 5.77, falls outside the critical region of 2.02, we can reject the null hypothesis that the two means are equal.

If there is no reason to believe that the two standard deviations are the same, by using equation (2.14) we estimate the pooled standard deviation to be

$$\sigma_{x_1 x_2} = \sqrt{\frac{(5.75)^2}{28 - 1} + \frac{(6.05)^2}{16 - 1}} = 1.91.$$

By plugging in 1.91 in equation (2.12), we get t value = 4.4/1.91 = 2.30. Again, this number is greater than 2.02, so we can reject the null hypothesis.

Unless there is some special reason to believe that the two standard deviations are equal, when comparing two series, you should not assume that they are the same.

Let us continue with our example of the school district. Suppose that we have two sets of schools that experimented with two different programs to reduce absenteeism. The question is whether the difference between the two schools is statistically significant. Therefore, our null hypothesis is

$$\overline{X}_1 \neq \overline{X}_2.$$

The individual average absenteeisms for the two sets of schools are as follows:

School	Rate of Absenteeism in Group A	Regional Average in Group B
1	4	9
2	3	5
3	4	6
4	5	4
5	3	9
6	9	9
7	2	7
8	3	3
9	3	4
10	8	10

The output of the t *test is as follows:*

Paired samples *t* test on GROUP A vs. GROUP B with 10 cases

Mean difference = –2.200
SD difference = 2.394

T = 2.905
DF = 9
Prob = .017
        56

> These results indicate that the difference between the two means is statistically significant at a 95 % level of confidence.
> The MYSTAT commands for getting these results are the same as comparing a sample mean with the population mean, described earlier.

The χ² (the Chi-Squared) test

From the preceding examples, you can see that if we are confronted with a problem such as determining whether a subgroup is significantly different from the larger population, we can use the *Z* test (provided, of course, that we know the population mean and the standard deviation). On the other hand, if we do not know the population values but are aware of two different groups, and we want to know if they are "truly" different from each other, we will use the Student's *t* test. In contrast to these two common forms of hypothesis testing, we frequently encounter the situation in which we may be interested in finding out whether an observed phenomenon is significantly distinct from its expected behavior.

Suppose the Metropolitan Transit Authority (MTA), which employs 300 drivers, has the task of training new recruits and periodically retraining older operators. The MTA used to operate an in-house driver training school. However, in a cost-cutting mood, it is experimenting with replacing trainers with a newly developed computer training method. By this method, trainees will sit in front of a terminal, go through each lesson, and at the end answer multiple choice questions. If they pass, they will move on to the next section, and will ultimately pass the entire theoretical portion of their training program. This computer-based program is attractive to management since it offers cost savings on salaries and benefits, and the training school can remain open 24 hours, thereby allowing the drivers of all shifts to come at their own convenience and train themselves. As a consultant, your task is to determine whether the system is acceptable to the drivers of MTA. You conducted a survey that asked the drivers whether they were

a. Enthusiastic about learning through a computer.

b. Indifferent between the computer and the training school.

c. Upset about the change and would prefer the old training school.

Since fear of computers is likely to be related to an individual's age, I decided to classify the trainees according to their age and then look at the survey responses. I have presented the data in the form of a matrix, which is known as a **contingency table** (see Table 2.12). In this table, the numbers next to the word *observed* represent the actual number of responses corresponding to the attitude toward computer assisted training, classified by the gender of the respondent.

You will also notice that below each observed frequency of responses there is an entry for the expected responses. This expected response is based on the hypothesis that there is no age bias in the acceptance of computer assisted training. Thus, the two figures are exactly the same proportion as the two classifying variables (sex and attitude toward computer). This expected number is derived by multiplying the column total (known as the *marginal*) with the row total for each cell and dividing by the overall total (the total number of trainees = 300). Thus, the expected value for the female trainees who like computers is calculated by

$$\text{Expected value} = \frac{\text{Column marginal} \times \text{Row marginal}}{\text{Total frequency}} = \frac{135 \times 55}{300} \simeq 52.$$

The logic for this operation is that if preference for the computer does not depend on the gender of the respondent, then the females will prefer it exactly in the same proportion as all those who prefer the computer.

After we have determined the expected value for each cell, we can look into the difference between the actual and the expected values. Similar to the other probability distributions, the sum of the squared differences between actual and expected values is also distributed along a theoretical probability distribution, called χ^2 or **chi-squared**. This is written as

$$\chi^2 = \Sigma \frac{f_o^{\ i} - f_e^{\ i}}{f_e^{\ i}}$$

where f_o^i is the observed value of the cell i, and

Table 2.12 Example of a Contingency Table

Sex of the Trainees	Likes Computers	Indifferent	Does Not Like Computers	Total
Females	Observed: 15	Observed: 10	Observed: 30	55
	Expected: 25	Expected: 13	Expected: 17	
Males	Observed: 120	Observed: 60	Observed: 65	245
	Expected: 110	Expected: 57	Expected: 78	
Total	135	70	95	**300**

f_e^i is the expected value of the cell i.

Thus we can write the formula as

$$\chi^2 = \Sigma \frac{(\text{Observed - Expected})^2}{\text{Expected}}$$

$$= \frac{(15-25)^2}{25} + \frac{(10-13)^2}{13} + \frac{(30-17)^2}{17} + \frac{(120-110)^2}{110} + \frac{(60-57)^2}{57} + \frac{(65-78)^2}{78}$$

$$= 14.25.$$

Like the t distribution, the χ^2 distribution varies with the degrees of freedom. For the χ^2 distribution, the degrees of freedom are calculated by (the number of columns −1) × (number of rows - 1). Thus the degrees of freedom for our example are

df = (column − 1) × (row − 1) = (3 − 1) × (2 − 1) = 2 × 1 = 2.

Now we can look up the chi-squared distribution given in Appendix E. As you can see for 3 degrees of freedom, the critical value at the .05 level is 7.815. Since our calculated chi-squared value 14.25 is greater than this number, we can safely conclude that the results show a definite sex bias in the acceptance of computer-based training for the MTA bus drivers. You may notice here that in this case, we did not need to know anything at all about the mean and the standard deviations of either the sample or the general population. This is the strength of this test. Also, you should note that whereas t and Z distributions compare the difference between only two values, the χ^2 distribution measures the significance of all the cells jointly. Therefore, it is called a *joint probability distribution*.

Testing for Correlation: Pearson's r

Often you may wonder if two sets of data are correlated. Throughout the ages, scientific knowledge has been gained by patient observers discovering close associations between two phenomena. Thus, the ancient astronomers noted that the tides change with the change in the lunar cycle. In the area of social science research, the *nature* and *extent* of association between two variables are often the subject of inquiry.

We may want to know if being a victim of child abuse is correlated with later criminal behavior. The nature of correlation between two variables is described as positive or negative. If the presence of abuse is linked with criminal behavior, it is called a **positive correlation**. On the other hand, if we find that a child's academic achievement is lowered with the presence of an abusive relationship, this is an example of a **negative correlation**.

The extent or the strength of correlation between two variables can be explained with the help of a diagram (Figure 2.17). The correlation between two variables, yellow and blue, is shown as the area of intersection. The larger the green area, the stronger the correlation. If the correlation is perfect, then the entire circle is green. In contrast, when they are not at all correlated, they will form two distinct circles, as in the right-hand panel. We can measure this area of correlation with the help of **Pearson's r**, or simply **correlation coefficient**. Suppose we have two sets of variables, X and Y. The correlation coefficient between them is measured by the formula

$$\text{Correlation coefficient} = \frac{\Sigma\left(X_i - \overline{X}\right)\left(Y_i - \overline{Y}\right)}{\sqrt{\Sigma\left(X_i - \overline{X}\right)^2 \Sigma\left(Y_1 - \overline{Y}\right)^2}}$$

The correlation coefficient is equal to 1 when there is a perfect positive correlation; is –1 when there is a perfect negative correlation, and is 0 when there is no correlation at all.

In reality, however, the relationship between two variables is seldom perfect. Therefore, you may wonder if the calculated coefficient is statistically significant. One of the advantages of the correlation coefficient is that it can be used to test the hypothesis that two variables are correlated. To test this hypothesis, r has to be converted into a t statistic by using

$$t = \frac{r\sqrt{n-2}}{\sqrt{1-r^2}}$$

where n is the size of the sample.

For example, the correlation between X and Y has been found to be .65, with a sample of 26 observations. Since the correlation is less than perfect, you can formulate the null hypothesis that there is no correlation between the two variables. That is,

Figure 2.17 The Extent of Correlation between Two Variables

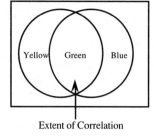

Extent of Correlation

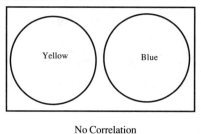

No Correlation

H_1: $r > 0$
H_0: $r \leq 0$.

By using the preceding formula, you can calculate the t as

$$t = \frac{.65\sqrt{26 - 2}}{\sqrt{1 - .4225}} = 5.51.$$

Since there are 26 observations, the degrees of freedom for the t test are $26 - 1 = 25$. The critical value for t at a 5% level of confidence for 15 df is 2.060. Since our calculated t statistic is greater than this critical value, we can reject the null hypothesis.

The Risks of Making a Mistake in Hypothesis Testing

While hypothesis testing under uncertain conditions, we run the risk of (1) rejecting the null hypothesis when it is, in fact, true, or (2) accepting a false hypothesis. If we reject a true hypothesis, we incur **type I error**; while **type II error** is created when a false hypothesis is accepted as true. This dilemma can be explained best with the following matrix:

Decision	Hypothesis Is True	Hypothesis Is False
Reject hypothesis	**Type I error**	Correct decision
Accept hypothesis	Correct decision	**Type II error**

Many public sector decisions affecting the health and welfare of citizens are based on the statistical reasonings of hypothesis testing. Therefore, the cost of an erroneous decision can be enormous. Suppose we are considering school funding based on the attendance record of pupils. A particular school shows a higher than average absentee rate, which puts it at risk for losing part of its revenue from the government. If we reject the hypothesis that the school is failing to provide a rewarding education system to keep students in class, and the hypothesis is indeed true, we will be wasting public funds on an inefficient (at least by this particular measure) institution. On the other hand, if we accept the null hypothesis and find the school negligent of its duties, when in fact its attendance record is not worse than the other schools in the district, then we will be inflicting undue pain on a school.

Therefore, in our determination of the decision rules we try to minimize these two errors. Unfortunately, the dilemma is that these two errors are inversely related. That is, when we want to reduce type I error, we create more of type II error. Thus, if we want to give the benefit of the doubt to the individual schools, we stand to encourage poor schools by failing to take punitive measures. On the other hand, if we become extremely strict about attendance records in determining school funding, we inflict unnecessary punishment on some otherwise deserving schools.

In statistics, the type I error is the chosen level of significance, or the alpha. Therefore, when we choose the alpha level .05, we make sure that we will falsely reject a true hypothesis only 5% of the time. If we lower the significance level to .01, we reduce the chance of accepting a false hypothesis but increase the probability that we will inadvertently reject a true one.

The choice of the significance level depends on the type of problem under consideration and the consequences of rejecting a true hypothesis. The criterion for accepting a hypothesis is rather conservative, and, given a choice, we would rather err on the side of the status quo than make a false move. An example may clarify the dilemma. In the early 1990s, the Food and Drug Administration (FDA) came under fire from two different groups for two diametrically opposite reasons. On the one hand, the FDA was accused of taking too long to test and approve for sale experimental drugs for AIDS. On the other hand, the FDA was heavily criticized for approving silicone gels for breast implants too quickly without proper testing. If we are dealing with a problem that requires utmost safety, we would be better off setting the level of significance as small as possible (say, at .001). However, it is matter of common practice to set the confidence level at 95% (alpha equal to .05) for most research and policy analysis.

Steps toward Hypothesis Testing

1. Check theories relating to the comparability of the variables for testing.
2. State the null hypothesis clearly, making sure of the opposite hypothesis.
3. Specify the significance level of α.
4. Specify whether to use a Z or a t test.
5. Compute the value of the test statistic.
6. Draw your conclusion regarding the rejection or nonrejection of the null hypothesis.

Subjective Probability

In our everyday lives, all of us make subjective judgments about uncertain situations. We appraise the future by assigning chance factors or odds. Although in life it is often sufficient to state that "it is likely that the task will be completed within the next week," or "there is a good possibility that the shipment will not arrive on time," in professional work, these vague chance factors must often be expressed in numerical terms. Thus, it is more useful to know that an expert assigns a 30% chance of a certain legislation passing Congressional scrutiny, or an 80% probability of a survey's results being completed by next Thursday, than simply knowing the odds in qualitative terms ("small chance" or "highly probable"). This assignment of numerical value gives more precision to the statement and, as such, can be compared to the assessment of some other expert. However, the question is, How do we assign probability figures to future events? While we assign probability value to an uncertain event in the future based on our individual experience and expertise, the process of correctly judging the probability is fraught with pitfalls resulting from personal biases. To understand subjective probability, we must know the sources of biases that may obscure our judgments.

Sources of Personal Biases

Sociopsychologists studying behavior under uncertainty observe that people rely on a limited number of principles to reduce the complex task of assigning probability.[5] Although these simple principles are extremely useful in the appraisal of an uncertain situation, they can sometimes lead to systematic biases that cause severe errors in judgment.

These principles, which Tversky and Kahneman call *heuristics,*[6] are similar to predicting the probability of rain by looking at the sky or judging distance by looking at the size of a distant object. Since we associate the darkness of clouds with a higher probability of rain, we may overestimate the probability during the fading daylight hours. Similarly, based on the heuristic principle that nearby objects are larger and clearer to vision than distant ones, we gauge distances with the naked eye. However, using this principle, severe errors in judgment can be made under poor visibility conditions, when objects may look farther away than they actually are. By keen observations, Tversky and Kahneman have reduced these heuristic principles for judging probability into three broad categories: **representativeness**, **availability**, and **adjustment and anchoring**. That is, when asked to make a judgment about an object or an event, people make their decisions on the basis of representativeness or how closely this event resembles another group of events. People also make subjective judgments based on availability of information when asked to predict the future development of an event. Finally, when the predictions are at variance with reality, the future appraisal is revised from the old numbers by considering the new information.

Representativeness

The first rule of assigning probability is association or representativeness. At the root of all scientific discovery is association. If we have experienced a connection between the thickness of coat in woolly caterpillars and the coldness of the coming winter, or the sunshine of a particular day when the groundhog comes out of its burrow and finds out if it can see its shadow, we predict the length of the remaining winter season. Associations such as these have led to scientific discoveries by causally linking events. At the same time, reasonings along these lines have produced old folk tales and prejudices. When we cringe at the sight of a group of youths in a subway and find comfort in a group of individuals wearing business suits, we are engaging in judgment based on representativeness. Since

---

[5] Amos Tversky and Daniel Kahneman, *Science*, September 1974, Vol. 185, pp. 1124–1131.

[6] Derived from the Greek word *heuriskein*—to find out—*The New Webster Dictionary* defines *heuristics* as "teaching principles which allow students to make their own discoveries."

these associations are often based on long-term observations, in many cases our predictions turn out to be correct. However, unless we are extremely careful, a blind adherence to association can lead us to the worst kind of policy decisions resulting from biases.

Bias of Irrelevant Information.   Biases may result from our insensitivity to prior probability of outcomes. In a psychological experiment, subjects were told that a group contained 70% farmers and 30% lawyers.[7] As you can readily see, if we pick an individual at random from this group, the probability that we will find a farmer is .7. The subjects in this experiment used this prior probability information to figure out the odds of getting one or the other group in a random pick. Subjects were given worthless information on a person from this group, such as

Dick is a 30 year old man. He is married with no children. A man of high ability and high motivation, he promises to be quite successful in his field. He is well liked by his colleagues.

After reading this passage, subjects were asked to estimate the probability that Dick is a farmer. Since this information carries no information regarding Dick's profession, the subjects should have stuck to the overall probability of 70%, since that is the ratio of farmers to lawyers. Yet they ignored the prior probability and proceeded to assign 50% probability of Dick being from either group. In life, we are often misled when confronted with useless information that triggers judgments based on heuristics of representativeness and, despite the presence of prior information, decide to ignore it.

Pay Attention to the Sample Size.   The second set of problems may arise from the erroneous use of representativeness heuristics because of our insensitivity to sample size. Suppose I ask you the following question:

There are two hospitals for child delivery in your city, one large, one small. As you know, the probability of having a boy or a girl baby is 50%. Now if each hospital records the number of days in a year when the percentages of boy babies exceeded 60% of the births, which hospital would expect to have the greater frequency of days with over 60% boy babies?

You would be incorrect to pick the large hospital, or to assume that both will have an equal number of days with a high number of boy babies. This is because, as we have seen in Figure 2.9, as the number of tries increases, the samples become less likely to stray from the average probability figure. Therefore, the larger hospitals, with more births, are less likely to show a higher frequency of days with more than 60% boy births. If you made the wrong choice, take heart in the fact that many people make decisions based on such faulty statistical reasoning—including the people whose profession it is to teach statistics.

---

[7] Tversky and Kahneman, ibid.

Chances Don't Self-Correct, They Merely Dilute.   Suppose you are playing a game of cards and are losing, or you are watching your favorite hitter in baseball strike out once again. In such cases, do you reason that since you have had a string of bad luck, your luck is due for a change? If you do, you are making a biased decision that is not backed by sound statistical reasoning. This is because you are making an erroneous inference about an independent probability distribution. Recalling our discussion of the independence of probability, if you have received four heads in a row in a toss of a coin, the chances of your getting a tail does not go up on the fifth try. We often make the mistake by thinking that the chances self-correct. But the anomalies of chances are not corrected over many many tries; they are merely diluted. This is especially true for small samples. You must remember that the smaller the sample size, the less its chance of being representative of the larger population. Therefore, less faith should be placed on results based on small samples.

If You Do Not Have The Relevant Information, Do Not Predict. Suppose your department wants to complete a project within a rather tight time frame. You have been asked to recommend one out of a number of applications from a group of vendors. Since the vendors were not aware of the time constraint at the time of application, there is no mention of their ability to deliver on time. Instead the applications contain the usual: the lists of projects they have been involved in, the qualifications of the project team, and, of course, the budget.

What would you do in such a situation? You may look into their relative experience and qualification and predict their ability to meet the accelerated time deadline. If you do, you may be committing an error of judgment, which Kahneman and Tversky[8] call the error of *insensitivity to predictability*. In an experiment, some of the subjects were asked to *evaluate* the quality of lessons prepared by a group of student teachers, while other subjects were asked to *predict* the probability of success of these student teachers after five years using the same materials. When the numbers were in, the match was identical. This meant that the second group of subjects was basing its prediction of performance in the distant future on some rather flimsy information. Interestingly, these subjects were perfectly aware of the limited predictability on the basis of the available information, yet they boldly proceeded to do so anyway. In our daily lives, we often make such mistakes in subjective judgment: We boldly predict on the basis of irrelevant information, when no prediction is logically warranted.

Therefore, going back to the example of choosing a vendor, you should know that the available information tells you practically nothing about the vendors' ability to complete the job in a hurry, since this capability will depend on their present work load and their ability to devote key personnel to the project. Therefore, facing such a situation, you should get more information relevant to their ability to complete the project within the time frame. Failing this, you would be better off refraining from any kind of prediction.

---

[8] Tversky and Kahneman, ibid.

Bias of Picking the "Right" Evidence. The heuristics of representativeness require that we match the closeness of association of an event with that of a cluster whose outcomes we are aware of. Since an event may be represented by a number of characteristics, you must choose the ones that are the most significant in determining this representativeness. Therefore, there is a high degree of possibility of self-selection of evidence, or picking evidence to suit your preconceived biases. These raise particularly tough issues, especially when discussing matters of deeply held values and biases.[9] Laboratory experiments in psychology as well as in real-life situations demonstrate ample evidence of predicting on the basis of self-selecting evidence.

The Unavoidable Draw of the Mean. Suppose you are an avid but an average golfer, and you know your handicap. This morning you teed off with a fantastic drive, and you nearly got a hole in one. However, in the very next shot, you bogied and failed to put the ball in the hole from a close distance. You are disappointed. Personally, you have every reason to be disappointed. However, statistically speaking, you should not despair, since your performance simply showed that you could not beat the mean. In other words, you are simply playing your average game. If an exceptional shot is followed by another, then you would be playing at a level that is much higher than your natural average. In fact, more than 100 years ago the French mathematician Galton noted that observations have a tendency to gravitate toward the mean. He called this the *regression toward the mean.*

Ignoring the regression toward the mean is another important source of error in subjective judgment. If there is a long history of past performance, you will be much better off by predicting along the mean than along a more optimistic or pessimistic line based on some minor variations in the external condition.

Limits to Objective Reasoning: the Allais Paradox. The precepts of objective reasoning state that when faced with an uncertain outcome, choose the option that maximizes your *expected returns.* The expected return of an option is defined as the probability of winning multiplied by its reward. Thus, if I offer you $10 for calling correctly on a coin toss, your expected return is .5 X $10 = $5. Therefore, facing two options, either winning $10 in a coin toss or $25 in a roll of dice, you should stick with the coin, since the expected reward of the coin toss ($5) is greater than the roll of a die (1/6 X $25 = $4.17). Unless you are a real

---

[9] I am tempted to narrate a story about two friends to exemplify this point of a self-selection bias. One person held an unshakable faith in astrology, while the other did not. All their lives they argued about the validity of astrology. One day, the believer learned that he would have to make a long trip across the state by car. Having consulted all the relevant astrological signs, he found the most auspicious day to start his journey, only to run into a serious accident within half a mile from his home. The poor man was removed to a nearby hospital, where his friend went to greet him with his best-rehearsed arguments against believing in such superstitious nonsense. However, even before the visitor was able to say anything, the injured man looked up from his hospital bed and asked, "Now, you believe in astrology don't you? Can anybody survive such an accident? I was lucky to have consulted my chart before I started my trip. What do you think of it now?"

gambler (a risk taker), the laws of probability dictate that despite the larger reward for the dice, you should choose the coin. This is a well-accepted principle in statistics and mathematics. The French mathematician Allais showed the presence of systematic biases in subjective reasoning even among the most astute statisticians and individuals who are keenly aware of the laws of probability.[10]

The *Allais Paradox* can be explained best with an example. Suppose you are being offered two options: In the first option, you have a 100% chance (certainty) of winning $1 million; in the second option, you have a 50% chance of winning $5 million. In experiments, most people tend to choose the first option in violation of the rules of expected returns (since 1.0 X $1 million = $1 million is less than .5 X $5 million = $2.5 million). Why do people ignore the laws of probability? Because when there is a certainty or near certainty of outcome, we tend to focus more on the probability factor.

In contrast, consider two other options. In the first option, you have a one in 10,000 chance of winning $1 million, in the second, your chance of winning $20 million is one in a million. Which one would you choose? Again, contrary to the principles of statistical rationality, when probabilities are small (one in 10,000 versus one in a million) people tend to focus more on the reward than on the odds of winning. Therefore, Allais in his paradox unearthed some important systematic biases in human reasoning that may indeed prove critical in the decision-making processes of a public organization.

Availability of Information

The probability of an event taking place is often judged by the frequency of occurrence of similar events. For example, your city is considering starting its own garbage recycling plant. By considering the available information on similar ventures, you appraise its probability of success. Tversky and Kahneman call this *availability* in their judgmental heuristics. Information on similar events yields valuable clues regarding future possibility by pointing toward a more certain outcome when similar examples are numerous, and uncertain when they are less frequently available. However, in the process of information gathering, biases may creep in to cloud judgment. These biases may come because of difference in **retrievability of information**, **effectiveness of a search, biases of imaginability**, and **illusory correlation**.

Biases of Relative Retrievability. Our memory functions in a way similar to a filing cabinet. If we know where to search, we can retrieve a stored item quickly. However, information that is quite important, if filed away in a wrong place, cannot be retrieved easily. Therefore, if we associate an event with some recognizable pattern or some other event, we may retrieve this information by

[10] M. Allais, "The Foundations of a Positive Theory of Choice Involving Risk and a Criticism of the Postulates and the Axioms of the American School." (Translation of *"Fondoments d'une théorie de choix comportant un risqueet critique des pustulates et axiomes de l'eloce Americane."* Paris, CNRS). In M. Allais and O. Hogan (eds.), *Expected Utility Hypothesis and the Allais Paradox: Contemporary Discussions of Decisions under Uncertainty with Allais' Rejoinder* (Dorchet, Holland: D. Reidel, 1952).

recalling the other pattern or event. For example, most people who were alive during the assassination of President Kennedy have a vivid memory of the day. We may not recall something important that happened during the past three weeks, but we will be able to remember a great deal of events that took place over three decades ago on that tragic day. These are common patterns of human cognition. Therefore, biases in judgment can easily come in as we recall more memorable events or events associated with some other facts that made a strong impression on us. This may lead to biases of availability, in which relatively unimportant factors were given a higher prominence than their importance warrants. Thus, we are aware of different life-threatening diseases that put us in peril every day. However, as soon as we hear that a celebrity has been inflicted with a particular disease, or we come to know about the illness of a friend or relative, our awareness regarding that disease goes up, along with fear and, often, hysteria. As a result, we may focus on the probability of getting that particular affliction more than is warranted by our personal habits, life style, or genetic history, and we may disregard some other more plausible source of illness.

Effectiveness of Search.   Have you ever conducted a computer search for information through a library information retrieval system? Suppose you are looking for information on a certain subject (say, drug abuse in North Carolina). If you are able to define the key words for this search, you will be rewarded with information on a number of highly relevant works. However, if your choice of key words is too wide (for example, simply *drugs*), you will be inundated with irrelevant information. On the other hand, if your key words are too narrowly defined, you may miss out on a large number of important works on the subject. Similarly, in our minds we formulate the key words to retrieve information effectively. Therefore, if our choice of reference points is not clear for a search for relevant association, we may not be able to recognize an important pattern for a good appraisal of future possibility.

Biases of Imaginability.   If you are considering undertaking a risky venture, you would start imagining the difficulties and the advantages of such an undertaking. Naturally, you would like to consider a full slate of possibilities before taking any action. Therefore, your considerations are restricted by the limits of your imagination. If there is a project for which the relative risks and payoffs are difficult to imagine, biases may creep in. These sorts of biases seem to be most prevelant when a decision must be made for an extraordinary event (such as disaster preparedness, which may include such catastrophic and unpredictable events as floods, tornadoes, earthquakes, or large-scale riots).

Illusory Correlations and Organizational Myths.   People often make decisions based on long-held beliefs born out of illusory correlations. For example, do you believe that you have a "lucky" article of clothing or a color that helps you during an uncertain situation? If you do, you may be guilty of illusory correlation, which is described in Latin as *post hoc, ergo propter hoc,* or "before this, therefore this." In other words, you are taking past cooccurrences as signs of correlation. For example, if I was wearing a shirt while scoring a decisive victory in a crucial tennis match, and I conclude that my win was due to the wearing of this particular shirt, then I am guilty of attributing *causality* between the two events where, in fact, there is none.

The errors in judgment caused by illusory correlation are often deep rooted and cannot be corrected easily. We create myths based on such assertions that affect not only our individual decisions but also decisions made at the organizational level. The classic case of organizational decisions made on the basis of a paranoid world view can be found in some of the taped conversations of President Richard Nixon and his aids during the Watergate crisis. Time and again, they seem to have made decisions that were rooted in this fortress mentality, and this contributed to the ultimate demise of the Nixon administration. Similarly, the vision of the decision maker in any organization can be clouded by myths of illusory correlation created by a single key member, or by the existence of collective myths created by a number of people within an organization.

Biases of Adjustment and Anchoring

In the process of gauging the subjective probability of an event, we are frequently influenced by the starting number. For example, in a popular television game show, a group of contestants are asked to judge the price of an item. If you notice, the first contestant's answer seems to have a great deal of influence over the answers of the rest of the contestants. Contestants appear to be calibrating their own answers by the previous answers. In real life, we often arrive at a quantitative judgment based on an initial number. This tendency can cause serious errors in assessment of an event's probability.

For instance, let us suppose that you and a colleague are trying to assess the probability that a proposed project will experience a cost overrun. The last project that you managed went over its allocated budget, while your colleague was able to keep expenditures down to the allowable level. Who do you think will have a more pessimistic appraisal of future cost overrun? Correcting for all the other external factors, one who starts out with a high initial estimation will be prone to have a higher appraisal of probability, and vice versa. Psychologists have conducted a number of interesting experiments that corroborate the fallacy in reasoning that occurs as a result of our natural proclivity to be influenced by the initial number.

Biases in Subjective Judgment: Some Concluding Thoughts

In this section, I have attempted to show some of the major sources of cognitive biases that can produce faulty assessment of subjective probability. The list presented here is long but by no means exhaustive. Thanks to the prolific work of social psychologists, we are learning more about these natural biases. The most important conclusion that we can draw from this discussion is that these distortions of judgment are not caused by self-serving motivations such as wishful thinking, reward, or punishment. Instead, they are rooted in our cognition and information processing. Therefore, these biases cannot be eliminated by making the process of decision making internally consistent. The rule of consistency tells us that if we are faced with the same situation twice, we should reach the same conclusion. As you can see, if the method of information processing contains systematic biases, we will merely be consistent in our erroneous judgments. Hence, most importantly, while embarking on a subjective assessment of probability, we should be highly aware of these internal biases.

Key Words

Adjustment and anchoring bias	Mutually exclusive probability
Asymptotic property	Normal distribution
Availability bias	Null hypothesis
Bias in probability	Objective probability
Central limits theorem	One-tailed test
Central tendency	Range
Confidence interval	Relative frequency
Critical value	Representativeness bias
Degrees of freedom	Skewness
Dispersion	Standard deviation
Hinge	Standard normal distribution
Hypothesis testing	Stem-leaf method
Independent probability	Subjective probability
Level of significance	t test
Mean	Two-tailed test
Mean absolute deviation	Variance
Median	Weighted median
Midspread	Weighted mean
Mode	Z test

Exercises

1. What is the implication of the name *descriptive statistics*? What are the measures of central tendency and dispersion? Explain the term *central tendency*. Why do we face controversies regarding the appropriate choice of a measure of central tendency?

2. Consider the following series, and choose the most appropriate measure of central tendency for each series. Explain your choices.

Series A	Series B	Series C	Series D
10	5	3	5
11	8	7	7
9	11	9	9
27	13	25	11
16	16	7	9
15	18	7	7
17	21	7	5

Suggestion: You may want to plot the data to determine the patterns.

3. What do we measure by the coefficient of variation? Give an example of its possible use in public sector decision making. Using this method, comment on the relative dispersions of the four series of data presented in the preceding table.

4. Which one of the measures of central tendency is most commonly used in mathematics and statistics? Why?

5. What is an objective probability? What is a bias in objective probability?

6. What is a subjective probability? What are the main sources of biases that an individual faces in assessing subjective probability?

7. With an appropriate example, discuss the use of the central limits theorem as the foundation of statistical reasoning. Explain how it helps build a model of hypothesis testing.

8. The average SAT score for your state is 850, with a standard deviation of 65. The high school in your area has an average score of 980. Is this school an exception? Justify your answer.

9. From the information given in exercise 8, provide a confidence interval to develop a criterion for identifying schools with exceptionally good and unususaly poor records.

10. Property tax is levied on the appraised market value of a property. However, it is often alleged that while for the lower priced homes the appraised value is quite close to the market value (revealed when the property is actually sold), for the upper priced homes the appraised values are significantly lower than their market values. To investigate this allegation, the city of Masters conducted a study that found that for the 40 lower priced homes the ratio of assessed value/market value = A/M = .89 with a standard deviation .09. For a sample of 40 high-priced homes this ratio was .65 with a standard deviation of .15.

   Do you agree that the poor home owners in the city are carrying an unfair property tax burden?

11. The financial manager for the city of Masters is considering a switch from the existing money market fund to a new one. On the basis of the presented data series, do you believe that the difference between the two is significant enough to warrant a change?

Year	Existing	New
1	7.5	6.7
2	8.0	9.3
3	7.9	5.5
4	8.5	10.9
5	7.0	5.3
6	9.2	12.6
7	8.2	6.7
8	7.4	4.3
9	8.8	10.7
10	8.0	12.9

12. The city of Masters has been conducting a survey of police response to an emergency call. For comparison purposes, a similar city has been chosen. The following table shows the distribution of response time during a typical week. Is there any reason to believe that there is any significant difference in the record of the two cities?

Distribution of Police Response Time

Response time (minutes)	Masters	The other city
1–3	23	45
3–5	62	72
5–8	41	59
8–10	38	43
10–15	16	32
15–25	3	21
25–35	0	13
35–60	0	7

13. Let us continue with the example of Metropolitan Transit Authority's new computer assisted driver training program. Having looked at the possible sex bias in the acceptance of the program, suppose you are trying to look at the possibility of age bias. Your survey resulted the following table. By using chi-squared distribution, determine whether age imposes an additional barrier to the use of computers in the MTA.

Age of the Trainees	Likes Computers	Indifferent	Does not Like Computers	Total
18–25	30	25	10	65
26–45	65	30	60	155
46 and over	15	10	55	80
Total	**110**	**65**	**125**	**300**

14. Suppose we have observed 10 individuals to establish the hypothesis that education has a strong correlation with income. Consider the following data, and test the hypothesis:

Education (years of schooling)	12	18	6	17	19	12	16	16	20	8
Income (000)	25	35	22	56	85	20	45	48	65	20

15. Write an essay on subjective probability. Suppose you are attempting to determine the odds of your favorite football team winning the Superbowl. What kinds of biases may cloud your judgment?

Chapter 3

Source of Data

Where Do We Find the Numbers?

The first question that confronts an empirical researcher is, Where do I get the necessary information? A recent survey by the library of a major university discovered what many in academia suspected: The vast majority of students do not know how to use library resources to obtain necessary information for writing a report or a term paper. In chapter 1, we discussed the framework of an objective analysis. We noted that the first rule of an objective analysis is the definition of goals or an objective. Similarly, *before* looking for data, you must define precisely the problem you want to investigate. Thus, if your task is to determine the effectiveness of a particular public policy, you need to decide precisely how you are going to measure the effectiveness of the program. If there are several measures, you will have to decide which of the alternate measures to use in the analysis. After deciding on the measure, you must collect the information. The required information may or may not be readily available. If the information is available in published form, it is called **secondary data** (that is, data collected by someone other than the researcher for the specific use of the project). If, on the other hand, you must collect the data on your own, you are using **primary data**. Therefore, this chapter is divided into two broad sections. The first section deals with the issues of measurement; while the second discusses primary and secondary sources of data.

What Are We Measuring?

We are quantifying animals. We express in number the degree of heat, the amount of rainfall, the speed at which we drive our cars. We attempt to express intelligence in terms of numbers. We collect information on income, unemployment, crime, political violence, even the extent of democratic values and the level of authoritarian personality. At times it seems that we tend to put a numerical value on everything except some of our innermost feelings, such as love, happiness, and anger, although quite often in various popular magazines we find interesting attempts at measuring things like sensuality, desirability, and so on based on answers to a set of questions. We aim to assign numbers to the properties or attributes of various phenomena, events, or other kinds of individual attributes according to some specific rules. Controversies, however, often arise regarding how good the measurements actually are. Therefore, let us first discuss the various types of measurements and then concentrate on the relative merits of these measuring units.

Types of Measurement

Phenomena to be measured can be assigned values according to nominal, ordinal, interval, or ratio scales. Of these measurements, the weakest form of assigning numerical value is called a **nominal** scale. For example, while filling out census or many other kinds of application forms, we are often asked to identify our ethnic background. Each ethnic group is assigned a number (1 through 5, say), numeral (I through V), or an alphabetic classification (A through E). These are the weakest forms of classification since these numbers are not amenable to mathematical treatment; they do not yield any insight to their relative comparability, such as group B is closer to A in any attribute or physical quality than is group E. Therefore, for these kinds of measuring scales, the assigning of numbers is devoid of any intrinsic meaning. In other words, while classifying individuals by gender, it would not matter if we assign the value 1 to male and 2 to female, or vice versa.

Some phenomena are comparable to each other such that we can arrange them according to some quality but are not able to tell precisely the distances among them. For example, we may rank order the presidential candidates according to their political philosophies or according to their chances of being elected, but we may not be able to tell that candidate A is 2.35 times more conservative than candidate B. This process of ranking is called an **ordinal** scale. It is important to note that since numbers for ordinal rankings do not carry any specific meaning, the direction of their assigned value does not make a difference. Thus among five candidates, the most conservative candidate may be assigned the value 1 or 5 without any consequence, as long as the ordering is in sequence. As you can see, ordinal rankings are stronger than nominal ones, since we can compare the relative position of the case in question (the conservativeness of the presidential candidates in this example).

Arrangement by **interval** scale offers us the maximum amount of flexibility in comparing the cases, both according to arrangement of ranking and the actual distance between any two cases. Thus, if the candidates are assigned a number in an interval scale, we can compare them not only by saying that A is more conservative than B, but that A is 2.35 times more conservative than B. Because of this desirable quality, the temptation to express orderings according to interval scale is strong. As a consequence, a great deal of effort has been directed toward constructing interval scale measures for various kinds of social, political, and economic phenomena. Thus, the various conservative and liberal Congressional watchdogs assign numbers to individual members of the Senate and the House of Representatives by their voting patterns. In other studies, countries have been given numerical values for their development potential, degree of democratization, and level of political violence.[1] The Amnesty International assigns numerical values to nations according to their adherence to human rights; the Federal Bureau of Investigation (FBI) releases data on crime index for various cities; Rand McNally has rated the relative desirability of the cities; and rent

---

[1] Professors Irma Adelman and Cynthia Morris created an index for measuring development potential. See "Performance Criteria for Evaluating Economic Development Potentials," *Quarterly Journal of Economics*, 1968, Vol. 62. Ted Gurr (*Polity II* database (Interuniversity Consertium), 1989) quantified the degree of "democratization" of countries. Among several others, Douglas Hibbs, Jr., *Mass Political Violence: A Cross-National Causal Analysis* (New York; Wiley, 1973) and Dipak Gupta, *Economics of Political Violence* (New York: Praeger, 1990) developed indexes of political instability.

control ordinances have been scaled according their degree of restrictiveness. These are but a few examples.[2]

The interval scale, however, may not have a fixed and well-defined zero at which point we may say that the quality we are measuring in the cases does not exist. For example, in the progressive assignment of points (the higher the number, the higher the level of liberalism) to classify members of the U.S. Senate according to liberal orientation, the Senator with a score of zero must show no traces of liberal value whatsoever, an attribute rarely seen in human beings. On the other hand, we may order various school districts by the percentage of minority enrollment, or airlines according to the ratio of delayed to total flight arrivals. In each of these instances, the value of zero will have a specific meaning (a school district with no minority students or an airline that is always on time). This is called a **ratio** scale.

How Valid Are the Measuring Scales?

The problems of measurement are many. If we want to measure a phenomena that has a physical manifestation and only one dimension, our efforts are largely free of controversy. For example, measuring an individual's height or weight is done without any trouble, as long as we are measuring a unidimensional phenomenon (either height or weight). However, we are likely to run into a bit more trouble if we attempt to quantify the "largeness" of a person, a measure that must encompass both height and weight. Therefore, if we want to express a phenomenon that has no obvious physical manifestation, such as an individual's intelligence, attitude, or quality of life, or the regional inflation rate, national growth potential, or international political instability, we are treading dangerous water. However, even measuring strictly physical single attribute phenomena can be controversial. For example, Gleick[3] gives an interesting example in a popular book on mathematical theory of chaos. In the encyclopedias and other reference books, one frequently encounters various measures of national geography, such as the total square miles of land area or the total shoreline. Gleick points out that measurement of the jagged shoreline must vary with the size of the yardstick. When cartographers do measure shorelines, they are only using an approximation. Consider Figure 3.1. Suppose I am using a long yardstick to measure the shoreline. By looking at Figure 3.1, you can tell that this is only an approximation, since this long stick is missing all the jagged edges that it cannot measure. Therefore, by using a smaller stick, I can try to be more precise. In so doing, the measurement of the shoreline will register an increase, as this more precise instrument will include areas that were

[2] Dipak K. Gupta and Louis M. Rea, "A Quantitative Comparison of Second Generation Rent Control Ordinances," *Urban Affairs Quarterly*, Vol. 19, No. 3, March 1984, pp. 395–408.

[3] J. Gleick, *Chaos* (New York: Viking Books, 1987).

Figure 3.1 Measuring the English Shoreline

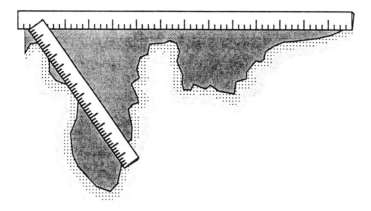

not measured before. However, this smaller stick does not give us a complete measurement, as it misses out on areas smaller than itself. Clearly, as we reduce the size of the yardstick, we increase the total shoreline. Therefore, when the size of the stick is very close to zero, the total shoreline of Great Britain becomes infinitely long!

We live in an imperfect world. Therefore, along with everything else, we must live with the shortcomings of our indicators. The only recourse we have is to be aware of their inherent biases and problems, and be extremely careful in their interpretation. With these words of caution, we may examine the types of data and their sources.

The Primary Data: Doing a Survey

Often, the kind of information you need is not available in archival records. In this case, you may want to engage in collecting information on your own; you need to conduct a survey. The study of collecting unbiased information in a systematic way is called **sampling theory**. Sampling theory helps us determine the most cost-efficient way to derive unbiased information. On the basis of this theory of sampling, a **survey** is **designed**. The study of sampling theory and survey design is a field unto itself, for which a voluminous literature exists. Therefore, in this section, I will introduce you to some of the most basic concepts.[4]

---

[4] For one one of the most easily readable explanations of survey design and survey methodology, see Louis M. Rea and Richard Parker, *Designing and Conducting Survey. A Comprehensive Guide* (San Fransico: Jossey-Bass, 1992).

The starting point in any survey design is the question of **population**. The term *population* is defined as the entire target group from which the necessary information is to be extracted. For instance, let us suppose that we are designing a survey to determine whether the residents of a small town are willing to accept a proposed prison facility in the town's outskirts. In such a case, we may define all the adult residents of the city as the *population* of this survey. Or, if we are trying to figure out the effect on the restaurant business of a new state policy of banning smoking, all the food-serving establishments in the state will form the population of the survey. As you can tell from these examples, the population of a survey will vary with the purpose of the study.

In a perfect world that does not impose any constraints on time and money, it is desirable to have a complete enumeration, or survey of each member of the population. However, in reality, we must confine our inquiry within a small group of representatives of the population, called the **sample population**. The single most important quality of the sample population is its *representativeness*. That is, how closely does this sample group represent the entire population? If it does not represent the population well, the sample population will give us biased (and therefore erroneous) information about the population, as shown in Figure 3.2.

These biases can be either **systematic** or **random**. The systematic sampling errors result from an inappropriate survey design and can be eliminated by proper understanding of the sampling theory. Random sampling errors, however, are caused by the random variations of the data, which cannot be completely eliminated but can be managed within a certain limit through proper survey design. Let us discuss these in detail.

Figure 3.2 Errors in Sampling

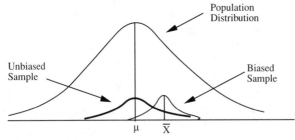

The purpose of sampling is to find the most cost-effective way to determine the attributes of a large population. For this, the sample must be representative of the population. The mean of the unbiased sample (drawn with a thicker line in this diagram) represents the "true" population mean (μ). However, as you can see, the biased sample mean ($\overline{X}$) is not representative of the population.

The Sources of Systematic Errors in Sampling

Systematic errors result from biased sampling of the population. There can be many sources of these biases. For our discussion, we identify the five most common sources of systematic sampling biases.

Inappropriate sample

If the sample group is inappropriate, it may cause the inferences to be drawn about the population to be biased. We have discussed the problem of *Literary Digest* predicting an election victory for Alf Landon in 1936, based on a telephone interview. The problem of infering with the help of a biased sample has been epitomized by an incidence in 1936. During the Presidential campaign, the now defunct *Literary Digest* conducted a telephone survey. Based on this sample of New York residents, the magazine predicted a comfortable margin of victory for Mr. Alf Landon against Franklin D. Roosevelt. However, when the actual poll results came out, FDR had won a decisive victory against his opponent. How could the survey be that wrong? The prediction was incorrect because it was based on a sample which did not properly represent the population. Since in 1936 telephone was still a novelty, restricted to the relatively affluent, it did not become a tool of universal communication as it is today. Therefore, a sample of telephone owners was an inappropriate sample for rest of the population.

This epitomizes the example of systematic bias resulting from the sample population being nonrepresentative of the actual population. Thus, if we poll the members of the Sierra Club on an environmental issue, it is highly probable that their responses may not represent the opinion of the entire population. The designer of a survey should always be on guard about this kind of systematic bias. For example, suppose you are to determine the opinion on a certain issue and you get the names of the individuals from the property tax roll. Your sample mean may diverge from your intended group, as the sample population will exclude the renter population. Also, some of the property owners may be absentee owners and may therefore inject a new twist into the problem. The elimination of this error requires an intimate knowledge of the population and the existence of biased "cells" or subgroups within it.

Self-selection Bias within the Sample

The problem of getting unbiased information will not go away even after correctly specifying the sample group. For example, you have correctly identified your sample group and have administered a detailed questionnaire. When the results come in and are tabulated, you find out that the results are biased. This may happen because of self-selection within the sample group. Thus, if I want to measure some aspect of intimate personal behavior or attitude, the respondents may be primarily those who are not squeamish about telling interviewers about their private lives. This group may turn out to be sociologically significantly different from the population. Therefore, to eliminate this problem, a researcher should always check the typical characteristics of the respondent groups with those of the population. Thus, we should make sure that the social and demographic characteristics such as age, sex, race, income, and other relevant factors of the two groups are not substantially different.

Collection Bias: Reporting and Collecting

Biases may often creep in due to the presence of some natural obstacles to reporting. For example, in several border states the issue of illegal immigration has been rather controversial. Since immigration has a tremendous impact on the region's economy, many policy analysts wished for a more accurate enumeration of the illegal immigrants and a more detailed knowledge of their socioeconomic attributes. However, for understandable reasons, samples of illegal immigrants have been underreported.

There can also be biases resulting from the mode of collection. For example, the *World Handbook of Political and Social Indicators* (1982) by Charles Taylor and Michael Jodice makes a significant contribution to scholarly research by compiling international social and political data. Yet, as the authors readily admit, much of the political data are collected from the *New York Times* and a few other published reports. Since it is obvious that these newspapers are more likely to report on events that take place in this and other Western nations than in some obscure nation in Asia or Africa, the reported series will contain systematic biases.

Errors due to Observation

In an experiment, physicist Heisenberg was trying to observe the position of subatomic particles. However, these particles were charged to make their presence known to the observer, and this charge caused them to change their original position. A social scientist or an organizational analyst is just as likely to encounter this problem, which is due to the subjects being observed. In other words, if we are told that we are being observed, we may behave differently under a laboratory scrutiny than we would in our day-to-day lives. The most celebrated example of this is the so-called Hawthorne experiment. In 1932, a group of researchers reported the results of an experiment they had been conducting for the past five years at the Hawthorne plant of the Western Electric Company. In a serendipitous finding, they discovered that people generally seem to work better and are more productive when their performance on the job is made the object of flattering attention by a group of university researchers.[5] Therefore, under such circumstances, inferences drawn from a laboratory experiment are likely to be different from reality.

---

[5] A group of researchers headed by Elton Mayo and F. J. Roelithsberger were trying to find out the level of lumination that will maximize production in a garment factory. They started with a very high degree of light and slowly reduced its intensity to see if it would influence the productivity of the workers. The workers, on the other hand, became aware of the fact that they were being observed. As the light got dimmer and dimmer, they took it as a matter of group pride and started to work even harder. Needless to say, their sensitivity toward being observed spoiled the original intent of the research. However, the results of this experiment made scholars of organizational behavior aware of the strength of group identity as a motivating force in the workplace and started the so-called humanistic school of organizational behavior.

Bias in the Survey Instrument

Survey results can be biased if the instruments (the quarters) are loaded with hidden values, which will elicit certain reaction from the respondents. For example, during the early days of the former Soviet Union's dissolution, then President Ghorbachev's government objected to a referendum in a breakaway republic that asked, "Would you like to be free or be willing to be dominated by the empirical forces of communist Russia?" Naturally, the election results were hardly ever in doubt. In public policy analysis, a faulty survey instrument can often distort the results. Thus, in a general context, few people would object to having public goods such as a clean environment, abundance of wildlife or safer and well-maintained infrastructure. When asked in a survey, people are likely to show their preference for such goods. However, this may not truly reflect the public opinion, as people are just as likely to change their minds when these same questions are asked with proper reference to their costs (especially if the marginal cost factor coming out of the individual respondents' pockets can be identified).

Further, biases will be introduced if the instruments call for subjective judgments on the part of the respondents. Thus, if asked to categorize something as "high," "low," "large," "small," etc., the subjective nature of people's judgment may stand in the way of determining the "true" opinion of the public.

Random Sampling Errors

Random or sampling errors occur because of unexplained random variations around the "true" population values. Because these variations are random (or are caused by factors that cannot be determined), they can fall in any direction around the true values. For instance, suppose you are throwing stones at the middle of a target. Some of the stones will hit the bull'seye, some will not. If you are aiming for this particular point, the stones will have a strong central tendency. Therefore, however poor a marksman you are, the stones will form a more or less normal distribution (unless, of course, your arm gets tired and creates a bias as a result), which will look like a Mexican sombrero. Similarly, if the errors are randomly distributed around the mean, in a three-dimensional situation, they will form normal distributions in any direction around the mean (μ). I have attempted to depict this in Figure 3.3. As you can see, the true population value (of, say, the

Figure 3.3 Random Sampling Errors

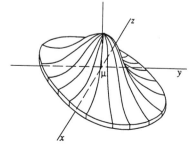

proportion of the population favoring handgun control) is μ. However, owing to the presence of random variations, the sample value may turn out to be different from this true value.

Since these variations are random, we cannot completely eliminate them. Instead, we can try to increase the precision of the sample results by reducing the random error factor. How can we do this? Recalling the discussion of the law of large numbers in the previous chapter, we can see that as the size of the sample increases, the domain of the error term will shrink, and when the number of samples approaches infinity or the sample size becomes the same as the entire population (in which case it no longer is a sample, but a complete enumeration), the sample value becomes equal to the true population value. Therefore, the problem of sampling error would prompt us to go for a census or a complete enumeration. Of course, a complete enumeration is often impossible because of the cost (both in terms of time and money). Hence, we need to design a survey that is within our financial means and provides us with a result with a tolerable degree of precision. For instance, you may notice that whenever the results of a survey are reported, they are accompanied by the corresponding error level. We will discuss this more at length when we tackle the question of sample size later in this chapter. Let us now discuss the various methods of choosing the sample population.

Survey Design

Armed with the knowledge of possible pitfalls, we may discuss the process of designing a survey. This process essentially centers around four questions: (1) Who gets to be picked? (2) How many get picked? (3) Which questions should be asked? and (4) What is the mode of polling?

Choosing the Sample Population

Before starting to poll the sample group of individuals, you must determine how you are going to pick them out of the total population. The determination of the process of choosing the sample is called *sample design*. Keeping in mind that the larger the sample, the closer you are to the true population values, you must determine the sample design with an eye to the cost of sampling and the ease of administration. Let us discuss these questions systematically.

There are numerous methods of choosing the group of subjects. In this section, I will present a number of such methods. These methods may be called *objective* or probability-based sampling, in which case the sample subjects are drawn according to some set rules to maximize the probability of achieving an accurate account of the population. In contrast, one may also engage in the *judgmental* method of sampling, in which one utilizes some specialized knowledge about the population to get to the correct answer.

For example, suppose that for an urban renewal project, your city needs to make an inventory of the buildings within a proposed redevelopment district. The task of compiling this inventory has fallen on a team of 10 people in the building inspection department. If you want to estimate how long it would take them to complete the task, you may poll all the members of the team and average their responses. However, suppose you know that within the group, there are two key members who are most knowledgeable about the process. Therefore, without wasting your time by chasing all 10 members of the group, you may simply poll the two most experienced members. This may actually give you a better appraisal of the time involved than by asking each member, which may, in fact, give a less than accurate measure as the voice of experience may drown in the pool of inexperienced members. However, as you can tell, this sort of judgmental method requires the pollster to possess some special knowledge of the group. Such knowledge is unusual, and since the judgmental method is inherently subjective, the objective methods are more commonly followed.

Random Sampling

The sample group is chosen by random sampling design when each element in the population has an equal chance of being picked. There are many ways of ensuring that the samples are drawn randomly, or each element has an equal chance of being picked. For example, you may use computer-generated random numbers to pick the subjects. Or, in a large metropolitan city, you may go by the listings in the telephone book (say, by choosing the tenth person on each page). You may devise many such procedures to ensure randomness. If you choose samples through a random number series, this is an example of pure random selection. However, if you choose every tenth person, this is frequently called a *systematic random sampling*, as you pick your subjects based on some preset rules. The two sample results would yield similar results, unless there is a systematic bias in the sample. For example, suppose we are checking for patterns of defect in widgets produced by a factory. We are checking every tenth widget that comes out of the production line. However, if there are a number of different machines that are manufacturing these widgets, the use of this kind of systematic sampling may inadvertently cause us to pick preponderantly from one machine. This type of unsuspected bias may cause severe problems in sampling.

A random sampling method is most likely to give us the desired results when the population is homogeneous. For example, if we are interested in gathering information on social norms and mores, a random sample may be the most appropriate design, since when it comes to determining individual attitude, each member of the society has an equal voice. However, on other issues a different kind of sample design may be in order.

Stratified Sampling

If the population is not homogeneous and is divided into distinct subgroups or *strata*, it may be better to use stratified sampling. An example may clarify the situation. Suppose a school district is considering switching from the traditional academic year to year-round schooling, with breaks distributed evenly throughout the calendar year. To assess the reaction to this proposed change, the school district wants to poll the residents of the district. If the population was homogeneous in its socioeconomic and ethnic composition, a random sample would have given the decision makers a good idea of the feelings within the community. But the population is far from homogeneous. It is fragmented along the traditional lines of income and race. Also, the district authorities are sensitive to the special needs of the single parents. In such a situation, we may identify each stratum of the society and poll the strata separately.

The design of stratified sampling faces three main challenges. For a proper sampling, we need to determine (1) how to identify the appropriate strata, (2) the method of choosing sample subjects within each stratum, and (3) the size of sample for each stratum. Of these, the most daunting problem is posed by the first question. Indeed, there is hardly a way of telling what the natural cleavages are within a community. This knowledge is derived from a deep understanding of the population under study. If you do not have that kind of a knowledge, you will be well advised to consult experts before designing the survey. Or you may recommend a small pilot survey to determine if there is any reason to believe that the population is indeed sufficiently heterogeneous (the individual group means are significantly different from each other) to warrant a stratified sampling. This pilot study may also be used to collect social, political, and demographic information on the population to identify the various strata within it.

The second and third questions are answered with relative ease. The subjects within each stratum are generally polled by the random sampling method, since the population within a stratum is likely to be homogeneous (if not, then the classification must be further fine-tuned to extract a more detailed classification of the population). Facing the third problem, researchers usually choose for a proportional representation for each stratum. Thus, if a population is characterized by five different groups, then the total sample must be divided into the five groups according to their proportion in the general population.

Cluster Sampling

When there is an extremely large population to be polled, a pollster may find it difficult (or too expensive) to include each member of the population in the list of potential subjects from which the sample is to be drawn. Instead, the pollster may decide to use a small area, which can reasonably be assumed to be the microcosm of the larger population, and concentrate on this cluster. Thus, suppose we need to examine some aspect of urban America, and we find that it is impossible to reach every city. In such a case, we may argue that a particular city (say Buffalo, New York) can serve as the "typical city." Hence, we can poll the residents of Buffalo and draw conclusions about the rest of the urban areas of the United States. This procedure begs the question of how representative the cluster is for the population. If this question can be adequately addressed, cluster sampling may provide a relatively inexpensive alternative.

When developing a cluster sample, the question may arise of whether it is better to have a large number of small clusters, or a small number of large clusters. Although there is some reason to believe that the former would yield more precise results, because of economies of scale (per unit prices go down with increasing size), the latter is often the more economical way to go.

Choosing the Size of the Sample

One of the most important questions relating to sampling is determination of sample size. You may recall our discussion of the biases of the mean. We mentioned that as the sample size increases, the sample mean tends to get closer and closer to the population mean. In other words, if we are interested in knowing average family income in the United States, the sample average will become more reliable as the sample size increases. Ultimately, total accuracy will be achieved if we were to interview each member of American society. Since only the decennial census comes the closest to complete enumeration, interested researchers and policy analysts wait eagerly for its results. However, doing a complete census is so expensive and time consuming that it can be justified only once every 10 years. For all other purposes one must achieve a balance between the need for accuracy and the cost of a sample survey. Therefore, the question of how many people to contact becomes paramount.

The development of theoretical statistics has given us some of the most powerful tools of quantitative decision making. One of these tools helps us in determination of the required sample size. The method of selecting the sample size is closely linked with the concept of confidence interval and sample error. Recalling our discussion from the previous chapter, confidence interval is calculated by using the following formula:

$$-Z_a \times \frac{\sigma}{\sqrt{N}} \rangle \overline{X} - \mu > +Z_a \times \frac{\sigma}{\sqrt{N}}$$

$$(2.9)$$

where Z_α is the value from the Z table at the desired level of confidence, α,

       σ is the population standard deviation,

       N is the population size,

       $\overline{X}$ is the sample mean, and

       μ is the population mean.

This formula tells us that we can be confident at any desired level of α that the difference between the sample mean and the population mean will fall within a particular band. We can rewrite this formula as

$$\overline{X} - \mu \rangle \pm Z_\alpha \times \frac{\sigma}{\sqrt{N}}$$

or,

$$\mu = \overline{X} \pm Z_\alpha \times \frac{\sigma}{\sqrt{N}}.$$

That is, the population mean will fall with a certain band around the sample mean. The problem with using this formula is that it uses the population standard deviation, which is unobservable. We can estimate the population standard deviation from the sample standard deviation as follows:

$$\mu = \overline{X} \pm Z_\alpha \times \frac{s}{\sqrt{n-1}}$$

(3.1)

where s is the sample standard deviation, and
         n   is the size of the sample population.

Let us take a specific example. Suppose, from a sample of 100 residents of a city, we learn that 67% of them support a proposed referendum. We also know that the survey has a standard deviation of .15. To be safe, we want a 95% accuracy. Therefore, we can look up the Z table for the value of $Z_{.05}$, which turns out to be approximately 1.96. Using these numbers in equation (3.1), we can be 95% certain that the population mean, which we cannot observe, will fall within the range

$$\mu = .67 \pm 1.96 \times \frac{.15}{\sqrt{100-1}} = .67 \pm .0295.$$

That is, we can be 95% sure that the opinion of the population of the city at large will vary within the range of approximately 70% and 64%. In other words, the sample result contains a **sample error** of ±3% (by rounding off .0295). If you study the formula given by equation (3.1) closely, you will see that there are two policy matters imbedded in it: the level of confidence and the sample size. Let us first look at the confidence level. If the desired level of confidence is increased to 99%, the corresponding value for $Z_{.01} = 2.57$. Replacing 1.96 by 2.57, the confidence interval becomes

$$\mu = .67 \pm 2.57 \times \frac{.15}{\sqrt{100-1}} = .67 \pm .0387.$$

We can be 99% certain that the actual population mean rests between the interval 63.3% to 70.9%, or the sample result contains approximately ±4% sample error (by rounding off .0387). Therefore, the results show that greater assurance must be accompanied by enlarging the boundary.

Let us now turn to the second policy variable, the sample size. What happens if we enlarge the sample size? For comparison purposes, let us suppose that we still want 95% accuracy, but this time we have increased the sample size to 500. We assume that the sample mean and the standard deviation have remained unchanged.

$$\mu = .67 \pm 1.96 \times \frac{.15}{\sqrt{500-1}} = .67 \pm .0132$$

As you can see, by increasing the sample size to 500 we have been able to narrow the confidence interval. We can expect that 95 times out of 100, the population mean will fall within the range of 66% to 68%. Therefore, as shown in Figure 3.4, the increase in sample size will be coupled by a greater degree of accuracy.

As Figure 3.4 demonstrates, the accuracy of estimating the true value of μ goes up with the increase in sample size. In the extreme case, the need for a confidence interval disappears as the sample size approaches the total population. It would be quite a task to determine the number of samples necessary to achieve a certain level of confidence. However, fortunately, statisticians have already calculated such tables for us (e.g., Table 3.1).

Table 3.1 provides a ready list of the minimum number of samples required to make estimates at a desired level of confidence. As shown in Figure 3.4, if you move across Table 3.1, say for a population of 10,000 people, you can see that as the desired level of confidence goes down, so does the required number of

Figure 3.4 The Relationship Between the Size of the Confidence Interval and Sample Size

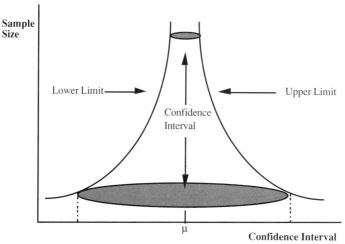

Table 3.1 Ninety-five percent confidence level (percent in population assumed to be 50%)

Size of population	± 1%	± 3%	± 4%	± 5%	± 10%
1,000	*	**500**	375	278	143
2,000	*	**696**	462	322	154
3,000	*	**787**	500	341	158
4,000	*	**842**	522	350	159
5,000	*	**879**	536	357	161
10,000	4,899	**964**	566	370	164
20,000	6,489	**1,013**	583	377	165
50,000	8,057	**1,045**	593	381	166
100,000	8,763	**1,056**	597	383	166
500,000 and more	9,423	**1,065**	600	384	166

* In these cases, more than 50% of the population is required in the sample.

subjects in the sample. You may also notice from Table 3.1 that for any specific level of confidence, the required sample size increases with the increase in the size of the population.

Therefore, given a certain population, the question becomes, What level of accuracy should we aim for? The usual practice among poll takers is to require a 95% level of confidence with a ±3% sampling error. For this widespread convention, this column is set in boldface in Table 3.1.

There are a few final words of caution, however. First, the numbers of Table 3.1 refer to an overall random sample. If you want, for example, to use a stratified or cluster sample, the numbers will have to change. For instance, suppose you want to draw conclusions about the opinion of a particular ethnic group within a city population of 500,000. By following the rule, you have drawn a random sample of 1,065 people, of which only a portion belong to the ethnic group in question. This sample size will not be appropriate, and you will have to determine the sample size corresponding to this particular ethnic population.

Second, when determining the sample size for a survey, you must keep in mind that Table 3.1 presents the minimum number of *actual responses* that are required to draw valid conclusions. While conducting a survey, you will encounter people who will refuse to answer the questions or will give inappropriate responses. Therefore, you must be sure to gather a sufficient number of valid responses.

Choosing the Survey Instruments

While choosing the size of the sample is mechanical, the real art (derived from experience and creativity) of conducting a survey lies in designing the questionnaire. In doing so, keep in mind two overarching concerns. First, like all scientific inquiry, questions should be asked with the main purpose of the survey in mind. Thus, before writing the questions, make sure that the objective of the survey is clear. If you are to elicit information about the respondent's opinion on a certain matter, make sure that the questions go directly to the heart of the matter. For example, if the purpose of a survey is to estimate the demand for new housing in an area, the answer to a question such as "Would you like to buy a new house now?" would be misleading since it does not put the question in the context of the respondent's ability to make the purchase. You may notice that when pollsters attempt to predict the outcome of an election, they often do not take a random survey of voters. Since many people do not vote, questions are raised in the context of the respondents' likelihood of actually casting ballots. Therefore, you will frequently hear the survey results preceded by statements such as "among those who are likely to vote."

However, for certain types of issues, the sensitivity of the respondents must be taken into account. For example, questions regarding intimate or embarrassing personal habits, morality, or civic duty can often draw elusive answers. For example, in answer to the question, "Would you vote in the upcoming election?" people may say yes either because they are embarrassed to admit that they would not carry out their civic duty or because they do wish to vote, but for one reason or another, they will not show up at the booth. In such cases, better results may be obtained by asking people if they did vote in the previous election and basing your judgment regarding future behavior on past action.

The second overarching concern to keep in mind while designing a questionnaire is the future use of the data. If the purpose of the survey is to simply convey the distribution of opinion, preference, or attitudes, then you may not have to worry about the survey's linkage with future research efforts. However, if the survey is directly linked with a research project, requiring some specific hypotheses testing or the survey's use in some other quantitative technique, then care must be taken to ensure that the derived data are appropriate for their future use.

While developing a questionnaire, many concerns pop up. We may classify them in five broad categories: (1) being on level with the respondents, (2) choosing the right format of answers, (3) avoiding questions with emotional overtones, (4) choosing the proper sequence of questions, and (5) choosing the proper length of the questionnaire.

Be on level with the respondents

Questionnaires must be developed with the respondent in mind. If you are to develop a questionnaire for middle school children to determine their awareness of some national and international issues, would you ask questions with words that are beyond their vocabulary? Certainly not. And since you are asking youngsters, you would be careful about the way you phrase your questions. However, this kind of care may also be neded when designing questionnaires for adults, many of whom, unfortunately, may not have a vocabulary beyond those of children in their early teens. While I was in London, huge advertisements in the underground railroad stations paid for by the *Times of London* caught my attention. To my surprise, these ads were simply giving out tips on how to write for a newspaper. One of the first suggestions was to keep the language simple. The ad suggested that while choosing a word, avoid the Latin-based ones or the ones that are more difficult. For example, instead of using *obtain* use *get*, or replace *propitious* with *lucky*, etc.

Also, unless the survey is intended for a specific purpose, avoid questions that may have different meanings to different people. For example, the question "Do you belong to the poor, middle, or wealthy class?" would draw a mixed reaction, since everybody's definitions of the boundaries of these classes are likely to vary considerably. Instead, you can get a much more specific answer by asking, "Which of the following income groups do you belong to—less than $10,000; between 10,001 and 20,000; . . ?"

Choose the right format of answers

Questions in a survey can be either open ended or fixed alternative. In an open-ended question, the respondents are asked questions whose answers can be long and descriptive. For example, to determine positions on handgun registration, questions may be phrased as, "What is your position on handgun control?"

On the other hand, questions may be put in within a fixed format, such as

"I believe all handguns within the State should be registered."
- ☐ Strongly Agree
- ☐ Agree
- ☐ Disagree
- ☐ Strongly Disagree

Both of these kinds of questions have their relative sets of advantages and drawbacks. Open-ended questions have the advantage of drawing out a full spectrum of responses without being restricted by specific choices mentioned in the questionnaire. For instance, in the preceding example of a fixed-alternative questionnaire, if some respondents feel neutral about the statement, or harbor no view at all on the matter, the aforementioned survey instruments do not provide an outlet for their point of view. Of course, this problem can be avoided by making the list as exhaustible as possible; but no matter how much you try, in a large sample, you are more than likely to come across a respondent whose opinion does not fit in any of the boxes. On the other hand, the answers to the open-ended questions, by virtue of being unstructured, cannot not be easily fitted into a specific coding system for quantitative analysis.

Avoid words provoking emotion

Certain words and phrases evoke strong emotion in people. If your goal is to derive an objective set of questions, you should avoid these terms. For example, you are trying to determine public support for the U.S. government's food aid to the drought-stricken parts of Africa. Consider three questions:

A. "Do you support U.S. aid to the drought-stricken parts of Africa?"

B. "Do you support U.S. aid to the starving people of Africa?"

C. "In view of all the problems facing this country, do you support U.S. food aid to Africa?"

Although, in general, few people are against food aid to a starving group of people, it is fairly obvious that the answers to these three similar questions are likely to be quite different. However, to an unsuspecting audience, you can report the results of this survey as "people's opinion on U.S. aid to Africa" by picking the one that suits your purpose best. You may agree with me that among the three questions, only A is phrased in an objective manner. B contains *starving people*, an emotionally charged phrase that is going to elicit a lot more favorable reaction to the issue of aid to Africa. In contrast, C changes the focus of the question by using another vague and emotionally charged phrase, *all the problems facing this country*. In this case, opinion is likely to swing in the other direction. There are many phrases in common, everyday use that convey to respondents that the interviewer expects a certain answer. An objective pollster must recognize their existence in a poorly designed set of survey instruments.

Choose the proper sequence of questions

Few surveys ask only a single question. If there are multiple questions, the sequence in which they are put to respondents can be crucial. The questions can be asked in a random sequence, where there is no particular order to the questions. They can also be asked in a funnel or an inverted funnel sequence. A questionnaire is said to have a funnel-like sequence when broadest questions are asked in the beginning, followed by more specific ones. Figure 3.5 shows examples of a funnel-shaped and an inverted funnel-shaped sequence of questions.

Figure 3.5 Sequence of Questions

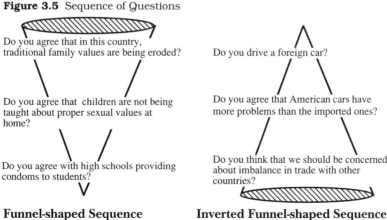

Funnel-shaped Sequence   **Inverted Funnel-shaped Sequence**

The general rule of sequencing the questions is that if the respondents are likely to be familiar with the broad issues, it is better to start with the most general question and then narrow down to a more specific one. In our example, most people hold some kind of an opinion on the state of family values in the United States. Therefore, we can start out by asking respondents to assess the state of family values and then, within that context, ask their opinion on the controversial issue of distribution of condoms in high schools.

In contrast, most people are not well informed about the problem of the external trade deficit and may require some help in framing the issue. Therefore, by starting out with a specific question, we can help them focus on the broader issue.

Choose the appropriate length of questionnaire

The final practical note about designing a questionnaire is its size. Since conducting a survey is an expensive and time-consuming affair, there is a tendency to load questionnaires with as many questions as possible. However, this tendency is to be resisted, as most people lose interest in answering questions if they are too long or there are too many. This is particularly true for surveys conducted through telephone or mail. A greater latitude is often possible when using a face-to-face interview.

Choosing the Method of Polling

All surveys require asking the subjects questions. Determining the mode of interview is an extremely important aspect of survey design. Much thought must be given to choosing this important aspect. Generally speaking, there are three methods of interview: (1) personal interview, (2) telephone interview, and (3) mailing of questionnaires. Each method has its own relative strengths and weaknesses.

Face-to-face interviews

Of the three methods, the personal, face-to-face interview is the most expensive, and probably the most accurate method of gathering information about the population. Face-to-face interviews are particularly appropriate when the questionnaire has a good number of open-ended questions. Frequently this form of personal interview is useful, as it can put the subjects at ease with the interviewer. However, personal contact may have its drawback, as the interviewer and the interviewee may find each other less than acceptable, and, as a result, the survey results may be skewed. For example, in a less educated minority community, sending predominantly white college students may cause distrust among the subjects. Therefore, the researcher should spend some time planning the type of poll taker to be sent for personal interviews.

Telephone interviews

Telephone interviews are a relatively inexpensive way of polling. Unlike in 1936 during the famous *Literary Digest* poll, when owning a telephone was restricted to the affluent, today telephones are part of our daily lives regardless of our income status. Generally speaking, in the United States the telephone can be used as the medium of interview without much fear of creating systematic biases. However, this may not be the case in many other countries, or even in some of the poor rural areas of the United States.

Although telephone interviews are quick and inexpensive, they are most effective in conducting a quick survey rather than in-depth interviews. People are often squeamish about opening up to a faceless voice over the telephone wire, and are guarded in their responses.

Mailed Questionnaires

Mailed questionnaires are frequently used mediums of survey. Since no real person accompanies the questionnaires, they are relatively inexpensive and are free of the influences of individual interviewer. Mailed questionnaires allow subjects to think over their responses, and can be used to elicit long, open-ended answers. Also, once the questionnaires are returned they can be processed and data can be recorded, tabulated, tested, and reported with relative ease. In many cases, surveys are conducted in which responses are recorded on paper that can be scanned by a computer. This process immediately creates computer files for subsequent testing.

However, mailed questionnaires often suffer from extremely low response rates. Since they are left to the initiative of the respondents to be filled out and mailed, they are often set aside and quickly forgotten. Nachmias and Nachmias[6] report that while for personal interviews response rates are typically around 95%, for mail surveys these numbers are between 2 and 40%. Therefore, unless we are careful, the results can exhibit a self-selection bias. In other words, if the rate of returns is extremely low, those who have taken the initiative to fill out the questionnaires and mail them may represent a special subset of the population. It may be that these individuals have a special agenda, strongly held beliefs, or possess some other special socioeconomic characteristics (such as being better educated and/or older). Therefore, any conclusion based on such a survey may be misleading. As a precaution against small group bias, every effort must be taken to increase the size of the sample (which, in this case, is the number of returned questionnaires). Hence, you should follow up a mailing with telephone calls or reminder letters.

[6] David Nachmias and Chava Nachmias *Research Methods in Social Sciences.* New York: St. Martin's Press, 1976, p. 107.

Quantification of Survey Data

Most frequently survey results are expressed in numbers. We are told of survey results in terms of percentages or means. If a survey consists mostly of open-ended questions, it is often difficult to report the results in terms of numbers. Therefore, most surveys use fixed-format answers. There are certain questions that are answered in numbers, such as income, age, years of education, size of family, etc. There are others that are expressed in terms of a nominal scale, such as sex, race, religion, national or linguistic groups, etc. Finally, there are data that relate to matters of attitudes and values, which cannot be readily translated into numbers. To express these variables in terms of numbers, we need to use predetermined scales.

Although there are several kinds of scales, in social sciences **Likert scales** are the most commonly used for measuring attitudes, values, and other matters of information that cannot be readily quantified. In a Likert scale, respondents are asked to express their feelings on a continuum varying from highly positive to highly negative. Thus, on a five-point scale, the respondents will be asked whether they "strongly agree," "agree," "are undecided," "disagree," or "strongly disagree" with a particular statement. These answers can then be assigned weight either in ascending (1, 2, 3, 4, 5) or descending (5, 4, 3, 2, 1) order. Based on their answer, the respondents will be given points, which will indicate their individual stance on a particular issue, or the average of the responses can be calculated for determining the "average" attitude or feeling.

Pretesting questionnaire

It is a good idea to pretest your survey questionnaire on a small group of people for both substantive and format issues. A pretest will give you a good idea about your survey's potential problems. Unless you are an experienced poll taker, you are likely to encounter problems, such as showing your personal bias in setting up the questionnaire, not extracting the answer needed for the survey, leaving out important questions, or including less than relevant ones. A pretest may effectively help you avoid these pitfalls.

Analysis of Survey Data

Analysis of survey data starts with descriptive statistics. The means, medians, and standard deviations are calculated to draw insights into people's attitudes, beliefs, and values. Then, depending on the purpose of the survey, hypotheses are tested regarding differences and similarities among the groups of respondents.

Perhaps the most commonly used technique of survey analysis is the **contingency table** (discussed in chapter 2). The results of a survey often go beyond simple reporting of average responses to a question. Often the results help us identify the causal linkage that binds two variables. For instance, a survey on computer use among middle-level managers in a public organization may reveal statistically significant differences based on gender, age, and education. Therefore, how much time an individual would spend working on a computer may be predicted on the basis of the three demographic characteristics. Since the extent of computer use is dependent on these factors, it is called the **dependent variable**, while those that influence the dependent variable are called **independent variables**. Notice that the direction of causality flows from the independent variables to the dependent variable, and not the other way around. That is, a person's age will determine how much time this person is likely to spend on a computer, but an individual's age is not determined by his or her computer use.

| Dependent variable | ← | Direction of causality | ——— | Independent variable(s) |

The contingency table allows the analyst to determine some of these causal linkages. For example, a survey of middle-level management found that on the average a manager spends 20% of the work day in front of a computer. Using a contingency table, we can retabulate the results by dividing the respondents into male, female, and other categories of age and education. Of course, it is tedious to recalculate all the numbers for each independent variable; computers can do such calculations without any difficulty. Using a contingency table, means are calculated for each specific group and the results are reported in a tabular form. Thus, for division along the sex line, we may get the following results:

Percent of Time Spent on Computer	Percent of Male Managers	Percent of Female Managers
0– 5%	20	25
6–10%	25	45
11–20%	40	25
21–40%	15	5
More than 40%	5	0
Total	100	100
N	60	45
Mean	11.3	8.3

From these results, we can test the hypothesis of whether there is a male/female difference in computer use. Contingency tables are extremely useful tools of research and are widely used for the analysis of survey results.

■■ **Analyzing by Contingency Table Using a Computer** ■■■■■■■

There are a number of softwares for applying a contingency table. However, of these, the best (and certainly the most commonly used) is SPSS (Statistical Package for Social Sciences). SPSS is a versatile software package and is available for mainframe/mini and personal computers. Once the data have been collected, MYSTAT can also analyze data using **Tables**.

Reporting of Survey Results

Surveys are conducted to gather information and to test a specific set of hypotheses. It is very important to report the results of a survey in a proper way. Most of the survey results are reported with tables, graphs, and charts. I discuss these techniques in chapter 4. However, since survey data can be misused and misinterpreted, you must spell out in detail the assumptions, sampling method, sample error, level of confidence, and often the questions themselves.

On the eve of the Republican convention in 1992, the *Los Angeles Times* conducted a nationwide opinion survey. At the end of the story, the newspaper added the following explanation of its polling method, which can serve as a good guide for you:[7]

■■ **How the Poll Was Conducted** ■■■■■■■■■■■■■■■■■■■■

The *Times* poll interviewed 1,146 registered voters nationwide, by telephone, from August 12 to 14. Telephone numbers were chosen from a list of all exchanges in the country. Random-digit dialing techniques were used to ensure that both listed and nonlisted numbers had an opportunity to be surveyed. Results were weighted slightly to conform with census figures for sex, race, age, education, and household size. The margin of sampling error for the total sample is plus or minus three percentage points. For certain subgroups, the error margin is slightly higher. Poll results can also be affected by other factors, such as question wording and the order in which questions are presented.

Survey Design: A Step-by-Step Approach

Designing a survey requires skills that can be acquired only through repeated experience. Since we have to live within the boundaries of our financial means and allocated time, often a compromise is required between what is the best way of gathering relevant information and what is feasible. Therefore, the entire survey design must be done within the context of feasibility. The following are important steps toward conducting a survey.

A. Determine the objective of the survey.

---

[7] *The Los Angeles Times*, Sunday, August 16, 1992, p. A6.

B. Determine the method of selecting samples for the survey.

C. Determine the minimum sample size, given the size of population and the desired level of accuracy.

D. Develop the questionnaire.

E. Pretest the questionnaire.

F. Given the allocated time and money, determine the method of interview.

G. Code survey data.

H. Analyze data.

I. Report survey results.

When the Polls Are Suspect

Advancements in communications technology have made it easy to get in touch with people. Increased ability of computers to compile vast amounts of data in split seconds and increased knowledge of statistical reasoning have created the science of polling. Polls are increasingly being used in public policy debates. Candidates for elected offices direct their campaigns according to poll results. Once in office, they often base their positions on various issues on the expressed opinions of their constituents. The use of polls in policy debate has become so pervasive that hardly a day goes by without the evening newscasts informing us about our collective positions on diverse issues of national and local importance. So it seems that we have finally perfected the art of polling and have elevated it to the hallowed position of a science. Or have we?

While survey results can give you important information, they can also be quite unreliable, even after you have followed all the rules for ensuring statistical accuracy and eliminating survey biases. We have discussed many of these problems in bits and pieces, but these issues are extremely important, so we now consider them separately.

These errors result from many sources. First, even the most "scientific" polls call for subjective judgments on the part of the poll taker. Second, when asked sensitive questions, people often lie. Third, polls can run into any one of innumerable self-selection biases. And finally, the survey design can influence the results. Here are a few examples.

The Problems of Subjective Line Calls and Pragmatic Solutions

The notion of a "scientific" methodology conjures up images of white-cloaked scientists plying their trade in sterile objectivity. Yet, in reality if you are conducting a survey, you will frequently be called on to make subjective judgments. For instance, we have stated that a random survey is appropriate only if the population is homogeneous in its characteristics. When there are reasons to doubt the homogeneity, a stratified sampling is warranted. However, the problem of carrying out a stratified sample is that you may not get enough respondents from a particular subgroup.

For instance, in a large metropolitan city, you do not have enough Asian respondents in the survey; you have only 50% of the required number. You may solve this problem by continuing to poll until you reach the target number. However, if the Asian population is not concentrated in any single area of the city, doing so may mean a considerable expenditure of time and money. In such a case, you may find a short-cut by simply doubling the weight on those who have responded to your questionnaire. This practical and convenient decision (frequently made by poll takers) can significantly bias your results.

When People Lie

If you ask a sensitive question, people often do not tell the truth. For instance, to a candidate for an elected office the most important results are from those who would actually vote. Since the proportion of people who go out and vote can be quite low, the opinions of those who actually do so take on a special importance. Therefore, all the poll takers aim at reaching this select group of individuals. Yet the question remains, How do you know who would actually show up at the booth on election day? The most renowned pollsters use different techniques. Louis Harris surveys, for example, screen the respondents by asking if they voted in the last election. Being embarrassed to acknowledge that they did not carry out their civic duties, many people would lie and thus bias the results. There are many other examples of such behavior. If there is a minority candidate or the issue involves a conflict between a morality and self-interest, people often mask their true preferences, so as not to seem racist or greedy.[8]

The Biases of Self-Selection

There are literally millions of ways the biases of self-selection can creep into the poll results. These biases can come from not knowing the opinions of those who refused to take part in the survey, or those who could not be reached during

---

[8] For example, in the 1990 U.S. Senate election in Louisiana, the incumbent Democratic candidate was widely predicted to score an overwhelming victory over David Duke, a former grand wizard of the Ku Klux Klan whose platform rested on opposition to affirmative action. Preelection polls projected that Duke would garner no more than 25% of the votes. Yet when the actual poll results were tabulated, he had managed to get 44%, including 60% of the white votes. See P. Thomas, "The Persistent 'Gnat' that Louisiana Can't Get Out of Its Face," *Los Angeles Times*, October 14, 1990, p. M1. Even the exit polls turned out to be inaccurate, suggesting that many people would not admit to having voted for Duke. Similarly, on the eve of the 1989 mayoral election in New York, polls gave David Dinkins, a black candidate, a 14 to 18% lead over Rudolf Giuliani (who is white). The exit polls predicted a 6 to 10% spread between the candidates. However, the actual margin of win turned out to be much smaller, a meager 2% margin. See A. Rosenthal, "Broad Disparities in Votes and Polls Raising Questions," *New York Times*, November 9, 1989, pp. A1, B14.

the survey period, or even those who *could* be reached. For instance, during the 1984 re-election campaign, the internal GOP polls showed Ronald Reagan well ahead of Walter Mondale, except when they were taken on Fridays. The panic in the Reagan camp was eased when it was pointed out that since the Republicans were more affluent, they were disproportionately not available during the Friday evenings. Similarly, the polls taken during a Republican political convention in 1992 showed a slight "blimp" in the support for President Bush. However, this was merely reflective of the fact that those who were home watching the convention were disproportionately Republicans.[9]

The Problems of Survey Design

Survey results can change dramatically depending on the way the questions are put or the sequence in which they are asked. We have discussed some of these problems. For example, if you ask people about a candidate you will get a certain reaction, which may alter drastically when the individual's party affiliation is presented (for instance, asking "would you vote for Bill Clinton?" as opposed to "would you vote for the Democratic nominee, Bill Clinton?"). Also, during the 1992 election, it was noticed that support for Bill Clinton went up significantly if those polled were asked to choose the presidential candidate after a few questions about the state of the economy.

The Secondary Data

The secondary data are collected by someone other than the researcher. Perhaps the best sources of secondary data are government publications. Governmental agencies in the United States are the most inveterate collectors of statistical information. It is therefore imperative that before starting an analysis, you be clear about your **data needs**. Your needs will be determined by the problem at hand and the type of model that you want to use to analyze a particular policy.

Suppose you are interested in evaluating the homeless problem in your city. Your first task would be to determine the data need. The data need will vary with the type of inquiry. If you are interested in the reasons for homelessnes, you will have one kind of need; on the other hand, if you want to ascertain the cost to the city of caring for the homeless, or you are attempting to forecast the size of the future homeless population, your data need will vary accordingly. Therefore, as the first step, you will have to think of the research problem vis-à-vis the type of analytical model that you would want to use to assess your data need.

---

[9] "The Science of Polling," *Newsweek*, September 28, 1992, pp. 38–39.

Library Search

Since there is so much available information, more and more efforts are being directed toward making information accessible to researchers. As a result, on-line computer-based data and literature searches are becoming part of standard research practice.

Computerized library search techniques generally involve the use of key words. Published articles and books are classified by the salient words, which describe their content most effectively. Thus, to continue with our example of looking into the homeless problem in your city, if you were to simply specify the search as "homeless," you may be inundated by everything that has been written on the subject. Therefore, you will have to narrow the field of search by adding another word such as the name of your city. If your research concerns only homeless children in Boston, you may begin the search as "homeless" and "Boston" and "children." This will enable the computer to provide you with information on those books and articles that are specific to your need.

It is worthwhile to familiarize yourself thoroughly with computer-based data search techniques. Most colleges and university libraries offer on-line services to users. Many governmental organizations are becoming part of this incredible information-sharing network. Although there are a number of extensive databases available and new ones are being created, I mention a few important ones at this point.

For any kind of research, the starting point should be a thorough understanding of the relevant literature. Therefore, if you are interested in bibliographic research, you may look into Bibliographic Retrieval System (BRS), Lockheed Information System (DIALOG), or Systems Development Corporation (SDC). A good literature search will point you to the type of quantitative data that you will need to conduct your research project. There are a number of private corporations that maintain excellent databases, that can be accessed for a fee. Among these, you may consult Chase Econometrics, Cyphernet, and Data Resources Inc. Also, for quantitative data needs for public policy analysis, many of the government documents are increasingly available on-line. For instance, the on-line data banks of *American Statistical Index* and *Public Affairs Information Service Bulletin* (PAIS) will give you a remarkable amount of detailed information on many areas of public policy analysis.

Traditional Library Search

If you do not have access to such technology for conducting a literature search, the traditional, time-honored places to start are the published versions of *Public Affairs Information Service Bulletin* (PAIS), the *Social Science Citation Index*, or the ABC index of *Political Science and Government.* If you are specifically interested in urban issues, there are selective publications like the *Index to Current Urban Documents.* There are a number of specialized indexes for various areas of social sciences, public policy, and planning. There are also subject-specific abstracts that publish selected abstracts or summaries of important articles in the fields of business, education, economics, law, political science, public administration, public policy, sociology, urban and regional planning, etc. Finally, for a thorough literature survey, you may also build on other students' unpublished work. This is an often overlooked area of literature search. Although the Ph.D. dissertations and Master's theses are not formally published, upon their acceptance for degrees they become part of public document. Since the students who wrote them have already spent a great deal of time developing the bibliography and a literature review, access to the relevant theses or disserations can be extremely useful for a you as a researcher, especially if you are not familiar with the topic.

Another important source of information for public policy research is newspapers. The major national and regional newspapers and magazines frequently provide excellent, well-rounded reviews of a particular topic. Libraries throughout the United States subscribe to many of the major newspapers. Also, with the advent of technology, local versions of major newspapers such as the *New York Times, The Wall Street Journal,* and *USA Today* are being printed simultaneously across the United States. You may also profitably look into weekly magazines such as *Newsweek, Time, US News and World Report,* etc.

Having gone through the relevant literature, you are now ready to collect numerical information on the topic. For this, you should start from the *Annual Statistical Abstract of the U.S.,* the annual *Report of the President,* the *Handbook of Labor Statistics,* and the *Census Catalog and Guide.* State and local government data are available in several excellent publications. For example, *Census of Governments, County and City Data Book, County Yearbook,* and *Municipal Yearbook* provide excellent sources of data.

There are also excellent sources for international data. However, the problem is that international data are often not comparable, as different governments may use different criteria for classifying information, which may make comparison between nations problematic. Nevertheless, a number of international agencies, such as the United Nations and the World Bank, compile the best available information cross-nationally. For example, you may start from the *U.N. Statistical Yearbook, Yearbook of International Trade Statistics,* and the *U.N. National Accounts Statistics.*

In addition to these vast amounts of economic, political, and social information, a huge array of data are available on attitudes and opinions. For example, the Institute for Social Research at the University of Michigan collects and compiles data on many aspects of social, political, and psychological attitudes.

Finally, if your research project involves a particular governmental agency, a great deal of information will be available in the agency's annual budget reports. Also, the agency may collect for its own internal use a good deal of information that may not be available in a ready-to-use form. However, you may be able to make effective use of these pieces of information by spending some time to arrange them in a proper way.

When Data Are Not Available

Having gone through all these numerous data sources, you feel frustrated. The specific information that you are looking for does not exist anywhere. This can happen if what you are looking for is too specific. Or it may be that for political or cultural reasons, such data have not been collected. For instance, if you are looking for time series data on the homeless population in your city, you may not find it because it is too specific. You may also find cases where the data for a few crucial years are missing from an otherwise complete series. Or, suppose your city is considering building a new convention center, and you are interested in estimating its possible impact on the city's economy. You will not find much information since the convention center has not been built yet. Or, suppose you are looking for data on smoking-related deaths on a crossnational basis. You may find that because of lack of awareness, such data have not been collected for many countries around the world.

In such cases, you may consider inferring the data. That is, if you can find a comparable city with the similar demographic, cultural, and economic background, you may draw a parallel. These kinds of inferences are often permissible when no data are available. However, if you must have a series prepared through inference or interpolation, you must make absolutely clear to the reader the nature of your data and the procedure by which they were obtained.

Key Terms

Cluster sample	Population and sample
Confidence interval	Primary data
Contingency table	Random sample
Dependent variable	Ratio scale
Independent variable	Sample design
Interval scale	Sample error
Likert scales	Sampling biases
Nominal scale	Secondary data
Ordinal scale	

Exercises

1. What are primary and secondary data? Discuss the various scales of data. What are their relative strengths and weaknesses? What are their respective uses?

2. The city of Masters (population 150,000) wants to enlarge its airport to accommodate a growing need for commercial airline landing. For this, the city

wants to conduct a survey to assess public opinion on the locational options. Specifically, the city wants to know who would support and who would oppose such an expansion effort in certain already identified sites. The survey must be completed within three months. Design a survey, specifying the sampling method (random, stratified, etc.), number of people to be surveyed, questions to be asked, and the mode of interview.

3. Write a short essay on the biases of sampling. Collect information from the real world to elaborate your points.

Chapter 4

Making Sense of Numbers

Managing Those Numbing Numbers

Much of a busy executive's work day involves making decisions. These days executives find themselves increasingly surrounded by information, which is often expressed in numbers. The introduction of electronic computers has generated a new era of information gathering. The advent of computing technology has made the collection and storing of data easy. Advancements in the field of computer software have also made the retrieval of data extremely simple. Yet a large series of numbers has a way of numbing our senses and pushing us beyond our limited cognitive capabilities. Therefore, when managers must make objective decisions, they increasingly consider arranging large sets of numbers in easily understandable form.

The purpose of this chapter is to provide students and practitioners with a guide for describing a particular social, political, or economic phenomenon either by using representative statistics or by using graphical renditions. You should be creative when presenting your arguments persuasively without misleading or deceiving the audience. As you can readily see, in our daily lives as well as in important legislative or boardroom hearings, ideas are most frequently conveyed through the methods of descriptive statistics or graphs and charts. The advantage of these techniques is in the simplicity of their presented message. In the age of quick dissemination of information, the importance of these simple techniques in shaping public policy debates, from presidential elections to the allocation of a neighborhood park, cannot be overstated. Therefore, I will take you through the familiar terrain and expose you to the advantages and pitfalls of the most commonly used and abused methods of numerical decision making.

Techniques of Statistical Assessment

Often we are concerned with assessing our present situation. This assessment can be done in two different ways. First, if we want to evaluate our present position in its historical context, we need to collect data over time. In statistical terms, this is called **time series** or **longitudinal** data. On the other hand, if we want to evaluate our relative position in comparison with relevant others, we collect data for one single time period for all the comparable units. This is called **cross-section** data. Thus, while attempting to evaluate the crime rate of a city, we can look at the time series data (e.g., covering the last 15 years), or compare the city's crime rate for this year with that of other cities of similar size and demographic characteristics.

A situation can be assessed using descriptive statistics or graphical techniques. These techniques are often neglected in statistics and operations research textbooks because they seem too simplistic. However, we know that an overwhelming number of decisions in both public and private organizations are made on the basis of simple decision rules. Think of how often the more complex methods of data analysis are used in testimony before legislatures or are presented in corporate board rooms. The most frequently used methods are those of

Table 4.1 Expenditures by Functions and Levels of Government, Fiscal 1983*

	I DISTRIBUTION BY FUNCTION AT EACH LEVEL				*II DISTRIBUTION BY LEVEL OF EACH FUNCTION*			
Functions	*Federal*	*State*	*Local*	*AS*	*Federal*	*State*	*Local*	*AS*
1. Defense	29.1	—	—	17.0	100.0	—	—	100
2. Internal	13.7	4.4	4.3	10.2	81.2	8.3	9.8	100
3. Human resources	39.9	98.5	59.4	49.3	49.1	24.3	28.8	100
4. Education	1.7	19.9	41.8	13.6	7.3	25.5	87.2	100
5. Welfare	3.2	19.9	4.9	6.5	29.8	53.5	16.7	100
6. Health	1.5	8.6	8.4	4.3	21.4	35.7	42.9	100
7. Housing	1.3	—	2.8	1.4	55.6	—	44.4	100
8. Social Insurance	32.2	19.9	1.7	23.3	83.5	14.8	1.7	100
9. Transportation	0.5	0.3	6.0	3.5	2.0	48.7	44.4	100
10. Natural resource	6.1	2.7	0.3	4.2	87.3	10.8	1.8	100
11. Police	0.3	1.5	5.0	1.5	10.0	15.0	75.0	100
12. Other	10.3	13.2	23.7	13.9	45.5	16.8	37.7	100
13. Total	100.0	100.0	100.0	100.0	60.5	17.4	22.1	100

* Expenditures to the public; with international games accounted for at the redpen level. Includes goods and service expenditures and translana.

Source: Rex Foundston, *Facts and Gigures on Government Finance*, 23d ed. 1988, Washington, D.C., p. 28.

Printed with permission from the publisher.

descriptive statistics and graphical techniques. Indeed, I cannot overemphasize the need for a decision maker or analyst to comprehend the power of the most simple of all statistical analysis and operations research.

Tabular Presentation of Data

A long series of numbers pushes us to the limits of our cognitive capacities. Therefore, the value of an effective table as a means of communication can not be overstated. Presenting data in a good tabular form is an art, which comes only through practice. An excellent example of a masterful use of a table can be found in the widely used textbook of public finance by Richard and Peggy Musgrave.[1] (See Table 4.1.)

Notice the incredible amount of information presented in Table 4.1. The table contains two sections: one showing the distribution of government functions among the three levels of government, and the other showing the percentage of each of those functions undertaken by each level of government. For example, by

[1] See R. Musgrave and P. Musgrave, *Public Finance in Theory and Practice*, 5th ed. (New York: McGraw-Hill, 1989).

looking at this table we can tell how important a particular function is within a particular level of government and how much of the total national burden it shares. Thus, for the state governments, education takes up 19.9% of their budgets, while expenditures on education comprise 25.5% of the total national outlay.

The preparation of an effective table requires considerable thought, time (and, therefore, money), and it comes with experience. Nevertheless, we can give a few suggestions for preparing a good table. First, have a clear idea of exactly what you want to communicate to the reader. Second, choose a title that, parsimoniously describes the contents of the table. Third, consider various ways of presenting the raw data so that they make the point you want to make most effectively. In the next section we discuss the depiction of numerical information by graphical methods.

The Worth of a Picture: The Graphical Methods of Analysis

Let us consider a hypothetical situation. Suppose the city manager of a medium-sized city, Masters, PA is interested in knowing how much the city depends on state and federal grants. The city manager is given yearly breakdowns of state and federal grants to the city for the last 10 years. The financial management division for the city produces Table 4.2.

Use of the Current Dollar Figure

The numbers in Table 4.2 convey the sense that state and federal funding for the city is growing every year. A better appreciation of the historical trend can be obtained by plotting the data. However, as you will soon discover, there is more than one way of making a picture.

Year	State and Federal Grants in Current $
1980	71,000
1981	75,000
1982	85,000
1983	89,000
1984	91,000
1985	91,500
1986	93,000
1987	95,000
1988	98,000
1989	102,000

Table 4.2 State and Federal Grants to Masters, PA

Figure 4.1 State and Federal Grants to Masters, PA

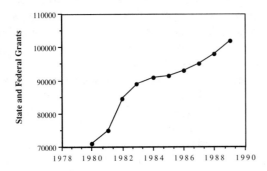

Of course, the plotted information shown in Figure 4.1 is a great improvement over the table. The diagram clearly shows the generosity of the state and federal governments to the city. The dollar amount of the grants has increased steadily over the years, with the greatest increase coming during the early 1980s. However, the city manager is skeptical; this diagram does not take into account the rate of inflation for the period. Therefore, the price deflator (the consumer price index for the United States) was obtained for the period, and the yearly numbers were converted to constant dollars. This is shown in Table 4.3.

It is obvious from the calculation of constant dollar figures that the city is not doing all that well with the state and federal grants as was assumed. In fact, the inflationary forces in the early 1980s have eroded so much of the purchasing power that they caused an actual decline in the grant money in *real terms* (see Figure 4.2).

Table 4.3 State and Federal Grants to the City of Masters

Year	State and Federal Grants in Current $	Consumer Price Index Number	State and Federal Grants in Constant $
1980	71,000	100	71,000
1981	75,000	110	68,182
1982	85,000	117	72,650
1983	89,000	122	72,951
1984	91,000	127	70,930
1985	91,500	129	67,883
1986	93,000	137	68,345
1987	95,000	139	68,534
1988	98,000	143	68,531
1989	102,000	147	68,388

Figure 4.2 Comparison of State and Federal Grants: Current and Constant Dollars

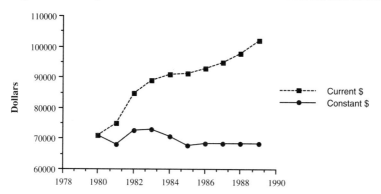

Therefore, we see that we obtain radically different conclusions each time we transform the data. Further transformations can be done with respect to many other variables such as population or the size of the city budget; the data may be compared to a national or regional average, or the series can be looked at by its rate of increase. Let us consider some other ways of looking at the same data.

For example, we can expand Table 4.3 to include information on total city revenue during the period of study. If we express the dollar amount of grants received by the city as a percentage of its total revenue, we will be comforted by the fact that we have done well over the years (see Table 4.4). We may be further comforted if we look at the national trend of the ratio of state and federal government assistance to cities as a percent of their total revenue. We can see that during our study period, compared to the early 1980s, the city is doing considerably better in terms of the national average. (see Figure 4.3)

Table 4.4 State and Federal Grants to Masters, PA 1980–1989

Year	State and Federal Grants in Current $	Total Government Revenue in Current $	State and Federal Grants as Ratio of Total Government Revenue	National Average of Grants as a Percent of Local Government Revenue
1980	71,000	360,000	19.7	35.5
1981	75,000	369,000	20.3	32.3
1982	85,000	382,000	22.3	30.2
1983	89,000	385,000	23.1	26.8
1984	91,000	398,000	22.9	22.8
1985	91,500	410,000	22.3	21.5
1986	93,000	419,000	22.2	20.2
1987	95,000	425,000	22.4	20.3
1988	98,000	432,000	22.7	19.8
1989	102,000	444,000	23.0	19.5

Figure 4.3 Comparison of State and Federal Grants as a Percent of Local Government Tax Revenue

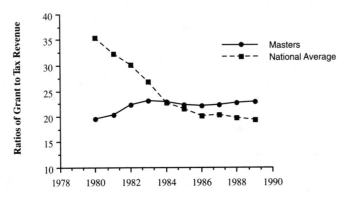

Each of these transformations tells a slightly different story. Through them we get glimpses of different facets of the situation. Therefore, the question is not which one is telling the "true" story, but which one contains the most important message from the perspective of the inquirer.

Percentage Change

You may want to look at the information in yet another way. For instance, you may calculate the yearly percentage change in constant dollar grants to Masters. This information has been presented in Table 4.5 and plotted in Figure 4.4, and it can be quite useful in discerning year-to-year changes in state and federal assistance to the city.

Table 4.5 Yearly Percentage Change in State and Federal Grants to Masters

Year	State and Federal Grants in Constant $	Yearly Percentage Change
1980	71,000	—
1981	68,182	-3.95
1982	72,650	6.55
1983	72,951	.41
1984	70,930	-2.77
1985	67,883	-4.30
1986	68,345	.68
1987	68,534	.28
1988	68,531	-.01
1989	68,388	-.21

Figure 4.4 Plot of Yearly Percentage Change in State and Federal Grants to Masters

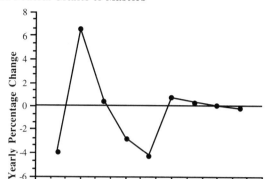

In the Perspective of a Base: Creating an Index

Finally, it may be useful to look at the data with the help of an index. An index is created when we take a particular figure as the **base** and then express the series in the perspective of this particular number. For instance, if we take the grants figure for 1980 as the base (expressed as 100), we can calculate by dividing each year's data by this number and then multiplying it by 100. That is,

$$\text{Index for } 1981 = \frac{1981}{1980} \times 100$$

or,

$$\frac{68,182}{71,000} \times 100 = 96.03.$$

Table 4.6 Yearly Percentage Change in State and Federal Grants to Masters

Year	State and Federal Grants in Constant $	Index with 1980 = 100
1980	71,000	100.00
1981	68,182	96.03
1982	72,650	102.32
1983	72,951	102.75
1984	70,930	99.90
1985	67,883	95.61
1986	68,345	96.26
1987	68,534	96.53
1988	68,531	96.52
1989	68,388	96.32

Figure 4.5 Plot of Index of State and Federal Grants to Masters (1980 = 100)

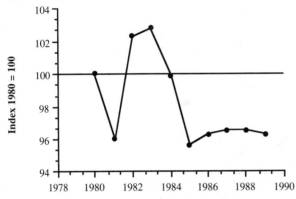

As you can see, each presentation of the same information tells a slightly different story. Therefore, you can choose the way you want to present your case depending on your need.

Choosing the Type of Graph to Use

In the previous examples we used only line graphs. Thanks to advancements in software technology, today's managers have at their fingertips the means to use various kinds of graphs, such as **scatter plots**, **line**, **bar**, and **pie charts**, and so on. Each kind of graph presents the information in its own unique way. You should be familiar with each kind of graph and be creative to determine which kind of pictorial rendition gets your intended message across in the most effective way.

Graphical Methods in Decision Making

Graphical presentations usually describe a situation. However, they should not be considered as passive tools of description; they can also be used as extremely powerful decision tools. Consider the following situation. The police department in Masters is trying to reach as many youngsters as possible to educate them about the perils of drug use. Last year the department expended considerable effort in arranging school appearances of officers and experts, and advertising on local radio and television. Suppose that last year the city had spent $7,500 on school lectures, $13,000 on radio advertisements, and $20,000 on television ads. A recent survey by the city shows that of the children who are aware of the city's drug prevention effort, 35% became aware of the issue through face-to-face contact with officers, 15% through radio ads, and the remaining 50% through watching television. Figure 4.6 shows expenditures and contacts using two pie diagrams.

Figure 4.6 Comparison of Relative Efficiency of
Drug Prevention Education Programs

Expenditures on Drug Prevention Program

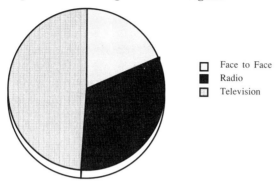

Contacts through Drug Prevention Programs

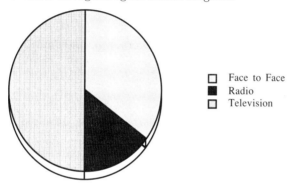

From these two diagrams the police department is able to discern that face-to-face contacts are the most cost-effective way to disseminate drug prevention information to school-age children. The same information could have been presented using a table with simple percentages. However, as is often the case, a picture is worth a thousand words.

To Tell the Truth and Nothing But the Truth

Over the years, statistics have been characterized in less than flattering ways. One of Disraeli's famous quips is, "There are three kinds of lies: lies, damned lies, and statistics." In addition, we have come to accept expressions such as "statistical artifacts" or "cooked-up statistics." However, when we talk about this intimate connection between a statistical series and lies, we must recognize that problems can arise due to *deception*, misunderstood *implication*, or the existence of a bias in the process of *collection* of information.

One source of the so-called lie may be outright *deception*. The deceptive use of numbers must be defined with respect to the intent of the user. Thus, if an individual or an organization puts out information knowing full well that the data have no real-life validity, this is a case of fraud or deception. Government agencies, during the time of national emergencies or war, routinely use data for propaganda purposes. For example, a nation at war may exaggerate or downplay claims about its military or industrial strength, or its war casualties, depending on its strategy. China, in the course of suppressing the prodemocracy movement, underreported the number of student casualties and released figures that were widely disputed by knowledgeable people and agencies (e.g., Chinese student groups in the United States or Amnesty International). Similarly, the figures for North Vietnamese war casualties were routinely inflated by Pentagon officials.

Another source of contention frequently centers around the "true" implication of a statistic. We often use the per capita Gross National Product (GNP) as a measure of the relative economic development of nations. However, it is obvious that the word *development* used in a national context should imply more than a measure of its per capita GNP, since development implies a certain degree of progress and maturity in social, political, and economic institutions. For example, the tiny oil-rich nations may have the highest per capita GNP, but one would be hardpressed to characterize those countries as the most developed in the world.

A statistic may also be misinterpreted because of biases caused by the influence of other factors. For example, there are valid questions about whether or not IQ tests measure relative levels of intelligence in children. Also, for years, entrance to the U.S. Civil Service was based on the scores on a multiple choice examination. However, it was eventually determined that such an examination was biased in favor of white, middle-class males. Therefore, the test score could not be accepted as the best measure of suitability of a candidate for a position.

Then there are data that, by their very nature, call for subjective judgment in the way they are defined and compiled. A good example of bias entering into the collection of data can be found in the Consumer Price Index constructed by the U.S. Bureau of Labor Statistics. The Consumer Price Index purports to measure the rate of inflation. Therefore, it looks at a "typical" basket of goods and services that an "average" American consumes yearly. However, we know that each of us has a unique consumption pattern, based not only on our individual tastes, but also on various factors such as age, income, race, and geographical location. Thus, for example, if the price of skateboards goes up, senior citizens are less likely to be affected. Similarly, an increase in the cost of health care may not affect single young adults as much as the increase in the index would suggest. So we see that whoever compiles this record faces two problems in making the index relevant to the majority of Americans. First, the compiler must choose a "typical" bundle of goods and services that a "typical" consumer will choose to consume. Second, a determination of the quantity of each commodity this "typical" consumer uses must be made. Thus, if the price of vegetables rises significantly, but vegetables do not form a major component of one's diet, then that person will be less affected by the rise in the Consumer Price Index. There are many examples of ways in which errors creep in during the collection of information that severely distort the data; not recognizing this means that the results of analyses may be meaningless, misleading, or even damaging.

You must be extremely wary of accepting data for analysis, and you cannot be too careful in looking at the possible sources of biases and errors. At the same time, remember that it is impossible to find a perfect set of data series in an otherwise imperfect world. Like the proverbial fastidious eater who (having vowed not to eat any food without looking at its entire production process to make sure that there was no potential source of contamination or lack of hygiene) died of starvation, a too cautious researcher will know all the flaws of the data and its analyses without being able to analyze and draw any useful conclusion from them.

The rule of thumb, then, is to evaluate carefully the sources of bias in the data and be aware of the cost of doing an incorrect analysis. Thus, if you are engaged in conducting medical research for a new type of vaccine as an antidote for a disease, or calculating trajectories for the reentry of shuttle craft into the earth's atmosphere, the margin of acceptable error is rather low. However, mercifully, in the areas of social science or public policy research the demand for numerical accuracy may not be that critical. Therefore, it is most important to be aware of the shortcomings of the data and the possible sources of bias in the analysis and interpretation, and be forthright about it.

Interpretation and Deception

The last source of skepticism with regard to the use of numbers to describe a situation or prescribe a public policy is that to most people, numbers portray a rigid, self-evident truth. In a cocktail party discussion, a friend of mine claimed that homosexuality was purely biological since every society seems to have homosexuals as 10% of its population. It is fairly obvious that this statement is the kind designed to end all discussions, as it purports to present a totally scientific, incontrovertible fact of life. To many people, numbers pose an immediate threat because of their appearance of "scientific" objectivity. However, closer scrutiny will reveal problems resulting from the various biases we have described; and a significant source of disagreement may be because any information (numerical or otherwise) about a complex social situation is bound to be open to interpretation.

In 1954 Darrell Huff wrote an extremely interesting, humorous book, *How to*

Lie with Statistics. In it he systematically demonstrated many ways to distort information to suit the purpose of the investigator. In his tongue-in-cheek introduction he states,

> This book is sort of a primer in ways to use statistics to deceive. It may seem altogether too much like a manual for swindlers. Perhaps I can justify it in the manner of the retired burglar whose published reminiscences amounted to a graduate course in how to pick a lock and muffle a football: The crooks already know these tricks; honest men must learn them in self-defense.

Huff's highly acclaimed book advanced understanding of the various ways one can use descriptive statistics among generations of undergraduate students. However, in all honesty, we may pose the question differently. If the manipulation of data is always suspected of "distorting" the picture, then there must be a truly undistorted version of real life. In other words, are we to assume the universality of truth? Does it always require a statistician to obfuscate an otherwise obvious situation? A famous turn-of-the-century Japanese play, *Rashomon,* by Ryunosuka Akutagawa, brings home the point of relativity of perception. In the play, a young woman traveling with her Samurai husband is raped by a bandit. A number of different individuals witnessed this terrible act of violence. When they are brought to trial (including her deceased husband, who speaks through a medium), the rape of the woman by a rogue is found to have variations of interpretation. Therefore, it is entirely possible that there may be honest differences of opinion in the way one looks at a most mundane fact of life, even when expressed in "cold, hard, objective numbers." We live in a complex world, where "truth" may have more dimensions than can be effectively captured by any one-dimensional measure. On the other hand, if we use multiple indexes to characterize a situation, our cognitive limitations will stand in the way of formulating any definitive picture. Therefore, like everything else in life, quantification of social phenomena would require a trade-off between the confusion of a total picture and the ease of cognition of a measure offering a limited view.

For example consider our hypothetical city of Masters, PA. The demographic composition of Masters, PA is typical of the region, with a large number of working-class people (some of whom have been hard hit by the recent economic slump) along with pockets of urban blight, characterized by persistent levels of high unemployment. However, in this city there are areas that house a number of extremely wealthy families. Let us focus on three individuals plying their trade in Masters: a real estate broker, a college professor, and a city planner. All three of these individuals want to present the "true" economic picture of this city with a single number—the average income of the city's people. However, a problem arises, as these three have different objectives. The real estate broker wants to portray a very favorable picture of the city to his prospective clients as a nice place to live and raise a family. Therefore, he mentions as "average" the mean income of the residents of the town. Since Masters has a small number of extremely wealthy households, the mean is influenced by their high incomes. Therefore, the prospective buyer gets a picture of the average affluence of the city, which is much rosier than that espoused by the professor. The professor is conducting research in the area of urban economics, for which he is using the figure of median income. Since median is the middle income from the highest to the lowest, his number is not affected by the presence of the wealthy sector of the community. However, even this number, which presents a less attractive picture of the economic well-being of the city, is far superior to the one used by the city planner. The city planner of Masters wants to respond to a request for a grant proposal from the state government to bring in money earmarked for the economically depressed areas. For this proposal, she uses the modal income of the town, which is the most frequently found income of the inhabitants.

Since these three individuals use three different measures of average income because of their different objectives, is it possible to pick out the one who is engaged in an act of deception? We would argue that none of them can be accused of such an act unless some other kind of deception is present. For example, when it comes to the definition of average, because of its intuitive appeal, most people use the arithmetic mean, median, and mode, in that order. Therefore, by convention, if one uses the term *average* for the mean, one can feel justified. The use of the median may require justification, and the use of the modal income would certainly require its mention in the report, to be ethically fair and aboveboard. However, the use of any of these measures cannot be called a deception. Therefore, we must conclude that without the *intent* of deception none of the figures can be characterized as a lie; there can be honest difference of opinion, even among those whose business it is to deal with numbers, as to which one of these three represents the most valid picture of the city.

Another source of bias, Huff claimed, comes from the deceptive use of pictorial information—graphs. A picture is often worth a thousand words. Therefore, the need to convey information by graphical means is rather strong. But in the process one might take advantage of certain trickery. Consider the example in Figure 4.7, where we have depicted nonwhite unemployment as a

Figure 4.7 Ratio of Nonwhite to White Unemployment Rate

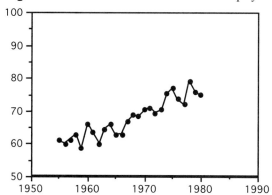

Source: U.S. Bureau of Labor Statistics

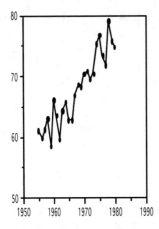

Figure 4.8 Ratio of Nonwhite to White Unemployment Rate

percentage ratio of white unemployment. In 1955, the unemployment rate within the nonwhite population was 62% higher than that within the white population.

Would it suit your purpose to present the information in the way we have done, or do you want to portray more dramatically the plight of the minority population in the United States? If you do, you can s-t-r-e-t-c-h the graph for added visual effect showing the same information (Figure 4.8). Obviously, in this case the difference between nonwhite and white unemployment is portrayed in a much more dramatic fashion.

What if you contend that the situation for the minority population is really not that bad, or that the situation has not changed appreciably over the years? In that case, you can add one more trickery. You can increase the range of the vertical axis, which allows you to present the same information in a different light. Against a much wider range of possible ratios of unemployment, the ethnic difference in the relative measure of economic deprivation does indeed look small (Figure 4.9).

Figure 4.9 Ratio of Nonwhite to White Unemployment Rate

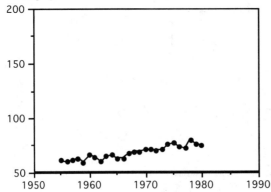

Figure 4.10 Ratio of Nonwhite to White
Unemployment Rate

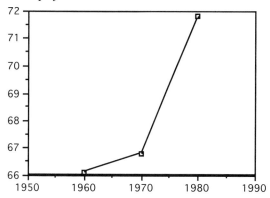

Yet another effective way of representing a series may be by using selective years for comparison. For example, you may want to present the same information contained in the three diagrams, but *even more emphatically.* You may want to show them in either of the following ways without "lying" with your statistics. In both of the next diagrams, we have selected only three years—1960, 1970, and 1980. This restriction removes the distracting effects of yearly fluctuations and allowed us to present the long term trend in the figures. Then, by simply manipulating the vertical axis I have presented my case with two radically different visual effects (See Figures 4.10 & 4.11).

Now that we have given you various ways of presenting the same information, which do you think represents the "true" picture? The answer is simple: We do not know which of these diagrams would be classified as a deceptive representation of the reality. However, if there are ones that might be interpreted as edging toward

Figure 4.11 Ratio of Nonwhite to White
Unemployment Rate

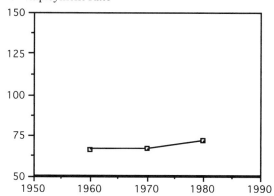

Figure 4.12 Ratio of Nonwhite to White Unemployment Rate

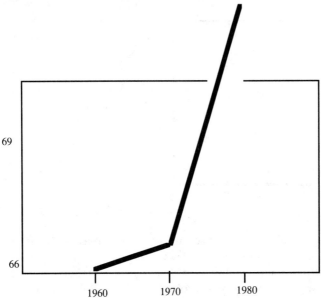

questionable practices, they would be Figures 4.9 and 4.11, since the vertical axis in these two figures has been made to have a wider range than is warranted by the data. But would you call that lying? In real life, truth, like beauty, lies in the eyes of the beholder.

In the preceding examples, the difference between interpretation and deception might have been subtle, but consider the rendition of the same information shown in Figure 4.12. In this diagram, you are not only presenting facts, but also trying a make a rather loud statement by the obvious analogy of the ratio going through the ceiling.

Darrell Huff pointed out that, intended or unintended, deception may creep in more readily when one uses graphics instead of lines and bars, which are drawn according to scale. Consider a diagram showing the plight of African elephants (Figure 4.13). It is shocking to realize that in 10 years the elephant population has diminished to one third of its 1980 size. However, the problem with this diagram is

Figure 4.13 African Elephant Population, 1980–1990

that the pictures are not drawn according to scale. Since our eyes catch the relative size differences in the picture more readily than the difference in magnitude between the numbers, we may not be able to catch that the 1980 figure is more than three times the size of the 1990 figure. These kinds of pictorial renditions are popular with presenters at various levels of legislative hearings and administrative decision making, as the message is direct and dramatic. With computer graphics so easy to use, the possibility of some creative minds deceiving the unwary has never been greater.

The power of strong visual presentation is well recognized and well documented. A 1985 *Wall Street Journal* story documents how the use of such a tool helped the cause of Caspar Weinberger, then Defense Secretary, to avert a cut in the Pentagon budget coming from David Stockman, director of the Office of Manangement and Budget. The story reports,

> In staving off Mr. Stockman's assault on the planned buildup, Mr. Weinberger turned to a tactic for which he has since become famous, the chart and easel. The defense secretary's charts, presented in a meeting with the president, showed large soldier's bearing large weapons, which were labeled "Reagan budget." They towered above small soldiers with small weapons labeled "OMB budget." President Reagan went along with the "Reagan budget."[2]

With the ever-increasing capabilities of personal computers, the ability to manipulate information is also increasing, as is our responsibility to present information as objectively as possible. Anyone engaged in public policy formation must not take this responsibility lightly because erroneous statistical information has often led to bad policies and inflicted suffering on innocent people.

Those Not So Innocent Numbers

We have argued that while it is relatively easy to define outright falsehood or lying by the measure of intent and the sheer fabrication of data, the line between deception and differences in interpretation is rather murky. However, often the intentions of the presenters of information are not obvious; nor do we have the capability to detect purposive contamination of data. Since we tend to place our faith in the objectiveness of numerical information more readily than in the qualitative statements, history is replete with examples of deceptive use of statistics bringing incredible misery to people. For example, in 1896 Frederick L. Hoffman, a nationally famous statistician for the Prudential Insurance Company of America, wrote a book titled, *Race Traits and Tendencies of the American Negroes*. Hoffman's thesis was that since their emancipation, black people (having come out of the

---

[2] Tim Corrigan, "Weinberger Finds His Wee-Worn Strategies Always Succeed in Blunting Defense Budget Ax," *The Wall Street Journal*, March 1, 1985.

protective care of their slave owners) were going back to their "basic racial trait" of "immorality of character." Hoffman based his theory on a number of different statistics that he had collected. He noted that in 1890 there were 567 Negroes in prison for rape, which constituted 47% of the prison population convicted on rape charges. Since this number was significantly greater than the proportion of the Negro population (about 10% at the time), according to Hoffman, rape and other sexual crimes were reflective of the "Negro racial trait." Hoffman thus concluded that

> All the facts brought together in this work prove that the colored population is gradually parting with the virtues and the moderate degree of economic efficiency developed under the regime of slavery. All the facts prove that a low standard of sexual morality is the main and underlying cause of the low and anti-social condition of the race at the present time.[3]

Hoffman then connected the "Negro racial trait of immorality" to the high mortality rate among the Negro population. On the basis of this causal linkage, disregarding the fact that the census of 1890 showed a steady increase in the size of the black population, Hoffman predicted that Negroes were doomed to face a "gradual extinction of the race." This statistical study was accorded an added dose of respectability as it was published by the American Economic Association and was widely used as a weapon in promoting white supremacy for decades to come. However, another important consequence of this study was that as a result of this and other internal statistical studies that judged blacks to be bad actuarial risks, Prudential promptly started to cancel all black life insurance policies. Within four years, by the end of the century, most insurance companies got out of the business of insuring African Americans.[4] In a similar manner, statistics have been used over the years to perpetrate many kinds of heinous crimes, or their faulty uses have led to extremely inefficient public policies.

Structure above a Swamp

Our discussions in this and the previous chapter may no doubt be confusing to you. On the one hand, we emphasize the relative nature of truth, and, on the other, we advocate objective analysis. The resolution of this contradiction may be achieved by quoting Karl Popper, the eminent philosopher of science:

> The empirical basis of objective science has thus nothing "absolute" about it. Science does not rest upon rock-bottom. The bold structure of its theories rise, as it were, above a swamp. It is like a building erected on piles. The piles are driven down

---

[3] Frederick Hoffman, *Race, Trait and Tendencies of America Negroes.* Quoted in Joel Williamson, *The Crucible of Race: Black-White Relations in the American South Since Emancipation*, New York: Oxford University Press, 1984, p. 329.

[4] For a detailed discussion, see Joel Williamson, *The Crucible of Race: Black-White Relations in the American South Since Emancipation* (New York: Oxford University Press, 1984).

from above into the swamp, but not down to any natural or "given" base; and when we cease our attempts to drive our piles into a deeper layer, it is not because we have reached firm ground. We simply stop when we are satisfied that they are firm enough to carry the structure, at least for the time being.[5]

Therefore, while "scientific laws" regarding the society can be empirically tested, their truth cannot be known. This ability of testing hypotheses has lent social sciences and policy science a considerable degree of credibility. Hence, in this shifting ground of an elusive "truth," we want to achieve objectiveness of analysis by being systematic in our definition of goal, consistent about our method of analysis, and forthright about our implicit assumptions.

In psychology it is often held that the strength of one's character can also be the source of one's weakness and fatal flaw. Similarly, the appeal of objective methods of policy analysis is their ability to present complex phenomena with simple, easy to understand numbers and figures. At the same time, the unquestioned acceptance of these statistical artifacts can lead to serious flaws. Therefore, since we know that statistics are extremely useful and powerful tools, we should also know how to use them skillfully. This skill is honed with practice and by knowledge of the methods of manipulation.

Plotting with a Computer

You can use a computer most profitably to generate graphs and plots. MYSTAT will allow you to do scatter plots and bar diagrams.

However, MYSTAT is not designed primarily for drawing graphs. Therefore, the graphs presented in this book are not drawn with the help of MYSTAT. There are some exquisite graphing softwares readily available. For DOS computers, Harvard Graphics, and for MacIntosh, Cricket Graphs can do excellent work. All the graphs in this book are drawn in Cricket Graph.

Your MYSTAT program allows you to draw scatter plots, stem-leaf plots, and histograms. Let us consider the data on state and federal grants to Masters in current dollars. I have drawn a line graph below.

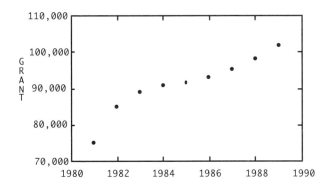

[5] Karl Popper, *The Logic of Scientific Discovery* (New York: Harper and Row, 1959).

You can draw this graph by the following procedure.
If you have a DOS-based computer, type in
PLOT GRANT*YEAR
The computer will know that the first term is the *Y*-axis variable (the dependent variable) and second one is the *X*-axis variable (the independent variable). You can manipulate the axis size by specifying axis height in the **YMAX, YMIN, XMAX,** and **XMIN** commands.
If you have a MacIntosh, drag down **Graph** and choose **Plot**. Then, click on your dependent variable and **Select** it. It will show up on the box below **Select**. Then identify the independent variable and by the same procedure. Click on **OK**.
MYSTAT will also allow you to plot a histogram for a quick look at the distribution. Below, I have drawn a histogram on the same variable series. To reproduce it, type
HISTOGRAM GRANTS.
If you have an Apple, follow the procedure for scatter plot, but choose the icon for **Histogram**.
You can alter the axes by choosing various sizes for special effects.

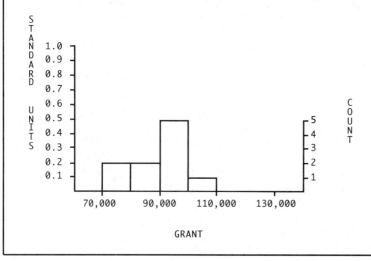

Exercises

1. Suppose we have two cities. The first has an average (mean) income of $18,000, with a standard deviation of 270,000; for the second city, the mean income is $53,000 with a standard deviation of 320,000. In which city is income more equally distributed?

2. Write an essay on truth and objectivity in quantitative analysis for public policy. Within this context, describe the relative advantages and disadvanteges of the various measures of central tendency and dispersion. Provide appropriate examples.

3. Collect data on the growth rate of per capita GNP, rate of inflation, and unemployment from 1950 (consult the *Economic Report of the President* and *Statistical Abstract of the United States*). First make the case that the nation has been better served by the Republican presidents, and then make the case for the Democrats based on the same set of data.

4. Consider the following table, which shows yearly data on percentages of the population living under poverty. Plot the data and derive as many different (and even contradictory) conclusions as you can from them.

Year	All	White	Black
1959	22.4	18.1	58.2
1960	22.2	17.8	56.4
1961	21.9	17.4	56.8
1962	21.0	16.4	56.1
1963	19.5	15.3	51.1
1964	19.0	14.9	49.8
1965	17.3	13.3	47.1
1966	14.7	11.3	39.7
1967	14.2	11.0	38.2
1968	12.8	10.0	32.8
1969	12.1	9.5	30.9
1970	12.6	9.9	31.6
1971	12.5	9.9	31.3
1972	11.9	9.0	32.4
1973	11.1	8.4	29.3
1974	11.2	8.6	29.7
1975	12.3	9.7	29.8
1976	11.8	9.1	29.5
1977	11.6	8.9	29.0
1978	11.4	8.7	29.4
1979	11.7	9.0	28.1
1980	13.0	10.2	29.9
1981	14.0	11.1	34.2
1982	15.0	12.0	35.6
1983	15.2	12.1	35.7
1984	14.4	11.5	33.8
1985	14.0	11.4	31.3
1986	13.6	11.0	31.1
1987	13.5	10.5	33.1
1988	11.6	8.8	29.1

5. Look at some of the recent news reports presented with quantitative data. See if you can derive a different conclusion by looking at the same set of information.

PART II

CAN WE FORECAST THE FUTURE?

Chapter 5

Projection Techniques: When History Is Inadequate

Projection Versus Causal Prediction

One of the most important functions for an organization is to plan for the future. If you were asked to predict the future course of any event, how would you begin the process? We begin to predict what may happen in the future by looking at what has happened in the past. It is not merely a cliché that it is impossible to predict the future without knowledge of the past. In history we look for **trends** and the **causal connections** that offer explanations of the events at hand. We may call the analysis of trends, **projection**. In contrast, we may call **prediction**, the inquiry into the causal relationship that binds the variable to be explained (the *dependent* variable) to a set of variables (the *independent* variables) that purport to explain it.

We call trend analysis *projection* because it contains an underlying hypothesis that whatever factor(s) had set in motion the past pattern of change, it will continue to operate in the future, leading to the same rate of growth or the same pattern of behavior. This postulate of continuation of the past trend into the future is called the *assumption of continuity*. This assumption is the underlying premise of all forecasting methods. Therefore, projection techniques aim at discerning the past trend and projecting it into the future. Of course, forecasting on the basis of past trend raises the philosophical question of whether history really repeats itself. Without getting embroiled in this age-old controversy, we can safely point out that since progress in the realm of social sciences is mostly evolutionary and incremental, the study of any long socioeconomic series would point to the existence of some sort of trend patterns.

The causal analysis, in contrast, hypothesizes that the future development of the dependent variable is not related to its past trend (at least not to any significant extent) and, therefore, its future behavior cannot be predicted solely based on its past pattern. Instead, it is determined by a complex causal linkage between the dependent variable and a set of independent variables.

An example may clarify the difference. If we want to know the extent of future health care needs, we can either estimate it by looking at the past trend and saying that since health care costs increase by a certain percentage every year, we forecast that in five years we will need a corresponding amount of money to meet health care needs. Or, we may try to explain future health care needs by looking at various explanatory factors, such as the percentage of children and elderly in the population, or expenditures on preventive medicine, food and nutrition, education, rate of growth of income, etc.

Both projection and prediction methods have their relative advantages and drawbacks. Projection methods often turn out to be easier to use for forecasting, while the predictive methods are better suited for policy analysis. For selecting the appropriate model, you must consider factors such as data availability, time, and resource limitations.

Inadequacy of History

If we want to forecast the future with the help of the past, we need a minimum amount of information going back in time to provide us with any kind of meaningful insight into the future. Unfortunately, however, researchers and policy analysts often face the problem of inadequacy of past information. This inadequacy may result from (1) lack of history itself, (2) the fact that nobody in the past cared to collect information, or (3) the fact that although past information exists in a scattered manner, its compilation in a series would require the expenditure of an unacceptable amount of time and money.

If the phenomenon under study is of recent origin, we may not have a past to look into. Thus, if we want to forecast the growth of the AIDS epidemic or the use of personal computers by public sector managers into the next decade, we will not find any information going back more than a few years. Also, during the course of an analysis, a researcher often comes across the problem that past data are rather sketchy, as no systematic effort was made to collect them. Thus, a city attempting to estimate the influx of tourists may find out that such data exist only for the last two years. Or it may find out that various agencies have collected the data over a number of years without a great degree of cooperation or cohesion. As a result, the compilation of the data in one continuous series would require a good deal of time and money. In such cases, where the analysts do not have the luxury of a long historical data series, projection can be made by using a simple method of forecasting on the basis of the past rate of growth. For these kinds of cases, I discuss a number of techniques that can be classified under two broad headings: single-factor projection and the judgmental method.

Single-Factor Projection

Suppose we are interested in projecting the number of cases of AIDS infection in our area. Since this virus has been recently identified, our town has data on the number of AIDS victim for only the last two years. Last year, there were 150 reported cases, while the year before, there were 138 cases. Therefore, the rate of AIDS infection in our area increased by nearly 9% last year. On the basis of this best available information, we may project the next year's infection by multiplying the number of this year's infected cases by 1.09. In symbolic terms, this can be written as

$$P_1 = (1 + r) P_0 \qquad (5.1)$$

where P_1 is the future year's population,

r is the rate of growth, and

P_0 is the present year's population.

Therefore, using this formula, we can predict that if the current population of AIDS victims is 150, then by one year later, this number is estimated to reach

$150 \times (1.09) = 163$. Using the same logic, we can see that the year after, this number is going to increase by another 9%. Thus, if P_2 is the population for the second year, then it can be estimated by

$$P_2 = (1 + r) \, P_1. \tag{5.1a}$$

Since we know from equation (5.1) that P_1 is equal to $(1 + r) \, P_0$, we can substitute this expression for P_1 to obtain

$$P_2 = (1 + r) \, (1 + r) \, P_0,$$

which means

$$P_2 = (1 + r)^2 \, P_0. \tag{5.2}$$

Therefore, it is obvious that if the population grows at a constant rate, to obtain the second year's population, we must multiply the current year's population by a factor of one plus the rate of growth to the power *two*. If the population keeps growing at this constant rate, in three years we can expect the number to reach the current year's population multiplied by the factor of one plus the rate of growth to the power *three*. Therefore, by generalizing this logic, we can write the formula as

$$P_n = (1 + r)^n \, P_0 \tag{5.3}$$

where n is any year in the future. Thus, if we want to estimate the number of people who might be inflicted with the deadly virus 10 years from now, we set the number of years equal to 10 in the preceding equation ($n = 10$). Thus, we write equation (5.4) as

$$P_{10} = (1 + .09)^{10} \, P_0 \tag{5.4}$$

Using this formula, we can estimate that 10 years from now, *if the present rate of infection continues*, we can expect to see 355 people coming down with the infection.[1] This is the formula of geometric growth, which is also used to calculate compound interest rate. The use of this formula can make the task of an analyst easy, as the size of any future population can be estimated simply by substituting the appropriate numbers in equation (5.3).

For policy analysis, it is often important to know not only the point estimate

---

[1] Those of you who have hand calculators with a button that says [y^x] can be spared of having to multiply 1.09 ten times. The [y^x] key raises a number to the desired exponent. To calculate this number, you need to (a) enter 1.09; (b) then hit the [y^x] button followed by (c) the number 10; (d) press the [=] sign to obtain the value for the expression $(1 + .09)^{10}$. By multiplying this number to the initial number of cases (P_0), you can estimate the value of P_{10}.

of the number of cases n years in the future, but also the total number of cases for the entire time span. Therefore, to estimate the total number of people afflicted with the AIDS virus during the next 10 years, we can estimate the size of the inflicted population for each year by using equation (5.5) and then adding them up. Since this process is cumbersome and time consuming, we can estimate the sum of any geometric series using the following formula:

$$\sum_{n=1}^{k} P_n = \frac{(1+r)^{n+1} - 1}{r} P_0$$

(5.5)

Using this formula, which can be calculated using a hand calculator, we can estimate the total number of patients needing treatment and public assistance to be nearly 2,634. (See footnote 2). Multiplying this number by the current level of medical costs and public funding per patient, for example, we can provide a rough-and-ready estimate of the total medical costs for the treatment of these 2,634 would-be patients and the amount of money that will be required in public assistance during the next 10 years for the city.

In the preceding example, we projected the future values of a variable on the basis of its past rate of growth. However, projections can be made on the basis of many other factors. For example, suppose a large parcel of vacant land within a city is being considered for rezoning. The new zoning ordinance will allow residential housing, apartments, or commercial buildings. Analysts may use past information on land use patterns and their fiscal impact to project the future needs of the new community. Thus, by looking at the prices of the proposed residential units, planners can get a good idea about the economic capabilities of the newcomers. From the data for the larger city or a similar neighborhood, projections can be made for detailed demographic characteristics of this group indicating, among others, the number of school-age children and elderly, commuting behavior, and recreational needs. For instance, if we expect 10,000 people to settle in the new neighborhood, by calculating the percentage for each demographic segment, we can project their numbers. These projections, in turn, would allow the projection of future resource needs for schools, libraries, recreational facilities, roads, sewer systems, and other necessary infrastructure. These data can also be used for projecting traffic congestion, crime rate, or the generation of various kinds of tax revenues for the city. This method of projection is often called **fiscal impact analysis**.

[2] To arrive at this number, we write equation (5.5) as follows:

$$\sum_{1}^{10} P_n = \frac{(1+.09)^{10+1} - 1}{.09}.$$

Figure 5.1 The Problems of Single-Factor Projection

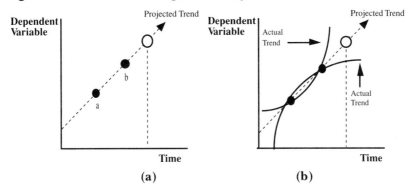

(a) (b)

Problems of Single-Factor Analysis

Using the single factor projection method, a forecast is performed by projecting past behavior into the future. This method is relatively inexpensive and provides a quick estimate of the future course of events.[3] Often, to avoid the high cost of conducting a detailed study, this quick projection technique is used at various levels of public decision making. We frequently come across it in public policy debate estimates of important social and economic phenomena, such as the crime rate, population growth, number of drug addicts, etc.

The problem with such an estimate is the implicit assumption that whatever happened during the previous period will continue to remain unchanged. However, in life, relationships hardly remain unaltered over time. Thus, if we project the rate of growth of the AIDS virus among the U.S. population, based on the last five year's experience, we can see that there is already some empirical evidence to suggest that the virus's rate of growth may have slowed down a little, at least among some target groups, because of greater public awareness through education and media exposure. Therefore, the reality of the future may not turn out to be as dire as predicted by our method.[4]

Figure 5.1 illustrates the predicaments of a single-factor projection. Figure 5.1a, the two black dots represent the two known points in history. On the basis of this meager knowledge, we are predicting the linear trend shown by the arrow. However, as you can readily see, an infinite number of nonlinear trends can be drawn through two points. In Figure 5.1(b), I have drawn two such nonlinear trends. If any of these is the actual trend, it is obvious from the illustration that a projection based on a straight line trend will cause serious errors.

---

[3] Although elaborate models of fiscal impact analysis are available, this method of projection is often less expensive than other methods we are going to discuss shortly.

[4] However, some other studies are claiming contrary evidence.

Single-Factor Analysis: The Fiscal Impact of Illegal Immigration in San Diego County

Because of the various problems associated with single-factor projections, they are always highly controversial. Yet, when there is no reliable information available, they can effectively serve as the starting points of policy debate and eventual policy formation. Since these techniques are extremely common in the public sector decision-making process, let me give you an example.

Located on the border with Mexico, San Diego County faces the problem of large numbers of illegal immigrants, mostly from Mexico and other central American countries. Since nearly all of these people are extremely poor, they impose a great deal of cost in health care, education, and law enforcement, which the County must bear. Therefore, in 1992, the state of California commissioned a study to estimate the number of illegal immigrants in San Diego County.[5] However, the researchers faced the problem that nobody had any information on the number of illegal aliens. Therefore, they used some simple but imaginative methods. The number of illegal aliens were estimated by the following procedure:

> During the 12 month period ended September 30, 1991, the INS (Immigration and Naturalization Services) apprehended 540,300 undocumented immigrants in San Diego County. It has been further estimated by the San Diego Border Patrol that between 1 in 3 and 1 in 5 undocumented immigrants are actually apprehended. This implies that from 1,080,600 to 2,161,200 undocumented immigrants succeeded in entering San Diego County during the year.[6]

The study estimated the cost to the state and county governments for the care of the illegal immigrants by calculating their proportion to the total population served by the health care services, education, social services, and criminal justice system, and then multiplied that number by the total expenditure. This was claimed to be the total cost to the state and local governments. Following a similar procedure, the researchers estimated the tax revenue contributions by the undocumented alien population of the region. The total net cost to the state and local governments was estimated to be $145,921,845.

---

[5] This study generated a lively controversy on the cost of illegal immigration in the region. Without taking any side in the controversy, I am simply reporting the results as an example of single-factor projection when no other data are available.

[6] *A Fiscal Impact Analysis of the Undocumented Immigrants Residing in San Diego County.* Report by the Auditor General of California, C-126, August 1992, p. 11.

Judgmental Methods of Projection

Frequently in life we encounter situations in which forecasting cannot be performed in a structured way, either because of a lack of knowledge of the past or because the causal linkages are too complex to be quantified properly. In such cases forecasts must be based on special insights and intuition. Let us consider an example. The passage of a piece of legislation through the U.S. political process is a highly complex affair. After it works its way through a maze of committees, it must pass both chambers of the Congress. After its passage, if the President signs it, it becomes the law. This process can be easily derailed if there is disagreement between the House and the Senate, or if the President decides to veto the legislation. However, it may be necessary to predict the future of a particular piece of legislation so that those with a stake in the matter can be prepared for a change in the course of action. Or, consider the case of policy makers in the State Department, who are waiting for a certain development to take place in a foreign country and want a reliable forecast of the situation. In such cases, one must depend on forecasts based on intuition or subjective judgment of the experts. Out of this necessity, over the years, a good number of techniques have been developed to deal with unstructured forecasting needs.

Many phenomena in society must be analyzed in a structured manner. Therefore, a forecast of their behavior must depend on the use of the most sophisticated computers on earth—the minds of the experts. In the previous section, we attempted to estimate the growth of the AIDS virus with the help of only two data points. We also saw the problems posed by such simple techniques. For example, in projecting the spread of AIDS, in the population, one must consider the impacts of the present sexual habits, practices, and mores. But these are not unchangeable. Therefore, one must also consider the effects of increased awareness and the development of curative and prophylactic drugs on its subsequent development. In such a complex issue, it is entirely possible that no single individual would possess all the necessary information to draw a realistic conclusion. In such cases we must depend on judgmental methods of projection based on collective wisdom and experience of the experts. In the following sections we will discuss a few of them.

The Delphi Technique

The name *Delphi technique* was coined after the famous oracle in the Apollo temple in the ancient Greek city of Delphi, where the oracle (in fact, the priests hiding behind it) used to forecast the future of the devotees. The Delphi technique is an important subjective predictive tool that was developed in 1948 by researchers at the RAND Corporation. Like most of the other techniques in the field of operations research, the Delphi technique owes its origin to attempts to solve problems of military strategy systematically. However, the last four and a half decades have seen a wide use of this technique in many countries around the world.[7]

The Delphi technique was developed to bring a systematic, unbiased reasoning process into subjective group forecasting. For example, we may form a panel of experts and let them sit around a table and come to an agreement about what may take place in the future. However, decisions made by a group may suffer from several sources of biases. Thus, if there is a well-known authority in the panel, the lesser members may become intimidated. The same would be true if there is a strong personality who approaches an issue with a particularly strong opinion based on emotion, if the rest of the panel is dispassionate about it, they may be swayed by this one individual. Also (as we discuss in the final chapter) research shows that most people are prone to be victims of "groupthink."[8] That is, most of us loathe being the odd person out with a different point of view from the rest of the group. As a result, more cogent points with differing points of view may never be raised in a group discussion.[9]

One way of solving this problem is to ask the experts to forecast independently. In this case, the problem of succumbing to a "groupthink" will be averted, but if the experts have differing conclusions, we will have no way of achieving a consensus. Therefore, to find a happy medium between preserving the individuality of opinion and a synthesis of ideas, the Delphi technique was developed. It is based on five principles:

1. *Anonymity:* The anonymity of the individual group membership is achieved through strict physical separation of the panel members. In some cases even the names of the members should be kept secret from each other.

---

[7] For a historical account of its development, see Harold Sackman, *Delphi Critique* (Lexington, Mass: D. C. Heath and Company, 1975). Also see Juri Pill, "The Delphi Method: Substance, Contexts, a Critique and an Annotated Bibliography," *Socio-Economic Planning Science*, Vol. 5, 1971, pp. 57–71. However, for an excellent discussion on Delphi and other techniques of subjective decision making, see William N. Dunn, *Public Policy Analysis: An Introduction* (Englewood Cliffs, NJ: Prentice-Hall, 1981).

[8] The term *groupthink* was made popular by psychologist Irving Janis. For a more detailed explanation and many more examples, see his *Groupthink: Psychological Studies of Policy Decisions and Fiascoes*, a revised and enlarged edition of *Victims of Groupthink*, 1972 (Boston: Houghton Mifflin, 1982).

[9] People often choose not to express their "true preferences" in public for the fear of possible peer pressure or social ostracization. If the need to be "politically correct" overwhelms your need to be truthful to your true beliefs and preferences, your publicly held views will deviate from what you may believe to be the truth or your true preference. From the standpoint of the society, the price of distortion of the citizens' preferences may be considerable, as public policies based on misconstrued views can lead to inefficiency or social conflict. Therefore, where sensitive issues are involved, we may have to grant people the opportunity to articulate their preferences in private. For an interesting discussion of this need for anonymous discourse for the articulation of genuine preferences, see Timur Kuran, "Mitigating the Tyranny of Public Opinion: Anonymous Discourse and the Ethic of Sincerity," *Constitutional Political Economy*, Vol. 4, No. 1, 1993.

2. *Iteration*: The judgments of the panel members are summarized and circulated for the group members to modify their original positions. Each round of individual deliberations and receiving information on others' opinions is called iteration. During the entire process, there may be two or three such iterations.

3. *Controlled feedback*: The members are given summary measures of the questionnaires given to each panel member.

4. *Distribution of statistical summary*: The individual responses are tabulated and the measures of their central tendencies and dispersion are provided to the members. To eliminate the extremes, often the median value is presented for the measure of central tendency. As for dispersion, various measures of range are usually provided. The members may also receive detailed graphs and charts specifying the shapes of the distribution of response.

5. *Group consensus*: Finally, on the basis of this process of iteration and feedback, efforts are made to achieve a group consensus on the issue.

The Delphi technique was created primarily for forecasting technical information from a largely homogeneous group of experts. The overall homogeneity in value creates a strong central tendency for the distribution in the forecast values (like the bell-shaped curve). In such a situation, the mean value is a fair representation of the group's judgment on a particular issue. However, when it comes to forecasting a sociological phenomenon, such unimodality of distribution of opinion may not exist. Let us, for example, consider an emotionally charged issue: the future of race relations in the United States. If you assemble a group of experts on the matter, there are likely to be strong disagreements reflecting diversely held value positions. In such a case, the group may not come together to form a consensus. In such cases, a slightly different method of **policy Delphi technique** may be more appropriate.

A policy Delphi technique starts with the initial assumption that the experts are not homogeneous in their points of view. In fact, the panel members may not even be experts, but are individuals who represent the various interest groups of the issue. Therefore, for policy Delphi technique, the original steps are modified to reflect the changed reality:

1. *Selective anonymity*: In policy Delphi, it is recognized that there will be subjectiveness in arguments based on interest or value positions. Therefore, frequently the participants are kept anonymous only during the initial stage of discussion. After everybody has a chance to state his or her view, the issue may be debated openly in the subsequent rounds of iteration.

2. *Informed multiple advocacy*: Unlike the original Delphi technique, the panel members are chosen not for their expertise on the matter, but for their interest or knowledge in this matter. Thus, while considering policy options on how to contain outbursts of racial or ethnic hostility, the panel may include the conservative advocates of strict law and order, the liberal advocates of social reform, and the members of the opposing ethnic groups.

3. *Multimodal response*: Since opinions are likely to reflect the multimodal distribution of opinion of such a panel, the statistical summary to be provided to the members for the subsequent iterations may not attempt to find the central tendency. Instead, the summary may attempt to provide as accurate as possible a picture of the multipolar distribution of opinion.

4. *Structured conflict*: While the original Delphi technique depends on the convergence of views, the policy Delphi is built around conflicts. In a contentious, well-staked-out world, it is often helpful just to be able to define opposing points of view. Therefore, policy Delphi does not always aim at a resolution, and it can end up showing the final unbridgeable gap between the parties.

Both Delphi techniques may seem deceptively simple. For a successful use of this technique, you must follow the same path of structured reasoning as we discussed in the first chapter.

- *Define the problem.* First, you need to define the problem. A major portion of a successful Delphi process depends on the definition of an issue. For example, facing a probable cut in funding, an agency may engage in planning its course of action through the Delphi technique. Before it assembles the panel, it must decide the perimeter of the issue at hand. It may attempt to forecast simply the amount of money available for the next fiscal year, or it may decide to tackle the question of specific cuts corresponding to certain levels of funding. An ill-defined issue can easily cause confusion and cost the organization a great deal in wasted efforts, time, money, and morale. The proper definition of issue is even more critical for a policy Delphi, since social issues are likely to be far more complex than a technical problem facing an organization.

- *Choose the right panel.* Choosing the right panel is equally critical for the success of a Delphi technique. Hard thinking must precede the selection of the panel members. Often the individuals designing a Delphi may not have adequate knowledge of the important personalities relevant to the issue. For this Professor Dunn[10] suggests a practical way. Frequently, the planners may not be aware of the full slate of experts but are able to name the most influential figure in the debate. In such a case, this individual may be approached to identify the two people with whom he or she agrees most closely or disagrees most vehemently. By asking these individuals the same question, you can be on the way to selecting an entire panel that shows a full range of opinion.

- *Develop the first-round questionnaire.* Having defined the issue and identified the panel members, the next problem that confronts a designer of Delphi is the questionnaire. Since the success of Delphi depends on the type of questions that

---

[10] William N. Dunn *Public Policy Analysis: An Introduction* Englewood Cliffs, N.J.: Prentice-Hall, 1981, p. 198.

are put before the panel, the analyst must decide on the types of questions that would be asked in the first and the subsequent rounds of discussion. The questionnaire for the first round must be developed with an eye for the next. There are no hard and fast rules about developing these questionnaires. Suppose the purpose of the exercise is to obtain a forecast, say of the number of AIDS victims in the next five years. In such a case, we can start off with some very structured questions regarding the future spread of the disease. Or, we can first discuss the trends in the factors that will determine the number of victims of the deadly virus. These factors would include trends in people's attitudes, sexual practices, changing social mores, and the attitude of the administration toward a frank discussion of unsafe sexual and intravenous drug use practices among the target groups and the distribution of prophylactic devices. In this case, the first-round questionnaire can be relatively unstructured and contain a number of open-ended questions. If the questions are not open ended, then the answers should be quantified according to some scale.

- *Analyze first-round results.* The results of the first round of questionnaires should be analyzed to determine the position of each panel member. These results should be tabulated, and for each question the measures of central tendency and dispersion should be calculated, which will be made available to the panel members for the subsequent rounds of deliberations. For example, if the question was, "How much do you expect teen-age sexual practices to change in view of an increase in awareness campaign?," and the answers were rated on a five-point scale (5 being significantly changed, 0 being no change at all), the panel members should be given at least the mean, median, standard deviation, and the range of distribution of the answers. If you have the graphics capability, it may not be a bad idea to show the panel visually the distribution of their answers. This may be a particularly good idea since you may not expect the panel members to be expert statisticians.

- *Develop questionnaires for the subsequent rounds.* Comparison of the group results with the individual responses paves the way for further discussion in the Delphi process. Therefore, the next round of questionnaires should be developed with the direction given in the first. For example, if the answers indicate a significant responsiveness of teen-age sexual behavior in response to a concerted ad campaign, forecasts (and future policies) can be developed through a more detailed discussion by pursuing this line further. Also, you may note that while the panel members do not have a chance to state their basic assumptions and the arguments for their positions, they are allowed to do so in the successive rounds. Since policy Delphis usually involve three to five rounds, there is ample opportunity for the members to evaluate each other's arguments in greater detail. These rounds of discussion may cause the members to modify their positions.

- *Arrange the panel discussion.* At the end of the process a group meeting is arranged so that the panel members can see if a consensus finally emerges through an open, face-to-face discussion. These group discussions can be particularly fruitful since by now each member of the panel is thoroughly conversant with the positions, arguments, hypotheses, and logic of others in the panel. Therefore, the group discussion can often take place in an atmosphere of mutual understanding, if not agreement.

- *Prepare the final report.*   The last step of a Delphi process is for the analyst to prepare the final report. This report should describe the entire process of discussion from step 1 of choosing the issue and selecting the panel members. If an overall agreement appears, the report should mention it, being careful not to ignore minority or extreme positions, if any. If there is no consensus, care must be taken to document the diverse points of view and the extent of divergence of opinion.

The Feasibility Assessment Technique

The *feasibility assessment technique* (FAT) is a commonly used judgmental method of projection. This method is particularly useful in forecasting the outcome of a contentious issue, fought by a number of interested parties. Therefore, FAT has found wide application in the forecasting of political, economic, military, and institutional outcomes of a conflict. It is a versatile technique and can be used at any phase of the policy-making process. For example, it can be used for predicting which issues are going to come to the forefront, what will be the legislative outcome, or how a policy will be implemented.

The technique can best be understood with the help of an example. Suppose we are trying to forecast the outcome of a bill for funding of AIDS information to high school students before a state legislature. To forecast the outcome of this debate, we need to make a list of the interested parties who play an active role in determining the outcome of the bill. We can make a list of the major players as follows: the governor, the liberal lawmakers, the media, the conservative lawmakers, the public health group, the conservative Christian church groups, and the gay activist groups. Let us assume that the governor is a moderate conservative who shows mild opposition for the bill. The liberal lawmakers strongly support the measure, while the conservative lawmakers are solidly opposed to it. The public health groups support the issue. Finally, the church groups are vehemently opposed to the public funding of explicit sexual education, and the gay activists are equally visceral in their support for the bill. In FAT terminology, the relative position of the "player" groups (those who exert some power and influence over the policy outcome) is called *issue position*.

The relative issue position is assessed by an analyst's (or a group of analysts') estimation of the probability that each player group is going to support the issue. This probability measure is assigned to each group, and it varies between +1 and –1. If a group is certain to support the issue, then its issue position will have a value of 1. If it is certain to oppose it, its issue position value is assessed to be -1. If the

Figure 5.2 Relative Issue Positions on Public Funding of AIDS Information

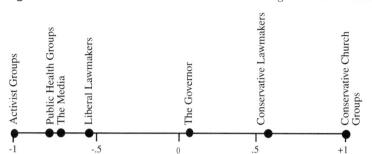

group is likely to be indifferent, then its value will be 0. Going back to the issue of spending public money for dissemination of sex education among high school students, you can readily see that we will not be too far from reality if we assign a +1 value to the gay activist groups and a -1 to the conservative church group. Let us assume that the support of the public health group is .9, the media .8, liberal lawmakers .6, the governor -.1, and the conservative lawmakers -.7. Figure 5.2 illustrates the relative issue positions.

Looking at Figure 5.2, you might think that since there are more groups to the left of the spectrum (right-hand side of the diagram) and with more passion, the issue is certain to be decided in favor of funding. However, reality is more complicated than that.

To begin with, not every player has equal influence over the outcome of the debate. Therefore, for the next step, we would want to measure the players' available resources on the issue. The resources within the disposal of each group would include prestige, legitimacy, money, time, administrative capabilities, and communication capabilities. The available resources are measured within the range of 1 (having a great deal of resources to bear) and 0 (with no resources whatsoever). Thus, looking at our lineup, we may hypothetically assign the values shown in Table 5.1.

Table 5.1 The Availability of Resources

The Governor	.9
The liberal lawmakers	.4
The conservative lawmakers	.5
The media	.8
The conservative church groups	.3
The gay activist groups	.1
The public health groups	.05

Table 5.2 Potential for Policy Influence

Groups	Issue Position (a)	Available Resources (b)	Potential for Policy Influence (a) x (b)
The governor	-.1	.9	-.09
The liberal lawmakers	.6	.4	.24
The conservative lawmakers	-.7	.5	-.35
The media	.8	.8	.64
The conservative church groups	-1.0	.3	-.30
The gay activist groups	1.0	.1	.10
The public health groups	.9	.05	.045
Total			+.285

The potential influence of each player can now be calculated by multiplying the issue position of each group with its total available resources. Thus, we can derive Table 5.2.

As you can see, the total potential of policy influences predicts a positive outcome for the measure. However, the potential does not often foretell the actual outcome. Every player faces a slate of issues it considers to be vital for its mission. For example, the governor has a number of agendas, of which fighting the funding of the AIDS information project is one. Therefore, facing an issue, every player must decide on the relative importance of the issue in relation to its other obligations. In other words, this particular issue, like all others facing each group, must have the group's commitment for investment of its resources. This is called the *ranking of resources.* Let us assume that the players have decided to allocate their total available resources as shown in Table 5.3.

In other words, the liberal lawmakers are willing to commit 15% of their resources, the gay activist groups are estimated to spend 80% of their resources, while the largely disinterested media is expected to commit no more than 2% in promoting this measure. In contrast, the governor has decided to spend no more than 10% of his resources in fighting this measure, but the conservative lawmakers have made this a hall-mark of conservative agenda and are expected to spend 30% of their available resources. Similarly, the conservative church groups are expected to commit 90% of their resources to fighting the public funding of what they consider to be offensive. This commitment factor added to the total potential determines the outcome. Thus, we may construct Table 5.4.

Table 5.3 The Ranking of Resources

The governor	.1
The liberal lawmakers	.15
The conservative lawmakers	.3
The media	.02
The conservative church groups	.9
The gay activist groups	.8
The public health groups	.6

Table 5.4 Potential for Policy Influence

Groups	Potential for Policy Influence (c)	Ranking of Resources (d)	Feasibility Score (c) x (d)
The governor	-.09	.1	-.009
The liberal lawmakers	.24	.15	.036
The conservative lawmakers	-.35	.3	-.105
The media	.64	.02	.0128
The conservative church groups	-.30	.9	-.270
The gay activist groups	1.0	.8	.08
The public health groups	.045	.6	.027
Total			-.2282

Table 5.4 gives us the total feasibility score, which shows that the opponents of the measure will have more than twice the support of the proponents (-.384 as opposed to .1558). Therefore, despite popular support (more groups in favor), the measure will be soundly defeated in the process.

You may find the conclusion of this hypothetical study somewhat surprising, especially in view of the initial assessment based on Figure 5.2 and Table 5.2. In fact, the ultimate outcome of any public policy depends on the relative issue position and the fraction of the total resources that the player groups are willing to invest to achieve a favorable outcome. Thus, you may notice that although the governor is the most resourceful person in this debate, his reluctance to invest a great deal of resources reduces him to the position of a minor player. On the other hand, by combining their total resources and a stronger determination, the coalition between the conservative lawmakers and the church groups becomes formidable in stopping public funding for AIDS information to high school students. This technique explains very well a number of social and political events. Consider, for example, the impact of the so-called Moral Majority, a coalition of right-wing religious groups and conservative politicians put together by the Reverend Jerry Falwell in the late 1970s and early 1980s. Although not supported by the majority of the American public, this group had a profound impact on the course of American politics that went far beyond its numerical strength.

Step-by-Step Method of Using the Feasibility Assessment Technique

Step 1:   Identify the issue.
Step 2:   Identify the player groups.
Step 3:   Estimate the issue positions of the groups.
Step 4:   Estimate the available resources for each group.
Step 5:   Estimate the resource rank within each group.
Step 6:   Calculate the feasibility assessment index.

The Expected Utility Model

Some analysts have found a variation of the expected utility model to be a useful forecasting tool for predicting the outcomes of an incredible variety of social phenomena, from international relations to banking regulations. Professor Bruce Bueno de Mesquita of Hoover Institution at Stanford University and his associates are at the forefront of such predictive efforts.[11] Their methodology for forecasting is far too complex to be discussed in this book, but I can give you the basic idea behind these prediction methodologies.

Suppose we are forecasting the probability of a change in a certain government policy. By scanning the political landscape, we can pick out the major players in the game. They may then be classified as proponents of a change and opponents of a change. Let us assume that the government and its allies do not want any change, while the opposition groups do. Those groups that are proposing a change are inviting a confrontation with those who prefer the status quo. Each group recognizes that just like investing in a risky project, the investment of resources to fight a rival has its own risks. For example, a loss might cause an embarrassment and may expose the group's vulnerability to its foes. On the other hand, a win will bring the usual and highly desired spoils. Therefore, a group's strategic move in determining whether to confront its opponent and how much to invest in the process will reflect its expectations about the future. The relative positions of the proponents and the opponents of a policy change can be shown with the help of the following example. Suppose opposition groups are proposing a change in the government's policy (e.g., in hand gun control, or increased funding for urban renewal, or conservation of open space, etc.), while the government and its supporters are opposing such a change. The expected payoffs of the two groups can be shown with the help of a diagram. Consider Figure 5.3. In this figure, the four *quadrants* created by the intersection of the two straight lines have been subdivided into eight *octants*. These octants are marked with boldfaced Roman numerals.

In Figure 5.3, we have plotted the expected payoffs of the two groups on a Cartesian plane. In the northeastern quadrant—comprising the two octants I and II—each contestant expects to gain by confronting the other. Therefore, if both the contenders feel that they can come out winners as a result of a confrontation, the chances of an open confrontation are extremely high. However, if the government's expectations of the outcome of a confrontation fall in the octant I, along the point *x*, then the government expects to gain more than what the opposition parties would gain. Therefore, we can expect the government to take an aggressive posture and start a confrontation. In an authoritarian regime, this confrontation may take the form of cracking down on the opposition. In a democratic system, it may be a presidential veto.

---

[11] See, for example, Bruce Bueno de Mesquita, David Newman, and Alvin Pabushka, *Forecasting Political Events: The Future of Hong Kong* (New Haven, CT: Yale University Press, 1985).

Figure 5.3 Expected Pay-off of the Government and Its Opposition

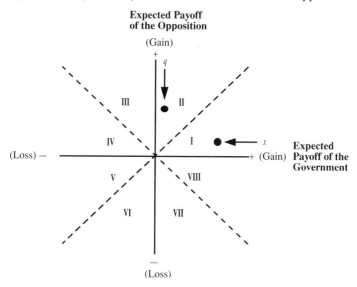

On the other hand, if the government's expectations of the outcome of a confrontation fall on a point, such as q on octant II, then it would expect to win but its win is going to be less than that of its rival. As a result, if mutual expectation patterns fall in this region, we can expect a reversal of role, where the opposition parties would more aggressively seek confrontation with the government. However, since both the parties expect to win, the chances of a confrontation are extremely high. In an international context, the disputes that fall within these two octants have escalated into war about 90% of the time.[12]

In the northwestern quadrant (octants III and IV), the opposition expects to win while the government expects to lose. In octant III, although the challenger expects to win, its gains will be smaller than the authority's loss. Therefore, seeing the prospect of a small loss, the government will sit down with the opposition and negotiate a compromise that gives the opposition an edge.

In octant IV, in contrast, the government is expected to suffer a heavier loss than what the opposition would gain. If the government's expectations match this kind of a pattern, we can expect it to accede to the demands of the opposition. In 1987, as a part of a wide-ranging budget compromise, President Bush decided to go along with the Democrats in increasing taxes. At that time the President had anticipated that he had more to lose by opposing a compromise. In view of his

---

[12] Douglas Beck and Bruce Bueno de Mesquita, "Forecasting Policy Decisions: An Expected Utility Approach," in Steven Andriole (ed.), *Corporate Crisis Management* (New York: Petrocelli Books, 1984).

earlier unequivocal campaign pledge of not increasing taxes ("Read my lips, no new taxes"), his action became a liability and came to haunt him later.

In the southwestern quadrant, both parties expect to lose. Therefore, if the expectations follow this pattern, there is little chance of a confrontation. You may note that in octant V the opposition's losses are expected to be greater than those of those in power. The situation is reversed in octant VI. Facing the prospect of a lose-lose situation, neither parties show much enthusiasm for a head-on confrontation.

Finally, the southeastern quadrant is the mirror image of the northwestern quadrant. That is, in this case, the government is expected to win in confrontation, while the opposition expects to lose. When the condition of octant VII prevails, the government perceives that it is making a legitimate demand on the opposition, and it has a good deal to gain from its position, but, more importantly, the opposition has a good deal more to lose. Situations such as these prove to be tranquil as the opposition is effectively shut off with the prospect of a heavy loss. For example, in the spring of 1984, President Ferdinand Marcos of the Philippines called for election. President Marcos often used the results of the highly corrupt elections to gain political legitimacy for his regime. As there was widespread disenchantment with his rule, many observers had predicted organized opposition to Marcos, or a call for the boycott of the elections and even violence. However, the leading opposition groups did not expect to defeat Marcos and expected to lose far more than the loss they could inflict on his regime by opposing him in the election. Based on their perception, Bueno de Mesquita correctly predicted no serious challenge to Marcos's presidency and a relatively uneventful election. We show the expected outcomes of confrontation in Figure 5.4.

The use of this expected utility model requires the identification of the major players and the estimation of their expectations with respect to the issue at hand. For these estimations, you can use the expertise of those who are directly knowledgeable of these groups. Having ascertained the groups' positions, you may first plot them in their respective octants to see if a pattern emerges. These results will tell you whether you can expect a confrontation.

Shortcomings of the Judgmental Methods

Often in life, issues are so complex that it is extremely difficult to capture all of their dimensions within the confines of structured techniques of analysis and forecasting. In addition, in real life you will encounter situations in which there is no history to depend on for predicting the future. In such cases, judgmental methods give us extremely useful alternatives. Time and again, the various subjective methods of prediction have proven their usefulness. However, like so many things in life, the very sources of their strength in one situation become their liability in another.

Although the techniques of judgmental methods offer more flexibility than

Figure 5.4 Dynamics of the Policy Outcome

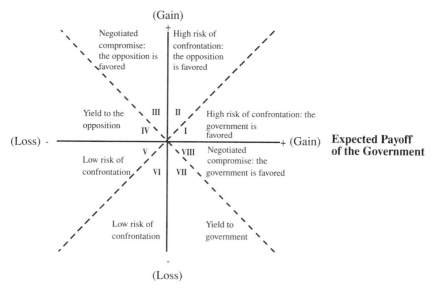

the other more rigorous statistical methods (which we will discuss in the following chapters), they still must operate within some structure. For example, in analyses of group interaction (say, between the government and the opposition), we assume that each group is making its decision independently and all at the same time. Yet it stands to reason that they are interdependent. Also, group interactions are part of a dynamic process in which groups communicate with each other, compromise, and form or break coalitions. Many of these complex behaviors cannot be accommodated even in the most flexible open-ended forecasting method.

However, the more serious problem with the judgmental methods is that since there is no systematic way of discussing the assumptions and arguments in the subjective assessments of the "experts," frequently judgments are contaminated by preconceived ideas, prejudices, nonarticulated agendas, self-interest, or other psychological pitfalls and cognitive limitations. For example, few experts (in and out of the government) had predicted the U.S. war with Iraq. Even at the last minute, most were willing to dismiss the threats and counterthreats (for example, Saddam Hussein's apocalyptic "mother of all wars") as simple bravado, posturing, or face-saving gestures. At the end, when all the pieces were put together, it seemed that most of the utterances of the rival sides were true. When President Bush ordered Iraq to get out of Kuwait or face war, he was not bluffing. On the other hand, when Hussein, facing incredible odds, said his army would never leave Kuwait on its own accord, he meant it. Yet the prospects of this strange war were so far fetched to most experts that almost until the first bullet was fired, they refused to believe the resolve of the two contenders. Similarly, because of these psychological impediments, the Central Intelligence Agency was caught off guard by the sudden collapse of the Soviet Union. Having poked and prodded, studied and analyzed the Soviet system for decades, the Agency experts completely failed to understand the fundamental fragility of the system.

Exercises

1. Consider the following facts in your community and explain how would you go about forecasting them for the next five years:
   a. The number of homeless population
   b. The number of child abuse cases
   c. The number of school-age children
   d. The number of violent crimes
   Explain your data needs, point out the possible sources, and choose the model for projection.

2. Suppose the indigent elderly population that depends on public assistance is growing at a rate of 4% per year in your county. At present there are 3,500 such individuals. How many such people would you expect to see at the end of three years from now? If it costs the county $2,300 per person for the health care of such people, estimate the total cost of indigent health care for your county.

3. Explain the problems of single-issue predictions. Despite these problems, single-factor projection remains one of the most commonly used techniques of projection. Taking a real life example, account for the wide-scale use of single-factor projection in public policy analysis.

4. Explain the process of policy Delphi technique. What are its strengths and shortcomings?

5. The city of Masters is facing a controversial issue. The marshland adjacent to a prosperous neighborhood is presently not being utilized. A developer has submitted a proposal to make it into a golf course. However, the marshland is the habitat for a number of migratory birds. Hence, the project is being opposed by the powerful environmental groups. The conservative, pro-business council members are supporting the project. Since this is a divisive issue, the mayor has expressed her mild opposition to the project, while the liberal members of the city council are in vehement opposition. The following table shows the relative position of the various parties, their available resources, and the ranking of resources. Predict the outcome of the debate.

Groups	Issue Positions	Ranking of Resources	Available Resources
Mayor	-.2	.3	.8
Developer	+1.0	.9	.3
Conservative city council members	.85	.6	.4
Liberal city council members	-.65	.8	.5
Environmental groups	-.9	.9	.9
The chamber of commerce	+.5	.4	.1

6. Take any current controversial issue facing your community, state, or the nation, such as gun control, abortion, the amount of national defense funding, etc. Then, as a group project, predict the policy outcome using the feasibility assessment technique. How accurate do you think your predictions are? What are the major weaknesses of your prediction? Would you feel comfortable using these techniques in a real-life situation? Explain. [Suggestion: The size of the group is often crucial to the success of projects like these. I have found it useful to keep the group size close to 5. A clan of larger size can be broken into several groups, attempting to forecast the same issue or different ones].

Chapter 6

Projection Techniques: Analysis of Historical Data

The Problem

Forecasting based on projection techniques requires understanding of the basic *pattern of behavior*. Without a pattern, variations are totally erratic or random, in which case the future behavior cannot be predicted. In the previous chapter we discussed methods of forecasting when we are faced with a paucity of past information. However, often we are fortunate to have a long history of behavior of the phenomena under study. When the past pattern is known, projection techniques aim at discerning the trend of past behavior and projecting it into the future. But availability of a good deal of historical data comes with its own set of problems. To understand the trend of a series (or the direction in which it is heading), one needs to plot the data first. Although it is an excellent idea to plot the data before you start to do anything with it, the scatter plot may not always reveal a strong trend. Consider, for example, a hypothetical series of tourists coming to visit our Pennsylvania town, Masters, which has a strong tourist industry that attracts vacationers primarily during the skiing and summer seasons. Masters's chamber of commerce has collected data on tourist influx quarterly (in three-month periods) for a 13-year period, from 1980 to 1992. We have plotted the data in Figure 6.1.

You may agree that the scatter plot of the quarterly tourist population looks quite confusing, and few conclusions can be drawn from it. The reason for this confusion is that the series contains a number of different elements which are obscuring our vision. In general, a data series contains an element of **trend**, or the general direction in which the series is heading. A series that tends to grow over time is called a **positive trend**, while a series that declines as time goes by is said to have a **negative trend**. Besides the trend, a data series may also reflect fluctuations resulting from the effects of **seasonality**. Further, a data series may exhibit effects of long-term economic **cycles**. As the economy expands and contracts during the

Figure 6.1 Number of Tourists in Masters, PA

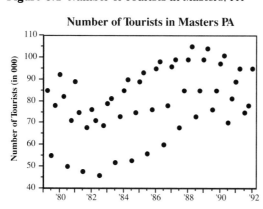

149

Figure 6.2 Linear Trend Patterns

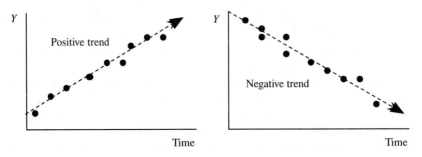

course of a business cycle, it affects many kinds of economic and social activities. Finally, a series contains the effects of pure random fluctuations, which are caused by factors outside our consideration. Natural calamities (like floods, earthquakes, devastating tornadoes), political events (like riots, assassinations of important political persons, election of a new chief executive or a political party) or institutional factors (such as changes in government regulations) can have an unpredictable effect on a series. For instance, the collapse of the Soviet Union had an extraordinarily important but unforeseen effect on the U.S. defense industry. Since these external factors cannot be factored in a model, their effects are called **random errors**. Therefore, time series data (data recorded over time) may contain the following:[1]

Data = Trend + Seasonality + Cyclical Effect + Random Error.

Let us examine these components in greater detail. Figure 6.2 depicts two **linear trend** patterns. Many aggregate social, economic, and demographic data (such as the per capita GNP of a country, population growth in a short term, etc.) show a positive linear growth when plotted over time. As shown in Figure 6.2, not all points of observations fall on the trend line. Since these deviations cannot be accounted for within the model, we assume that aberrations reflect the effects of the random error component.

In the cases presented in Figure 6.1, the rate of growth does not seem to change over the time period under consideration. This trend can be upward or downward. For example, despite little peaks and valleys for economic booms and recessions, the GNP per capita, measured in constant dollars, has shown an upward trend over the years in the United States. A series may also exhibit a

---

[1] Also, in reality, a series can assume a much more complex trend pattern. For a more detailed discussion, see Spyros Makridakis, Steven Wheelwright, and Victor McGee, *Forecasting: Methods and Application* (New York: Wiley, 1983).

Figure 6.3 Horizontal or No-Trend Pattern

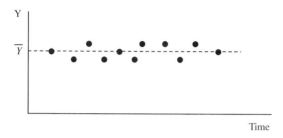

negative or a downward trend. For instance, during the 1980s, federal government assistance to state and local governments demonstrated a steady downward trend.

When data values fluctuate around a constant mean, a **horizontal trend pattern** is developed. This is characteristic of a series in which there is *no trend* and the data seem to fluctuate in a random fashion. In technical terms, such a series with no discernible trend is called a **stationary** series. In a stationary series, a trend line will go through the mean ($\bar{Y}$). Since there is no seasonality in the human reproductive process, for example, the daily number of births in New York City hospitals within a year will depict such a series. Figure 6.3 demonstrates a horizontal pattern of fluctuation.

The **seasonal trend** is shown in Figure 6.4. The quarterly fluctuations of a series are plotted, and it is apparent that the quarterly data depict a trend of regular fluctuations of peaks and valleys during the course of a year. Home construction, unemployment, crime, and the highway accident rates often tend to show this kind of seasonal variability.

A **cyclical trend** exists when the data are influenced by long-term economic fluctuations associated with the business cycle. Thus, during a period of slow

Figure 6.4 Seasonal Trend Pattern

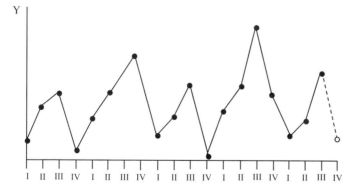

Figure 6.5 Effects of Economic Cycles

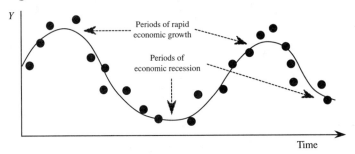

economic growth, housing construction will go down. Most of the economic data tend to be sensitive to the business cycle and fluctuate according to the phase of the cycle. Figure 6.5 reflects the cyclical variability of a series.

Going back to our example of quarterly tourist data, we can plot the data again (Figure 6.6) according to the effects of various elements in a series. As you can see, now the patterns are quite clear. The series reflects an overall positive trend over time, although it shows strong seasonal fluctuations along with effects of the economic recession of the early 1980s and 1990s and rapid economic expansion of the mid-1980s. Now that we have succeeded in showing definite patterns, our task of forecasting becomes a lot more manageable.

Patterns of Trend

The trend of a data series can take a wide variety of patterns. In this section, we discuss a few important trend patterns. Figures 6.7a and 6.7b show patterns of **quadratic trends**. The reverse U-shaped relationship is typical of a situation in

Figure 6.6 Discerning the Components of the Number of Tourists in Masters, PA

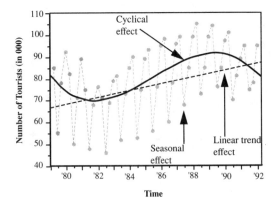

Figure 6.7 Quadratic Trends

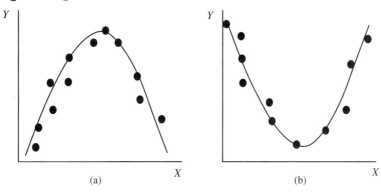

(a)   X   (b)   X

which the dependent variable shows an increasing pattern followed by a declining trend. Data on the percent of Americans living under the official poverty line demonstrate this kind of quadratic structure during the period 1950 to 1990. In terms of a causal linkage, we may consider the relationship between agricultural production and the application of fertilizer. As one increases the use of fertilizers, the level of production tends to go up. However, after the point of saturation, overuse of these chemicals reaches a toxic level and, consequently, begins to have a deleterious effect on production.

The U-shaped relationship, on the other hand, is typical of a per unit cost curve in a situation of increasing inefficiency as the scale of operation increases. Consider the operation of a county sheriff's department. If the sheriff's department operates at a very small scale, its cost of operation will be extremely high, because it will have to bear a large fixed cost for its administration and other necessary operations. However, as its size of operation increases (maybe because other small, incorporated cities will start contracting the sheriff's department and will not have a separate police department of their own), its per unit cost of operation (whichever way it is measured) will go down. But this downward trend cannot continue forever, and after a certain stage the department is going to be so huge that its efficiency will be hampered. Beyond this point (which in economics is regarded as the point of maximum efficiency), the unit cost of operation will start to increase. Therefore, if one measures the efficiency of an expanding organization over time, such a quadratic relationship may be discerned.

A series may also depict an **exponential** growth path, as shown in Figures 6.8a and 6.8b. For example, viewed over time, data on life expectancy in the developed world depict a negative exponential pattern close to Figure 6.8a. Advancements in medical technology have increased people's life expectancies at a fairly rapid rate. However, it seems that we are approaching a biological limit on how long we can survive, and the rate of growth is slowing considerably. The reverse, a positive exponential form (Figure 6.8b), is found for infant mortality.

A series can also depict a rather complex pattern of growth. For example, a

Figure 6.8 Exponential Trend

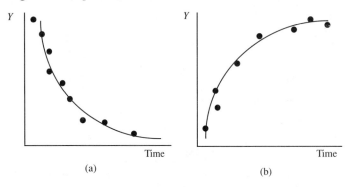

series can have a **logistic** or an S-shaped trend, such as the one shown in Figure 6.9. This trend shows a changing pattern of growth. The rate of growth is slow at the beginning of the series but changes during the transition period, at which time the rate of growth becomes quite rapid. However, after a certain point, this rate slows as the series reaches a steady state or an upper asymptote (a ceiling). This behavior is considered typical of a learning situation. When we try to learn something new (say, a foreign language), at the beginning our progress is painfully slow. However, after we have mastered the basics our pace of absorbing material accelerates, only to reach a point of saturation when we reach the upper limits of learning.

A series is said to have demonstrated a **catastrophic** trend when there is a sharp discontinuity (Figure 6.10). This kind of a precipitous rise or fall can come as a result of a war or some other kind of national calamity. For example, if one

Figure 6.9 Logistic Trend

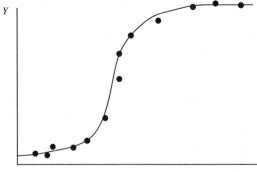

Figure 6.10 Catastrophic Trend

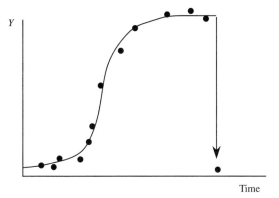

examines the growth of German per capita GNP prior to the second world war, the catastrophic impact of the war is apparent as the GNP plunges after the war. The technique of catastrophic trend analysis is still in its infancy and, therefore, is not commonly used in social science research or public policy analysis.

Methods of Seasonal and Trend Adjustment

Frequently the true nature of a trend is lost in the seasonal fluctuations of the data. In such cases, you may want to examine the data by filtering out the effects of seasonal fluctuations. Similarly, the pure effects of seasonal fluctuations can be muddled by the presence of a strong trend. Unless this trend factor is eliminated, the effects of the seasons on the data may not be apparent. Perhaps the simplest way of eliminating the effects of seasonal fluctuations and trends is the method of seasonal and trend adjustment.

Suppose the chamber of commerce in Masters, a small mountain resort town known for its winter and summer recreational facilities, is trying to understand the nature of tourist demand for its facilities. The town has been keeping records of quarterly figures of tourist populations for only the last three years. These are shown in Table 6.1.

As you can see, the data presented in Table 6.1 do not reveal a great deal of

Table 6.1 Tourist Population (in 000)

Year	1990				1991				1992			
Quarter	I	II	III	IV	I	II	III	IV	I	II	III	IV
	45	35	42	33	46	36	44	38	49	38	45	42

Figure 6.11 Plot of Number of Tourists per Quarter

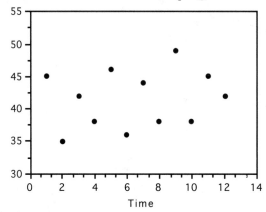

information regarding the nature of the town's tourist industry. Neither does their plot shown in Figure 6.11. Indeed, we would be hard pressed to draw too many conclusions from the information we have at hand.

Seasonal Adjustment

The method of seasonal adjustment can lend a helping hand. The reason for this apparent confusion regarding the data is that there are two factors at play: the seasonal effect and the trend effect. The presence of these two factors is obfuscating the picture presented by the raw data. To begin with, we may want to suppress the effects of seasonal variations to accentuate the effects of the trend. If you look at the data carefully, you will see that the first and the third quarters tend to bring in more tourists, as these two quarters cover the peak skiing and summer seasons. If there were no seasonal variation whatsoever, the quarterly totals would have been the same. Therefore, we can adjust for this variation by forcing each season to be the same. Table 6.2 shows the process of seasonal adjustment.

Table 6.2 The Calculation of Quarterly Adjustment Factors

Quarter	Quarterly Totals (1990-1992)	Quarterly Average	Quarterly Adjustment Factor (quarterly averages minus grand average)
I	140	46.7	+5.6
II	109	36.3	-4.8
III	131	43.7	+2.6
IV	113	37.7	-3.4
Total	493	41.1	

Table 6.3 Seasonally Adjusted Quarterly Tourist Population (in 000)

Year		1990				1991				1992		
Quarter	I	II	III	IV	I	II	III	IV	I	II	III	IV
	45	35	42	33	46	36	44	38	49	38	45	42
Adjustment factor	-5.6	+4.8	-2.6	+3.4	-5.6	+4.8	-2.6	+3.4	-5.6	+4.8	-2.6	+3.4
Adjusted figures	39.4	39.8	39.4	36.4	40.4	40.8	41.4	41.4	43.4	42.8	42.4	45.4

The quarterly totals were calculated by adding the number of tourists for each of the four quarters during the three-year period. Thus, during the first quarter, 45,000 tourists visited the town in 1990, 46,000 in 1991, and 49,000 in 1992. Therefore, during the first quarters, the town had a total of 140,000 visitors during these years. By dividing the quarterly total by 3, we calculated the average quarterly figure for the study period. You may notice that during this period there was a total of 493,000 visitors, which calculates to about 41.1 thousand tourists per quarter. This is the average of tourists that we could expect if there were no seasonal effect. Therefore, we can calculate the **seasonal adjustment factor** by subtracting the grand average from each quarterly average. This is the adjustment factor, which, subtracted from each individual quarter, will give us a seasonally adjusted figure. We show the seasonally adjusted figure in Table 6.3.

Armed with this new series of numbers the chamber of commerce can plan more effectively for the future knowing that at least for the last three years, there has been a definite upward trend in the number of visitors coming to town. By comparing Figure 6.11 with Figure 6.12, you can see how this process of seasonal adjustment has subdued the quarterly variations, and has emphasized the trend pattern.

Figure 6.12 Plot of Seasonally Adjusted Quarterly Data

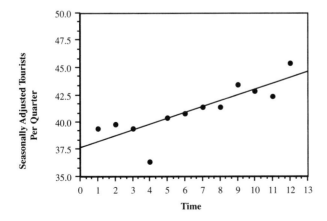

■ Using a Computer to Make Seasonal Adjustments

Business MYSTAT will make seasonal adjustments for a series. For DOS machines, the general command for seasonal adjustment is

ADJSEAS[<Var1>/SEASON=<#>,ADDI|MULT]

The # in the **SEASON** option will specify the periodicity, or the number of seasons in a year. For example, if the data are quarterly, there are four seasons; if you are working with biannual data, there are two seasons, etc. If you do not specify the number of seasons, the machine will assume that there are 12 seasons. In other words, you are working with a monthly data series. For creating the adjustment factor, data are generated either through an additive (**ADDI**) or a multiplicative (**MULT**) model. The default is a multiplicative model.

If you have a MacIntosh, drag down the **Forecast** icon and select **Smooth**. Then, by using the Select box, select the variable(s) to be seasonally adjusted. Click on the **Seasonal decomposition** box to ask for seasonal adjustment. Then specify the number of seasons in a year in the **Seasonal periodicity box**. Click on the **Save smoothed variables** box. Then click on **OK**.

Trend Adjustment

The chamber of commerce may also want to understand the patterns of seasonal fluctuations without the distorting effects of a trend. This can be done simply by adjusting the data for yearly variations. Again the logic is the same. If there were no trend pattern, there would be no variation across time. Therefore, in such a situation, fluctuations will be caused solely by seasonal factors. We can calculate the yearly totals for the three years and then subtract them from the yearly average to get the yearly or **trend adjustment factors**. We have done this in Table 6.4. These yearly adjustment factors show the average change from the mean. Therefore, by adjusting the data for each quarter by this factor, we will be able to suppress the influence of the trend. This will accentuate the seasonal variations. Table 6.5 shows this adjustment process.

Figure 6.13 emphasizes seasonal changes and has filtered out the trend factor. This diagram will help the policy makers in Masters visualize the seasonality

Table 6.4

Year	Yearly Total	Yearly Average per Quarter	Yearly Adjustment Factor (yearly average minus grand average)
1990	160	40	-1.5
1991	164	41	-0.5
1992	174	43.5	+2.0
Total	498	41.5	

Table 6.5 Trend Adjusted Quarterly Tourist Population (in 000)

Year	1990				1991				1992			
Quarter	I	II	III	IV	I	II	III	IV	I	II	III	IV
Adjustment	45	35	42	33	46	36	44	38	49	38	45	42
factor	+1.5	+1.5	+1.5	+1.5	+0.5	+0.5	+0.5	+0.5	-2.0	-2.0	-2.0	-2.0
Adjusted figures	46.5	36.5	43.5	34.5	46.5	36.5	44.5	38.5	47.0	36.0	43.0	40.0

of the tourist trend and plan for the future. Although the methods of seasonal and trend adjustment are not methods of forecasting per se, they can shed a good deal of light on the behavior of a seemingly chaotic data series. For instance, in this case, by looking at the seasonal fluctuations, we can make some useful observations. As you can see in Figure 6.13, the trend adjusted data show that the number of tourists visiting Masters has remained stable for the first two quarters. On the other hand, the numbers have gone up steadily for the third quarter, while they have declined for the fourth quarter. This insight into the data can be a powerful planning and analysis tool for the Masters chamber of commerce.

Smoothing Out the Fluctuations

In a time series data, the trend line is often obscured by the presence of seasonal and other kinds of cyclical and random fluctuations. If these distractions can be *smoothed out*, the trend pattern will be revealed. In this section, I discuss a few simple methods of smoothing out fluctuations and making a very short-term projection.

Figure 6.13 Plot of Trend Adjusted Tourist Data

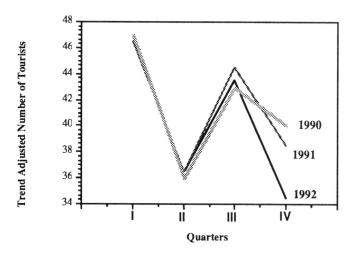

Let us consider the quarterly time series data on tourists visiting Masters, PA during the 13-year period from 1980 to 1992. As you can see from the plotted data presented in Figure 6.1, the trend line is hidden behind fluctuations caused by the seasonal variations. The quarterly data has been presented in Table 6.6.

Table 6.6 Quarterly Series on Number of Tourists Visiting Masters, PA

Year	Quarterly Data	Lag (1 year)	Moving Average (2 years)	Moving Average (4 years)
1980.1	85			
1980.2	55	85		
1980.3	78	55	70.0	
1980.4	92	78	66.5	
1981.1	82	92	85.0	77.50
1981.2	50	82	87.0	76.75
1981.3	71	50	66.0	75.50
1981.4	89	71	60.5	73.75
1982.1	75	89	80.0	73.00
1982.2	48	75	82.0	71.25
1982.3	68	48	61.5	70.75
1982.4	76	68	58.0	70.00
1983.1	71	76	72.0	66.75
1983.2	46	71	73.5	65.75
1983.3	69	46	58.5	65.25
1983.4	79	69	57.5	65.50
1984.1	81	79	74.0	66.25
1984.2	52	81	80.0	68.75
1984.3	73	52	66.5	70.25
1984.4	85	73	62.5	71.25
1985.1	90	85	79.0	72.75
1985.2	53	90	87.5	75.00
1985.3	75	53	71.5	75.25
1985.4	89	75	64.0	75.75
1986.1	93	89	82.0	76.75
1986.2	56	93	91.0	77.50
1986.3	76	56	74.5	78.25
1986.4	95	76	66.0	78.50
1987.1	98	95	85.5	80.00
1987.2	60	98	96.5	81.25
1987.3	78	60	79.0	82.25
1987.4	96	78	69.0	82.75
1988.1	99	96	87.0	83.00
1988.2	68	99	97.5	83.25
1988.3	85	68	83.5	85.25
1988.4	99	85	76.5	87.00
1989.1	105	99	92.0	87.75
1989.2	73	105	102.0	89.25
1989.3	85	73	89.0	90.50
1989.4	99	85	79.0	90.50
1990.1	104	99	92.0	90.50
1990.2	76	104	101.5	90.25

1990.3	85	76	90.0	91.00
1990.4	97	85	80.5	91.00
1991.1	101	97	91.0	90.50
1991.2	70	101	99.0	89.75
1991.3	81	70	85.5	88.25
1991.4	89	81	75.5	87.25
1992.1	95	89	85.0	85.25
1992.2	75	95	92.0	83.75
1992.3	78	75	85.0	85.00
1992.4	95	78	76.5	84.25
Forecast for 1993.1	-	95	86.5	85.75

Projecting the Immediate Past: Naive Projection

If I were to ask you to predict your earnings for the coming year, your prediction would probably be based on what you earned this year. Prediction based on last period's performance is often called the *naive* method of projection. In Table 6.6, we have written the quarterly data by pushing them down one row. In statistics, this process is called *lagging*. If we lag a column by one period, we express it in terms of what happened in the immediately preceding period. Similarly, a three-period lag would present the series in terms of what happened three periods ago. When we write in algebraic symbols, the periods are expressed in subscripts. For example, X_t would mean the value of the variable X in period t, which in this case is the current year. Similarly, X_{t-1} would mean last period's value (or value lagged by one period), and X_{t-10} would be value lagged by 10 periods.

Although forecasting on the basis of the last period's data is called the naive method of projection, since within an organization decisions are almost always made on the basis of incremental reasoning (an argument like, "Last year, this program cost $150,000; therefore, this year we expect it to cost. . . ."), forecasting on the basis of what happened last period is probably the most frequently used method. This method yields a reasonably good forecast if the trend is steady and there are few fluctuations. Therefore, if you have steady salaried employment, your current year's earnings would serve as a good proxy for the future year's prediction. On the other hand, if your income tends to fluctuate, this method will not give you a very good prediction. For instance, since there are ample variations caused by seasonality, the lagged data presented in Table 6.6 act as a poor predictor for the next quarter.

Projecting by the Mean

Another method of projection is calculating the mean. For instance, consider a series:

$$X_1\ X_2\ X_3\ X_4\ X_5\ \ldots\ X_{t-1}\ X_t$$

In this case, we can make a prediction for the following period, X_{t+1}, simply by taking the mean of the series—that is, by calculating

$$\overline{X} = \frac{\left(X_1 + X_2 + \ldots + X_{t-1} + X_t\right)}{T} = X_{t+1},$$

where T is the total number of observations.

Therefore, the forecast of X_{t+1} is given by $\overline{X}$. You may note that by using the mean for the future period's prediction, we can extend the series ad infinitum by projecting the value for the period X_{t+2} as:

$$X_{t+2} = \frac{\left(X_1 + X_2 \ldots + X_{t-1} + X_t + X_{t+1}\right)}{T+1}.$$

You might wonder when this simple method is appropriate for forecasting a series. This method is useful only if you have a stationary series with no observable trend (see Figure 6.3). In such cases, the mean of the series may be your best bet. For instance, while predicting fluctuations in rainfall you may do best by taking the yearly average. The same may be true for predicting price movements for a specific period in the stock market. Therefore, if there is no discernible trend, the mean value would give you the best possible forecast for future behavior.

Moving Average

When there is a clear trend, the variations within a series can be ironed out by what is known as the method of **moving average**. By this method, we would predict for X_{t+1} as follows:

$$X_{t+1} = \frac{X_t + X_{t-1}}{2}.$$

Since we are lagging the data by one period, this is called the moving average of order (1)—first order moving average. This is called a moving average because we keep on doing the same procedure for the entire series of data, as shown in Table 6.6. As you can see, while calculating moving average of order 2, we lost information on the first two observations since these were used to calculate the forecast for the third period. We can increase the order by taking the average of a larger number of lagged data. Thus, if we want to calculate a fourth-order moving average, X_{t+1} will be computed as

$$X_{t+1} = \frac{X_t + X_{t-1} + X_{t-2} + X_{t-3}}{4}.$$

Figure 6.14 Tourists Visiting Masters, PA 1990–1992

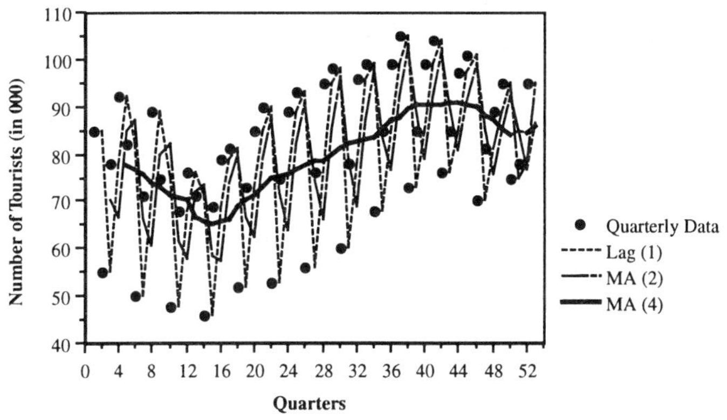

If you have quarterly data which reflect a strong seasonal effect, a four-period moving average would essentially iron out the seasonal fluctuations. This has been shown in Figure 6.14. As the order of moving average increases, we lose more information at the top of the series. Also, the effect of an increase in the order of the moving average is a greater degree of smoothing of the series.

Analyzing Trend: A Step-by-Step Approach

1. Specify the objective of your study.
2. Plot the data.
3. Look for trend pattern.
4. If the series is monthly or quarterly, look for seasonal variability.
5. For a long yearly series, look for cyclical effects.
6. Correct for seasonality or trend depending on the purpose of the study.
7. If there is no trend, use the mean for forecasting.

Using a Computer to Get Moving Average

Business MYSTAT will allow you to smooth a series by using moving average. For a DOS-based machine, this is done by using the following general command:
SMOOTH[<Var1>,<Var2>.../MEAN = <#>,WT = <#,#,...>]
After the **SMOOTH** command, you specify the variables that you want smoothed. MYSTAT smoothes a series either by the mean or by the median. It is by far more common to use a mean. In the examples in this chapter, we have created moving average series by using the mean. That is, for calculating the next period's value (X_{T+1}), using a three-period moving average, we have taken the average of the current period and the two before it: $\left(\dfrac{x_T + x_{T-1} + x_{T-2}}{3} \right)$. Therefore, if the three

numbers are 5, 6, and 14, the mean will be 8.33. However, if we take the median, it will be the middle value between 5 and 14 = 10. If for any reason you want to use the median to calculate your moving average series, you will have to specify it as
SMOOTH[<Var1>,<Var2>.../MEDIAN = <#>,WT = <#,#,...>]
The **WT** option is to be used only when you want some specific weight to put on the past period's value. For our purposes, you should ignore these and specify it simply as
SMOOTH[<Var1>,<Var2>.../MEAN = <#>]
It is important to note here that MYSTAT smoothes the variables by using a different formula from ours. It calculates the smoothed value for the current year (X_T) by averaging $\left(\dfrac{x_{T-1} + x_T + x_{T+1}}{3} \right)$. This procedure will yield a slightly different result and, as you can tell, cannot be used for prediction. However, if you specify **MEAN = 2**, MYSTAT will give you a two-period moving average according to our formula. To calculate moving average (rather than smoothing), you will have to (a) use the **LAG** command to lag the variable to the desirable period and create separate series of lagged variables, and then (b) use the **MATH** command to calculate the average.
If you have a MacIntosh, drag down the **Forecast** icon and select **Smooth**. Then, by using the **Select** box, select the variable(s) to be smoothed. If you want a two-period moving average, change the default 3 to **2** in the **Window** box. Click on the **Save smoothed variables** box. Then click on **OK**.

Markov's Chain

The Problem

Suppose a recent survey of freshmen on a medium-sized urban college campus indicates that of 6,500 freshmen, 15% use drugs. A previous survey had revealed that of those students who do not use drugs, 90% are expected to remain that way, while 10% are likely to become users of drugs. On the other hand, if a student is presently a user, it is 80% likely that he or she will remain a user during sophomore year. Only 20% of the users are expected to become drug free in the successive year. For the purpose of determining the extent of the campus drug problem, we want to forecast the number of users as this group of students goes through college.

Markov's Chain

From the preceding information, we may be able to project the magnitude of the future drug problem for this group of students by following a simple but surprisingly powerful predictive tool developed by W. W. Markov, a turn-of-the-century Russian mathematician. As you can see, the total number of drug-free students can be calculated by adding the fraction of those who will remain drug free with those who are present users but will stop using drugs within a year. Similarly, the number of drug users for the next year will comprise those who will start using drugs in their sophomore year plus the fraction of the users who will continue to take them. In equation terms this can be written as

Nonusers$_2$ = .9 x (Non-users$_1$) + .2 x (Users$_1$)   (6.1)
Users$_2$ = .1 x (Nonusers$_1$) + .8 x (Users$_1$)   (6.2)

In these equations, the subscripts 1 and 2 refer to this and the coming year, respectively. Since we know that 90% of the 6,500 freshmen are nonusers, we can calculate the number of users and nonusers for the next year by plugging these numbers in the preceding equations:

Nonusers$_2$ = .9 x (.85 x 6,500) + .2 x (.15 x 6,500) = 5,167
Users$_2$ = .1 x (.85 x 6,500) + .8 x (.15 x 6,500) = 1,333.

This tedious process of calculating the number of future user and nonuser population can be made much simpler by using a matrix operation. If you are familiar with matrix operations, you may skip the next section. If you are not, do not be alarmed. They are fairly simple.

A matrix is a tabular arrangement of numbers in rows and columns. For example, we may write the information imbedded in equations 6.1 and 6.2 as follows:

		Sophomore year (Next year)	
		Nonusers	Users
Freshman year	Nonusers	.9	.1
(Current year)			
	Users	.2	.8

If you go across the first row, you may read it as 90% of the nonusers in the freshman year are likely to remain nonusers in the sophomore year, while 10% of the current nonuser population will become users in the next year. The second row reads, 20% of the current users will become drug free next year, while 80% will continue to use drugs. In matrix notation, this table can be written as

$$\mathbf{T_1} = \begin{bmatrix} .9 & .1 \\ .2 & .8 \end{bmatrix}.$$

This matrix, which we call $\mathbf{T_1}$, is also known as the **transitional matrix**. It is called transitional because it chalks out the way the present population is transformed in the future. To understand the workings of Markov's chain, it is desirable to know the process of matrix multiplication. The elements of the transitional matrix are called **transitional probabilities** when written in matrix. From this transitional matrix we can calculate the number of projected nonusers and users as follows:

Nonusers$_2$ = .9 x (.85 x 6,500) + .2 x (.15 x 6,500) = 5,168
Users$_2$ = .1 x (.85 x 6,500) + .8 x (.15 x 6,500) = 1,332.

A Lesson in Matrix Operation

A matrix is an arrangement of numbers in rows and columns. Suppose we have two matrices, A and B. We can write them as

$$\mathbf{A} = \begin{bmatrix} a_{11} & a_{12} \\ a_{21} & a_{22} \end{bmatrix}_{2\times2}$$

$$\mathbf{B} = \begin{bmatrix} b_{11} & b_{12} \\ b_{21} & b_{22} \end{bmatrix}_{2\times2}$$

The element a_{11} of matrix **A** is read as value row 1 and column 1, and a_{21} is read as the value of row 2 and column 1. Since there are two rows and two columns, we call this a 2 x 2 ("two by two") matrix. We have written the size of the matrix in subscript (2 x 2 in these cases). Similarly, if there are four rows and six columns, we would call it a 4 x 6 matrix. If we have a single row or a single column of numbers, this is called a **vector**. For example, **K** and **Q** are vectors, while **M** is a 3 x 4 matrix:

$$\mathbf{K} = \begin{bmatrix} a_{11} \\ a_{21} \\ a_{31} \\ a_{41} \\ a_{51} \end{bmatrix}_{5\times1} \quad \mathbf{Q} = \begin{pmatrix} a_{11} a_{12} a_{13} a_{14} \end{pmatrix}_{1\times4} \quad \mathbf{K} = \begin{pmatrix} a_{11} & a_{12} & a_{13} & a_{14} \\ a_{21} & a_{22} & a_{23} & a_{24} \\ a_{31} & a_{32} & a_{33} & a_{34} \end{pmatrix}_{3\times4}.$$

When adding or subtracting two matrices, we add or subtract each corresponding element. For this, we have to have matrices of equal sizes. Thus, we can add **A** and **B** as

$$\mathbf{A} + \mathbf{B} = \begin{pmatrix} a_{11} & a_{12} \\ a_{21} & a_{22} \end{pmatrix}_{2\times2} + \begin{pmatrix} b_{11} & b_{12} \\ b_{21} & b_{22} \end{pmatrix}_{2\times2} = \begin{pmatrix} a_{11} + b_{11} & a_{12} + b_{12} \\ a_{21} + b_{21} & a_{22} + b_{22} \end{pmatrix}_{2\times2}.$$

Let us consider some concrete numbers. By adding the following two matrices, we get

$$\mathbf{A} + \mathbf{B} = \begin{pmatrix} 3 & 4 \\ 1 & 5 \end{pmatrix}_{2\times2} + \begin{pmatrix} 1 & 6 \\ 7 & 2 \end{pmatrix}_{2\times2} = \begin{pmatrix} 4 & 10 \\ 8 & 7 \end{pmatrix}_{2\times2}.$$

The same rule goes for subtraction. You may note that we can add or subtract only matrices of similar dimensions. In the preceding case, since both matrices are

2 x 2, we could add them. However, when multiplying we use a slightly different rule. We multiply the element of the first row of the first matrix with those of the first column of the second matrix. Thus, if we want to multiply **A** by **B**, we will have to do the following:

$$\mathbf{A} \times \mathbf{B} = \begin{bmatrix} a_{11} & a_{12} \\ a_{21} & a_{22} \end{bmatrix}_{2 \times 2} \times \begin{bmatrix} b_{11} & b_{12} \\ b_{21} & b_{22} \end{bmatrix}_{2 \times 2} = \begin{bmatrix} (a_{11}b_{11} + a_{12}b_{21}) & (a_{11}b_{12} + a_{12}b_{22}) \\ (a_{21}b_{11} + a_{22}b_{21}) & (a_{21}b_{12} + a_{22}b_{22}) \end{bmatrix}_{2 \times 2}.$$

By using numbers, we can do the same operation as follows:

$$\mathbf{A} \times \mathbf{B} = \begin{pmatrix} 3 & 4 \\ 1 & 5 \end{pmatrix} \times \begin{pmatrix} 1 & 6 \\ 7 & 2 \end{pmatrix}_{2 \times 2} = \begin{pmatrix} (3 \times 6) + (4 \times 7) & (3 \times 6) + (4 \times 2) \\ (1 \times 1) + (5 \times 7) & (1 \times 6) + (5 \times 2) \end{pmatrix}_{2 \times 2} = \begin{pmatrix} 31 & 26 \\ 36 & 16 \end{pmatrix}_{2 \times 2}.$$

For multiplying two matrices, the matrices must have compatibility. Thus, you can multiply a 2 x 2 matrix by a 2 x 3 matrix, but it is not possible to multiply a 2 x 3 with a 2 x 2. Between the two multiplicants the middle number must be the same. If you multiply a 2 x 2 by 2 x 3, this will give you a 2 x 3 matrix. A 5 x 4 multiplied by a 4 x 1 vector will give you a 5 x 1 vector. For a proper understanding of matrix operation, you should do a few multiplications.

Projection by Markov's Chain

Now that we've gone through the technical aspects of matrix operation, we can proceed with the projection of trend with Markov's chain. The projections for the junior year of the student population can be obtained by transitional matrix $\mathbf{T}_1$ by itself. Therefore, $\mathbf{T}_1 \times \mathbf{T}_1$ would give projections for the third period ($\mathbf{T}_2$); the projection for the fourth period ($\mathbf{T}_3$) will be given by multiplying $\mathbf{T}_2 \times \mathbf{T}_2$. The projection for the junior year is calculated by

$$\mathbf{T}_1 \times \mathbf{T}_1 = \mathbf{T}_2 = \begin{pmatrix} .9 & .1 \\ .2 & .8 \end{pmatrix} \times \begin{pmatrix} .9 & .1 \\ .2 & .8 \end{pmatrix} = \begin{bmatrix} .83 & .17 \\ .34 & .66 \end{bmatrix}$$

In other words, we can write

		Junior year (Third year)	
		Nonusers	Users
Freshman year (Current year)	Nonusers	.83	.17
	Users	.34	.66

That is, by the junior year, 17% of the nonusers will become users, while 66% of the current users will remain users. Hence, the total number of projected users and nonusers is calculated as

$$\text{Nonusers}_2 = .83 \times (.85 \times 6{,}500) + .34 \times (.15 \times 6{,}500) = 4{,}917$$
$$\text{Users}_2 = .17 \times (.85 \times 6{,}500) + .66 \times (.15 \times 6{,}500) = 1{,}583.$$

If you are now comfortable with matrix operation, you can obtain these preceding results by multiplying the transitional matrix (**T**) by the category proportion vector (**S**) and the vector of the total number of freshman population (**P**):

$$\mathbf{T} \times \mathbf{S} \times \mathbf{P} = \begin{pmatrix} .83 & .17 \\ .34 & .66 \end{pmatrix} \times \begin{pmatrix} .85 \\ .15 \end{pmatrix} \times (6{,}500 \quad 6{,}500) = \begin{pmatrix} 4917 \\ 1583 \end{pmatrix}$$

By following the same logic, we can see that during the senior year, the corresponding figures are likely to be

$$\mathbf{T} \times \mathbf{T_2} = \mathbf{T_3} = \begin{pmatrix} .9 & .1 \\ .2 & .8 \end{pmatrix} \times \begin{pmatrix} .83 & .17 \\ .34 & .66 \end{pmatrix} = \begin{pmatrix} .781 & .219 \\ .340 & .660 \end{pmatrix}$$

Again, by multiplying **T₃** by the vectors of student population and the percent of nonusers and users, we estimate the number of drug-free and drug-using seniors to be

		Senior year (Fourth year)	
		Nonusers	Users
Freshman year (Current year)	Nonusers	.83	.17
	Users	.34	.66

These numbers translate into the following projection of drug users on campus in the senior year:

$$\begin{pmatrix} .781 & .219 \\ .340 & .660 \end{pmatrix} \times \begin{pmatrix} .85 \\ .15 \end{pmatrix} \times (.6500 \quad .6500) = \begin{pmatrix} 4{,}529 \\ 1{,}971 \end{pmatrix}$$

The number of projected campus drug users shows an alarming growth trend over time and has been plotted in Figure 6.15. As you can see, this brief analysis can give policy makers a quick picture of what may lie ahead if the present trend continues.

Figure 6.14 Projected Trend of Campus Drug Use

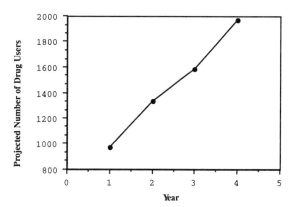

In Markov's chain we are not restricted to a simple 2 x 2 matrix. We can make the transition process as realistic (and complicated) as we want to. For instance, there is no reason to assume that the student population is divided in a binary fashion between users and nonusers. Let us hypothesize that there are three groups: the nonusers, casual users, and the regular users. The following is the transitional matrix for the freshman class:

		Sophomore year (Second year)		
		Nonusers	*Casual Users*	*Regular Users*
Freshman year	Nonusers	.80	.15	.05
(Current year)	Casual users	.30	.40	.30
	Regular users	.10	.20	.70

The preceding information is written as the transitional matrix **T**:

$$\mathbf{T} = \begin{pmatrix} .80 & .15 & .05 \\ .30 & .40 & .30 \\ .10 & .20 & .70 \end{pmatrix}.$$

Again, by multiplying **T** x **T**, we get **T₂**, and by multiplying **T₁** by **T₂**, we get **T₃**:

$$\mathbf{T}_1 \times \mathbf{T}_1 = \mathbf{T}_2 = \begin{pmatrix} .69 & .19 & .12 \\ .39 & .27 & .34 \\ .21 & .23 & .56 \end{pmatrix}$$

$$\mathbf{T}_1 \times \mathbf{T}_2 = \mathbf{T}_3 = \begin{pmatrix} .621 & .204 & .175 \\ .426 & .234 & .340 \\ .294 & .237 & .469 \end{pmatrix}.$$

The Absorbing State

Another important dose of reality that can be introduced to the Markov process is what is known as the *absorbing state*. The absorbing state can be defined as the condition which, when reached, cannot be reversed. That is, if a subject enters the absorbing state, it gets out of the system. For example, in this case of projecting drug use among an entering batch of college students, an absorbing state can be dropping out of college (although perhaps only death is the ultimate absorbing state, you may note that if students drop out, even if they are readmitted, they do not get promoted to the next higher status, such as from freshman to sophomore. Therefore, dropping out can be considered a realistic absorbing state for this example). Accordingly, let us formulate the transitional matrix with an absorbing state:

		Sophomore year (Second year)			
		Nonusers	*Casual Users*	*Regular Users*	*Dropouts*
Freshman year	Nonusers	.80	.14	.05	.01
(Current year)	Casual users	.30	.30	.30	.10
	Regular users	.05	.20	.40	.35
	Dropouts	0.0	0.0	0.0	1.00

The preceding table indicates that of those freshmen who do not use drugs, by the sophomore year 80% will maintain their current status, while 14% will occasionally experiment with drugs and 5% will turn into regular users. The table also states that 1% of these students will drop out of college. Among those entering college, if they are casual drug users now, 30% will become nonusers, 30% will become regular users, and 30% will continue to use drugs on occasion. Of this group, 10% are expected to drop out. Forty percent of the current regular users are likely to remain that way, while 5% of them will give up the habit and 20% will reduce their use to be classified as occasional users. From this group of students, 35% are likely to drop out before next year. You may notice that the first three elements of the dropout row are zeros. This is because if someone has dropped out, he or she cannot go back and join the ranks of any of the other classifications. The diagonal element is one, indicating that the group that chose not to go to college this year will not advance the following year. This information is written as the transitional matrix T_1, from which we can derive the following information:

$$T_1 = \begin{pmatrix} .80 & .14 & .05 & .01 \\ .30 & .30 & .30 & .10 \\ .05 & .20 & .40 & .35 \\ 0.0 & 0.0 & 0.0 & 1.0 \end{pmatrix}$$

Let us assume that of the 6,500 freshmen, 40% are nonusers, 30% are casual users, 20% are regular users, and the dropout rate is 10%. By multiplying the vector of proportion of freshmen in each category, we get

$$
\mathbf{T_1} \times \mathbf{S} = \begin{pmatrix} .80 & .14 & .05 & .01 \\ .30 & .30 & .30 & .10 \\ .05 & .20 & .40 & .35 \\ 0.0 & 0.0 & 0.0 & 1.0 \end{pmatrix} \times \begin{pmatrix} .4 \\ .3 \\ .2 \\ .1 \end{pmatrix} = \begin{pmatrix} .42 \\ .19 \\ .17 \\ .22 \end{pmatrix}.
$$

In other words, these results indicate that among the sophomores, we can expect the percentage of nonusers to increase while the percentage of casual and regular users decreases. This is good news, but notice that the dropout rate has registered an alarming increase. This is because over a third of the users have been found to drop out of college before the year is over.

Policy Analysis with Markov's Chain

Markov's chain allows us to look at the possible impact of alternate policies. For example, looking at the results given in the preceding calculation, we are alarmed by the dropout rate. We may extend this analysis further to look into the possible impacts of alternate programs of drug rehabilitation for the regular users or an extensive educational program for the nonusers so that the fraction of them becoming either casual or regular users drops significantly.

When Is It Appropriate to Use Markov's Chain?

As you can tell from the preceding example, Markov's chain offers us a simple but powerful tool of prediction. This procedure is particularly useful when we do not have a long history to go back to. If we did have data going back in history, we could have used different methods, shown in the following two chapters. But when we are faced with inadequacy of back data, a method such as Markov's chain may be the answer. Notice that for this method the data need is minimal. As long as we are able to define the transitional matrix, and we know the total population and the share of each condition within it, we are able to project the future numbers. Also, as you can see, this process allows for rather complex interrelationship among the various states or conditions, which may help explain several kinds of nonlinear trends across time.

However, like any other method of mathematical prediction, Markov's chain is bound by its own sets of assumptions. By studying these assumptions you will be able to gauge its relative advantages over other methods as well as understand its shortcomings. First, Markov's chain assumes the existence of well-defined, mutually exclusive categories, which are collectively exhaustive. Thus, in our previous example, we must be able to classify all the respondents of the survey into categories of "users" and "nonusers," and an individual cannot be classified as both (mutually exclusive). Further, this division must exhaust all the possible conditions. However, since there will be those who cannot be classified in any of these two categories, we created an added state called "casual users." Even that may not classify everybody accurately. For that, we created yet another category of "dropouts." As we strive to achieve mutual exhaustiveness, we keep on increasing the number of categories. Hence, care must be taken to ensure that these categories are mutually exclusive and that we do not keep any group outside of our consideration.

The second assumption of Markov's process is that the relationships shown by the transitional matrix remain unchanged from one period to another. Since this assumption is not typical of Markov's chain and is the basic building block of all trend analysis, we must guard against the possibility that the trend may change due to the influence of some external factors.

The third restrictive assumption of Markov's chain is that the individuals do not have any memory from one period to the next. That is, based on common experience, it makes sense to assume that an individual who has been hooked on drugs for a long time will find it more difficult to get rid of the habit compared to someone who has started only recently. Yet, as you can see, the probabilities of a freshman user quitting remain the same as those of a junior. In certain cases, this may be a restrictive behavioral assumption and, unless we are careful, may cause the predictions to be severely flawed.

Finally, when we talk about a change in time period, we must assume that these periods are of equal length. Since we were concerned with the status of college students, this was not an unrealistic assumption; however, suppose we are attempting to forecast unemployment, homelessness, or other kinds of social phenomena for which there are no fixed time intervals. For these cases, we may have to resort to some rather artificial divisions.

If these four conditions are met, at least in the short term, Markov's chain provides us with an extremely useful forecasting tool.

Computer Application

If you try to multiply matrices, especially if they are larger than 2 x 2, you will have to do a large number of tedious calculations for which our brains are typically not well suited. Therefore, you would be better off using computers. If you have purchased the OPTIZE/MATRIX software, it will perform matrix operations. To solve a Markov's chain problem, you need to create a file for the transition matrix. By multiplying the vector of the initial population with the transition matrix, you will receive the prediction for the next period. For prediction of the following period, you will multiply the transition with itself to get the transition matrix for next period. This new transition matrix will have to be multiplied by the population vector to get the prediction for the following period. You can keep on doing this operation until the steady state is reached.

To use the MATRIX program:

1. Copy it in your hard drive from the Master Disk.

2. Type in **MATRIX** to access the program.

3. After the logo, the program will respond with a prompt >.

4. Now you are ready to enter the data. You have to create a file for the transition matrix and the population vector. Unlike many other programs, MATRIX does not require you to specify the dimension of a matrix. You simply enter each element of the row and at the end of each row hit (return). This will automatically take you to the following row. Close the matrix with a square bracket. Then save your matrix. Thus, suppose we are creating a 2 x 2 transition matrix with the data from the first example. We are calling the transition matrix **T**$_1$. We are calling the population vector **P**.

5. At the prompt, write

>**MATRIX T1=[.9 .2** (return)

.1 .8]

6. Save matrix by typing

SAVE T1 (return)

7. Create the 2 x 1 population vector the same way:

> **Matrix P=[6500** (return)

6500]

8. **SAVE P**

9. Multiply the two matrices to get the projection for the next period:

>**MATRIX B=T1*P**

Save the new matrix **B**.

10. Now if you print matrix **B**, you will get the predicted values.

For creating the transition matrix for the next period, multiply **T**$_1$ with itself.

> **MATRIX T2=T1*T1**

You may notice that you can create the transition matrix for the nth period by raising the transition matrix to the nth power. Thus, if $n = 10$, you can get the results by typing:

>**MATRIX T10=T1**10**

If you choose not to purchase the OPTIZE/MATRIX software, there are several programs designed for personal or minicomputers which allow matrix operations. Although most of these programs are simple to use, I have found MINITAB to be particularly useful and possibly the simplest.

WHICH PROJECTION TECHNIQUE TO USE?

1. Define the objective of projection.

2. Plot the data.

3. If there is a great deal of seasonal variability, for comparison purpose, do seasonal and trend adjustments.

4. If there is no trend, use the mean of the series.

5. If there are seasonal fluctuations, use moving average. Remember, the higher the

order of the moving average, the greater the smoothing effect.

6. If there is no time series, but there are data on transition matrix, use Markov's chain.

Key Words

Absorbing state	Negative trend
Catastrophic trend	Positive trend
Cyclical trend	Prediction by the mean
Exponential trend	Quadratic trend
Horizontal trend	Random error
Linear trend	Seasonal adjustment factor
Logistic trend	Seasonal trend
Markov's chain	Trend analysis
Moving average	Trend adjustment factor
Naive projection	

Exercises

1. Write an essay on trend analysis when the past behavior is known. Give examples from real life for the various kinds of trend patterns discussed in this chapter.

2. A typical time series contains wide-ranging fluctuations. Explain, with examples, various sources of fluctuations in a data series. How can you adjust for such fluctuations?

3. In 1987, several states increased the speed limit on their highways in sparsely populated areas. Suppose a county analyst is trying to see if the change caused a discernible change in accident fatality rate. The following table of quarterly fatality data has been compiled:

Quarters	1985	1986	1987	1988
I	85	76	88	92
II	43	42	52	48
III	51	57	71	78
IV	98	97	110	121

What kinds of conclusions can you draw for policy prescription?

4. You are in charge of investing your agency's liquid cash. You are considering investing in a particular security portfolio which has yielded the following monthly returns. How would you predict its behavior for the next three months?

Month	Yield
1	7.0
2	3.7
3	1.8
4	0.5
5	9.5
6	0.1
7	2.3
8	6.3
9	3.2
10	0.9
11	4.1
12	9.3
13	7.3
14	7.8
15	6.6

5. The number of auto thefts in the city of Masters for the last 15 years is given in the following table. Use the moving average technique to discern the overall trend and predict the number of auto thefts for the coming year.

Year	Auto Thefts
1	98
2	87
3	110
4	112
5	108
6	121
7	132
8	125
9	127
10	130
11	145
12	153
13	148
14	151
15	149

6. Collect a series of data on any event of national, state, and local importance. Write a report on its trend pattern and predict its value for the next period.

7. You are trying to predict the number of homeless population in the downtown area of the city. A survey of the homeless population shows that if a person is currently without a home, the probability that he or she will remain so six months from now is .75. The survey also shows that 2% of the local residents who have an address will join the ranks of the homeless in the next six months.

The size of the current homeless population is 350, while the number of residents in the area is 10,000. The preceding information indicates the following transition matrix:

This period	Next period	
	Homeless	Living in home
Homeless	.75	.25
Living in home	.02	.98

Project the number of homeless population two years from now.

8. In the preceding example, add the absorbing state condition that 20% of the currently homeless population will no longer be in the area in the next period (either through migration or death). Now assume that 65% of the currently homeless population will remain homeless in the next period (six months from now), 15% will have a home life once again, and 20% will drop out from the population. Project the number of homeless population for the next two years.

9. In a brief essay, explain the strength and weakness of the Markov's chain method of projection. Provide at least one real-life example of when it may be feasible and useful to employ this method of forecasting.

Chapter 7

Projection Techniques: The Method of Least Squares

The Problem

The need for forecasting is integral to the process of planning. In the previous chapter we discussed the problem of projecting trend when a long history is unavailable. However, in this present Information Age, we frequently encounter a long series of past information. When such information is available, the task of forecasting becomes much more systematic, or "scientific" if you will, than forecasting on the basis of a single rate of growth.

We do not have to look far to find examples of forecasting in the public sector. State and federal governments routinely forecast revenues from various sources for the preparation of budgets. Local governments, unless they are extremely large, do not generally get involved in projecting tax revenues, as they depend primarily on state governments to provide them with such information. However, local government agencies frequently engage in forecasting needs for their services. For instance, the financial management department may write a report to ask for permission to raise money from a bond issue for enlarging the existing children's recreation facilities. This may call for a forecast of the number of children in the community for the next five years. In addition to these government agencies, branches of federal reserve banks, research institutes and information consultants (such as Data Resources, Inc., or Chase Econometrics), and many other groups get involved in the business of forecasting the future. In this chapter, we will examine the tools of their trade, the **method of least square** or the **regression** models.[1]

Building a Least Squares Model

The task of forecasting becomes considerably easier when we have a long history with which to see if there is any definite trend. When the trend is readily apparent, we can build a model which can project it to forecast the future. For example, by looking at the **time series data** (a series of data over time) of per capita gross domestic product (GDP) of the United States, we can hypothesize that GDP per capita is growing in a linear trend pattern over time. In other words, the level of per capita income is determined by the elapsed time since the beginning of the study period. In Figure 7.1, the straight line drawn through the yearly data approximates the trend line. By our model we hypothesize that the per capita GDP of the country will continue to grow along this line and, by extending it into the future, we can forecast the future levels of per capita GDP.

While building a model for the projection of trend, we hypothesize that the fundamental direction in a data series can be explained by the functional relationship proposed by the model. I can best explain the basic idea of a trend model with the help of Figure 7.2. In this figure, we have built a model which states that the

[1] There are numerous books on regression analysis and the least squares method. However, for one of the best explanations of the method, see Peter Kennedy, *A Guide to Econometrics*, 2nd ed. (Cambridge, MA: The MIT Press, 1985).

Figure 7.1 U.S. Per Capita Gross Domestic Product (in 1972 constant dollars)

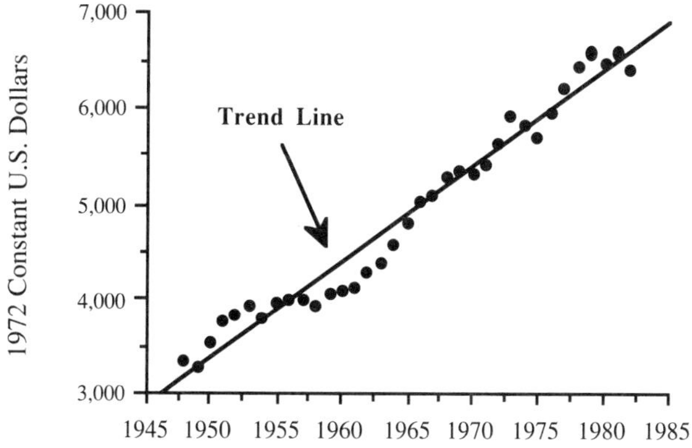

Frequently a data series exhibits a pattern or trend in its development. In this case, U.S. per capita GDP is showing a linear, upward (growing) trend over a 40-year span.

dependent variable (in this case, per capita income) as an input is being transformed by the internal logic (or the functional relationship) of the system. An input stimulus (a change in the independent variable—in this case, the passage of time) in the system produces the output (the new level of per capita GDP).

As you can see, not all the actual observations fall on this trend line. If they did, we would have a perfect relationship, which in the realm of social sciences is seldom seen. Some data points do not fall on this line because of the effects of random events. We build our model with the implicit assumption that all the observed points would have fallen on the trend line if it were not for the presence of shocks created by the effects of random elements, which impel the observations to stray from the projected line. These random shocks are considered to be external to our model and may be caused by diverse factors such as international relations (war and peace), social and political factors (riots, presidential elections, etc.), or even the climate (hurricanes, earthquakes, droughts, etc.). In sum, we hypothesize that the difference between what we *predict* and what we *actually observe* is caused by random shocks to the system. We call this difference **error**.

Figure 7.2

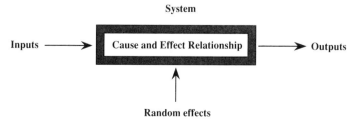

Therefore, we assume that the observed system contains two components: the explained and the unexplained. That is,

Data = trend + error.

Hence the primary purpose of trend analysis is to uncover the pattern which will allow us to project the pattern into the future. Therefore, in this endeavor, we look for the *best line* which can approximate the trend in a data series. Consider, for example, Figure 7.3. In this figure, we are measuring the values of the dependent variable *Y* on the vertical axis, while the horizontal axis measures the independent variable *X*. The plotted observations show a linear trend pattern. By extending the trend (shown by the dashed line), we can project the future value of *Y* based on *X*. Then the question becomes how to derive the trend line. It should be obvious that for us to obtain the line that best explains the trend, we must obtain the one that *lies closest to the observations.*

Since the line closest to the data points is the best representative of the trend in the series, our object is to obtain the line that leaves us with the least amount of unexplained error. However, in our quest to find the line that minimizes the errors we encounter a problem. Consider, for example, Figure 7.3. Suppose we have five observations on the dependent variable *Y*, the trend of which we are trying to estimate by deriving a line as close as possible to the data points. Suppose we have obtained the trend line for the data series. The points on the trend line are the esti-

Figure 7.3 Errors of Estimation

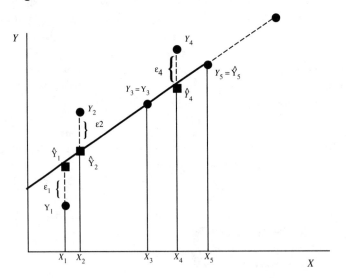

The differences between the projected trend line and the observed data points are called errors. The best line must be the one which is closest to the data points—in other words, one with the minimum amount of errors.

mated values. Thus, for the observation Y_1, we estimate it to be $\hat{Y}_1$ (called "Y hat"). Since our estimate falls short of the actual value, the difference between the actual and the estimated value is the **error of estimation**, which we call, ε_1.

It is obvious that drawing the line of estimation by hand (as we have done in Figure 7.3) will not do, since we can never be sure that it is, in fact, the closest line to the data. Since it is axiomatic that the distance from the mean is the least, the best possible line should go through the mean of the series of observation.

However, while the deviation from mean is always the least, we face the problem that the sum total of deviation from the mean is always equal to 0. This problem can be shown with the help of Figure 7.4. Suppose I have only two observations and I want to draw the line which lies closest to these two points of observation. Clearly, as shown in Figure 7.4a, the line drawn through the two points will be best line since for each observation the error terms are equal to 0. However, suppose I draw this line in the opposite direction, as shown in Figure 7.4b. Let us assume that the distances from the trend line to the observed points are +3 and –3, respectively. If we want to choose the best line on the basis of least amount of errors, we are at a loss to choose between these two lines, because the sum of errors for both of them is equal to 0. Therefore, how do we choose between the two lines when the sum of errors is zero in both cases?

In chapter 4, we discussed the problem of deviations from the mean being equal to 0. Recalling our discussion, we can see that this problem can be avoided if we *square the deviations* from the line. By following this method, the line in Figure 7.4a still gives us an error value of 0, while the sum of the squared deviations for the second line is $(+3)^2 + (-3)^2 = 9$. Clearly, now we can choose the first line over the second.

Figure 7.4 The Problems of Summing the Errors

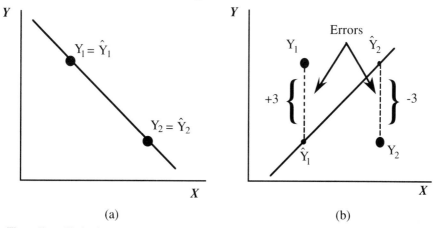

(a)   (b)

The problem with simply summing the errors is that the positive errors cancel out the negatives. As a result, you will not be able to choose between (a) and (b), since for both of them the sum of errors is zero.

Therefore, we can lay down our criterion for choosing the best line as *the one that gives us the least amount of squared deviation from the observed points.* This is the notion behind the **method of least squares.**[2] The equation derived through the method of least squares is called the **regression equation.** If the equation contains one independent variable, it is called a **simple regression**, while if it contains more than one independent variable, it is called a **multiple regression**.

Straight Line Trend

The method of least squares can be used to estimate various kinds of trend lines. Let us consider the straight line. The regression model for a straight line is given by

$$Y = \alpha + \beta X + \varepsilon \tag{7.1}$$

where Y is the **dependent** (the one to be explained) variable, α is the **intercept**, β is the **coefficient for trend**, X is the **independent** (the one that explains the dependent variable) variable and ε is the error of estimation (or the residual difference between actual Y and estimated $\hat{Y}$). Figure 7.5 explains the meaning of a straight line equation. The intercept term measures the point at which the trend line meets the vertical axis. Quite often, the intercept term has interesting interpretations. For example, in fitting a Keynesian aggregate consumption function (the relationship between consumption and income), the intercept term measures the level of consumption one must have even when income is zero. This is the subsistence level of consumption which presumably must be met either through government transfer (welfare payment) or private charity.

The trend coefficient (β) measures the extent of interdependence between the dependent and independent variables. Thus a higher value of β' would signify a steeper line—implying that a small change in the independent variable will cause a great deal of change in the dependent variable. The reverse will be true for a

---

[2] The method of least squares has a long history, with the names of some of the most illustrious mathematicians attached to its development. This method was first proposed in 1806 by Legendre. Shortly afterward Laplace and Gauss justified its use and demonstrated some of its useful properties. In 1812 Laplace offered proof that every unbiased linear estimator is asymptotically normal when the number of observations tends to infinity. Further, Laplace demonstrated that for the least squares estimators the asymptotic variance is minimal. In a series of articles (1821–1823), Gauss showed that among all unbiased linear estimates, the least squares estimators minimize the mean square deviations between the true value and the estimated value. Most importantly, Gauss established that this relationship holds for any distribution of the errors and for any sample size. Later corroboration of his findings came through the work of Markov (1912). Subsequent developments in the least squares method were the work of mathematicians such as Aitkens and R.A. Fisher from the late 1920s through the 1940s. This method forms the basic building block of the field of econometrics.

Figure 7.5 Explanation of a Straight Line Equation

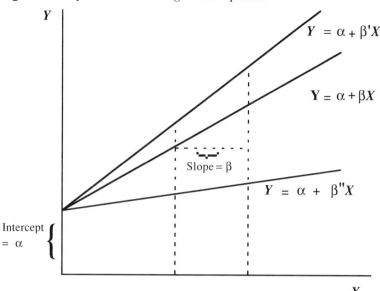

*A straight line trend is defined by the intercept (α) and the slope (β). These terms are alternately called **constants**, **coefficients**, or **parameters**.*

smaller trend coefficient (β'').[3] A positive trend coefficient implies an upward slope; a negative coefficient, a downward slope; and a 0 coefficient implies the absence of any relationship between the dependent and independent variable.

An estimated equation for a straight line contains three components: the coefficient for the intercept and the coefficient for the slope, and the error term:

$$\hat{Y}_i = a + bX_i + e_i \tag{7.1a}$$

where $\hat{Y}_i$ is the estimated value of Y_i,
    a is the estimated intercept coefficient,
    b is the estimated slope coefficient, and
    e is the estimated error term.

---

[3] If you are not well versed with the algebra of a straight line equation, you may engage in the following exercise. Consider two sets of equations:

a) $Y = 2 + .5X$
b) $Y = 2 + 2.5X$.

By substituting values of 0, 1, and 2 for X, you can see the implications of the intercept and trend coefficient. [Y is equal to 2, 2.5, 3 for (a) and 2, 4.5, 7 for (b)].

It is important to note the difference between the "true" coefficients and their estimated values. The true values are conceptual in nature and, as such, cannot be known. The best we can hope for is to obtain their best estimated approximation. Since it is important to understand this difference, *we are denoting the true values with Greek letters, and their estimated values with Roman letters.*

The error term is the difference (the residual) between the *actual* and the *estimated* values of Y:

$$e_i = Y_i - \hat{Y}_i$$

By replacing $\hat{Y}_i$ with a + bX (from equation 7.1a), we get:

$$e_i = Y_i - a - bX_i \tag{7.2}$$

As explained earlier, by the method of least squares we estimate the coefficients of *a* and *b* such that we minimize this sum of errors:[4]

$$\text{Minimize } \Sigma(e_i)^2 = \Sigma(Y_i - a - bX_i)^2 \tag{7.3}$$

From the preceding expression (7.3) we can devise the following formula for the estimated coefficient of *b*:

$$b = \frac{\Sigma\left(Y_1 - \overline{Y}\right)\left(X_1 - \overline{X}\right)}{\Sigma\left(X_1 - \overline{X}\right)^2} \tag{7.4}$$

where $\overline{Y}$ and $\overline{X}$ are the means for Y_i and X_i variables.

---

[4]For those of you who are interested in the logic of derivation of the formulae for *a* and *b*, they can be derived by the use of differential calculus. Thus, we are trying to minimize:

$$S = \Sigma(e_i)^2 = \Sigma(Y_i - a - bX_i)^2.$$

Therefore, the sum of squares is minimized with respect to the values of *a* and *b*. Hence, we have

$$\frac{\delta S}{\delta a} = -2\Sigma\left(Y_i - a - bX_i\right) \tag{7.2a}$$

$$\frac{\delta S}{\delta b} = -2\Sigma X_i\left(Y_i - a - bX_i\right). \tag{7.2b}$$

By setting equations (7.2a) and (7.2b) equal to 0, we get two equations which can be solved for the two unknowns, *a* and *b*. Since this exercise falls slightly beyond the scope of this book, it may suffice here to indicate the logic behind the derivation of formulae for the two coefficients.

Table 7.1

Population (000)	Year
5	1
8	2
10	3
15	4
17	5

The intercept term is estimated by

$$a = \overline{Y} - b\overline{X}. \tag{7.5}$$

Let us consider the following example. Suppose we are estimating a linear trend line to the population data of a small community experiencing a steady rate of growth (see Table 7.1). To estimate the coefficients a and b, for a straight line equation, we need to work out Table 7.2. Recall the formula for calculating b:

$$b = \frac{\Sigma(Y_i - \overline{Y})(X_i - \overline{X})}{\Sigma(X_i - \overline{X})^2}.$$

By inserting the calculated numbers from Table 7.2, we estimate $b = 31/10 = 3.1$.

Similarly, we can calculate the intercept term a as

$$a = \overline{Y} - (b\overline{X}) = 11 - (3.1 \times 3) = 1.7.$$

Therefore, the estimated equation can be expressed as

$$\text{Population } (\hat{Y}) = 1.7 + 3.1 \text{ Year } (X). \tag{7.6}$$

The plot of the actual data and the trend line are shown in Figure 7.6.

Table 7.2 Calculations for a Straight Line Regression Equation

Population (Y)	Year (X)	$(Y_i - \overline{Y})$	$(X_i - \overline{X})$	$(X_i - \overline{X})^2$	$(Y_i - \overline{Y})(X_i - \overline{X})$
5	1	-6	-2	4	12
8	2	-3	-1	1	3
10	3	-1	0	0	0
15	4	4	1	1	4
17	5	6	2	4	12
Total		0	0	10	31

Note: $\overline{Y} = 11$, $\overline{X} = 3$.

Figure 7.6 Population Trend

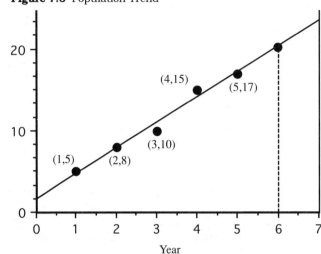

Projection into the Future

We have plotted the estimated and actual values of population in Figure 7.6. From this derived equation we can project the future population of the city. For example, we can see that population for the sixth year can be estimated by

$$1.7 + 3.1 \times 6 = 20.3.$$

Similarly, to obtain the projected figure for the seventh year, you need to substitute the value for the independent variable (X) with 7. This arithmetic calculation will provide you with 23.4, the projected population figure for the seventh year.

How Good Are the Results?

Having estimated the trend line, you can legitimately ask, "How good are my results?" There are two parts to this question: First, you may ask whether your model is offering a significant explanation of the variations within the series. Second, you may ask, "How confident am I in my estimation of the coefficients?" That is, are the estimated values reflective of the "true" relationship between the dependent and independent variables, or is what we have obtained by chance—a spurious correlation?

How Much Is Being Explained?

To tell how much we are explaining, we need to recall Figure 7.3. We can see that while estimating the relationship between the dependent and independent variables, we are able to explain part of it, while the remainder is unexplained. A perfect explanation explains all the variations within a series. In contrast, in the absence of any relationship between the two variables, none of the variations will be explained. Hence, the measure of goodness of fit is the proportion of explained variance within the total variance. Again, since we want to get rid of the problem of having to add positive deviations with negative deviations, we square the deviations and then sum the results.[5] This ratio is called the **coefficient of determination**, or R^2, and is written as

$$R^2 = \frac{\text{Squared sum of explained variations}}{\text{Squared sum of total variation}} = \frac{\Sigma(\hat{Y} - \overline{Y})^2}{\Sigma(Y_i - \overline{Y})^2} \tag{7.7}$$

where $\overline{Y}$ is the mean of Y,

$\hat{Y}$ is the Y values predicted on the basis of regression line (calculated by using the estimated equation, $\hat{Y} = a + bX$), and

Y_i is the actual values for Y observations.

You may note that when all the Y values are correctly predicted, then the predicted values are the same as the actual values. In that case, $\hat{Y}$ is equal to Y_i, which means that the numerator is equal to the denominator, or the value of R^2 is equal to 1. This is the situation of a perfect explanation. On the other hand, when a model is totally unable to explain the variation (or when the variations are random), then the term $\hat{Y}$ is a horizontal line (such as the one shown in Figure 6.3) which goes through the average value of the distribution. In such a case, $\hat{Y}$ is equal to $\overline{Y}$, which makes the numerator equal to 0 and consequently, $R^2 = 0$. Therefore, the value of R^2 will always fall within the limit 0 (no explanation) and 1 (perfect explanation): $0 \geq R^2 \geq 1$.

Let us calculate the R^2 for our example (see Table 7.3). We can calculate R^2 by using equation (7.7):

$$\frac{96.1}{98.0} = .9806.$$

[5] The squared sum of explained variations is also known as the error sum of squares (ESS), and the squared sum of total variation is also referred to as the total sum of squares (TSS).

Table 7.3 Calculation of R^2

Population (Y_i)	Year (X_i)	Predicted Values* ($\hat{Y}$)	($\hat{Y} - \bar{Y}$)²	($Y_i - \bar{Y}$)²
5	1	4.8	38.44	36.0
8	2	7.9	9.61	9.0
10	3	11.0	0.0	1.0
15	4	14.1	9.61	16.0
17	5	17.2	38.44	36.0
Total			96.1	98.0

*Note that the predicted values are calculated with the help of the estimated equation (7.6).

In other words, our model is predicting slightly over 98% of the variations.

Although R^2 is widely used as measure of goodness of fit and as a measure for choosing among the alternate specifications, it contains some important drawbacks. The most important problem with R^2 is that it measures how much of the total variation is being explained by the model. Therefore, in a multiple regression model (one with more than one independent variables), if one keeps on adding variables which are only marginally relevant, the total explanation will go up, or at the very least will remain unchanged. Thus, in a model, if we include an independent variable which adds nothing to the explanation of the dependent variable, the R^2 measure *will not go down* to reflect the inclusion of an irrelevant variable.

To correct this problem, we use the measure of $\bar{R}^2$, which is also known as **adjusted** or **corrected** R^2. $\bar{R}^2$ can be calculated either independently or from the calculated value of R^2. Since it is easier to calculate it from the calculated value of R^2, we provide the following formula:

$$\bar{R}^2 = 1 - \left(1 - R^2\right)\frac{N-1}{N-K}$$
(7.8)

where N is the number of observations, and
K is the number of coefficients in the regression equation.

If you examine this formula carefully, you will note the following features:

1. When we have just one independent variable,[6] that is, $K = 1$, $R^2 = \bar{R}^2$. Otherwise, if there is more than one independent variable ($K > 1$), then $\bar{R}^2$ will be less than R^2 ($R^2 > \bar{R}^2$).

---

[6] You can have only one independent variable if you run a regression equation without the intercept term. That is, you are estimating an equation $Y_i = bX_i + e$. This is a special form of equation which makes a rather stringent assumption that the intercept term is equal to zero. Although there may be some reason to formulate such a model, in general you should not specify a model without the intercept term.

2. If you include an additional independent variable in the model, unlike the R^2, $\overline{R}^2$ may go up *up* or *down*. As can be seen, $\overline{R}^2$ will go up *if and only if* the change in R^2 resulting from the inclusion of this additional independent variable is able to offset the dampening effect of the fraction $(N-1/N-\mathrm{K})$. Therefore, for this highly desirable property, it is advisable to choose correctly the independent variable by noticing the change in the adjusted R^2 value.

From our example of estimated regression equation, we can calculate the value of $\overline{R}^2$ as follows:[7]

$$\overline{R^2} = 1 - (1-.98)\frac{5-1}{5-2} = .97.$$

What Is a High R^2?

There is no universally acceptable answer to this question. Generally speaking, if you are dealing with an *economic time series data*, you are likely to find a high degree of correlation, since most of the economic variables tend to move in the same direction. In an interesting study, Ames and Reiter showed that even when unrelated time series data were chosen at random and regressed against each other, R^2 values exceeded .5.[8] However, for cross-section and even time series sociological or political events data, the R^2s are typically smaller.

How Relevant Are the Estimated Coefficients?

Now that we've determined how much of an explanation of the data the model is providing, we may want to know the following: (1) How relevant are the *individual coefficients*? and (2) How relevant are the coefficients, *taken as a whole*? To answer these questions, we need to look back on the development of theoretical statistics. One of the most remarkable theorems of the entire field of mathematics and mathematical statistics was derived nearly 200 years ago and provides the basis for hypothesis testing. Suppose you know the average (mean) height of the American male population (μ) and the standard deviation (σ). You are conducting a **random** survey, whereby you are collecting groups of men, noting their average height. At every try, you are getting this small sample group together and are noting their average height, subtracting it from the **population average** (μ), and dividing by the **pop-**

---

[7] Note that for us $K = 2$, since we have two coefficients, *a* and *b*.

[8] E. Ames and S. Reiter, "Distributions of Correlation Coefficients in Economic Time Series," *Journal of American Statistical Association*, 1961, Vol. 56, pp. 637–56.

ulation standard deviation (σ).[9] You continue with this process, which symbolically can be written as

$$\frac{\left(\overline{X}_i - \mu\right)}{\sigma}. \tag{7.9}$$

As we have discussed in chapter 2, if you repeat your experiments, the plotted results will approach a normal distribution. This distribution will have a mean = 0 and standard deviation = 1. The remarkable aspect of this theorem is that it does not matter what the distribution of the variable X_i is. Unless there are some systematic biases (like measuring only the basketball players to arrive at the average height of the general public), the repeating of this procedure will give us the normal distribution as the number of samples increases. This theorem is known as the **law of large numbers**. The derivation of a normal distribution is particularly fortuitous since by the property of this standardized distribution we know how much of the values will fall within what range. For example, we know that approximately 95% of all the values will fall within ±1.96 standard deviation, and nearly 99% of all values fall within ±2.57 standard deviation. Therefore, in our example, suppose we come across a group of Pygmies with an average height which is more than 1.96 standard deviation less than the average for the U.S. men. Then we can state with a 95% level of confidence that the members of this particular sample are not Americans. Let us explain this with the help of Figure 7.7.

You may, notice, however, that we have emphasized the term *random*. A variable is considered random if its values are determined by the outcome of a *chance experiment*. That is, in our example, if we confined our search within a particular ethnic group, or a group of basketball players, then the outcomes are not being determined by chance. In such a case, whether the selection is done by design or by some unrecognized bias on the part of the researcher, this theorem of the law of large numbers will not apply; the resulting distribution will not approximate a normal distribution regardless of the number of experiments. As a result, none of the results that we will be describing below will hold true. We will discuss the implications of this bias in detail in chapter 8.

---

[9] You should note that we are using two different sets of symbols for mean and standard deviations. They are μ and $\overline{X}$ for mean and σ and S for standard deviation. This is because we want to distinguish between the population or the "true" mean and standard deviation, and sample or "observed" mean and standard deviation. The true values have only conceptual validity since we can never observe them. Yet, in statistical theory, theorems such as the one shown by equation (7.9) are valid only when we have the true values. Therefore, to get around the problem, we use the estimated or sample values with some necessary modifications.

Figure 7.7 Curve of Normal Distribution

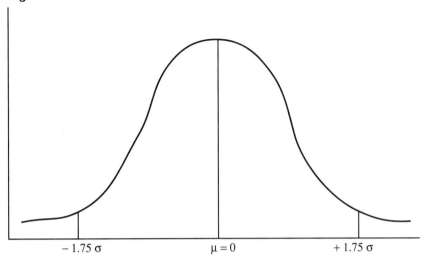

One of the most important assumptions of a regression model is that the model includes
all the relevant explanatory variables. Therefore, the variation in the observed data that is
not explained is caused by random factors, which are distributed normally around the
mean of 0.

The Significance of Individual Coefficients

As can be seen in Figure 7.7, if the average for a group is sufficiently different from
the mean, it may indicate that the two populations are indeed different. Hence, this
theorem serves as the basis for testing validity of hypotheses. For our purpose, we
can use this result to test the **null hypothesis** that our coefficients are results of
chance and, in fact, there is no relationship between the dependent and the independent variable. For example, if we want to know the level of statistical significance
for our estimated trend coefficient (b), this can be done by calculating

$$\frac{b - \beta}{\sigma} \qquad (7.10)$$

where b is the estimated coefficient, β is the true coefficient, and σ is the true standard deviation of the distribution. Since we are testing the null hypothesis that
there is no correlation between the dependent and independent variables, we set β
equal to 0. Also, since we do not know what the true standard deviation is for population, we approximate it with the estimated standard error of coefficient, which we
may call SE_b. Therefore, the expression (7.10) can be written as

$$t_b = \frac{b}{SE_b}. \qquad (7.11)$$

Similarly, for testing the statistical significance of the coefficient a, we need to calculate the t ratio given by

$$t_a = \frac{a}{SE_a}.$$

(7.12)

From (7.11) and (7.12), we can see that the larger a coefficient is in relation to its standard error of estimate, the farther out the calculated ratio will be on our normal distribution chart. The farther out it is, the more convinced we will be that the coefficients are not equal to 0. Therefore, the value of this ratio will tell us that the coefficients are **statistically significant**.

Before we get into the process of actually testing the null hypotheses regarding the validity of the coefficients, I would like to repeat a few important properties of hypothesis testing from our discussion in chapter 2. First, as the name suggests, by the law of large numbers, the normal distribution is achieved only in the limit—that is, only when the number of observations becomes extremely large. In such cases, one can use the Z table for testing hypotheses. However, when the number of observations is relatively small, an approximation of the normal distribution is used to ascertain the critical values. This is called the **Student's t distribution**, named after a statistician who used to write under the pseudonym *Student*.

Since we do not know the true standard deviation of an estimator (an estimated coefficient), we need to approximate it with our sample results. Let us take a concrete example. In our population projection, we estimated two coefficients: $a = 11.0$ and $b = 3.1$. On the basis of that result, we can use the following sample estimate of the true variance σ^2:

$$SE^2 = \frac{\Sigma e_i^2}{N-2} = \frac{\Sigma\left(Y_i - a - bX_i\right)^2}{N-2}$$

(7.13)

where SE is the standard error of estimate.

You can see that the numerator of equation (7.13) is the sum of squared errors of estimate. This sum is being divided by $N-2$ (the number of observations minus 2) to approximate the true variance.[10]

With an estimate of Σe^2, we can estimate the variance *associated with the estimated coefficients*, a and b. The respective standard errors are calculated by

---

[10] The theoretical justification of dividing the sum of squared errors by $(N-2)$ lies in the fact that there are N data points in the estimation process but the estimation of the intercept and the slope introduces two constraints on the data. This leaves $N-2$ unconstrained observations with which to estimate the errors of estimate. Hence, the number $N-2$ is referred to as the number of degrees of freedom.

$$SE_a = \sqrt{SE^2 \frac{\Sigma X_i^2}{N\Sigma(X_i - \overline{X})^2}}$$

(7.14)

$$SE_b = \sqrt{\frac{SE^2}{\Sigma(X_i - \overline{X})^2}} \cdot$$

(7.15)

From the preceding formula, we can see that to calculate the standard errors of the coefficients, we need to add a few more columns to Table 7.2 (see Table 7.4).

From (7.13), the estimate of $SE^2 = 1.9/3 = .63$. Substituting the numbers in (7.14 and 7.15), we derive the estimated standard error of coefficients a and b as

$$SE_a = \sqrt{.63\left[\frac{55}{5 \times 10}\right]} = .83$$

$$SE_b = \sqrt{\frac{.63}{10}} = .25$$

Substituting the respective values in (7.11) and (7.12), we get

$$t_a = \frac{1.7}{.83} = 2.05$$

(7.14a)

$$t_b = \frac{3.1}{.25} = 12.4$$

(7.14b)

For an interpretation of these results, we can resort to Figure 7.7. We noted that if the estimated coefficient is located farther than the critical value of it, we can be reasonably certain that the estimated value is different from true value proposed by our null hypothesis.

Table 7.4 Calculations for Tests of Significance

Population (Y_i)	Year (X_i)	Predicted Values ($\hat{Y}$)	$(Y_i - \hat{Y})^2$	$(X - \overline{X})^2$	X^2
5	1	4.8	.04	4	1
8	2	7.9	.01	1	4
10	3	11.0	1.0	0	9
15	4	14.1	.81	1	16
17	5	17.2	.04	4	25
Total			1.9	10	55

These values (t_a and t_b) are distributed as t, with $N-1$ degree of freedom. Since we have five observations, our degree of freedom is $5-1=4$. If we can check a t table for four degrees of freedom, we can see that for a .05 level of significance (95% confidence level), the t ratio is equal to 2.13. Therefore, if the ratios are greater than this number, we can state with a great deal of confidence that our estimated coefficients are indeed significantly different from zero. In other words, there is a significant relationship between the dependent and the independent variable.

Since the intercept term is less than this critical number (2.1), we *cannot reject* the null hypothesis that the intercept is equal to 0. In contrast, since the t ratio for the slope (b) is greater than this number, we *can be sure* that this number is *statistically significant.*

The Significance of Coefficients Taken Together

A multiple regression model contains a number of independent variables, most of which are statistically significant on an individual basis. However, questions may still be raised as to their significance as a set. For this test, we test the null hypothesis that *none* of the explanatory variables helps to explain the variation of the dependent variable around its mean (that is, $b_0 = b_1 = b_2 = \ldots b_n = 0$). In our previous attempt to establish statistical significance of individual coefficients, we used the t distribution. For this test, known as the *joint probability test* (since we are testing the collective significance of the all the independent variables), we have to use the F distribution. We calculate the F value for the equation by

$$F_{(K-1,N-K)} = F_{[1,3]} = \frac{R^2}{1-R^2}\frac{N-K}{K-1}. \tag{7.16}$$

The F test is closely linked to the R^2. This is because, while testing the null hypothesis that none of the independent variables is relevant, the F test, in fact, is testing the null hypothesis that $R^2 = 0$. Therefore, for a two-variable linear equation, the null hypothesis is that the slope of the regression line is horizontal (such as in Figure 6.3).

From our example, we can calculate the F statistics as follows:

$$F_{(2-1,5-2)} = \frac{.9806}{1-.9806}\frac{5-2}{2-1} = 151.64.$$

The subscript for F, $(K-1, N-K)$, denotes the degrees of freedom. If you look at the F table, you will see that the table is arranged in a matrix form, where the coordinates are specified by the row and column numbers. For our test, the first number of the subscript $(K-1)$ refers to the denominator (the row) and the second number $(N-K)$ refers to the numerator (the column) of the table. Consulting the table (Appendix C), we can find that the critical value for $F_{(1,3)}$ at a 5% level of significance is 10.13. Since our F value 151.64 is greater than 10.13, we can reject the null hypothesis and conclude that the model is indeed relevant.

■ Estimating Regression Models Using a Computer ■

Business MYSTAT is designed for a quick and easy estimation of regression equations. To estimate a simple regression with a DOS-based computer, use the following commands:

MODEL <dep. var> =CONSTANT+<indep. var.>
ESTIMATE

For estimating a multiple regression with n number of independent variables, type in

MODEL <dep. var> =CONSTANT+<indep. var.#1>+<indep. var.#2>+.... <indep. var.#n)
ESTIMATE

To estimate the regression equation for our preceding example, type

MODEL POPULATION =CONSTANT+YEAR
ESTIMATE

If you have a MacIntosh, choose **Regression** from the menu, and formulate your equation by **Select**ing the **dependent** and then the **independent** variables. Click on **OK**.

This will generate the following output table:

DEP VAR:POPULATION N: 5 MULTIPLE R: .990   SQUARED MULTIPLE R: .981
ADJUSTED SQUARED MULTIPLE R: .974 STANDARD ERROR OF ESTIMATE: 0.796

VARIABLE	COEFFICIENT	STD ERROR	T	P(2 TAIL)
CONSTANT	1.700	0.835	2.037	0.134
YEAR	3.100	0.252	12.318	0.001

ANALYSIS OF VARIANCE

SOURCE	SUM-OF-SQUARES	DF	MEAN-SQUARE	F-RATIO	P
REGRESSION	96.100	1	96.100	151.737	0.001
RESIDUAL	1.900	3	0.633		

Presentation of Estimation Results

Once a regression equation is estimated, the results have to be presented to the readers. There are, of course, many ways of presenting. I am suggesting the following:

$$Y = 1.7 + 3.1\ X$$
$$t = (2.05)\ (12.4)*$$

$$R^2 = .98$$
$$\text{Adjusted}\ \ R^2 = .97$$
$$N = 5$$
$$F(1,3) = 151.\ 64*$$

where: Y = Population
         X = Year
*Significant at .05 level

I have presented the estimated equation (7.6) above. The numbers within the parentheses are the respective t-values for the individual coefficients. The asterisks (*) point out the significant t-values and F-value. You may notice that while the t-value for the slope coefficient and the F-Statistic are significant, the t-value for the intercept term is not significant at .05 level.

What Happens If the Trend Changes?

In a straight line model, we make a hypothesis that the trend has remained unchanged during the study period. However, it is entirely possible that the data may reflect a changing pattern. This change can be abrupt or can be part of a gradual process. An abrupt change in trend can result from sudden catastrophic events like war, changing of a law, a significant invention resulting in a change in technology, or a change in policy resulting from a change in political leadership. These events introduce a **qualitative** change in a series. For example, if we note the trend of per capita GNP in a country like Iraq, we may notice dramatic downward shifts in trend following Iraq's two devastating wars with Iran and the United States-led coalition. Similarly, several data series (such as national debt) for the United States will show signs of abrupt changes brought about by significant wars throughout U.S. history. Studying immigration patterns, the results of changes in the law will be apparent. Similarly, the invention of many modern drugs, such as penicillin, caused shifts in the trends of infant mortality in the late 1940s and 1950s.

Abrupt Changes in Trend

An abrupt change in trend is shown in Figure 7.8. You may notice that during the middle of the series, a vertical shift has taken place without affecting the trend pattern itself. It is clear from this figure that a broken trend line would produce less errors of estimation than an unbroken straight line fitted through the entire series.

These sorts of shifts are typical of series on which an extremely important external event has taken place or there is a large gap in the data set. Let us take a concrete example. Suppose we are studying the trend in the per capita expenditure by the local government in a community which incorporated itself as a new city in 1985. The achievement of its city status has enabled it to access more state and federal grants, which has caused a vertical shift in the series. Table 7.5 provides the series of per capita government expenditures for this hypothetical city.

For a better visual presentation, we have plotted the data in Figure 7.9. From this figure, we can see the result of a vertical shift. This vertical shift can be

Figure 7.8 An Abrupt Shift in a Series

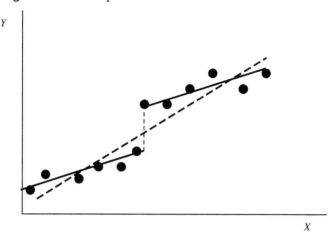

Abrupt shifts in trend take place as a result of significant changes in the external world, such as war, natural disaster, or a change in government policies. A shift may also be caused by missing data points in the middle of a series.

accounted for if we are able to draw a trend line based on our preincorporation (before 1985) data, and then add a constant to the estimated values for the postincorporation data (1985 and after). This can be done if we have *two* intercept terms, one for before, and one for after the incorporation. We can accomplish this with a trick: We can introduce what is known as an **intercept dummy variable**.

An intercept dummy introduces an additional intercept term to account for this kind of a shift in the intercept term of a regression equation. This takes the form of adding an extra independent variable, which has 0 for the observations prior to the time of shift, and 1 for periods afterward. Therefore, the equation to be estimated is written as

Table 7.5 Per Capita Federal Grant Expenditures

Year	Expenditure (Constant $)
1980	105.0
1981	110.0
1982	116.0
1983	120.0
1984	125.0
1985	180.0
1986	187.0
1987	193.0
1988	200.0
1989	213.0

Figure 7.9 Shifts in the Expenditure Pattern

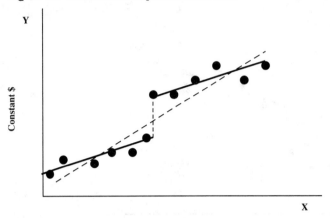

$$Y_i = a + a' + bX_i + e_i \qquad (7.17)$$

where a' is the dummy variable, which is $= 0$ for years prior to the shift, and is $= 1$ for years after.

Let us take the example of our newly incorporated city. Since we want to introduce an additional independent variable a', we have to add a new column to Table 7.5 in Table 7.6.

You may realize now that as we introduce an additional independent variable a', we will be using **multiple regression** instead of simple regression. The problem with the estimation of the coefficients of multiple regression is that they are a bit too complicated for their calculation by hand. Even though generations of students of statistics and econometrics were subjected to this torturous exercise of having to calculate the coefficients of multiple regression by hand, the proliferation of comput-

Table 7.6 Setting Up an Intercept Dummy Variable

Year	Expenditure (Constant $)	Dummy (a')
1980	105.0	0.0
1981	110.0	0.0
1982	116.0	0.0
1983	120.0	0.0
1984	125.0	0.0
1985	180.0	1.0
1986	187.0	1.0
1987	193.0	1.0
1988	200.0	1.0
1989	213.0	1.0

ers has relegated this tiresome exercise to redundancy. Therefore, we will simply ask you to use a suitable statistical package to derive the coefficients for this equation.

The use of this dummy variable gave us an excellent predictive model as shown by the results of the estimated equation:[11]

$$\text{Expenditure} = -12,074.7 + 6.15 \text{ Year} + 49.25 \text{ Dummy}$$
$$t \text{ ratio} \quad (7.9)^* \quad (9.4)^* \quad (11.1)^*$$

$R^2 = .995$, adjusted $R^2 = .994$
$N = 10$
F $(2,7) = 371.2^*$
*Significant at .05 level

where the dummy variable is 0 for years prior to 1985 and 1 for the years 1985 and after.

We have placed the calculated t ratios under the corresponding regression coefficient. As you can tell from this equation, we are explaining 99.4% of total variance in the series. The dummy variable tells us that as a result of incorporation, an average resident of the city gained $49.25 in government funding. If we want to predict the level of per capita government expenditure for 1990, we will have to write the equation as follows:

$$\text{Expenditure} = -12,074.7 + 6.15 \times 1990 + 49.25 \times 1.0$$
$$= 213.05.$$

For estimating values for years prior to 1985, we will have to set the dummy = 0, and therefore the equation will contain only the intercept and the slope terms. Thus, we may estimate the value for 1983 as follows:

$$\text{Expenditure} = -12,074.7 + 6.15 \times 1983$$
$$= 120.75.$$

We have plotted the predicted versus the actual values of expenditure in Figure 7.10. The estimated line with the dummy variable has been drawn with a solid line, whereas the straight line equation has been drawn with a dotted line. You

---

[11] You may notice that here we have estimated the time trend by using the values of the years (such as 1980, etc.) as the independent variable. For ease of computation, you may also use numbers 1, 2, 3, etc. for the actual values of the year. This will not change the basic relationship between the dependent and the independent variable; only the values of the estimated coefficients will change. If you have access to a computer, try estimating the same equation both ways, and then calculate the predicted or estimated values for the dependent variable. They will not change.

Figure 7.10 Comparison between a Straight Line and a Dummy Variable Estimate

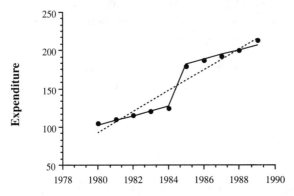

This diagram demonstrates the effectiveness of the introduction of a dummy variable when there is an abrupt shift in the observed data. As you can see, the estimated line with an intercept dummy variable is clearly superior to the one without.

may notice the close approximation of the actual values as a result of the use of the dummy variable.[12] The use of the dummy significantly improves the quality of the estimated equation.

Abrupt Change in Slope

In the previous example, we discussed the situation in which there is a parallel shift in the trend line. In reality, there can also be an abrupt change in the slope. But this change is more dramatic, since this new situation has altered the entire direction of the trend line. There are many examples of this abrupt change in trend. For example, the discovery of gold in California in 1849 caused a huge influx of population; the initiation of the Great Society Program caused a sudden increase in the trend of social expenditure; the successful launching of the Soviet Sputnik caused a big increase in expenditure for NASA for a decade; during the presidency of Ronald Reagan, federal assistance to state and local governments took an abrupt change in the opposite direction. Let us consider a hypothetical example of government expenditures on drug rehabilitation programs for a period of 15 years. Assume that

---

[12] Without the dummy variable, this equation is estimated as

$$\text{Expenditure} = -26{,}868.65 + 13.61 \text{ Year}$$
$$t \qquad (8.8)* \qquad (8.9)*$$

$R^2 = .91$, adjusted $R^2 = .896$
$F_{(2,7)} = 78.7.*$
$N = 10$

*Significant at .05 level.

■ **Using a computer to estimate a model with an intercept dummy variable** ■

For estimating this model with MYSTAT, it is best to enter into your data set the binary dummy variable. Then, for DOS-based machines, type in:
MODEL EXP = CONSTANT+YEAR+DUMMY
ESTIMATE
For MacIntosh, after **Select**ing the **dependent** variable, **Select** the two **independent** variables. Then click on **OK**.

due to increased awareness and a change in political leadership during the eighth year of the study, society has decided to spend at an increasing rate on drug rehabilitation programs. This is shown in Table 7.7 and is plotted in Figure 7.11.

From this figure, it is clear that the trend pattern changed after the seventh year. While for the first seven years of the study government expenditure was increasing at a slow rate, the rate of change accelerated greatly from the eighth year on. This change in trend cannot be accommodated simply by adding an intercept dummy. Therefore, in our projection of trend, we need to account for this change. This abrupt change in the trend pattern can be captured adequately by using dummy variables for the two different slopes. Imagine holding a stick at an angle approximating the trend shown at the beginning of a data series. If we break the stick at the point where the change in trend pattern took place to account for the new trend, we can visualize this procedure. To split the series into two distinct trend lines, we introduce two dummy variables, D_1 and D_2, with D_1 having the value 1 for all the points for which the old trend applies and 0 for the rest. D_2 has 0s and 1s in the reverse order. Then, by multiplying the independent variable by these two dummy variables, we can create two new sets of independent variables. By running a multi-

Table 7.7 Expenditures on Drug Rehabilitation Programs

Year	Expenditure (in $000)
1	76
2	75
3	78
4	76
5	80
6	81
7	80
8	96
9	97
10	102
11	109
12	114
13	116
14	125
15	129

Figure 7.11 Plot of Trend in Government Expenditures

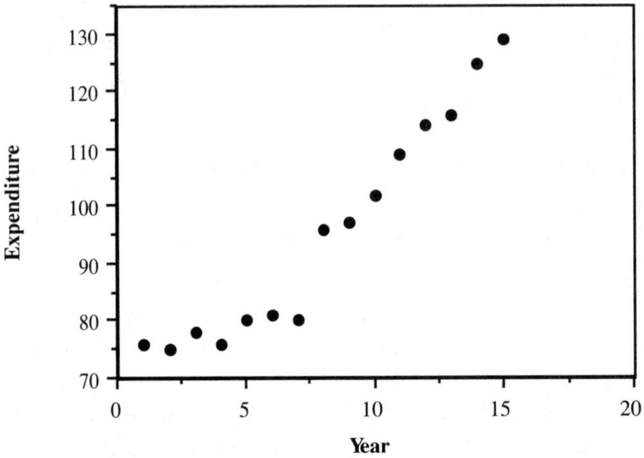

A data series may often exhibit a shift in the slope. This situation takes place when there is a qualitative change in the behavior prompted by some external factors.

ple regression on the dependent variables against these two newly created variables, we can estimate the equation containing two different slopes (Table 7.8).

By using the data shown in Table 7.8, we estimate the trend equation for government expenditure, which yields the following results:

$$\text{Expenditure} = 70.61 + 1.663 \ D_1 \times \text{Year} + 3.568 \ D_2 \times \text{Year} \qquad (7.18)$$
$$t \qquad (27.5)* \quad (2.8)* \qquad \qquad (15.0)*$$

Table 7.8 Setting Up Slope Dummy Variables

Year	Expenditure	D_1	D_2	$D_1 \times$ Year	$D_2 \times$ Year	Predicted Expenditure
1	76.000	1.000	0.000	1.000	0.000	72.263
2	75.000	1.000	0.000	2.000	0.000	73.926
3	78.000	1.000	0.000	3.000	0.000	75.589
4	76.000	1.000	0.000	4.000	0.000	77.252
5	80.000	1.000	0.000	5.000	0.000	78.915
6	81.000	1.000	0.000	6.000	0.000	80.578
7	80.000	1.000	0.000	7.000	0.000	82.241
8	96.000	0.000	1.000	0.000	8.000	99.144
9	97.000	0.000	1.000	0.000	9.000	102.712
10	102.000	0.000	1.000	0.000	10.000	106.280
11	109.000	0.000	1.000	0.000	11.000	109.848
12	114.000	0.000	1.000	0.000	12.000	113.416
13	116.000	0.000	1.000	0.000	13.000	116.984
14	125.000	0.000	1.000	0.000	14.000	120.552
15	129.000	0.000	1.000	0.000	15.000	124.120

$R^2 = .974$, adjusted $R^2 = .969$
$F(2, 12) = 222.75.*$
$N = 10$
*Significant at .05 level.

From this equation, we can see that the trend coefficient for the second period (3.568) is 2.15 times larger than that of the first period (1.663). This equation can be used to estimate the amount of government expenditure for every year within the study and can be used for predicting the values for future time periods. We have given the estimated values for the dependent values in the last column of Table 8.8. We have plotted the actual versus the predicted values in Figure 7.12.

A Word of Caution

If you estimate an equation with a slope dummy, you may run into a problem. If you estimate an equation with two slope dummies to account for the two phases of a trend, you may have to include an intercept dummy as well in your model. If you do not include an additional intercept dummy, the model will force each slope to compromise on a common intercept, which will make both the slope lines deviate from their actual positions. If, on the other hand, you allow for the slope dummies to have their own intercepts, then the estimated results will be far superior. The problem has been explained in Figure 7.13.

You can understand the point I am making with the help of our model. Consider once again the estimated equation (7.18). We can make a significant improvement by including an intercept dummy D_1 in the model. The model is estimated as

Figure 7.12 Plot of Actual versus Predicted Values of Government Expenditure

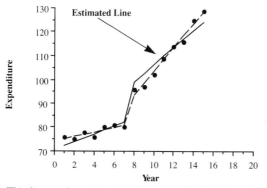

This diagram demonstrates the effectiveness of a slope dummy in approximating the observed behavior of a data series. Clearly, the introduction of the dummy has enabled us to be true to the trend pattern.

$$\text{Expenditure} = 74.29 - 20.51 \text{ D1} + .929 \text{ D1 x Time} + 4.976 \text{ D2 x Time} \qquad (7.19)$$
$$t \qquad (53.37)* \quad (6.24)* \qquad (2.98)* \qquad\qquad (19.58)*$$

$$R^2 = .994, \text{ adjusted } R^2 = .993$$
$$N = 10$$
$$F(3,11) = 630.47.*$$

* Significant at .05 level.

If you compare the estimated results of (7.18) with those of (7.19), you will notice that all the statistics have improved. However, the real improvement can be seen when the predicted values based on the two equations are plotted side by side against the actual values. I have done this in Figure 7.14. The line Pred1 is based on equation (7.18), and Pred2 is based on equation (7.19). You can see that the line Pred2 is clearly superior (closer) to the actual values. You may also note that the slope of the second phase (4.976) is nearly 5.4 times the slope of the first phase (.929).

Best Linear Unbiased Estimator (BLUE)

The least squares method promises to provide us with the estimated coefficients (the estimators) which will give us the least amount of variation from the observed points ("best") and which, when the sample size is increased, will get progressively closer to the population values ("unbiased"), provided that the model meets certain

Figure 7.13 Slope Dummies with Their Own Intercepts

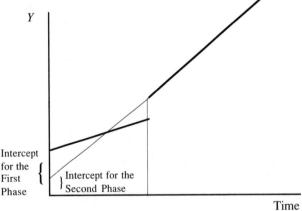

If you are trying to estimate an equation where there has been a shift in the trend, you may need to introduce an intercept dummy as well so that you do not force the two slopes to go through the same intercept.

Figure 7.14 Change in Slope with and without a Change in Intercept

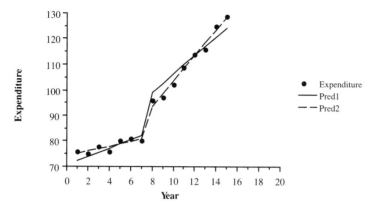

criteria. These criteria are called the basic assumptions of the classical least squares method[13] and are as follows:

1. The model is linear.
2. The error terms are randomly distributed with a population mean of zero.
3. The error terms are normally distributed.
4. The error terms have a constant variance (σ).
5. The error terms are uncorrelated with each other.
6. The independent variables are not perfect linear functions of each other.
7. All the independent variables are uncorrelated with the error terms.

If any of these assumptions are violated, the method of least squares will not be able to give us BLUEstimators. We will discuss the implications of these assumptions in the following chapter.

Gradual Changes in Trend: Estimation of Nonlinear Trends

Many data series relating to society and economy can be approximated by a straight line. However, there are cases in which the trend is fundamentally nonlinear. In such cases the use of a straight line will cause severe problems in forecasting. There are many nonlinear forms that can be captured by regression equations (thanks to

[13] The term *classical* does not mean ancient Greece, or the early theories of economics. It simply refers to the assumptions of ordinary least squares methods of estimation.

■ **Using a computer to estimate equations for a change in slope** ■

For estimating equations with slope dummies, you will have to include variables which are derived by multiplying a dummy variable with an independent variable. Once you have entered the dummy variables, you ask MYSTAT to create this new variable (such as our **D1*YEAR** variable). MYSTAT will perform all kinds of algebraic transformation of data (see your manual). To transform a variable in DOS machines, you need to name the new variable and set it equal to the form of transformation (expressions such as **multiply var1 with var2, divide var2 by var3**, etc.). For instance, to create a new variable (let us call it **D1Y**), we set it equal to the variable **D1** multiplied by the variable **YEAR**. In DOS commands a transformation operation is performed by

LET <variable> = <expression>

Therefore, in this case, we write

LET D1YEAR = D1*YEAR

This command will create a new column of the transformed variable under the heading **D1YEAR**.

For Apple computers, the transformations are done as follows:

1. Select **Math...** command from the Editor menu.

2. Type **D1YEAR** in the **Set Variable** box.

3. Click on the **Variable or expression** box.

4. Double click on the **D1** variable in the variable list box.

5. Type the multiply sign (*).

6. Double click on the **Year** variable in the variable list box.

7. Click on **OK**.

After the variable is created, go to the regression option and estimate the equation with the two independent variables.

advancements in computer technology) without a great deal of computational problems. Some of the non-linear trends can be estimated easily by transforming the data, in which case we do not need to use any special nonlinear estimation techniques (which are beyond the scope of this introductory book). Let us consider a few examples.

Polynomial Forms

A polynomial form expresses a dependent variable as a function of a number of independent variables. Some of these independent variables may be raised to powers greater than 1. The degree of a polynomial is known by the highest power among the independent variables. Thus, a quadratic form, expressed as $Y_i = a + bX_i + cX_i^2$, is called a second-degree polynomial, or the equation $Y_i = a + bX_i + cX_i^2 + dX_i^3$ is called a third-degree polynomial, etc.

It is common to find examples of a quadratic relationship in nature. We can think of applying fertilizer to plants. As we apply fertilizer, plants grow at a rapid rate, and we get more flowers, fruits, and vegetables. However, after a certain point, the application of more fertilizer damages the growth. As another example, within a short period of time, if we start consuming something we highly desire, our utility or satisfaction goes up, but after a point of saturation, we tend to lose interest. Or, after an initial period of lowering of per unit cost as we increase our scale of operation, inefficiency creeps in and unit costs reverse the trend and start climbing up. All of these are examples of quadratic relationships. A quadratic form can be U shaped or inverted U shaped. Figure 7.15 shows the two forms.

The quadratic equation is specified as

$$Y = a + b_1 X - b_2 X^2 \qquad (7.20)$$

for a U-shaped relationship (Figure 7.13b), and

$$Y_i = a - b_1 X_i + b_2 X_i^2 \qquad (7.21)$$

Figure 7.15 Quadratic Forms

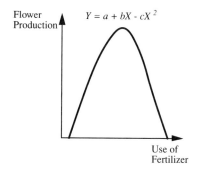

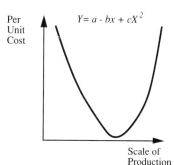

Figure 7.16 Publicly Held Federal Debt as a Percentage of GDP

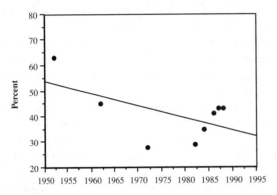

Source: Economic Report of the President, 1989.

for an inverse U-shaped relationship (Figure 7.13a).[14]

Let us see how these nonlinear forms are estimated. Consider the following data series for the federal debt held by the public as a percent of U.S. GDP:

Year	Percent
1952	63
1962	45
1972	28
1982	29
1986	41
1988	43

When we plot the data (Figure 7.16), we can readily see that the trend is not a linear one. During the 1950s and 1960s, federal debt as a percentage of U.S. Gross Domestic Product showed a trend of steady decline. This trend stabilized during 1970s, and then showed a rapid rate of increase. Therefore, if we try to fit a straight line trend, the approximation of the actual data will be

---

[14] If you want to see how these equations specify a quadratic relationship, consider the two equations:

(a) $Y = 10.0 - 2.0X + 0.5X^2$ and
(b) $Y = 2.0 + 2.0X - 0.5X^2$.

If you start substituting values 0, 1, 2, 3 for X (and squaring them for X^2) and then calculating and plotting the resulting values of Y, you will see the shapes of quadratic curves.

rather poor. This is demonstrated when a linear estimation yields the following result:

$$\text{Percent Debt} = 1138.86 - 0.553 \text{ Year} \qquad (7.22)$$
$$t \qquad (1.66) \quad (1.6)$$
$$R^2 = .389.$$

We have placed the calculated t ratios in parentheses beneath the coefficients. Since the critical value for t at a .05 level of significance is 2.0, we cannot reject the null hypothesis that the coefficients are, in fact, equal to 0. Also, as can be expected, you may notice that the R^2 is somewhat low at .389. In other words, we are explaining only less than 40% of the variations. Any prediction based on an estimated trend line such as this is going to yield highly unlikely values. Thus, based on this equation, the predicted value of the percentage of publicly held government bonds for 1995 is $1138.86 - 0.553 \times 1995 = 35.62$.

The situation changes dramatically, however, when we try a quadratic fit. To do that, we need to add one more column of independent variables, Year^2 (see Table 7.9).

Now that we've made the necessary data transformation, we can estimate the desired equation. Since we have three coefficients (a, b, and c) to estimate, we will not attempt to calculate these by hand. The computer can accomplish this much more quickly and accurately. Therefore, we can use our software to estimate this equation the same way we estimated the straight line equation. In this case, we will have to indicate that we have two independent variables (Year and Year^2) instead of one.

The estimated values of the coefficients are

$$\text{Percent Debt} = 280,320.87 - 283.938 \text{ Year} + .071908 \text{ Year}^2 \qquad (7.23)$$
$$t \qquad (5.0) \qquad (5.0) \qquad (5.0)$$
$$R_2 = .934 .$$

The critical value for t at a .05 level of significance = 2.0.

As you can see from Figure 7.17, the estimated quadratic equation (7.20) is

Table 7.8 Transformation of Data for the Estimation of a Quadratic Equation Form

Percent	Year	Year²
63	1952	3,810,304
45	1962	3,849,444
28	1972	3,888,784
29	1982	3,928,324
41	1986	3,944,196
43	1988	3,952,144

Figure 7.17 Publicly Held Federal Debt as a Percentage of GDP

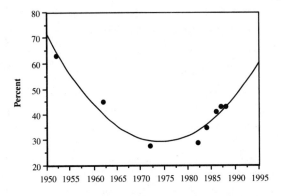

clearly superior to the straight line equation (7.21). From this equation, we can estimate the forecasted value for 1995 to be 54.21%.[15]

Higher-Order Polynomials

Although the regression results indicate that the quadratic form (7.20) seems to be a definite improvement over the linear form (7.17), can we not improve the results even more by using a third-degree polynomial? If we run a third-degree equation, we get the following result:

$$Y = 17,704,000 + 271,050 \text{ Year} - 13.83 \text{ Year}^2 + 3.0 \text{ Year}^3 \qquad (7.24)$$
$$R^2 = .983.$$

Indeed, as equation (7.24) as well as Figure 7.18 indicate, the third-degree polynomial is a better fit than a second degree. In fact, if we keep on increasing the degree of polynomial, the resulting curve will get closer and closer to the observed points and, when we use $n - 1$ (the number of observations minus 1) degree, there is no residual. A perfect fit! However, unfortunately, such an exercise reduces our result to a mathematical tautology. In fact, it is extremely rare for researchers in social sciences to use higher than a second-degree polynomial. This is because,

---

[15] In a previous footnote, I mentioned that you could use the actual figures for the years. However, you should be careful, because this makes the value of the independent variable Y^2 extremely large. Therefore, any rounding of the estimated coefficient will cause your projection to fluctuate wildly. For instance, if you round off the estimated coefficient for Y^2 at .072, the estimated percent of publicly held government bonds become 411. That is why, in this equation, I had to report the coefficient up to six decimal places.

Using a Computer to Estimate a Quadratic Equation

The fitting of a second degree, or a quadratic, form of equation to the data requires raising the independent variable to the second power. To do this, follow the steps for transforming a variable. You can square a variable simply by multiplying it with itself. Thus **YEAR**^{2} is created by multiplying **YEAR x YEAR**. After creation of the new variable, use it in the estimation of the regression equation.

apart from the tautological reasoning, the use of a higher-degree polynomial imposes undue restrictions on the data. For example, in a third-degree polynomial, the predicted values of Y may increase for the initial range of the value of X, then decrease rapidly, and finally increase at a dramatic rate. In the final stage, when the coefficient of the extremely large third-degree term becomes dominant, predictions outside the sample range will give you a highly inflated figure, as you can see in Figure 7.18.

Even the simpler quadratic form is not free from structural biases. Due to its strict mathematical structure, it forces a symmetric specification, which can lead to faulty predictions. The result of this bias is shown in Figure 7.19. If the dependent variable shows a symmetric distribution, then you are safe. However, if the distribution is skewed, the predictions will be suspect. Unfortunately, this bias may not be apparent from the regression results, as you will see a fairly decent fit. Yet if you plot the actual observations against the predicted values, the quadratic form will reveal its shortcomings.

Figure 7.18 Prediction With A Third Degree Polynomial

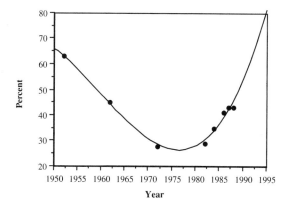

Figure 7.19 Symmety Forced by a Quadratic Form

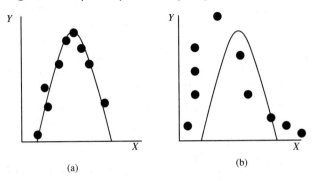

(a)

(b)

One of the problems with a quadratic specification is that its mathematical form assumes a perfect symmetry, as shown in (a), however, if the data are

Log Transformed Forms

If you look at the segment of social science research which uses regression analysis, you will find that after the linear form, perhaps the most common functional specification is the log-log form. To understand the log-log functions, you should know what a log is.

A log transformation expresses a number by the exponent of its base. That is, suppose we are using 10 as the base. Since 1,000 is 10^3, we write $\log(1,000) = 3$. By following this logic, $\log(100) = 2$, $\log(10) = 1$, and since any number raised to the power 0 is equal to 1, $\log(1) = 0$. For numbers less than 1, their log values become less than 0 or negative. However, there is one problem area for log. As the logs of numbers become very close to 0, they produce very large negative numbers and, therefore, the log of 0 is an infinitely large negative number. *So you cannot take the log of 0.* Logs can have any base, but the most commonly used base is 10. Hence it is called the **common log**. If the base of log is e (a commonly used number in mathematics, which is equal to 2.71828), it is called a **natural log**. If you want to get the original values from the log transformed values, you have to use **antilog**. Thus, the common log of 10 is 1, and the antilog of 1 is 10. The common log is written as **log**, while the natural log is expressed as **ln**. For a better understanding of logarithm, you may try log transforming a few numbers with the help of your hand calculator.

Although you can use either 10 or e as the base, in statistics it is more common to use the e-based natural log. Therefore, in this section, we will use the expression ln for log transformed variables. By log transforming the dependent and independent variables, a log-log functional form is written as

$$\ln(Y_i) = a + b\ln(X_i) + e_i.$$

After this brief introduction to logarithms and the transformed functional form, we can explore the question, Why log transform a variable? The log transformation of the data offers us a few attractive features. First, a series may exhibit a nonlinear form such as the ones shown in Figure 7.20a. If the coefficient b is greater than 1, the series would grow exponentially. Although you would be hard pressed to find examples in the realm of social sciences of a series with such an explosive growth pattern, over a short period of time a series (for example, housing prices in the boom areas of the United States) may exhibit such a pattern. The British political economist Thomas Malthus (without the help of any reliable statistical series) hypothesized that population growth is exponential. However, data on world population do not show such an explosive pattern. Many series in social sciences, however, come close to the lines shown where $0 < b < 1$. For example, cross-national data show that as nations become affluent, their aggregate rate of growth rate, after a period of rapid expansion, tends to slow. Also, it is relatively easy to find examples where b is negative (< 0). For instance, contrary to Malthus's conjecture, we know that as nations become affluent, their rate of growth of population registers a steady rate of decline. In such cases log-log functions will offer better fits than linear forms.

Second, as you can tell, the log transformation of a very large number makes it small. For instance the $\ln(85{,}790) \cong 11.36$. Therefore, if there is a great deal of variation in your data (which often is the case when the numbers are large), the log

Figure 7.20 Double-Log Functional Forms

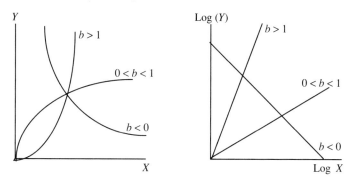

If the data show a nonlinear form such as the ones shown in (a), a log-log form may be better suited than a linear form. If you have regular graph paper, the plotted data will resemble one of the lines in (a). However, if you plot the data on a log-log form, they will show linear patterns (b). The value of the regression coefficient (b) determines the shape of the log-log curves. If b is greater than 1, the series will show an explosive growth rate. However, if b is less than 1, but is greater than 0, the rate of growth will slow. If b is negative, the rate of growth will progressively decline with time (or X).

■ **Using a computer to estimate log-log functions** ■

MYSTAT will transform your data into logs. Make sure you do not have any 0s in the series, since you cannot take the log of 0. You may transform the data in DOS machines by typing the command

LET (new variable name) = LOG(name of the variable to be transformed)

For MacIntosh, name the new variable, click on **LOG( )**, and then click on **Select**. Then place the cursor between the two brackets in the "variable or expression" box, and double click on the variable you want log transformed.
Log transform both the dependent and the independent variables. Use the new variables in your regression model.

---

transformation gives you a better fitted equation. You should note, however, that if you estimate a log-log curve, the predicted values will be in log forms. To change to actual numbers, you will have to take their antilog.

Inverse Forms

The inverse functional form expresses Y as a reciprocal (or inverse) of the independent variable X. An inverse functional form can show a positive or a negative relationship between the dependent and independent variables. You may notice that since it is an inverse relationship, the following expression will give you a negative relationship:

$$Y_i = a + b\frac{1}{x_i} + e_i$$

while

$$Y_i = a - b\frac{1}{x_i} + e_i$$

will show a positive relationship, as shown in Figure 7.21. While using an inverse form, you should remember that since you cannot divide any number by zero, there must be no 0s in the independent variable.

You should use the inverse functional form when the value of the dependent variable falls (or rises) sharply and then approaches a certain number without actually ever being equal to it as the value of the independent variable gets larger. Figure 7.21 illustrates the asymptotic nature of a typical inverse functional form.

Figure 7.21 The Inverse Form

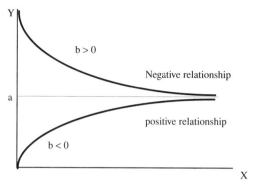

The reciprocal or inverse functional forms show typical asymptotic behavior. In a negative functional relationship, the value of the dependent variable falls precipitously to approach the value of the constant (a), which constitutes the "floor." For a positive relationship, it rises rapidly only to slow down to approach the "ceiling" set by the constant term (a).

Other Nonlinear Forms

All of the nonlinear forms discussed so far can be transformed into a linear form for estimating with regression models. However, there are many complex nonlinear forms (such as a logistic or a catastrophic form) which cannot be so transformed. They fall outside the scope of this book.

Using a computer to fit an inverse functional form

For fitting an inverse functional form, you need to take the reciprocal of the independent variable and then use this newly created variable to estimate the equation. The reciprocal of a variable can be calculated by using MYSTAT. You should make sure that the variable to be transformed does not have 0s. For DOS-based commands, type

LET (variable name) = 1/(independent variable name)

For MacIntosh, after naming the new variable, type "**1/**" in the "variable or expression" box, and then select the independent variable from the variable list.

How Do I Choose the Correct Functional Form?

So far we have discussed quite a few functional forms for regression models. Choosing the correct functional form is essential for good forecasting. Yet the books on econometric theory are of little use to a researcher when it comes to choosing a particular functional form. However, I can offer you this word of advice: *Unless theory, common sense, or your experience tells you otherwise, use a linear form.* Before using any model, read theoretical literature on its behavior, plot the data to see if there is any reason to believe that a form other than a linear one is more appropriate, and draw on your or an expert's experience in choosing the functional form.

Forecasting and Its Problems

The purpose of estimating a regression equation is to forecast. We depend on forecasting in every facet of modern life. The stock market reacts to the projected future of the economy, revenue and expenditures are forecasted for government budgets, students often choose their career moves based on expected remuneration of their chosen fields, orders are placed on the basis of forecasted demand, and investments are made on the basis of expected future trends in the market. Therefore, from many private decisions to public policies, forecasting has become an integral part of our lives. However, someone once sarcastically commented that "It is extremely difficult to predict, especially the future." Indeed, there is a great deal of truth to this cynicism. However, since we are in the business of forecasting, let us go about it in a more systematic fashion.

First, a definition. A forecast is a quantitative estimate of the likelihood of an event taking place in the future, based on available data on past history. There are two kinds of forecasts. A forecast can be either a **point forecast** or an **interval forecast**. A point forecast predicts a particular value for our dependent variable, which is likely to take place at a certain point in time in the future. An interval forecast, in contrast, indicates a band within which the future value is likely to lie.

Point Forecast

Since most of our predictions turn out to be point forecasts, let us discuss these first. While interval forecasts make clear the probability factor associated with the predicted value, point forecasts do not always do so. However, whether it is made explicit or not, all forecasts contain an element of probability. Thus, when we forecast the government revenue to be $1.6 trillion for the year 1994 or population of a city to be 123,758, despite the apparent precision to the last decimal point, we are engaging in predicting a probable occurrence by extrapolating from the past trend. In a sense, an economic forecaster has a certain handicap compared to a weather forecaster. We associate weather forecasting with probabilistic outcome, even though the actual outcome is always binary—it is either going to rain or it won't. Thus, when we are told that there is a 40% chance of showers, we are not terribly disappointed with the forecaster whichever way the actual event goes. Yet the results of forecasts based on a regression model, with its numerical precision and its omission of the probability factor, can be awfully deceiving, as they convey a certain sense of determinism. Therefore, it is important to inquire into the factors that make a forecast good or poor.

The true test of pudding is in its taste; the worth of a forecast is in its accuracy. Yet it is possible to have a good predictive model provide an inaccurate prediction, or a prediction based on a poor model turn out to be astonishingly close to reality. However, before we delve deep into the questions of accuracy of prediction and sources of possible error, it is important to clarify certain useful terminology of the trade.

Forecasting can be either **ex post** or **ex ante**. Suppose we are predicting on the basis of a series of past data, which ends last year. Since we know the value of the dependent variable for this year, we may compare the accuracy of our prediction against this known data. This is called an ex post prediction, where we know with certainty the values of the dependent and independent variables. It is still a prediction since the model is providing us with values outside of the study period (which had ended the previous year). It is called *ex post* or *after the fact* because the event has already taken place. In contrast, an *ex ante* forecast predicts values which are not yet known.

We can also distinguish between **conditional** and **unconditional** forecasts. An unconditional forecast is made when we know with certainty the values of all the independent variables. Thus, if we are predicting on the basis of time alone, measured in years, then for the forecast of the year 2002 we know the value of the independent variable. Therefore, this is an example of an *unconditional* forecast. However, if we do not know the values of the independent variables with any certainty, then the forecast is called *conditional*. An ex post forecast is always an unconditional forecast, since we know the values of the dependent and independent variables. But an ex ante forecast may be either conditional or unconditional. Clearly, if we do not know for sure the values of the independent variables in the future, this will be an example of both an ex ante and unconditional forecast. However, like the example of time series for the year 2002, or when the independent variable is the past year's dependent variable (for example, when we hypothesize that how we will perform next year will depend on how we do this year),[16] then a forecast can be both ex ante and conditional.

Interval Forecast

An interval forecast is made when a boundary or band is provided, within which the actual value is likely to lie. For this kind of forecast, we need to use the law of large numbers again. Recalling that we can test the validity of our null hypothesis by calculating how many standard deviations away the estimated parameter is from its

---

[16] We will discuss these types of prediction models in chapter 9.

"true value," by using the same logic, we can predict with a given level of certainty that the actual value of the predicted variable will fall within a particular range. Thus, for example, we are testing at a .05% level of confidence the null hypothesis that our estimated parameter b is the same as the "true" parameter β. We write this as

$$t_{.05} \leq \frac{b - \beta}{\sigma} \leq t_{.05} \tag{7.25}$$

where $t_{.05}$ is the value of the t ratio (derived from the t table) at a .05% level of confidence, and σ is the standard deviation.

We reject the hypothesis if the calculated value of this ratio is greater than or equal to, or less than or equal to, the critical value of the t ratio. Now it is easy to see that we can use the same logic to state that

$$b - \sigma \, t_{.05} \leq \beta \leq b + t_{.05} \, \sigma.$$

The preceding equation states that we are 95% confident that the actual value of the parameter β is going to between $b \pm \sigma \, t_{.05}$. Therefore, we can use the same technique to derive the band within which we predict with a certain degree of confidence what the future value of our dependent variable will be. This is given by

$$\hat{Y} - \sigma_f \, t_{.05} \leq Y_f \leq \hat{Y} + t_{.05} \, \sigma_f \tag{7.26}$$

where $\hat{Y}*$ is the predicted value of Y,
σ_f is the standard deviation associated with forecasting, and
Y_f is the future value of Y.

This formula would provide us with the necessary interval for our predicted value if we knew the value of σ_f. Since we do not know this value, we estimate it. For estimating the *errors associated with prediction* (S_p^2), we need to adjust the *standard error of estimation* (SE^2) derived in equation (7.13) with the following factor:

$$S_f = \sqrt{S_f^2} = \sqrt{SE^2 \left[1 + \frac{1}{N} + \frac{\left(X_{T+1} - \overline{X}\right)^2}{\Sigma \left(X_i - \overline{X}\right)^2} \right]} \tag{7.27}$$

where X_T is the terminal period of the study. Thus, if our study period includes 25 years, then X_T is 25, and when we predict for the next year, X_{T+1} is 26. Therefore, by using this measure, we can rewrite the equation (7.27) as

$$\hat{Y} - S_f \, t_{.05} \leq Y_f \leq \hat{Y} + t_{.05} \, S_f \tag{7.28}$$

It is interesting to note from the formation of equation (7.27) that because of the expression $(X_{T+1} - \bar{X})^2$, as the prediction moves away from the mean ($\bar{X}$), the error of prediction flares out in an exponential manner. In other words, the farther into the future we want to predict, the greater is our chance of committing error and, therefore, the larger the band of prediction interval. This is shown in Figure 7.22.

Looking back at our example, we had already calculated the values of S (which is 1.9) and $\Sigma(X_i - \bar{X})^2$ (which is 10). Hence, for us, the standard error of prediction is

$$S_f = \sqrt{1.9\left[1 + \frac{1}{5} + \frac{(6-3)^2}{10}\right]}$$

$$= 2.0.$$

This error of prediction is distributed with $N-2$ degrees of freedom. Since we had five observations, the relevant t value is 3.182. We can derive the prediction for the sixth year from our estimated equation, which is 20.3. Therefore, the interval of prediction is given by

$$20.3 - 2 \times 3.182 \leq Y_f \leq 20.3 + 2 \times 3.182$$

or

$$13.94 \leq Y_f \leq 26.66.$$

Figure 7.22 Errors of Estimation

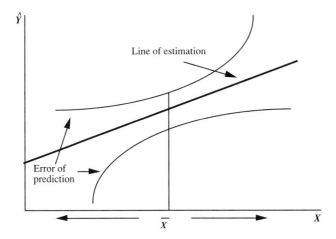

We are 95% confident that the future population for the sixth year will fall between the band 13.94 and 26.66. To check out the flaring effect of the prediction errors, you may calculate it for a few more years in the future.

Explaining the Present with the Past: Lagged Dependent Variables

In real world, once an incident has taken place, its effects linger for a considerable amount of time. For instance, we can argue that the level of crime that a city is presently experiencing will largely be dependent on the extent of criminal activities of last year. This kind of a lingering relationship is particularly true when the relationship between the dependent and independent variables is shaped by long-term factors such as culture, poverty, education, etc. Therefore, it may be true that for a forecast of a city's future year's crime rate, we have to look at its own past records of criminal activities. In econometric analysis, this is accomplished by running a regression treating the past year's observation as the independent variable for this year. Thus,

$$Y_t = a + b Y_{t-1}$$
(7.29)

In technical terms, this use of the past year's data as the independent variable is called a **lag dependent** or an **autoregressive** model. An example may clarify this model for you. Suppose we are trying to forecast the number of violent crimes for future years. We have the data presented in Table 7.10.

Table 7.10 Yearly Crime Statistics

Year	Current year's crime rate (Y_t)	Previous year's Crime rate (Y_{t-1})
1	10	—
2	13	10
3	13	13
4	16	13
5	15	16
6	18	15
7	19	18
8	25	19
9	24	25
10	26	24
11	27	26
12	29	27
13	30	29
14	31	30
15	35	31

In Table 7.10, the yearly crime statistics for the city (Y) are presented in column 2. In column 3, the data are lagged by one period (Y_{t-1}). Using this information in equation (7.29), the model for the lagged dependent variable is estimated to be

$$Y_t = 1.192 + .981\ Y_{t-1}$$
$$t \qquad (1.26)\ (12.53)*$$
$$R \text{ squared} = .929$$
$$F \text{ statistic } (1,12) = 48.11*$$
$$N = 14.$$

* Significant at .05 level.

You may notice that as a result of lagging, we are missing the first year's data. Hence, the number of observations has become 14 instead of 15. You may also notice that the results of this equation can be used to forecast the future year's crime rate. For instance, for the sixteenth year, we need to plug in the data for the fifteenth year in the equation. That is, the estimated figure for the sixteenth year is

$$\hat{Y}_{t+1 \text{ (16th year)}} = 2.192 + .981 \times 35 = 36.53.$$

This equation can be used add infinitum to generate future forecasts. For the seventeenth year, we need to plug in the forecast for the sixteenth year; for the eighteenth year, we need the forecast for the seventeenth year, and so on. As we discussed in the previous section, the farther we move into the future years (and, therefore, away from the mean of the actual series), the progressively larger will be the errors of estimate.

The use of a lagged dependent variable in a regression equation carries some rather important implicit assumptions. You must be aware that by accepting the previous year's observation as the independent variable, you are assuming that all the external forces that shaped last year's crime rate will continue to have the same impact in determining future values.

■ Forecasting by Curve Fitting: A Step-by-Step Approach ■

Review literature. First, understand the underlying relationship linking the dependent variable with the independent variables. If there is no literature available, prepare the appropriate arguments for your postulated hypothesis.

Collect data. Second, collect data arranged in a series. Make sure there are no missing or otherwise "contaminated" data.

Plot the data. Once you have the data, the first step in forecasting by curve fitting is to plot the data. A scatter plot will show you the nature of the underlying trend.

Formulate a projection model. Decide on the appropriate model of forecasting. When in doubt, use parsimony as the guiding principle. If there is a strong quadratic or exponential trend, use an appropriate nonlinear form. If in doubt, use a linear form. If there are a number of distinct trend patterns, or there are a great deal of fluctuations in the series, use the moving average model.

Estimate the model. Use appropriate computer software to estimate the parameters.

Present your findings. Present your findings with all the estimated parameter values and their corresponding t values. Report R^2 and the F statistic. Then verbally explain the full implications of the estimated model. If the report is to be read by a nontechnical person, consider placing the results of your estimation in a footnote or in the appendix. Make sure that the reader is fully aware of your methodology, assumption, and the data.

For using a trend model, you must remember that the trend method assumes the existence of a continuing trend and, therefore cannot predict turning points. If the trend pattern changes or is expected to change, you are better off using a causal model of prediction.

Exercises

1. The county health authority data show a 3% annual increase in the number of indigent emergency care cases. According to a recent survey of area hospitals, there were 3,500 such cases last year. Using a deterministic model, estimate the number of cases of indigent emergency care in your county for the next five years. If the county is paying $1,500 per case for treatment, estimate the total money requirement during this period of time. Having made the estimate, comment on the reliability of your result.

2. A similar method can be used to estimate the numbers of homeless people, teen-age pregnancies, illegal immigrants, etc. As a part of your project, select a specific issue in your area and forecast its course for the next three years.

3. The following table presents three different distributions, all showing a quadratic structure. Explain which one (Y, K, or Z) will be best explained by a quadratic specification.

Dependent Variables			Independent Variable
Y	K	Z	Time
2	2	2	1
4	3	10	2
7	5	15	3
10	12	8	4
8	16	4	5
3.5	10	3	6
2	2	2	7

4. Consider the hypothetical yearly data of garbage collection for the town of Masters, PA. Estimate the tonnage for 1993 and 1994. Use various models of forecast. Which one of these models would you choose and why?

Collection of Garbage for Masters, PA (in 000 tons)

Year	Garbage
1970	1,325
1971	1,356
1972	1,386
1973	1,402
1974	1,435
1975	1,495
1976	1,550
1977	1,597
1978	1,645
1979	1,701
1980	1,756
1981	1,810
1982	1,899
1983	1,967
1984	1,998
1985	2,030
1986	2,780
1987	3,134
1988	3,753
1989	4,004
1990	4,139
1991	4,356

5. By using an inverse functional form, forecast the tax rate from the preceding table for the data from 1980 to 1990.

6. The following table shows per capita chicken consumption (in pounds) for the period 1966 through 1980. On the basis of this information, forecast the per capita demand for the years 1981, 1982, 1983, and 1984. For these years, the actual numbers were 51.6, 53.0, 53.8, and 55.6. Comment on the accuracy of your model.

Year	Consumption
1966	35.6
1967	36.5
1968	36.7
1969	38.4
1970	40.5
1971	40.3
1972	41.8
1973	40.4
1974	40.7
1975	40.1
1976	42.7
1977	44.1
1978	46.7
1979	50.6
1980	50.1

Source. U.S. Department of Agriculture, *Agricultural Statistics.*

7. Predict the value of Y for X equal to 16, 17, 18, 19, and 20.

X	Y
1	35
2	28
3	25
4	20
5	18
6	16
7	15
8	16
9	21
10	27
11	32
12	35
14	45
15	53

8. Write a brief essay explaining why it is difficult to predict the course of the economy even with the most sophisticated methods of trend analysis. Give specific examples.

9. Collect any time series data (for example, government debt as a percent of GNP, population, sales tax revenue, etc.), and, with the help of a regression model, project it for the next five years. Estimate the errors of projection for each year's projection and calculate the confidence intervals.

10. Explain various trend patterns discussed in this book, and give appropriate examples of when such patterns may be appropriate.

11. The passage of the Property Tax Limitations Act (Proposition 13) in 1978 caused a dramatic shift in local government finances for California. The following are the property tax rates per $100 of assessed valuation for the city of San Diego. Estimate the tax rate for 1991 and 1992. Also estimate the intervals for those two years.

Year	Tax rate	Year	Tax rate
1971	1.959	1981	.0860
1972	1.809	1982	.0195
1973	1.774	1983	.0170
1974	1.753	1984	.0160
1975	1.753	1985	.0147
1976	1.733	1986	.0130
1977	1.548	1987	.0117
1978	1.357	1988	.0112
1979	.131	1989	.0103
1980	.088	1990	.0099

Models of Causal Prediction: Multiple Regression

The Problem

Models of trend projection assume that whatever the present trend is, it is going to continue, at least for the period of prediction. The problem with the assumption of continuity is that the past trend may not hold true for any length of time. Also, there may not be any discernible trend pattern in the data. For forecasting cases like these, we need to think about the causal relations that may link the dependent variable with a set of independent variables. Consider a simple example. Suppose you are new in town. You are looking for a house to buy in the fashionable section of the town. You have found a house for which the owner is asking for $265,000. The price seems rather stiff to you. However, before making a bid on it, you would like to know if the asking price is within the norm of the neighborhood.

In such a case, trend analysis would be futile in predicting housing price, since you would have to track the price of the particular house or at least similar houses over time, which is not possible. Similarly there are many instances in which past behavior will not provide much clue to future behavior. Suppose we are interested in predicting the expected tax revenue for a state government for the next fiscal year. The magnitude of tax revenue depends on various factors of current economic conditions. If the economy slows down, the lower level of economic activities will produce less tax revenue, and vice versa. This complex relationship cannot be predicted on the basis of past trend alone. In such cases, we will have to build a causal model for predicting the future.

Building a Causal Model

Building a causal model requires establishing the causal linkage between a dependent variable and a set of independent variables. Therefore, as the first step, we must select a list of independent variables. In the second step, we must determine how these independent variables are related to the dependent variable. In technical literature, these two steps comprise the **specification** of the model.

Let us go back to our example of predicting the price of a house. With the help of a number of characteristic variables which determine the price of houses in the market, we can forecast the expected price of this particular house. As the first step toward specification, we hypothesize that the price of a house depends primarily on the type of structure and location. We assume that the type of structure has one component: the size of the covered area. The location factors include two separate variables: whether the house has a view and whether it is located on a cul-de-sac. Therefore, you can write your model of forecasting housing price as

$$\text{Price} = f\,(\text{Area, View, Cul-de-Sac}). \tag{8.1}$$

The expression (8.1) is read as "price is a function of (or depends on) area, view, cul-de-sac." This expression is also known as an **implicit function** or **implicit model**.

It is called implicit because we are not making any explicit hypothesis regarding the nature of the relationship between the dependent variable and the independent variables. If we express the model by specifying the relationship, it is called an **explicit function** or **model**. Thus, the implicit function written in (8.1) can be made explicit by writing

$$\text{Price} = \beta_0 + \beta_1 \text{ Area} + \beta_2 \text{ View} + \beta_3 \text{ Cul-de-Sac} + \varepsilon \tag{8.2}$$

where β_i's are the coefficients for the independent variables, and
$\quad$ ε is the error term.

The explicit model (8.2) states that we expect the price to go up with the size and relative desirability of the location factors. Also, the model states that we are hypothesizing a linear relationship between price and the other independent variables.

Causality, Co-occurrence, and Acts of Trivial Pursuit

One of the most difficult problems of statistical analysis based on regression or a correlation coefficient is that these results can never establish **causality**, they can only demonstrate **co-occurrence**. That is, the empirical results can only establish that the dependent and the independent variables moved in the same direction, but cannot say whether one was caused by the other. The actual causality must be established by the behavioral theory of human interaction. An example may clarify this point. Data show that productivity in the United States, measured in per capita gross national product and adjusted for inflation (real per capita GNP), is increasing steadily over the years. So is the population of Lima, Peru. If we regress U.S. per capita GNP against the population of Lima, we will find a high degree of statistical significance, leading to the claim that an increase in Lima's population adds to U.S productivity. Yet it is fairly obvious that no such causal connection can exist. On the other hand, a statistical finding correlating expenditure on education, health care, or research and development with U.S. productivity will raise fewer eyebrows.

This is the very essence of establishing causality with the help of regression analysis alone. This problem is amply demonstrated in the field of medical research. Hardly a day passes without medical researchers linking some food or personal habit with some form of human ailment. These findings, of course, cannot claim causality, and only point out close association. Sometimes some of these findings can be misused by asserting a causal connection where there is none. On the other hand, some people can take advantage of the fact that these results do not *prove* causality, and deny a significant relationship. Thus, lobbyists for the tobacco industry have tried to dismiss the results linking lung cancer with smoking as a mere co-occurrence. However, in the face of overwhelming evidence, increasing public awareness prompted public policies that limit tobacco use.

Another important mistake is using trivial variables to find a causal linkage.

Table 8.1. Housing Prices and Characteristics

	Price	AREA (Square Feet)	View	Cul-de-Sac
1	310,000	2200	1.000	1.000
2	233,000	1800	.000	.000
3	400,000	3500	1.000	.000
4	430,000	3200	1.000	1.000
5	210,000	1800	.000	.000
6	240,000	1700	1.000	1.000
7	300,000	2200	.000	1.000
8	350,000	2100	1.000	1.000
9	385,000	2600	1.000	1.000
10	368,000	3000	.000	.000
11	200,000	2000	.000	.000
12	298,000	1750	1.000	1.000
13	275,000	1900	.000	1.000
14	198,000	1800	.000	.000
15	253,000	2200	1.000	.000
16	278,000	2100	1.000	1.000
17	320,000	2170	1.000	1.000
18	178,000	1200	1.000	1.000
19	225,000	2000	.000	.000
20	212,000	1900	.000	1.000
21	288,000	2800	.000	1.000
22	315,000	2300	1.000	1.000
23	255,000	2600	.000	1.000
24	284,000	2700	1.000	.000
25	189,000	1640	1.000	.000
26	220,000	2600	.000	.000
27	248,000	1900	1.000	.000
28	276,000	2000	1.000	1.000
29	210,000	2300	.000	.000
30	205,000	2200	.000	.000

For example, if we are trying to predict the level of production in a clothing manufacturing plant, and we find a strong correlation between the output and the amount of fabric bought by the plant, we will establish a trivial link. Similarly, if, in trying to explain expenditure in the criminal justice system, we take the number of law enforcement officers as the independent variable, we will be engaging in a trivial pursuit.

In the case of establishing a causal link or avoiding the inclusion of trivial independent variables, the lines of judgment can be quite fine. As we have attempted to establish throughout this book, these problems cannot be solved by the techniques of statistical manipulation. They must be resolved outside of statistical analysis through a deep understanding of human behavior linking the dependent with the independent variables.

Estimation of the Model

Having specified the model, we proceed to estimate the relevant coefficients. For this we need to determine how each of the variables is to be measured. In our example, the dependent variable is the sale price of the houses in the neighborhood during the last six months. We can measure the covered area by square feet. The locational factors also include two qualitative variables, showing whether the house has a view and whether it is located on a cul-de-sac (which is desirable for privacy and the absence of fast-moving traffic). The location variables are measured as intercept dummies, with the value of 1 if the house has a view and is located on a cul-de-sac.

Suppose your real estate agent has provided you with information on 30 houses in the neighborhood sold during the last six months. The information is presented in Table 8.1. You can estimate the model with the help of this data.

Since I discussed the procedure for using MYSTAT in estimating regression equations in chapter 7, I refrain from repeating the instructions here. However, it will be worthwhile to look at the MYSTAT output to understand its various aspects. The output is shown in Table 8.2.

Using information from Table 8.2, you can write the estimated equation as follows:

Price = 6,767.87 + 100.04 Area + 40,603.07 View + 42,607.31 Cul-de-Sac (8.3)
t value   (0.233)   (8.18)*   (3.23)*   (3.38)*
R^2 = .786, Adjusted R^2 = .761
F (3,26) = 31.77*
N = 30.
* Significant at .05 level.

Table 8.2. MYSTAT Output of Estimated Regression Equation

DEP VAR: PRICE N: 30 MULTIPLE R: .886   SQUARED MULTIPLE R: .786

ADJUSTED SQUARED MULTIPLE R: .761 STANDARD ERROR OF ESTIMATE: 32456.030

VARIABLE	COEFFICIENT	STD ERROR	STD COEF	TOLERANCE	T	P(2 TAIL)
CONSTANT	6767.872	29038.679	0.000		0.233	0.818
AREA	100.039	12.224	0.746	0.9934159	8.184	0.000
VIEW	40603.074	12587.715	0.310	0.8903693	3.226	0.003
CULDESAC	42607.314	12625.776	0.32	0.8850094	3.375	0.002

ANALYSIS OF VARIANCE

SOURCE	SUM-OF-SQUARES	DF	MEAN-SQUARE	F-RATIO	P
REGRESSION	.100391E+12	3	.334637E+11	31.768	0.000
RESIDUAL	.273882E+11	26	.105339E+10		

Interpretation of the Estimated Results

The estimated equation (8.3) tells an interesting and convincing story about how home prices are determined. For example, it states that each square foot of covered land area adds $100.04 to the price of a home. The estimated results also point out that locational variables contribute heavily to the determination of price. Thus, if the property is located on a piece of land with a view, it increases its price by $40,603.07, while being on a cul-de-sac boosts the price by another $42,607.31.

The interpretation of the intercept term is often problematic in a regression equation. For example, equation (8.3) indicates that if there is not a single square foot of covered area, there is still price. Therefore, the temptation to interpret the intercept term as the price of land is great. For example, using this logic, we can state that if a piece of vacant land (square feet = 0) does not have a view (view = 0) or is not located on a cul-de-sac (cul-de-sac = 0), it will carry a price of $6,767.87. With a view, this price is going to change to $47,370.94. If it is located on a cul de sac but has no view, it is worth $49,375.18. Finally, when a plot of land in this particular neighborhood has a view and is located on a cul de sac, it should command a price of $89,978.25. However, there may be a good deal of danger in such an assertion. This is because we can interpret the intercept term to be the land price if we accept the model to be perfectly specified. If not, we may have left out one or more significant independent variables, the impacts of which will then be captured by the intercept term. For instance, we did not use the lot size (or the total land area) for the houses. Since this is a potentially important variable which was left out, we cannot readily interpret the intercept term. Therefore, unless the model is fully specified (no important variable was left out), any interpretation of the intercept becomes open to questions.

How Significant Are the Estimated Results?

The estimated results indicate that the four independent variables explain 78.6% of the variations (R^2). Since there are 30 observations, at 29 degrees of freedom, the relevant t value for evaluating the significance of the five estimated coefficients (including the constant) at a 95% level of confidence is 1.697. Since all the coefficients except for the constant, have t values greater than this, all are statistically significant. The critical F value at 4 and 25 degrees of freedom is 2.76. Since the calculated F value is 31.768, we can safely conclude that the equation as a whole is statistically significant.

The Uses of the Estimated Results

Now that you are satisfied with the quality of the estimated model, you can predict the price of the house you are interested in. The equation states that each square foot of housing area adds $100.39 to the base price of $6,667.87 (value of the intercept). Also, if a house has a view its price goes up by $29, 641.68. Finally, its location on a cul-de-sac increases its value by $38,889.36.

The house you are interested in has 2,200 square feet of covered area and, although it does not have a view, it is located on a secluded cul-de-sac. Armed with the information derived from the estimated model, you can forecast the market price as follows:

Estimated price = 6,767.87 + 100.039 x (2,300) + 40,603.07 x (0) + 42,607.31 x (1.0).

Notice that since this house does not have a view, the value of the dummy variable is zero. But, as it is located on a cul-de-sac, its value is equal to 1. By using this equation, the estimated price for the property turns out to be approximately \$279,465. Since the owner is asking for \$265,000, it does seem like a bargain.

How Good Is the Model?

Multiple regression is probably the most commonly used technique of statistical research and econometric prediction. While regression analysis offers a powerful tool for prediction, the quality of prediction depends on the model—how close it is to the "true" relationship. Again, as we have mentioned before, we cannot observe the "truth." Therefore, we have no objective way of knowing whether we are sufficiently close to the desired specification. Since the process of specification contains two separate parts—(1) choosing the right set of independent variables and (2) postulating the correct functional form—let us first discuss the problem of selecting the right set of independent variables.

What Happens When We Leave Out Important Explanatory Variables?

When choosing the independent variables, we might omit important variables or include some which are irrelevant. The **error of omitted variables** occurs because one never knows which variables are truly relevant. This omission leads to some rather serious problems of estimation. Let me explain.

Suppose in our housing price example that the true relation is captured by the specification of (8.2); that is, housing price depends on three variables: area, view, and cul-de-sac. In such a case, the estimated coefficients will reflect their true values. For the purpose of exposition, suppose we did not include in our model the variable, area. As a result, equation (8.2) is improperly specified and written as

$$\text{Price} = b'_0 + b'_1 \text{View} + b'_2 \text{Cul-de-Sac} + \varepsilon \qquad (8.4)$$

Since the true relationship includes area, the omission will cause the effects of the omitted variable to be distributed among the remaining independent variables and error terms. This will create a twofold problem. First, the estimated coefficients for the independent variables, by illicitly incorporating fractions of another coefficient, will deviate from their true value. Second, the error term will now contain bias due to contamination by the residual factors of the omitted variable, causing the regression to violate the precepts of the classical least squares method and the estimated coefficients not to be the best, linear, unbiased estimators (BLUE).

Let us see what happens to our estimated equation as a result of this error of omission. By estimating equation (8.4), we get

$$\text{Price} = 230{,}560.4 + 43{,}030.87 \text{ View} + 34{,}230.87 \text{ Cul-de-Sac} \qquad (8.5)$$

t value (12.72)*   (1.84)   (1.47)

$R^2 = .234$, Adjusted $R^2 = .177$

$F(2,27) = 4.11$

$N = 30$.

* Significant at .05 level.

If you compare the results of equation (8.5) with those of equation (8.3), you can see the obvious differences. First, you may notice that both the R^2 and adjusted R^2 have dropped significantly in magnitude, implying that less is being explained by the new model. Also, quite significantly, the variable cul-de-sac is no longer statistically significant. To a researcher, these are the telltale signs of a poorly specified model. Therefore, any prediction based on such a model would be erroneous.

How to Detect the Error of Omitted Variables

The errors of specification are the most difficult to detect. If you have omitted some important explanatory variables, the first indication may be a lower than expected R^2 value. Since R^2 measures percentage of explained variance, leaving out important explanatory variables will cause it to be low.

Since the omission of an important variable causes its effect to be absorbed by the error term, the second probable sign of omission of important variable(s) is a high serial correlation. I will discuss the problem of serial correlation later in this chapter. It may suffice at this time to point out a few important facts regarding serial correlation.

You may recall that one of the fundamental assumptions of the classical least squares method is that the error terms are randomly distributed. Now suppose the true model of housing price contains a variable X, which we have failed to include. In that case, the true model is

$$\text{Price} = b''_0 + b''_1 \text{ Area} + b''_2 \text{ View} + b''_3 \text{ Cul-de-Sac} + b''_5 X + e \qquad (8.6)$$

Since I have omitted X, its effects are now incorporated in the error term (e), which, in effect, has become (e + $a_5 X$). As you can imagine, since the variable X is causally linked with price, its effects will not be random, and its inclusion in the error term will cause a bias. This bias in the error term can cause **serial correlation**. If there is evidence of a high degree of serial correlation, you should look for important explanatory variables that you may have inadvertently left out.

How to Correct the Error of Omitted Variables

The error of omitted variables can be corrected not by resorting to any statistical technique, or through any statistical artifacts, but through an understanding of the nature of the dependent variable. This understanding must come from theoretical literature. Thus, if we are attempting to build a model for predicting the crime rate of a city, we must have a deep understanding of the sociological factors that determine the overall crime rate. For forecasting revenue for the state government, we must look into economic theory and understand the state's fiscal structure.

What Happens When We Include Irrelevant Independent Variables?

The second source of specification error is the inclusion of irrelevant variables in a model. What happens when we include independent variables which are not relevant in explaining the dependent variable? The error of **irrelevant variables** is easier to detect and even simpler to correct for (simply by eliminating them from the model). Let us see what happens when there are irrelevant variables in the model.

Suppose, in estimating housing price, we decide to include a fifth variable, which measures the ease of access from the homes. This is measured by the minutes of travel time to reach the nearest highway. I have added this new variable to Table 8.1 and have shown it in Table 8.3.

When we include this new variable and reestimate our model, we get the following results:

$$\text{Price} = 9{,}291.11 + 99.78 \text{ Area} + 41{,}495.06 \text{ View} + 43{,}182.0 \text{ Cul-de-Sac} - 180.5 \text{ Time} \tag{8.7}$$

t value   (0.30)   (8.0)*   (3.15)*   (3.32)*   (-0.29)

$R^2 = .786$, Adjusted $R^2 = .752$
$F_{(4, 25)} = 23.01$*
$N = 30$.

* Significant at .05 level.

As you can see from the preceding results, the new variable turns out to be statistically insignificant. This lack of statistical significance may be because while some people prefer easy access to the highway, others prefer seclusion and distance from it. Therefore, these conflicting preferences do not show up in the determination of demand for housing.

How to Spot a Redundant Independent Variable

The inclusion of irrelevant variables poses less of a specification problem than the omission of important variables. Thus, if the new variable is totally random, it will impose no bias on either the estimated coefficients or the error term. However, unless you are deliberately choosing a random series, few data sets in nature will be randomly distributed with respect to some other, especially when a researcher has chosen a particular variable as an independent variable (which means that there is

Table 8.3. Variables for Determining Housing Price

Price	AREA (Square Feet)	View	Cul-de-Sac	TIME (minutes)
310,000	2200	1.000	1.000	25
233,000	1800	.000	.000	3
400,000	3500	1.000	.000	17
430,000	3200	1.000	1.000	8
210,000	1800	.000	.000	2
240,000	1700	1.000	1.000	35
300,000	2200	.000	1.000	7
350,000	2100	1.000	1.000	33
385,000	2600	1.000	1.000	35
368,000	3000	.000	.000	21
200,000	2000	.000	.000	10
298,000	1750	1.000	1.000	1
275,000	1900	.000	1.000	15
198,000	1800	.000	.000	4
253,000	2200	1.000	.000	15
278,000	2100	1.000	1.000	13
320,000	2170	1.000	1.000	9
178,000	1200	1.000	1.000	32
225,000	2000	.000	.000	22
212,000	1900	.000	1.000	25
288,000	2800	.000	1.000	1
315,000	2300	1.000	1.000	7
255,000	2600	.000	1.000	19
284,000	2700	1.000	.000	20
189,000	1640	1.000	.000	20
220,000	2600	.000	.000	4
248,000	1900	1.000	.000	3
276,000	2000	1.000	1.000	15
210,000	2300	.000	.000	10
205,000	2200	.000	.000	25

some reason to believe that there is *some* causal link between the dependent and the independent variable). This largely irrelevant variable will impose some biases. The results will be as follows:

1. If the included variable is not significantly correlated with the dependent variable, it will show up as an insignificant *t* value for its estimated coefficient. As can be seen (equation 8.7), the variable Time has a statistically insignificant *t* value.

2. While R^2 will remain unchanged or may even go up, the adjusted R^2 will register a decline. You recall our discussion of R^2 and adjusted R^2 in chapter 7. The R^2 is the measure of total explanation. Therefore, even if you add an utterly irrelevant variable, the worst it can do is to add nothing to the explanation. In such a case, R^2 will remain the same (unchanged) when you include this variable in the original list of independent variables. However, as the formula for adjusted R^2 implies

$$\left[\overline{R^2} = 1 - \left(1 - R^2\right)\frac{N-1}{N-K}\right],$$

unless the new variable adds more to the value of R^2, than the correction factor [N - 1/N - K] made for the inclusion of an additional variable, the value of $\overline{R^2}$ will decline.

By comparing the estimation results of (8.3) with (8.5), we can see that the R^2 value has remained unchanged at .786 as the irrelevant variable, Time, was included. However, since this marginal increase could not compensate for the adjustment factor, the adjusted R^2 declined from .761 to .752.

3. The inclusion of irrelevant variables also tends to increase the variance of the estimated coefficients. This increased variance reduces the magnitudes of the t values of the coefficients.

As you can see, the inclusion of an irrelevant variable has caused a slight reduction in the t values of all three independent variables.

How to Search for the Proper List of Independent Variables

Advances in computer hardware technology and innovations in software have opened up new opportunities for those who want to conduct quantitative research. One of the largest beneficiaries of this technological advent has been econometricians. Thanks to the increased computing capabilities of modern computers, the most sophisticated techniques of estimation are available to prospective users at the touch of a button. As a result, the temptation to replace thoughtful but time-consuming effort to build a theoretically sound model with one of empirical convenience is strong. This can often lead to serious but undetected problems of specification error. Since there is no substitute for good understanding of the causal interrelationship, I will discuss some of the most commonly misused techniques for solving the specification problem.

Fishing Expedition

Suppose I am trying to build a causal model for forecasting a complex sociological phenomenon: the cases of drug abuse among high school students. Being industrious, I have found information on various social and economic characteristics of the general population in the surrounding areas of the school district. However, not being conversant with the scholarly literature on the subject, I do not have a clue as to which variables are important and which are not. It is easy to run a regression when the data are already in the machine, so there is no stopping me. I proceed to run a large number of equations and then choose the combination that gives me the highest R^2 and best t values. This is called a "fishing expedition" or "data mining." The problem with this is that since the model has been built without a deep understanding of the causal linkages, what we are observing is a simple case of co-occurrence. Therefore, this model is likely to give us a misleading forecast, as the future development of these less-than-relevant independent variables will have little bearing on the course of the dependent variable.

Fishing Expedition with Stepwise Regression

Stepwise regression is a statistical technique which minimizes the tedious job of having to choose manually the best set of independent variables. Instead, given a list of variables, it will search for the variable that gives the highest R^2. After that, it will pick from the list the second variable which adds the most to this R^2 value, and then go on the third, and so on. Many of the statistical packages come with this stepwise option. The problem with stepwise regression is the same as choosing variables manually: It selects independent variables based solely on the strength of association and not on causality.

Sequential Searches

Most conscientious statistical researchers tend to stay away from fishing expeditions. However, for building a statistical model, they often rely on what are known as "sequential searches." For these, a primary model is constructed based on theoretical understanding of the variables, and then other variables are added and modifications are made in a sequential order. However, as you can see, the differences among the three techniques of fishing expedition are a matter of degree. Even sequential searches are not free from the possibility that we might include variables which have a strong association with the dependent variable without a compelling causal link, while leaving out variables which are truly relevant for understanding the behavior of the phenomenon we have set out to explain.

There is no substitute for hard-nosed theoretical research for building an empirical model. A model which is based solely on the expedient premise of the highest R^2 and t values is likely to contain serious problems of specification.

Predicting on the Basis of Wrong Functional Forms

Even if we have selected the "correct" set of independent variables, serious errors of specification can arise if we do not choose the right functional form. For example, suppose we have a data set in which the true relationship is a quadratic one, as shown in Figure 8.1. If we assume that the relationship is linear and fit a straight line, obviously we are going to get a terrible predicted value. Figure 8.1 shows the huge differences that can result between actual and predicted values if incorrect functional forms are chosen.

The only way to avoid the problem of misspecifying the functional form is to graph each independent variable against the dependent variable. Although a linear form is recommended over a more complicated nonlinear one, you cannot take a linear functional form for granted. If the data are arranged in a way which quickly reveals, say, a quadratic form, you may not have to spend time plotting the data. However, in most cases you cannot be sure until you have plotted them. Consider

Figure 8.1 Errors of Functional Misspecification

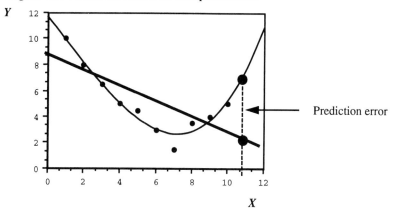

We have a huge error in prediction due to the misspecification of the functional form. Clearly, in this case, the polynomial form is more appropriate. The choice of a straight line causes prediction error.

two sets of data presented in Table 8.4. From the table it is fairly obvious that the variable P has a quadratic relationship with the independent variable, Time. But can you tell the relationship between X and Y just by looking at the data? If not, you will be better off making a quick plot of the data. We have shown the scatter plot Y on X in Figure 8.2.

Figure 8.2 strongly suggests a nonlinear relationship. However, this does not solve the problem completely. You can see in Figure 8.3 that you may still be undecided about the type of polynomial to use. You may try either a second- or a third-degree polynomial.

The estimation of the second-degree polynomial gives us the following result:

$$Y = -190 + 2.03 \text{ x } X - .034 \ X^2 \tag{8.8}$$
$$t \quad (.27)* \quad (3.6)* \quad (4.0)*$$
$$R^2 = .80 \text{ Adjusted } R^2 = .71$$
$$F(2,4) = 8.3$$
$$N = 7.$$
*Significant at .05 level

Table 8.4

Time	P	X	Y
1	0	7	9
2	5	19	30
3	10	25	35
4	15	3	5
5	10	52	3
6	5	36	25
7	3	60	5

Figure 8.2 Scatter Plot Y on X

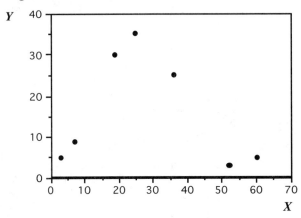

The estimated results look fine, with high R and significant t and F values. The estimated curve has been plotted with a heavy line in Figure 8.3. However, we may also try a third-degree curve, since by inspecting Figue 8.3, we can see some sign of the series turning the corner and going up again. In that case, the results are as follows:

$$Y = -10.74 + 4.408 \times X - .135 \times X^2 + .001 \times X^3 \qquad (8.9)$$
$$t \quad (1.8) \quad (4.4)* \quad\quad (4.0)* \quad\quad (2.6)*$$
$$R^2 = .94, \text{Adjusted } R^2 = .88$$
$$F(3,3) = 15.4$$
$$N = 7.$$
*Significant at .05 level.

The preceding results indicate that although the second-degree curve gives us a good fit, the third-degree one gives us a slightly better fit. We have plotted the expected values based on the preceding formulation in Figure 8.3. However, aside from the question of fit, as you can see, for most X values within the sample range of 60 and 3, there is a significant difference in projected values based on the two curves. But the problem of model specification becomes truly critical when we attempt to project outside the sample range. For example, if we want to project for $X = 85$, the expected value for the quadratic form is -263.1, while for the third degree polynomial it is 2.68. Therefore, unlike the case of a fishing expedition for the right set of independent variables, there is no real harm in looking for the proper functional form by running several equations and then choosing the one with the best fit.

It is extremely important to remember that the functional form you choose may give you forecasts which are significantly different from each other, especially for the independent variables *outside of the sample range* considered in the model (the

Figure 8.3 Projection and Model Specification

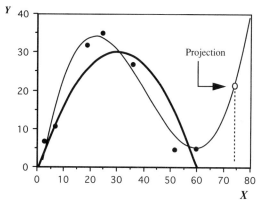

The forecasts outside the sample range can be highly sensitive to the functional form, especially, if we are attempting to forecast outside the sample range (3–60). The figure shows the predicted value for the third-degree specification. You may note that a great deal of variation in the predicted value will take place depending on the choice of the functional form.

range between the highest and the lowest values of the independent variable), and you may not have any objective way of choosing among the different functional forms.

However, even if a higher-order functional form may give you an apparently good fit, there are few instances in social sciences which conform to the explosive growth of a higher-order polynomial. Therefore, to repeat my previous suggestion, always use a linear form when in doubt, and never use a functional form higher than second order.

Figure 8.4 Plot of Home Prices and Covered Area

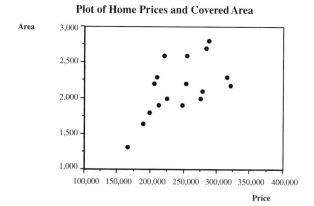

Going back to our example of predicting home price, to specify the functional form, we plotted price against Area in Figure 8.4. From the plotted data, we decided that linear was the best functional form.

When Regression Results Are Suspect: The Errors of Estimation

While using regression analyses, a researcher, like the heroes of the Greek epics, can be misled by a number of different errors or may forfeit sound reasoning and be seduced by empirical results which appear to be gorgeous at the first blush. However, a more careful scrutiny reveals their deceptive nature. Let us discuss the major errors of regression analysis.

When the Independent Variables Are Highly Correlated

One of the premises of the classical least squares method is that the independent variables are not *collinear* (or are not correlated). In statistical terms this is called being *orthogonal*. When two variables are perfectly linearly dependent, in a plot they show up as parallel lines. For example, take any series of numbers (e.g., the square foot measure of the various houses in our example). If another variable is created by adding, multiplying, dividing, or subtracting a constant, then these two are perfectly correlated and are called perfectly collinear with each other. Hence, in our housing price equation, if we add another variable which measures the covered area in square meters, then we have created a situation of perfect **multicollinearity**, since this new variable is a multiple of the old variable.

The presence of perfect multicollinearity prevents us from deriving any estimate of the slope coefficients.[1] Let me explain why. Let us suppose that we are trying to estimate the following equation:

$$Y = a + bX + cZ + e \tag{8.10}$$

where X and Z are two perfectly collinear independent variables.

Since the computation of a multiple regression is extremely time consuming, we did not include the formulae for calculating regression coefficients for multiple regression models in this book. However, for the purpose of exposition I may point out that when there is more than one independent variable, the estimated standard error of slope coefficients is obtained using the following formula:

---

[1] You may test this by creating a linearly dependent variable and then including both the independent variables in a regression model. Most software will give you an error message stating that the coefficients cannot be computed. There may be a few softwares which, due to some rounding error, will give you highly imprecise estimates.

$$SE(b) = \sqrt{\frac{\sum\limits_{i=1}^{n} e_i^{2} / (N - K)}{\sum\limits_{i=1}^{n} (X_i - \overline{X_1})^{2} (1 - r^2_{XZ})}}$$

where e_i^2 is the error sum of squares,

N is the number of observations,

K is the number of independent variables, and

r^2_{XZ} is the square of the correlation coefficient between the two independent variables, X and Z.

From the preceding formula, you can see that when there is no correlation between X and Z (that is, when $r^2_{XZ} = 0$), the term $(1 - r^2_{XZ})$ in the denominator is equal to 1. Therefore, the estimated standard error of the estimated regression coefficient b is at its minimum.

However, as the correlation between X and Z becomes stronger, the correlation coefficient r_{XZ} becomes close to 1. If there is a perfect correlation, this term is equal to 1. In such a case, the denominator of the estimated standard error becomes equal to 0, which makes the standard error infinite. This makes the estimation regression of the coefficients impossible.

In real life, we seldom encounter perfect collinearity between two independent variables unless they are the same variable, simply expressed in two different measurement units. If we accidentally use two perfectly collinear independent variables, our computer software will be able to warn us about it by posting an error message. However, what the software cannot tell is where there is less than perfect correlation. This, as we can deduce from the preceding equation, will make our estimated standard error more widely dispersed, as shown in Figure 8.5.

What is the immediate effect of this increasing dispersion of the error term of the estimated coefficients? If you may recall, the t values for the estimated coeffi-

Figure 8.5 The Effects of Severe Multicollinearity

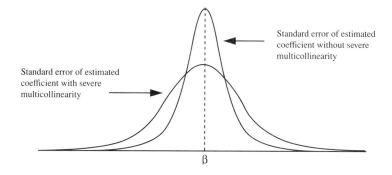

Standard error of estimated coefficient without severe multicollinearity

Standard error of estimated coefficient with severe multicollinearity

β

cients are calculated by dividing the coefficient by its standard error (see equation 7.15). Therefore, this increase in error term will reduce the t value, causing the researcher to reject an otherwise significant independent variable as insignificant.

However, you may note that despite multicollinearity, as Figure 8.5 indicates, the estimated coefficients will remain unbiased. In other words, going back to our example of housing price, we estimated the regression coefficients with the help of 30 observations. This gave us an estimate of the true value of β. If we get another sample group of houses and reestimate the same equation, we would get another estimate of this elusive β. If we continue to repeat this experiment, the distribution of the estimated values of b will have a mean which will get closer and closer to the true value of β. You may recall that this is the property of unbiasedness in the classical least squares method. The presence of multicollinearity does not make our estimated coefficients biased. Therefore, this property of classical least squares is not violated.

Since the variance of the distribution of the estimated coefficients goes up with increasing levels of multicollinearity, the inclusion of a collinear variable will cause the estimates to fluctuate widely. Thus, if we include an independent variable which is highly correlated with another independent variable in the model, their estimated coefficients will become extremely sensitive and will change dramatically each time the equation is run with a slightly different set of independent variables. *However, this extreme sensitivity will not affect those independent variables which are not highly correlated with this new variable.*

The presence of multicollinearity does not affect the measures of overall goodness of fit, either. That is, R^2 and F values in an equation with a high degree of multicollinearity will be unaffected. Consider our example of estimating home prices. Suppose we include two other variables to model, number of bathrooms (Bath) and the total land area (Land) (as opposed to the area under the structure) for each of these units. Suppose that these homes are all located in the same tract-home development and, therefore, the total land area is highly correlated with the covered area. So is the number of bathrooms. These new variables are presented in Table 8.5. Let us explore the effects of the inclusion of these highly correlated independent variables in the model.

The results of the newly estimated equation are as follows:

Price = 33,257.061 + 29.589 Area + 31,877.21 Bath + 30,145.55 View
t values   (1.10)   (0.19)   (2.28)*   (2.24)*
+ 38,593.03 Cul-de-Sac + 10.425 Land   (8.11)
    (3.15)*   (0.12)
R^2 = .825, Adjusted R^2 = .788
$F(5,244)$ = 22.58*
N = 30.
* Significant at .05 level.

By comparing the results of equation (8.11) with those of (8.3), we can see the results of severe multicollinearity. As you can see, the most affected variable is Area,

Table 8.5

Price	Covered Area (square feet)	Bath	View	Cul-de-Sac	Land (square feet)
310,000	2200	3.5	1.000	1.000	4170
233,000	1800	2.5	.000	.000	3330
400,000	3500	5.0	1.000	.000	6175
430,000	3200	4.0	1.000	1.000	6000
210,000	1800	2.0	.000	.000	3330
240,000	1700	2.0	1.000	1.000	3045
300,000	2200	3.0	.000	1.000	4090
350,000	2100	3.0	1.000	1.000	3885
385,000	2600	4.5	1.000	1.000	4810
368,000	3000	4.5	.000	.000	5650
200,000	2000	2.5	.000	.000	3777
298,000	1750	2.0	1.000	1.000	3237
275,000	1900	2.5	.000	1.000	3500
198,000	1800	1.5	.000	.000	3330
253,000	2200	3.0	1.000	.000	4100
278,000	2100	3.0	1.000	1.000	3885
320,000	2170	3.5	1.000	1.000	3999
178,000	1200	1.0	1.000	1.000	2220
225,000	2000	3.0	.000	.000	3700
212,000	1900	2.0	.000	1.000	3515
288,000	2800	3.5	.000	1.000	5280
315,000	2300	4.0	1.000	1.000	4255
255,000	2600	3.0	.000	1.000	4810
284,000	2700	3.5	1.000	.000	4995
189,000	1640	2.0	1.000	.000	3034
220,000	2600	3.0	.000	.000	4810
248,000	1900	2.5	1.000	.000	3515
276,000	2000	3.5	1.000	1.000	3700
210,000	2300	3.0	.000	.000	4255
205,000	2200	2.5	.000	.000	4070

which is highly correlated with the newly introduced variables Land and Bathrooms. While the estimated coefficients and their respective t values for the other two independent variables (View and Cul-de-Sac) remained relatively unchanged, the estimated coefficient for Area was significantly reduced, and its error term increased greatly, causing a precipitous drop in the t value. You may also notice that the R^2 value was not affected by the inclusion of this correlated variable.

Once you understand the problems caused as a result of multicollinearity, the question becomes how to detect it and what to do about it. You should note that

the presence of multicollinearity should be suspected if you have high R^2 but lousy t values.

For detecting which independent variables are collinear, you should also calculate the correlation matrix among the independent variables. For example, if you indi-

Table 8.6 Correlation Matrix

	Area	Bath	View	Cul-de-Sac	Time	Land
Area	1.000					
Bathrooms	0.867	1.000				
View	-0.003	0.208	1.000			
Cul-de-Sac	-0.078	0.060	0.330	1.000		
Time	-0.079	0.035	0.289	0.237	1.000	
Land	0.997	0.864	-0.022	-0.069	-0.092	1.000

cate that you want the correlation coefficient to be calculated among the independent variables, most software packages would provide you with the matrix shown in Table 8.6.

You may read this diagonal matrix as each entry showing the correlation coefficient between the row and the column variables. For example, the correlation between Bathrooms and Area is .867. You may notice that the diagonal numbers are all 1.00. This is because, by definition, each variable has a perfect correlation with itself. From this table you can see that the three independent variables, Area, Bathrooms, and Land, are highly correlated with each other. This would account for the presence of multicollinearity in the estimated equation.[2]

What to Do about Multicollinearity

The presence of multicollinearity poses a dilemma for the analyst. If there is severe multicollinearity between two independent variables, one of the best ways to resolve the problem is to eliminate one of them. However, if the eliminated variable happens to be an important variable in explaining the dependent variable, then by eliminating it we will cause specification error, with its accompanying problems. Further, as we have noted, multicollinearity among a partial list of independent variables will not affect the other variables, nor will the error term be biased.

Therefore, researchers often choose not to do anything about multicollinearity unless the problem is acute. For example, looking at the correlation coefficients of our previous example, I would be inclined to include the number of bathrooms in the model, as this happens to be one of the vital considerations in determining the price of a home. On the other hand, I would reason that having a correlation coefficient of .997, the variable Land is not adding much to the explanation of market price beyond the area of the structure (Area). Hence, I would specify the model by including Bathrooms but eliminating Land. As you can tell, this is purely a line call based on subjective judgment.

Econometricians have attempted to walk the tight rope between being com-

---

[2] The presence of multicollinearity is best determined by the test of variance inflation factor. However, this test is a bit too complicated for inclusion in this book. See D. E. Farrar and R. R. Glauber, "Multicollinearity in Regression Analysis: The Problem Revisited," *Review of Economics and Statistics*, 1967, pp. 92–107; D. A. Belsley, E. Kuh, and R. E. Welsch, *Regression Diagnostics, Identifying Influential Data and Sources of Collinearity* (New York: Wiley, 1980). For an excellent overall discussion, see A. H. Studenmund, *Using Econometrics: A Practical Guide*, 2nd ed. (New York: HarperCollins, 1992).

prehensive in including all the important information, and at the same time avoiding severe multicollinearity. Although this is a matter of subjective judgment and comes through years of practice, I suggest a few practical steps for eliminating multicollinearity among the independent variables:

1. In certain circumstances, the two independent variables can be added together. This newly created variable will contain information from both variables, and may add to the explanation without having the problems of multicollinearity. This trick may work provided that the two variables do not have opposite expected signs, or are not significantly different in magnitude. Suppose we are adding two highly correlated independent variables X and Z to form a new variable K. If X is positively related to the dependent variable Y while Z is negatively related (X and Z are negatively correlated with each other), the newly created variable will be found to have little explanatory capability as the positive relationship is going to be offset by the negative. The addition of the independent variable also will not work if one of the variables has a substantially higher mean than the other. In this case, the smaller variable is going to be lost in the larger variable and the linear combination of the two will not provide any more insight into the variation of the dependent variable. Further, the newly created variable may not have any intuitive meaning. For example, for a completely different purpose, economist Arthur Okun created an index by adding unemployment rate with the rate of inflation, which he called the "misery index." As you can see, this composite measure has a readily understandable meaning. In contrast, if we add the variable Area with Land, this variable may not convey any definite meaning for policy makers (in this case home buyers).

2. For a time series data, the problem of multicollinearity can also be solved if you take the first difference. That is, you create a new variable by subtracting the preceding time period's data from that of the current period. For example, suppose we are trying to forecast the sales tax revenue for a state government. We have chosen as independent variables the rate of growth of per capita state income and the rate of unemployment. But in formulating our model we find that there is a strong negative correlation between the rate of growth of per capita income and unemployment rate (that is, during prosperous times when the rate of growth of income is high, unemployment is low, and vice versa). Therefore, we cannot add these two together. Hence a way out may be to take the yearly difference in unemployment rate, which may not have as strong a correlation with the rate of growth of per capita income as does the absolute level of unemployment. However, even this method is not a panacea for correcting multicollinearity. Similar to the problem of creating a composite variable, the yearly difference of a variable may not have the same meaning (or even any meaning) as an independent variable. Therefore, even after getting a high t value and R^2, we may be at a loss to explain our results in a meaningful way.

3. Finally, another (and probably the least controversial) way of dealing with the problem of multicollinearity is to increase the sample size. If it is a viable alternative, it is certainly worth pursuing. This is a remedy because if the two vari-

ables are not simply multiples of each other (perfectly correlated), then as the number of observations increases, the natural variations within the series will sufficiently distinguish themselves from each other to allow the proper estimation of the model. Thus, in our example of housing price, if we can increase the sample size from 30 to, say, 300, the variations within the two series may sufficiently distinguish themselves from each other and allow us to estimate the model properly.

Serial Correlation: When the Successive Error Terms Are Correlated

Serial correlation (which is also known as **autocorrelation**) means that the order in which the observations are arranged has some implication on the estimation of the regression coefficients. In other words, serial correlation exists in an estimated model if the observations are arranged in a way by which the error of one observation depends on that of the previous one.

An example may clarify the point. Suppose every year I purchase boxes of Girl Scout cookies for subsequent sale to my friends and colleagues. Every year I place an order for those cookies by anticipating their demand. If there are unsold boxes of cookies (in which case I have to eat them, albeit reluctantly!), next year I will reduce the size of my order. On the other hand, if, after placing the order, I find out that there are more people who are interested in the tasty treats, my order in the subsequent year will reflect this year's underpurchasing of cookies. Therefore, the magnitude of my last year's error will closely relate to this year's error.

If you plot random error terms with no serial correlation, they will reflect a random quality, shown in Figure 8.6.

In contrast to the situation of a random distribution of the error terms, Figure 8.7 shows the existence of serial correlation, both **positive** and **negative**. If the current period's error term generally shows the same sign as the previous ones, then the series is said to have a positive serial correlation. Thus, if a public policy keeps

Figure 8.6 Distribution of Errors Showing No Serial Correlation

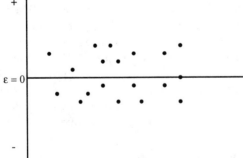

The plot of the error term showing a random distribution.
The errors show no particular trend or pattern.

Figure 8.7 Serial Correlation

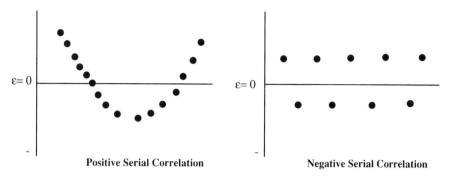

The basic assumption of hypothesis testing is that the errors are randomly distributed. However, if the errors exhibit a pattern of trend, then they violate the principle of randomness. This is called serial correlation. As a result, none of the hypothesis tests is operable.

on affecting the course of the economy for a number of years (for example, the passage of the property tax cut initiative—Proposition 13—in California on property tax revenue and on areas of local government expenditure), the series shows positive serial correlation.

In contrast, if a series shows alternate positive and negative error terms, this is called negative serial correlation. In this case, the error terms oscillate back and forth like a pendulum. This is typical of a series with seasonal variations. For example, quarterly data on the sale of umbrellas will show such a pattern.

The existence of a correlation between the successive error terms violates one of the fundamental principles of the classical least squares method. The most widely used method for detecting serial correlation is the **Durbin-Watson** d test.[3] This test is applicable only when

1. The regression model includes an intercept term.
2. The error terms have a first-order correlation. That is, each year's error is only correlated with the one preceding it, and not to the ones of two or three years prior. In symbolic terms, this can be written as

$$e_t = \rho e_{t-1} + \varepsilon$$

where e_ts are the residuals (estimated error terms),
ρ is the correlation coefficient, and
ε is the true random error term, t is the year (or time period).

3. The regression model does not include a lagged dependent term.

---

[3] This test is based on J. Durbin and G. S. Watson, "Testing for Serial Correlation in Least-Square Regression," *Biometrica*, 1951, pp. 159–177.

The Durbin-Watson d statistic is defined as

$$d = \frac{\sum_{i=2}^{n}\left(e_t - e_{t-1}\right)^2}{\sum_{i=1}^{n} e_t^{\ 2}}$$

(8.12)

The d statistic varies between 4 and 0. If there is perfect positive serial correlation ($\rho = 1$), e_t is the same as e_{t-1}. Therefore, notice that the numerator becomes zero. If there is perfect positive correlation, the d statistic = 0. If, on the other hand, there is a perfect negative correlation ($\rho = -1$), then the numerator becomes equal to $4\Sigma e_t^2$. Hence, in such a case the expression (8.12) becomes $4\Sigma e_t^2/\Sigma e_t^2 = 4$. If there is no serial correlation at all, the d statistic is equal to 2. Hence, if the d statistic is close to either 0 or 4, you should suspect the presence of serial correlation.

Unfortunately, the correction for serial correlation is beyond the scope of this introductory textbook. In fact, the abbreviated Business MYSTAT does not even estimate the d statistic. If you are interested in knowing more about these problems, you may consult one of many excellent texts on econometrics.[4]

Heteroskedasticity: The Problem of Scaling of Variables

One of the important conditions for the classical least squares method is that the error term of the observations is constant. This is the condition of **homoskedasticity**. Figure 8.8 demonstrates the implication of this assumption. As you can see, the variance of the error term corresponding to the three observations of the dependent variable X falls within the same band. However, this happy situation may not hold true if the dependent variables vary a great deal in magnitude. In that case, as the magnitude of the dependent variables increases so does the variability of the error term. This situation of increasing variability of the error term is called **heteroskedasticity** and is shown in Figure 8.9.

Heteroskedasticity, therefore, is caused as a result of essentially mixing apples with oranges in the data set, and is typically encountered in cross-section models. For example, suppose we are attempting to account for urban crime in America. If our data set contains the numbers of high crimes committed in large metropolises along with those in small towns in primarily agricultural states, we are likely to encounter heteroskedasticity. Heteroskedasticity can be either pure or impure. If the model is not properly specified, then there can be difference in the variance of the error terms. This is called **impure heteroskedasticity**. If, on the other hand,

---

[4] For example, see Harry H. Kelejian and Wallace E. Oates, *Introduction to Econometrics: Principles and Applications* (New York: Harper & Row Publishers, 1981); A. H. Studenmund, *Using Econometrics: A Practical Guide* (New York: HarperCollins Publishers, 1992).

Figure 8.8 Homoskedastic Distribution of Errors

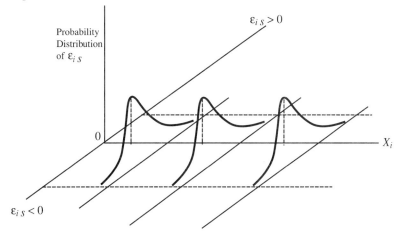

By the precepts of classical least squares analysis, the error terms must have the same standard deviation. This diagram shows the error terms with constant standard deviations.

despite the best specification of the model the error terms show signs of heteroskedasticity, this is known as **pure heteroskedasticity**.

Figure 8.9 Heteroskedastic Distribution of Errors

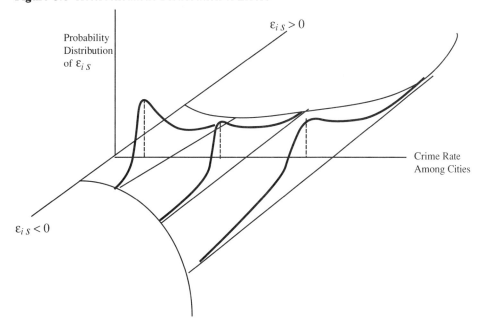

Figure 8.10 Hypothetical Plot of Errors Showing Heteroskedasticity

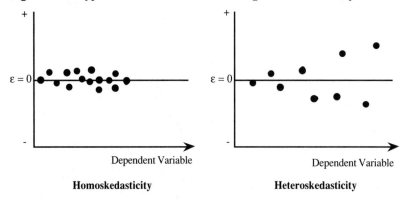

The distribution of error terms cannot be readily observed. However, we can test whether there is heteroskedasticity by saving the residual from an estimated model and then plotting the error terms against the dependent variable. However, a more precise degree of heteroskedasticity can be calculated with the help of some sophisticated measures.

How to Detect Heteroskedasticity

The presence of heteroskedasticity can be visually inspected by plotting the error terms. If we do not have heteroskedasticity, the errors will be distributed randomly around 0.0. However, if there is heteroskedasticity, the errors will show a flaring-out pattern as in Figure 8.10.

To explain the point, let us go back to our old example of estimating housing price in a neighborhood. Using the results of equation (8.3), we have obtained the predicted value for each of the homes in the sample. The difference between the actual and the predicted is the error terms, which have been plotted in Figure 8.11.

Figure 8.11 Plot of Error Terms of Housing Price Data

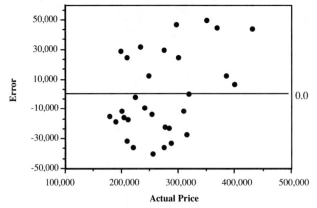

As a demonstration of the problem of heteroskedasticity, we have plotted the residuals from our housing price model. As you can see, the estimated errors show a discernible pattern.

The plot in Figure 8.11 does not indicate any overwhelming presence of heteroskedasticity. This is because the housing prices are fairly close to each other. Now suppose we have included in the sample data from an adjoining but dissimilar neighborhood. While the original sample contains data from an upper-middle-class area, the next one is decidedly from a more affluent one. The expanded data set, with 10 new entries of extremely high-priced homes, has been presented in Table 8.7. In this table we have included a column of predicted values of house prices by

Table 8.7 Series on Housing Price by Including a Dissimilar Neighborhood

Observations	Price	Predicted Price	Error (residuals)
1	310,000	320,733	-10,733
2	233,000	168,067	64,933
3	400,000	422,349	-22,349
4	430,000	436,803	-6,803
5	210,000	168,067	41,933
6	240,000	262,698	-22,698
7	300,000	263,770	36,230
8	350,000	309,126	40,874
9	385,000	367,161	17,839
10	368,000	307,351	60,649
11	200,000	191,281	8,719
12	298,000	268,501	29,498
13	275,000	228,949	46,051
14	198,000	168,067	29,933
15	253,000	271,458	-18,458
16	278,000	309,126	-31,126
17	320,000	317,251	2,749
18	178,000	204,663	-26,663
19	225,000	191,281	33,719
20	212,000	228,949	-16,949
21	288,000	333,412	-45,412
22	315,000	332,340	-17,340
23	255,000	310,198	-55,198
24	284,000	329,493	-45,493
25	189,000	206,458	-17,459
26	220,000	260,923	-40,923
27	248,000	236,637	11,363
28	276,000	297,519	-21,519
29	210,000	226,102	-16,102
30	205,000	214,495	-9,495
31	535,000	548,433	-13,433
32	648,000	640,217	7,783
33	656,000	606,468	49,532
34	802,000	814,322	-12,322
35	735,000	724,313	10,687
36	546,000	658,699	-112,699
37	762,900	944,846	-181,946
38	485,000	546,637	-61,637
39	942,000	979,667	-37,667
40	1,250,000	898,418	351,582

using the specification of equation (8.3) but adding a dummy variable for the two communities. The newly created dummy variable for community (Com) is = 0 for the moderately priced one, and = 1 for the wealthy community. The estimated equation is as follows:

Price = – 40,859.71 + 116.07 Area + 56,963.41 View + 49,275.54 Cul-de-Sac
t value   (0.94)   (6.20)*   (2.11)*   (1.88)*
+ 275,903.98 Com   (8.13)*
(6.73)*
R^2 = .905, Adjusted R^2 = .894
$F(4,35)$ = 83.57*
N = 40.
* Significant at .05 level.

The column "Predicted Price" was created using this formula. The error terms were calculated by subtracting the predicted price from actual price (Price).

The error terms, shown in column 4 of Table 8.7, have been plotted against the actual price (Price) of the homes in Figure 8.12. By comparing this figure with the previous one (Figure 8.11), you can clearly see that the introduction of high-priced homes in the sample has created heteroskedasticity.

What Are the Effects of Heteroskedasticity?

If there is pure heteroskedasticity, it can increase the variance of the estimated coefficients in a way that will cause the t and F values to come out stronger than what is warranted by the data. Therefore, while the estimates remain unbiased, all

Figure 8.12 Error Terms Showing Heteroskedasticity

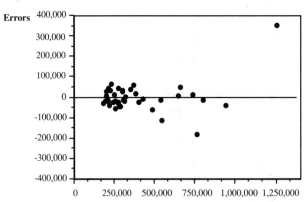

When the original series of housing prices is combined with data from a highly affluent neighborhood, we encounter the problem of heteroskedasticity. As you can see from the plotted residual values, there is a pronounced flaring-out pattern, implying the presence of heteroskedasticity.

the measures of hypothesis testing will be suspect. On the other hand, if there is impure heteroskedasticity resulting from a poor specification of the equation, its impact on the estimators will be similar to those of serial correlation discussed earlier.

How Can Heteroskedasticity Be Corrected?

The error of heteroskedasticity is primarily a result of having a variable which is simply too diverse. Hence, the presence of heteroskedasticity should be suspect in cross-section data with samples varying greatly in size, or in time series data over a long period of time or in a situation where the magnitude of the dependent variable is increasing at a very high rate with time. Thus, if we are attempting to predict the number of homicides for our city based on the number of homicides for this year among a large number of diverse cities and towns, we are likely to encounter heteroskedasticity. Also, heteroskedasticity is likely to exist in a time series data showing the number of individuals infected with the deadly and rapidly spreading AIDS virus, since the actual numbers of infected individuals keep on increasing in size every year.

Heteroskedasticity can be detected with the help of some of the more sophisticated tests, which are beyond the scope of this introductory book. However, we may say a few words about correcting heteroskedasticity at this point. First, if heteroskedasticity is impure, it can be corrected simply by specifying the model better. To repeat our discussion of proper specification, this requires a great deal of hard work in thinking through the proper theoretical structure.

If, on the other hand, heteroskedasticity is pure, the very nature of the data causes the variance of the error terms to change, and we need to think about the dependent variable. For instance, if we encounter strong heteroskedasticity in trying to work with data on the number of homicides in cities and towns across the nation, we may separate out the sample in two groups: large cities and small towns. Or we may express the absolute numbers in ratios, such as homicide rate per 1,000 inhabitants. Sometimes these kinds of data transformation can reduce the variance to such an extent that the extent of heteroskedasticity can be significantly reduced.

When the Data Are Imperfect

Finally, a serious source of error in forecasting with regression models occurs when the data are spurious. In statistics, this is known as the **error in variable** or the measurement problem. The problem can creep in due to various factors. For example, many sociological data, when available, often contain severe measurement errors. Thus, information on child and wife abuse, rape, incest, etc. are significantly underrepresented. Even economic data, such as unemployment or inflation, are often criticized for containing biases of all sorts. The unemployment data are typically collected by adding the numbers of all those who registered at unemployment offices. This list, then does not include those whose unemployment benefits have run out, the students or homemakers seeking employment for the first time, and the underemployed (those who are working at levels far below their capabilities, such as an engineer working as a waiter in a restaurant). The data on inflation are computed by comparing the prices of a basket of goods a "typical" consumer would buy. Since there are wide differences in consumption habits, the inflation figures published by the Bureau of Labor Statistics are likely to affect individuals differently.

Therefore, when data containing biases are used in a regression model, the accuracy of statistical explanation and prediction are affected. These errors can occur if the dependent variable is biased or if there is measurement error in the independent variable as well. If the dependent variable contains measurement error but the independent variable is generally free of it, and the bias is random, then the measurement error will increase the errors of prediction while the estimated coefficients will remain unbiased. Therefore, the predicted results will have more variation, although the estimated coefficients will be unbiased. In other words, if we were to repeat the experiment a sufficient number of times with different samples, the average of all the estimated coefficients will approach the actual coefficient. Theoretically at least, this is a lesser problem than the one caused by the existence of error in the independent variable.

If the independent variables contain measurement biases, bias spreads through the error term in the estimated equation (e), which cannot be corrected easily. In its effect, this bias in the independent variable will cause the independent variable to be correlated with the error term (e).[5]

◼ Summary: Step-by-Step Suggestions for Building a Model of Causal Prediction ◼

1. **Develop theory.** The first step toward building a causal model is to have an excellent understanding of the causality. Do a thorough job of reading the existing literature on the issues. Then, based on theoretical understanding of the relationship between the dependent and independent variables, develop your hypothesis in terms of an implicit model.
2. **Operationalize variables.** Having developed your hypothesis, think how you can measure the relevant variables. You have to make sure that you are measuring what you intend to measure and nothing else.
3. **Collect clean data.** If there are built-in biases, make sure you are aware of them and can make the necessary adjustments in your model.
4. **Plot the dependent variable against each independent variable.** To formulate the explicit functional form, plot the dependent variable against the independent variables. Determine which is the most appropriate form.

---

[5] This will be a situation close to the simultaneous bias. However, the bias of simultaneity has been deliberately left out of this introductory book. Without explanation, I will simply state that this bias can be corrected by using the instrumental variable approach. If you are interested in learning more about this problem, see Studenmund, *Using Econometrics*, or R. Pindyck and D. Rubinfeld, *Econometric Models and Econometric Forecasts* (New York: McGraw-Hill, 1981).

5. **Estimate** the regression equation and make necessary adjustments to omit unnecessary variables or include necessary ones.
6. **Check for multicollinearity.** Calculate the correlation matrix. If the problem is not acute, leave it alone. Otherwise, see if you can pick one variable among the collinear ones to represent the set. Also see if adding the variables or taking the first difference makes theoretical sense.
7. If there is reason, check for **heteroskedasticity**.
8. Check for **serial correlation**. Use Durbin-Watson statistics, if available.
9. Present estimation results clearly, and draw conclusions.
10. Explain all the assumptions and point out the possible sources of biases in your conclusions.

Tips: Go for parsimony. If two models explain approximately the same amount, choose the one with fewer variables.

Keep it simple. Unless a more complicated functional form is truly necessary, choose the simpler one.

While forecasting the future, remember that the error of estimation is going to flare out as you move away from the sample mean. Therefore, the problem of making accurate predictions increases exponentially as you go farther into the future.

EXERCISES

1. What is causal prediction? What are its advantages over the methods of trend projection? What are its relative shortcomings?

2. Based on our estimated model of housing price given in equation (8.3), comment on the following four units presently on the market:

	Area	View	Cul-de-Sac	Asking Price
a.	2,500	yes	no	$295,000
b.	3,200	yes	yes	$325,000
c.	1,500	no	no	$162,000
d.	1,950	no	yes	$182,000

To explain the housing prices more thoroughly, what are some of the other variables you would include in the model?

3. Suppose you have been asked to forecast the crime rate of your city. For this, you have decided to use a cross-sectional model of 55 cities across the nation.
   a. What measure of the dependent variable would you use?
   b. Which variables would you include as the independent variables, and what signs for their coefficients would you postulate?
   c. What would be the source(s) of your information?
   d. Explain the various statistical problems that you will face while estimating this model.
   e. What actions would you take to correct these problems?

4. Suppose your state legislature is considering legalizing a state-run lottery. One of the aspects of lottery that is under scrutiny is the demographic profile of the prospective players. A survey of total monthly purchases of lottery tickets by 450 participants in a neighboring state shows the following relationship:

Total purchase = 10.51 - .086 PI + 1.23 Age - .162 ED + 2.59 Min
t value   (6.78)   (3.67)   (2.46)   (2.01)   (3.52)
R^2 = .68, Adjusted R^2 = .668
F (4, 445) = 189.95
N = 500

where   PI is personal income in $000,
        Age is dummy variable = 1 for participants over the age of 65 and
                              = 0 otherwise,
        ED is years of school, and
        Min = dummy variable = 1 for minority players and
                             = 0 otherwise.

   a. Write a detailed report explaining the results.
   b. What are the important policy implications that the legislators should be aware of?
   c. What are some of the other independent variables that could have been included?
   d. Based on this estimated model, how much are you expected to spend on lottery per month?

5. The water utility department of your town has estimated the following model of water use per capita:
   PWU = 15.64 + 1.86 Y - .0059Y^2 + 3.29 CH + 2.87 AD + .029 SQ + .009 LS
   t values (7.89) (6.86) (-9.32) (2.85) (1.98) (3.16) (2.88)
   R^2 = .867, Adjusted R^2 = .850
   F (6, 343) = 297.89
   N = 350

   where   PWU is per capita water use,
           Y is income per household,
           CH is number of children in the house,
           AD is number of adults in the house,
           SQ is square feet of covered area, and
           LS is lot size (land area).

   Interpret this equation and write a report explaining the significance of these findings.

6. What are the possible sources of bias in the estimation of a classical least squares method? Explaining the terms *multicollinearity*, *heteroskedasticity*, and *serial correlation*, discuss how you would detect their presence in an estimated relationship. What are some of the ways of eliminating multicollinearity and heteroskadasticity?

7. Following is the record of the total number of medals (gold+silver+bronze) won by the participating nations in the Barcelona summer Olympic games of 1992. You may note that among the participants with a large population, India and Bangladesh failed to win a single medal.

Nation	Medals	Nation	Medals	Nation	Medals
*CIS	112	Czechoslovakia	7	Austria	2
United States	108	Norway	7	Namibia	2
Germany	82	Turkey	7	S. Africa	2
China	54	Denmark	6	Israel	2
Cuba	31	Indonesia	6	Mongolia	2
Hungary	30	Finland	5	Slovenia	2
S. Korea	29	Jamaica	4	Switzerland	1
France	29	Nigeria	4	Mexico	1
Australia	27	Brazil	3	Peru	1
Spain	22	Morocco	3	Taiwan	1
Japan	22	Ethiopia	3	Argentina	1
Britain	20	Latvia	3	Bahamas	1
Italy	19	Belgium	3	Colombia	1
Poland	19	Croatia	3	Ghana	1
Canada	18	Independent*	3	Malaysia	1
Romania	18	Iran	3	Phillippines	1
Bulgaria	16	Greece	2	Pakistan	1
Netherlands	15	Ireland	2	Puerto Rico	1
Sweden	12	Algeria	2	Qatar	1
N. Korea	9	Estonia	2	Surinam	1
Kenya	8	Lithuania	2	Thailand	1

*CIS is the Confederation of Independent States—the former Soviet Union.

Form a causal model to explain the distribution of medals among these diverse nations. Comment on the quality of your estimated model. Based on your model, estimate the number of medals each country was expected to win. Which of these did significantly better and which did significantly worse? How would you explain these countries' performance? (Hint: Performance in the Olympics may be closely linked to the overall development of the individual countries. Also government policies of expenditure on sports is an important variable. Use a dummy variable for communist nations).

PART III

THE LOGIC OF EFFICIENT MANAGEMENT

Chapter 9

How to Plan a Large Project: Gantt, PERT, and the Critical Path Method

The Problem

Your department is embarking on a new project. You just received the good news that the federal grant that you had applied for has been approved. Now you will have to complete a need analysis for the homeless population in your city within eight months (32 weeks) from the sanction of the money. As the project manager, you feel slightly bewildered, considering different tasks you will have to complete within the next eight months. In your mind are three primary questions:

Will we be able to complete this job within the time period?
Which jobs are the most critical for the project?
How should the scheduling be done?

Large projects often pose problems for planning. With so many interconnected things to do, you are likely to seek help. This help may come in the form of a **Gantt, PERT** (Program Evaluation Review Technique) and **CPM** (Critical Path Method). The strength of these techniques lies in the fact that they allow you to visualize the entire project as a string of interconnected activities. PERT is a visual representation of a series of interrelated tasks. CPM is a further extension of PERT and is used for analyzing time, cost, and the probability of completing a project on time.

PERT was developed for the U.S. Navy in the mid-1950s during the construction of Polaris missile program, when innumerable tasks had to be performed in a technologically determined sequence. Around the same time, CPM was developed by the DuPont Corporation for the construction of its new plastic plants. Both the projects were eminently successful. The Polaris program was completed nearly two years prior to its scheduled time. A good part of this enhanced efficiency was attributed to planning with PERT. DuPont also found CPM to be extremely helpful in reducing bottlenecks and shutdowns by 37%, at a savings of nearly a million dollars (in 1957 dollars). This impressive debut launched these techniques for a wide range of applications in the private and public sectors.

Gantt Chart

The more complex depiction of interrelated activities in a PERT network was developed from its earlier and simpler version, called a Gantt chart or Gantt's Milestone chart. A Gantt chart simply breaks down a project into its crucial components and shows them in chronological order. For example, if we are going to conduct a survey for estimating the number of homeless in our city, we may breakdown the essential tasks as (a) prepare a questionnaire, (b) hire personnel to conduct the survey, (c) conduct survey, and (d) write a report. The Gantt chart for the project is shown in Figure 9.1.

In Gantt terminology, the circles are called "milestones," which represent the accomplishment of a specific phase of the project. The rectangles represent indi-

Figure 9.1 Gantt's Milestone Chart

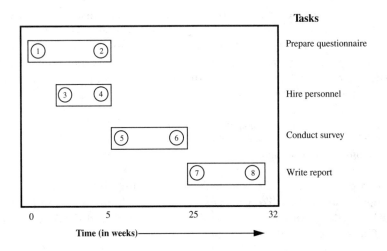

Gantt chart showing the chronological sequence of the major tasks. The circles represent the accomplishments (starts and finish) of a specific phase, and the rectangles show individual tasks.

vidual tasks. The strength of this representation is its simplicity. It visually shows a manager, in clearly defined terms, the various phases and tasks of a project.

Simplicity of presentation, however, is not an asset when it comes to the planning and managing of a complex project. Out of this concern evolved the PERT network. In contrast to a Gantt chart, PERT is not concerned with phases of the project. Rather PERT defines each activity with a project in sequence and with individual duration time. Therefore, the rectangles showing tasks are dropped in PERT along with the horizontal depiction of time.

PERT Network

In the PERT network, a visual representation of the sequence of activities within a project is drawn in terms of **activities** and **events**.

> An **activity** is a time-consuming element in a project, which is usually represented by an arrow, and an **event** is a point in time corresponding to the start and the end of an activity. Events are shown as circles in a network.

Thus, if my project in the morning is to get ready for work, then "brushing teeth" would be a time-consuming element, with a starting event (the time I start brushing my teeth) and an ending event (when I finish it). The diagrammatic representation of an activity with a starting and an ending event is shown in Figure 9.2.

Figure 9.2 Activity and Events

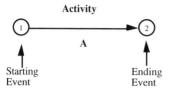

An activity, a time-consuming element
in a project, is shown with an arrow.
The activity (A) has a starting event
(1) and an ending event (2), which are
drawn as circles.

In this figure, we have drawn an activity, (A), with starting event (1) and ending event (2). For the sake of consistency, we will denote activities with letters and events with numbers.

The morning does not end with brushing teeth; it continues with getting dressed. We have shown this in Figure 9.3 as activity B, with the starting event 2, and ending event, 3. You may notice the logic of this sequencing: Activity B starts only when A is completed, and cannot start until that point. However, what happens when more than one activity can start at the same time? When I start making coffee, I do not have to wait for the coffee to be brewed to start my eggs and toast. In fact, after getting dressed, I can immediately start my coffee machine and, while it is brewing, I can put slices of bread in the toaster and begin boiling eggs. Such a sequence has been drawn in Figure 9.3; as soon as activity B (getting dressed) is completed, I can start activities C (making toast), D (brewing coffee), and E (boiling eggs).

Soon after all three of the activities (C, D, and E) are completed, I can start my breakfast. However, when I try to draw the next sequence of activities, I run into a

Figure 9.3 Branching Out of Activities

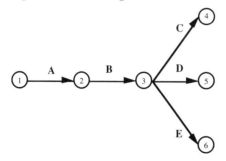

Several activities are started at the same point in a
project. Activities C, D, and E can start as soon as
activity B is completed.

Figure 9.4 Example of Including Unnecessary Activities

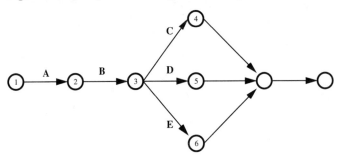

slight problem. I can draw lines to show the activities of bringing the toast, eggs, and coffee to the table, but my kitchen area is rather compact, and it would not serve any purpose to draw separate activity lines for each of these activities. Therefore, my problem boils down to the fact that I have activities, but they do not take any measurable amount of time to complete. Since an activity is defined as a time-consuming task within a project, drawing activity lines such as in Figure 9.4 would not do. At the same time, if I do not draw these lines, the three activities are going to dangle without logically coming to an end for the next activity (eating) to begin.

The way out of this dilemma is provided by **dummy activities**. Dummy activities are defined as those elements in projects which perform the function of a logical linkage, but take no time of their own. These activities are drawn with dotted lines, as shown in Figure 9.5.

Now we have a logically complete sequence of events, with a starting event for the entire project (1) and an ending event (7). Figure 9.5 shows that as soon as the activities C, D, and E are done, F can begin.

Figure 9.5 The Inclusion of Dummy Activities

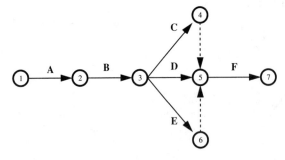

Dummy activities are used to depict those activities which do not consume any time, yet are needed for the proper sequencing of activities. These non-time-consuming activities are drawn with dotted lines.

Estimation of Time

The next step toward completing a PERT network is the estimation of time for completing each of the activities. Going back to our example of getting ready in the morning, I can ask myself, How much time do I need to do each of the activities? From my past experience, I can say that brushing my teeth usually takes me four minutes. However, the quickest I can do it in is three minutes. On the other hand, if I am really being slow in the morning, it can take me as long as eight minutes. In terms of PERT terminology, these three **expected** durations of time are known as the **optimistic time**, **most likely time**, and **pessimistic time**. Therefore, I can construct the chart shown in Table 9.1 describing the sequence of activities and their expected times of completion.

From the three expected times (optimistic, pessimistic, and most likely), we can **estimate** the duration time for an activity. This can be done by taking an average of the three expected times. However, you may notice that in such a case, we will give an equal weight to the expectations. Since the distribution of time is biased toward the most likely time, we should give it the most weight. This is done by calculating a weighted average given by the following formula:

$$\text{Estimated time } = \frac{\text{Optimistic time } + \left(4 \times \text{Most likely time }\right) + \text{Pessimistic time}}{6} \tag{9.1}$$

As you can see, we have given a weight of 4 to the most likely time, which will create a bias for the estimated time to be close to this number; but at the same time, the estimated time will also be influenced by the expectations of the optimistic and pessimistic times. Thus, the estimated time for the activity "brushing teeth" will be

$$\text{Estimated time for brushing teeth } = \frac{3 + \left(4 \times 4\right) + 8}{6} = 4.5 \text{ minutes.}$$

Table 9.1 Activities and their Expected Times of Completion (in minutes)

Activity	Description	Depends upon	Optimistic time	Most likely time	Pessimistic time
A	Brushing teeth	None	3.0	4.0	8.0
B	Getting dressed	A	8.0	10.0	12.0
C	Making toast	B	2.0	3.0	4.0
D	Brewing coffee	B	4.5	5.5	6.5
E	Boiling eggs	B	1.5	2.0	2.5
F	Eating breakfast	C, D, E	7.0	15.0	17.0

If you are wondering why you are dividing by 6, you may note that by multiplying the most likely time by 4, we have six different expectations of completion time. Therefore, the mean of the weighted average is calculated by dividing the sum by 6. This procedure is directly derived from the asymptotic property of the mean, subject to all the possible biases, discussed in chapter 2. To be sure, there will be some wild guesses. However, if these guesses do not have any specific bias, the extremes on both ends are going to cancel each other out and leave us with a value close to the reality. Let us suppose that for a particular activity the optimistic time is two weeks, most likely time is four weeks, and pessimistic time is six weeks. In such a case, we have a symmetric distribution of expected time, as shown in Figure 9.6a. In this case, when we estimate the duration time, it is going to be equal to the most likely time indicated by the experts.

The distribution of expected time, however, is often not symmetric. If, for example, an activity is expected to be completed in two weeks optimistically, four weeks most likely, and eight weeks pessimistically, then the distribution of expected time is skewed to the left, with a long tail to the right (see Figure 9.6b). In this case, the estimated duration time is influenced by the fact that if things do not go the right way, the activity can take much longer to complete. This is reflected in the calculation of the duration time of 4.33 weeks, which is a more pessimistic appraisal than the most likely time.

In contrast, if the distribution of expected time is skewed to the right, with a long tail extending to the left (Figure 9.6c), then the duration time is going to be influenced by the rosy expectations of the optimistic prediction, and the calculated duration time will be less than the most likely time. You can readily see this by considering an activity with 2 weeks of optimistic expected completion time, 8 weeks of most likely time, and 10 weeks of pessimistic time. For this activity, the duration time is 7.33 weeks, which is less than the assessment of the most likely time.

The deviation of the estimated duration time from the most likely time may seem simple minded to you, but a number of studies have been conducted on the

Figure 9.6 Distribution of PERT Estimated Time

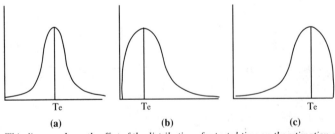

Te	Te	Te
(a)	(b)	(c)

This diagram shows the effect of the distribution of expected time on the estimation of duration time. If the distribution is symmetric (a), the estimated duration time is equal to the most likely time (drawn as the line T). However, if the distribution is skewed, the estimated duration time is more pessimistic than the most likely time in (b) and more optimistic than the most likely time in (c).

accuracy of the estimation of duration time based on the distribution of expected time. All of these studies indicate that the error in calculating the expected duration time was too small to have any significant effect in real- life application.

Calculation of Critical Path

Going back to our example of preparing breakfast, we can calculate the estimated time for each activity by the weighted average formula given in equation (9.1). We have placed these figures in Table 9.2 in the third column, "Estimated Time." Once we have the estimated time, we can fill out the rest of the table by calculating the **earliest start**, **earliest finish**, **latest start**, and **latest finish**. The earliest start refers to the earliest possible time for a particular activity to begin. If an activity depends on another, it cannot start until that one is completed. For instance, since activity A does not depend on any other activity, it can start at time 0. However, as B cannot start until A is completed, the earliest it can start is after three minutes into the project, since it would take me at least that long to brush my teeth.

By following this process, *adding the duration time to the earliest start*, we can calculate the earliest finish time for the activity at hand, which is the earliest starting time for the subsequent activity. Therefore, we can see that activities C, D, and E can start as soon as B is completed, which, at the earliest, is 14.5 minutes into the project.

The calculation of activity F is a little more complicated since it cannot start till C, D, and E are completed. Since among these three activities, D takes the longest, I must wait to start my breakfast until my coffee is brewed. Therefore, activity F will start, at the earliest, 20 minutes after I start brushing teeth. Since my estimated time for eating breakfast is 14 minutes, the total time for the project is 34 minutes. This is called the **project time**, which is calculated by following the most time- consuming activities in the project.

The latest start and latest finish for each activity (which does not delay the project) within a project can best be calculated by working backward through the PERT network. For example, if C, D, and E are completed at the twentieth minute, F must start right at that time; otherwise the entire project will be delayed. Therefore, F has no choice but to start at the twentieth minute at the latest.

Table 9.2 Calculations for Critical Path Analysis

Activity	Depends upon	Estimated time	Earliest start	Earliest finish	Latest start	Latest finish	Slack time
A	None	4.5	0	4.5	0	4.5	0.0
B	A	10.0	4.5	14.5	4.5	14.5	0.0
C	B	3.0	14.5	17.5	17.0	20.0	2.5
D	B	5.5	14.5	20.0	14.5	20.0	0.0
E	B	2.0	14.5	16.5	18.0	20.0	3.5
F	C, D, E	14.0	20.0	34.0	20.0	34.0	0.0
				Project time		34.0	

Activity E (boiling eggs), however, does not need to start as soon as I get dressed (activity B, on which it depends). Since boiling eggs takes only two minutes, and the eggs must be ready when I actually start eating (activity F), it has some leeway. That is, I can start it at eighteenth minute at the latest and can still meet my deadline for starting the subsequent activity.

> Therefore, the **latest start** for an activity can be calculated by subtracting its duration time from the earliest start time of the following activity.

By following this logic, we can calculate the latest start and latest finish columns in Table 9.2. You may notice another by-product of working backward on the PERT table. You may check in the first two columns of Table 9.2 whether the sequence of events is in order. Although we did not label the dummy activities in Table 9.1 or in the figures, for the sake of logical consistency you should always label them and include them in your table showing 0 duration time. This is especially important if you are working with a computer to calculate the critical path, since without these specifications the computer algorithm will fail to recognize the dummy activities and will reject them as unlinked activities.

Slack Time and Critical Path

If you look carefully at Table 9.2, you can see that there are some activities which are critical for the project, in the sense that if they do not start exactly when the predecessor event ends, the entire project will be delayed. Therefore, for these activities, there is no difference between earliest start and latest start. These are the activities which are on the **critical path** of the project.

In contrast, the noncritical activities are those that have slack time, defined as the difference between the earliest starting time and latest starting time. Thus, consider Table 9.3. In this table, we have shown the activities and the slack time. The ones with asterisks are on the critical path of the project.

In PERT diagrams, the critical path of a project is traced by etching out the relevant activity lines. This has been shown in Figure 9.7.

The critical path is defined as

> the path within a network, which takes the longest amount of time to complete.

Table 9.3 Activities and Slack Times

Activity	Description	Slack time
A	Brushing teeth	0.0*
B	Getting dressed	0.0*
C	Making toast	2.5
D	Brewing coffee	0.0*
E	Boiling eggs	3.5
F	Eat breakfast	0.0*

Figure 9.7 The Critical Path

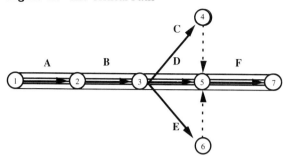

This path is called "critical" because any reduction in project time must be achieved by cutting the duration time on the activities on this path. For instance, in our example, if I want to get out of the house faster than I usually do (within 34 minutes from the time I start brushing my teeth), it should be readily apparent that boiling eggs faster or eating half-toasted bread will not help. I can reduce my project time only by reducing the duration time of the activities on the critical path.

Can We Finish This Project Before a Certain Time? The Use of Variance

Although we cannot know the future for sure, we can take calculated guesses at the chances of completing a project or an individual activity within a certain time. This can be done by figuring out how dispersed the distribution of expected completion time is. From our discussion in chapter 2, we know that the more closely bunched up a distribution is, the greater is the probability that our sample mean will reflect the actual mean. This dispersion, of course, is measured by variance and standard deviation. The variance of the distribution of possible completion time of an activity (i) can be approximated by

$$\sigma^2_1 = \left(\frac{\text{Optimistic time - Pessimistic time}}{\text{Most likely time}} \right)^2.$$

(9.2)

For example, our activity of brushing teeth will have a variance = $(3 - 7/4)^2 = 1$. Therefore, the standard deviation is: $\sqrt{1} = 1$. You may notice that since standard deviation (σ) is the square root of variance (σ^2), standard deviation can be calculated simply by

$$\sigma_1 = \left| \frac{\text{Optimistic time - Pessimistic time}}{\text{Most likely time}} \right|$$

Figure 9.8 The Use of Calculated Variance in Estimating Completion Time

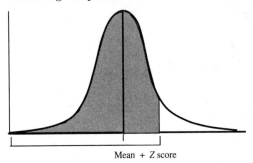

Mean + Z score

From this information, we can calculate the probability of completing this activity at a particular time (let us call it the "desired time") by calculating the Z score. Thus, if we want to calculate the odds of completing brushing within five point five minutes, by using the **central limit theorem** (or the **law of large numbers**) we can calculate the Z score as:

$$Z = \frac{\text{Desired time - Expected duration time}}{\text{Standard deviation}} \qquad (9.3)$$

Therefore, if we want to know the probability that I will finish brushing within five minutes, we can use the following formula:

$$Z = \frac{5.5 - 4.5}{1} = 1.0.$$

The corresponding one-tailed probability is .3413.

Since we posed the question as, "What is the probability that the task will be completed within five point five minutes?" we add the left-hand probability of the normal distribution with the probability of .5. This gives us the probability measure .5 + .3413 = .8413. In other words, we can be 84% certain that this task will be completed within the specified time limit (see Figure 9.8).

The logic of this analysis can be extended to the completion of the entire project. That is, the total variance for the project (*P*) can be calculated as the summation of the variances of the activities on the critical path. For me to complete my breakfast, activities A, B, D, and F are on the critical path. Therefore, the standard deviation for the entire project can be calculated as

$$\sigma_p = \sqrt{\left(\frac{3.5 - 7.5}{4.0}\right)^2 + \left(\frac{8.0 - 12.0}{10.0}\right)^2 + \left(\frac{4.5 - 6.5}{5.5}\right)^2 + \left(\frac{7.0 - 17.0}{15.0}\right)^2}$$

$$\sigma_p = \sqrt{1 + .16 + .132 + .444} = 1.32.$$

Since the expected duration of my project to have breakfast is 34 minutes, with a standard deviation of 1.32 minutes, we are able to calculate the probability that I will be able to complete my breakfast within 32 minutes. By using formula 9.2, we can calculate the probability as

$$Z = \frac{32 - 34}{1.32} = -1.51,$$

with the corresponding probability as .4345. Subtracting from .5, we can see that the probability of my finishing breakfast two minutes before the expected duration time is less than 10% (.0655 to be exact).

As you can see, the use of this technique can give us some rather strong analytical tools. However, a few words of caution. Extending the asymptotic properties of mean to the calculation of expected time for a particular activity is somewhat problematic, as the very idea of asymptote implies that if this particular activity is performed innumerable number of times, the mean of the sample distribution would reflect the "true" mean. But these activities are frequently one-shot affairs, and are certainly not repeated time and again, and therefore chances are that the actual completion time will be either greater than or less than the expected. Also, while calculating the probability of completing a project within a certain time, you should remember that each activity is assumed to have an independent probability of being completed on time. In other words, the cause of delay of one activity is not assumed to affect the other ones. However, if there is a crippling national labor strike, or some other natural catastrophe, the delay may be injected into most of the activities, which may cause an unforeseen delay for the project.

Things to Avoid in Preparing PERT and Critical Path

As you can see, the PERT network develops the sequence of activities in a logical fashion. Therefore, anything that upsets this logical structure must be avoided. Take, for example, cyclical activities, as shown in Figure 9.9. This figure implies that activity B must precede activity C, and that activity C must again precede activity B. This is logically inconsistent. Of course, in a small diagram this is readily apparent. However, in a large network, this may not be so. Also, if you are trying to solve critical path with the help of a computer which only understands strings of sequential activities, such mistakes may not be caught quickly.

Figure 9.9 Circular Reasoning

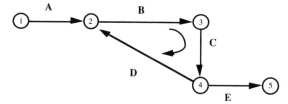

Figure 9.10 Broken Activity Lines

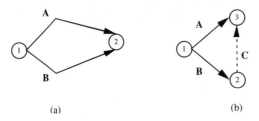

(a)   (b)

Since PERT networks are drawn to represent a complex sequence of tasks as simply as possible, you should always economize on choosing the number of arrows or guard against making the diagram unnecessarily complicated. As a simple diagram attracts attention, a too complex and cumbersome diagram detracts people's attention. One of the ways of making the diagrammatic representation simple and coherent is to use dummy activities. For example, the activity lines should not be broken or drawn as curves (Figure 9.10a). Instead, when two or more activities have the same starting and ending events, dummy activities have to be used (Figure 9.10b).

Finally, a common logical mistake occurs when a project is shown to have multiple starting and multiple ending events and to have dangling activities which do not link up to any other activity. This has been shown in Figure 9.11.

Figure 9.11 has been correctly drawn in Figure 9.12. You can see that by the use of appropriate dummy activities, we have been able to construct the sequence of tasks in a proper way. To facilitate comparison with Figure 9.11, I did not change

Figure 9.11 Dangling or Out-of-Sequence Activities

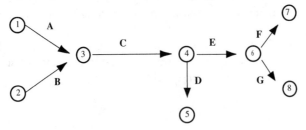

This PERT network has two starting events, 1 and 2. The activity D is dangling, without a link with any other activity. Also, the network shows two ending events, 7 and 8.

Figure 9.12

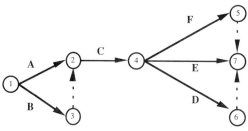

Proper representation of the sequence of activities shown in Figure 9.11. Now there is a unique starting event (1), a unique ending event (7), and all the activities are properly linked.

the names of the activities, and hence did not label the dummy activities. However, I encourage you to think of dummy activities as activities without any duration time. Therefore, they should be labeled.

Survey of the Homeless Population: An Example

Let us consider the example of preparing a survey to assess the extent of the homeless population in a city. Suppose your agency has received a grant to conduct such a survey within eight months (32 weeks) from the start of the project. The first step toward preparing a PERT network is to list all the activities within the project. The second step is to determine the sequence of activities (that is, which preceding activity or activities does the successive activity depend on?). Table 9.4 shows such a list.

Table 9.4 List of Activities for the Survey

	Activities	*Depends on*
A	Hire surveyors	None
B	Prepare a list of areas and agencies to be contacted	None
C	Prepare questionnaire	None
D	Conduct survey	A, B, C
E	Hire personnel for data entry	None
F	Enter data in computer	D, E
G	Analyze data	F
H	Prepare report and present findings to the granting agency	G

Figure 9.13 PERT Network for the Survey Project

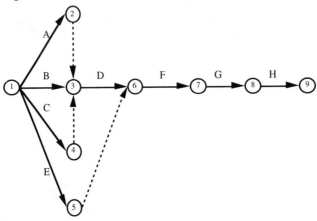

From the information given in Table 9.4, we can draw the PERT network shown in Figure 9.13.

You may check the consistency of the network by going backward through the sequence of activities. The third step for preparing the PERT network is to estimate time. This was done by surveying experienced individuals within the organization. The results are shown in Table 9.5.

Table 9.5 shows the estimated time for each activity. By transferring this information to Table 9.6, we can see that the estimated completion time for the project is 30 weeks, which is two weeks prior to the project deadline.

Table 9.6 also shows the activities on the critical path of the project. We can see that the personnel to be hired for conducting the survey do not have to be hired immediately, and by hiring them on a time coinciding with the appropriate activity, the city can save money on salaries. The critical path for the project is shown in

Table 9.5 (in weeks)

Activities	Optimistic Time	Likely Time	Pessimistic Time	Estimated Time
A	1	2	6	2.5
B	0.5	1	4.5	1.5
C	2	5	8	5
D	8	10	15	10.5
E	0.5	1	1.5	1
F	4	6	8	6
G	2	2.5	3	2.5
H	3	6	9	6

Table 9.6 Calculations for the Critical Path

Activity	Depends upon	Estimated time	Earliest start	Earliest finish	Latest start	Latest finish	Slack time
A	None	2.19	0	2.5	2.5	5	2.5
B	None	1.5	0	1.5	3.5	5	3.5
C	None	5	0	5	0	5	0.0*
D	A, B, C	10.5	5	15.5	5	15.5	0.0*
E	None	1	0	1	4	5	4.0
F	D, E	6	15.5	21.5	15.5	21.5	0.0*
G	F	2.5	21.5	24	21.5	24	0.0*
H	G	6	24	30	24	30	0.0*

Figure 9.14. This diagram can be further modified by drawing it to match the scale of time in order to flag any delay in the critical path of the project. For a complicated project, it is a good idea to draw the PERT diagram and post it in a visible place so everyone connected to the project can monitor its progress.

Crashing Time on the Critical Path

A major strength of PERT and CPM is that they allow the manager to control the course of a complex project. They also allow the manager to determine the most efficient way to reduce the project duration time. For example, a project may have to be completed ahead of schedule. Or, because of time overrun in the earlier part

Figure 9.14 The Critical Path

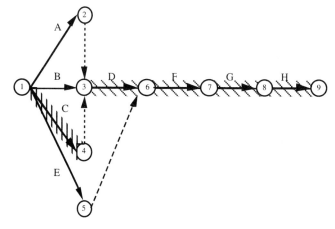

of the project, the duration time for the subsequent activities may have to be reduced. In PERT jargon, this is known as "crashing" time. In other words, to meet the new deadline, the time of certain activities must be "crashed." Then the question arises, which activities should be targeted for crashing, and at what cost?

Clearly, the activities which are not on the critical path should not be crashed, as their completion ahead of schedule will have no bearing on the total duration of the project. Of course, if the crashing of one activity on the critical path makes some other activity which was not critical to be on the critical path, we will have to consider reducing the second activity's time as well. To assess the most cost-effective way of reducing project time, we need to calculate the chart shown in Table 9.7.

In Table 9.7, we have placed an asterix next to the activities on the critical path for easy detection. From this table, it is clear that the most cost-effective way of crashing time is by reducing time on activity C, followed by F, H, and G. However, the problem is that we cannot crash activity C to the full extent of three weeks, because we will run into the problem that activity A will become critical. The cost of crashing activity A turns out to be extremely expensive.

Therefore, we can devise the strategy that up to 2.5 weeks, activity C will be crashed. After that we will look at activity F for another half a week. If we want to reduce the project time even more, the most cost-effective strategy would be to reduce the duration time for activity C to 3 weeks, A to .5, and F to .5. Beyond this 4 weeks of crashing, you may notice, project time can be further collapsed by 1.5 weeks by crashing activity H, and by 1 week by crashing activity G. The results of these strategies of crashing are presented in Table 9.8.

Based on Table 9.8, we can calculate Table 9.9 showing the trade-off between time and cost. As you can see, as time is crashed, workers will have to be paid overtime, or other nonproject tasks will have to be pushed aside, and added personnel must be included in the project. The increased cost figures reflect all of these costs: the increased personnel, the overtime payments, and the opportunity cost of devoting time away from other non-project activities.

However, when a project is completed ahead of schedule, it not only causes the costs to go up, but also creates some cost savings. These savings come in terms of the fixed cost of running the operation, from supplies to salaries, fringe benefits,

Table 9.7 Crash Time and the Costs of Crashing

Activities	Depends Upon	Normal Time	Normal Cost	Crash Time	Crash Cost	Crash Cost per week
A	None	2.5	$1,500	2.0	$2,000	$1,000
B	None	1.5	$750	1.25	$850	$400
C*	None	5.0	$4,000	2	$6,250	$750
D*	A, B, C	10.5	$15,000	9	$18,000	$2,000
E	None	1.0	$400	1	$400	—
F*	D, E	6.0	$5,000	5.5	$5,450	$900
G*	F	2.5	$10,000	1.5	$12,200	$2,200
H*	G	6.0	$12,000	4.5	$14,000	$1,333

*Activities on the critical path.

Table 9.8 The Strategies of Crashing Project Time

Change in Project Duration Time	Crash strategy	Cost	New Critical Path(s)
30 to 27.5 weeks	Crash C for 2.5 weeks	$1,875	C,D,F,G,H
27.5 to 27 weeks	Crash F for .5 week	$900	C,D,F,G,H
27 to 26.5 weeks	Crash A for .5 and C for .5 week	$875	C,D,F,G,H & A,D,F,G,H
26.5 to 25 weeks	Crash H for 1.5 weeks	$2,000	C,D,F,G,H & A,D,F,G,H
25 to 24 weeks	Crash G for 1 week	$2,200	C,D,F,G,H & A,D,F,G,H

and other fixed items. Let us assume that for our organization, this cost saving amounts to $800 per week. The results of reduction of fixed costs are shown in Table 9.9.

Table 9.9 indicates that it is more cost effective to try to finish the project by crashing time by two and a half weeks than to complete it in the normal course of time. This is because the fixed cost saving per week is greater than the cost of crashing the project time at this phase. However, as we try to cut project time even more, the fixed cost saving is offset by the increasing rate of the cost of crashing project time.

When to Use PERT

PERT is an extremely useful tool of project management. The preparation of a PERT network allows a manager systematically to plan the entire course of operation, by ensuring the logical connections of all the interconnected aspects of the project. Since PERT emphasizes the planning of time, it forces managers to be aware of time constraints and be prepared for unforeseen snags.

The visual representation of the entire project allows the members of various departments to review the project in a systematic way, on commonly understood grounds. Reviews such as these can identify the weak links and the possible problem areas, and facilitate project coordination. The sharing of responsibilities can be made clear, with a specific expectation of time for each participant.

Table 9.9 Comparison between Time Saved and Costs Incurred

Types of Costs	Completion Time (weeks)					
	30	27.5	27	26.5	25	24
Normal Costs	$48,650	$48,650	$48,650	$48,650	$48,650	$48,650
Total Crash Costs	0	1,875	2,775	3,650	5,650	7,650
Average weekly cost	1,622	1,837	1,905	1,974	2,172	2,354
Total costs	$48,650	$50,525	$51,425	$52,300	$54,300	$56,500
Weekly fixed cost savings ($800 per week)	0	-$2,000	-$2,400	-$2,800	-$4,000	-$4,800
Total adjusted costs	$48,650	$48,525	$49,025	$49,500	$50,300	$51,700

The analysis of critical path provides detailed knowledge of the most vital areas of project execution. By providing information on the minimum time in which the project can be completed, the manager can get valuable insights into the costs of crashing time and the problems that can occur in the process (especially by some other path becoming "critical"). This information leads to a more efficient use of resources.

Finally, PERT is an extremely useful tool for monitoring a large project, where delay in one of the critical activities can jeopardize the entire time table. If properly used, PERT can raise warning flags in time for the manager to take proper corrective actions.

Although quite versatile in its use, there are certain areas in which the PERT technique can be used most fruitfully. For example,

1. PERT is primarily designed for one-time large projects, such as building construction, large survey projects, product planning, and start-up activities in a plant or a factory. Since PERT allows a planner to scan visually the development of a project and the efficient use of resources, it is particularly useful for projects with a definite completion time and a cost for time overrun.

2. PERT is particularly adept in planning and scheduling of interdependent activities. Therefore, a project with many such activities can be greatly facilitated by the use of PERT network analysis.

3. For the proper utilization of PERT, activities and events must be well defined, with clearly identifiable starting and ending events.

4. The value of PERT is best realized in projects for which there is little or no past experience and many uncertainties. In such a situation, PERT brings order to a seemingly chaotic process.

Words of Caution

Although PERT is one of the most useful techniques for planning projects, there are areas for which it is clearly not well suited. Like any other method of management, PERT demands a certain amount of discipline and acceptance, which may not be forthcoming from all the participants. Apart from employee resistance, there are some important areas of concern.

First, PERT is concerned solely with the process. It aims at making the process the most efficient it can be. For this, it requires good estimations of time and cost. Therefore, if a project is particularly nebulous or experimental, the estimation of time becomes extremely difficult, making PERT less effective. PERT is designed for goal-oriented, physical planning, and it is particularly useful for engineering project and other scheduling problems. On the other hand, in the area of social work or community health, for example, where projects are intimately connected with the so-called human elements, PERT loses its effectiveness.

With regard to cost estimation, PERT poses some rather difficult problems. The internal accounting of cost based on time spent on a project or an activity creates various kinds of problems. If an employee is dividing time between a project activity and nonproject activities, the proper accounting of time spent on a project requires keeping of meticulous records. This problem is compounded when an employee's project activities are very close in nature to the nonproject activities. This difficulty often results from questionable accounting practices. For example, during the late 1980s, defense contractors, working on a "cost plus" basis, were found to have charged an inordinate amount of money for the most mundane of activities. Apart from greed and avarice, this can partly be accounted for by the difficulty in keeping track of time spent on project activities. Therefore, while considering the most cost-effective way of crashing time, the results can be less than optimal.

The most vexing problem of developing PERT network analysis is the difficulty in determining the proper sequencing of activities. The level of detail in the sequencing of activities will pose problems for any project. For instance, you can see that sequencing activities for preparing breakfast in our earlier example can be made infinitely more complicated by introducing many more subtle activities, such as taking the pieces of bread to the toaster, getting the toast out, spreading butter and jam on the toast, etc. Hence, the decision of the appropriate cut-off point for activities must be regarded as an art rather than a science, which must be derived based on a number of definable and undefinable criteria.

Exercises

1. Draw PERT networks for the following data, calculating the project time and showing the critical path.

   a.

Activities	Depends on	Optimistic time	Most likely time	Pessimistic time
A	—	5	7	9
B	—	7	10	13
C	B	10	11	12
D	A	6	12	18
E	C,D	4	5	14

   b.

Activities	Depends on	Estimated time
A	—	10
B	A	7
C	A	3
D	A	19
E	A	5
F	C,C,D,E	8

c.

Activities	Depends on	Estimated time
A	—	1
B	—	17
C	B	7
D	A	5
E	A	11
F	D,E	3

d.

Activities	Depends on	Estimated time
A	—	2
B	—	5
C	—	7
D	A	10
E	B,F	3
F	C	5
G	B,F	7
H	D,E,G	10
I	C,G,F	3
J	H,I	9

e.

Activities	Depends on	Estimated time
A	—	10
B	—	6
C	A	6
D	A	2
E	B	5
F	B	7
G	C,D	15
H	E,F	3
I	G,H	5
J	I	7
K	I	10
L	I	3
M	J,K,L	9

2. Write an essay on the types of problems in public sector management for which PERT is ideally suitable. What are some of the main pitfalls of PERT network analysis?

3. When should you choose to use a Gantt milestone chart over a PERT network? Explain.

4. What criteria would you use for determining the optimal strategy crashing time? What kinds of data would want to have to make such an analysis, and where would you look for such information?

5. Suppose you are managing a project, given in Exercise1.c. You have been instructed to reduce the project time by four days. The costs of crashing for each activity are:

Activities	Cash cost/per day (in $000)
A	4
B	5
C	4
D	6
E	4
F	4

Find the most cost-effective way to shorten the project time by four days.

6. Do one of the following projects(these projects are also appropriate for group work):

If you work for a public organization, take an appropriate project and, by drawing a PERT network, conduct critical path analysis.

Your best friend has decided to get married six weeks from now, and you are in charge of planning the ceremony and a formal reception afterward. Help your friend by drawing up a PERT network and analyzing the critical path. Be as realistic as you can be.

Write a report.

Chapter 10

Inventory and Cash Management

The Problem

The City Manager's office wants to increase efficiency by cutting costs. The purchasing department is reviewing the way it orders and holds supply in the inventory. In addition, the finance director wants to look into the amount of cash that is held in non-interest-bearing accounts to meet the city's day-to-day and other unexpected expenditures. The problems of these two departments seem quite different at the outset. However, the basis of both problems boils down to the same thing and can be solved using the same type of model. These days, when cost cutting and increases in government revenue are on everyone's mind, the optimal solution to these problems can save government agencies a great deal of money. The need for inventory and cash management has kept pace with increases in the size of government at all levels. Therefore, more efficient management of inventory and liquid cash is needed.

Inventory Management

In our personal lives, we all make decisions about the optimum size of inventory when we go grocery shopping. We keep in mind the storage capacity of our refrigerator and kitchen. We want to buy enough so that we do not have to make too many trips to the grocery store, which is inconvenient in terms of lost time and money (especially if you have to drive to the supermarket). Although you shop for everyday needs, unless you are a die-hard survivalist or live in an area prone to natural disaster, you probably do not stock pile essential life-sustaining supplies like food, medicine, and matches in your home. The reasons for not stocking these items are threefold: first, you do not anticipate their sudden demand; second, you are reasonably certain that if the need arises, you will be able to go out and make the necessary purchase without a problem; and third, you have to balance between the cost of having to go to the store and paying for purchases which do not have immediate use. However, if you hear of an approaching hurricane or a huge snowstorm, you will make an effort to keep these items in stock. In a world of perfectly reliable and instant suppliers and no unanticipated demand, nobody would need to keep an inventory. But in a world where demand is uncertain and supply is reasonably reliable but time consuming, the need for keeping inventories is undeniable. Therefore, inventory management has two important components: the anticipation of demand and the lag time in receiving supply.

The Concept of Average Inventory

At the heart of inventory management is the concept of average inventory. This simple notion provides us with the first stepping stone for a rational analysis of inventory size. Figure 10.1 explains the concept.

Figure 10.1 Reserve Stock and Average Inventory

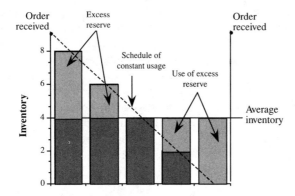

*When orders are received at the beginning of the working week, there is
100% stock in the inventory. During the next five days, the stock is
used at a steady rate of 20% each day. At the end of the five days, a
new shipment comes in as the inventory is completely depleted.*

Suppose an organization uses 20 units of an inventory item during the five
working days of a week. Therefore, if this item is used at a steady rate, the inventory
manager should be prepared to see the daily use of four units, which is the average
inventory. Since the ordered goods arrive at the beginning of the week, there is an
excess inventory during the first two days of the week. This excess inventory is used
up during the second half of the week. Average inventory acts as the anchor for
analysis of inventory size.

Posing the Problem of Inventory Management

Now that we understand the concept of average inventory, let us pose the problem
of inventory management more formally. A generalized model of inventory management has been presented in Figure 10.2. This figure shows that at the beginning
of the period when we have received our ordered goods, we have 100% stock in
inventory. Throughout the period, the goods are being consumed at a steady rate
(shown by the diagonal line), and at the end the entire stock is consumed. You
should note that the average level of inventory is half the amount of the ordered
stock. During the first half of the period, the stock level is in excess of the average,
which is depleted in the second half.

The situation shown in Figure 10.2 is a particularly happy one, since the
demand for the period is known and stable. In this case, the beginning inventory is
consumed during the period at a steady rate, and there is no excess or shortage of
inventory at the end of the period.

This ideal situation, however, is seldom seen in reality, although demand for

Figure 10.2 Single-period Inventory Management with Stable Demand

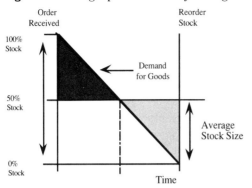

This figure is a generalized version of Figure 10.1 and shows a steady rate of consumption and the average inventory size.

items for regular use (such as paper, pens, and other stationery goods) within an organization can be fairly stable over time. Undoubtedly, when the demand varies between order periods it imposes a certain amount of complexity on the problem of efficient management of inventory. For instance, variation in demand by itself is not the factor that causes this complexity; rather it is the unknown which tests the limits of the manager's experience and ability to forecast the future. We have discussed the issues of forecasting in the previous chapters. When there is uncertainty in the flow of demand, you should carefully choose the appropriate model of forecasting to estimate future demand.

The Problems of Reordering

The process of reordering and its associated problems can be best explained with the help of Figure 10.3. Suppose your agency's annual demand for a product is 2,000 units. You can order these units (Q) biannually, in which case, you will be keeping an average inventory $Q/2$ of 500 units. On the other hand, you may place orders of 500 units every three months, which will reduce your inventory size to 250.

How frequently you would order would depend on several cost factors. In effect, the problem of inventory management is one of minimization of costs of reordering resulting from the uncertainty of demand and supply. These costs can be placed in three major categories:

1. *Reordering costs.* There is a certain amount of cost attached to the process of ordering goods. This cost is analogous to making trips to the supermarket. Every time you go, it costs you time and money. For an organization, it can include costs resulting from clerical time spent on ordering to the handling and shipping costs charged by suppliers.

Figure 10.3 The Frequency of Reordering

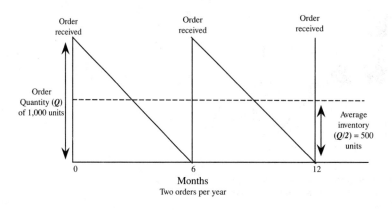

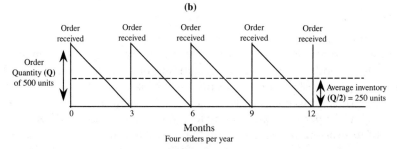

This figure shows the relationship between the frequency of ordering and the average inventory size. As we double the frequency of ordering from twice a year to four times a year, the average inventory size is cut in half.

2. *Storing costs.* When you buy a lot of groceries at one time to save you trips to the store, you incur the costs associated with storing. For instance, the perishable food may spoil, or (especially if you have children) your tastes may change and you may not feel like eating the food you fell in love with at first bite. Similarly, for an organization, these costs include the costs of spoilage, deterioration, and obsolescence. Costs are also attached to storing, having to buy insurance, and, most of all, having to tie up funds for something that may not be used immediately. Table 10.1 shows the approximate range of costs associated with holding an inventory.[1]

3. *Stockout and Shortage Costs.* While running a small business, one of the most

[1] See Robert J. Thierauf, *An Introductory Approach to Operations Research* (New York: John Wiley & Sons, 1978). Also see Eli Schwartz, "Inventory and Cash Mangement," in J. Richard Aronson and Eli Schwartz (eds.), *Management Policies in Local Government Finance*, 3rd ed. (Washington, DC: International City Management Association, 1987), pp. 342–363.

Table 10.1 Components of Inventory Costs

Items	Approximate Range
Storage costs (including heat, lighting, etc.)	0–3%
Insurance	1–3
Taxes	1–3
Interest (on money invested in inventory)	6–14
Obsolescence and depreciation	4–20

dreaded situations is having to tell your valued customers that the item of their choice is sold out. The cost attached to running out may not be directly measurable, but its lingering effects may be considerable over a long period of time. You may remember the airline which ran out of your favorite dish as the passenger next to you ordered the last one, or the shoe store that did not have your size of the most attractive shoe on display. You may feel so frustrated that you avoid the offending establishment the next time around. These days, when public agencies are trying hard to shed their image of inefficiency and are facing increased levels of competition from private industry, a public sector manager would be well advised to avoid the political costs of shortages. Beyond these political costs, if supplies are not available on time, construction projects may be delayed and normal operations will be hampered. These situations may have serious economic implications for an organization as they may cause significant cost overruns.

In addition, shortage costs are closely linked with the type of function an agency performs. For example, inventories in the fire, police, or paramedic department will have a high shortage cost since they may affect the health and safety of citizens. In contrast, inventories in the parks and recreation department may have a lower shortage cost.

There are a number of different models to determine the optimum size of inventory. In the following sections I introduce some of them.

The Safety Stock Model

Of all the models of determining the optimum level of inventory, perhaps the safety stock model has the greatest intuitive appeal. Since holding an inventory is expensive, the safety stock model (SSM) wants to minimize cost by maintaining a "safe" level of inventory, which is the *minimum level required to meet the unexpected demand*. The size of inventory which can be considered safe will depend on the degree of unpredictability of demand and supply, and the political and economic costs of shortage. If the demand and supply are fairly predictable, and the cost of shortage is fairly low, then the safety level of stock would be close to zero (or you will get by

Figure 10.4 Expected Costs of Shortage

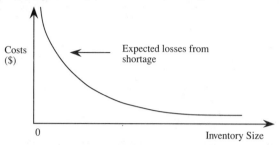

The possibility of a shortage goes down as the inventory size increases.

without much of an inventory). In contrast, as the erratic nature of demand and supply increases and the cost of shortage becomes considerable, the level of safety stock will increase precipitously. One example of this kind of reasoning is the U.S. government's storage of gasoline, a contingency measure in case of a war or other national emergency. Due to the oil embargo of the late 1970s, which exposed U.S. vulnerability to the unpredictable oil supply from the volatile regions of the Middle East, the level of storage that was considered safe was upgraded significantly.

The basic principle of SSM starts with the expected costs resulting from a shortage. These are shown in Figure 10.4. This figure postulates that the expected cost of a shortage is negatively related to the size of the stock. That is, as the stock size increases, the chance that we will accidentally run out of the stored item will diminish.

In contrast, the total cost of holding an inventory is a positive function of the size of the inventory. This is shown in Figure 10.5.

Together, Figures 10.4 and 10.5 spell out the trade-off. On the one hand, there are significant benefits attached to keeping a large inventory. On the other hand, the larger the inventory, the larger the cost. This trade-off is shown in Figure 10.6. The difference between the expected loss from a shortage and the cost of

Figure 10.5 Cost of Holding Inventory

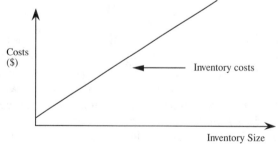

As the size of the inventory goes up, so does the cost of storing the additional amount of goods in the warehouse.

Figure 10.6 Determination of Optimal Size of Inventory

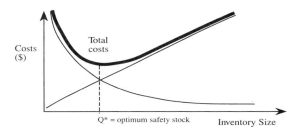

Figure 10.6 is drawn by combining Figures 10.4 and 10.5. The total cost curve has been derived by adding the two cost figures. The lowest point of the total cost curve shows the optimum safety stock.

holding an inventory is the total cost, shown in Figure 10.6 as a bold line. The point (Q^*) at which this curve reaches its lowest point is the optimal size of inventory. To the left of this point, the marginal expected loss from a shortage is higher than the marginal cost of holding the inventory. Therefore, we can derive positive net benefits by increasing the size of the inventory. To the right of the optimum size of inventory, Q^*, the cost of holding cannot be justified by the aversion of costs of a shortage. Hence, Q^* turns out to be the optimal point for the safety stock model.

The major problem of determining the optimal point with SSM is the estimation of the cost of shortages. Since this is a subjective cost, its estimation may be controversial. Also, for smaller cities, determination of the exact point of minimum cost of inventory using a complicated computer program is often not considered worth the effort. In such cases, the safety margin is often maintained by following certain rules of thumb, such as

- Keeping inventories to cover approximately 15 days of usage
- Keeping raw materials to cover 30 days of normal service
- Turning over inventories at least four times a year.

Although these rules of thumb give a fairly good approximation of the safety level of stock, in light of the ready availability of computers there is hardly a reason for not trying to save money through optimum control of the size of the inventory. Therefore, let us look at a slightly more complicated model of determining the optimum level of holding.

The Economic Ordering Quantity Model

A more sophisticated model of determining the optimum level of inventory and the frequency of reordering can be found in the economic ordering quantity (EOQ) model. This technique requires knowledge of incremental ordering costs, the costs of carrying, and the average size of inventory in terms of the EOQ model. First developed by F. Harris in 1916, this model focuses on the trade-off between carrying costs and the costs of reordering. However, this model assumes that the demand for the inventory item and the related costs are known.

The Tabular Approach

The easiest way to determine the optimum level of inventory using the EOQ model is to write out the costs for every frequency of ordering. These costs can be calculated by (1) deciding the total amount to be purchased; (2) either selecting lot sizes to be purchased at each time or selecting the number of orders to be placed during a fixed time period; and (3) choosing the optimum size of ordering. This model can be used in conjunction with the safety stock model by making sure that the inventory level does not drop below the minimum safety margin. The model is shown in Figure 10.7.

Figure 10.7 shows that following the recommendations of model 1, we can reorder five times during a span of 10 time periods, or we can double the frequency of ordering (thereby cutting the lot size ordered each time by half) following model 2, all the while making sure that the level of inventory does not drop below the predetermined safety level. You may notice that by doubling the frequency of ordering, the average size of inventory has been cut in half. Now the question is, Which of the two models is more desirable?

Let us start with a simple numerical example. Suppose, during the course of a

Figure 10.7 Economic Ordering Quantity Model

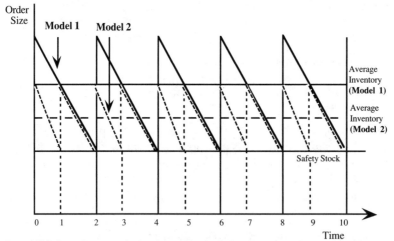

Figure 10.7 shows that even after keeping a safety level of stock, inventory size can be cut by ordering more frequently. Once these options have been determined, they can be evaluated for their respective cost effectiveness.

year, your agency consumes 2,000 units of a certain item. The cost of average inventory holding is $2 per year of average holding, and the fixed cost of ordering is $15 per shipment. This information is shown in Table 10.2.

Table 10.2 indicates that for this particular example, the optimal solution is reached when four shipments (every three months) of 500 units are ordered during a year. You may note that we do not need separate calculations for the frequency of order and the lot size, since the determination of one will give us the other. Therefore, if we need a total order of 2,000 units, knowing the optimal order size of 500 will automatically indicate four orders, and vice versa.

Solving EOQ by Algebraic Method

The simple tabular method of solving for the most economical size of inventory is not as economical when it comes to the calculation, neither does it give a precise point. For instance, in the preceding example, we calculated only a few points along the total cost curve. It may be that the point of minimum cost is either between 2 and 4 or between 4 and 8. To make a quick and yet more precise calculation of the optimal solution, we need to solve the problem with the help of an algebraic formula.

We can write the basic requirements of the EOQ model with the help of the following symbols:

R = Total annual quantity requirements
I = Annual average inventory cost per unit
C = Fixed cost per order
Q = Quantity (or lot size) per order
N = Number of orders.

You may note that for the preceding example, $R = 2,000$; $I = 20¢$; and $C = 15.

Table 10.2 Calculation of Optimal Order Size by Tabular Method

Orders per year (1)	Lot Size (2)	Average inventory (3) = $^1/_2$ (2)	Carrying costs ($.20 per unit) (4) = (3) x .20	Ordering cost ($15 per shipment) (5) = (1) x 15	Total costs (6) = (4) + (5)
1	2,000	1,000	$200	15	$215
2	1,000	500	100	30	130
4	500	250	50	60	110*
8	250	175	25	120	145
12	166.7	83.3	16.7	180	196.7
16	125	62.5	12.5	240	252.5
32	63	31.5	6.3	480	486.3

* Optimal frequency of ordering.

Since the optimum point lies at the point where ordering costs are equal to the inventory carrying cost, we can set these two as equal and then solve for the optimum value for Q. In algebraic terms, this can be written as

$$
\underset{\substack{\text{(average} \\ \text{size of} \\ \text{order)}}}{\underset{2}{\dfrac{Q}{2}}} \times \underset{\substack{\text{(inventory} \\ \text{cost} \\ \text{per unit)}}}{I} = \underset{\substack{\text{(number of} \\ \text{orders}}}{\dfrac{R}{Q}} \times \underset{\substack{\text{(cost} \\ \text{per} \\ \text{order)}}}{C}
$$ (10.1)

Rearranging equation (10.1), we get

$$
QI = \frac{2RC}{Q}
$$

$$
Q^2 I = 2RC
$$

$$
Q^2 = \frac{2RS}{I}
$$

or,

$$
Q = \sqrt{\frac{2RC}{I}}.
$$ (10.2)

Equation (10.2) gives us the optimal solution for the size of orders per year. By plugging our data in this equation, we get

$$
Q^* = \sqrt{\frac{2(2,000)(\$15)}{(.20)}} \cong 548.
$$

That is, the optimum size per order is 548 units. This translates into

$$
N = \frac{2,000}{548} = 3.65, \text{ or } 4 \text{ orders per year.}
$$

The derivation of this solution is shown in Figure 10.8.

The problem with the EOQ model presented here is that it is a restricted version of reality. To reduce the sterility of the restrictive assumptions, we may first assume that the cost of placing an order is not fixed, but variable. Then we consider the case of a discount for larger orders, and finally we include the possibility of a

Figure 10.8 The Optimal Solution for EOQ Model

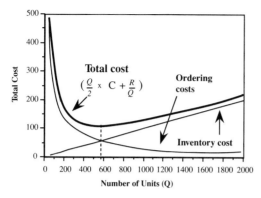

The point of equilibrium for the EOQ model is reached at the point of minimum total cost, which is the sum of inventory costs and ordering costs.

necessary lead time for placing an order. We will see that the introduction of greater realism will make the computation of the optimal solution a bit more complex. However, in some other cases, this will have little effect on the final solution. The amount of realism that you want to introduce will depend on your need and the relative cost calculations.

Variable Ordering Costs

In the previous example, we hypothesized that the cost of ordering is fixed per order. Let us make a more realistic assumption that while there is a fixed handling and processing fee, the cost of ordering takes into account the number of units ordered. In that case, the total cost C will have two components, k_0, (the fixed cost) and k_v, (the variable cost). Therefore, the total cost (TC) of placing n number of orders is

$$n\left(k_0 + k_v Q\right) = \frac{R}{Q}\left(k_0 + k_v Q\right) = \frac{R}{Q}k_0 + Rk_v$$

Since the total cost (TC) is the sum of the cost of ordering plus the inventory cost, it is calculated as

$$TC = \text{total cost} = \left\{\frac{R}{Q}k_0 + Rk_v\right\} + \frac{Q}{2}I$$

$$(10.3)$$

From equation (10.3), we can calculate the minimum point of the cost curve, Q.[2]

Solving for the optimum amount Q^*, we get

$$Q^* = \sqrt{\frac{2k_0 R}{I}}$$

(10.4)

Since the fixed cost component k_0 is the same as our fixed cost of ordering (C), it may interest you to note that the inclusion of a variable cost did not change the determination of the optimum point in the cost curve. In fact, you can see that equation (10.2) is the same as equation (10.4). The reason for this is that since we need the total amount R during the year, and it costs the same per unit whether we order now or later, the inclusion of the variable component of the cost of ordering does not influence the point of optimality.

Quantity Discounts

Determination of the optimal point for ordering may be affected when we consider the possibility of discounts for buying at a larger quantity. Suppliers often give large discounts to entice buyers to place large orders. Placement of large orders can save a public agency a good deal of money. Frequently, these deals are presented as steps—the price varies if you buy more than a certain amount, and changes again after a certain threshold is reached.

You may notice that in our calculation of total cost for determination of the optimum inventory size, we did not include the price of the item to be purchased. This may come as a surprise to you, but if you think about it, the price decisions of a product are not made at the inventory level. Once the need for a certain item has been determined, it is the task of an inventory manager to ensure that these supplies can be stored in the most cost-efficient manner. The question of a quantity discount is relevant only in the context of cost saving by ordering in bulk.

Let us suppose the supplier of the item in question is offering the discount schedule shown in Table 10.3.

One way of solving this seemingly vexing problem is to include the cost factor in the formula. However, the presence of abrupt, steplike changes would make the task cumbersome. A better way of choosing the optimum size is to conduct a two-

---

[2]The minimum point Q^* is calculated by differentiating total cost by quantity, setting it equal to 0, and then solving for Q^*. Thus,

$$Q^* = \frac{\delta TC}{\delta Q} = \frac{K_0 R}{Q_2} + \frac{I}{2} = 0$$

Table 10.3 Discount Schedule

Quantity Ordered	Discount	Unit Purchase Price
0–99	-	$1.00
199–100	2%	$ .98
499–200	3%	$ .97
999–500	4%	$ .96
1,000 or more	6%	$ .94

stage inquiry. First, calculate the optimum point by using the formula (10.2). In the second stage, compare the cost advantage of ordering at the next slab by pitting the bulk discount against the increased cost of storage. We can then recalculate Table 10.2 and choose the optimum order size. This is done in Table 10.4.

Table 10.4 shows the result of a significant quantity discount. The point of optimal order shifted from 500 units (four orders per year) to 1,000 units (two orders per year). This change took place because for an additional 500 units of order from the original point of minimum cost, the discount rate of an extra 2 cents per unit calculated to $40 of savings. This increased saving was able to offset the added inventory cost of $20.

When Usage and Supply Are Uncertain

In our discussion so far, we have assumed that the demand or usage within the organization is constant and certain. Similarly, we have assumed that supply is adequate and, given a constant lead time, we will be able to replenish our inventory on schedule. Given a world of certainty, the inventory manager orders the item with a constant lead time preset by the supplier. This ideal situation is shown in Figure 10.9.

Unfortunately, however, reality often stands in the way of a nicely developed model and makes it messy and complicated. Let us first consider uncertainty with regard to demand or usage.

Table 10.4 Recalculation of Cost by Including Quantity Discounts

Number of Orders (1)	Lot Size (2)	Calculated Total Cost (from Table 10.2) (3)	Cost Saving from Quantity Discount per unit ($) (4)	Recalculated Costs (5) = (3) - (4) x (1)
1	2,000	$215	.06	95
2	1,000	130	.06	70**
4	500	110*	.04	90
8	250	145	.03	137.5
12	167	196.7	.02	193.4
16	125	252.5	.02	250
32	63	486.3	0	486.3

Figure 10.9 Inventory Management with Constant Demand and Lead Time

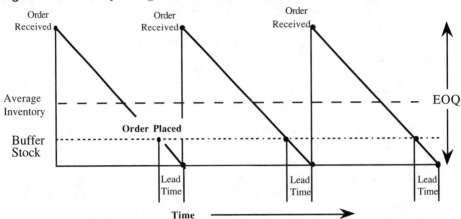

Figure 10.10 shows the problems of an uncertain flow of demand. In this figure, the dotted line shows the projected usage expected to occur at a constant rate. The heavy curved line is the actual usage, measured in terms of inventory size at any one particular time. The usage at this level causes the inventory to deplete sooner than expected. The shaded area is the area of stock shortage due to an unusually high level of usage during the reorder period. Since the normal lead time for reordering would prevent the agency from purchasing through normal channels, it will either have to face the prospect of not meeting the demand or purchasing the item at a higher than normal rate (perhaps paying retail prices).

Figure 10.10 The Case of Uncertain Demand

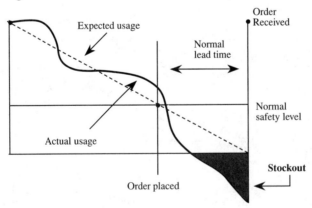

The problem of inventory management gets complicated when there is uncertainty in the usage of stocked items. This problem can be addressed by analyzing the probability of a stockout at various levels of inventory stock and then arriving at an equilibrium where the costs of carrying in the inventory are equal to the costs associated with a stockout.

Table 10.5 Actual Three-Month Usage for the Last Three Years

Actual Usage	Number of times this quantity was used	Probability of usage
450 units	2	$^2/_{12}$ x 100 = .17
475 units	3	$^3/_{12}$ x 100 = .25
500 units	4	$^4/_{12}$ x 100 = .33
525 units	2	$^2/_{12}$ x 100 = .17
550 units	1	$^1/_{12}$ x 100 = .08
Total	12	1.00

The possibility of a shortage resulting from uncertain demand can be remedied logically by following a procedure similar to the one prescribed for considering quantity discount. In this case, we should once again start from the calculated optimal point of four orders of 500 units per year. We should start by putting probability values on the various levels of usage. Let us assume that our agency has data on the last three years of quarterly usage. These twelve observations are presented in Table 10.5.

Table 10.5 illustrates the process of calculating probability to the various levels of usage. For instance, from this table we can see that by ordering 500 units, there is approximately (owing to rounding error) a 76% probability (calculated by adding .17 + .25 + .33) that we will not face an unforeseen shortage. That leaves us with a probability of 24% that we may actually run out of the item in stock before the new shipment arrives.

This added complexity calls for yet another trade-off, the relative comparison of the cost of a shortage versus the cost of ordering extra and carrying a larger inventory. Let us assume that in the case of a shortage, we will have to buy the item at a retail price, costing $.60 per unit extra. If we order 500 units, and the actual usage is 525, we have a shortfall of 25. Hence, this number multiplied by its probability and the extra cost of buying the items at retail each ordering period would give us the cost of a shortage. This expected annual cost of shortage is then calculated as probability **x** number of items short **x** added cost of ordering **x** number of items ordered during the year. Notice that in our example, the number of orders per year is 4 (derived from equation 10.2). Table 10.6 calculates the total annual cost of stockout for ordering amounts of 500, 525, and 550.

Table 10.6 Calculation of Annual Stockout Cost

Lot size per order (1)	Stock safety level (2)	Shortfall (3)	Probability of stockout (4)	Expected annual cost (5) = (3) x (4) x $1.5 x 4 (5)	Total annual cost of shortage (6)
500	0	25 when usage is 525	.17	25 x .17 x $.60 x 4 = $10.2	
		50 when usage is 550	.08	50 x .08 x $.60 x 4 = $9.6	10.2 + 9.6 = $19.8
525	25	25 when usage is 525	.08	25 x .08 x $.60 x 4 = $10.2	$4.8
550	50	-	0	0	$0

Final determination of the trade-off between the cost of a shortage and the added cost of ordering a larger quantity can be calculated with the help of Table 10.7. In this table, I have calculated the cost of ordering at 500, 525, and 550 unit levels by considering only the inventory cost for one year. If there are other costs that can be associated with a larger order, then they should be included in this calculation. The added costs of carrying excess inventory have been added to the previously calculated costs of shortage (Table 10.6) in the column labeled "Total Cost." This column indicates that it would be cost effective to order a lot size of 525 units instead of 500, the original point of optimal order size.

The preceding example illustrates the problems associated with uncertain levels of demand or usage of an inventory item. Uncertainty can creep in through the supply side as well. The flow of supply can be hampered as a result of vendors' normal production processes. The importance of a possible delay due to the normal working of a supplier's production plant will depend on the degree of dependence that the agency has on one particular vendor. If there is a good deal of competition among suppliers, this delay is likely to be of less importance. However, if the item purchased is produced overseas, or the domestic market faces a large-scale union action, the supply schedule can be affected badly. In such cases, the experience of the inventory manager in anticipating breaks in supply will become of crucial importance. When there is uncertainty with regard to supply, the problem can be solved in the same way as that of demand. In the long run, however, the best solution for the problem of supply uncertainty is to develop a network of suppliers who can be reached quickly if one of them fails to supply on time.

Inventory Classification: The Place of Maximum Saving

The simplified model of inventory management makes one drastic assumption: There is only one inventory item. However, typically an inventory will contain hundreds of different items. It will be impossible to seek points of optimality for each individual item. Instead, the inventory manager should seek points of maximum impact. The technique of **inventory classification** may aid the manager significantly.

If you look at a typical inventory, you will find that it carries a small volume of high-priced items, a large volume of low-priced items, and some which fall in between the two. The first task of a manager is to classify the stocked items in three categories: high-priced low volume items (A), intermediate items (B), and low-

Table 10.7 Determining the Trade Off Between Stock Shortage and Safety Stock

Lot Size per order	Stock safety level	Total annual cost of shortage	Added annual inventory cost (extra units x $.20)	Total cost (shortage cost + added inventory cost)
500	0	$19.8	0	$19.8
525	25	4.8	5	9.8
550	50	0.0	10	10.0

priced high-volume items (C). Then the manager can look for the percentage of space that the three categories of items occupy. The manager's efforts at classification can be illustrated with the help of Table 10.8.

By looking at this table, you can see what a powerful planning tool inventory classification can be. If the manager wants to make the most impact, the place to do it is in the items classified in the A category. These items, which occupy only 10% of the inventory space, account for 70% of its value. Therefore, the models of inventory control would result in the biggest saving when applied to this category of goods. However, although this classification may point to the place of maximum saving in terms of relative value, a relatively inexpensive, high-volume item (such as sterilized cotton balls in a public health agency) may be critical to the functioning of the agency. Therefore, special care must be taken in preparing a reordering schedule, regardless of items' classifications.

How Useful Is the EOQ Model?

At first glance the EOQ model seems exceedingly restrictive in its assumptions and, therefore, in its practical use. The original model assumes constant usage, certain supply, and no economies of scale resulting from placing a large order. In most circumstances, these assumptions are likely to be far from reality, and hence an optimal solution, calculated on the basis of the original model (equation 10.2), may be of limited value to a public agency's inventory manager.

However, as we have noted, realism can be injected into this sterile model with relative ease by relaxing many of its strict assumptions. We can consider, for instance, the possibility of a quantity discount or effectively take into account uncertainty affecting either the level of usage or the supply of the inventory item. These amendments can be incorporated directly into the formulae and can be solved for the optimal point. Or, the optimal point can be evaluated against the alternate situation, as shown in our preceding examples.

Cash Management

The cash manager in the city of Masters has a problem. The city receives its share of the property tax revenue, its largest source of tax revenue, from the state of Pennsylvania twice a year, on the first of January and the first of July. These large amounts of money coming in at six-month intervals present the line of the basic trade-offs for the cash manager. This money is needed for paying all the bills

Table 10.8 Classification of Inventory Items and Their Relative Space and Value

Classification	Number of items	Inventory value
A	10%	70%
B	25%	20%
C	65%	10%

throughout the year. On the other hand, the excess cash that is not needed immediately can be invested profitably in bonds, notes, securities, and certificates of
deposit. In an ideal situation, when the expenditures come in at a regular pace, the
cash manager can plan the strategy perfectly by making investments at the highest
amount of returns that mature the day the expenditures come due. This situation of
perfect certainty is analogous to the problem of inventory management illustrated
in Figure 10.3. I have redrawn this situation with respect to cash management in
Figure 10.11.

As you can see in this figure, the first installment of tax revenue is received in
January, and the money is used at a constant rate until the end of June, after which
the next receipt is due. During the first half of the period from July 1 through
September 31, the cash requirement will be less than the average cash reserve,
which can be profitably invested. These investments will mature at the middle
point, shown as t_1 in Figure 10.11. From this point on, the excess receipt of the previous period is going to pay for the excess demand of this period.

Figure 10.11 demonstrates a situation in which there is only one transaction
within a specific period. Clearly, this creates a large portion of time in the second
three-month period when the excess cash is not being invested. Therefore, as
shown in Figure 10.12, if there are four transactions during a pay period following
Model 1, a greater efficiency (interest earning for the city) can be achieved by following Model 2, which invests the excess cash *in between* the two transaction periods,
for a total of eight transactions. Since there are bonds of various maturities from
overnight to 30-year maturity, a cash manager can have most of the idle cash
invested at any single time.

Figure 10.11 The Logic of Cash Management

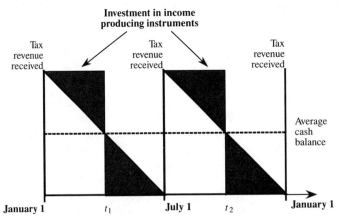

The total revenue received at the beginning of a period is expended at a steady rate.
Half of the reserve cash is invested in interest-bearing accounts during the first half of
the period. These reserve funds are consumed during the second half.

Figure 10.12   Efficiency In Cash Management

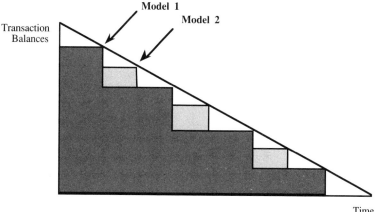

Since more money can be earned by keeping it invested as long as possible, a greater efficiency in cash management is achieved by increasing the number of transactions and thereby keeping the money invested longer.

The efficient investment of idle cash can generate an important and painless source of revenue for state and local governments without having to impose a new tax or licensing fee. In fact, there has been a significant increase in efficiency in cash managment, as shown in Figure 10.13. This figure indicates that while in the early 1950s nearly 40% of state and local government cash was held in checking accounts or other non-interest-bearing instruments, by the 1990s this figure dropped to about 4% (which means that 96% of cash holdings is invested at all

Figure 10.13 Trend in the Percentage of Idle Cash Held in Non-Interest-Bearing Accounts by State and Local Governments

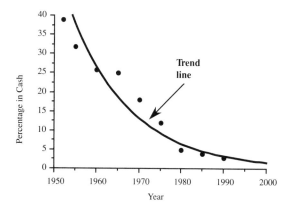

times during the course of a year).[2] A number of factors have contributed to this dramatic change in the efficiency of cash management. In the 1950s, real interest rates (interest rate divided by the rate of inflation) were much lower than they were in the 80s and 90s. This made investment much more lucrative. Also, thanks to researchers, the techniques of cash and inventory management have been made sharper, pointing to the optimum size of cash holding. Furthermore, government decision makers realize that they must hire better educated financial managers, which has contributed to greater efficiency in cash management. Finally, advancements in computer technology have made it easy to keep track of diverse portfolios and predict accurately the timing of cash demands to meet everyday expenditures, and the process of electronic transfer has facilitated the process of deposits and withdrawals.

The Elements of Cash Management

The successful cash manager, in essence, perfects a juggling act between two sets of opposing concerns. The first juggling act consists of determining the optimum number of cash transactions by balancing between the costs of transaction and the returns on investment. As the rate of return increases, given the same transaction cost, so does the need to keep a larger sum of money invested at all times. This calls for an increased number of transactions. On the other hand, if the transaction costs go up with respect to the rates of return, the cash manager will be wise to limit the number of transactions to a minimum.

The second, and decidedly more complex, balancing act is to select a portfolio of investments which balances the concern for high rates of return with that of minimizing the risks of investment. In this chapter we are concerned only with the first trade-off. The second trade-off concerns balancing the risks of investments with the rates of return. This problem is at the heart of portfolio management, which happens to fall outside the scope of this book. However, at this point, I clarify a term I use a number of times in this chapter. To a cash manager in the public sector, there are a number of options when it comes to choosing instruments of investment. Since most governments prohibit their agencies from dealing in commercial papers, the idle cash of public agencies is invested in federal, state, or municipal bonds, notes, and bills (whose names vary by the length of maturity), and certificates of deposits in commercial banks. For the sake of simplicity, we will call all these instruments *bonds*.

Determining the Optimal Number of Withdrawals

To determine the optimal number of transactions, let us start with a simple case. Suppose that at the initial point (t_0) we start with a balance of $\$B$, *held in bonds*. Since the payroll and other day-to-day financial obligations cannot be met with illiquid bonds, the cash manager will have to cash this portfolio of bonds to meet these

---

[2] Data collected from John Mikesell, *Fiscal Administration: Analysis and Application for the Public Sector* (Pacific Grove, CA: Brooks/Cole Publishing Co., 1991).

expenditures. The manager can cash the entire portfolio at one time or may do so over a number of transactions over time. As noted earlier, the longer the money stays in the form of interest-bearing bonds, the more money it makes for the agency. On the other hand, each time a transaction is made, a number of different costs are incurred. These include fixed costs resulting from the necessary paperwork, notification of sale, etc. Besides these fixed costs there are some variable costs which depend on the size of the transaction. These costs are typically assessed as a percentage of sale and include items such as brokerage fees or any penalties for early withdrawal.

Let us denote a withdrawal by W. If $\$B$ is the total portfolio of bonds, then the number of withdrawals, W, is determined by the size of the cash requirement at each regular interval:

$$W = \frac{\$B}{\$C}$$

For instance, suppose we have a total portfolio of $10,000 ($B$). If we need $1,000 ($C$) to meet expenses at regular intervals, this would call for 10 transactions (W). At the time of each transaction, there will be two kinds of costs, which we can express as

$$a + b \cdot C \tag{10.5}$$

where a is the fixed and b is the variable cost.

Let us suppose that the fixed cost is $5 ($a = 5$) per transaction, and the variable cost is 3% ($b = .03$). Therefore, the total cost of transaction is

$$\text{Transaction cost} = \frac{\$B}{\$C} \times \left(a + b \cdot c\right) \tag{10.6}$$

The total cost of keeping money in cash (or in non-interest-bearing checking accounts) has another important component: the interest income lost for not investing the money, or its *opportunity cost*. The total *opportunity cost* is the average cash balance multiplied by the interest rate ($C/2 \times r$). Therefore, by adding these two costs, we can determine the total cost as

$$\text{Total cost} = \left\{ \frac{\$B}{\$C} \times \left(a + b \cdot C\right) \right\} + \left(\frac{C}{2} \times r \right) \tag{10.7}$$

(transaction cost) + (forgone interest earning)

From equation (10.5), we can deduce the size of the optimum cash balance as[3]

$$C^* = \sqrt{\frac{2B \cdot a}{r}}$$

(10.8)

Equation (10.6) indicates the optimum size of cash withdrawal. You may note that similar to the derivation of the optimum inventory size with a constant variable cost (without any quantity discount), the variable cost b does not feature in the determination of the optimum size of cash withdrawal, since without a quantity discount, no matter when the money is withdrawn, we will have to pay this amount at a constant rate. By assuming a rate of return of 6.5%, we can calculate the optimum size of cash withdrawal to be

$$C^* = \sqrt{\frac{2 \times 10000 \times 5}{.065}} = \$1,240$$

which translates to about eight withdrawals per year (10,000/1,240).

The Trade-Off between Investments and Withdrawals

As the rate of return on investment goes up, it becomes more profitable to keep the surplus cash invested and, at the same time, it becomes worthwhile to go for a larger number of transactions. For instance, for our numerical example, if the rate of return reaches 10%, with everything else remaining the same, the cash manager of Masters, PA would be advised to make 10 transitions. On the other hand, if the market rate of returns declines to 5%, transaction costs will become paramount. In such a case, the manager should aim at seven withdrawals during the pay period. This relationship between the number of transactions and the interest rate has been plotted in Figure 10.14 for the preceding example.

Similarly, the path of a trade-off between fixed transaction costs (a) and the optimal number of withdrawals (C^*) can also be traced with the help of equation (10.6) for the preceding example. We calculated that when the rate of return is

---

[3]Derivation of the optimum size requires a rudimentary knowledge of differentiation. Since it is not essential for you to know calculus to use this technique effectively, I will refrain from a lengthy explanation. It will be sufficient to note at this point that the point of minimum cost is derived by differentiating the total cost function with respect to the cash size, then setting the derivative equal to zero, and finally solving for C^*. That is,

$$C^* = \frac{\delta \text{ Total cost}}{\delta C} = \frac{Y}{C^2}a + \frac{r}{2} = 0; \text{ or } C^* = \sqrt{\frac{2Y \cdot a}{r}}$$

Figure 10.14 Trade-off between Rates of Return and
the Optimal Number of Transactions

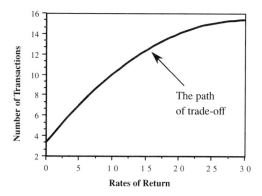

*The interest earnings of an organization go up if money is invested
longer. Therefore, these earnings can be maximized by making a
large number of transactions.*

6.5%, and we have an investment portfolio of $10,000, for the transaction cost of $5
per withdrawal, the optimal number of transactions is 8. You can check on your own
that when the transaction cost is reduced to $2, the optimum number goes up to 13,
and when the cost rises to, say, $20, the optimal frequency of transaction becomes 4.
By tracing these points, I have drawn the path of trade-off between transaction costs
and the optimal number of transactions in Figure 10.15.

Figure 10.15 Trade-off between Transaction Costs
and the Optimal Number of Transactions

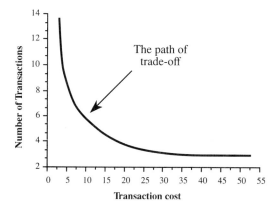

The Miller-Orr Method

Clearly, the most simplified model of cash management takes serious liberties with reality. In the complex world of unforeseen expenditures and wildly fluctuating interest rates, the rules of optimum cash balance, derived by fitting reality in a straight jacket, seem of limited use. Yet, like the original model discussed with regard to inventory management, this simple model can often give a cash manager a useful marker against which to evaluate a number of options. However, when it comes to cash management and investment criteria, much more sophisticated models abound. Among these models the Miller-Orr model is perhaps the most widely used.[4]

Due to the uncertainty in predicting actual day-to-day expenses, the liquid cash reserve for an organization is likely to fluctuate in a random fashion, as illustrated in Figure 10.16. You can see in Figure 10.16 that the cash reserve is fluctuating wildly without any trend or cyclical pattern. Without a pattern, future cash demand cannot be predicted. Therefore, Merton Miller and Daniel Orr suggested that the optimal cash balance held in non-interest-bearing assets should be determined with respect to a band that consists of an upper and lower limit. As the cash balance increases to the upper limit, cash is transferred to bonds, and when the cash reserve is depleted and comes close to the lower limit, bonds are converted back to cash. As long as fluctuations take place within these two limits, no transactions are recommended.

Therefore, in the Miller-Orr model, the trick is to determine the optimum location of the upper (H) and lower (Z) control limits. If these limits are set are too narrow, too many transactions will be taking place, costing the agency more than they should. On the other hand, if they are set too wide, then the agency risks running out of cash to meet unexpected expenditures.

In the Miller-Orr model, the control limits are determined with the help of fixed transaction costs, the rate of return, and (to take into account the random fluctuations of cash flow) the variance of daily net cash flows (σ^2).[5] Although I will not go into the somewhat complicated derivation of the equations, the lower control limit (at which the securities are transacted for cash) is given by

$$Z = \sqrt{\frac{3b\sigma^2}{4r}}$$

(10.9)

where b is the fixed cost of transaction,

---

[4] Merton H. Miller and Daniel Orr, "A Model of the Demand for Money by Firms," 1966, *Quarterly Journal of Economics*, pp. 413–35.

[5] The significance of dispersion in measuring uncertain fluctuations will be discussed at length in chapter 15.

Figure 10.16 Random Fluctuation in Cash Reserve and the Miller-Orr Method of Cash Management

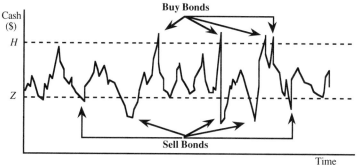

σ^2 is the variance of cash flows, and
r is the rate of return on investment.

The optimal value for H is $3Z = 3\sqrt{\dfrac{3b\sigma^2}{4r}}$.

Due to the presence of random fluctuations, without the help of a long history the average cash balance cannot be calculated easily. However, it can be approximated by $(Z + H/3)$. As the experience of the cash manager develops, and a more detailed record of cash demand is kept, the average cash flow can be calculated according to the mean, since the characteristic of a random series is that it fluctuates without any discernible pattern around its mean.

Practical Steps toward Efficient Cash Management

The use of quantitative techniques can certainly improve the odds of making more money for the agency by keeping cash invested in interest-bearing accounts. There are plenty of good models for determining the optimal size of cash holding and the frequency of transactions. However, regardless of the type of model used, there are a few practical steps which every cash manager should take. Before discussing the practical aspects of cash management, the most important thing to remember is *never to be surprised by an unexpected need for cash.* This calls for an accurate forecasting of the needs for cash and detailed information on the time of maturity and transaction costs corresponding to each investment. This information should be kept over time for proper comparison and forecasting, and it can be stored in a computer data bank and accessed easily for regular perusal. Keeping this general word of advice in mind, and in light of the important components of efficient cash management indicated by the preceding models, we can briefly examine the three practical aspects of cash management: **cash budgeting**, **safety cash balance**, and keeping information on the market **rates of return** and the **transaction costs**.[6]

Cash Budgeting

Finance officers in charge of cash management (especially in a large organization with a complex portfolio) would be well advised to prepare a periodic cash budget showing sources and amounts of future revenue and cash demand. Property taxes are the most important source of tax revenue for local governments. Since property tax is a stable revenue generator, coming in at predictable intervals, the task of a local government cash manager is comparatively easier than his or her counterpart in industry. The other tax receipts also come in more or less evenly throughout the fiscal year. On the side of expenditures, even if there are wide swings (which are relatively infrequent in the government sector), a cash manager should be able to determine the expected cash demand on a monthly (or even daily) basis. Therefore, our cash manager for the town of Masters can prepare a cash budget similar to the one shown in Table 10.9.

As you can see by looking at this table, the cash manager will be able to plan future investments, liquidation of bond holdings, or (if cost effective) borrowing with short-term tax anticipation bonds, which will be paid off when revenues come in at the beginning of July.

The Safety Cash Balance

No organization should be lured by returns on investment to reduce its cash holding to lower than its minimum safety level. This minimum safety level should be determined in the context of the organization's past experience. Also, for effective planning, the cash manager should keep accurate information on the minimum balance required for maintaining interest-free checking accounts, the transaction costs, and the financial consequences of early withdrawals from investment accounts.

Commercial Banks and Fees

The cash manager must be knowledgeable about the various investment opportunities, rates of returns, and their associated risks. In the competitive market of financial investment, with virtually an unlimited number of options, this is a full-time job. It is certainly worth the money to hire a qualified financial manager.

---

[6] See Aronson and Schwartz, *Management Policies*, and John Mikesell, *Fiscal Administration*.

Table 10.9 An Example of a Cash Budget (in $000)

Items	January	February	March	April	May	June
Expected revenues	155	45	32	43	42	46
Expected expenditures	65	72	68	51	55	49
Net revenue	90	(27)*	(36)	(8)	(13)	(3)
Net cash reserve at the beginning of the month	(13)	77	50	14	6	(7)
Net cash position	77	50	14	6	(7)	(10)

* The numbers within parentheses represent negative balance.

Exercises

1. Explain the fundamental trade-offs of inventory management. How are they similar to the issues of cash management?

2. Although the basic model of inventory management is quite restrictive in its assumptions, explain how it can be used even in complex problems. How would you handle quantity discount?

3. Discuss the Miller-Orr method of cash management. Do you believe that the Miller-Orr method would give a cash manager a better set of rules than a standard model of inventory management? Explain.

4. Explain the use of inventory classification in minimizing costs.

5. Contact an inventory manager in a public or a private organization. Write a report on the actual use of inventory modeling in real life. The inventory management experts suggest a few practical rules of thumb. Find out how helpful these are to the manager.

6. The inventory manager of the public works department of Masters needs to purchase 22,000 gallons of paint every year at a cost of $2.20 per gallon. The fixed ordering cost per shipment is $35. The inventory manager has also determined that the average cost of storing is 25¢ per gallon. With the help of the EOQ model, determine

    a. The optimal quantity of ordering
    b. The optimal number of orders per year
    c. The optimal number of days of supply per order.
    d. Rework a, b, and c when the ordering costs increase to $45, $50, and $70.
    e. Rework a, b, and c when the inventory carrying costs increase to 30¢, 50¢, and 75¢ per gallon.

7. During the summer months, the parks and recreation department operates the public pools in Masters. For the maintenance of the pools, the city purchases pool-cleaning chemicals. Since the usage of the pools varies with the prevailing weather conditions, there is a wide variation in the usage of cleaning chemicals.

The inventory manager has compiled the following table of usage from last year's record of 16 weeks of summer:

Weekly usage (pounds)	Number of times this quantity was used
450	2
475	4
500	6
550	2
575	1
650	1

The lead time of ordering is 15 days. Also, if the warehouse runs out of stock, it will have to purchase in the open market for 50¢ a gallon extra.

a. How would you determine the size of the optimal weekly order?

b. Assume that the supplier offers the following discount rate for lot size:

Lot size	Discount rate (¢ per pound)
0–399	0
400–449	5
450–499	10
500–549	15
550–600	20
600 and above	25

8. Suppose the cash manager of Masters is starting the fiscal year with $120,000 in cash reserve, which will be spent during the first six months of the year at a steady rate. The excess cash can be invested in one-month Treasury bills, which are currently paying 6.50%. The (variable) cost of investing is 0.15% of the money invested. In addition, the city will have to pay a $60 fee in fixed cost for each transaction.

a. How much should the cash manager invest in Treasury bills, and how much should be held in cash?

b. What is the optimum number of transactions for the six-month period?

c. How much money did the city make by following your advice?

PART IV

HOW TO CHOOSE THE BEST ALTERNATIVE

Chapter 11

Elements of Social Choice

What Is Best for Society?

As individuals, we make innumerable choices during our lifetimes. When I choose something, I understand that given all the other feasible choices, this particular one is going to provide me with the maximum amount of benefit, enjoyment, or satisfaction, after considering the respective costs. In fact, the process of choosing the alternative which maximizes net benefit is so fundamental that often it is accepted as the very definition of human rationality. For instance, Nobel laureate economist Gary Becker has argued that the concept of rationality implies that an individual, having understood the relative costs and benefits of different alternatives, chooses the one that has the maximum benefit in relation to cost.[1] Without getting bogged down in a quagmire of discussion on human rationality, it is sufficient to note the fundamental nature of cost-benefit analysis in the decision-making process. So pervasive has been this notion of maximization of net benefits that researchers have used this concept to analyze areas of human behavior which are normally assumed to be beyond rational explanation. In fact, the birth of systematic behavioral analysis dates back to the work of Emile Durkheim at the turn of the century, who found that suicide, the quintessential act of emotion rather than rationality, has a close connection with systematic human reasoning. Similarly, statistical evidence is piling up to indicate that even when we choose our mate in marriage,[2] decide to join an act of political rebellion,[3] or even choose to join a particular religious order, our decisions are amenable to explanation by external factors, which indicates a systematic process of decision making. To elaborate a bit more, if these acts were completely random (if the probability that Cinderella would marry the Prince were the same as the probability that her ugly stepsisters and the rest of the unmarried women in the kingdom would do so), then we would expect no definite pattern to correlate the social and economic status of brides and grooms. But, instead, statistical analyses point to a close correlation between their income, education, and other social status factors, indicating a conscious ("rational") choice on the part of prospective brides and grooms.

Therefore, we may take a quantum leap to say that when choices are being made for the entire society, we must also choose the alternative that maximizes the net benefit. This statement would not raise too many eyebrows—unless, of course, we wonder what is the measure of social benefit. In the romantic philosophy of Jean Jacques Rousseau, the existence of a "general will" is beyond question. This is supposed to be the will of the people, which is considered to be so fundamental that it

---

[1]Gary Becker, *Economic Approach to Human Behavior* (Chicago: University of Chicago Press, 1976).

[2]See, for example, Amyra Grossbard-Sechtman, "A Theory of Allocation of Time in Markets for Labor and Marriage," *Economic Journal*, Vol. 94, 1984, pp. 863–82.

[3]See, for example, Dipak K. Gupta, *The Economics of Political Violence: The Effect of Political Instability on Economic Growth*, (New York: Praeger, 1990). For a more comprehensive discussion of hegemony of economic rationality in various aspects of human behavior, see Jack Hirschleifer, "The Expanding Domain of Economics," *American Economic Review*, 1985.

is self-evident. Thus, recall the lofty list of inalienable rights in the Declaration of Independence—"We hold these truths to be self-evident. . . ." This sentence unabashedly assumes that "we" includes everybody in the newly found nation, and that everybody holds certain rights as self-evident and inalienable. Yet time and again history shows that not everybody in the nation was in the same mind; nor did they all hold the fundamental rights to be inalienable for everybody regardless of race, religion, sex, or national origin.

Similarly, we frequently hear of the "welfare of the society," "the good of the people," or "the will of the nation" in political rhetoric or in social discourse. Yet in a secular, pluralistic political culture, such confident assertions reveal their fragility to a thoughtful reader of public policy analysis. We can hardly think of a policy which is an unmixed blessing—a boon to every individual in the society. Instead, we are apt to find cases where there are winners and losers, victors and the vanquished, benefits and costs. How then can we adopt policies which will not benefit everybody, but instead will help some at the expense of others? This fundamental question has survived the ages of scholarly discourse. From the recorded dialectics of the ancient Greeks to the modern-day social scientists, this question has bewildered anyone who has cared to take a deeper look. Since every public policy aims at maximizing the elusive "collective welfare," as practitioners in the field we must find our way out of this intellectual labyrinth, often by taking help from frustrated pragmatists who, like Alexander the Great, have cut the confusing knot not by painstaking (and impossible) unraveling of the yarn, but by using a hatchet.

Choosing the Best Alternative

To analyze rationally the process of choosing the best alternative, we must set the rules of rationality straight. To begin with, let us assume that we *can* define **social welfare**, which can be expressed in terms of **attributes** or desirable qualities. Thus, the effect of a public policy can be expressed in terms of its desirable attributes, such as reduction of unemployment, a greater equality in the distribution of wealth, etc. As policy makers and analysts, we strive to maximize social welfare. Social welfare, expressed in terms of desirable attributes, is called the **objective function**.

Problems of Multiple Attributes

However, the problems of choosing on the basis of an expressed social welfare are many. Let us start with a simple personal example. While looking for a job, you may simply look at the salary. In such a case, your welfare objective is composed of a single attribute—salary. However, in reality most of our choices involve multiple attributes. Thus, when looking for a job, we look at the salary, location, job security, prospects for advancement, work environment, prestige, etc. All of these attributes form our overall welfare objective. The shorter the list of attributes of the objective, the easier it is for us to settle on an **optimum** choice (the one that provides the maximum value for the objective function). The easiest problem to solve is the one that has only one attribute. However, since most of the choices in real life comprise more than one attribute, we will be at a loss to choose without a systematic approach.

When we buy a house, a car, or take a new job, we are not required explicitly to articulate each aspect of the selection process. Therefore, we can keep our objective function hidden (often even from our own selves) until the point when we make the final decision. Thus, I tell my family and friends that I want to buy an inexpensive but reliable car. However, having seen and priced all the functional cars which "make sense," on impulse I choose a flashy sports car. In this case, I probably was not being truthful to my most cherished attribute—the need to own a sports car. Or, maybe that I had all the other functional attributes in mind, but I simply gave this one the greatest weight.

However, as analysts working for a public organization, we must be explicit about the process by which a policy decision is made. Therefore, we must proceed in a systematic way. Parts of this process may seem like an exercise in obfuscating the obvious. In that case, I would invite you to explain the reasons why you purchased your particular car, home, or some other personal item. You will soon realize the complexity of the process and the need for a step-by-step approach when making a choice for the community.

In a simplified case, when we are aware of community preference, we can extend the standard microeconomic analysis of individual utility maximization to society. Let us assume that in our imaginary Pennsylvania city of Masters, we are considering several alternatives for a fleet of police cars. Suppose that all the different makes of vehicles under consideration cost about the same. The distinguishing factors for the various models are the presence of two desirable qualities or attributes: reliability (measured in average maintenance cost) and fuel efficiency (measured in terms of miles per gallon of fuel).

Figure 11.1 demonstrates the process by which you can choose among various cars offering different degrees of reliability and fuel economy. Suppose we are comparing two types of cars, brand A and brand B. Car A is more reliable than car B, but B is more fuel efficient. If the gains in reliability in one car are exactly offset by the increase in economy by the other, we are indifferent between the two. We can draw a downward-sloping curve, which will go through points A and B showing all the combinations of reliability and fuel economy along which we will be indifferent. In other words, this curve shows all the types of cars among which we will be hard pressed to choose the best, because they all keep us at the same level of utility. In plain English, this means that we consider both cars to be *equally good*. The plotting of these equally good combinations of the two attributes is called an **indifference curve.**

An indifference curve shows the combination of the two desirable attributes which will keep us on the same level of utility, and we will be indifferent among the points along this curve. However, suppose we come across another vehicle (C),

Figure 11.1 Choice Involving Two Attributes

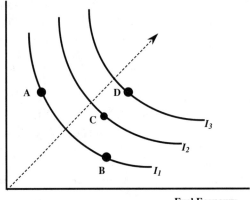

The indifference curves show the ordinal preference structure of an individual or a society. The chooser is indifferent between points on the same curve (i.e., A and B). However, the levels of the indifference curves show a higher level of desirability. Thus, D would be preferable over C, which, in turn, would be preferred over either A or B.

which provides us with less reliability than A and less fuel efficiency than B, but the loss of one is more than compensated by the gain in the other when compared with either A or B individually. Thus, although C is less fuel efficient than B, it is so much more reliable that we would certainly prefer it over B. Similarly, the increase in reliability of C over B overwhelms the small loss of fuel efficiency, which makes C preferable to B. In such a case, if we are able to obtain C, we move up to a higher indifference curve (from I_1 to I_2).

Problems of Inconsistency in Choice

It is important to note that indifference curves are arranged by layers—the higher the level, the higher the level of utility, and vice versa. Therefore, starting from any point on an Euclidean space, a move upward in the northeasterly direction gets us to higher and higher levels of utility. There are three important features of these indifference curves. Since we assume that both of these attributes give us positive utility (as opposed to disutility from factors such as pollution, noise, etc.), there has to be a trade-off to keep us on a level utility plane. In other words, an increase in one good must be compensated by a decrease in the other, or we will move up to a higher plane of utility. This implies that the indifference curves should always be downward sloping. If we further assume that a consumer is affected by the **law of diminishing utility** (the more we consume one good at the expense of the other, the less willing we will be to give up the former good to receive an additional unit of the

Figure 11.2 Relative Preference on a Fixed Ratio

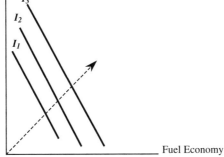

Under normal circumstances, the choice between two infinitely divisible, utility-producing goods would be subject to the law of diminishing marginal utility, showing a slow downward curve as in Figure 11.1. However, at certain times the choice will be between goods which can be had only in fixed ratios. In such cases, the indifference curves will take on the straight line forms shown in this figure.

latter), the shape of the indifference curves are going to be concave to the origin, as shown in Figure 11.1. In contrast, if we disregard the law of diminishing utility and prefer the two alternatives in a fixed proportion, then we are going to get straight line indifference curves (Figure 11.2).

Finally, it is logically inconsistent for indifference curves to intersect one another. Consider Figure 11.3, which shows a situation of logically inconsistent choice. From this figure we can see that one is indifferent between A and B, and between C and D as these points fall on their respective indifference curves.

Figure 11.3 Inconsistency of Choice

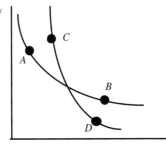

Indifference curves do not intersect, since this would mean an inconsistent choice. Thus, being on the same curves, I am indifferent between A and B, and between C and D. Yet by looking at this figure, you can see that I prefer C over A and B over D, since C and B are located at higher planes of utility than A and D. This is clearly illogical.

However, since C is at a higher utility plane than A, C should be preferred over A. But at the same time, since B is at a higher plane than D, B is preferred over D. In simple terms, suppose I am indifferent between a popsickle and a packet of candy. Also, I am indifferent between a bag of potato chips and a bag of peanuts. To be logically consistent, if I prefer a popsickle over peanuts, I should also choose candy over potato chips. If not, I will be irrational in my preference structure. In technical terms, this is called **transitivity** of choice. By using symbols, the principle of transitivity can be written as follows:

a. If $A > B$, and $B > C$, then $A > C$.
b. If $A \sim B$, and $B \sim C$, then $A \sim C$.
c. If $A > B$, and $B \sim C$, then $A > C$.

In the preceding expressions, the symbol $>$ implies preference. The expression $A > B$ means that A is preferred over B. The symbol $\sim$ is used to denote indifference. Thus, $A \sim B$ implies that the chooser is indifferent between A and B, and considers both to be equally good.

The first rule of transitivity implies that if A is preferred over B, and B over C, then one must choose A over C. The second rule states that if one considers A to be equally as good as B, and B as C, then one must accept A to be just as good as C. Finally, if A is considered better than B, but one is indifferent between B and C, then A should be considered preferable to C.

Laying Down the Rules of a Logically Consistent Social Preference

To a reader with a practical bend of mind, the preceding discussion may seem self-evident or even trivial, but often in public debate or in private preference, rules of logical consistency are broken. However, if we want to conduct a systematic analysis, we must lay down the rules of rational choice.

Drawing diagrams on a piece of paper is certainly easier than making a choice in real life. When I draw an indifference map, such as in Figure 11.2, I clearly show the relative desirability of all the possible points in the diagram in relation to the points on the curve; all the points above the curve are more desirable while those below it are inferior. In contrast, real life situations rarely offer such clearly defined points of preference. In such cases, the process of rational decision making must start with a clear understanding of what we know and do not know about the relative desirability of the possible choices. For instance, suppose we have a particular choice in mind (e.g., a particular brand of car as in the previous example). We show this choice as point A in Figure 11.4. This point A represents a combination of two desirable attributes, I and II. Since both these attributes are desirable, any alternative to A, which offers more of one attribute without any sacrifice of the other (greater fuel economy with the same level of reliability, or vice versa) will be strictly preferable to A. Naturally, an alternative, which offers more of both the attributes (greater fuel economy and higher relia-

Figure 11.4

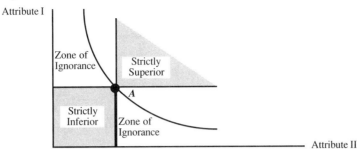

One of the fundamental problems of economics as a social science is that it can shed no light on the process of an objective choice between two goods when there is a trade-off involved. In choosing among positions, if we unilaterally sacrifice one good without gaining any in the other, we are strictly worse off. On the other hand, if we get more of one good without losing any of the other, we are better off. However, objectively speaking, we have no way of knowing our relative position when we gain one only at the expense of the other, without a prior knowledge of our relative preference for the two attributes.

bility) will be considered superior to A. Figure 11.4 shows this area as the zone of strict superiority over A.

The reverse is the case with the lower left-hand region, where all the alternatives falling in this area have a lower value for at least one of the attributes without any compensating increase in the other. This area has been marked the zone of strict inferiority.

However, a problem arises if we are to compare the desirability of two alternatives when there has been a trade-off(that is, when the loss in one attribute is coupled with a gain in the other). If we knew the position of the indifference curves, as shown in Figure 11.1, we could have made a determination regarding the relative attractiveness of the two alternatives. However, since we do not have any information about the relative strength of preference for the two attributes (for example, "I would prefer an additional increase in reliability twice as much as an additional increase (or decrease) in gas mileage"), we must call these the "zones of ignorance."

This may be clarified with the help of an example. Suppose we are considering five models of cars for the Masters police department. Table 11.1 provides the average reliability index and gas mileage data for the models.

Table 11.1

Model	Reliability Index	Gas Mileage
A	3	15
B	2	30
C	3	16
D	2	10
E	4	16

Figure 11.5 Alternative Models of Automobiles

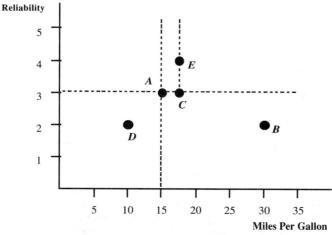

The dominant alternatives are those which are strictly superior. While choosing among various combinations, you should concentrate only on those alternatives which are dominant. In this case, since A and D are strictly inferior to E and C, for the sake of economy of time, you should discard them from consideration. Since you cannot make any prejudgment about B (because it falls in the zone of ignorance), you should consider only E, C, and B.

If we were to choose a model from the data presented in Table 11.1, we may be a bit confused. However, when we plot the data we get a clearer picture (Figure 11.5). From Figure 11.5, we can see that starting with alternative A, D falls in the strictly inferior zone and therefore can be eliminated as a relevant alternative. Alternatives C and E fall in the zone of strict preference and thus are superior to A. Again, compared to C, E is strictly preferable. The ones which fall on the strictly superior zone, compared to an alternative, are called **dominant alternatives**.

We can state that alternative E is superior to A, C, and D. But how about B? We can see that B falls in the zone of ignorance. While B offers higher gas mileage, E is a more reliable automobile. In such a situation, which one should we go for? It is obvious that unless there is information regarding the relative desirability of these two attributes, we cannot proceed. Suppose a cost analysis shows that one unit of increase in reliability should be valued as much as a five-mile increase per gallon of fuel. In that case, we can draw fixed ratio indifference curves to find out which one of the two would be preferable. This has been done in Figure 11.6. This figure shows that alternative B is the one that maximizes the utility of the city. Notice, of course, that we profess to know the preference of the city—measured in terms of dollars saved between reliability and gas mileage.

There is another important qualification—the ability to afford the alternative. It is obvious that the farther up we climb on the indifference curves, the better off

Figure 11.6 The Choice of the Best Alternative

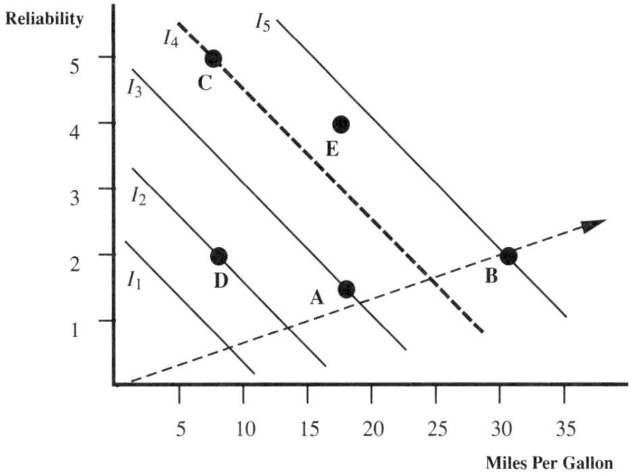

The direction of the indifference curve tells us about the relative weight that we place on the alternatives. Therefore, if we know our preference, we may be able to settle on a unique choice which will be considered optimal or the best. Thus, knowing the direction of the indifference curves, we can choose B as the optimal point.

we are. However, the problem is that we cannot afford many of the things that can take us to higher utility planes. After seeing the Hearst Castle in California, George Bernard Shaw quipped that God would have created paradise exactly like this, if He had enough money. Thus, looking at Figure 11.6, suppose that the total allocation of money for this project will allow us to go up to indifference curve I_4. In such a case, although tempting, alternatives E and B would fall outside of our feasibility set, defined by our budgetary allocation. Therefore, under the circumstances, we will have to settle for alternative C. The implications of the process of utility maximization given a set of constraints will be explored in detail in chapter 13.

In the preceding example, the process of social preference seemed simple enough. However, controversy will soon ensue if we consider the possibility of a change in social preference. Suppose our city has become more cost conscious and is willing to bear the added cost of environmental pollution if cars are more mechanically reliable. During the late 1980s and early 1990s, many U.S. cities experimented with cars that run on alternate fuel, such as electricity or methanol. For the most part these experiments turned out to be more expensive than the communities were willing to bear. This change in social preference is shown in Figure 11.7. By tilting the direction of the indifference curves, the greater weight placed on reliability has been depicted. This shift in preference will result in the selection of alternative E.

Figure 11.7 A Change in Social Preference

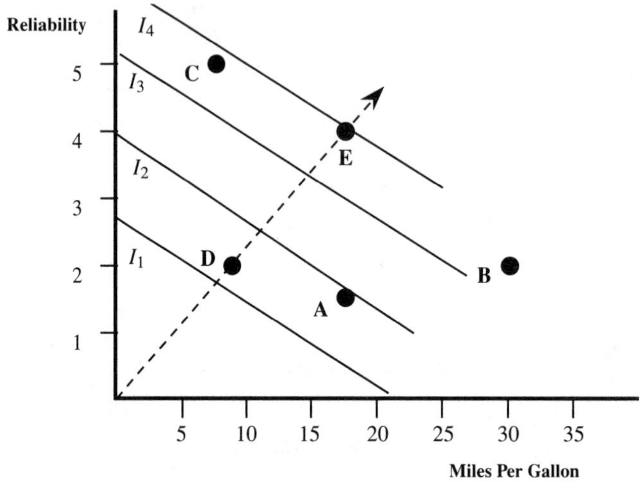

The direction of the indifference curves indicates social preference. In this case, society has decided to place a greater weight on reliability than on gas mileage. Reflecting this change in the direction of social preference, option E now turns out to be the optimal choice.

The Problem of More than Two Attributes

The solution to the previous problem was relatively simple, since we had to contend with only two attributes. This allowed us to seek a graphical solution on a two-dimensional plane. If there were three attributes, we could have tried to solve the problem graphically, although the depiction on a three-dimensional scale would have been exceedingly cumbersome. If there were more than three attributes, the problem could not have been shown with the help of a line drawing. Yet, as we discussed earlier, most real-life problems are multidimensional. What can we do in such cases?

The best way to handle a multidimensional problem is to collapse the dimensions preferably to a single attribute, and then compare. For the most part, this attribute turns out to be money. Consider, for instance, that you must choose between accepting a job in a small town or in a large metropolitan city. The job in the city pays $10,000 more than the one in the small town. As you sit down to calculate the pluses and minuses of the two positions, you come up with the list shown in Table 11.2.

You must confront choices with multiple attributes. Looking at Table 11.2, you are likely to be confused as to which one would be your optimum choice. You may proceed by asking yourself the following question: How much are these attributes worth to me in monetary terms? Thus, if you have a choice between working in a good work environment as opposed to an excellent environment, how much of

Table 11.2 Choice of Alternatives with Multiple Attributes

Attributes	City Job	Small Town Job
Work environment	Good	Excellent
Prospect for quick promotion	Good	Not very good
Possibility of buying a house	Poor	Very good
Possibility of further education	Excellent	Poor
Cultural diversity	Excellent	Fair
Personal security	Fair	Excellent
Scenic beauty	None	Excellent
Cost of living	High	Moderate

compensation would you want for the inferior job? Suppose, after a bit of soul searching, you come up with the figure $500. That is, if there are two identical job offers, one with a good work environment, and the other with an excellent environment you will be indifferent between the two if the former were to offer you an extra $500 per year. If the offer were more than this, you would go for the former job, and if it were less than that, you would prefer the latter. Since the "price" of a difference in work environment is $500, you may subtract this figure from the $10,000 salary difference.

For the sake of brevity, you may choose to consider only those attributes which are better for the small-town job. If, after going through the list and subtracting all the compensations, the salary difference remains positive, you should choose the city job. On the other hand, if the sum turns out to be a negative number, you should take the small-town job.

By proceeding in this manner, you will come up with a rational choice. Does this mean that your choice will be beyond reproach? Does this mean that you will not regret your decision later in your life? Certainly not. Having followed this procedure, all you will be able to claim is that given the set of objectives, information, and your subjective judgment of the time you made the best possible choice. In the very least, you have laid bare your assumptions and the process of choice. If this turns out to be a poor decision, the next time you face a similar situation, you will know where you made a mistake previously. This is the foundation of objective analysis.

In this part of the book we explore how to choose the best alternative. We offer the two most frequently used techniques: benefit-cost analysis (chapter 12) and linear programming (chapter 13).

Exercises

1. Write an essay on the process of determining social preference. How do indifference curves help us in our theoretical determination of the optimal choice? Discuss the problem of inconsistency of choice when two indifference curves intersect.

2. Suppose you have a free choice of your mate on the basis of two attributes: money and looks. You have identified five prospective mates. Their relative rankings are presented below. Graphically show your choice when you (a) place equal emphasis on the two attributes, (b) place twice as much weight on looks, and (c) place twice as much weight on money.

Prospective mates	Looks	Money
A	3	2
B	1	4
C	4	3
D	5	1
E	2	5

How would you determine your optimal choice when there are other attributes to be compared?

Explain how this process may aid the decision process in public policy debate, especially when the choice involves multiple attributes.

Chapter 12

Choosing the Best Alternative: Benefit-Cost Analysis

The Problem

Your city is considering the best possible way to ease traffic congestion in the down-town area. There are several options on the table: (1) a reconfiguration of traffic flow through a series of one-way streets; (2) cordoning off the entire area to private vehicles and allowing shuttle bus service; and (3) adding parking facilities for private automobiles by constructing three city-run parking facilities. Or, consider the example of a fire district about to choose a fire engine from three different makes and models. In another example, the U.S. Park Services is pondering the feasibility of acquiring new park land, or is pondering the possibility of selling off some parcels of park land for private development. In another case, the World Bank is evaluating funding a hydroelectric plant in Costa Rica. The question is, How do you determine the relative desirability of the various projects in these diverse examples?

Keeping in mind the discussion in chapter 11 regarding social choice, we now consider **benefit-cost** analysis. The simple principle behind such analysis is as follows:

> Choose the alternative with the highest net benefit (the difference between total benefits and total costs).

Suppose we have three alternatives, A, B, and C, with the costs and benefits shown in Table 12.1. From this table, we can see that of the three alternatives, B offers the most net benefit. Therefore, according to the principle of benefit-cost analysis, we should choose B. However, in actuality, costs and benefits of public projects are not well defined. The problem is further complicated by the fact that within a complex society, the gains and losses are seldom easy to define and are even harder to measure. Let us proceed by first considering the theory behind this seemingly simple and almost intuitive analysis.

The Theory of Social Benefit-Cost Analysis

Before delving deep into an explanation of benefit-cost analysis, it is important to understand the notion of **consumer surplus**. Suppose you are traveling through a desert on a hot summer day and you are lost. After some time you come across the

Table 12.1 Choosing the Alternative with the Highest Benefit

Alternatives	Benefit	Cost	Net Benefit
A	110	60	+ 50
B	100	45	+ 55
C	125	73	+ 52

welcome sight of a restaurant. You need a drink badly. Suppose you are so thirsty, that you are willing to pay up to $20 for the first glass of your favorite beverage. After the first drink, your thirst is somewhat quenched. Therefore, you feel that for the second glass, you could pay up to $10. For the third, you are willing to pay $2.00, and for the fourth, the most you would be willing to pay is 50¢. However, the drinks at the restaurant sell for $2.00 a glass. This should prompt you to stop after consuming the third glass, since before this point, you were gaining in utility or having a surplus utility from each drink, as you were getting more utility than what you had to pay out. This surplus utility is called consumer surplus in economic literature, and it is shown in Figure 12.1. In this figure, we indicate the highest prices you would have agreed to pay for each drink. The difference between the maximum price that you would have paid and the actual price ($2.00) is represented as a bar. Thus, for the first drink, you are willing to pay up to $20, but since the actual price is only $2, your consumer surplus is worth $18. Therefore, by buying three drinks, you get a total surplus utility of $26 ($18 for the first glass [$20 - $2], $8 for the second [$10 - $2], and 0 [$2 - $2] for the third).

The concept of individual consumer surplus can be extended to the aggregate society. Suppose a large metropolitan city is considering building a new convention center at its presently decaying center city area. The idea of a convention center has been promoted to bring new life into the crime- and poverty-ridden downtown. The construction of the convention center is going to add to the existing stock of hotel and motel rooms for out-of-town visitors.

Let us suppose, that the present state of aggregate demand and supply for the hotel and motel industry in the city (without the proposed convention center) is

Figure 12.1 Individual Consumer Surplus

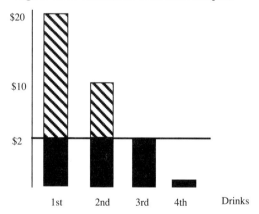

This figure shows consumer surplus (the difference between the price reflecting the true utility to a consumer and the actual price) for an individual consumer. The black boxes measure the size of consumer surplus for each drink.

shown in Figure 12.2. In this figure, we are measuring the average room price on the vertical axis, and the quantity of available rooms on the horizontal axis. At present there are a number of different hotels and motels in town which accommodate out-of-town visitors and conventioneers. With the present supply of rooms, the equilibrium between demand and supply is reached at the point b, at a price of P_0 of average room rate. Since the average price is P_0, the rectangular area bounded by $OP_0 bQ_0$ (price x quantity) is the gross receipt of the hotel and motel industry.

However, the society's benefits extend beyond the benefits of the producer group. Since the demand curve is the aggregate of the individual demands, each point on the curve represents the demand of some individual(s), or the amount they are willing to pay to consume a unit of the product. For instance, along the demand curve in Figure 12.2, consider a point close to the point a. These consumers (presumably affluent and eager to visit the city) are willing to pay a very high price for their hotel room. However, since the price was lower than what they were prepared to pay, they find it a bargain. This difference between what one is *willing to pay* and one *actually pays*; is called **consumer surplus**. In the aggregate, consumer surplus measures benefit to the consumers at large. Thus, the area bounded by the demand curve and the price line—abP_0 in Figure 12.2—is the extent of aggregate consumer surplus for the city's visitors.

The effect of the proposed project on society is shown in Figure 12.3. The construction of the proposed convention center would increase the supply of rooms. Increase in supply lowers the average room rate while accommodating many more

Figure 12.2 Consumer Surplus

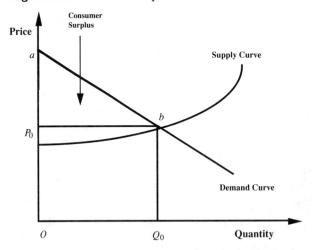

This figure shows aggregate consumer surplus. Each point on the demand curve represents the maximum price some consumers are willing to pay. Therefore, the difference between their willingness to pay and the actual price of a hotel room reflects aggregate consumer surplus.

Figure 12.3 The Benefits Resulting From A Change in Supply

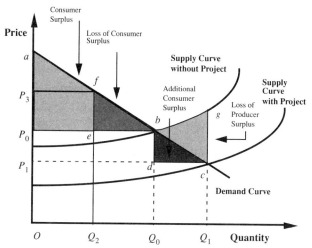

With the price P_0, the area $P_0 bQ_0 O$ is the total revenue of the hotel and motel industry. The triangle $aP_0 b$ is the consumer surplus. The new project lowers the price of rooms from P_0 to P_1. Now $aP_1 c$ is the new consumer surplus, bdc is the additional consumer surplus, and cgb is the loss of producer surplus. The rectangle $P_0 bdP_1$ shows the pecuniary effect. In contrast, when there is a restriction in the supply to Q_2, the loss of consumer surplus (dead weight loss) is efb.

of those who could not come to the city because of the high price of lodging. In Figure 12.3, it can be seen that the supply curve shifts to the right, reflecting an increase in the availability of rooms as a result of construction of the new convention center. This increase in supply lowers the average price of rooms to P_1. In response to this cheapening of room price, demand increases, as those who could not afford to come before start filling up the hotel rooms. As a result, the area of consumer surplus enlarges from the original $aP_0 b$ to cover the space bound by $aP_1 c$.

However, the entire area of the consumer surplus is not the sole contribution of the new project. The consumers were getting consumer surplus to the amount of $aP_0 b$ even before the new project. Further, note that although the rectangle $P_0 bdP_1$ is an added surplus to consumers as a result of lowering the price of lodging in the city, their gain is a dollar-for-dollar loss to the producers—the hotel and motel owners—as they had to lower their rates to fill the added capacity. This is called the **pecuniary effect** in economic literature, and it represents a change in the welfare of one group of individuals at the expense of some other. Since the gains of the gainers exactly match the loss of the losers, for the society as whole there is no change in welfare, unless we want to value one group's gain differently from the other group's loss. This is really a question of society's value in regards to a redistribution of income. We will discuss this at length later in this chapter.

Since from the enlarged consumer surplus area $P_0 bdP_1$ we subtract abP_0 as the old surplus, and P_0bdP_1 as the pecuniary effect, we are left with the true added benefit of the new project, the triangle *bcd*. This is the additional consumer surplus resulting from the project.

However, an unmixed blessing is rare in life, and the increase in the supply creates a condition of further loss to the producers beyond the pecuniary effect, which is not covered dollar-for-dollar by a corresponding gain for the consumer group. That is, this project has created a group of losers whose losses are not necessarily being backed by a corresponding gain for someone else. For example, the new convention center might take prospective clients away from those establishments which now find themselves to be located in less desirable areas. Their loss is represented by the triangle *bgc* and is called the loss of **producer surplus** or the **dead weight loss** for the producers. Therefore, we can see that the difference between the additional consumer surplus and the loss of producer surplus is the **net social benefit**. If the net social benefit is positive, we recommend the project; if not, we reject it.

Public projects not only produce tangible goods; frequently they are designed to restrict the supply of a socially undesirable good. For instance, suppose we want to save a habitat for a certain species and stop commercial development in that region, so we restrict the supply of hotel rooms(presumably by refusing to grant new permits, and closing down some old hotels). In such a case, the reverse takes effect. The loss of consumer surplus or the dead weight loss for the consumers (measured in terms of lost consumer goods, jobs, etc.) must be evaluated against the gain in producer surplus (gain of the habitat, and the increase in price of the existing goods, now in scarce supply).

The actual size of the benefit to the consumer depends on the **elasticity of demand** for the particular good. The term *elasticity of demand* means how responsive the demand is to a change in the price. For example, if the price of salt goes down, you will not start sprinkling your french fries with more salt. On the other hand, if the price of a luxury good (for instance, the price of tickets for the Super Bowl) goes down, there will be an explosion of new demand. Those goods whose demands do not change significantly in response to a price change are said to have **inelastic** demand; and those whose demand changes a great deal in response to a small change in price are said to have **elastic** demand curves. Typically, the necessity goods tend to have inelastic demand curves and the more luxury goods tend to have elastic demand curves. Figure 12.4 shows the difference in demand as a result of a change in price for these two types of goods. As can be seen, for a good with an inelastic demand curve a change in price causes a small change in demand. As few consumers change their consumption habit because the good is now cheaper, the size of the consumer gain is also limited. In contrast, since for the goods with an elastic demand a small change in price causes a huge change in demand, a lot more consumers gain from such a change. Therefore, the size of consumer surplus for these items is correspondingly larger.

Similarly, the term *elasticity of supply* measures the relative change in supply in response to a change in price. There are goods which are produced with relative ease, and therefore, if their prices go up, producers are able to flood the market in

Figure 12.4 Elasticity of Demand and Consumer Surplus

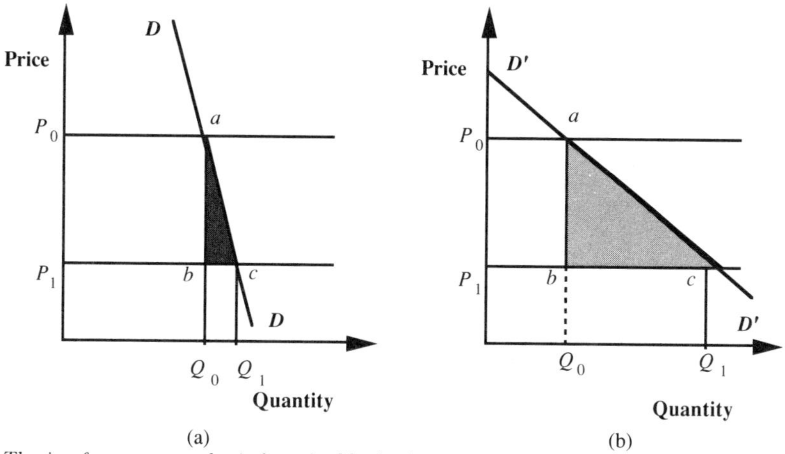

(a)   (b)

The size of consumer surplus is determined by the elasticity of the demand curve. If the demand curve is inelastic as in (a), the increase in consumer surplus as a result of a reduction in price is going to be small since the demand is inelastic, and consumers will not increase their demand in response to this price cut. However, for goods with elastic demand curves (as in b), such a reduction will result in a large increase in consumer surplus.

no time. For these goods, the supply curve is **elastic**. However, due to technological, resource, and time constraints, goods may have a reduced elasticity of supply. For example, due to long delays in preparing environmental impact reports and other legal and procedural constraints, the nuclear power industry faces a virtual inelastic supply curve. Similarly, because of its low availability, the production of gold cannot be increased significantly, even in response to a sharp increase in price. In fact, due to its ability to hold its price during periods of economic uncertainty (because of its inelasticity of supply), throughout history investors have sought security in gold holding. Also, most goods would have an **inelastic** supply in the short run. Therefore, the size of producer surplus will vary with the elasticity of supply. That is, the producer surplus will be higher for a commodity with an elastic supply and will be lower for one with a lower level of elasticity. (See Figure 12.5.)

External Effects on Costs and Benefits

The external benefits and costs, also known as **"externalities,"** are measured by the effects of a project on the surrounding communities. The beneficial effects (e.g., creation of jobs, generation of new tax revenues, etc.) are called positive externalities or benefits to the society at large. In contrast, the harmful effects (e.g., added pollution, traffic congestion, etc.) are called negative externalities or external costs to a project. The inclusion of external (indirect) costs and benefits in the calculation separates benefit-cost analysis performed for the private sector from that for

Figure 12.5 Elasticity of Supply and Producer Surplus

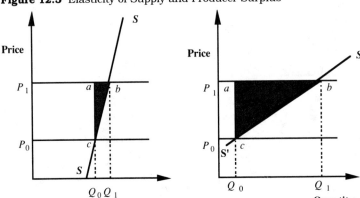

Just as elasticity of demand determines the size of the consumer surplus, the extent of supply elasticity determines the magnitude of producer surplus, or the gains to producers as a result of an increase in prices. Since products with low supply elasticity cannot change their supply in response to a price increase (a), in comparison with the ones with a greater elasticity of supply (b), they are unable to take advantage of the market and have a smaller producer surplus.

the public sector. The project itself cannot benefit from all the indirect benefits it generates for the surrounding communities. Therefore, the extended costs and benefits do not enter into the accounting sheets of a for-profit project funded by private money. For example, the social benefit (as a primary source of help for the development of trade and commerce in the region) of an airport far exceeds the private (or direct) benefit, comprised of landing fees from the aircrafts and other sundry revenues. Therefore, in such a case, the private sector will not find it a viable business proposition, while the government may consider subsidizing the operation. Figure 12.6a depicts the situation in which social benefit exceeds private benefit. Suppose, at present, the airport is handling Q_o volume of traffic per day. However, at this rate the social benefit is surpassing the private benefit, and in order for the private benefit to come in line with the social benefit, the authorities are considering a grant to expand the capacity to Q_o. In this case, *abc* is the area of added benefit to society. The triangle *dcb* is the zone of pecuniary effect, and *deb* is the loss resulting from increased noise and loss of business to neighboring cities (as more passengers fly directly to your city). The government would find it justified to subsidize an expansion plan to accommodate Q_o amount of air traffic, if *abc* exceeds *deb*.

The private sector investors are not concerned with the indirect benefits or gains to society. In their calculation of profits and loss, the private investors do not worry about the costs that their operation anonymously imposes on the community. When the costs are traceable to the project, the society will attempt to exact compensation, which may come in terms of increased fees or the imposition of fines or enforcement of standards. Thus, all U.S. manufacturing plants must adhere to environmental standards, pay fees for legal dumping of wastes in designated areas, and

Figure 12.6 External Benefits and Costs

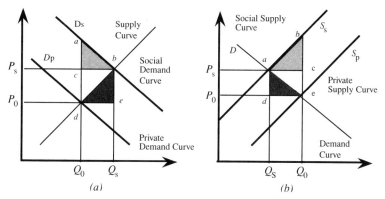

(a) *The effect of a positive externality: the social demand exceeding private demand. The triangle* abc *is the gain for the society for increasing the supply;* dcb *is the pecuniary effect; and* deb *is the loss.*

(b) *The effect of a negative externality: the social cost exceeds private cost. The triangle* abc *is the gain for the society for restricting the supply;* ade *is the loss; and* ace *is the pecuniary effect.*

pay fines when caught dumping illegally. When the costs imposed on society at large cannot be traced to one individual organization, the society may impose a blanket fine for all potential imposers of external cost. The so-called Super Fund set up by fees collected from chemical companies to clean up illegal dumpsites across the United States is an example of such an action by society. The costs imposed on private individuals can be redeemed through litigation, with juries imposing fines and compensation for the aggrieved parties. Thus, in the 1970s, Ford Motor Company was found liable for improperly designing the gas tank in its Pinto model cars, which caused a severe fire hazard when the car was hit from the rear. This resulted in horrible burns for a number of passengers. The jury, particularly incensed to learn that the manufacturer was aware of the danger but thought the cost of redesigning the fuel tank was higher than the potential danger to its users, awarded a punitive amount beyond the expectations of even the litigant. The intention of the jury was to make sure that in the future, when a manufacturer conducted a benefit-cost analysis, it would weigh the costs of safety more heavily.

Steps Toward Conducting a Benefit-Cost Analysis

Conducting a benefit-cost analysis is a complicated operation. However, with the aid of the previous discussion, we can chalk out the following steps toward a benefit-cost analysis:

1. Define the goal(s) of the project.
2. Identify the alternatives.

3. Make an exhaustive list of all benefits and costs, present and future.

4. Estimate and express in monetary terms benefits and costs as much as possible.

5. Choose the alternative with the largest net benefit.

Defining the Goals

The first task of a benefit-cost analysis is to identify the goals of the project. For example, goals can include the provision of a sports complex for a community, the determination of effectiveness of a rate increase for an electric company, or the feasibility of removing trade restrictions with a foreign country. The clearer the goals are, the easier it will be for an analyst to select the best course of action for achieving those goals. An example may clear up this point. Suppose I am thinking about buying a car. I will have many choices, ranging from an old jalopy to a brand new Rolls Royce. If I do not define my goal, such as buying a car to serve a specific function (e.g., providing me with a reliable mode of transport, or enhancing my image), I can theoretically spend the rest of my natural life looking for the best alternative. Thus, if I am looking for a functional automobile, I will restrict my search appropriately among certain segments of the market. On the other hand, if the purpose of buying this car is to project an image of a successful executive or businessperson, my choice set will comprise of a different group of vehicles.

Identifying the Alternatives

The second step toward preparing a benefit-cost analysis is to identify the alternatives. Again, since we are bound by a world with limitations, in choosing our best course of action we face the ultimate constraint of life—*time*. We cannot go on looking for the best option, and we need to restrict our search among the most relevant alternatives. Scholars debate what should be the extent of the search. Professor Herbert Simon has rightly pointed out that time and information both cost money. Thus, in my search for the ideal car, I may find one in the next town, or in a car dealership across town or even across the national border. However, to conduct a search of that magnitude would require an expenditure of time and money, which are not in abundant supply. Therefore, in view of time constraints, we will not engage in looking for "the best" alternative, which, like the holy grail, may never exist. Instead, we will engage in **satisficing**, a term which Simon coined to signify two attributes—satisfying and sufficient.[1] Thus, we will look for possible alternatives until we determine that the search has been of sufficient intensity; and that intensity, given all the other restrictions, will suffice. As a part of this process to economize time, we need to eliminate the irrelevant, *strictly inferior,* or clearly infeasible alternatives.

---

[1] Professor Herbert Simon's work is vast and varied. However, you may enjoy reading one of his more recent articles, "Human Nature in Politics: The Dialogue of Psychology with Political Science," *American Political Science Review.* 1979 (2), pp. 293–304.

Let us make a few points clear in this respect. In real life we engage in satisficing behavior, as it is impossible to consider all of the relevant alternatives that exist in the world. However, the extent to which a decision maker will engage in taking a shortcut and call off the search for an even better alternative will depend on the cost of delay and the cost of making the wrong decision. While choosing among mundane, everyday alternatives, we would be more apt to restrict our search to a few alternatives. Thus, while buying a simple T-shirt, we may make a quick decision, but buying a new home will call for a wider search and a deeper evaluation of the relative merits. In the area of public policy we find a similar pattern. An organizational decision maker will make a quick decision if the cost of delaying is outweighed by the cost of making a wrong decision. For instance, if I, as project director in a public organization, am hiring a graduate student as an intern, when the job is temporary, low paying, and of relatively little importance, the cost of making an elaborate search would take too much of my valuable time. Since the cost of hiring a bad intern is small, I will be apt to go through a short list of possible applicants. In contrast, consider an extreme case in the opposite direction. In the 1940s, a Bedouin boy on the shores of the Dead Sea stumbled on a bunch of 4000-year-old manuscripts detailing the early periods of Judaism and the birth of Christianity. Since the cost of making a wrong decision was enormous, considering the implication for the great religions of the world and the corresponding social and political ramifications, the decision was made to restrict access to these manuscripts to a small group of respected scholars, who would come up with the best possible translation of them. By 1991, after waiting over 40 years, the patience of those who were not allowed to see the manuscripts wore thin. As a result, the manuscripts, were surreptitiously published by a group of impatient scholars.

Listing the Costs and Benefits of the Alternatives

After selecting the alternatives, the next step toward conducting a benefit-cost analysis is to make as exhaustive a list as possible of the costs and benefits of the various alternatives. When making a list, it may be useful to delineate costs and benefits into the scheme shown in Figure 12.7.

Figure 12.7 Classification of Benefits and Costs for the Alternatives

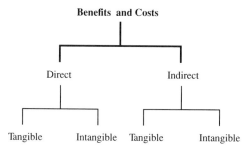

Costs and benefits of a project can be broadly classified into two categories: direct and indirect. The direct costs and benefits are those that are associated directly with the project itself. In contrast, the indirect or external costs and benefits are those that affect the surrounding community but do not show up in the ledger of the project. In economic literature, the indirect effects are known as the externalities. Externalities can be positive or negative. Thus, if the local NFL team hires a high-priced (and, therefore, well-known) football player, this brings in new enthusiasm for the team, which translates into higher receipts at the gate. This increase in revenue, along with revenues for increased sales in the concession stands, parking fees, and royalties from all the sundry paraphernalia around town through various retail outlets, will constitute the direct revenues for the franchise.

The benefits of an improved image for a team and the possibility of a winning season will not be confined within the stadium, however, and will spill into the outside community. Larger audiences will also mean more business for the surrounding area. There will be increased levels of economic activity, which will be felt from the local watering holes (either to celebrate the victories or to drown the agonies of defeat) to the hotels and motels and will generate income for the private sector as well for the local government, in terms of increased levels of sales tax, transient occupancy tax (levied on guests in the hotels and motels), fees and fines (for traffic violations). All of these benefits would be part of the indirect benefits accruing to the community. On the cost side, the possibility of having a winning team can bring about anxieties for the residents of the surrounding areas, as their neighborhoods suffer from increased traffic congestion, crime, pollution, and lack of parking facilities. Local governments also must spend more on police overtime to fight an influx of out-of-town visitors.

Intangible Costs and Benefits

Not all costs and benefits are measurable in monetary terms. There are many costs and benefits which are primarily qualitative in nature, and as such cannot be readily expressed in dollars and cents. For example, the benefits of having a winning team can include the intangible benefit of new-found pride for the city. Or the construction of a new city hall can bring about a change in attitude in the downtown area. Similarly, if the project is considered a source of embarrassment, it can be a blow to the civic pride of the citizens. These are the intangible costs and benefits of a project. Analysts should be extremely careful to be as comprehensive (without being absurd) as possible to enumerate all the costs and benefits of a public project, both intangible and tangible. In the following section we discuss ways of attributing monetary value to intangible costs and benefits.

Estimating and Valuating Benefits and Costs

A number of benefits and costs may not be readily available for comparison and, instead, have to be estimated. For example, it is not enough to state that the construction of a new convention center would increase revenues for the city. We need to come up with a reasonable estimate of the future increase in revenue for the city. (For doing so you may find our discussion of projection in the previous chapters useful.) Let us carry on with our example of constructing a new convention center.

The construction of a convention center would bring in groups of people from various organizations, who would want to use the city as a venue for their convention. The proposed convention center would provide large rooms for various meetings during the convention, as well as hotel space for participants and their guests. Let us suppose that at present, the total available hotel rooms can accommodate 300,000 guests per year. The construction of the new center would increase this capacity to 350,000. The average cost of renting a room in the city is $50, which is expected to drop to $45 with the increase in supply of rooms. Also, the new convention center will be built by selling municipal bonds, the service charge for which is $500,000 per year (a cost to the city taxpayers). We can analyze this case using Figure 12.8.

In Figure 12.8 we can see that the total consumer surplus is the sum of the rectangle *abdc* and the triangle *deb*. The area of the rectangle is calculated by height x width = {($50 - $45) x 300,000} = $1.5 million. Using the Pythagorean theorem, the area of the triangle is

$$\frac{\text{height} \times \text{width}}{2} = \frac{(50 - 45) \times 350,000}{2} = \$875,000.$$

Therefore, the total consumer surplus generated with the increased capacity is

Figure 12.8 Valuation of Benefits

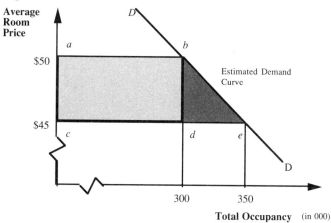

The rectangle abdc *and the triangle* deb *measure added consumer surplus, which is equal to (300,000 x $5) + (350,000 x $5)/2 = $1.5 million + $.875 million = $2.375.*

The rectangle abdc *is the pecuniary effect (= $1.5 million), and the gain in consumer surplus is $.875 million.*

$1.5 million + $.875 million = $2.375 million. We know that the area of pecuniary effect is really a transfer of payment from the hotel industry to consumers, and, therefore, can be ignored as a "wash" from society's standpoint. Hence the net gain in consumer surplus is $875,000. Since the city taxpayers pay for the cost of borrowing money to finance this project to the order of $500,000 per year, the net gain to society is the difference between the net consumer surplus and the cost of servicing the loan ($875,000 - $500,000) = $375,000.

Thus, we can complete the score card for this project as follows:

Total consumer surplus	$2,375,000
Loss to the other hotels	- $1,500,000
Net gain in consumer surplus	$ 875,000
Cost to the taxpayers	- $ 500,000
Net social gain	+$ 375,000

The preceding example was an easy one to solve. In real life, calculations of costs and benefits are rarely as simple. Controversy can arise from many sources. For example, errors in the calculation of net social benefit may arise because the shape of the demand or the cost curve is not known, the market may be distorted or nonexistent, and there may be a great deal of uncertainty with regard to the outcomes of the proposed projects.

Estimating the Demand and Supply Curves

We noted previously that the size of the benefit to consumers of the products of a public project—consumer surplus—is dependent on the shape of the demand and supply curves. Therefore, before we make any statement regarding society's gains or losses, we need to know the shape of the demand curve. In the preceding example we assumed a straight line demand curve based on our knowledge of two points. However, while only one straight line can go through two specific points, an infinite number of non-linear curves can pass through them. Therefore, imagine a situation in which we know two points A and B, and on the basis of this meager knowledge we are evaluating a project where the supply will be increased up to the point C (Figure 12.9). An example may clarify the point. In our example of the construction of a convention center, we had estimated the level of increased demand corresponding to a lower average room price. But the question is: How did we arrive at this estimate? Our estimation efforts can begin if we have at least two points average price and the corresponding level of demand. Based on these two points we can hypothesize a straight line demand curve to estimate the average price in response to an increase in the supply of hotel rooms. However, even the ready availability of two reference points showing demand and supply does not make our estimates beyond question. This is because, for the sake of convenience we had assumed a linear demand curve. However, there is no certainty that we had made a valid assumption. As Figure 12.9 shows, if the "true" shape of the demand curve is non-linear, the assumption of linearity can introduce severe distortion in the estimation of the mar-

Figure 12.9 Distortion in the Estimation of Consumer Surplus

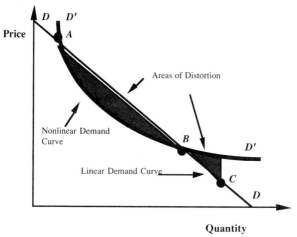

The demand curve DD is the linear demand curve, going through points A and B. Any number of nonlinear curves can go through these two points. D'D is one such curve. If this is the "true" demand curve, its approximation with DD will cause underestimation in the shaded area between A and B, and overestimation between B and C.

ket-clearing average price corresponding to the increased level of supply of hotel rooms at point C.

The above qualifications with regard to the estimation of the demand curve are equally applicable to the estimation of the supply curve. Since the estimation of the supply curve is crucial for the correct measurement of the producers surplus, any error in estimation can seriously undermine the accuracy of our benefit-cost analysis.

Nonexistent Market

One of the most important aspects of conducting a benefit-cost analysis is the valuation of intangibles, which are not bought and sold in the market. Yet for the sake of comparison, an analyst must impute monetary values to these items. Let us consider a few examples.

Can We Put a Price Tag on Life or Limbs?   How would you value the life of a human being, or the risk of injury which may result in physical disfigurement, or irreparable damage to the environment? As you can readily see, putting a value on such matters would evoke controversy. Indeed, it may seem abhorrent to you to put a specific monetary value on the life or limb of an individual. Yet this is done frequently around the world. For example, when a jury hands down an award for pain and suffering, loss of face, disability, or loss of life, it is imputing a value to the most intangible aspects of life. The recent case of the State of Alaska versus Exxon Corporation, resulting from an oil spill in the pristine and ecologically fragile Prince William's Sound, is an example of people putting a specific monetary value on the loss of habitat and pollution. Therefore, it is indeed legitimate to consider how you would value these intangibles while conducting a benefit-cost analysis.

The need to consider the value of a human life arises because often projects involve tasks with risks attached for the loss of life. For example, a large construction project would carry the possibility of accidents resulting in severe injuries and even death. In such circumstances, it is essential to include the costs of such accidents. There are several methods of calculating the incalculable, but as you will see, they all have their advantages as well as serious defects.

There are three general approaches to the calculation of human life: **the face value of life insurance**, the **discounted future earnings**, and the **required compensation**. The face value of life insurance measures the monetary worth of one's life by the amount of life insurance that one carries on one's own life. The idea behind this approach is that I would buy insurance to cover exactly the amount I think the insured item is worth. However, the problem with this approach is that people buy insurance for many different reasons (for example, to some, it is a form of forced saving), and as such their purchase may have little to do with their perception of the value of their own lives.

The discounted future earnings approach is often used to value human life in court cases. Thus, a person's life is worth the discounted value of future income. The future earnings are discounted because a dollar in the future is worth less in today's money. We discuss the methods and implications of discounting later in this chapter.

All three of these methods carry their own sets of advantage and drawbacks. For example, although the concept of discounted future earnings is easy to understand, it suffers from some serious shortcomings. First, since it evaluates life by one's earning potential, it will undervalue the lives of those individuals whose talents are not sold in the market or have stopped earning money. Therefore, it will fail to place much value on homemakers, retirees, and people with disabilities who cannot work.

The market valuation of life does not ask, How much of the added risk is compensated by the income differential in the perception of the worker involved? This is an important question, since the answer would imply how much an individual perceives his or her life to be worth. Thus, there are jobs (e.g., teaching in an elementary school, working as a clerk in a bank) which carry no risk of death based on the nature of the jobs. On the other hand, there are jobs (e.g., fire fighters, members of a bomb disposal squad) which carry an inordinate amount of risk resulting from the nature of their tasks. Therefore, if we take an individual's education, age, experience, and other relevant factors of earning determination as constant, we will arrive at a margin of payment that goes to the risky jobs to compensate the workers for their added risk. The calculation of this margin of compensation for risk is called the **required compensation principle**. This is an important issue, and a number of economists have attempted to estimate the size of this margin. From their studies it seems that this value varies from a lower bound of $2.5 million to $5 million in 1988 constant dollars. This value turns out to be, on the average, 5 to 10 times the value of life calculated under the discounted future earnings principle.[2]

As you can imagine, the imputing of a higher value for human life would make many projects less than economically viable. Therefore, you may think of these numbers as quite excessive, until you ponder that the individual who took this job might not have been totally aware of the risk involved. This is particularly true in the high technology field (such as an atomic power plant), where workers used for sealing radiation chambers have complained that they were not adequately apprised of the risk by management. Also, as technology improves we come to realize the deleterious effects of substances such as asbestos, whose risks most people were not aware of only a few years ago. Also, even if the person was aware of the risk involved, this individual did not have the bargaining power to cover adequately against such a loss. Finally, this measure does not take into account the externalities of such a loss. The death of an individual can destroy a family and cause irreparable damage to the welfare of those who were dependent on this person for financial and emotional security. In light of these kinds of externalities, the U.S. military often exempted the only son from draft, or two brothers from serving in the same ship.

Valuation of most of the intangibles in life is extremely problematic. Therefore, the numbers can vary to absurd ranges. For instance, we mentioned the case of environmental damage caused by an oil spill by the Exxon *Valdez*, a ship operated by Exxon Corporation off the coast of Alaska in 1989. In 1991, in a compromise, Exxon Corporation agreed to settle criminal and civil complaints brought by the state of Alaska and the federal government for $1.25 billion. Yet, within a relatively short period, the result of a study commissioned by the state and federal government was released, which put the damage to the ecology at $15 billion.[3] In another interesting example, the *Wall Street Journal* reported the following story:[4] While considering the site for a third London airport, a twelfth-century Norman church in a small village was marked for demolition. Since the parishioners had fire insurance of about a few thousand dollars, the value of tearing down the church was put at that level. The report of this government analysis angered an antiquarian, who suggested an alternate method of valuation. He estimated that if the original cost of building the church was £100, and the property went up in value at an annual rate of 10%, then the church is worth no less than a decillion pounds (1 fol-

---

[2] For an excellent discussion, see Edward Gramlich, *A Guide to Benefit-Cost Analysis*, 2nd ed. (Englewood Cliffs, NJ: Prentice Hall, 1990), pp. 67–70.

[3] "Secret Studies Put Spill Damage at $15 Billion," *Los Angeles Times*, October 8, 1991, p. 1.

[4] December 9, 1971. Reprinted in John L. Mikesell, *Fiscal Administration: Analysis and Application for the Public Sector* (Pacific Grove, CA: Brooks/Cole, 1991).

lowed by 33 zeroes). In other words, to this individual, the church was simply price-less. Indeed, as a society we may at times place such high prices on projects. For example, if a project threatens a species with extinction, or destroys a place of national interest or veneration, then we may assume that the cost of its destruction is too high for any conceivable monetary compensation. For example, to prevent extinction of spotted owls, a moratorium on logging was declared in Oregon in 1991.

How Can We Measure Future Capita Loss or Gain?   The prospect of future capita loss poses one of the most difficult obstacles to public projects. In popular terminology, this is the dreaded NIMBY factor (Not In My Backyard), which community groups can effectively use to stop construction of items which have widespread indirect benefits but impose specific costs on a certain community. Thus, while the construction of a new airport may prove to be a boon to a region's economy, the question remains of where to locate it. Although small in proportion to the total gain to the region, the cost of increased noise can have disastrous effects on property values in nearby neighborhoods.

The problem for the analyst is that the loss of property value has not yet occurred and therefore, must be estimated. This estimation can typically be carried out using a causal regression model, discussed in the previous chapter. We can form a regression model in which the price of property will be a function of

$$\text{Price} = f(\text{Noise, Pollution, Travel Time, Other Factors}). \qquad (12.1)$$

In this case, we hypothesize that the price of property will depend on the level of noise (measured in decibels) and pollution (measured by standardized various emission units) which will have a negative effect on the price of a piece of property. A decrease in travel time (measured in terms of minutes to the airport), on the other hand, is likely to increase the price. The other factors are those which we would want to include to approximate the price of property, such as size, location, view, etc. Since the construction of the airport will not change these factors, for the model these will be taken as given.

Taking a cross section of city properties, we can estimate the relevant coefficients for noise, pollution, and travel time. Since the coefficients for each term measure the impact of a one-unit change in the independent variable on the dependent variable, by multiplying that with the expected change in that variable as a result of the construction of the airport, we can estimate the total loss to the property. For instance, suppose our regression coefficient for noise on the price of property terms out to be $5,000. This would mean that a one-unit increase in decibel level would reduce the price of a piece of property by $5000. Suppose the environmental impact statement estimates that the new airport would add 5 decibels to the already existing noise level of a particular neighborhood. Then we can estimate the loss of property value for that neighborhood to be $5,000 x 5 = $25,000. Similarly, other coefficients can be used to measure the total impact on property value from the new airport.

The problems of this kind of estimation are many. The property owners are likely to dispute the estimated results, as they certainly will not cover all the costs associated with increased noise and other kinds of pollution (such as the impact on the physical and psychological health of the residents). Although theoretically the regression coefficient showing the lowering of property value includes all the potential pain and suffering, the potential losers are often dissatisfied by the estimates. It is interesting to note that frequently there exists an asymmetry in information between the gainers and losers of large public projects. In some instances a small group of potential losers tend to know and care about their losses a lot more than the large numbers of potential gainers. In such cases, well organized groups are often able to stop a project through political protests or obstructive legal actions. Conversely, in other cases, where the potential for individual gains are strong, a handful of powerful interest groups are able to get approval for a project which may inflict costs on a wide segment of the society.

Placing Monetary Value on the Intangibles of Life.   It should be obvious to you by now that inferring the value of nonmarketable items is not an easy task and often creates controversy. Yet as an analyst you may have to estimate the value of time saved as a result of a traffic diversion or the emotional cost of destroying a community as a result of building a freeway through it. You have to approach such matters boldly, but with a lot of caution. For example, a recent report suggested that the construction of high-occupancy vehicle lane (the highway lanes which are set aside for vehicles carrying more than a certain number of passengers) on the perennially clogged Los Angeles freeways reduced commuting time by 15 minutes. You may be tempted to put a value on the time saved by multiplying it by the average wages of the commuters multiplied by their number, until you realize that the time saved is not likely to increase the commuters' working hours. Instead the 15 minutes which would have been spent sitting in a traffic jam, will now be spent pursuing enjoyable activities which carry no commercial value. You may instead consider the amount of gasoline saved by having to run the car engine for 15 minutes and then calculate the money saved by commuters. In addition, you may look for the environmental benefits of reduced auto exhaust emissions.

In the previous pages we discussed the problems of imputing monetary values on nonmarketable items. If you find items which are simply not translatable in money, you may do well not to overstretch your imagination. As we have seen, unless you are extremely careful, the valuing of nonmarketables can quickly veer toward the ridiculous. Therefore, in such cases, an analyst should report accurately the intangible effects of the proposed project so political decision makers can make an informed decision.

Choosing the Best Alternative

After valuating the various alternatives, we are in a position to compare the alternatives. The usual decision rule that we adopt is to choose the alternative that provides us with the largest amount of net benefit. Thus, if we are considering project A with project B, with the corresponding net benefits 10 and 8, we would choose the former project. However, this simple process of choosing gets bogged down in controversy because of time constraints and uncertainty.

Introduction of Time: Present Value Analysis

In the preceding example, we have a relatively simple choice to make between two alternatives based on their one-time, lump sum net benefit. However, for most projects, the benefits and costs do not occur at one time. Instead, they come in a stream over a period of time. This inclusion of time adds one more dimension to our problems.

To begin with, if we are getting our money over a long period of time, a dollar received a number of years down the road is not worth as much as a dollar already in our pockets. While discussing the problems of inclusion of time, I am always reminded of a local television commercial for an annuity program. In this commercial, the announcer asked viewers to join a "millionaires' club." If a young adult would save a certain amount of money per month, then at the end of nearly 35 years this individual would receive $1 million from the annuity plan. Of course, during the dreamy announcement part of this commercial, the camera lens panned over all the trappings that are commonly associated with the lives of millionaires—a fancy home, a limousine parked in the driveway, etc. However, ask yourself, Would a million dollars 35 years from now be worth a million dollars in today's money? Obviously, the answer is that the two are not equal. But the question, How different are they? (a dollar in my pocket today versus one in the future) can be answered only if we understand the process of discounting.

The process of discounting can be best explained by first explaining the process of compounding. Suppose I have invested $100 in a certificate of deposit, maturing at the end of the year, at a 10% interest rate. At the end of the year, I will receive $110. Thus,

$$\$10 \text{ invested @ } 10\% \text{ for a year will yield } \$100 \times (1 + .1) = \$110.$$

The preceding formulation is perfectly obvious. If I keep this one more year at the compounding interest rate of 10%, then at the end of the second year I will get back, not another $10, but $11, as I will earn interest on the previous year's interest. Therefore, at the end of the second year, I will receive

$$\$110 \times (1.1) = \$121.$$

By inserting into the preceding equation the formula by which we obtained the result of $110, we get

$$\$100 \times (1.1) \times (1.1) = 121,$$

which can be rewritten as:

$$\$100 \times (1.1)^2 = 121.$$

If you are observant, you will note that keeping the money for *two* years requires us to multiply the original amount of money invested by 1 plus the interest rate (10%, or .1 in this case), the quantity raised to the power of *two*. Therefore, if I had kept the money for three years, the exponent of the term within the parentheses would have to be raised to 3. Then, by extending this logic, we can generalize by stating that the original investment of P_0 amount invested at $r\%$ rate of interest for n number of years will give us $\$P_n$ amount of money:

$$P_n = P_0 \times (1 + r)^n. \tag{12.2}$$

Using an electronic calculator, we can determine that \$155, invested at a 6.5% rate for 17 years, would yield $\$155 \times (1.065)^{17} = \$452.14$. This is the formula for the computation of compound interest. This formula, therefore, tells you how much a dollar invested today at a certain interest rate would be worth in the future.

In contrast, a dollar in the future may not be worth to you its full face value in today's currency, because much of its value could be eaten away by the forces of inflation, uncertainty, risk, and the plain fact that you would rather have your money now than at a later date. In other words, I may pose the question from the opposite direction: How much would a dollar be worth to you in the nth year in the future? In such a case, without *compounding* your initial investment, you would have to *discount* your future income. Let us take a specific example. Suppose I were to receive \$100 a year from today. Since I will be getting it in the future, if I use a discount rate (which measures the intensity with which I want my money in the present) of 10%, then the \$100 will be equal to

$$\frac{100}{1.1} = \$90.91.$$

Like our previous example, if we are considering n years in the future, our future gain will have to be discounted by 1 plus the rate of discount, raised to the number of years we have to wait for it. Thus, we can generalize the formula as

$$P_v = \frac{P_n}{(1+r)^n}. \tag{12.3}$$

Going back to our example of the millionaires' club, we can see that if the discounting factor is 10%, then \$1 million dollars received 35 years from now will be equal to

$$\frac{\$1,000,000}{(1+.1)^{35}} = \$35,584.10.$$

Figure 12.10 Time Preference and Discount Rate

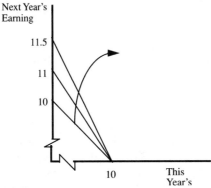

If I am given a choice between having some money now or a year later, I will choose the same amount ($10 now versus $10 a year from now) if I am indifferent, or have no time preference. The stronger my time preference (the more urgency I feel to have my money now), the more I will have to be compensated for.

Alas, by using this analysis, it appears that the dream associated with the receipt of $1 million has to be curtailed quite a bit. In other words, the *present value* of $1 million received 35 years in the future is worth only about $35,000 dollars. With this amount, one certainly cannot expect all the trappings required for membership in a millionaires' club. This is called the **present value analysis**. We can use this formula to calculate the present value of a stream of benefits and costs to arrive at the net present value of a project. Notice that the larger the discount rate, the lower the present value of future dollars. For example, if we were to discount a million dollars at a 15% rate, we would arrive at the paltry sum of $7,508.89 for the same time period.[5] You can see that as we increase the discount rate, the future dollars look smaller and smaller. As a result, gains to be made in the future look increasingly less attractive; similarly, the prospects of losses in the distant future look less ominous. Therefore, the discount rate captures the strength of the desire to have money now as opposed to sometime in the future. This is called **time preference**.

The relationship between time preference and the discounted future value of

---

[5] As we explained in chapter 3, you can calculate the present value by using a simple hand calculator. If you have a y^x button on your calculator, you can make the necessary calculation. For calculating the present value of $1 million 35 years later, at a discount rate of, say, 5%, punch in the numbers in the following sequence: 1000000 / (1.05 y^x 35) =. This sequence will give you the answer: 181,290.29.

a dollar is shown in Figure 12.10. In this figure, we have plotted this year's earnings on the horizontal axis and next year's earnings on the vertical axis. If we do not have a time preference, then we will be indifferent between $10 today or $10 next year. The line connecting $10 on the two axes shows an indifference map with no time preference. However, if we discount the future earnings at a 10% rate, then to be on the same utility plane, we must earn $11 next year. If we have an even higher time preference, equal to a 15% rate of discount, unless we earn $11.50 in the following year, we would prefer to have $10 today.

Let us consider a concrete example. Suppose we are evaluating two projects with the streams of benefits and costs shown in Table 12.2. From Table 12.2, it is clear that Project A provides us with double the net benefit ($80) provided by Project B ($40). So should we automatically choose Project A over B? If we were to jump to this conclusion, we would be remiss, since we would fail to consider that while A yields more net benefit, the benefits come at a later stage in the project's life. In contrast, Project B yields benefits at an earlier stage of its life. Our choice between the two projects will depend on the strength of our time preference—the willingness to wait for the future returns. Therefore, to compare the two projects on a level ground, we must translate these future streams of benefits and costs into their present values. The formula is written as

$$PV = \sum_{t=0}^{n} \frac{\left(B_t - C_t\right)}{\left(1 + r\right)^t}$$

(12.4)

where B_t is the benefit and C_t is the cost at t. This expression can be opened up to write

$$PV = \frac{B_0 - C_0}{\left(1+r\right)^0} + \frac{B_1 - C_1}{\left(1+r\right)^1} + \frac{B_2 - C_2}{\left(1+r\right)^2} + \ \cdots \ + \frac{B_n - C_n}{\left(1+r\right)^n}.$$

Table 12.2 Comparison of Benefits and Costs for Alternatives A and B

Year	Project A Benefit	Project A Cost	Project B Benefit	Project B Cost
0	0	30	15	5
1	0	15	15	5
2	0	10	15	5
3	10	5	15	10
4	20	5	15	10
5	120	5	15	15
Total	150	70	90	50

Since any number raised to the power 0 is equal to 1, the expression can be written as

$$PV = \left(B_0 - C_0\right) + \frac{B_1 - C_1}{\left(1+r\right)} + \frac{B_2 - C_2}{\left(1+r\right)^2} + \ldots + \frac{B_n - C_n}{\left(1+r\right)^n}.$$

(12.5)

You may notice that since the number of years (t) varies from 0 to n, the 0th year's net benefits are not discounted. This makes eminent sense, since the current year's dollar is equal to its face value and hence, does not need to be discounted.

If we are willing to wait (i.e., it does not matter to us whether we receive our payments today or tomorrow), our time preference is said to be nil. In such a situation, we discount the future stream of net benefits with a 0 discount rate and, therefore, do not discount at all. Thus, if we do not have any time preference, the net benefits for Projects A and B are $80 and $40.

On the other hand, suppose we do have a definite time preference, and we want to evaluate the future stream of net benefits for the two projects at a 10% discount rate. In such a case, we can write the present values of A (PV_A) and B (PV_B), discounted at 10%, as

$$PV_A = \left(0 - 30\right) + \frac{0 - 15}{\left(1+.1\right)} + \frac{0 - 10}{\left(1+.1\right)^2} + \frac{10 - 5}{\left(1+.1\right)^3} + \frac{20 - 5}{\left(1+.1\right)^4} + \frac{120 - 5}{\left(1+.1\right)^5}$$

$$= -30 - 13.64 - 8.26 + 3.76 + 10.24 + 71.41 = 33.51$$

$$PV_B = \left(15 - 5\right) + \frac{15 - 5}{\left(1+.1\right)} + \frac{15 - 5}{\left(1+.1\right)^2} + \frac{15 - 10}{\left(1+1\right)^3} + \frac{15 - 10}{\left(1+1\right)^4} + \frac{15 - 15}{\left(1+1\right)^5}$$

$$= 10 + 9.09 + 8.26 + 3.76 + 3.41 + 0 = 34.52.$$

From the preceding calculation, we can see that discounted at a 10% rate, Project A is less preferable to Project B, as it carries a lower present value. We can also see that the present value of the two projects will depend on the rate of discount, which will determine the relative desirability of the two projects. We have plotted the present values as functions of the rate of discount in Figure 12.11. From this figure, it can be seen that the two projects become equally desirable at a discount rate slightly less than 10%. For discount rates below 10%, Project A is preferable to B. However, the relative desirability changes for discount rates of 10% and above. This change, of course, reflects that although Project A gives twice as much net benefit as Project B, the benefits in the former project come at the end of the project life. In contrast, Project B yields positive net benefits from the first year of its inception. Therefore, if we can afford to wait (and have a small discount rate), we would prefer Project A. However, if we are in a hurry to get back the returns on

Figure 12.11 Plot of Present Value as a Function of Discount Rates

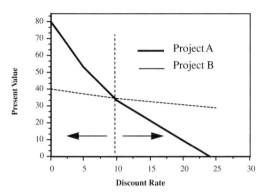

The relative desirability of a project depends on the choice of discount rate. In this case, it can be seen that for discount rates less than 10%, Project A seems more desirable; however, for rates higher than 10%, Project B is preferred.

investment (and, therefore, have a stronger time preference), we should choose Project B.

Finally, if the present value is negative (as Project A is for a discount rate close to 24%), we should reject the project.

Choice of Time Horizon

The choice of appropriate time horizon is of crucial importance for a benefit-cost analysis. The relative desirability of a project is intrinsically connected to the question, When is this project coming to an end? Those projects which are long-term in nature, when compared to a short-term project will be found lacking when the time period is short. In contrast, an essentially short-term project will be considered less desirable to a long-term project when evaluated over a longer time period. For instance, many of the projects for drug interdiction are designed for short-term results. In these projects, the problem of drug use is considered primarily as a law and order problem, and efforts are made to lower the supply of illicit drugs by police action. In contrast, programs of treating drug abuse as a public health problem requires expenditure on education, rehabilitation and employment opportunities. These demand side efforts (trying to reduce the drug demand) offer longer term solutions to the problem. Therefore, unless they are given a longer time horizon, their impact on drug use will not be fully realized. This impact of project desirability on the choice of time horizon has been shown in Figure 12.12. You can see that before the critical point in time, Tn, the short term project (Project I) yields higher net present value. However, beyond this point, the long-term project (Project II) becomes more attractive.

Figure 12.12 The Effect of Choosing Time Horizon

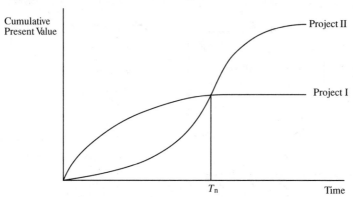

The choice of time horizon can be an important element in the choice of a project. As you can see here, Project II produces more in the long term than Project I. If we restrict the time horizon to less than the point T_n, we are apt to prefer I over II. However, when the time horizon is extended, II looks more favorable than I.

Choice of Discount Rate

The results shown in Figure 12.11 demonstrate how sensitive the assessment of desirability of a project can be to a change in the discount rate. Therefore, it is essential that we come up with the "correct" choice of discount rate in evaluating a public project. In fact, the sensitivity of a public investment decision to the choice of discount rate was underscored by a proposed joint water project between Canada and the United States. While the United States analysts, who used a lower discount rate, recommended the project, their Canadian counterparts, who used a higher discount rate, rejected it. The last few decades have produced voluminous literature on benefit-cost analysis. Yet there is no mention in this literature of a specific "appropriate" discount rate. However, at times you can learn important lessons from a state of prevailing confusion and lack of a definite answer.

The reasons for this confusion may be explained with the help of a simple personal example. Suppose I am thinking of investing in a project. This project yields a certain amount of money over a period of time. While considering the desirability of this investment I may consider my alternate investment uses for this money. I find out that the best return on available investment is 8%. In such a case, I would discount the future net benefits of the project at an 8% rate. If this discounting provides me with a positive net present value, I should invest; otherwise I should not. This process of considering alternate uses of money provides the **opportunity cost** or the **shadow price** of money.

However, the opportunity cost of money may not be the only guiding principle for investment. For instance, I may choose to discount my investment with a rate which reflects my own time preference. People may use many different rates of discount representing differing time preferences. Thus, if I want my money right now (or, in other words, I have a strong time preference), I would use a very high discount rate. On the other hand, if I have a long-term perspective, I would be willing to wait for a higher return in the future, in which case, the rate of discount will be quite low. In fact, in an extreme case, my time preference can even be less than zero. Consider yourself to be a dictator of a small but wealthy country. You have all the money you want for the present. However, what you do not have is security for the future—you may find yourself deposed by a coup or a revolution. In such a case, your discount rate can even be negative, and hence you will be willing to put your money in a Swiss or otherwise secret bank account, where the bank will charge you for the safekeeping of your (presumably ill gotten) assets and will not pay you interest. In other words, depending on my circumstances, it may be perfectly reasonable for me to use a discount rate different from the opportunity cost, in conformity with my personal time preference.

Similarly, in the case of the society, economists have argued back and forth regarding the optimum rate of discount on the basis of opportunity cost and **social time preference**. The proponents of opportunity cost for investment argue that since government pays for its investments by taking money away from private citizens, unless the returns of these investments are at least equal to those of the private sector, it does not make any economic sense for the government to invest. Therefore, according to this point of view, while evaluating a public project, the analyst should take into account the opportunity of alternate investment opportunity in the private sector, and hence discount the project by a rate equal to the private rate of return. For instance, suppose that the U.S. Space Agency is proposing building a new kind of space vehicle which will be able to deploy satellites with a greater degree of efficiency than the existing space shuttles. Money for this project must be raised from private taxpayers. If the market is yielding 10 cents on a $1 investment, unless it can be shown that the return from this project is going to be at least 10% (i.e., the project carries a positive net present value, when discounted at 10%), the project should not be undertaken.

This rule of discounting seems reasonable. However, upon further consideration, it turns out to be unsatisfactory. Problems arise because like all other markets, the capital market is characterized by various kinds of imperfections. For example, the existence of monopoly can significantly distort security prices.[6] Also, the government may face several political constraints in its investment decisions, which can make any comparison with the private sector invalid. Therefore, by looking at the vast and imperfect capital market, an analyst is likely to be confused about the "appropriate" rate of yield in the private sector.

The comparison of government rate of return with that in the private market

---

[6] Recall the security exchange fraud during the late 1980s and early 1990s by the giant trading houses such as Drexel, Burnham and Lambert, and Solomon Brothers, which had a significant impact on the market. Similar irregularities in Japan caused widespread concern over the integrity of Japanese financial institutions.

is further complicated by the fact that the source of government revenue is often not well defined. Thus, if tax money comes out of the taxpayers' savings, the consideration of opportunity cost may be valid. However, if it comes from the money which was allocated by the taxpayer for consumption, the comparison would not make much sense.

In addition, the source of government revenue is diverse. The government may get its money from taxes, tariffs, licenses and fees, or from selling bonds or government property. Not all of these moneys have the same opportunity cost, and when financing a project it is impossible to pinpoint the exact source of the funding.

Finally, the outputs of government projects may be intangibles and as such cannot be measured in monetary terms. Thus, it will be impossible to convert the benefits of subsidized school lunch programs into strict monetary units. Also, many government programs can generate long-term positive externalities which are extremely difficult to measure. For example, the development of computer technology, to a large extent, has been a by-product of the space program. Yet, at the time of the inception of the program, nobody could have predicted this fortuitous outcome, which has changed the entire course of human development.

The recent literature in economics suggests the use of a discount rate that reflects the subjective time preference of the society.[7] Unfortunately, the scholars who have spent a great deal of time contemplating the appropriate discount rate are unable to tell us exactly which number to use. Therefore, the issue of the appropriate discount rate is still very much disputed.[8] However, the insights derived from these discussions can at least point out the follies of using grossly inappropriate rates. Given the enormous complexity of our world, we may consider that to be a giant step forward.

The Internal Rate of Return

Since it is so difficult to settle on a universally acceptable discount rate for public projects, a decision maker can often be tempted to use what is known as the **internal rate of return** for judging the desirability of a project. The internal rate of return is defined as *the rate of discount at which the present value of a project is equal to zero*. Thus, from Figure 12.13, you can see that the present value for a hypothetical project approaches zero at about 24%, which is its internal rate of return.

The advantage of using an internal rate of return is that it reduces the decision maker's burden of having to choose based on a single discount rate. Instead, a

---

[7] See David F. Bradford, "The Choice of Discount Rate for Government Investments." In Robert H. Haveman and Julius Margolis (eds.), *Public Expenditure and Policy Analysis*, 3rd ed. (Boston: Houghton Mifflin Co., 1983), pp. 129–144.

[8] If you want a precise figure for discounting, Edward Gramlich suggested that the social time preference for federal government, corrected for inflation, in 1988 was about 4% for projects financed by tax revenue and 6% for those financed by bonds. *A Guide to Benefit-Cost Analysis*. 2nd ed. Prentice-Hall: Englewood Cliffs, N.J., 1990.

Figure 12.13 The Internal Rate of Return

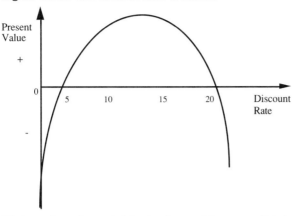

The internal rate of return is defined as the rate of discount at which the present value of a project is equal to zero. If you can show that the internal rate of return is higher than the opportunity cost, the project in question should be adopted. This may serve as a good indicator for determining the viability of a single project, but it offers no help in comparing two or more projects. It also becomes ineffective as a guide if there is more than one internal rate of return for a single project, as shown in this figure, where the net present value is 0 at 5% and 20%.

project can be accepted if the returns are larger than what can be reasonably obtained in an alternate investment. Going back to our example, if the internal rate of return for a Project is 24%, it is so much higher than what can be reasonably expected in other possible investments that a decision maker will be hard pressed to reject it.

However, despite this intuitive appeal, the internal rate of return suffers from some important shortcomings. First, while the internal rate of return is useful in pointing out the desirability of a single project, it is ineffective when choosing between more than one. Also, depending on the configuration of streams of net benefits, projects can often have more than one internal rate of return, as shown in Figure 12.13.

Since there are two rates (5% and 25%) at which the present value of the project becomes equal to zero, our decision maker is likely to remain confused about the desirability of the project. Stokey and Zeckhouser[9] point out that the internal rate of return can point to the correct public policy decisions under some rather unrealistic circumstances, such as when there are no budgetary constraints, no comparisons with other alternate projects, and when the stream of returns is first negative and then positive.

---

[9] Edith Stokey & Richard Zeckhouser, *Primer for Policy Analysis.* New York: W.W. Norton, 1978, p. 167.

Some Additional Considerations

The preceding discussion of benefit-cost analysis leaves out a number of important problems. In this section, we consider three of them: redistribution of income, uncertainty, and benefit-cost ratio.

Redistribution of Income

The basic problem with government projects in a zero-sum society is that one group of individuals almost always comes out on top at the expense of some others. In society there must be some valuation of the relative merit of this redistribution of income. For example, it will be relatively easy to show the benefits of massive highway construction in the United States, especially during the 1950s. Trade and commerce received a tremendous boost with ease of transportation. Yet such construction did not come without a long list of those who were adversely affected by this development. Many small towns by the now abandoned but previously well-traversed roads were simply wiped out of existence; many communities lost their identities as the highways cut through their heart, causing dislocation, isolation, and a general deterioration of neighborhoods. As the highways were built for motor traffic, the trucking industry gained at the expense of a much more energy efficient railroad industry; suburbs gained at the expense of the center cities.

Yet, as a reflection of the state of the art in social sciences and social philosophy, benefit-cost analysis is singularly unable to answer the question, How do we value the gains of the gainers versus the losses of the losers? Social philosophers have been attempting to grapple with this problem for centuries, with surprisingly few answers. Recalling our discussion of determining social preference from the previous chapter, I can safely paraphrase Sir Winston Churchill to state that rarely in the entire field of social philosophy and social sciences have so many spent so much effort to produce so few results.

Uncertainty

In the previous discussion, we assumed that the estimated net benefits are certain to accrue. However, since there is hardly any guarantee in life, these figures can be based on probability. That is, we may say that "we expect with 60% certainty that the project will yield this much revenue." We can accommodate such uncertainty, which we will discuss in the following chapter.

Benefit-Cost Ratio

When choosing among alternatives, you may want to consider the ratios between benefits and costs, instead of their difference. In many cases, the use of any of these two criteria will lead to the same conclusion. However, a conflict may arise because of a difference in the scale of operation. Consider the problem shown in Table 12.3.

Table 12.3 Contradictory Decision Based on Net Difference and Benefit-Cost Ratio

	Benefit	Cost	Net Benefit	Benefit-Cost Ratio
Project A	10	3	+7	3.33
Project B	50	25	+25	2.00

From this table, you can see that we are really comparing apples with oranges, as the two projects are qualitatively different by the sheer difference in their size. Therefore, while using the ratio method we are apt to choose Project A, and by following the difference method we will be compelled to choose Project B.

Although the ratio method is intuitive and is often used in the personal decision-making process, the analytical literature seems to be unanimous in its preference of the net benefit approach over the ratio method.

Cost-Effectiveness Analysis

The Problem of an Ill-Defined Objective Function

The basic principle of benefit-cost analysis is simple enough: *Choose the alternative that gives you the maximum net benefit.* However, in many cases of public expenditure we find that the benefit schedule is ill defined or impossible to measure. For instance, the local department of fire protection wants to buy fire engines which can accomplish more or less the same task; an organization is planning to purchase a number of personal computers of similar capabilities. In such cases, if it is reasonable to hold that all of the alternatives are substitutes of each other, then we can explicitly assume that the benefit levels for all of them are equal and, hence, can be regarded as constant. Thus, we can choose the least expensive alternative.

Alternately, suppose money has been allocated to support an outreach program to teach children of the homeless families, and proposals are being evaluated for choosing the best alternative. In this case, the costs are the same, and hence for comparison we need only concern ourselves with maximizing the benefits. In this circumstance we can use a truncated version of benefit-cost analysis. This is called **cost-effectiveness analysis**. The two simple rules for cost-effectiveness analysis are as follows:

■ **Using a Computer to Calculate Present Value** ■

The are a number of excellent spreadsheet programs which can easily perform a present value analysis. Unfortunately, MYSTAT is not equipped to handle such programs. For computing the present value of a series of numbers, you should look into LOTUS, QUATROPRO, and EXCELL.

1. If the benefits are the same, choose the alternative with the least cost.
2. If the costs are the same, choose the alternative with the most benefits.

For instance, suppose we are planning to purchase a fire engine for our city. We are considering two different makes. Since they both serve the same function, we can concentrate on various aspects of costs of purchase and operation and then choose the less expensive one. This is called a cost-effectiveness analysis. As we will soon find out, even the path to this seemingly straightforward analysis is frought with conceptual pitfalls, ambiguity, and the need to make heroic assumptions.

■ Fitting Seat Belts in Texas School Buses: An Example ■

Adapted from "Cost-Benefit Analysis of Safety Belts in Texas School Buses." Charles E. Bagley and Andrea K. Biddle, *Public Health Reports*, Vol. 103, September-October 1988, pp. 479–88.

The Problem

In 1985, Texas was confounded by the problem that more adults and children were injured in school bus accidents (635 total in 1985) than in any of the previous eight years. Since Texas did not require school buses to be equipped with seat belts, only a very small fraction of the injured children (1.7%) were wearing seat belts.

The Goal

The goal of the study was to evaluate the potential reduction in serious injury and death to the school children resulting from the installation of safety belts.

The Alternatives

The study considered two alternatives: (a) Install seat belts on all the school buses, and (implicitly) (b) do nothing.

Assessment of Costs and Benefits

Benefits: Avoidance of serious injuries to children
Costs: Cost of refurbishing the existing school buses

Imputing tangible values on intangible benefits

Data on the effectiveness of seat belts in the prevention of serious accidents were not available for school buses. Therefore, it was assumed that seat belt effectiveness in buses was the same as in autos, for which data were available. These data were used to calculate the percentage of preventable injuries. The severity of injuries was calculated by the Multiple Abbreviated Injury Scale (MAIS). The results are as follows:

Types of Injuries and Preventable Numbers for Texas, 1983–1985

Age and injury category	Number of Accidents Belted	Not Belted	Preventable fraction	Number of preventable cases
MAIS 0 No injury	4	354		
5–14 years	3	297	.00	0
15–18 years	1	57	.00	0
MAIS 1 Minor injury	3	253		
5–14 years	2	212	.00	0
15–18 years	1	41	.00	0
MAIS 2 Moderate injury	1	150		
5–14 years	1	126	.01	1
15–18 years	0	24	.23	6
MAIS 3 Serious injury	0	91		
5–14 years	0	76	.07	5
15–18 years	0	15	.39	6
MAIS 4 Severe injury	0	37		
5–14 years	0	31	.20	6
15–18 years	0	6	.64	4
MAIS 5 Critical injury	0	32		
5–14 years	0	18	.25	5
15–18 years	0	4	.71	3

MAIS 6   Fatal injury (no fatal injuries were reported)

Discount Rate

A social discount rate of 6% was used to calculate the present value of net benefit over time.

Recommendations

The results indicate that the economic benefits from mandatory seat belts would not be cost effective for all the existing buses. However, mandatory seat belts may be cost effective for new buses.

Discussion

This result is surprising given the widely accepted social benefits resulting from automobile seat belts. The authors explain this discrepancy by noting that the number of injuries per mile of school bus ride is significantly less than for autos. Also, the severity of injuries is much higher in autos. Second, since the injury victims are children, who do not start earning income for years (in contrast to an income-earning adult), the use of their discounted earning capability reduces the size of the benefits. Third, the indirect benefit that the habit of wearing seat belts may carry over to the private autos, as the children learn to use them, was not included in the study. Finally, the study did not consider the cost effectiveness of requiring seat belts for only the newly acquired buses.

Key Words

Benefit-cost analysis	Opportunity cost
Compensation principle	Pareto optimality
Consumer surplus	Pecuniary effect
Cost effectiveness	Present value
Dead weight loss	Producers' surplus
Discount rate	Required compensation
Discounted future earning	Satisficing
Elasticity of demand and supply	Shadow price
Externality	Social time preference
Face value of life insurance method	Time horizon
Intangible costs and benefits	Time preference
Internal rate of return	Utilitarianism
Net social benefit	

Exercises

1. Suppose your friend is considering buying a new home or renting a bigger apartment. In a report, define your goal, the feasible set of alternatives, and the set of desirable attributes. Then, given your budgetary limitations, write a report describing the process by which you arrived at the optimum choice.

2. Consider a project in your area which is proposing to increase the supply of any public good. Indicate the benefits and costs, pointing out the possible area of consumer surplus, pecuniary effect, and the loss of producer surplus. You may also think of a project that proposes some new government regulation to bring social cost in line with private cost. In such a case, point out the area of possible dead weight loss in consumer surplus, pecuniary effect, and the gain in producer surplus. Explain your choice of discount rate (you do not need to show any actual calculation of present value).

3. What is a social discount rate? Why is there so much confusion in defining social discount rate? Why is it important to determine this rate while calculating the relative desirability of a public project?

4. What is a cost-effectiveness study? How does it differ from a full-blown benefit-cost analysis? Give examples of when it is more appropriate to use a cost-effectiveness analysis.

5. Calculate the net social benefit of the following two projects by evaluating them at 0%, 5%, 10%, and 20% discount rates.

Year	Project A Benefit	Cost	Project B Benefit	Cost
0	10	10	0	55
1	15	10	5	25
2	20	10	15	25
3	30	10	50	15
4	20	10	65	15
5	10	10	95	15

Linear Programming: Choosing the Optimal Mix of Alternatives

Introduction

We discussed the problem of choosing the best from a number of alternatives in the previous chapter. However, often the question of optimum choice does not involve accepting the best one over the others. Frequently we must determine the optimal mix—spread out our efforts or resources among a number of competing alternatives in a way which best serves our purpose. Thus, if we have a fixed amount of money which we want to invest, we may not want to put all our eggs in one basket. Instead, we would like to spread the risk and choose an optimum mix of investments which will maximize our return by keeping within reasonable bounds the concerns for risk, uncertainty, and liquidity of assets.

The technique of linear programming grew out of similar concerns. Developed by a number of mathematicians and economists, linear programming is one of the most sophisticated tools of operations research. This technique lends itself to a wide variety of problem solving that involves maximization of some specific goals given the limitations of inputs or minimization of costs with the specification of some minimum levels of benefits. Since linear programming is best understood in the context of an example, let us start with one.

Facilities Planning: An Example

Suppose you are the director of facilities planning for a small college. You are in charge of constructing dormitory units for the students. You are considering two types of units: single student unit and married student unit. Your survey shows that there are 4,000 married and 6,000 single students seeking dormitory rooms. This situation is shown in Figure 13.1. On the vertical axis we measure the number of married students in units of 1,000. On the horizontal axis we plot the number of single students. Each point on the surface of this figure represents a specific combination of housing for the two groups of students. For instance, the point A represents a combination of 2,000 units of housing for the married students and 3,000 for the single students. Since there are 4,000 married students, we draw a straight line through 4 on the vertical axis. Since there is no more demand for married student housing beyond this point, it would not make any sense to build at point B. Therefore, we etch out the area above the line showing 4,000 married students. We call this a **constraint** or a limitation, since our choice of combination of units will be limited by the demand for those units.

Similarly, we can draw another line showing the demand constraint for single student housing. Now consider the point C. This point shows a combination of 1,500 married student units and 6,000 single student units. Should we recommend that we build at that combination? Obviously not. By constructing at that point, we will leave out a great deal of unmet demand from the single student population. Therefore, we should ideally construct accommodations for all 9,500 students, at point D.

Figure 13.1 Demand Constraints for the Two Kinds of Housing

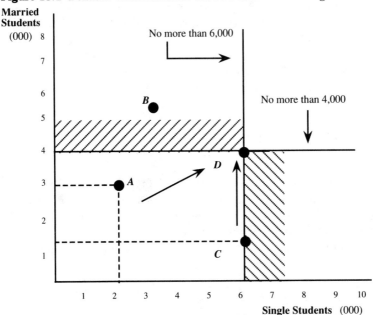

This figure plots the two demand constraints and shows that we should not build beyond the demand for each type of housing (that is, no more than 4,000 married and 5,500 single student units). Ideally, we should build at point D to accommodate fully the total demand for housing.

However, as with everything else in life, unconstrained choices are rarely available. Suppose we come across an additional constraint: space. Let us assume that single student accommodations require 700 square feet of land area per unit; married student units require 900 square feet. The college has 6,300,000 square feet of developable land for the project. To draw this constraint in our diagram, we need to find the extreme points on the two axes. That is, you can see that by utilizing all the available land, one can construct 9,000 single student housing units (obtained by dividing the total available land by the square footage required per unit of single student housing—700 square feet). This is the extreme point on the vertical axis. Similarly, if all the space was allocated for married student housing, we can build 7,000 units (6,300,000/900 = 7,000). Having obtained these two points, we simply join the two points with a straight line. By the laws of geometry, any point on this line represents a combination of the two kinds of units, which would exhaust the total allocated space for the project.

Therefore, in Figure 13.2, we have been able to etch out an area within the confines of which it is possible to construct the two types of housing units. Thus, we may build at any point within the bounded region, including points *A, B, C, D, E,* or *G*. Unfortunately, as you can see, the point *F* falls outside this area. Therefore, it is

Figure 13.2 The Addition of Space Constraint

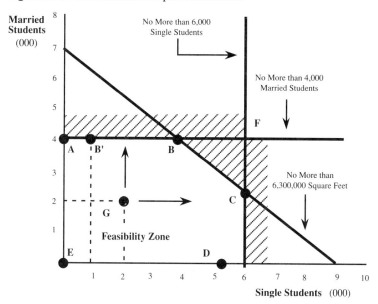

In this figure, we added the space constraint. There are 6.3 million square feet of land available for construction. The constraint shows all the combinations of the two types of housing
that can be built by utilizing fully the available space. The area marked by the constraint is
called the feasibility zone. It is feasible to build on any point within the zone. Therefore, it is
no longer possible to provide housing for everybody (point F), as this falls outside the feasibility zone.

not possible to build that combination of housing. Since the point *F* represents the
complete satisfaction of demand for housing, it is clear that we cannot accommodate the entire student demand, as we come up against the space constraint. The
area bordered by the three constraints is called the **feasibility zone**, since it is feasible to build any mix of housing within this area. No points outside this area are
feasible.

It is important at this point to understand some distinct features of the feasibility zone. Notice that although it is feasible to produce at an interior point, such as
G, it does not make sense to build at that combination, since at that point we have
an excess capacity and can expand our production of housing units without any
trouble. Therefore, the first feature of linear programming is that

> *the optimal or the best possible combination should always be within the borders of the feasi-*
> *bility zone.*

You may also note that while it is possible to build at a point on the boundary
between points *A* and *B* or between *C* and *D*, it does not make sense to do so. This is

because from that point, we can always move to another point, at which we will be able to achieve more of one good without having to give up any portion of the other. Thus, consider a combination in between points *A* and *B*. Let us call it *B'*. At this point, we are considering a combination of 4,000 married student housing units and 1,000 single student units. It is obvious from the figure that this combination would not utilize all the resources to the fullest, as we will still have space left over for more single student housing. Therefore, we can move to the right of this point, until we bump against the space constraint at point *B*. Therefore, the second feature of linear programming is that

> *the optimal solution will always be located at the corner—at the points of intersection between at least two constraints.*

You may, of course, wonder, What about points between *B* and *C*, where there is a trade-off? Thus, while moving from point *B'* to *B'* the choice was obvious since we could get more single student units without any sacrifice in the married student units. However, in moving between *B* and *C*, we trade one type of housing for the other. Therefore, to judge which combination is the best, we must know about our preference or the relative weight we place on the two variables. We will address this question formally during our discussion of the direction of the objective function later in this chapter. Assume for the moment that the optimal solution for a linear programming problem must be found at one of the corner points of the feasibility zone.

You may also wonder, If we are going to consider only the corner points on the boundaries of the feasibility zone, then would it not be trivial to consider the point *E*, although it satisfies both of the aforementioned criteria of being on the border and being a corner point? It may be so in this case, where you can visually inspect the diagram of an extremely simple example. However, in actuality, you are likely to encounter problems with many more than two variables and constraints, in which case it is impossible to plot them on a two-dimensional graph for a quick visual inspection. Therefore, the computer must go through the time-consuming iteration process of evaluating each corner point for the one that maximizes the objective.

Let us proceed further with our example and introduce a few more constraints. The one constraint that we have not considered so far is the financial constraint. Suppose it costs $10,000 to build a unit of married student housing. A unit of single student housing costs $6,000. The total budget for the project is $60 million. Consider a couple of legal or policy constraints: We must build at least 1,000 units of married and 1,000 units of single student housing. These kinds of constraints arise due to some government regulations or policy decisions within an agency to ensure a fair minimum or to place a ceiling for the allocation of resources among the competing groups.

In Figure 13.3, the budgetary constraint is drawn in the manner just described. We joined the two extreme points on the two axes to find out the maxi-

Figure 13.3 The Introduction of Budgetary and Legal Constraints

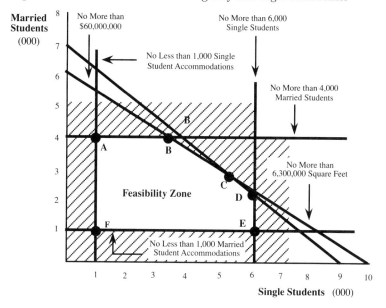

mum number of units of each kind which can be built by diverting the entire allo-cated sum to the production of one kind of housing only. Then a connecting straight line would mark the constraint. The two policy constraints are the vertical and horizontal straight lines.

The rules of linear programming suggest that the optimal solution for our problem lies within the feasibility zone and that it would be one of the corner points, where two or more constraints intersect. By visually examining the feasibility set, we can determine that the optimal solution must lie on one of the points, *A, B, C, D,* or *E.*

Optimality of solution begs the question of the determination of desirability. Therefore, to choose among the various possible mixes, we must specify what we want. This clearly is a policy matter which is often determined within an organiza-tion at a level higher than the analysts'. In technical terms, this is known as the **objective function**. We introduced the concept of objective function during our dis-cussion of social choice in chapter 12. We may specify it for our problem in many ways. Suppose we are not concerned about the relative desirability of building hous-ing units for the two kinds of students, and instead are interested in maximizing the total number of units built. In such a case, we can look at the possible combinations of the two kinds of housing for each corner point and choose the one with the high-est number of units built. This is shown in Figure 13.4.

The coordinate values for points *A, E,* and *F* are easily discerned by visually inspecting the graph. For other points, you may get approximate values if you plot

Figure 13.4 The Feasibility Zone

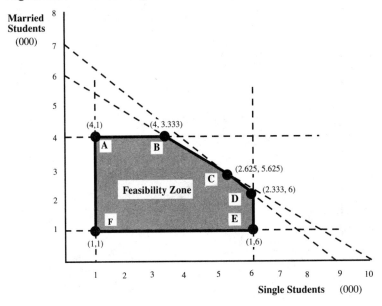

The feasibility zone and the corner points. The coordinate values for each of the corner points are in parentheses.

on graph paper. However, these points are not going to be the exact values. Since we can see that the corner points are the points of intersection between two straight lines, we can obtain the exact values by solving simultaneously the equations for the two intersecting lines.[1] By inspecting Figure 13.4, we can see that the five corner points suggest the following combination of housing units shown in Table 13.1.

The values in Table 13.1 are given in the units of 1,000. Therefore, we can see

[1] In case you need a refresher on solving a simultaneous equation system, let us consider the following example:

$$2X + 3Y = 7 \tag{1}$$
$$10X + 10Y = 20. \tag{2}$$

To solve this set of simultaneous equations, you have to set the value of one variable equal to zero and then solve for the other. Let us set $X = 0$. This can be done by multiplying the first equation by 10 (the coefficient of X in the second equation) and the second equation by 2 (the coefficient of X in the first equation). These operations will make the values of X equal:

$$20X + 30Y = 70 \tag{1'}$$
$$20X + 20Y = 40 \tag{2'}$$

By subtracting equation (2') from (1'), we get

$$20X + 30Y = 70$$
$$\underline{-20X - 20Y = -40}$$
$$0 + 10Y = 30.$$

Since $10Y = 30$, we find $Y = 3$. Now substituting the value of $Y = 3$ in the first equation, $2X + 3 \times 3 = 7$, we solve for the value of $X = -1$. You may want to double check your answer by plugging in these values of X and Y in the second equation to see if they satisfy the equation.

Table 13.1 The Feasible Solution of the Corner Points of the Feasibility Zone

Corner point	Married Student Units (000)	Single Student Units (000)	Value of the Objective Function
A	4.000	1.000	5.000
B	4.000	3.333	7.333
C	2.625	5.625	8.250
D	2.333	6.000	8.333
E	1.000	6.000	7.000
F	1.000	1.000	2.000

that at point *A*, we can build 4,000 units of married student housing and 1,000 units of single student housing. The figures for point *B* are 4,000 units of married student and 3,333 units of single student housing. From this table, you can see that the optimal mix of housing is reached at point *D*.

To demonstrate the logic of choosing the mix that maximizes the objective function graphically, we need to draw the indifference maps. Since we have assumed that the policy makers place equal value on the two types of units, we are able to draw a series of indifference maps by joining two equidistant points on the vertical and horizontal axes. This allows us to move on a 45° direction. By moving in this direction, you can see that the highest indifference curve touches point *D* in the feasibility zone. Therefore, this is our optimal choice, and we would recommend that the college builds 2,333 units of married student and 6,000 units of single student housing. This situation is shown in Figure 13.5.

Figure 13.5 The Process of the Optimal Choice

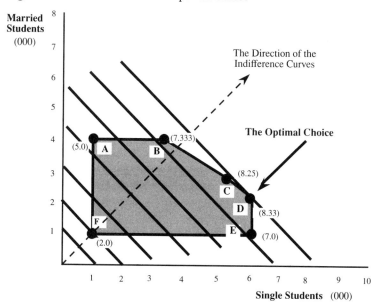

A series of indifference maps showing equal importance of the two types of housing points and the selection of point D *as the best possible mix of housing units, since it maximizes the total units built. The value of the objective function (which, in this case, is the total number of units built) for each point is written next to it.*

Expressing Linear Programming in Algebraic Form

The linear programming problem in algebraic terms is written as

$$\text{Maximize: } Z = M + S \tag{13.1}$$

subject to the constraints

M		$\leq$	4,000	(13.2)
	S	$\leq$	6,000	(13.3)
$900M$	$+ 700S$	$\leq$	6,300,000	(13.4)
$10,000M$	$+ 6,000S$	$\leq$	60,000,000	(13.5)
M		$\geq$	1,000	(13.6)
	S	$\geq$	1,000	(13.7)
M		$\geq$	0.0	(13.8)
	S	$\geq$	0.0	(13.9)

where M is married students, and
S is single students.

Let us examine the algebraic representation closely. The objective function, which we call Z, is equal to $M + S$. This implies that both kinds of housing carry an equal weight of 1. Therefore, both of these two types of units are equally important to us.

Now the constraints. The first two constraints (13.2 and 13.3) represent the market limitations of demand for housing. They state that the total number of units to be constructed should *be less than or equal* to 4,000 for the married students and less than 6,000 for the single students.

The third and the fourth inequalities (13.4 and 13.5) represent the space and budget constraints for the project. The third constraint may be read as follows: It takes 900 square feet of land area for married student housing and 700 square feet for single student housing, with a total allocation of 6.3 million square feet of land area. The budget constraint implies that it costs $10,000 and $6,000 per unit of married and single student units, respectively, with a total allocation of $60 million.

The next two constraints (13.6 and 13.7) represent legal or policy constraints, which states that the optimal mix must contain *at least* 1,000 units of each type of housing. And finally, constraints (13.8) and (13.9) are introduced to ensure that we do not get a trivial optimal solution with negative values for the variables.

You may note the analytical strength of linear programming. As long as the logical consistency of the formulation is maintained, linear programming is able to consider any kinds of disparate constraints, measured in units of money, time, weight, space, or any other quantifiable unit. It is also able to accommodate various kinds of legal and policy considerations, as long as they are articulated in numbers.

Accommodation of Policy Considerations

Policy considerations can be accommodated within the linear programming framework in two ways: through weights in the objective function or as constraints. We discussed policy constraints earlier and will introduce a few others later in this chapter. Let us look into the issue of other policy considerations introduced through the objective function. In popular discourse, it is often heard that the strict logical formulation of quantitative techniques of decision making is unable to consider the political aspects of decision making. However, as long as the political authorities are able to articulate their preferences, it is not a problem to include them within a logical construct. Of course, you may question the prudence of fully articulating the preferences of a political decision maker. In such a case, as an analyst you may show the results of a change in the weights of the objective function on the optimal mix of housing units.

When Social Preferences Change

For some reason, which may be political or simply reflective of the fact that the married students find it more difficult to find housing, the college has decided that it place a higher weight on married student housing, to the order of 3 to 1. That is, one unit of married student accommodation is valued three times more than a corresponding construction of a single student unit. This causes a rewriting of the objective function (13.1) as

$$\text{Maximize } Z = 3M + S. \qquad (13.10)$$

Reflecting this change of weight, we have redrawn the indifference curve in Figure 13.6. Since we are placing more importance on married student housing, the optimal solution now turns out to be point B. Notice that since we are putting three times the weight on married student housing, we need to recalculate the value of the new objective function for each point by multiplying the number of married units times 3 plus the number of single units. Thus, the value of the objective function for point A is calculated by 3 x 4 + 1 = 13. We have recalculated the objective function value of each point in Table 13.2 and have shown them next to the corresponding points in Figure 13.6. From Table 13.2, you can see that as a result of a change in the objective function, the new optimal point is B.

The preceding results point to the importance of proper specification of the objective function for arriving at the right optimal solution. For instance, if we change the weight to $Z = X + 1.5Y$, we will see that C has become the most desirable mix of two kinds of housing. You may calculate the value of Z for this latest specification and verify the result.

Figure 13.6 A Change in the Objective Function

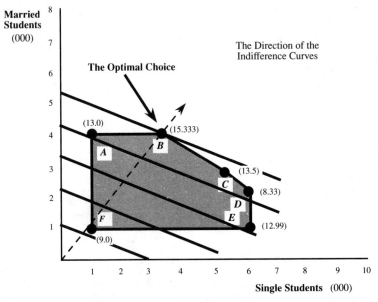

A change in social preference is reflected in the direction of the objective function. As a result of such a change, the position of the optimal solution within the feasibility zone also changes.

Having discussed the effects of the direction of the objective function, we can go back to the question we raised at the beginning of this chapter: Why is it not possible to have an optimal solution in the middle of a trade-off line, such as between points B and C in Figure 13.2? The answer is simple. If the objective function is tilted with reference to this constraint, you can see that we will settle at a corner solution. However, if the objective function is parallel to the constraint, there will be no unique solution as the objective function will satisfy an infinite number of combinations.

Table 13.2 The Feasible Solution of the Corner Points of the Feasibility Zone: The Recalculated Values of the Objective Function

Corner points	Married Student Units (000)	Single Student Units (000)	Value of the Objective Function
A	4.000	1.000	13.000
B	4.000	3.333	15.333
C	2.625	5.625	13.500
D	2.333	6.000	12.999
E	1.000	6.000	9.000
F	1.000	1.000	4.000

Mathematical Solutions for Linear Programming Problems

Although linear programming can trace its origins to the work of eighteenth-century French economist Quesney and his *Tableau Economique,* which presented a rudimentary form of an input output model, linear programming in its present form was developed largely by the Russian economist W. Leontieff in the 1930s. Later in 1941, F. L. Hitchcock analyzed a "transportation type problem." Later development of the solution of linear programming came during the late 1940s as a result of some of the brightest economists and mathematicians of the time. For example, in 1945 Professor Joseph Stigler studied the "diet problem"; in 1947, Tjaling Koopmans further developed the transportation problem. In the same year, George Danzig developed the formal mathematical method of solving linear programming problems.

In our example, we solved our linear programming problem by graphical means. There will rarely be a situation in real life when we will be able to obtain the solution to a problem graphically. The mathematical solution to problems of linear programming is obtained through the **simplex method**, developed by George Danzig. This method algebraically reaches the optimal point through iterations, as it searches for the optimal solution by calculating the values of the objective function for all corner solutions. It is an extremely laborious process which, for most practical problems, can take weeks or even months to work out. Fortunately, we need not learn this tedious technique for our present purpose, as we can always summon the help of a computer.

Through the efforts of many scholars and practitioners, and spurred by progress in computer technology, linear programming has become one of the most widely used quantitative methods of decision making. However, the problem with the simplex method is that it is extremely time consuming, even for computers. If you have a situation in which there are large numbers of variables and constraints, the iterative process of a simplex method would require an enormous amount of computer time. Since computer time directly translates into money, efforts have been made to find a more direct and less time-consuming way of deriving solutions for linear programming models. In 1984, Narendra Karmarkar of Bell Laboratories developed an innovative approach which allows the computer to avoid evaluating all the corner points and move directly to the optimal solution from a given point within the feasibility zone.[2]

[2]Narendra Karmarkar, "A New Polynomial-Time Algorithm for Linear Programming," *Combinatorica,* Vol. 4(184), pp. 373–95.

Logical Inconsistency and an Empty Feasibility Zone

Results obtained through sophisticated techniques such as linear programming are only as good as the formulation of the problem and the reliability of the data. We will take up the question of data reliability during our discussion of sensitivity analysis later in this chapter. At this point, let me make a couple of points about the logical consistency of the formulation.

If we make a logical error by which we specify that the value of a factor A must be less than or equal to 10, then later on, in the context of another constraint, we specify the requirement to be $A \geq 13$. In such a case, we are committing a logical error, and therefore the feasibility set will be an empty set. This can be a critical point to remember, especially if you are using a computer to solve a linear programming problem, since it is easy to get mixed up between a greater than and a less than sign. Therefore, if you get an error message to the effect that the feasibility set is an empty (or a "null") set, you may check all the signs. If they turn out to be consistent with your formulation, then there must be a logical inconsistency with which you have set up your problem.

The Consideration of Shadow Price

Solutions to a linear programming problem provide a policy maker with a number of extremely useful insights into the complex problems at hand. For instance, government in its regulatory role frequently imposes constraints on economic activities. In our public debate, we often hear that "this added restriction will cost the consumers [somehow this is always the ultimate target group!] this much money." The lumber industry, for example, in response to a proposal for saving the natural habitat of the spotted owls in the northwestern states, warned consumers that this restriction would translate into higher prices for all kinds of wood products. The cable television industry, facing the imposition of new regulations to hold down costs, cautioned viewers that the regulations would do just the opposite of what they purported to do. Therefore, it is legitimate to ask, What is the cost of a particular constraint? Or, we may put the question a little differently: How much do we gain (measured in terms of an increase in the value of the objective function) if we were to allow the constraint value to go up by 1%? We are able to answer such questions within the framework of linear programming. The answer to this question is called the **shadow price** of a constraint.

For example, we may want to examine the shadow price of the space constraint in our facilities planning model. That is, How much of a gain in the value of the objective function can be obtained by, say, a 1% increase in the space allocation? A 1% increase in total available space would give us 63,000 square feet of land area. The availability of this additional land would shift the constraint to the right, thereby allowing us to build more houses. We show the impact of this shift in Figure 13.7. As can be seen, the shift in the space constraint affects point D. At this point, we are already at the limits of the demand for married student housing. Therefore, as a result of this relaxation, we would be able to construct 90 additional units of single student housing.

Figure 13.7 The Shadow Price

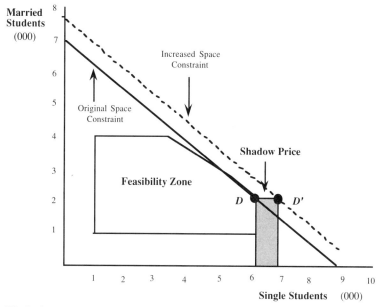

The shadow price *in a linear programming model measures the change in the value of the objective function as a result of a small shift in a constraint. If a constraint (or a resource) is non-binding (meaning there is already more than enough supply), the relaxation of that constraint will not change the optimal solution. Therefore, the shadow price for that constraint is zero. In this case, if we increase the space constraint, the optimal solution changes, showing a positive shadow price.*

Think of how useful this information can be to a policy maker. Since a single student unit costs $6,000, the construction of these additional 90 units would cost $540,000. The policy maker can then determine if it is worthwhile for the college to purchase the additional land to meet the residual demand. If the cost turns out to be less than the gain, then it is surely not worth it. On the other hand, if the cost is less than the gain, then it is desirable that we go ahead with the additional acquisition. Of course, in this particular example, there is no advantage to be had by increasing the single student housing since there is no more demand for single student housing. This is a case of zero shadow price, or a **nonbinding constraint**. In other words, for the facility planners of the college, building space is not the constraint. The most desirable aspect of the calculation of shadow price is that it allows a decision maker to evaluate the relative costs of each constraint.

However, the calculation of shadow price by graphical method can be tricky. as we relax one constraint, we may run into some other constraint. In that case, this new constraint may become critical and not allow us to move beyond a certain point. As we relax one constraint, if it runs into another constraint which was not critical before and had a zero shadow price, the new one will show a positive shadow price. However, almost all the computer-based linear programming algorithms are designed to give shadow prices for the constraints.

These shadow prices are calculated as part of what is known as the **dual solution**. The original problem, as we have posed it, in linear programming literature is called the **primal**. The dual solution of a maximization problem is a minimization problem. The solution of the dual problem does not provide any more information than the primal solution. However, by generating shadow prices, it places the imputed prices of the relevant constraints under sharper focus.

The Logic of Minimization Problems

Frequently, problems arise regarding determination of the optimal combination of variables which aim at minimizing cost rather than maximizing benefit, as shown in the previous example. The logic of the minimization problem is similar to that of the maximization problem. However, in this case, the direction of the preference is downward sloping. That is, we prefer the point which has the least value for the objective function. Minimization situations arise when we try to choose a mix which will provide us some minimum amount of benefit with the least amount of expenditure. The logic of a minimization problem is shown with the help of a hypothetical feasibility zone in Figure 13.8. As you can see from this figure, the optimum point turns out to be *A*, which is tangential to the highest indifference curve indicating the least costly option.

Figure 13.8 The Logic of a Minimization Problem

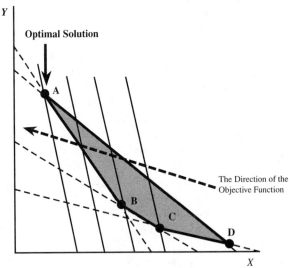

A minimization problem aims at deriving the point where the value of the objective function is the least. Therefore, for these problems, the direction of the objective functions is reversed, as shown in this figure.

Example of Another Application of Linear Programming

Linear programming is a versatile technique and lends itself to the analysis of a variety of problems. For example, the original problems tackled by linear programming were transportation problems. The typical transportation problem is concerned about finding the shortest routes among a number of delivery points. A diet problem might aim at finding the least-cost diet program given a certain minimum level of nutritional needs. There are numerous other cases in which linear programming can be of great help to decision makers. These may involve portfolio management (maximizing total return subject to risk constraints), personnel problems (finding the least expensive combination of personnel of various grades to complete a job), and scheduling problems (filling the slots of various shifts with the optimum number personnel), to name a few. Since there are so many possibilities, it is not feasible to discuss them all here. However, to show the versatility of the technique, I discuss prison planning, which shows one possible use of linear programming in the public sector.

Prison Planning

With increasing levels of crime, the number of criminals that state governments must place in state penitentiaries has increased as well. State governments face the problem of limited prison space, budgets, and other institutional constraints. Suppose a state's planners are considering the following problem. The state has three categories of inmates: the hardened (or the most dangerous ones, requiring incarceration with maximum possible security), the violent criminals, and the nonviolent criminals. Since the hardened criminals require the maximum amount of security measures, they are the most expensive to incarcerate. The cost goes down for the violent criminals, and of course the nonviolent prisoners are the least expensive to accommodate within the prison system. Let us suppose that there are three state penitentiaries, A, B, and C. A is the minimum security prison, B is the medium security, and C is the maximum security facility.

While allocating the total population of convicted individuals, the state planners face a few more constraints. First, the three facilities have maximum capacities of 3,000 inmates in prison A, 4,500 in prison B, and 5,200 in prison C. In algebraic form these three constraints can be written as

$$X11 + X12 + X13 \leq 3,000 \qquad (13.11)$$
$$X21 + X22 + X23 \leq 4,500 \qquad (13.12)$$
$$X31 + X32 + X33 \leq 5,200 \qquad (13.13)$$

where: $X11$ is hardened criminals placed in prison A
$X12$ is violent criminals placed in prison A
$X13$ is nonviolent prisoners placed in prison A

$X21$ is hardened criminals placed in prison B

$X22$ is violent criminals placed in prison B,

$X23$ is nonviolent prisoners placed in prison B,

$X31$ is hardened criminals placed in prison C,

$X32$ is violent criminals placed in prison C, and

$X33$ is nonviolent prisoners placed in prison C.

There are 1,500 hardened, 4,500 violent, and 10,000 nonviolent criminals who require incarceration in the state. Constraints (4), (5), and (6) show the total numbers of the three types of prisoners requiring accommodation:

$$X11 + X21 + X31 \leq 1{,}500 \qquad (13.14)$$
$$X21 + X22 + X23 \leq 4{,}500 \qquad (13.15)$$
$$X31 + X32 + X33 \leq 10{,}000. \qquad (13.16)$$

The prison faces certain structural constraints. Thus, for the minimum security prison A to keep its character, it cannot let the ratio of hardened criminals to exceed 5% of its total inmate population. For symbolic expressions of these constraints, we need to do a bit of algebraic manipulation. Since the hardened criminal population in prison A ($X11$) cannot exceed 5% of its total inmate population ($X11 + X12 + X13$), we can write the constraint as

$$X11 \leq .05 \, (X11 + X12 + X13),$$

which can be rewritten as

$$(X11 - .05 \, X11) - .05 \, X11 - .05 \, X13 \leq 0,$$

or

$$.95 \, X11 - .05 \, X12 - .05 \, X13 \leq 0. \qquad (13.17)$$

Further, the minimum security prison would not want the ratio of violent criminals to the total population to exceed 40%. Similarly, the medium security prison introduces similar structural limitations on the distribution of its prison population. It does not want the more hardened criminal population to exceed 20%, or the violent prisoners to exceed 40% of its total. By following the logic used to derive constraint (13.17), we can write these three constraints as

$$-.4 \, X11 + .6 \, X12 - .4 \, X13 \qquad (13.18)$$
$$.8 \, X21 - .2 \, X22 - .2 \, X23 \qquad (13.19)$$
$$-.4 \, X21 + .6 \, X22 - .4 \, X23 \qquad (13.20)$$

Finally, there are budget constraints. Since the minimum security prison is not equipped to handle the hardened prisoners, it is quite expensive to place them there. The cost structure for a month is given in Table 13.3, with a total allocation of $100,000,000 million of the yearly state prison budget.

Table 13.3 Cost of Incarceration in State Prisons

Prison	Hardened criminals	Violent criminals	Non-violent criminals
A (minimum security)	$2,500	$900	$560
B (medium security)	$1,800	$1,000	$900
C (maximum security)	$2,000	$1,800	$1,700

The budget constraints can be written as

$$2,000X11 + 900X12 + 560X13 + 1,800X21 + 1,000X22 + 900X23 +$$
$$2,000X31 + 1,800X32 + 1,700X33 \leq 100,000,000. \qquad (13.21)$$

Since the state places the utmost weight on the incarceration of the hardened criminals, and then on the violent ones, let us assume that the policy makers' preferences are translated into weights of 30 for the hardened criminals, 5 for the violent ones, and 1 for the nonviolent felons. The state does not have any preference for the relative desirability of the location of these inmates. Therefore, the linear programming problem is written as

Maximize $Z = 30X11 + 5X12 + X13 + 30X21 + 5X22 + X23 + 30X31 + 5X32 + X33$

$$X11 + X12 + X13 \leq 3,000 \qquad (13.11)$$
$$X21 + X22 + X23 \leq 4,500 \qquad (13.12)$$
$$X31 + X32 + X33 \leq 5,200 \qquad (13.13)$$
$$X11 + X21 + X31 \leq 1,500 \qquad (13.14)$$
$$X21 + X22 + X23 \leq 4,500 \qquad (13.15)$$
$$X31 + X32 + X33 \leq 10,000 \qquad (13.16)$$
$$.95 \ X11 - .05 \ X12 - .05 \ X13 \leq 0 \qquad (13.17)$$
$$-.4 \ X11 + .6 \ X12 - .4 \ X13 \leq 0 \qquad (13.18)$$
$$.8 \ X21 - .6 \ X22 - .6 \ X23 \leq 0 \qquad (13.19)$$
$$-.4 \ X21 + .6 \ X22 - .4 \ X23 \leq 0 \qquad (13.20)$$
$$2,000X11 + 900X12 + 560X13 + 1,800X21 + 1,000X22 +$$
$$900X23 + 2,000X31 + 1,800X32 + 1,700X33 \leq 100,000,000. \qquad (13.21)$$

The computer solution to this problem is given in Table 13.4
The slack values and the dual prices are given in Table 13.5.

Policy Analyses and Recommendations:

1. The optimal allocation accommodates all the hardened but cannot find accommodation for 694 violent and 6,200 nonviolent criminals.

2. The space constraint is most critical for the minimum security prison, followed by the medium security facility.

Table 13.4 Optimal Mix of Prisoners in the Three State Penitentiaries

Prison	Hardened criminals	Violent criminals	Nonviolent criminals	Total
A (minimum security)	0	1,200	1,800	3,000
B (medium security)	700	1,800	2,000	4,500
C (maximum security)	800	806	0	1,606
Total	1,500	3,806	3,800	

3. The structural constraints of the mix of inmates within the three prisons are limiting, and efforts should be made to change them. Of these four constraints, the most critical are the provisions that the ratio of violent criminals must not exceed 40% of the total in the medium security facility and minimum security prison. Also, the rule that the ratio of hardened criminals cannot exceed 20% of the total prison population in the medium security prison should be reviewed.

4. Presently, because of the cost factor, the maximum security prison is running below capacity. Therefore, appropriate policies need to be developed.

Table 13.5 Slack and Shadow Prices

Constraints	Description	Total Available	Optimal Allocation	Slack	Shadow Price
13.11	Space in the minimum security prison (A)*	3,000	3,000	0	.667
13.12	Space in the medium security prison (B)*	4,500	4,500	0	.309
13.13	Space in the maximum security prison (C)*	5,200	1,606	1,394	0.0
13.14	Total number of hardened criminals	1,500	1,500	0	24.44
13.15	Total number of violent criminals	4,500	3,806	694	0.0
13.16	Total number of nonviolent criminals	10,000	3,800	6,200	0.0
13.17	Ratio of hardened criminals in prison A*	5%	0%	5%	0.0
13.18	Ratio of violent criminals in prison A*	40%	40%	0	3.06
13.19	Ratio of hardened criminals in prison B*	20%	15.5%	4.5%	2.28
13.20	Ratio of violent criminals in prison B*	40%	40%	0	3.95
13.21	Budget constraint	$100 million	$100 million	0	2.78

*Policy variables for the prison planner.

Sensitivity Analysis

Sensitivity analysis involves analyzing the results of the optimal solution by changing some of the important parameter values. For instance, in the preceding example of prison population distribution among the various facilities, we may not be satisfied with just the derived results. Instead, we may want to know the impact of cost changes and other policy changes on the optimal solution. Sensitivity analysis has become extremely useful as a result of increased computer capabilities. For a decision maker, it may be more useful to receive a series of optimal solutions corresponding to a number of probable scenarios than to be informed of a unique optimal solution.

For example, we may want to know what happens if the minimum security facility is turned into a medium security prison. In that case, we would experiment with the possibility of housing more hardened criminals in that prison. Or, we may want to study the impact of the maximum security facility becoming a facility exclusively for the hardened criminals. If these are real concerns, sensitivity analysis is able to provide extremely useful answers for policy makers.

The Limitations Of Linear Programming

From the discussion of linear programming, you can tell that this technique can be useful in reaching an optimal mix of alternatives. However, it also carries some important limitations. First, as the name suggests, the objective function and the constraint are all linear. It is entirely possible that they would be nonlinear. Indeed, in actual life, we seldom come across relationships which are linear. Consider, for example, that we are trying to determine the optimum size of the jurisdiction of a fire service department. As the size of the area to be covered increases and along with it the number of taxpayers supporting the department, the per household cost for obtaining fire protection goes down. However, after a certain point, as the department becomes too large, inefficiency creeps in, and as a result the price of providing fire protection goes up.

For the most part, actual relationships can be approximated with the help of a linear form. However, when the nonlinearity of a relationship is strong and cannot be approximated by linear forms without a significant loss of information, we must resort to nonlinear programming. These techniques are extremely complicated and therefore, are beyond the scope of this book. However, we should note that unlike problems of engineering or physics, many relationships within the area of public policy making can be safely approximated with appropriate linear forms.

Another important limitation of linear programming is that the solutions may indicate fractions, whereas such division for the factors may not be possible. In such cases, we must resort to integer programming, whose solutions come only in whole numbers. The solutions to the integer programming are fairly close to linear programming. Therefore, let us now discuss integer programming.

Integer Programming

The optimal solution of a linear programming problem often does not come in whole numbers or integers. Instead, frequently we get optimal solutions in fractions. However, many of the items of public policy discussions may be indivisible. Consider, for example, our first problem in this chapter: planning to construct housing for two kinds of students. When we solved the linear programming problem, many of the corner solutions were in fractions. Since it does not make sense to recommend the construction of, say, 2.93 units of housing, we merrily discarded the fractions (since by rounding we would go over the constraints). However, shedding the fractional part of a solution can give us misleading results. Therefore, we use **integer programming**, by which we place an additional constraint on the solution by specifying that we would want the answer only in integers.

Let us consider a simple example. Suppose we are trying to maximize the following:

$$\text{Maximize } Z = X + 6Y$$
$$\text{Subject to } 2X + 3Y \leq 11.5$$

and

$$X, Y \geq 0.$$

We have drawn this problem in Figure 13.9. Since we have only one constraint, we can readily see that the two relevant corner points—ignoring the obviously inferior (0,0) point—are A and B. At point A, we have no X and 3.83Y, and at point B we have no Y and 5.75X. By inserting these values in the objective function,

Figure 13.9 Integer Programming Problem

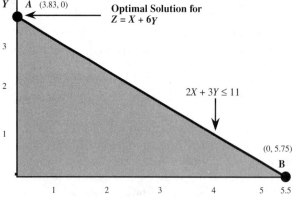

The linear programming solution for this problem is at point A *with* X = 0 *and* Y = 3.83.

we can see that *A* has a value of 23, with 5.75 for *B*. This obviously makes *A* the optimal choice.

Suppose both *X* and *Y* are indivisible. Therefore, we cannot have a 3.83 amount of *Y*. Since we cannot round it off to 4, as it will exceed the limitation imposed by the constraint, we have to choose the integer 3 by ignoring the fractional part of the solution for *A*. Within the linear programming logic, this is done by introducing a new constraint: $Y \leq 3$. This is called a **cut**. Therefore, we may recommend 3 *Y*s and no *X*, shown as point *C* in Figure 13.10. But you can readily see from Figure 13.10 that the choice of the point *C* would be a suboptimal, interior solution, as from this point we can move to the border of the feasibility zone to obtain more *X*. In fact, by moving as far as possible within the feasibility zone, we can get 1.25 *X*. (We get this by substituting 2 for *Y* in the constraint $2X + 3Y = 11.5$, which gives us $X = (11.5 - 9/2) = 1.25$). This is the point *D* in Figure 13.10. But again the problem remains that *X* cannot be divided into fractions either. Therefore, we introduce another cut or a constraint, $X \leq 1.0$, which gives us the optimal integer solution of $X = 1$ and $Y=3$.

Thus, integer programming is a special variation of linear programming, where we introduce successive constraints as a part of the iterative process to obtain the optimal solution. This creates more computing space. However, with ever-increasing computing capabilities available at our finger-tips, this should not pose any special problem. If the factors are not divisible, we should always test the solution with the help of integer programming.

Figure 13.10 Integer Programming Solution

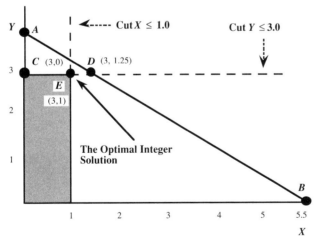

Since X *and* Y *are indivisible, a new constraint (cut) was introduced,* Y ≤ 3.0, *which took us to point* C. *Since* C *(with* X=0*) is an inside solution, this cut takes us to the corner solution* D. *But the value of* X *is a fraction at* D *(X=1.25), therefore, another cut,* X ≤ 1, *is introduced. This leads us to the optimal integer solution at* E *(Y=3, X=1).*

Using a Computer to Solve Linear Programming and Integer Programming Problems

There are several software packages on the market for analyzing linear programming problems. Since we are not concerned with the numerical accuracy of a solution or the ability to handle a huge amount of data, our only criterion for choosing a software package is its user friendliness. On that basis, I chose a software package called OPTIZE. Unfortunately, at the time of writing, this software is available only for DOS-based operating systems. If you are able to operate a DOS-based system, you will be able to use this software with a great deal of ease.

For solving our first example of facilities planning using OPTIZE, proceed as follows:

1. Install the OPTIZE program in your hard disk or access it through the floppy.
2. Create a DOS file for the data. Let us call it "FACILITY.CMD." This file will contain the following information. First, there will be the objective function, specified by **MAX** for maximization problems and **MIN** for minimization problems. Second, the constraints will be introduced by **CON**. The data file is concluded with the command **OPT**.

```
MAX Z=M + S
CON M < 4000
CON S < 6000
CON 10000*M + 6000*S < 60000000
CON 900*M + 700*S < 6300000
CON M > 1000
CON S > 1000
CON M > 0
CON S > 0
OPT
```
Having created the data file, go into the OPTIZE program by typing
```
> OPTIZE
```
Then type
```
> submit FACILITY.CMD
```
For getting an integer programming result without typing **OPT**, *type* **INT** *in your data file.*

Steps Toward Setting Up a Linear or Integer Programming Problem

1. Determine the goal of the problem. For example, "Determine the optimal mix of personnel which will maximize a certain objective," etc.

2. Quantify the objective function, making careful note of the variables under consideration. For example, if four categories of workers are needed to carry out this job, then identify them and determine their relative effectiveness. These will specify the arguments of the objective function.

3. Find out the bottlenecks or the constraints. If there are several constraints with

different units of measurement, make sure that the constraints are logically consistent in terms of the problem at hand.

4.   If there are more than two variables, use a computer to calculate the optimal solution. Otherwise, you may try to solve it graphically.

5.   Ask if the results make sense. If they do not, or if the computer warns you that there is no solution to your problem, look for logical inconsistencies.

6.   If the results make sense, analyze the shadow prices and think about their policy implications.

7.   If the results make sense, conduct a series of sensitivity analyses to determine policy implications.

8.   Write a report analyzing the results, making sure to mention the implications of assumptions regarding the linearity of the constraints and the objective function.

Key Words

Constraints	Nonbinding constraint
Cut (in integer programming)	Objective function
Dual solution	Optimal choice
Feasibility zone	Primal solution
Integer programming	Sensitivity analysis
Linear programming	Shadow price
Maximization problem	Simplex method
Minimization problem	

Exercises

1.   What is linear programming? Describe a typical problem in the public sector that can be analyzed using this technique. Under what conditions can you use linear programming and when can't you? Explain with appropriate examples.

2.   Graphically solve the following problems and then, if possible, check your answer with the help of a computer:

   a.   Maximize $Z = 3X + 7Y$
        subject to the following constraints:
        $5X + 6Y \leq 30$
        $20X + 100Y \leq 200$
        $X \geq 0$
        $Y \geq 0$.

   b.   Minimize $Z = X + .5\,Y$
        subject to the following constraints:
        $15X + 8Y \geq 120$

$$3X + 7Y \geq 21$$
$$X \geq 0$$
$$Y \geq 0.$$

c. Maximize $Z = X + Y$
   subject to the following constraints:
   $$3X + 4Y \leq 120$$
   $$X + .5Y \leq 60$$
   $$X \geq 0$$
   $$Y \geq 0.$$

3. What is the shadow price? What are its implications in economics?

4. Why do we need a separate algorithm for integer programming? If we need solutions in integers, would it not be easier simply to round off the standard linear programming outputs to integer values? Explain.

5. Recalculate all the problems of Exercise 2 using integer programming. Compare the integer programming results with those derived from linear programming.

6. What is sensitivity analysis? Explain with an appropriate example how it can help in the decision-making process.

7. The Metropolitan Transport Corporation (MTC) of your city wants to maximize savings by servicing its buses in an in-house repair and shop. The buses it cannot service will have to be sent to private garages, where the costs are substantially higher. The MTC runs a comprehensive shop. However, for analytical reasons its operations have been classified into four categories: routine maintenance, minor repairs, major repairs, and body work. Each category requires the work of mechanics and their supervisors, as well as the purchase of materials. Routine maintenance requires one hour of mechanic time, but no time for the supervisors. It also requires, on the average, $65 for the purchase of spare parts per unit. The minor repair jobs take up two hours of a mechanic's time and one hour of a supervisor's time. The spare parts required for minor repairs are $175 per unit. An MTC study that major repairs require 15 hours of mechanic work and 5 hours of supervisor work time per unit. The material purchase required for a major repair job is $250. A typical body shop job requires 12 mechanic hours and 2 supervisor hours. The available time for mechanics is 440 hours per week, and for supervisors 80 hours. The MTC has decided to limit the material purchases to $10,000 per week. The estimated saving for doing the jobs in-house and the maximum demand for each kind of service are as follows:

Type of work	Savings per unit	Maximum demand (units)
Routine maintenance	$120	280
Minor repairs	$265	55
Major repairs	$300	15
Body work	$220	33

Set up the linear programming model and solve for the optimal solution. The manager of the shop wants to hire 10 mechanics at a cost of $550 a week. The assistant manager thinks that MTC should hire five mechanics and promote two mechanics to the post of supervisor, while the MTC accountant recommends increasing the purchase of spare parts by another $5,000 per week. Analyze the results for the shadow prices of each of the constraints and take a position in the debate.

8. Think of a problem within a public agency that may be amenable to a linear programming analysis. Develop the problem, and interview the relevant officials to gather information. Analyze the data and find the optimal solution. Write a report explaining your success and failure.

9. Linear programming is widely used by management analysts in the private sector. Write an essay on the relative strengths and weaknesses of linear programming as an analytical tool for policy analysis. In your estimation, what are its prospects in the public sector? Explain.

PART V

HOW TO DEAL WITH UNCERTAINTY

Chapter 14

The Elements of Strategic Thinking: Decision Tree and Game Theory

The Problem

In March of 1976, President Gerald Ford had a problem. Epidemiologists were concerned about a particularly virulent form of influenza virus, called the Swine Flu virus, which broke out at Fort Dix, New Jersey. Experts feared that this new strain was going to hit the larger population of the United States in the fall, during the flu season. Many scientists suggested that the flu was related to a strain that caused a worldwide epidemic and took 20 million lives in 1918-1919. Quickly mutating flu viruses are nightmares for health care professionals. To counter the threat of influenza, every year manufacturers must reproduce these strains in laboratories, incubate them in eggs, and then make them harmless to humans by a certain process. When injected in human bodies, these harmless viruses become part of the shield which protects the body from the ravages of the natural viruses of their kind. But the problem is that the viruses engage in a hide and seek game with the researchers by mutating themselves, which makes them impervious to the protection of the inoculation. To compound the problem, the protective virus must be produced *before* the actual infestation takes place, as the time to produce the protective virus is considerable and, if people get infected with the invading virus, there is not much a doctor can do. Therefore, for President Ford the problem boiled down to making a decision on whether to start a massive inoculation program for the entire population, especially those who fall in the high-risk category (e.g., the elderly, and people with lung or other kinds of chronic health ailments), or do nothing. If he chose to do nothing, and the worst fears of the experts materialized, the nation would face a public health catastrophe of unparalleled proportion. But if the experts were wrong, the President would save a great deal of money. On the other hand, the President could decide to play it safe with the health of the American people, and inoculate the population. In such a situation, if the Swine Flu virus did show up, the President's prudence would be admired by a grateful public (which translates into a considerable amount of political goodwill for the President). However, if the threat failed to materialize, the President's policy was likely to be widely ridiculed, and his wisdom for wasting public money would be questioned.

Place yourself in the position of the President. What would you have done? At the root of President Ford's problem is **uncertainty**. He does not know for sure the future course of development of the unpredictable virus. As the old adage goes, there are two things in life which are for sure: death and taxes. Therefore, it is natural that a decision maker will frequently face uncertainty. So far in our discussion of quantitative techniques to aid the decision process, we have put the question of uncertainty in abeyance. Let us now see how the introduction of one more quark affects our decisions.

Uncertainty and Expected Payoff

The question of how to make the best possible decision under uncertainty has come under intense scrutiny. The first analytical breakthrough of the question was derived by John von Neumann and Oscar Morgenstern, two Princeton mathematicians, and has been developed further by a great number of mathematicians and economists over the years. Let us explain the basic precepts of this line of analysis.

Suppose someone offers you a choice. If you predict correctly, you may win $2 in a toss of a coin, or $5 in a roll of a dice. Which one would you choose? Theoretically, you should choose the coin toss. In the coin toss, your chances of winning are $1/2 = .5$. On the other hand, in the roll of dice, your chances of calling the right number is $1/6 = .167$. The **expected payoff** in an uncertain situation is calculated by

$$\text{Expected payoff} = \text{probability of winning x amount of reward.}$$

That is, in our case, the expected payoffs are

$$\text{Expected payoff for coin toss} = .5 \times \$2 = \$1$$
$$\text{Expected payoff for roll of a dice} = .167 \times \$5 = \$0.83$$

The expected payoff for a coin toss is $1 and for the dice, 83 cents. Therefore, you will be better off by betting on the coin toss—that is, unless you are a real gambler and a risk taker. In this case, you may still prefer the higher reward of dice regardless of the chances of winning. For the moment, let us assume that you are neither an undue risk taker, nor are you a risk averter; you are a risk-neutral decision maker. You may note here that if you want to maximize your chances of winning in the long run, you will be better off by following this law of rational decision making under uncertainty. In fact, in every kind of uncertain situation, including gambling or playing card games, good players are going to depend primarily on the proper calculation of the odds. For example, at Black Jack tables in the casinos, the House realizes its profits solely by playing the odd, which is in its favor. Therefore, while there are winners among the players, the House always cleans up the table at the end of the day.

The Decision Tree

We can use the insights which were formally developed by von Neumann and Morgenstern and proceed further to show the options and the optimal course of action. The branch of social science and applied mathematics that is dedicated to the study of decision making under uncertainty is called **game theory**. These strategies can also be shown with the help of a diagram, which draws the sequence of events and the corresponding probability figures. This is known as a **decision tree**.

Let us go back to the uncertain public policy problem of President Ford. Let us suppose that the experts at the Centers for Disease Control (CDC) have estimated the odds of the deadly virus reaching the United States to be 40%. Let us also suppose that the President appraises the benefits of his decision on a scale of +10 through -10, with +10 being the most desirable and -10 being the most undesirable outcome. Since we do not know the exact process of President Ford's reasoning, we hypothesize that if he decides to do nothing, and the epidemic becomes real, it would be the least desirable of his options, and we would rate it as -10. But if he decides to take no action and the epidemic does not show up, then he has remained calm in the face of an unjustified doomsday prediction and has saved a considerable amount of public money. On his scale, this would rate a +5. On the other hand, if he decides to inoculate, the most desirable situation from his perspective would arise if the threat of epidemic turns out to be real. In such a case, the President would be hailed as the savior, and deliver political goods, worth +10 in his rating. However, if the epidemic does not show up, the decision to have a mass inoculation program may turn out to be a political liability, which is assessed by a -5 rating. Having put numerical values on the probabilities and payoffs, we can draw the decision tree facing the President. This is shown in Table 14.1 and Figure 14.1. The branches of a decision tree can be divided into *actions* and *outcomes*. You may note that while actions are deliberate and reflect the conscious decision of an individual, the outcomes are uncertain. In Figure 14.1 I have drawn the actions with small squares, and the outcomes with circles.

We can see that facing an uncertain situation, President Ford had an option between an expected payoff of -1 (for "Do nothing" option) and +1 (for "inoculate" option). Therefore, given the logical construct, he should have chosen the option to inoculate the entire population against a probable Swine Flu infestation. As an anecdotal postscript to this analysis, President Ford did choose inoculate, and the virus failed to show up in the United States.

To Tell or Not to Tell Your Boss

John is currently working for Jane in a large organization. Recently he has found out about an opening in a sister department, which is more to John's liking than the position he is currently holding. He wants to apply for the position, but does not know whether to ask Jane for a letter of recommendation. The problem is the fol-

Table 14.1 Hypothetical Expected Payoff Matrix for President Gerald Ford

Action (1)	Situation (2)	Probability (3)	Payoffs (4)	Expected Payoffs (5) = (3) x (4)
A (Do nothing)	Epidemic starts	.4	-10	-4
	Epidemic does not show up	.6	+5	3
B (Start mass inoculation)	Epidemic starts	.4	+10	4
	Epidemic does not show up	.6	-5	-3

Figure 14.1 Decision Tree for Action on Swine Flu Threat

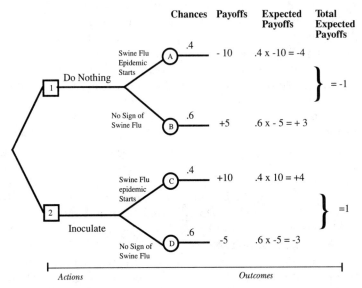

| | Chances | Payoffs | Expected Payoffs | Total Expected Payoffs |

The expected payoffs are drawn in this decision tree. The expected payoffs for the actions
(A and B) are derived by adding the payoffs for the two probable scenarios.

lowing: Without a letter from Jane, John thinks he has a 50–50 chance at the job. But Jane is on very good terms with Conrad, the head of the other department. Therefore, John figures that her letter is likely to carry a great deal of weight in Conrad's decision. However, what John does not know is how Jane feels about him. She may write a good letter, which will substantially increase his chances of getting the new job; or she may write a neutral letter, which will leave his chances essentially the same; or she may write a nasty letter, which will substantially reduce his chances of future employment in Conrad's department.

With the basic rule of decision making in mind, let us lend John a helping hand in analytically sorting out his problem. Since John faces two decision alternatives—to ask for a letter of recommendation or not—the tree starts off with two branches, as shown in Figure 14.2.

Figure 14.2 simply shows the paths of the decision scheme. John has two decision alternatives: (1) Do nothing, and do not ask for a letter of recommendation; and (2) ask for a letter of recommendation. If John does ask for a letter of recommendation, Jane can write a good one, a neutral one, or a poor one. John's chances of getting the new position, in that case, vary with the quality of the letter. Therefore, in choosing his best alternative, John faces two different probabilities if

Figure 14.2 John's Decision Scheme

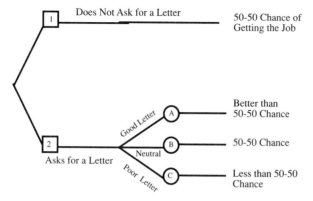

he asks for the letter. The first set of probabilities relates to the quality of the letter. If he does not have a clue about Jane's opinion of him as a worker, he may assign equal probability for three options, which is $1/3 = .33$. The second set of probabilities relates to his chances of getting the job on the basis of the letter. Suppose John estimates his chances of getting the job if Jane writes a good one to be 80%, 50% if she writes a neutral one, and a mere 2% in case she decides to write a poor letter of recommendation. Also, let us assume that John attributes the value (reward) 1 for getting the job and 0 for not. We have written these probability measures in Figure 14.3.

Figure 14.3 John's Payoff Structure

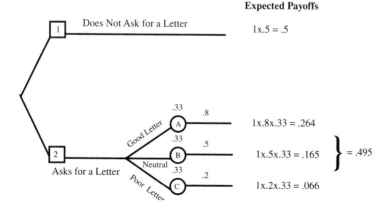

Following our decision criteria for determining the payoff, we can write the payoffs for the two strategic actions:

Actions	Expected Payoffs	
1) Do not ask for a letter.	.5 x 1	= .5
2) Ask for a letter.		
Gets a good letter	.33 x.8 x 1	= .264
Gets a neutral letter	.33 x.5 x 1	= .165
Gets a poor letter	.33 x.2 x 1	= .066
	Total payoff	= .495

Therefore, by comparing the payoffs for the two strategic actions, we may advise John that given the conditions, it would be prudent for him *not* to ask for a letter of recommendation from his boss. However, you may notice that the situation will change if John has any kind of inkling (in our terms "expectations") about the way his boss is going to respond. If there is a slightly higher chance than .33 that she would write a good letter, you can readily see that the balance is going to tip in favor of asking her for the letter.

Therefore, to make use of this technique, we need quantifiable measures of probability and measurable payoffs. Once again, for policy assessment, the best measure of probability can be obtained by asking the experts within an organization.

Playing the Dominant Strategy

The most important aspect of analyzing the future course of action is the identification of **dominant** and **dominated** strategies. In comparison, a strategy is called dominant if:

> by following this strategy you win *at least some of the time*, but never lose.

In contrast, by following a dominated strategy you are worse off at least some of the time, but never better off than when following the dominant strategy. The difference in strategies can be made clear by expanding our example.

Suppose that John has further courses of action with regard to his boss. If he can time his request properly, he can narrow the odds for a good letter of recommendation. John figures that he has three possible times: in the morning, in the afternoon, and during the after-work happy hour in nearby bar. John reasons that his boss is likely to be rather busy in the morning, and if he asks then, she is 25% likely to write a good letter, 40% likely to write a neutral letter, and a 35% likely to write a poor letter. The corresponding chances for after lunch are 35% good, 55% neutral, and 10% poor. Finally, he can corner her during happy hour. John argues that during happy hour, in keeping with the time, he may find her in a pretty good mood, and in that case she will be 45% likely to recommend him well to Conrad. But, at the same time, if he spoils her cherished free time, she may be furious and give him a poor letter of recommendation. John is afraid that the possibility that this will take place is 40%. As you can figure out, in this case there is only a 15% chance of John's getting a neutral letter. Again, we can give John a helping hand and calculate his expected payoffs.

Figure 14.4 shows John's decision tree and his strategic options. From this, we can see that now John has four different options. (1) He may not ask his boss for a letter of recommendation, or he may choose to ask her for one. If he does ask her, he may bring up the request (2) in the morning, (3) in the afternoon, or (4) during happy hour. When we compare strategy 2 with 3, we see that the expected payoff for asking her in the morning is .45, while that of asking her in the afternoon is .585. Therefore, between these two strategies, 3 is dominant. We have eliminated the dominated strategy (2) by drawing the symbol (‖) through it in Figure 14.4. Similarly, we can readily see that between 3 and 4, 3 is dominant. Therefore, if John decides to ask his boss, he should ask her after lunch. Now we can compare the expected payoff of this strategy with the strategy of not asking her at all. Again, we can see that between these two, 3 is dominant. Hence, on the basis of our analysis, we conclude that John should ask his boss for a letter of recommendation during the afternoon to maximize his chances of getting the job in Conrad's department.

Figure 14.4 Decision Tree Showing Dominant Strategy

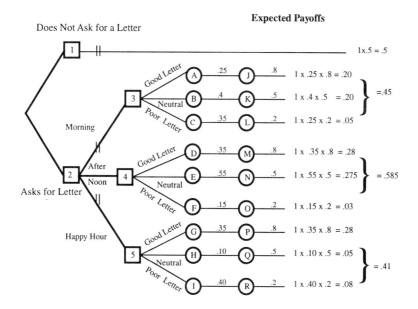

Two Active Players: The Game Theory

The decision tree is a schematic representation of decision making under uncertainty. It falls under the more general area of study called **game theory**. Game theory is particularly adept at studying strategic decision making when one is uncertain about the moves of the opponent(s). The literature on game theory is extremely varied and rich. The beauty of this technique is that it can be used to explain strategies from chess games to corporate takeovers, from bargaining with labor unions to international treaties. Also, because it lends itself to mathematical modeling, literature about it varies from simple to extremely complex, from eminently practical to highly esoteric.[1] The rules of strategic decision making have been researched by psychologists such as Kahneman and Amos Tversky and their associates, who have found extremely interesting, often amusing, yet frequently encountered fallacies about uncertainty.[2] Scholars of international relations have analyzed the strategic moves of countries, which sometimes push them toward conflict and war.[3] Students of corporate strategies have studied the ways corporations interact with each other.[4] Social scientists and policy analysts have analyzed the ways of strategic decision making within a social and political context.[5] Students of negotiations and bargaining have attempted to come up with rules for a resolution of conflict.[6] These diverse inquiries have significantly advanced our knowledge in the area of strategic decision making and sometimes have inflated expectations beyond what these techniques can deliver.[7]

Let us start with a very simple two-person game. While decision trees are shown with a diagram, two-player games are usually written as a matrix. With the help of game theory, let us analyze the Gulf crisis, with a cautionary note that this is a highly simplified rendition of a rather complex international crisis. The sole purpose of this exercise is to illustrate game theory, rather than to provide any new insight into international diplomacy. Let us begin with our scenario. Saddam Hussein's Iraq has attacked and occupied Kuwait. Now the United States has two options: Pursue a diplomatic resolution under the rubric of a so-called Arab solu-

[1]For a most informative, and yet highly entertaining, explanation of game theory, see *Thinking Strategically*, by Avinash Dixit and Barry Nalebuff (New York: W. W. Norton, 1991).

[2]Thomas Gilovich, Robert Vallone, and Amos Tversky, "The Hot Hand in Basketball: On the Misconception of Random Sequencing," *Cognitive Psychology*, Vol. 17, 1985, pp. 295–314.

[3]See Bruce Bueno de Mesquita, *The War Trap*.

[4]See, for example, David Krep *Game Theory and Economic Modelling* (Oxford: Oxford University Press, 1990). Also see, Paul Kemperer "Multimarket Oligopoly: Strategic Substitutes and Compliments," *Journal of Political Economy*. Vol. 93; 1985, pp. 488–511.

[5]Ken Binmore, *Fun and Games*. (Lexington, MA: D. C. Heath, 1991).

[6]See Roger Fisher and William Ury, *Getting to Yes* (New York: Penguin Books, 1981). Also see Howard Raiffa, *The Art and Science of Negotiation* (Cambridge, MA: Harvard University Press, 1982).

[7]For example, *Newsweek* magazine, in reviewing Fisher and Ury's (1981) book *Getting to Yes*, stated that "A coherent 'win-win' negotiation which, if it takes hold, may help convert the Age of Me to the Era of We." Quoted on the back jacket of *Getting to Yes*.

tion, or threaten and go to war with Iraq. Facing the peaceful initiative or a military action, Iraq can either retreat from Kuwait, or stay in the occupied country. If the United States has chosen a military option, the latter option will bring Iraq to a direct confrontation with the United States. Since there are two strategic options open to the two adversaries, there are four combinations of events. These are shown in Table 14.2, with the resulting outcomes. The numbers in the cells show preference ranking from the point of view of the two countries.

In this table, the numbers in parentheses represent the payoffs of the two contenders. The first number represents the U.S. payoff, and the second, the Iraqi payoff. From this matrix, you can see that from the U.S. perspective, peaceful negotiation is preferable to a military threat, if Saddam Hussein is expected to retreat from Kuwait (the payoff for a peaceful negotiation is 4 and military threat, 3). However, if Mr. Hussein decides to remain in Kuwait, U.S. would prefer to play its military card. Therefore, in that case, the payoff for a military threat is higher than that of opting for negotiations (2 and 1, respectively).

On the other hand, consider the situation from Saddam Hussein's point of view. By already occupying Kuwait, he has put himself in a box. For him a retreat is, by all means, less preferable to remaining in Kuwait. Although, he would rather retreat as a result of a negotiation (payoff is 3 as opposed to 0), his payoff is greatest, if he can remain in Kuwait despite a military threat from the U.S.

In sum, for George Bush, the path of minimum regret (or loss) is to opt for a military threat, and for Saddam Hussein, it is to defy international condemnation and to remain in Kuwait, despite the possibility of an armed conflict with a vastly more powerful allied force. Therefore, by following the logic of the two rational actors (George Bush and Saddam Hussein), we can see that given this scenario, the inevitable outcome is war.

This position, the lower-right hand corner of the matrix, is called an equilibrium solution after the work of a noted mathematician John Nash. This is called the **Nash equilibrium**, and it simply means that

it is an outcome from which neither player can gain by switching to another strategy.

That is, if the United States has chosen to confront Saddam Hussein militarily, Saddam does not gain by switching to a compromise option of getting out of Kuwait, since this would lower his payoff from 4 to 0. Similarly, since Iraq has chosen to remain in Kuwait, the best option that is open to the United States is to engage Iraq in warfare, otherwise, its own payoff is reduced from 4 to 0.

Table 14.2 Matrix of Payoffs for United States and Iraq

		Iraq's Options	
		Retreat from Kuwait	Remain in Kuwait
United States' Options	Peaceful Negotiation	(4,1)	(0,2)
	Military Threat	(3,0)	(4,4)*

* Point of Nash Equilibrium.

The Golden Rules of Decision Making under Uncertainty

The optimal strategic moves under a veil of uncertainty have come under a great deal of academic scrutiny. Based on this lengthy discourse, we can identify some sound advice.[8] Rule 1 is

Rule 1: Look ahead and reason back.

Behind most successful strategies (unless, of course, they are attained through sheer luck or serendipity) lies a conscious forward thinking. This action is the very essence of planning. However, while planning, one must think about the possible reaction of the opponent or the opposing course of action. The old native American adage of learning to walk a mile in someone else's moccasin does have a considerable degree of validity. This knowledge of putting yourself in your opponent's shoes requires drawing lessons from past experience to anticipate where your moves will ultimately take you. Thus, if John is a keen observer of human behavior, then the chances that he will be able to gauge his boss's mood are higher than if he were totally oblivious of her nature. Like the master chess player who anticipates several future moves of the opponent, the number one strategy for making decisions under uncertainty is to be informed and be able to anticipate the rival's move.

The second golden rule of decision making is

Rule 2: If you have a dominant strategy, play it.

It may not win you many friends, but if there is a dominant strategy open to you, you must play it regardless of the situation. This is especially true in **zero-sum games**, or where the player's interests are strictly opposed and one's gain is the other's loss. Thus, in poker or chess, both players cannot be winners. In such cases, players should be relentless in pursuit of the dominant strategies.

However, life outside of a card game frequently does not present zero-sum games. In other words, in a competitive situation, you can often find strategies which make both the contenders better off in a compromise, especially when a longer term perspective is taken. We will discuss this in the following section.

The third golden rule of strategy is

Rule 3: Successively eliminate all dominated strategies from consideration.

If there are a number of possible alternatives, you should compare the outcomes and eliminate the dominated strategies. The continuation of this process may bring you to a unique alternative which is better than all others. Choose it. As you can see, facing uncertainty, John proceeded to eliminate the dominated strategies one by one. This ultimately, led him to the best alternative within the given circumstances.

[8]Avinash Dixit and Barry Nalebuff, *Thinking Strategically.*

However, it may happen that the game does not have a unique dominant strategy but has a point of equilibrium, from which no deviation in strategy makes any of the contenders better off. In such a case, the golden rule of strategy is

Rule 4: In the absence of a unique dominant strategy, look for an equilibrium.

In the absence of a dominant strategy, settle for a point which is the best response under the circumstances, given the players' positions. However, the situation can be quite complicated. Game theorists have pointed out that there may be situations where there is more than one equilibrium position, or even none at all. Since the discussion of these complicated scenarios is likely to take us beyond the scope of this book, for the sake of parsimony we will hold these questions in abeyance and will simply refer the more curious readers (and certainly the adventuresome) to other books and articles.[9]

The Pitfalls of Dominant Strategy: The Prisoner's Dilemma

The existence of uncertainty often causes us to take actions which are not in our best interest. This is true for individuals, organizations, and even for nations engaged in international strategic moves. Often people get locked into a situation which is a poor solution for them; however, given the circumstances, there seems to be no way out.

Thus, in our example, if John knew for sure what his boss would do, his life would have been a whole lot simpler. Since he can only guess her feelings toward him, he may be completely wrong in his estimation. For example, he may be underestimating his own charm and may squander away an excellent shot at a more desirable job, as his boss is more favorably inclined to give him a good letter of recommendation than he thinks. Or alternately, she may be more than happy to get rid of him by writing a good letter. In either case, John has lost a great opportunity. Similarly, Jane, who is either a friend and a well-wisher for John or is keen on getting rid of an unwanted colleague, has lost an opportunity which is preferable to the status quo.

A situation such as this is known as the **prisoner's dilemma**. The name comes from a game that exemplifies a situation in which due to a lack of mutual trust, understanding, and cooperation, both parties must settle for a less than satisfactory resolution to a game. Let us consider the following scenario. You and your best friend have committed a crime. But there are no witnesses to this act. Therefore, the only way the district attorney can get a conviction is if either (or both) of you

---

[9]For a discussion of multiple equilibrium, see John C. Harsanyi, "Advances in Understanding Rational Behavior," in R. E. Butts and J. Hintikka (eds.), *Foundational Problems in the Special Sciences* (Dordecht, Holland: D. Reidel, 1977). For an application of this kind of a situation and its resolution, see Frank C. Zagare, "Rationality and Deterrence," *World Politics*, January 1990, pp. 238–60. Again, for the most readable explanation, see Dixit and Nalebuff, *Thinking Strategically*.

confess and turn state witness. Knowing this, the police have kept you in two different cells, with no possibility of communication. Your attorney tells you that you have two options: you can either confess or not confess. If you choose to confess, you will face two alternate scenarios. If your unrepentant, bull-headed friend does not confess, you will be rewarded by the witness protection plan, which, allows you to start your life over again. However, in such a case, your friend languishes in jail for 15 years. If, on the other hand, your friend (being gutless, as he is) decides to confess as well, both of you draw a five-year prison term.

If you decide not to confess, you face two consequences. If your unscrupulous friend betrays you by confessing to the crime, he is accorded the witness protection plan, and you would be sent to prison for a very long 15 year-term. However, if he turns out to be equally trustworthy, he will remain steadfast in not confessing, in which situation, the prosecution has no case, and both of you are acquitted.

What should you do? Before answering this question, let us consider the payoffs for each strategy, shown in Table 14.3.

You can see that if both of you confess, you each draw five years of imprisonment. If you confess and your friend does not, you get a reward in the form of a witness protection plan, while your friend gets a 15-year sentence. The situation is reversed if you choose not to confess, while your friend does. If neither of you confesses, both of you are set free.

Looking at this matrix, you can readily see that *collectively* both of you will be better off by choosing not to confess. However, you will reach this desirable position (from both of your viewpoints), only if you have *trust* in each other. Without the trust, you will reason this way: I have two strategies. I can confess or not confess. If I confess, the maximum I risk is five years in prison. But if I do not confess, the maximum I risk is 15 years in jail. Therefore, by following the decision rule of trying to minimize my maximum loss, I should choose to confess. This is called the **mini-max** rule. Following the same rule, your friend will arrive at the same conclusion, leading to a joint confession and a five-year prison term for both of you. You may also notice that in this case, confessing is the dominant strategy for both players.

Strategies to Overcome the Prisoner's Dilemma

You can see that following the rules of rational decision making under uncertainty can get you in an undesirable situation. There is no trust between you and your friend. If there were trust, you could have been free. We will discuss some of the ways of building trust and engineering cooperation in the subsequent section.

Table 14.3 Prisoner's Dilemma

Your Strategy		Your Friend's Strategy	
		Confess	Do not confess
	Confess	5, 5	Reward, 15
	Do not confess	15, Reward	0,0

However, often in life we have to proceed without trusting our adversaries. In international relations, nations get into wasteful arms races, (even those that can least afford to do so). By engaging in destructive labor disputes, industries around the world have been forced to shut down, causing unemployment for workers and economic hardship and loss of capital for owners and management. Many interpersonal disputes remain unresolved because of lack of trust.

However, trust is not developed in a vacuum. It can evolve through the players' trustworthy actions. If I know an individual to be reliable, I can expect cooperative behavior in response to my cooperative gesture. However, this balance of reciprocity of cooperative behavior can be broken because of greed or fear. In the example of a prisoner's dilemma, I can truly win if my comrade is made to trust me not to confess, while I turn star witness for the prosecution. This is greed. If I know that I can really win by an unexpected defection, like all other swindlers and con artists, I would slowly develop trust and then defect at the most opportune time. Or, I may defect out of fear—I may believe that you are about to break the trust, so I do it on my own. From violent ethnic strifes in Eastern Europe and Africa to relationships between friends and relatives, life is full of examples of such defections and the subsequent settlement for a suboptimal payoff for the players.

Greed and fear can be minimized if there is avenue for punishment for defection. The Mafia in southern Italy was able to maintain its ironfisted grip over the society by the use of *olmert*, the universal code of silence. Regardless of the situation, a defector was sure to face the fearsome wrath of the organization. This has kept the system of organized crime going for years. In the case of the larger society, punishment for the breach of contract comes from the established court system, with clearly understood and vigorously enforced tort laws. If the players are aware of the costs of defection, which are higher than the expected gains from defection, they can be assured of a cooperative game.

However, in many cases, such enforced cooperation is not viable. Therefore, a great deal of effort has gone into discerning the best strategies under complete uncertainty when cooperation between two players cannot be guaranteed. In the early 1980s, Robert Axelrod, a University of Michigan professor of political science, organized a tournament.[10] Game theorists from around the world submitted computer programs for strategies. These strategies were matched against one another in pairwise competition in games which were repeated 150 times. The strategies varied from extremely nasty (defection on every move) to saintlike (cooperation regardless of the opponent's action), from simple to highly complex systems of calculated cooperation and punitive defection. However, the game that received the highest number of points was one that was submitted by a professor of mathematics at the University of Toronto, Anatol Rappaport. This surprising winner had a simple strategy to follow, tit-for-tat. It started out by cooperating (that is, not confessing in our example). After this it simply repeated the last move of its opponent. In other

---

[10]The results of this tournament have been published by Robert Axelrod. See Robert Axelrod, *The Evolution of Cooperation* (New York: Basic Books, 1984).

words, if the opponent cooperated, tit-for-tat did the same. However, if the opponent defected, the strategy was quick on retribution to defect immediately. But if the opponent, having defected, went back to cooperation, it was quick to forgive after the necessary subsequent round of defection.

Axelrod attributed the success of tit-for-tat to four desirable qualities: clarity, "niceness," provocability, and forgiveness. The rules of this strategy are simple and, therefore, *clear* for everybody to see. The strategy is *nice* in the sense that it does not defect unprovoked. While it is quick to exact retribution for a breach of trust (*provocability*), it is equally quick to *forgive* and go back to the cooperating mode. Axelrod claimed great possibilities for tit-for-tat, and saw through it the evolution of a cooperative system. During the period of the renewed cold war (after the "evil empire" speech by Ronald Reagan), to many this simple strategy symbolized the hope for a new trusting world order.

However, despite the early hopes for greatness, later scrutiny found some damaging flaws in the universality of this strategy. First, we should remember that tit-for-tat was the winner only in cumulative score; it could not beat any strategy on a pairwise game. The best it could do was to tie with the cooperative (the saintly) games, or games following a strategy close to its own, starting with cooperation. It won overall because, since it echoed the opponent, it always came close, regardless of strategy—a quality which could not be matched by any other strategy.

The strategy of tit-for-tat also suffers from some other serious flaws. Dixit and Nalebuff (1991) point out that if two are playing this strategy, and one defects by mistake, or the move is seen as defection, the tit-for-tat strategy will kick in and the two will not be able to extricate themselves from the predicament of an ever-lasting cycle of retribution. Instead, they suggest a more forgiving strategy.

It is fairly obvious that no one would want to get mired in a game of "getting even." Mahatma Gandhi often quipped that the strategy of "a tooth for a tooth and an eye for an eye" ultimately leaves both the contenders toothless and blind. Across the United States a great deal of academic energy is being devoted toward finding ways to resolve seemingly intractable disputes. The key to the resolution of conflict lies in developing trust. When trust is lacking, participants need external enforcement of compliance through the imposition of cost for noncompliance, and always, in a conflict situation, should rely on bargaining. In their widely read book *Getting to Yes*, Roger Fisher and William Ury of the Harvard Negotiation Project attempt to spell out a number strategies to achieve agreement in dispute situation.[11] Although these stratetegies make extremely useful and lively debates, and I strongly recommend becoming familiar with them, their full discussion falls outside the scope of this book.

---

[11]See Roger Fisher and William Ury, *Getting to Yes* (New York: Penguin Books, 1981). Also see Roger Fisher and Scott Brown, *Getting Together: Building Relationships as We Negotiate* (New York: Penguin Books, 1988).

However, a final word of caution. By the very nature of disputes, not all of them have peaceful resolutions. For many different reasons, open hostility can often be deemed by the contenders to be more desirable than a negotiated compromise. In such cases, the problem lies with the basic values of the contestants, and the loser is destroyed and the victor has a hollow victory.

Key Words

Decision tree	Mini-max rules
Dominant strategy	Prisoner's dilemma
Expected payoff	Uncertainty
Game theory	Zero-sum game

Exercises

1. What is an expected payoff? How does the concept of expected payoff help analyze a situation of uncertainty? In this context, explain dominant strategy and the mini-max rule.

2. What is a zero-sum game? With an appropriate example, explain how conflict arises in the area of resource allocation (resulting from a public policy) because of a zero-sum situation.

3. What is a prisoner's dilemma? What are its outcomes for the participants? How can its development be prevented in real life?

4. In July, the parks and recreation department in your town wants to organize an exhibition of local arts and crafts. The department is considering whether to hold the exhibit inside the downtown sports arena or outside in its open air parking lot. However, the problem is that while planning the location of the exhibition, the planners face uncertainty with respect to the weather. The weather bureau reports that there is only a 20% chance of rain. If you hold the event inside the sports arena, after paying for the use of the facility, the town expects to break even if it rains. If it does not rain, the town makes a profit of $15,000 from the event. On the other hand, if the exhibition is held outdoors, it can be either a great success or a real failure depending on the weather. If it does not rain, the town will make a tidy profit of $35,000, but if it rains, it stands to lose $10,000. Draw a decision tree and explain the options open to the decision makers. What would be your recommendation?

5. Your town is located on the shores of Atlantic Ocean, directly in the line of devastating hurricanes. You are evaluating a policy to invest $10 million in emergency preparedness. It is estimated that the chance that a moderate to strong hurricane (categories 2 and 3) will come your way next year is 30%. The chance of being hit by a devastating category 4 hurricane is 5%. Right now, without this

additional preparation, the town can handle small tropical storms without much problem or property loss. If there is a category 2 or 3 hurricane, however, the estimated loss is going to be about $15 million, and for a fierce category 4, the estimated figure of property loss rises to as much as $50 million.

The financial administration department estimates that with the $10 million invested, the town will be able to withstand a strong hurricane of category 2 or 3 with a minimum damage of $5 million. Even if there is a giant hurricane of category 4, the damage estimate goes no higher than $20 million. Should the town invest the money in disaster preparedness? Draw the decision tree and write a report explaining your recommendation.

6. Suppose you are an aide to the governor of your state. Due to a much publicized story of a mentally deranged person killing a number of innocent victims in a crowded restaurant with an automatic weapon, the governor is considering a proposal to ban all sales of automatic guns within state borders. This is an emotionally charged issue, and the governor is keenly aware of the political cost of an unpopular decision. Facing this controversial problem, the governor sees three options: to do nothing, to propose a mild law banning the sale of a few such weapons, or to establish a commission. If the governor does nothing, there would be a political cost, to which the governor's advisors assign a value of -3. If a mild ban is unilaterally imposed, it will cause a net loss of popularity, valued at -2. On the other hand, if an independent commission is set up, the governor may be able to circumvent this lose-lose situation. However, the governor has no control over the recommendations of an independent commission. The commission may come up with a "do nothing" recommendation, which would absolve the governor for not doing anything (value = 0). On the other hand, the commission may recommend a mild ban, or a strict ban on the ownership of automatic weapons. The governor, however, retains the right to go along with the commission and reject its recommendations. If the commission recommends a mild ban, the governor can accept it for a political payoff +3, or may reject it and do nothing for a small loss of -1 (the commission has take the edge off the governor's inaction). The real problem may arise if the commission recommends a radical plan of gun control. If the governor accepts it, there will be a loss of -10, and by rejecting it the governor will incur a loss of -4. The governor's advisors think that the commission, which will have a broad-based support, will have a .3 chance of recommending to do nothing, a .5 chance of recommending a mild ban, and a .2 chance of going for a strict gun control measure. As a political analyst for the governor, what would be your recommendation and why?

7. Many social conflicts arise when rival factions place themselves in a prisoner's dilemma situation. With an appropriate example, discuss the prisoner's dilemma, pointing out the reasons for intractability of problems and suggesting some possible measures which may help generate cooperation among the parties involved.

Chapter 15

Queuing Theory and Simulations

Queuing Theory

The Problem

The director of the Youth Summer Employment Program of the Pennsylvania town of Masters needs help. As part of the Federal effort to keep urban youth busy during the idle summer months, the city has received money to employ 1,500 youngsters. Since it is expected that the program will attract a large number of applicants—by some accounts about 8,000—the city wants to find the optimal number of people to hire to interview and help fill out the forms of the applicants. It is estimated that, on the average, this will take about 15 minutes per applicant. If the city opens only one booth, it will take 8,000 x 15 minutes = 120,000 minutes, or 2,000 working hours. With a normal 40-hour week, it would take an individual at the booth 50 weeks, or a year (with 2 weeks of vacation time) to process all of the applications. On the other hand, if the city opens 50 booths, the entire job can be completed within a week. Therefore, facing a wide-ranging choice, the director wants an analysis on the optimum number of booths.

The Elements of Rational Queuing Model

This is a typical problem for the so-called queuing theory, which gets its name from the analysis of queues. The process of choosing the optimum number of queues is conducted within the context of two separate costs. If the city wants to hire 50 individuals for this job, it could be done in a week, or if it wants to hire 100 persons, the processing would take only 2 1/2 working days. Therefore, the more people are hired (or queues are opened), the more smoothly and quickly the whole job will be done. But hiring of personnel costs the city money. Hence, if too many are hired, public funds would be wasted. On the other hand, no body likes waiting in lines. Making people wait in lines has its own cost factor, especially in a democratic nation, to which elected officials and bureaucrats are sensitive. The lines to buy essentials in the former communist countries were legendary. Situations even remotely close to that in the delivery of public service would be simply untenable in the United States. Therefore, we can safely assume that the cost of keeping people waiting in line would depend on the length of time in waiting. That is, the longer people have to wait the greater will be their ire, and hence the cost to the organization. The optimum number of booths, therefore, will be at the point of intersection of these two cost curves. This is shown in Figure 15.1.

Figure 15.1 shows the equilibrium point at the intersection of the two cost curves. The cost of waiting in line is somewhat complex since it embodies two different factors. First, as we discussed earlier, the cost of waiting in line is a positive function of the duration of wait: the longer a client has to wait in line, the greater is the cost to the organization. On the other hand, the extent of wait is inversely related to the number of personnel hired to service the clientele—the length of the waiting period goes down as more people are hired. This line is derived by combin-

Figure 15.1 The Optimal Solution of a Queuing Problem

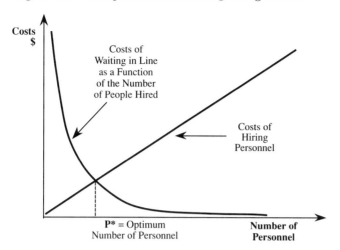

The optimal choice of a queuing model rests at the point where the cost of keeping the clients waiting is equal to the cost of hiring additional personnel to attend them.

ing these two ideas. That is, this line is expressed as the cost of waiting in line, as a function of the number of employees. You can see that when the number of personnel hired is low, the cost of waiting is high. This cost comes down as more people are brought in.

In contrast, the cost of hiring personnel is straightforward: the cost goes up as more people are hired. The point of intersection between these two curves is P^*. At this point, the cost of waiting in line to the clients is the same as the cost of hiring workers for the city. To the left of this point, too few people are hired. At that point, since the benefit of hiring additional workers outweighs the cost of their hiring, the city should employ more people. To the right of this point, the costs of hiring exceeds the benefit of lowering the waiting time.

The Diverse Structure of Queues

In queuing theory, the entire process starting with the arrival of a client, waiting in line, getting serviced, and then exiting is called the **queuing system**. The system consists of **arrival**, **waiting**, **service**, and **exit**. Queuing theory also talks in terms of **arriving units**, defined as the smallest entity that is handled by the system at a time. This unit can be a teenage job applicant, as in our current example, or can be a family of six applying for a visa to visit a country. While designing a queuing model, you must define your structure carefully, since it will have a definite impact on the time of service.

If the service is provided in one shot, it is called a **single-phase** system. For instance, the applicants get the necessary forms, fill them out, and get interviewed for a job in one single booth (as in a "one-stop-shopping"). On the other hand, if there are multiple points at which service is provided, it is called a **multiple-phase** system. In designing a queuing model, you must determine the queue structure and the number of phases.

Figure 15.2 illustrates three of an infinite variety of queue structures. In this figure, the lines show the direction of the channel, the circles are the clients, and the shaded squares are the service areas. The most elementary form of a queue is shown in Figure 15.2a where the queuing units stand in a single-channel, single-phase structure. Usually supermarket checkout counters are operated in this way. Another common form of queue is where the clients form one line up to a certain point, beyond which they split among a multiple of booths for service (Figure 15.2b). Finally, Figure 15.2c illustrates a two-phase system, where service is provided at two separate points. The design of the queues determines the level of complexity in the theoretical analysis and can save clients a great deal of annoyance and consequent costs to the service-providing organization.

A Deterministic Solution

The problem of choosing the optimum number of booths or queues can be solved simply if we are to assume that people are going to line up exactly on time, spacing themselves evenly on the line, like the bottles in an automated bottling plant, ready

Figure 15.2 Examples of Queuing Structures

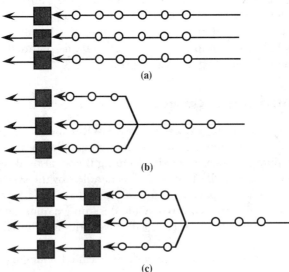

to be filled up with mechanical precision. "Totally unrealistic," you might think, but the assumption might be more useful than you think.

Going back to the example of the youth summer job program, let us assume that each working day the city expects 240 applicants to show up. If we assume that they will arrive at regular intervals during the eight-hour day, we will see 120/8 = 15 youths every hour. This pattern of arrival of 15 individuals per hour translates into one arrival every four minutes. It takes 15 minutes per applicant to provide the necessary service, and a single processor can serve 60/15 = 4 applicants per hour. Therefore, if there is only one window open at the start of the day, before the processing for the first client is completed, there will be a line of three. By the time the second person exits the system, the line has extended to seven. You can see that with only one person in charge of serving the applicants, the second one in line has to wait for 11 minutes (15 minutes service time - 4 minutes of arrival delay). The third applicant, who arrives within eight minutes of the opening of the doors, has to wait for 22 minutes {(15 x 2) - (4 x 2)}. If you are unfortunate enough to arrive half an hour after the beginning of processing, you will have to wait for 7 1/2 hours before being served. And, if you happen to arrive during the middle of the day (four hours after the doors open), you will be the sixty-first person to arrive that day, and you will have to wait for 13 hours for your turn at the booth!

The waiting time can be reduced significantly if there are two open windows. As you can see from the calculations presented in Table 15.1, the first two arrivals do not face any waiting time, since now there are two windows open. The third person walks in at the eighth minute and has to wait until the first window is available, which is going to be in the fifteenth minute. Therefore, for this individual, the waiting time is 15 - 8 = 7 minutes. The fourth applicant also has to wait for seven minutes. This is because, although window B gets free at the nineteenth minute (15 + 4 = 19 minutes since the second applicant arrived in the fourth minute), the applicant arrives in the twelfth minute. By following this logic, we can see that the luck of our mid-day arrival, the sixty-first applicant, is improving considerably as his waiting period has been cut to 240 minutes, or 3 1/2 hours.

By following this logic, we calculate that if the city hires three persons to process the applications, then the situation improves even more dramatically. Since

Table 15.1 Calculation of Waiting Time with Two Windows Open

Applicant	Arrives at nth minute	Goes to window #	Waiting time		
1	0	A			0
2	4	B			0
3	8	A	15 - 8	=	7
4	12	B	(15 + 4) -12	=	7
5	16	A	(15 x 2) - 16	=	14
6	20	B	{(15 x 2) + 4} - 20	=	14
7	24	A	(15 x 3) - 24	=	21
8	28	B	{(15 x 3) + 4} - 28	=	21
61	240	A	(15x30) - 240	=	210

we have taken the sixty-first arrival as the point of evaluation, calculations show (you can do it yourself) that this individual will have to wait for (only) an hour. This number is reduced to zero (no waiting) if there are four windows open (since it takes 15 minutes to process each applicant, with four windows open and applicants arriving at regular intervals of four minutes, one window will always be open for the next arrival). I have plotted the waiting time against the number of open windows in Figure 15.3.

Queuing Theory in an Uncertain World

To design the best configuration of queues, we must examine in detail the essential elements of the model, the arrival of the clients, the nature of the queues, and the service time. Let us discuss them systematically.

Arrivals

As you can tell, unless the arrivals can be completely controlled (which is scarcely seen in life), predicting the arrival of clients should be based on probability. That is, we should be able to plan on the basis of predictions such as, "The probability of 10 people showing up at the same time is 15%." The derivation of these probability measures, must depend on the past experiences of arrivals. To get this information, we must collect data on actual arrivals in either of two ways.

First, we can pick a time period (such as an hour, half an hour, of every 10 minutes, etc. depending on the nature of the operation) and record the number of people coming through the door during this time interval. A substantial database can be built by observing the arrival pattern over a number of "typical" days. Let us

Figure 15.3 Waiting Time and the Number of Windows

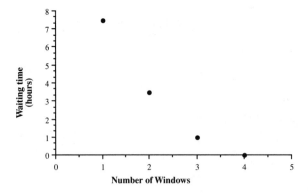

Table 15.2 Hypothetical Hourly Arrival Pattern
Within Hourly Intervals

Number of arrivals	Frequency	Probability of arrival (col. 2)/40
0 – 2	8	.20
3 – 5	10	.25
6 – 9	12	.30
10 –14	6	.15
15 –19	3	.075
20 –24	1	.025
Total	40	1.00

suppose we have observed the arrival pattern on an hourly basis over a 40-hour work week. This information is shown in Table 15.2.

Alternately, we may collect data by the time in between arrivals. Table 15.3 illustrates such a method of tabulating information. You may note that the time interval 0 implies a simultaneous arrival. The length of the interval depends on the analyst's judgment. However, the shorter the interval, the more detailed is the information. Also, since while calculating the average of grouped data we use the midpoint of each interval, a long time interval would make the average less reliable. Let us suppose that, with the help of a stopwatch and a counter, we have recorded the arrival pattern of 200 people during the course of a week. These data are presented in Table 15.3.

Although the arrivals can take any kind of shape, a number of studies indicate that actual arrival rates over a fixed period of time (as shown in Table 15.2) usually conform to a theoretical probability distribution called **Poisson probability distribution**. On the other hand, if we do not simply look at the time of *arrival*, but calculate the time gaps (interval space) between arrivals, it follows another theoretical probability distribution, called a **negative exponential**. Figure 15.4 illustrates the pat-

Table 15.3 Hypothetical Data on the Space
of Arrival within a Time Interval

Time interval (minutes)	Frequency	Probability (Col. 2)/200
0– 5	75	.375
6–10	62	.31
11–15	39	.195
16–20	13	.065
21–30	7	.035
31–45	3	.015
45–90	1	.005
Total	200	1.00

Figure 15.4 Poisson Distribution

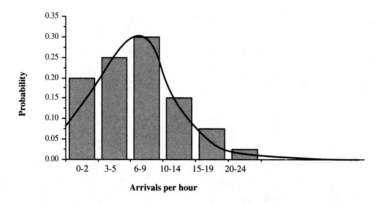

Arrivals per hour

tern of Poisson distribution, while Figure 15.5 shows a negative exponential distribution.

In this figure, The Poisson distribution assumes that the arrivals are random. This assumption of randomness implies that an arrival can occur at any time and that its probability is the same regardless how long the current waiting period is. That is, the clients do not adjust their behavior based on some external factor. For example, people living around the international border of United States and Mexico near San Diego have to contend with long lines at the border checkpoint, where at certain times waiting periods can extend to

Figure 15.5 Negative Exponential Distribution

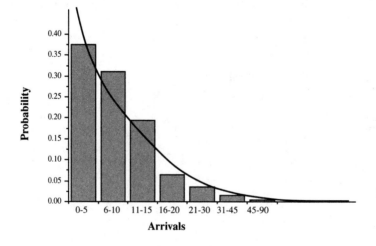

Arrivals

hours. Since there are several crossing points across the border, the local radio stations periodically announce the length of current waiting periods. People frequently change their plans either by hurrying up or delaying their departure to minimize waiting time. If this behavior substantially affects the traffic pattern, then we can assume that the arrivals at the border points are no longer random, as the future numbers are dependent on the current ones in the queue.

The arrival rate can also be calculated by looking at the interval space between arrivals. As Figure 15.5 illustrates, this pattern can often be approximated by a negative exponential curve.

The information that the arrival rates over a fixed period closely follow a theoretical probability distribution is of enormous value, since this can help us calculate the various results of a queuing model with a great deal of ease.

The Queuing Structure and Discipline

The proper functioning of a queuing model depends to a large extent on the configuration, length, and discipline in the lines. For instance, Figure 15.2 shows a number of different types of queue structures. The choice of the most appropriate structure will reduce the waiting time to a significant extent. In contrast, an ill-conceived design of queues will clog up the system and cause nightmarish waiting periods for service delivery.

The length of the potential line can be an important consideration. For example, a service establishment that routinely creates a log jam of traffic waiting in line will be considered a nuisance by its neighbors. Such establishments may often be kept away from neighborhoods by the use of zoning ordinances. If there is an artificial limit (imposed by the law), the mathematical queuing model will be able to handle it, but this will make the formulae quite complicated.

The final point about the queue is its discipline. If those waiting in line keep order, both the service delivery and its proper planning can be greatly helped. If people tend to break the line, either because they are culturally not used to standing in orderly lines (there are many places around the world where people are not used to standing in long, orderly lines) or because those who are in charge of running the operation routinely break the lines to accommodate important persons, members of their own family and friends, or those who might offer a bribe, no amount of sophistication in model building will be of much help.[1] Examples of smooth-functioning lines can be seen in large amusement parks, such as Disney World, where despite the huge lines, the park officials' experience in handling large crowds and the crowd's willingness to follow direction help considerably, even during the peak visiting periods. On the other hand, a small but rowdy and unruly

---

[1]An example of a legitimate breaking of the line is the operation of a medical emergency room. Similar kinds of line breaking can also be permitted in police work, fire prevention, and other emergency services, where need takes precedence over the time of arrival.

crowd (such as people waiting on line to buy beverages at some rowdy college foot-ball games) can make service delivery inefficient.

Service Time

The time spent in getting service can have a great degree of variability or can be totally fixed. At the one extreme are medical emergency rooms, where service delivery time can vary widely. At the other extreme are services which are doled out with mechanical precision, such as in our example of shows at Disney World and other large amusement parks. If the services do not fluctuate in duration, this helps the cause of planning with a queuing model immensely. However, even if the service varies in duration, one can find distribution patterns similar to those associated with the probability of arrival (Figures 15.4 and 15.5). When such patterns are pronounced, prediction becomes easier and the use of a model becomes more precise.

The Use of Theoretical Distributions in a Queuing Model

We applied the logic of a deterministic queuing model to the problem of processing applications for a youth summer job program. Since the assumptions of a deterministic model are totally unrealistic, we can introduce realism by assuming uncertainty in arrival and service delivery. We can safely assume that the probability pattern of arrival follows a Possion distribution, while service delivery time varies negative exponentially.

The most important impediment to the use of a theoretical model is mathematics, which can be quite involved. Since the level of mathematics required is generally beyond the scope of this introductory book, we can make use of a number of useful formulae without proof.

Let us reconsider our simple example of a single-channel, single-phase problem. This time, we assume that the arrivals follow a Poisson distribution, while service delivery follows a negative exponential form. The use of a mathematical distribution requires the assumption of independence. That is, the current arrival rate is not influenced by the length of waiting in the previous period. The assumption of independence also implies an infinite, or at least a very large (8,000 youths in our example), source of arrival. We will also assume away balking (not entering the queue because of its size), reneging (nobody leaves the queue before being served), and any limits on the length of the queues. Finally, it is extremely important to note that for the queuing theory to operate so that we do not get into a totally unrealistic situation where the lines spiral out to infinity, the mean arrival rate must be less than the service rate.

In queuing theory literature, the use of the following symbols is fairly consistent:

$$A = \text{mean rate of arrival}$$
$$S = \text{mean service rate.}$$

These two averages are calculated on the basis of their respective distributions. Once they are calculated, the entire gamut of results can be calculated using this information.

The expected number in the system: $\dfrac{A}{S-A}$ .... (15.1)

The expected number waiting in line: $\dfrac{A^2}{S(S-A)}$ .... (15.2)

The expected time waiting in line: $\dfrac{A}{S-A}$ .... (15.3)

The utilization factor, or the probability that when the next person

arrives he/she will have to wait in line. $W = \dfrac{A}{S}$ .... (15.4)

Probability that the system is idle: $1 - W$

Going back to our example, let us assume that the mean rate of arrival of youths is 15 per hour ($A = 15$). Also, if there are four booths open, then the average service rate is 4 per every 15 minutes, or 16 applicants per hour ($S = 16$). Armed with these two bits of information, we can estimate the following results:

The expected number in the system $= \dfrac{15}{16-15} = 15$

The expected number waiting in line $= \dfrac{(15)^2}{16(16-15)} \simeq 14$

The expected time waiting in line $= \dfrac{15}{16(16-15)} \simeq 94$ hours

The probability that the next arrival will have to wait in line $\simeq \dfrac{15}{16} = .94$.

We can calculate these numbers for any number of windows, as long as they are greater than 3, so that the arrival rate is less than the service delivery time. You may notice that unlike in the deterministic system, the waiting time does not go to 0, since we never know how these young men and women are going to come in. Therefore, as we increase the number of windows, the expected waiting time comes

Table 15.4 Results of a Queuing Model Based on Probability Distribution

Number of windows (1)	Number waiting in line (2)	Waiting time in hours (minutes) (3)	Probability of waiting in line (4)	Probability of an idle system (5) = 1 - (4)
4	14	.94 (56.4)	.94	.06
5	2.25	.15 (9)	.75	.25
6	1.04	.069 (4.14)	.625	.375

down drastically but does not become 0. Table 15.4 shows the results when 4, 5, and 6 windows are open for comparison.

Table 15.4 indicates that as the number of booths increases, the expected time spent on the line gets reduced to a significant extent, but at the same time, the probability that the system may be idle climbs steadily. As you can imagine, information such as this can be of great help to a decision maker trying to decide on the number of booths to open.

The Use of Simulations

The use of a mathematical model to derive the optimal solution works fine as long as the process is not terribly complicated. However, if there are complicated considerations, the mathematics can be harrowing and, indeed, may not even be solvable. For instance, the preceding example of solving a queuing model with Poisson distribution yielded quick results. After the mathematics were solved and the formulae were derived, we simply plugged in the two mean values and got the optimal solution. Yet, for all its apparent convenience, the problem of a single-channel, single-phase model in real life may not require the use of complicated mathematics, since the results may be obtained by a bit of logical thinking. On the other hand, if the problem at hand is more complicated (e.g., it has multiple lines and multiple phases, and the arrival pattern and service time do not conform to the theoretical distributions), we will be in deep trouble trying to solve the system mathematically. Therefore, in such cases, a better method of solving a queuing model is to employ a simulation model. Simulation models do not require a mathematical solution and, hence, are flexible enough to accommodate any kind of random pattern. However, they do require tedious calculations, best performed by a computer. As computer technology has improved, so has the use of simulations models in policy analysis.

Although I am discussing simulations in the context of a queuing model, they have wide-ranging uses in policy analysis, wherever there is an uncertain outcome.

There are many kinds of simulations, which vary from simple to highly elaborate. However, they usually fall in one of four categories: **system simulation**, **heuristic**, **game**, and **Monte Carlo**.

System Simulation

A system simulation attempts to reproduce the process with a number of equations. It is also known as "what-if" simulation. For instance, a city-run electric company expresses the demand for its product as

$$R = a + pQ$$

where R is total revenue,
a is fixed amount of demand,
p is price per kilowatt, and
Q is quantity consumed.

On the other hand, the cost curve for the production of electricity is

$$C = b + qQ$$

where C is total cost,
b is fixed cost of production, and
q is variable cost of production.

Since the city has a mandate to run its production at a break-even point (with no loss or profits), the point of optimal quantity to be produced can be determined by setting total revenue equal to total cost, and then solving for the quantity:

$$a + pQ = b + qQ$$
$$qQ - pQ = b - a$$
$$Q = \frac{b - a}{q - p}.$$

With this algebraic description of the process, the management of the plant can run various scenarios under which the various cost and revenue factors change, and then analyze their implications for the quantity to be produced. For example, the manager may ask, "What if the fixed cost goes up by 20%? In such a case, how much electricity should we produce?" This is a typical example of a simple system simulation. For a much more complex simulation, there can be many more equations of much more complex forms. These are extremely useful tools for analyzing the impact of a new tax on the economy, or discerning the role of the relaxation of a particular regulation on the market. A system simulation can be applied to a queuing problem by describing the system algebraically and then finding out the potential "choke" points, or the areas where the system can get clogged up if there is an unexpected number of arrivals.

Heuristic Simulation

Where a mathematical description is impossible because of extreme complexity of the system or the presence of a high degree of uncertainty about the relationships, a heuristic simulation may be the solution. A heuristic simulation involves expert judgment of developing various scenarios by using rules of thumb instead of precise numbers. Although a mathematical model can aid a heuristic simulation, it is typically done as a verbal process, the kind we discussed in judgmental forecasting chapter 5).

Game Simulation

A situation of conflict (such as the prisoner's dilemma, discussed in chapter 14) can be effectively simulated with the help of a game model. These models are ideally suited for uncertain situations involving strategies to deal with a potential threat. Although game simulations are widely used in many areas, their usefulness to the analysis of a queuing problem is limited.

Monte Carlo Method

A Monte Carlo model (name taken from the island city in Europe famous for its gambling casinos) deals with the probabilistic process of using random values to explore the nature of relationships within a system. Since Monte Carlo models require repeated iterations with numbers generated through random processes, the proliferation of computers has seen their extensive use in various fields of study, wherever there is a need to look into a **stochastic** or a probabilistic process. When dealing with a complex queuing problem, for which a mathematical solution is problematic, simulation based on a Monte Carlo model may provide the answer. This model is best described with the help of an example.

Let us go back to our original example of the Youth Summer Employment Program. Table 15.3 provides us with results of observation of actual arrival patterns for 200 applicants. These arrival data are expressed in terms of relative frequency or probability. We can generate the probabilistic arrival pattern by taking these probabilities. Let me explain how this is done.

Suppose, in a game, I have to take certain action if it rains. The game sets the chance of rain at 40%. If we want to simulate the chance factors, we may fill a bag with 10 balls, 4 of which will be, say, red. If I draw a ball without looking, and I get a red ball, I will assume that it has actually rained. By following this process, I have kept the chance of rain equal to its predicted value.

The Monte Carlo model uses this concept of simulation over and over again. By looking at Table 15.3, which has been replicated in Table 15.5, we can see that the probability that an applicant walks in the summer employment office within 10

Table 15.5 Simulating the Probability of Arrival by Using Random Numbers

Time interval (minutes) (1)	Frequency (2)	Probability (Col. 2) 200 (3)	Cumulative probability (4)	Random numbers (5)
0– 5	75	.375	.375	000–374
6–10	62	.31	.685	375–684
11–15	39	.195	.880	685–879
16–20	13	.065	.945	880–944
21–30	7	.035	.980	945–979
31–45	3	.015	.995	980–994
45–90	1	.005	1.000	994–999
Total	200	1.00		

minutes of the previous arrival is .685 (derived from the cumulative probability column). If we want to simulate the arrival of the next arrival within 10 minutes, we can do so by a process which is analogous to filling a bag with balls. For simulating probability, we can make use of a random number series.

Random numbers are generated by computers for these kinds of applications. We have reproduced a small segment of such a series in Table 15.6. You can start from any square on this table. Suppose we start from the top. Since we are considering probability figures up to three decimal points, by following the cumulative probability column, we have designated the corresponding three-digit numbers in the random series. Thus, if we start from top left-hand square, we can see that the first number is 044. Referring to Table 15.5, we see that 044 (in column 5) corre-

Table 15.6 An Example of Random Number Series

04433	80674	24520
60298	83456	72648
67884	05674	67533
89512	86497	51906
32653	59651	12506
95913	15405	45614
55864	21694	12085
35334	34127	01547
57729	78089	89154
86648	55639	76397
30574	72976	65812
81307	12875	85428
02410	98642	65835
18969	76912	37672
87683	89453	54353

■ **Solving a Queuing Problem in Real Life** ▬▬▬▬▬▬▬▬▬▬▬

1. Define the problem.
2. Design various queuing structures.
3. Observe and gather data on arrival patterns.
4. Observe and gather data on service delivery times.
5. Tabulate the data to generate the probability figures.
6. Write a computer program to simulate a "typical" day.
7. Run many iterations and then analyze the data.

---

sponds to the probability that the next applicant has arrived within five minutes of the previous one. The next set of numbers in the series is 602, which corresponds to the probability that the third arrival is between 6 and 10 minutes of the second. We can carry on this process of generating arrivals and then look at how the system is behaving, whether any bottleneck is being created, or whether there are idle resources.

This is a tedious process. Therefore, we can gladly delegate this task to our mechanical friends—computers. Once we have defined the system by specifying the number of windows and the configuration of the lines, and have provided the arrival probabilities based on actual observations, we can simulate a typical day with the help of a computer. If you know some computer programming, you can write a program which will generate random numbers and simulate arrivals of clients to the system. As the computer simulates many "typical" days, clear patterns should emerge as to the relative efficiency of the design of the queues. This information can then be profitably used for future planning of a service delivery system.

Key Words

Arrival	Queue structure
Arriving unit	Queuing system
Exit	Random number series
Game simulation	Service
Heuristic simulation	Simulation
Monte Carlo simulation	Single-phase queue
Multiple-phase queue	Stochastic process
Negative exponential distribution	System simulation
Poisson distribution	Waiting
Queue discipline	

Exercises

1. What is a queuing model? Give two examples of its possible use in the public sector.

2. Why is it difficult (but by no means impossible) to apply a queuing model in the emergency service delivery area? In this context, discuss the importance of queue discipline and consistency in service delivery time in the formulation of a queuing model.

3. Suppose you are to build a queuing model for a service delivery organization. What kinds of information would you need, and how would you go about collecting them?

4. Give an example where the queue size may be limited. What impact does it have on the formulation of a queuing model?

5. When is it appropriate to use a theoretical probability model to solve a queuing problem mathematically? When it is not possible to have a mathematical solution, what recourse does an analyst have? On an a priori basis, can you give real-life examples of when you can use a mathematical solution, and when it will be virtually impossible to do so?

6. In a city-run repair shop, the work crew comes in at a steady rate of 12 per hour to service equipment. On the average, it takes 45 minutes to service a single piece of equipment. With a five-person team, the shop can handle nine services per hour.

   a. What would the size of the queue be at end of four hours?
   b. What will be the waiting time for the sixth person in line?

7. Assume that for the same problem, the arrival of the work crew resembles a Poisson distribution, with the mean arrival of 12 per hour. The service delivery, on the other hand, follows a negative exponential distribution, with a mean of 16 per hour. With this information, calculate the following:

   a. The expected number in the system
   b. The expected number in the waiting line
   c. The expected time in the waiting line
   d. The probability that the next arriving work crew will find a queue
   e. The probability that the next arriving work crew will not have to wait in line
   f. Why is it essential to have the service delivery time greater than the arrival rate, for an analytical solution for a queuing model to exist?

8. For the model in the preceding question, suppose it costs $12.50 to hire an additional mechanic to service the equipment. On the other hand, it costs $15.00 an hour to hire a skilled work crew (who must remain idle while their equipment is being repaired). Should the city hire one additional mechanic? How many mechanics should the city be hiring optimally?

9. What is a simulation? Describe a system simulation, heuristic simulation, game simulation, and a Monte Carlo simulation.

10. Consider once more the example of a city repair shop. After observation of the actual arrival pattern of 300 individuals, the following table has been compiled. Using the random number series given in Appendix D, construct a typical eight-hour day, assuming service delivery time of 10 per hour.

Arrival Time (per hour)	Observed Frequency
0–4	49
5–9	66
10–14	125
15–17	45
18–20	13
21–23	2
Total	300

If this exercise were to be conducted over many iterations of "typical" days, explain how the information derived from this process could be used in decision making.

Chapter 16

Decisions by the Numbers: Problems and Solutions

The Princes, The High Priests, and Public Policy

My analyst friend looked dejected. Shaking his head, he told me that he had spent a great deal of time preparing an analysis on a particular issue. The results, based on a sophisticated mathematical model, clearly showed the "correct" course of action, yet the politicians rejected his recommendations and made an "obviously wrong decision." As I sympathized with my friend, I thought, Should this individual feel so dejected? Indeed, if you have spent a lot of time on a project, it is often impossible to separate your emotions from it. This leads me to the question of an analyst's role in a public organization.

From the days of prehistoric antiquity, the relationship between the princes and the pundits has been like a perfect marriage, with alternate periods of gleeful bliss and contentious acrimony. Unrecorded history is mute about the struggles between the chiefs and the shamans; the relationships between Alexander the Great and Aristotle, or Kautilya and his king Chandragupta Maurya of India, and Machiavellli and the Medici Prince are matters of myth. History, however, records that king Henry VIII, although respectful of his advisors Cardinal Wolsey[1] and Sir Thomas More,[2] did not let his admiration for these two men stand in the way of virtually imprisoning Wolsey and beheading Thomas More.

The economist's claim to the position of the high priest of policy formation came to fore during the Great Depression. Unable to account for the catastrophic swing of the business cycle, President Roosevelt (albeit reluctantly, and with much trepidation) sought the help of the famous British economist John Maynard Keynes. Contrary to the prevailing philosophy of the day, which looked at the free market as the ultimate arbiter of resources within society and minimized the role of government, Keynes, the father of modern macroeconomics, prescribed a strong activist role of the government to correct the course of market failure. Roosevelt's reservations about Keynes did not stem from the fact that he disagreed with the economist; rather he did not quite grasp what he was talking about. Robert Lachman reports that after the first meeting, an exasperated FDR grumbled to Frances Perkins, his Secretary of Labor, "I saw your friend Keynes. He left a whole rigamarole of figures. He must be a mathematician rather than a political economist." In his turn, Keynes expressed dismay to Ms. Perkins; he had "supposed the President was more literate, economically speaking."[3] The eventual ebbing of the

---

[1] In 1514, Henry requested Pope Leo X to perform the highly unusual but not entirely unprecedented action of making Wolsey (then a Bishop) a "caldinal sole" by himself. In his letter to Leo on August 12, 1514, Henry claimed that he "esteemed Wolsey above his dearest friends and could do nothing of importance without him." Jasper Ridley, *Statesman and Saint: Cardinal Wolsey, Sir Thomas More and the Politics of Henry VIII* (New York: Viking Press, 1982), p. 48.

[2] Henry showed deep personal respect and friendship for More, and often stated that he valued no one's approval more than his. See Carolly Erikson, *Great Harry: The Extravagant Life of Henry VIII* (New York: Summit Books, 1980), p. 120.

[3] Robert Lekachman, *The Age of Keynes* (New York: Random House, 1966) p. 123.

Great Depression accorded Keynes and his followers unprecedented access to the inner sanctums of politics. The pinnacle of the economic profession as the shaper of public policy came during the Kennedy-Johnson administration, when the theories of market manipulations were formally put to test. In an act of egregious hubris, the economic profession claimed to possess the analytical key which would stave off the ups and downs of the market cycles, and it laid claims to a universally acceptable road map for social engineering.[4]

The impacts of these exaggerated claims were amply reflected in the public policy literature of the day. Rapid development in the techniques of operations research (a number of which are included in this book) pushed expectations way beyond the realms of possibility. The compelling simplicity of analytical logic snared its biggest catch, the President of the United States. President Johnson pushed the Planning Programming and Budgeting System (PPBS), which sought to proclaim the primacy of analysis over politics.[5] The application of PPBS was imbedded in the larger context of a systems approach, which attempted to view the process of policy formation as an integrated system in which the "correct" course of action followed from the setting up of an overall goal and then the logical construction of the problem. For instance, a budgetary process is one of allocation of scarce resources among competing uses. We can go about it through the usual process of political give and take, based on fragmented (incremental) perception of the problem, or (perhaps by using something like a linear programing model) set up goals and the constraints, and then solve the problem mathematically to reach the optimal solution. In this book I have presented you with techniques which exude an overwhelming sense of cool objectivity. The appeal of the systems approach is so compelling that until recently, many textbooks on public policy and public administration called the systems approach the *rational* approach. If you call something rational, the flip side is irrational.

The unbridled exuberance of the 1950s and 1960s regarding the application of quantitative techniques in public policy analysis was tempered by scholars like Aron Wildavsky and Charles Lindblom. Their cogent criticisms and the years of failed experiments of application of objective techniques in "messy" reality have

---

[4] See Robert Carson, *What Economists Know* (New York: St. Martin's Press, 1990).

[5] Frederick C. Mosher, author of *Program Budgeting* (Chicago: Public Administration Service, 1954, pp. 48–49), defined PPBS as follows:

Planning involves first the conceiving of goals and the development of alternate courses of future action to achieve the goals. Second, it involves the reduction of these alternatives from a very large number to a small number and finally to one approved course of action, *the program*. Budgeting probably plays a slight part in the first phase but an increasingly important and decisive part in the second. It facilitates the choice-making process by providing a basis for systematic comparison among alternatives which take into account their total impacts on both the debit and the credit sides. It thus encourages, and provides some of the tools for, an increasing degree of precision in the planning process. Budgeting is the ingredient of planning which disciplines the entire process.

You may note the obvious emphases on comprehensive analysis in this definition of PPBS.

given way to pragmatic compromises.[6] In this concluding chapter, we explore this ongoing controversy in the study of public policy formulation.

My friend's woes, described at the beginning of this chapter, exemplify one of the deepest chasms in policy analysis. The problem at hand has three essential components: the first relates to the choice of proper methodology of analysis, the second relates to the presence of biases in human perception, and the third is concerned about the relative weight given to economic analysis vis-à-vis political concerns in the process of policy adoption. The methodological debate centers around the question of using the proper method of analysis to discern the *correct causal linkage* between the dependent and the independent variables. However, even when the correct methodology has been chosen, the cogency of the analysis may be clouded by the presence of *systematic biases*. These biases can result from the personal prejudices of the person conducting the evaluation, or they may be due to "group think" resulting from the environment within an organization. This area of policy making is possibly the least understood and, thanks to the work of social psychologists, is beginning to emerge as the focal point of much of the recent theoretical literature.

Finally, even after a policy has been analyzed with the best possible methods of analysis, with no discernable biases, a storm of controversy swirls around the issue of who *should have* the last word (the princes or the pundits) for its adoption as the official public policy. Therefore, this concluding chapter discusses the aspects of these three fundamental issues of public policy analysis and offers a few solutions.

The Methodological Question

The purpose of policy analysis is to choose the proper methodology which will determine the **causal linkage** between the dependent and the independent variable, **generalize** the results, and establish the **control** or the policy direction. This complex process may be described by drawing an analogy from the game of pool, shown in Figure 16.1. In this figure, the direction in which the 8-ball (the dependent variable) moves is linked to the movement of the independent variable, the Q-ball. Once we establish this causal linkage, we can think of the desired **goal**, which in this case is the direction (and also speed) in which the 8-ball moves. From the policy standpoint, we have a set of **control** variables (in this case the cue stick). As

---

[6] To continue with the saga of princes and high priests, the economic profession hit its lowest point when President Reagan, unable to make his chief economic advisor Martin Feldstein (a widely respected economist) see the efficacy of the "supply side economics," started to ignore the Council of Economic Advisors. A frustrated Feldstein resigned. The Council was brought back to its old glory by President Clinton, although much to the chagrin of the profession, Clinton passed over the recognized gurus and chose the relatively unknown Laura Tyson from Berkeley.

Figure 16.1 Methodology for Policy Analysis

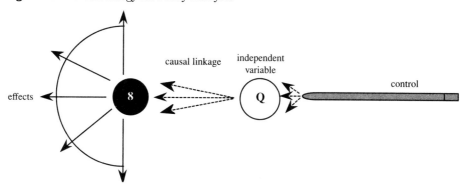

you can see, as an advisor to the pool player, we can recommend that to send the 8-ball in the desired direction, she should apply a certain amount of force at a particular angle on the Q-ball with the stick.

Similarly, suppose we are concerned about teenage pregnancy. Our policy goal is to reduce it by 15% within the next three years. If our analysis demonstrates the causal linkage between pregnancy (the dependent variable) and the dissemination of reproductive information through television advertising (the independent variable), we can estimate the amount of money (the policy or control variable) that will be needed to accomplish the policy goal. Therefore, in this process, our first task is to establish the causal relationship between the dependent and independent variable. For this we need to choose the appropriate research design. This choice research method will only point us to the pertinent technique, and we will still need to worry about whether the quantitative model contains sufficient analytical capability for the results to be generalized for practical use. Hence, I first address the question of research design, and then discuss generalization of the study results.

Designing Research

Research design, or the plan of inquiry into the string of causality that links the dependent variable with a set of independent variables, can take a number of forms, which vary in scientific rigor. Broadly speaking, research designs can be classified under the headings **experimental** and **quasi-experimental**. In experimental designs, the subjects of the inquiry can be assigned randomly across experimental groups and control stimulus, and the independent variable can be manipulated at the will of the experimenter. On the basis of the controlled experiment, the researcher is able to draw the necessary inference regarding the shape of the causal linkage, which can then be generalized for the purpose of designing appropriate policy to achieve a certain goal. In contrast, the quasi-experimental research design lacks one or more of these necessary criteria. Let me explain this with appropriate examples.

Experimental Design

The classic experimental design is found in controlled group experiments, mostly in the fields of medicine, natural sciences, and experimental psychology. The most rigorous of all designs is the so-called Solomon Four-Group design.[7] In this experiment, the subjects were randomly assigned to four groups. Then they were further divided into two more groups. One from each of the broad groups was introduced to the control stimulus. (Thus, to determine the effectiveness of a new drug, the patients can be separated into two groups.) Then within each group, they were further divided into two groups, one given the medicine and the other a placebo. This experimental design is shown in Figure 16.2.

After the administration of the new drug, the researcher would look into the progress of the patients' ailments. If the differences between the control groups $(a_1 - b_2)$ and $(b_1 - a_2)$ were significant, the researcher could experimentally establish a causal linkage between the new drug and the disease.

We can think of numerous examples in medical or biological research where it is possible to exert such an amount of control over the subject population, where inferences are experimentally drawn and proven with repeated experiments. New drugs come on the market; evidence is gathered about various carcinogens; human behavioral patterns are established in clinical tests.

Posttest-Only Control Group Research Design

Although it is evident that one should establish causal linkages with the help of Solomon Four-Group tests, conducting these elaborate tests can be extremely expensive, time consuming, and in most cases virtually impossible. Therefore, frequently a researcher must be satisfied with posttest-only control group experiment design. This less restricted research design is shown in Figure 16.3.

As you can see, in this case, without creating four groups, we have assigned subjects randomly into two groups: one exposed to the stimulus and one not. If the difference between the two groups is found to be statistically significant, we can establish the string of causality.

The criterion of random assignment of the subjects for the experiments is important. If they are not assigned in random order, some other forms of systematic biases may creep in to contaminate the experimental results. If the groups are separated by sex, for instance, the results may be invalid since the division along the gender line would introduce another independent variable along with the independent stimulus variable.

---

[7] For a more detailed discussion of research design, see David Nachmias and Chava Nachmias, *Research Methods in the Social Sciences* (New York: St. Martin's Press, 1976). Also see, Carl V. Patton and David S. Sawicki, *Basic Methods of Policy Analysis & Planning* (Englewood Cliffs, NJ: Prentice-Hall, 1986).

Figure 16.2 Solomon Four-Group Experimental Design

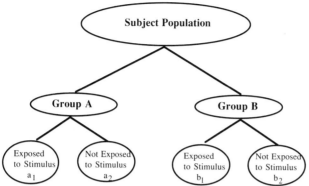

Quasi-experimental Design

The problem with the real world facing the policy researcher in social sciences is that it can rarely be controlled. Experimental research designs require the random distribution of the subjects, separation into distinct groups, no effect of lapsed time to dilute the effect of the stimulus, and ambiguity about the nature and extent of the independent control variable. Yet, in the frequently confusing and highly overlapping world of human interaction, such divisions or strict interpretations are problematic. For instance, if we want to test the hypothesis that strength of family ties has a direct bearing on a student's educational performance, we should be able randomly to assign family stability to the subject group, which is clearly not possible. Similarly, when the control variable is not amenable to change, we may have to make do with comparison between groups which are not strictly similar. Second, contrary to research in the fields of medicine, natural sciences, and experimental psychology, research efforts in social sciences are seldom directed toward discerning a stimulus-response reaction among the subject population. Instead, social sci-

Figure 16.3 Posttest-Only Control Group Design

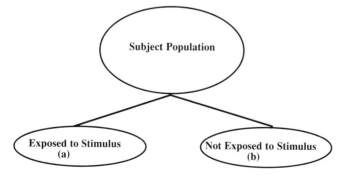

ence is primarily interested in understanding the causal linkage between a set of preexisting social or economic characteristics and the revealed dispositions of preference, attitude, values, and orientation. Thus, for policy purposes, we may want to predict housing demand based on the demographic and economic characteristics of the city population. Finally, even the nature of the independent variable may be open to question, and as such cannot be defined with a great degree of specificity. In sum, these are the stuff the nightmares of the quantitative analysts are made of. Yet this is the world of satisficing endeavor, quasi-experimental research design.

When Control Groups Are Not Strictly Equivalent.   During the course of conducting research, you will frequently encounter situations in which pre- and postcomparisons have to be made on groups which are not the same in the strict sense of the term. Yet there is sufficient commonality between the two that allows you to draw conclusions provided the distinctive features are isolated and their possible effects on the stimulus response are analyzed. For instance, a school district has embarked on a new program to increase the SAT scores on mathematics. To ascertain the success of the program, you may want to compare two schools which have experimented with this new program. Since no two schools are identical, for a valid conclusion to be made, you must control for the social and economic differences (such as parents' income, percentage of minority and bilingual population, etc.) which may contaminate the results.

When Time Influences the Outcomes.   The experimental design assumes that the stimulus response is instantaneous or is free of the influence of passing time. For example, suppose you are conducting research in microbiology and are interested in the impact of a certain chemical compound on the growth of a particular class of bacteria. If the results of the application of the chemicals on the bacteria dish are instantaneous, you have no problem and can clearly see the test results right before your eyes. However, if the gradual growth of the culture over a period of time is required, you will certainly not keep the dish exposed to the outside environment. You will take the precaution of keeping it free of the environment because you do not want the results to be contaminated by some other external agents. However, in society no such protection from the outside elements can be provided. This creates a number of interesting problems.

Suppose you are trying to establish a causal relationship based on time series data of dependent and independent variables. You are monitoring these two variables periodically over time. If the two series move in sequence, by observing their correlation you can hypothesize that the dependent variable is being influenced by the independent variable. But can you prove it? No. Unfortunately, without a controlled experiment, there is no way you can definitively prove a causal connection between the dependent and the independent variable in social sciences.[8] With time,

---

[8] Statistics are fairly truthful in calling the quantitative treatment "correlation" rather than causality; a strong correlation between two variables simply implies co-occurrence. From the strength of this relationship a social scientist would infer a causal linkage.

the dependent variable is influenced not only by the independent variable but a host of other factors. Therefore, theoretical controversies in social sciences are seldom resolved. For instance, every undergraduate macroeconomics textbook will tell you that if you increase the money supply in the economy, prices will increase. In fact, some of the best-known monetary economists of our time have spent their entire academic careers trying to establish this relationship. But if you simply plot the data, they will not exhibit any systematic correlation.

Then how can we discern a causal relationship between the dependent and the independent variable based on time series information? First, we look at the strength of the correlation and with the help of statistical tests try to minimize the error of accepting a false hypothesis as true. Second, if there are influences of other external variables, the research plan should be carefully designed to eliminate their contaminating influences.

Choosing the Right Model: How Much Abstraction?

Our problems do not end with the choice of a research design. The next problem that confronts us is the choice of a particular model. The fundamental problem is that we are trying to match two dissimilar worlds; the quantitative techniques are based on objective, structured, scientific reasoning which is superimposed on a largely unstructured, subjective world of public policy analysis. Can or should the two meet? The incongruity between the two separate worlds can be broadly classified in two categories: (1) A model, by definition is a truncated version of reality. Therefore, can we trust models to shed light on real-world problems? (2) The models of optimization assume uniformity of social objectivity. How relevant is it to assume singularity of purpose in a pluralistic democratic society?

Quantitative techniques of decision making encapsulate complex reality into *abstract models*. Hence, a model *always* deviates from reality. This deviation from reality inevitably makes quantitative models suspect. As reality is truncated with a series of assumptions, the questions about the relevancy of the model become paramount. In a highly controversial essay, economist Milton Friedman contended that[9]

> Truly important and significant hypotheses will be found to have assumptions that are wildly inaccurate descriptive representations of reality, and, in general the more significant the theory, the more unrealistic the assumptions.

Professor Friedman argues that a model should be judged not on the basis of the nature of its assumptions or hidden values, but on the basis of its capability to predict accurately. Friedman's spirited defense of building abstract models has been taken to heart particularly by economists. Because of the extensive use of models which often reduce reality to unrecognizable forms, economists have been subjects

---

[9] Milton Friedman, *Essays in Positive Economics* (Chicago: University of Chicago Press, 1953), p. 3.

of much derision, scorn, and, at the same time, awe.[10] In fact, for nearly half a century since its publication, Friedman's arguments (known as the F-Twist theory) have generated one of the longest academic debates regarding assessment of the validity of abstract (and often patently unrealistic) models.[11] I will not get embroiled in the controversy, but only remind you that a model should not be rejected simply because it makes simplifying assumptions about the real world. Because of the extreme complexity of the outside world, we frequently need these restrictive assumptions to separate fundamental global patterns from local, particular, or ephemeral effects. These restrictive assumptions help us define the domain where results are expected to hold. The boundaries of this narrow domain can then be expanded by systematically removing some of the restrictive assumptions to make the results more proximate to reality. Another important reason for building models is that they help us examine the internal consistency of reasoning. As a result of this structured logic, models frequently explain behavior and reveal unsuspected relationships. Finally, the use of a model eliminates the need for ad hoc reasoning and helps us understand our mistakes when our predictions go awry.

Let us consider a specific example. In chapter 6, while discussing Markov's chain, I gave an example of projecting the number of drug users on a college campus. My projection was based on a survey showing how many students used drugs last year and are continuing to do so and how many nonusers have started to use drugs. On the basis of this finding, I explicitly assumed that these relationships would persist throughout the four years of the freshmen entering college. Along with this explicit assumption, I also implicitly assumed that no other external factors were going to have a significant effect on this trend pattern. It is clear that these were bold assumptions, and it is easy to find reasons to question their validity. For instance, we did not include the transfer students coming in with a possible different behavioral trend; neither was the effect of education or psychological maturity on the student population considered. The inclusion of these factors may alter the projection in a significant way. But in support of the model, I may argue that first, given the set assumptions, this is the likely trend, which I might not have been able to guess without a formal model. Second, if there are reasons to believe that as the students mature and are better educated their level of addiction goes down, we can modify the model to allow for this change of relationship. Finally, at the end of four years, if I find that my projections were seriously flawed, I can go back to my original set of assumptions and try to correct the mistakes. The explicit assumptions and structured reasoning allow me to process feedback information in a way which would have been impossible if I had made the projections based solely on "gut feelings," intuition, and ad hoc reasoning.

---

[10] You may have heard the story of an economist in a group that is stranded on a desolate island, with only a can of beans. The economist suggests, "Let us assume a can opener."

[11] For a concise history of the relevant arguments, see A. Musgrave, "Unreal Assumptions in Economic Theory: The F-Twist Untwisted," *KYKLOS*, Vol. 34, 1981, pp. 377–78.

Whose Goals to Maximize?

Philosopher Karl Popper has spent his life examining various aspects of social sciences. As I mentioned in chapter 4, he likened the building of a theory in social sciences to the construction of a structure above a swamp. You dig deep enough for the posts to hold the structure, but not deep enough to reach the solid ground as absolute truth, which may or may not exist. In a similar fashion, while constructing a scientific theory, you attempt to make the structure internally consistent on the basis of testing "falsifiable hypotheses" (you don't make hypotheses, such as the existence of the eternal soul, which cannot be proven or disproven) with empirical data. Therefore, ideas which are held as self-evident truths, often disappear like morning fog under the microscope, exposing the vacuous nature some of the most cherished goals of our organized society. Upon scrutiny, truth, justice, liberty, and equality reveal their relative nature.

When using the quantitative techniques discussed in this book, the first and foremost assumption we make relates to their goals. As we use these techniques to look for the "best" possible solution to allocate scarce resources, we attempt to maximize *social welfare* or net benefit. At the outset, this seems like a simple and innocuous assumption. But the question quickly becomes, What is social welfare? For instance, any public policy—whether regarding global warming, national defense, or local zoning ordinances—must begin by stating the goal which it wants to achieve for the betterment of the community. Let us first consider the problem of defining what is best for the community.

Terms like *the people* or *the nation* are staples of political rhetoric. Politicians of all shades, from democrats to the demagogues, have taken utmost liberty with these terms. The President sets national agendas and boldly declares what the nation needs. The opposition, on the other hand, claims to know what "the people" want. But the question of who is "the nation" or "the people" has occupied some of the best minds of our intellectual history. French revolutionary philosopher Jean Jacques Rousseau, the most celebrated proponent on "general will," assumed its existence as a self-evident truth. As George Sabine points out,

> The general will . . . presented a unique fact about a community, namely, that it has a collective good which is not the same thing as the private interests of its members. In some sense it lives its own life, fulfills its own destiny, and suffers its own fate. In accordance with the analogy of an organism, which Rousseau had developed at some length in the article on political economy, it may be said to have a will of its own, the "general will (*volenté général*)."[12]

However, the problem with accepting the existence of an overarching social objective is that it comes directly in conflict with individual freedom and individual

---

[12] George H. Sabine, *A History of Political Theory*, 3rd ed. (New York: Holt, Rinehart and Winston, 1961), pp. 588–89.

rights. If you assume the existence of a collective will or, in economic terms, **social objective**, you implicitly assume its predominance over individual aspirations. For instance, if you believe that for the collective good of the entire world the hunting of whales must stop, the interests of the whaling industry and the people dependent on it must be sacrificed for the greater good of the community. In fact, the irony of the matter is that even Rousseau, the most vociferous promoter of general will, could not reconcile its contradiction with individual rights, and got hopelessly entangled trying to show that the general will of the community is the origin of all individual rights, liberty, and justice.

Nearly a century later, Karl Marx proclaimed the eventual triumph of communism, when the dictatorship of the proletariats would impose the will of the working class on society. Vladimir I. Lenin and the leaders of the Communist party put the Marxian concept in practice. Unfortunately, the practical application of the general will did not fare much better than its theoretical conceptualization. Despite a strong ideological base among the leaders, the French Revolution degenerated into a bloody anarchy, and the Soviet Union turned out to be a dictatorship of the communist party rather than of the proletariat. In fact, during the last 50 years, scholars looking into the notion of social welfare have come to a general agreement about the impossibility of defining these terms in any coherent fashion.[13]

Conflict between individual objectives and the collective good arises because every public policy ultimately affects how resources are distributed within a society. When whaling is banned, the whalers lose; antipoverty programs are funded by money taxed away from the rich and the middle class; the construction of a freeway helps some (communities on the freeway, the trucking industry, the motorists, the suburbs, etc.) while hurting others (communities bypassed by the freeway, the railroad industry, the center city, etc.). Why should those who would lose be willing to bear their losses? They should bear these costs for the greater good of the community, of course.

Concerned about the totalitarian implications of the "collective will," a group of social scientists began to stress individual rights. The most notable proponent of this view was the turn-of-the-century social scientist Vilfredo Pareto. In search of a definable social objective, Pareto developed the following scenario and then asked a question: Suppose a society is composed of two individuals, one fabulously wealthy, the other a starving destitute. If the government forces the wealthy to part with a small fraction of his fortune to share with his impoverished brethren, can we say that the society is better off? You can make this wealthy person as wealthy, and the unfortunate soul as deserving of public assistance, as you can imagine.

A happy compromise for the dilemma posed by Pareto was attempted earlier by a group of British social thinkers called the **utilitarians**. Jeremy Bentham, the best-known member of this group, argued for the maximization of total utility with

---

[13] See Kenneth Arrow, *Social Choice and Individual Values* (New York: John Wiley and Sons, 1951).

the society. The utilitarians, in effect, had argued that the marginal utility of a dollar diminishes with a person's level of income. Thus, the loss of one dollar is likely to get less attention from a wealthy person than a similar loss by a poor person. Therefore, by extending this logic, you can argue that if you take away, say, $1,000 from the wealthiest individual on earth and give it to a starving person, the rich person's loss will be felt less than the increase in benefit by the poor. As a result, the redistribution of income will result in an increase in the total utility of the society. By following this formula, we can keep on taxing the rich to pay for social programs until the point is reached where the two marginal utilities (one negative and one positive) are equal. However, the problem with such a position is that interpersonal utilities are not measurable. We cannot put numbers on personal feelings of utility. Therefore, if we encounter a miserly rich and a rather happy-go-lucky poor person, the redistribution of income may not affect the total utility of the society at all. In fact, the strict adherence to this rule can even lead you to some rather odd policy prescriptions. For example, if you assume that an individual with severe physical limitations or of old age is less capable of enjoying life than a healthy, young person, then it can be deduced that the marginal utility of a dollar, beyond what is needed for meeting the basic care and health needs, is less for the elderly or physically handicapped person than for the healthy and young ones. In such a case, the utilitarian solution may be a redistribution of wealth in favor of the young and healthy. These examples are, of course, designed to demonstrate the problems of attempting to make interpersonal comparisons of utility.

Following this line of logic that interpersonal utilities cannot be made, Pareto argued that under no circumstances is a society's welfare increased by a redistribution of income from the rich to the poor. The only way the society can be considered better off is if any one of its members gets more income (stumbling on an oil well, for instance) without taking anything away from the others. This is known as the **Pareto principle**. Therefore, public projects which benefit one group at the expense of some other cannot be justified in the name of aggregate social welfare. Extending this line of reasoning, around the turn of the century Swedish economist Knut Wicksell proposed the **unanimity law.**[14] Under his scheme, every elected member in the legislature should have veto power, and no legislation could be passed without unanimous approval. Or, at least, to prevent the tyranny of a simple majority, Wicksell proposed that the requirement to be no less than, say, five sixths of the members of the assembly.

Since it is almost inconceivable to have a public policy which has no redistributive component, clearly both the Pareto principle and the unanimity law are incompatible with any sort of government activism. Therefore, these two principles imply a system of free market without any government intervention. In economic

[14] Knutt Wicksell, "New Principles of Just Taxation," in Richard A. Husgrave and A. T. Peacock (eds.), *Classics in the Theory of Public Finance* (New York: Macmillan, 1958).

theory, free markets carry some strict characteristics. A perfectly competitive market embodies some of the most utopian concepts of eighteenth- and nineteenth-century liberalism.

A perfectly competitive market must have numerous buyers and sellers, free entry into and exit from the market, free flow of information and resources, no transaction costs, and must be free from externalities. The condition of numerous buyers and sellers implies that there is no concentration of market power for any individual or group of individuals to manipulate market outcomes. Monopoly causes the market price to increase (to account for the added monopoly profit) and supply to go down (the only way to maintain a high level of profit). The presence of monopoly also prevents other prospective competitors from entering the market by putting up all kinds of barriers. Similarly, the market process breaks down if there is no free flow information. For instance, Coca-Cola closely guards its secret formula from its competitors. If the formula is made public, it will lose its monopoly hold on those customers who are loyal to the taste of the fuzzy drink and will have to compete with others with exactly the same taste. The presence of barriers to entry and exit from the market causes the development of monopoly. In economic literature, these factors are called *indivisibility*. For instance, automobile manufacturing in this country consists of three giants: General Motors, Chrysler Corporation, and Ford Motor Company. In contrast, there is a lot of competition among, say, plumbing contractors. The reason new companies cannot just spring up in auto manufacturing is that this industry requires huge amounts of capital investment. Therefore, because of this indivisibility (the capital requirements cannot be chopped up into small parts), consumers are forced to deal with huge oligopolists (a handful of sellers). Similarly, the presence of high transaction costs (such as the cost of litigation) prevents people from challenging businesses, or each other, violating an important condition for a perfectly competitive market. Also, a free market gets distorted because of the presence of externalities. For example, a company which pollutes the environment does not pay for the full costs of its products, which must include price of the cleaning up. Without interference from the government, firms are less likely to take steps to produce in an environmentally safe way, since there is hardly an incentive within the market process for doing so.

Because of these market failures, the government must step in to correct the situation. In broad terms, a government must take the leadership in providing public goods, reducing poverty and extreme concentrations of income, reducing the swings of business cycles, and planning for the future growth of the economy. Public goods are those which we tend to consume jointly without worrying about their utility going down because of the sharing. For instance, when we breath in clean air, tune in to public radio and television signals, or are protected from external enemies by the armed forces, we are enjoying the fruits of public goods. However, these goods cannot be provided by the private sector because, typically, these goods do not offer quick profits and have huge indivisibilities (for example, it requires an enormous amount of money to develop a network of national freeways). Second, and most importantly, these goods suffer from the *free-rider* problem, expounded by Mancur Olson.[15] That is, since these goods are for joint consumption, everybody can enjoy their benefits regardless of contribution. For example, if I have not earned enough money to pay high taxes, this would not prevent me from driving down the highways or feeling safe from external military intervention. Therefore, since my share of benefits has no link with my contribution, it would be foolish (at least by economic reasoning) to want to contribute to it. Hence, if each individual takes this "rational" approach, no public good will ever be provided.

Similarly, left to its own, the market tends to concentrate income in the hands of a few. The traditional neoclassical economists and the proponents of the so-called trickle-down theory would argue that the true solution to a nation's poverty and income inequality lies in the rate of economic growth. That is, poverty is reduced as the economy goes through a sustained level of economic expansion, and not through a forced redistribution of wealth by the way of a welfare state. Although there is a great deal of truth to the proposition that long-term poverty is reduced through overall economic growth, it is doubtful that without active government intervention the level of disparity between the have and have-nots is lowered.

Left to the ebbs and tides of the market, the economy is likely to have wild swings of inflations and recessions. As Keynesian economics argues, active government involvement is needed to inject anti-inflationary and antirecessionary fiscal and monetary policies.

Finally, the role of government planning in shaping the course of the economy has been an anathema at least in political rhetoric in the United States. Although planning has been part and parcel of development of many sectors of the U.S. economy (such as zoning, transportation, the space program, education, etc.), the ideology of free market has often viewed such involvement with a considerable degree of suspicion. However, recent success stories from Japan have put government involvement in the planning of industrial development in a different focus. There has been a good deal of talk about a joint partnership between government and industry.

Endemic to all these discussions of government activism in the economy is the question, Whose interest should government maximize? For example, in the United States debate continues unabated as to the desired level of allocation of public goods, such as national defense, health care, access to free education, or environmental protection. The level of effort at reducing income inequality is often questioned in the egalitarian societies of the Scandinavian countries. Even in Japan, the prudence of a close relationship between government and industry through the fabled MITI (Ministry of International Trade and Industry) is not beyond reproach.

However, except for ardent libertarians, the need for government as an active participant in the economy is universally accepted. The question remains as to the level of this involvement. Recognizing the importance of the issue, a group of economists has tried to come up with a theoretical compromise between the needs of

---

[15] Mancur Olson, *The Logic of Collective Action* (Cambridge, MA: Harvard University Press, 1971).

society and the needs of individuals. Two British economists, Nicholas Kaldor and Sir John Hicks, argued that if a particular project creates so much gain for those who stand to benefit from it that they can compensate the losers for their losses and still remain better off, then we can argue that the entire society is better off as a result of the project. In other words, suppose a particular project causes A to gain $10 while costing B $7. Then A can pay B $7 as compensation, which leaves him with $3 of net gain. This does not violate the Pareto principle that a society should be considered better off only if at least one person gains without taking anything away from anybody else in the community. But the question remains as to how to compensate the losers. If the losers can be clearly identified (such as in declaring eminent domain for acquiring land for building roads), laws in all democratic nations guarantee the payment of adequate compensation. Yet in many cases the losses are diffused over a large part of the society and the losers cannot be identified or their losses adequately measured. In such cases, Kaldor and Hicks argued that we should not worry about the actual payment of compensation. As long as we can demonstrate that the benefits outweigh the costs, we can proceed with the project with a clear conscience. Such a position ultimately rejects the Pareto principle in favor of a greater "social good," but, more importantly, turns a blind eye to those who may suffer losses as a result of a public project but have no recourse to receive adequate compensation. There are many examples of even the most well-meaning public policies creating intolerable misery for a small group of individuals. Much-needed highways cut through the heart of a community. River dams, while producing electricity and irrigation, flood land of immeasurable value to inhabitants. However, as long as we can show that the net social benefits are positive, Kaldor and Hicks feel justified in ignoring the plight of the losers, who often turn out to be the least resourceful members of the society.

In contrast, philosopher John Rawls offers a different set of criteria for judging social welfare. For deducing the fairest rule of distribution, Rawls poses the following question: Suppose I have a pie which I am going to distribute to the class. However, I can cut the pie either in unequal portions (with one person getting the lion's share, while others literally get the crumbs) or I can divide the pie equally among the students. These portions are going to be distributed by a random draw over which you have no control. Rawls calls this random draw "the veil of ignorance." You have to choose whether you want the pie to be cut in equal portions or unequally. Rawls argues that by the precept of rationality, you should opt for an equal distribution, since in that way you minimize your chances of maximum loss. By extending this logic, Rawls claims that since we cannot choose our parents, if we were asked how the wealth in society should be distributed, we would opt for a way that protects the share of the most unfortunate lot. Hence, according to the **Rawlsian criterion**, a distribution of income should be judged by the absolute level of well-being of the least fortunate ones of the community. Suppose there are two communities, A and B, with the following sets of income distributions: A = [$10, $25, $8] and B = [$200, $150, $5]. The figures within the brackets show the levels of wealth held by the six members of the two communities. According to the Rawlsian criterion, one should prefer the distribution of A since the worst-off member of the community is better off than the poorest member of community B. Therefore, the Rawlsian principle throws its entire weight on the well-being of the poor and disregards the welfare of the others in the community. The Rawlsian criterion seems extremely interesting at the outset. However, we all know our relative positions in society. Therefore, it is highly unlikely that people would be willing to forgo their privileged position without some serious prodding.

We are back to square 1 once again with regard to the question of assessing an overall goal for society. Let us summarize the discussion. The use of the quantitative techniques covered in this book calls for the definition of a goal to be maximized. However, despite centuries of intensive search, the process of constructing a true social welfare function remains elusive. Any definition of one single objective inevitably requires the trampling of contradictory individual aspirations. On the other hand, a total dependence on the individual leaves us with an anarchic system of no government. Efforts at compromise are tantamount to a theoretical copout.

Defining the Social Goal: A Pragmatic Compromise

It is obvious from our discussion that there is no easy and elegant escape from this theoretical quagmire. As professors Edith Stokey and Richard Zeckhauser eloquently put it,

> Philosophers and economists have tried for two centuries to devise unambiguous procedures for measuring and combining welfares of two or more individuals to provide a measure of total social welfare. Their quest has been as successful as the alchemists' attempt to transmute lead into gold. The occasional flickers of hope have all been extinguished; not only have no feasible procedures been developed, none are on the horizon.[16]

The theoretical quest may not have been able to find a perfect solution, but it certainly has been able to define clearly our zones of ignorance with regard to public policy analysis. In ultimate analysis, knowing what we can know may be just as important as knowing what we cannot know. Hence, government policy makers all over the world keep on doing their jobs by setting up community goals. Parks and fire stations are built, excess cash is invested, endangered species are protected, and the effects of public policies on the target population are evaluated. Therefore, solution to the problem of setting goals for social programs must be sought not from those who have made this problem their lifetime preoccupation (and have gone nowhere), but from those who have attempted to define it from a practical standpoint.

In ancient Greece, the battle of ideologies was waged between the elitist

---

[16] Edith Stokey and Richard Zeckhauser, *A Primer for Policy Analysis* (New York: W. W. Norton, 1978), p. 276.

Sparta and the democratic Athens. In Sparta, there was hardly a debate over the will of the people. In contrast, the Athenians (in their experimentation with direct democracy, through endless fine-tuning) made sure that each of their 10 tribes was properly represented in the council and that every male citizen of Athens had a chance to be on a jury and to express his opinion in a court of law. In a representative form of democracy, the articulation of overall goal is impossible. Therefore, in such a system, we must accept the directions set by the majority of the elected representatives as the expression of the wishes of the people, an expression of their collective will.[17] At the federal level, for example, the President sets the tone for budgetary allocation through the Office of Management and Budget, and expresses it through the State of the Union message. Similarly, the governors set the overall goals for the states, and at the local level, depending on the form of government, either the mayor or the council provides direction. These goals are transformed through the legislative process and, in their final form, are articulated in the enabling legislations. Therefore, for the want of a better method, as practitioners we must accept these as the goals for specific government programs and projects.

The Test of Pudding: Suggestions for Framing an Analysis

The true test of pudding lies in its taste, and a model, in the final analysis, must be judged by its analytical capability. However, since we all operate within a limited time span, our quest for a model must *satisfice*—our effort must be satisfactory and it should be considered sufficient given all the constraints. Professors Edith Stokey and Richard Zeckhauser (pp. 277–86) have given pragmatic advice which is probably the best we can come up with. These solutions essentially suggest that the analyst takes a limited and more practical view and attempts to find the optimal solution within a limited boundary instead of trying to find an unbounded, global solution.

Limit the Number of Alternatives

The first practical suggestion toward formulating a policy relates to the number of possible alternatives. When buying a car, if you are determined by get the best buy, you may have to spend the rest of your life looking for it. Yet, without clairvoyance, the first option that you had (and passed on to look for an even better deal) might have been the best one to come your way. Therefore, as an analyst, you should keep the number of alternatives for evaluation within limits.

---

[17] Although once again Professor Kenneth Arrow has thrown a cold blanket on the assertion that the outcome of a democratically set-up vote should be accepted as the "will of the people" by demonstrating that under certain conditions the outcome of a vote may not reflect the "true" preference of the majority, for the most part we have no alternative but to accept this less than perfect outcome.

Consider Only Changes in Social Welfare

Suppose you are considering a program to provide summer jobs to inner city youths. Evaluate the program incrementally from the point of view of how much this program is going to change the youths' economic condition, rather than getting hopelessly entangled by the question of inner city poverty and the total picture of social deprivation. In doing so, you can keep the evaluation within a manageable framework by concentrating only on the marginal rather than the total change in social welfare.

Use Income as a Proxy for Welfare

"Money cannot buy happiness," goes the proverb, implying that the relationship between wealth and happiness (or utility) may not be a direct one. Yet in practice, we have no recourse but to accept money as the measure of individual utility. Thus, in a situation where one gains at the expense of another, we must be able to compare the gains and the losses in monetary terms. The acceptance of this proposition leads us out of the theoretical quicksand of utility measurement into the confusion of imputing monetary values to gains and losses. As we saw in chapter 12, this is by no means an easy task. But we can be assured that this is a practical problem with practical solutions rather than a theoretical problem with no solution at all.

Determine Aggregate Social Welfare

In the previous pages we looked at some of the theoretical reasons why it is impossible to arrive at an objective function for an entire community. Since every stated goal carries implications for redistribution of income, we as practitioners must have some rule for judging between two sets of income distribution. For instance, at the outset it seems like a noble idea to spend money on educating the nation's children. However, since the bulk of school funding in the United States is generated from property tax revenue, those who do not have school-age children (those without children or with grownup ones) share the tax burden with those who do, without deriving any direct benefit for the expenditure. Of late, this has set the stage for some rather notable confrontations.

To recapitulate, the utilitarian position provides an unworkable set of criteria since it is impossible to measure interpersonal utility. The Pareto principle turns out to be equally unhelpful, since it only builds barriers against government interventions. The Kaldor-Hicks proposal does not address the problems of those who might lose as a result of a public project, while the Rawlsian criterion is only concerned with the welfare of the poorest members of the community.

Politically, the easiest projects to accept are those that benefit a specific group of people while distributing the cost over a large, diffused populace. Most of the so-called pork barrel projects passed by legislators to benefit a few specific segments of their constituents falls in this category. Since the burden of these programs fall on the faceless masses of taxpayers, most of these projects go unopposed. When the benefits are diffused but the costs are specific, despite wide-spread popular support it is extremely difficult for the political process to allocate resources. The gun control issue would fall in this category. Polls consistently indicate that a solid majority of Americans support some kind of measure which makes it difficult for people to own a gun. However, the beneficiaries are diffused with no single powerful group of constituents fighting for such measures, while the small but powerful gun lobby is vociferous in their opposition to any kind of restrictions on gun ownership. Thus the legislation is extremely difficult to pass. In the third category, where both the beneficiaries and losers are diffused, inaction is the most likely outcome. For example, almost everyone agrees with the need to have an education reform. But it is extremely difficult to pinpoint the winners and losers since both of them come from the citizens at large. Therefore, it is hardly surprising that for all the talk, precious few actions are undertaken. The final set of possibilities arises when there are clear winners and losers. These are the most controversial redistribution issues. Cases like those for and against a new airport in London, the environmentalists versus the timber industry in the Pacific Northwest, or the issues relating to redressing past injustice such as the Affirmative Action program are examples of projects with clear winners and losers. I have presented these four categories of winners and losers in Table 16.1.

As indicated in Table 16.1, conflict and controversies arise when there are clear winners and losers. Since the theories of social welfare are of little help, pragmatic principles may be developed for accepting or rejecting a project. These principles call for value judgments on the part of analysts. This is all right as long as the basis for these judgments is made clear so the political decision makers can arrive at their own conclusions. Therefore, as a practical guide, you may make your recommendations on the basis of the following criteria.

Accept the project if

1. *The gains are significantly larger than the loss, the two groups are roughly equal in their social stature, and the loss poses only a minor problem for the losing group.* For instance, suppose you are evaluating a project to build an access road for linking two major thoroughfares. The vast majority of the inhabitants are going to benefit from the project; however, a small group of people living near the project is complaining about an increased level of traffic with all its accompanying problems. The commissioned environmental impact report fails to detect any significant loss to the environment or to the community. In such a case, you may rec-

Table 16.1 The Effects of a Public Project

Losers		Winners	
		Diffused	**Specific**
	Diffused	Inaction	Easy passage
	Specific	Difficult passage	Conflict

ommend the project over the objections of the affected community group on the basis of the aforementioned principle.

2. *If the benefits to the society are overwhelming compared to the cost to a specific group, or alternately the cost of inaction is enormous.* Consider, for example, the plight of the whales. It is fairly clear that without a moratorium, the whales would soon be extinct. However, the imposition of such restrictions would cause significant losses among the whaling communities in countries like Japan, Iceland, Russia, and Norway. Similar examples are banning the trade of ivory or rhino horns. In each of these cases, the cost of inaction is an irreversible loss to the global ecology. On the other hand, the banning imposes severe economic hardship on communities dependent on whaling or the families of the poachers, who are attracted to this lucrative trade and are driven by extreme poverty. Yet the decision to ban hunting of these endangered species is made because of the overwhelming nature of the net benefit. To be fair, the human plight of those dependent on these trades should be compensated whenever possible. In fact, some of the poorer countries like Brazil are demanding compensation from the developed nations for preserving their rain forests.

3. *If the benefits to the winners of a proposed policy are greater than the loss to the losers, and the gains are designed to equalize some of the losses resulting from past discriminatory policies.* Many affirmative action plans and other projects to remedy racial inequality, such as forced school desegregation and busing, would clearly fall in this category. Also, if community A has received some special benefits (such as California benefiting from increased defense expenditures during the 1980s), when the time comes for the second round of allocation, cases may be made for equalizing the beneficiary effects of public investment for communities who did not receive the benefits the first time.

In contrast, a proposed project should be rejected if

1. *The net benefit is positive but the cost imposed on a specific group is significant.* In the late 1980s, the government of India proposed a giant river project to provide much-needed electricity to urban centers and to meet the needs of India's growing industrial sector. The project was also to provide irrigation to a large area of farmland, to allow farmers to be independent of uncertain rainfall. However, the project was also to flood an area inhabited largely by a group of tribal people, who stood to lose their ancestral homes and their identities. A group of social workers and environmental advocates took up their cause and convinced the World Bank to withdraw its support for the project since the costs to these hapless people were going to be immeasurably high.

2. *The effect of redistribution is highly desirable but it does not pass the test of positive net social benefit.* We frequently encounter cases when the cause is noble but the costs do not justify the action. It is indeed desirable to provide the most comprehensive health care to everybody in the country regardless of income, age, or the level of

care needed. Yet the costs of doing so are prohibitive. Therefore, government agencies are being forced to come up with plans to prioritize their program.

These criteria are, by no means, perfect. However, given the practical needs of the public agencies, these are probably the best we can come up with. An objective analysis backed by a generally accepted guideline of fairness can make decision making more efficient and acceptable to the vast majority of people.

Make Sure that the Process Is Fair

During our discussion of social welfare, I briefly described the centuries-long effort to come to grips with the question of the ethics of redistribution of income. As I have noted, these impressive efforts have yielded little. At this stage, I add a caveat to this age-old debate.[18] Professor Kenneth Arrow pointed out, the quest for a universally acceptable social welfare object is futile, and it stands to reason to abandon a fresh new expedition to find the holy grail. Instead, we may concentrate on the issues of justice and fairplay from the standpoint of procedural justice. The objective of procedural justice is not to alter the final outcome to achieve fairness, but to ensure that the process by which the resources are being allocated is fair. The use of quantitive techniques can often help promote the notion of fairness in the allocation of resources by exposing hidden assumptions and values.[19]

The concept of procedural justice can be explained with the help of an example. The rewards of a lottery are unfair, since one ticket wins the bulk of the money with small amounts given to other winners. But for the vast majority of the players, the lottery yields nothing. Why then do we not complain about the gross inequality? We do not complain because we know that *the process of choosing the winner is fair.* That is, we accept the final outcome because we believe that each person buying a ticket has an equal shot at the prize money. We know the process by which a winner is determined (that is why the actual drawings are often done in front of a television camera), and when purchasing the ticket we agree to play by the rules of the lottery. If these conditions were violated, we would be extremely dissatisfied with the outcome. When people go over the speed limit and get a ticket, they seldom complain about the ticket itself, but they may complain about the way they were treated either by the police or the court system.

The concept of procedural justice has a number of important components. Political scientist Robert Lane points out that the concept of procedural justice

---

[18] See Kenneth Arrow. *Social Choice and Individual Values,* New York, John Wiley & Sons, 1951.[19]

For a classic exposition of essentially the same set of arguments, see Allen Schick, "System Politics and Systems Budgeting," *Public Administration Review,* Vol. 29, March-April 1969, pp. 139–150. The flip side of this argument is that frequently an agency might use these quantitative techniques either to rationalize its preordained decisions or as a public relations device to placate critics and ward off outside intereference. As an example, a later study by Harvey Sapolsky, *The Polaris System Development: Bureaucratic and Pragmatic Success in Government* (Cambridge, MA: Harvard University Press, 1972), has claimed that contrary to the much touted stories of success, the use of PERT network analysis had virtually nothing to do with the real progress and problems of the Navy's Polaris project development.

must include dignity, relief from procedural pain, uniformity of standard of justice, and the outcome of justice itself.[20] The dignity aspect of procedural justice has three components: the recognition, protection, and preservation of self-esteem of every individual in the society; a sense of controlling one's own destiny; and an understanding of the justice process. If an individual is stripped of his or her dignity, even the most equal distribution of wealth will seem oppressive, arbitrary, and capricious. The second aspect of procedural justice is the relief from procedural pain by which every individual is assured of a speedy disbursement of justice without a great deal of cost of justice procedure. If the process of seeking legal justice is cumbersome and time consuming, justice cannot be preserved. The third aspect of procedural justice is the resonance between the standards of justice of the judge and the judged. If one is being judged by a standard that is completely alien, one cannot accept the verdict as just. The sense of justice, therefore, must include the convergence of value and the notion of ethical standard. The final aspect of procedural justice refers to the actual justice itself, or the provision of some minimum economic safety net. This aspect of procedural justice may come close to the Rawlsian concept of distributive justice. Since it is hard to convince a starving individual of the fairness of the distributive process, the notion of procedural justice must include some minimum guarantee of economic well-being. Therefore, when it comes to the question of reallocation of resources, a public agency may do well to engender a sense of fairplay among the affected parties to minimize conflict.

Decisions Within an Organization: How Objective Is the Analysis?

In 1962, President John F. Kennedy confronted the Soviets in a direct showdown of force during the Cuban Missile crisis, and won. The mighty Soviets blinked. The word got out to the farthest corners of the world that President Kennedy had won the contest. However, a torrent of evidence coming out of Moscow after the dissolution of the Soviet Union demonstrated how this much celebrated stance of the young President brought the world to the brink of the ultimate failure of public policy—a full-scale thermonuclear exchange between two superpowers. The experts were wrong in almost every aspect of judging both the capability and the resolve of the Soviet Navy stationed in Cuba to confront a U.S. invasion. Had this information been known at the time, would there have been any difference in the policy of the White House? We can only guess. If the conflict had escalated into a third world war, how would any possible survivors have viewed this "bold decision?"

The answers to these speculative questions do not exist. However, the fact of the matter is that the experts were wrong in estimating the enemy's capability. Of course, this was not the first time that the experts had been wrong in their assess-

---

[20] Robert Lane, "Procedural Justice: How One is Treated vs. What One Gets." Paper presented at the Annual Meeting of the International Society of Political Psychology, Amsterdam, 1986.

ment for the formulation of public policy, nor will it be the last time. The experts, after all, are human. During the last half a century, a considerable effort has been made toward understanding the process of human reasoning and the sources of possible biases and pitfalls.[21] Broadly speaking, we can identify the possible sources of biases as the perceptions of an individual conducting the analysis, and the external constraints imposed by an organization on its analysts.

The Individual Biases

The quality of decision making can be seriously impaired by the presence of systematic biases in our own reasoning processes. I discussed the problems created by relative perception of the world in chapters 4 and 13: Biases and prejudices creep into the analysis either unconsciously or by deliberate design. However, recent discoveries by cognitive scientists cast a much darker shadow on the assumed objectivity of human rationality. These discoveries have come primarily in the area of individual decision making under uncertain conditions. The fundamental rule of decision making under uncertain condition assumes that we calculate the expected net reward of our action. In other words, this simply means

Take action if: (Probability of success x Reward) - (Probability of failure x Cost) > 0.

However, research in the human reasoning process has uncovered the existence of a number of psychological biases which stand in the way of making rational decisions based on the aforementioned criteria. In fact, recent research in human rationality has raised doubts about human beings as competent statisticians in their everyday lives. In his famous novel *The Rebel*, French writer Camus argued that humans are not smart enough to be rational.[22] In a different way, Nobel laureate economist Herbert Simon made the same points in his analysis of *satisficing* behavior. Over the decades, this has become a staple term of analysis in organizational decision making.

The Organization and the Question of Objective Rationality

Since policy analysts work within an organization, in addition to their own inability to remain objective, they face the problem of the organization imposing its biases on them. As we interact in a group, we inevitably create our group persona, complete with its own mythology of heroes and villains—a tunnel vision often shaped by the needs of the group rather than the needs of the larger society. The problems that are created in the process can be classified in four categories. The first set of

---

[21] For an excellent survey, see John D. Mullen and Byron M. Roth, *Decision Making: Its Logic and Practice* (Savage, MD: Rowman and Littlefield Publishers, 1991).

[22] A. L. Camus, *L'Homme Révolte* (Paris: Gallimard, 1951).

problems arises because of our inherent need to conform and be accepted as team players. As a result, decisions which are contrary to conventional wisdom are pushed aside. The second set of problems relates to the psychological need to avoid confronting our deep-rooted values even in the face of a changing world that offers contrary factual evidence. Therefore, to avoid the stress of decision making, we may often opt for stalling a decision, hoping that in time the problem will go away. This ostrich solution of burying our head during a sandstorm may create a deeper problem for the decision maker in the long run. Problems may also arise from the experts having a stake in their theory, choosing to ignore reality which does not conform to the theory. This process of rationalization can lead to serious policy problems. The fourth set of problems arises as we confront a complex world which does not lend itself to a quick and simple solution. As our cognitive capabilities are taxed, we try to deal with the problem by "stuffing" the complex reality into a simplified model, which can cause serious errors in judgment. Unless we are aware of these psychological impediments, policies based on judgment (with or without the aid of quantitative analysis) should always be suspect. Let us discuss these points in detail.

The Odd Man Out: The Fear of Nonconformity

Decision making within an organization is often fraught with the danger of being subjected to organizational thinking. In our lives we look for harmony and the warm feeling of being part of a group. In the process, we may often reject courses which may upset the established norm and "rock the boat." In the famous hierarchy of needs proposed by psychologist Abraham Maslow, the need for belonging is one of the most powerful fundamental human needs, and ranks immediately after the basic physiological needs. The strength of this *groupthink*—a term developed by Irving Janis,[23] who has written extensively in this area—even in the most mundane of matters has been demonstrated in numerous laboratory experiments. For example, researcher Solomon Asch asked his subjects to judge which of three lines on a card was closest in length to a standard line. To discern the effect of social pressure on individual judgment, Asch stacked the groups with "plants," who gave the wrong answers. Not wishing to be different from the overwhelming majority (seven "plants" out of groups of eight), nearly 80% of the subjects agreed with the majority and picked the obviously wrong answer. However, the experiments also found that the subjects were much more apt to provide the correct answer if they had even one ally in the group.

Therefore, while using judgmental methods, we should guard against groupthink of all kinds. The history of public policy making is full of examples of analysts who went along with the conventional wisdom and failed to inspect the signs of a changed market, social, or political climate. Detroit auto makers failed to realize that the American love affair with oversized cars could be over due to a steep

---

[23] Irving Janis, *The Victims of Groupthink* (Boston: Houghton Mifflin, 1972).

increase in gasoline prices. This put them years behind in the production of smaller and more fuel efficient cars. President Johnson failed to read the mood of the American people and got deeper into the quagmire of the Vietnam war.

Groupthink can be avoided by following the practice of collecting anonymous opinions during a Delphi session discussed previously in chapter 5. However, care must be taken to preserve anonymity so that the decisions are not contaminated by groupthink.

Subjective judgment can also be clouded as people tend to defer to an authority figure. Psychological experiments have shown that individuals, especially when working alone, are particularly prone to the influence of an authority figure.[24] However, the extent of this influence can be significantly reduced when subjects work in a group.[25] Therefore, from these psychological studies, we can extrapolate that analysts working alone (especially in small organizations) are more likely to be influenced by the larger group and authority figures within the organization than ones working in large groups (presumably in larger organizations). However, the size of team will be no guarantee against biased analysis due to the presence of its own groupthink. Instead, an enlightened management interested in getting independent assessments from its analysts, would do well to encourage dissent and different points of view.

The Challenge to the Basic Values: The Solution of an Ostrich

Max Weber, the classical organizational theorist, envisioned a perfect bureaucracy where decisions emerged from the process alone. In the Weberian model, all authorities emanate from rules from above.[26] Therefore, an organization can work like a well-oiled machine, where decisions are made with mechanical ease as part of a routine operation. However, the essence of the world is change. Change imposes uncertain choices on decision makers by depriving them of choices based on process alone. The presence of uncertainty poses risks of making the wrong decision, so decision making is a stressful process for the decision maker. One of the most common reactions to stress is to bury our head in the sand and wait for the storm to be over. This ostrich mode of decision making can create serious problems. By careful studies psychologists have been able to chart the course of various conflict situations resulting from uncertainty.

In a classic study, Kurt Lewin systematically categorized the stress resulting from making a decision under uncertainty.[27] By using our terminology of benefits and costs, we can explain Lewin's exposition of the stress of decision making. Each

[24] Stanley Milgram, *Obedience to Authority* (New York: Harper & Row, 1972).

[25] William Gamson, B. Fireman, and S. Retina, *Encounters with Unjust Authorities* (Homewood, IL: Dorsey Press.)

[26] There are five sources of law—the Constitution, legislative actions, judicial rulings, executive orders, and organizational rules.

[27] Kurt Lewin, *Dynamic Theory of Personality* (New York: McGraw-Hill, 1935).

decision represents a set of goods which are considered beneficial. These can be revenue from a project, victory on a battle field, or the accomplishments of a social program on poverty. Similarly, a decision clearly involves the risk of incurring costs, which can be anticipated or unanticipated. An anticipated cost involves such items as the costs of procuring goods and services, creating environmental pollution, or creating political protest. Unanticipated costs can cover a wide range of economic, political, or social costs. In choosing between alternatives, a decision maker faces four combinations, discussed next.

Benefit-Cost Conflict. This is the quintessential problem of deciding whether the net benefit (benefit minus cost) is positive or negative. The logic of choice states that if the net benefit is positive, the decision ought to be made to go with the proposed project. If, on the other hand, it is negative, the decision maker should do nothing and choose not to embark on the project. We are lured by the benefits, but are repelled by the cost. Like the Danish Prince Hamlet, this dilemma causes us to vacillate between wanting to be or not to be. This vacillation is likely to increase with the size of the cost.

For example, geologists have been warning the residents of California of the impending catastrophe caused by a huge earthquake. Although they cannot forecast the exact time of its occurrence, they are certain that "the big one" is surely going to come. When it does come, the toll from death and destruction is likely to be enormous. However, as the experience of earthquake-prone Japan shows, careful planning and large-scale preparation by individual citizens can significantly reduce the costs of an earthquake. Yet Californians largely go about their business oblivious of the Damocles's sword that is about to drop on them. If we plot the number of legislations passed by the California legislature, an interesting pattern will emerge. Soon after the news of a devastating earthquake somewhere in world, there is a flurry of activity. New legislations are proposed, studies are conducted, and money is allocated for various earthquake preparation work. As time goes on, the news fades from memory and the evening headlines, and enthusiasm wanes. The general public reacts in exactly the same way. Soon after an earthquake, insurance agencies are inundated with calls from customers wanting to buy earthquake insurance, which drops off precipitously with each passing week. This is a common human reaction to a problem when there is a significant benefit attached to an action, but the cost of the action is also considerable. As soon as legislators are confronted with the costs of preparing for an earthquake, or individual home owners are informed of the costs of buying earthquake insurance, hesitancy sets in. Time passes without any significant steps being taken.

Benefit-Benefit Conflict. Sometimes we are confronted with alternatives which are almost equally attractive. A school district, for example, having received a grant for acquiring a new computer lab, may take a long time in making up its mind regarding the type of computers to purchase. The grant may allow the district to purchase a certain number of more expensive but easier to use MacIntosh computers. Or, with the allocated money the district may acquire a larger number of MS

DOS-based machines. Both of these are attractive alternatives with no real cost to the district. Yet situations such as these can produce stress among decision makers and cause undue hesitation. This hesitancy stems from the fact that while both alternatives seem attractive, the outcomes are not entirely certain. Therefore, the decision maker is trying to minimize future regrets for not choosing the right alternative. The MacIntosh products are more user friendly and support excellent graphics but they are relatively more expensive and their limited quantity would restrict computer use among the students. On the other hand, the DOS-based products, while supporting a larger number of users, may not be as successful in promoting actual use as the MacIntosh computers.

Cost-Cost Conflict. The third situation arises when a decision maker is confronted with a Hobson's choice of choosing the lesser of two evils. Finding sites for the disposal of nuclear or other hazardous materials is an example of such a choice. Keeping hazardous waste materials at the point of production does not seem to be viable a solution. On the other hand, arranging an alternate site inevitably causes mounting political pressure from the concerned citizens living near a proposed site. In this case, both alternatives pose costs, and the problem boils down to the minimization of the costs. Unattractive alternatives such as these are likely to produce stress in decision making and can cause years of delay in carrying out the mission of an organization. There are unused or severely underutilized nuclear waste dumps in thinly populated states like New Mexico and Nevada, built at enormous costs to federal taxpayers. Stiff political opposition from the environmentalists and the residents of these states have caused decision makers to flee the field and postpone decision making for a very long time.

Defensive Avoidance. The psychological impediments to action imposed by the stress of decision making have been called **defensive avoidance**.[28] Defensive avoidance takes place when, confronting a stressful situation precipitated by a change, an analyst stops looking for facts which are in direct conflict with the basic values held individually by the analyst or collectively by the organization.

In their extensive study, Janis and Mann identified a number of common reactions to the stress of decision making. These include what they call *unconflicted adherence*, *diffusion of responsibility*, and *hyper vigilance*. A common reaction to uncertainty and serious threat is denial of facts and maintenance of status quo, which Janis and Mann call the unconflicted adherence. For example, the war planners of Imperial Japan were aware of the economic disparity between Japan and the United States, which determined the relative capability of sustaining war efforts. Yet they went to great lengths to avoid even discussing this obvious mismatch in their war plans. Diffusion of responsibilities implies shifting responsibilities where individual responsibilities are not as clearly delineated. For example, facing the prospect of an unpleasant confrontation with reality, an analyst in a large organization may try to

---

[28] Irving Janis and Leon Mann, *Decsion Making: A Psychological Analysis of Conflict, Choice, and Commitment* (New York: Free Press, 1977).

"pass the buck" to the others for writing the report. As a result, either the report will not be completed or its integrity will be seriously compromised. Another common reaction to threat is hypervigilance. That is, facing an imminent threat, one may develop a fixation over trivial details of a minor activity rather than focusing on the large picture. The proverbial rearrangement of deck chairs on the Titanic is an example of this kind of frantic behavior.

If the Theory Does Not Fit, the Reality Must Be at Fault

If you have conducted an intensive analysis of a problem using sophisticated analytical tools, you have invested a great deal in the study. You have developed an impressive, logically coherent model. But there is a problem. The complex reality is stubbornly refusing to agree with your model. While trying to understand the highly complex social and economic world, all of us develop models, theories, or viewpoints, which Thomas Kuhn calls **paradigms**.[29] Facing limited cognitive capabilities, it is the only recourse open to us—to shrink the world within a manageable proportion. It is the same process of building a theory or a model or a paradigm that leads to ideology. Therefore, this model building consciously or unconsciously allows us to reduce the infinitely complex to something handy. This cognitive process lets us derive quick conclusions. If it is a formal model, spelled out in great detail on paper, it may give quick predictions about the future course of the economy or the direction of a tropical storm. But there are infinite numbers of models that we have developed which allow us to find coherence within the maddening confusion of the outside world. In terms of sociopsychology, this process of model building or developing an ideology lets us be **cognitive misers**. That is, the models enable us to pick miserly what we perceive to be "relevant" from the infinite cornucopia of information. Therefore, having heard somebody speak, we quickly determine that "she is a liberal," or "he is part of the Eastern establishment," or "this is a conservationist viewpoint." Once this determination has been made, we feel relieved not having to deal with the complexity of the issue, and can comfortably file away the necessary information under the proper stack. These acts of "pigeon holing" of information reflect years of conscious or unconscious model building throughout our lives. However, like any model, these are but truncated versions of reality, like a blind person describing what an elephant *ought* to look like with the help of feeling the limited body surface of the huge animal. This process of internal theorizing or model building is what Lewin calls a **cognitive map**.[30] Since a cognitive map is prepared with limited information, it is not surprising that the map will often be at variance with reality. If this variance is relatively insignificant, we are able to live with it. However, if the gulf between what we hypothesize and what happens is wide, we are threatened. Through years of study, sociopsychologists have developed impressive lists of human reactions to such threats. Let us discuss some of them.

[29] Thomas Kuhn, *The Structure of Scientific Reasoning* (Chicago: University of Chicago Press, 1970).

[30] Kurt Lewin, *Dynamic Theory of Personality* (New York: McGraw-Hill, 1935).

Cognitive Dissonance. Cognitive dissonance is a term coined by Leon Festinger.[31] Cognitive dissonance arises when an inconsistency in the cognitive map threatens an individual's long-held values or much-invested models. For example, few people are neutral on the issue of welfare payments to the nation's poor. Some argue that these transfer payments help alleviate the problem of abject poverty seen in Third World countries, while others argue that this creates welfare dependence by sapping from a group of individuals their incentive to find gainful employment, thereby turning them into "welfare junkies." Suppose an individual is conducting a study to judge the success of a particular federal program to assist the poor. While conducting the study, this individual may face the prospect of cognitive dissonance if his deep-seated values are threatened by facts presented to him. Cognitive dissonance, in such cases, may cause people to **rationalize** their actions by simply reinterpreting the information. Frustrated by the lack of congruence between his cognitive map and facts before him, the analyst may also find himself being angry and transferring this anger to something else other than the gap between theory and reality, as a part of the rationalization process.

Other Individual Biases. Individual biases can introduce significant distortions in an analysis. While cognitive dissonance causes an individual to rationalize his or her mistakes, **confirmation bias** causes people to pick and choose among evidence to suit their theory.[32] Thus, if I am predisposed to some ideas I will only select the evidence which fits my theory. We can find innumerable examples in policy analysis where analysts have consistently biased their studies by selectively picking through evidence. During the Bay of Pigs invasion, the CIA analysts assumed that Castro's hold on power was tenuous and that the Cubans, chafing under Castro's communist rule, were ready to revolt. Therefore, the entire invasion plan was formulated with the notion that the Cubans were going to rise up in support of the invading force. Ideologically biased CIA analysts never considered the possibility that the Cubans might have separate considerations and might not aid the invading force. This bias led to a serious policy debacle for the Kennedy administration.

Biases can also creep in due to our tendency to judge by association. I may be associated with my friend's ideology without sharing anything but companionship with him. During the MacArthy era witch hunt, many people were hastily judged by their association. People are judged by their appearances, as we tend to associate appearance with many unrelated social, economic, and political characteristics. In a recent newspaper account, a defendant in a rape trial was described as "clean-cut, looking the least bit like a rapist," which presumes that most rapists are unshaven or

---

[31] Leon Festinger, *A Theory of Cognitive Dissonance* (Evanston, IL: Row Peterson, 1957).

[32] Lee Ross and Craig Anderson, "Shortcoming in the Attribution Process: On the Origins and Maintenance of Erroneous Social Assessments," in Daniel Kahneman, Paul Slovic, and Amos Tversky (eds.), *Judgment Under Uncertainty: Heuristics and Biases* (Cambridge, England: Cambridge University Press, 1982).

like to keep facial hair. Attempts to correlate preference for facial hair with proclivity to rape are ludicrous, until you notice that many of the defendants in criminal trials turn out in business suits. This is done purposefully to make the jury associate the defendant with the kind of people who go around town in business suits. In psychology, this is called the **halo effect**, or attribution of characteristics by association. Policy makers are, after all, human. Therefore, policies associated with respectable names are far more likely to get a fair hearing than those which are not. In fact, political scientist Aron Wildavsky, in his classic study of budgetary allocation, noted that the first and foremost task of an agency head is to promote confidence among the legislators in order to ensure continuing funding of the agency projects.[33]

An analysis can also be biased because of **self-serving biases** of the analyst. It is common human nature to prefer that which is going to serve one the best. A great deal of financial arrangements within the savings and loan industry during the 1980s were conducted within an incestuous framework, without the safeguard of excluding those who were to evaluate loan applications for possible conflicts of interest. The lack of regulations within the industry caused huge amounts of fraudulent or simply inefficient loans. Therefore, an agency which does not watch out for possible conflicts of interest may suffer the consequences of biased analyses.

Biases can also result from individuals or organizations having stakes or having incurred **sunk costs**. The old story goes that if you let the camel put his nose inside the tent on a cold desert night, soon you will find yourself shivering outside, while the pushy camel enjoys the cozy comfort of the tent. Indeed, one of the biggest contributors to the so-called uncontrollable items in a public agency budget are those which have a certain amount of sunk cost. In fact, many of the largest ticket items in the defense department budget started out with small allocations for research and development. But at every successive step, the argument of having already invested money was used to leverage ever-increasing amounts of money. The problem with the sunk cost argument is that it can preempt an objective analysis with the simple argument that "since we have invested the money, we should not let those past dollars go to waste."

Complex Problems, Simple Solutions

Someone once said that for every complex social problem, there is a solution which is simple, neat, but absolutely wrong. Yet, for our own survival, we must reduce the vast complexity of the real world into a manageable model. As professor Herbert Simon pointed out, there is a tremendous cost attached to information processing and, therefore, we cannot go on endlessly looking for the best solution.[34] The search process is limited by various constraints. Professor Simon calls it the **bounded rationality**. The process can be likened to a hungry horse looking for the

---

[33] Aron Wildavsky, *The Politics of Budgetary Process* (Boston: Little Brown, 1964).

[34] Herbert Simon, *Models of Man: Social and Rational* (New York: Wiley, 1957).

greenest pasture. It would be futile to try to find the "best" grazing spot in the world, since the animal is bounded by the fences of its corral. Similarly, we find ourselves fenced in by limitations of time, money, and political and social constraints. Therefore, facing the need to make a decision, we tend to "frame" the problem at hand. A decision maker will make a decision within the frame of the context, time, social considerations, and moral values. Social psychologists have pointed out the traps of systematic biases that await a decision maker. Some of these are amusing, yet they pose real dangers for sound decision making.

Framing within a Context.   We often frame our decisions within a context. What appears to be perfectly reasonable in one context appears to be silly in another. Suppose you are buying an expensive television set, costing $1,500, and a pair of shoes priced at $60. If you are informed that you could get the same items for $10 less at another store a few miles away, would you be willing to make the trip? Amos Tversky and Daniel Kahneman, in their experiments on anomalies of the rational decision-making process, found out that most people would think the trip worthwhile for the shoes but not for the television, although they are saving an identical amount of money in each case.[35] Similarly, Mullen and Roth pointed out that while buying a $15,000 car, we may be perfectly willing to "throw in" an additional $1,500 for optional leather seats, while we may never agree to pay that much for a sofa for our home.[36]

There are many such examples of contextual framing. If you think about it carefully, you will realize that we are violating the rules of rationality because we have framed our choices within the context. While buying a television set, we are more focused on the desired features of the set than saving an additional $10. Yet, while buying a pair of shoes, we are more mindful of saving money because within the context of the shoes, saving money is a primary concern. We view decisions within a limited context, which can often come in conflict with the basic precepts of rationality and lead to "penny-wise, pound-foolish" decisions.

Framing within Time.   Time is an extremely important consideration for framing a problem. The typical conflict is between the maximization of short- and long-run goals. For example, studies of employee compensation structures have pointed out that while those employed in the public sector tend to make less immediate income compared to their counterparts in the private sector, they are often rewarded with far more generous retirement benefits. One of the most crucial reasons for this is that the political decision making takes place within the context of the terms of office. Thus, if a mayor is elected for a two-year period, his focus may not extend beyond his term of office. Therefore, while granting pay increases poses

[35] Amos Tversky and Daniel Kahneman, "The Framing of Decisions and the Psychology of Choice," in George Wright (ed.), *Behavioral Decision Making* (New York: Plenum Press, 1985).

[36] John D. Mullen and Byron M. Roth, *Decision Making: Its Logic and Practice* (Savage, MD: Rowman and Littlefield Publishers, 1991).

immediate fiscal repercussions, the granting of retirement benefits does not, because they relate to future dollars when the present political leadership is out of the present position. This conflict between short- and long-term goals is often telling on policies requiring continuity over the terms of the elected officials. As a result, frequently projects with long-term benefits are pushed aside for those bearing fruits more quickly. It therefore should not come as a surprise that projects requiring long-term investments (such as the maintenance of infrastructure—roads, bridges, sewer systems, etc.) remain neglected until their deteriorated state requires immediate (and often expensive) attention.

Framing within the Social and Political Context. This is probably the most commonly understood barrier of sound decision making. Political expediency is often the reason behind making decisions which may turn out to be disastrous for an organization. However, there are two aspects to this problem. The first refers to the question of making a public policy decision on the basis of the constituent interests of the elected officials. In a democratic society this poses some unique problems, which are typically manifested by repeated polling results which consistently show that while the American public harbors a rather negative attitude toward the body of Congress, it tends to hold its own elected representatives in a much more favorable light (which contributes in no small measure to the overwhelming probability of reelection of incumbents).

The second aspect of framing a policy question within a social and political context results from personal attributes of the decision makers, their ambitions, perceived relative standing in comparison with their reference groups, etc.[37] After all, decision makers are human. Therefore, such psychological impediments to sound decision making often pose critical problems for organizations.

Moral Dilemmas and Decision Making. Under a democratic system, public goods are provided by the elected representatives of the people. However, only a small fraction of the actual allocations are done by elected officials, who can only draw the major outlines within which specific amounts of goods are allocated. For example, although the President and the members of Congress determine the size of the various departmental budgets, the actual allocation decisions are made by nonelected bureaucrats. This often raises the question, Whose interests do the bureaucrats look after? Conservative critics of bureaucracy have argued that in their decisions, bureaucrats attempt to maximize their goal of achieving power, prestige, and a bigger share of the budget pie.[38] However, a responsible nonelected decision maker must weigh the conflicting interests of many groups. The process of making

---

[37] On the question of relative standing clouding economic decisions, see Robert H. Frank, *Choosing the Right Pond: Human Behavior and the Quest for Status* (New York: Oxford University Press, 1985).

[38] See James Buchanan, *Public Finance in Democratic Process* (Chapel Hill: University of North Carolina Press, 1967). Also see William Niskanen, *Bureaucracy and Representative Government* (Hawthorne, NY: Aldine Publishing, 1971).

decisions on public policy becomes complicated as the decision maker often faces organized, well-articulated, and well-heeled interest groups, which may attempt to hijack the process for their own benefit. The temptation to give in to the interest group pressure must be tempered by the need to look after the interest of those who are not represented. For example, in recommending an experimental drug treatment, the Food and Drug Administration (FDA) must consider the need of the unrepresented patients along with those of the drug manufacturers and the physicians' lobby group. In this process, the decision maker may often be the conservator of people who are not even in the picture at the time of decision making. Thus, in choosing methods of storage of hazardous materials, a decision maker must consider the interest of the future inhabitants, including the ones yet to be born.

Such questions frequently pose moral dilemmas for decision makers. In an uncertain and continuously changing world with shifting moral standards, decision making can be excruciatingly complex and painful, especially for conscientious decision makers. Although there is no easy answer to this dilemma, we can only point out that the efficacy of our decisions is limited by our present state of knowledge. Therefore, if the question has been properly framed, and all reasonable alternatives have been explored, a decision maker with a keen sense of morality can rest easy.

Avoiding the Psychological Impediments to Objective Analysis

In any organization, we can find examples of behavior that matches, in varying degrees, the aforementioned behaviors. A few people within an organization may become aware of the pressure of groupthink and its consequent pressure for conformity. For these individuals find their outlet either through a whispering campaign or, if the situation becomes serious, through whistle blowing.[39] Both of these actions carry costs to the individual as well as to the organization. However, frequently the members of an organization remain completely oblivious to the problem until it is brought to the fore in a period of crisis. At that time, although the problem of a distorted shared view of the world becomes apparent to most outside observers, the organization goes through a tormented period of denial and anger.

Organizations can avoid the pitfalls of groupthink by creating an atmosphere where a free flow of ideas, regardless of the level of popularity both within the organization and outside among the client group, is promoted. The use of management by objectives and periodic examination of the basic goals and objectives of the organization may help shake up the deeply held status quo within an organization. At a personal level, safeguards against groupthink start with objective analysis, sharp analytical tools, and pride in professionalism.

---

[39] The term *whistle blowing* was coined by consumer advocate Ralph Nader. See Ralph Nader, Peter Petkas, and Kate Blackwell (eds.), *Whistle Blowing* (New York: Bantam Books, 1972).

In Analysts Do We Trust?

Problems do not go away even after all of the individual and organizational biases have been accounted for. Sometimes you may come across forecasts based on elegant econometric procedures done by conscientious and enthusiastic research analysts which go against your own "horse sense." Should you question the results or, since they were derived through a complicated statistical procedure, should you hold back your doubts? This is an extremely important question, since public policies are based on future expectations. There are a number of highly regarded outfits, such as Data Resources Inc. (DRI), Chase Econometrics, and the government's own Office of Management and Budget and the Congressional Budget Office, that routinely provide forecasts of future economic behavior based on highly complex econometric models. How they compare with the subjective forecasts made by field experts has been the subject of inquiry in recent economic literature. Based on a well-known framework used in psychological research by Egon Brunswick[40] called the *Lens Model*, a number of studies have attempted to show the relative reliability of subjective and objective estimations.[41] The empirical results based on controlled experiments show that although subjective estimations appear to be less accurate at first blush, when the level of structural uncertainty is held constant both tend to offer forecasts with equal amounts of variability. Second, when the subjective forecasts are based on a group concensus, the results tend to show a greater degree of consistency, implying that the group as a whole is better able to weed out random disturbances more effectively. Finally, as the field experts gain more experience in forecasting and develop a deeper understanding of statistical analysis, the quality of their subjective forecasts improves. These results point out the need for mutual understanding between statisticians and the field experts in producing better forecasts. Therefore, if my analyst friend's results were thrown out because they had contradicted the expert's own sense of what lie ahead, a better prediction could have emerged if they sat down together and arrived at a concensus.

Whose Ball Is It, Anyway? Playing the Political Game

The most common complaint heard among those who make it their profession to analyze public policy with quantitative data is that their work often seems futile, since they don't seem to influence the final outcome of a public policy debate. To them and to many others outside the government, the gulf between analysis and adoption only shows the ugly side of politics—the injection of irrational political

---

[40] Egon Brunswick, *Perception and the Representative Design of Experiments* (Berkeley: University of California Press, 1956).

[41] See Harinder Singh, "Relative Evaluation of Subjective and Objective Measures of Expectations Formation," *Quarterly Review of Economics and Business*, Vol 30, No. 1, 1990, pp. 64–74.

compromise on an otherwise rational process. They argue that if only we could keep the politics out, the public sector could run as smoothly and rationally as its private counterpart.[42]

PPBS attempted to elevate the process of budgeting, which until then was considered mainly a tool of control against pilferage and waste, to systematic planning and efficient management. It proposed to start with an explicit goal or a maximand, set by the chief executive or the prescribed political process. Then by attributing productivity indicators to measure the relative efficiency of a limited number of specified alternatives, it purported to allocate funds in an optimal fashion much in the same spirit as linear programming or benefit-cost analysis. President Lyndon Johnson was so taken by its scientific approach that he directed all federal agencies to adopt PPBS. Yet for all its noblesse and promise, it failed miserably to deliver.

Of all the thousands of pages written on PPBS, none came closer to explaining this failure than the analysis of Professor Aron Wildavsky.[43] Wildavsky pointed out that the primary reason PPBS failed to work in the government sector is because it stressed *economic rationality* while completely ignoring *political rationality*. In a democratic system, the primary emphasis is not on economic efficiency but on political compromise. It is indeed strange to apologize for the political process in a democracy. However, Paul Diesing points out the primacy of political rationality in a democratic system as follows:

> The political problem is always *basic* and *prior* to the others. . . . This means that any suggested course of action must be evaluated first by its effects on the political structure. A course of action which corrects economic or social deficiencies but increases political difficulties must be rejected, while an action which contributes to political improvement is desirable even if it is not entirely sound from an economic or social standpoint.[44] (emphasis mine)

Therefore, you should not take it to heart if your analysis, based on economic rationality, is discarded in favor of judgment based on political rationality. It is not only to be expected but always accepted as fundamental to the democratic process. In fact, Professor Wildavsky claims that trying to run the government as business, based solely on economic rationality, is undemocratic and un-American. As an analyst, your job is simply to demonstrate the economic costs and benefits of the various alternatives. You should perform your task with utmost integrity and professional probity. In rejecting PPBS Professor Wildavksy did not, however, reject the need for sound analysis based on economic principles. He simply pointed out the folly of ignoring political rationality in a democratic system.

---

[42] See Peter W. House and Roger D. Shull, *Rush to Policy: Using Analytical Techniques in Public Sector Decision Making* (New Brunswick, NJ: Transaction Books, 1988).

[43] Aron Wildavsky, *The Politics of the Budgetary Process* (Boston: Little Brown, 1964).

[44] Paul Diesing, *Reason in Society* (Urbana, IL: University of Illinois Press, 1962), p. 228. Quoted in Aron Wildavsky (ibid.), 3rd ed., 1979, p. 193.

As an analyst, you should remember that the adoption of a policy falls outside of your job description. Having spent a great deal of time and effort, you may not always agree with this assertion; but as Sir Winston Churchill quipped, "Democracy is the worst system men have devised, except for all else."[45]

Say It with Numbers

"The pen is mightier than the sword." So goes the old saying proclaiming the power of verbal articulation over that of brute force. Again, within the range of verbal articulation, the strength of numbers is formidable. People of all walks of life have buttressed their arguments with numbers. Numbers seem to have a mystical quality about them. They have the appearance of being precise, objective, and irrefutable. In the popular 1960s television series *Star Trek*, the character of Mr. Spock, a totally rational (and hence, devoid of emotions) half-human from the planet Vulcan, spouts the probabilities of survival in five digit precision. Even in our most earthly conversations, if we can phrase our arguments in terms of numbers, our chances of scoring points are higher. A most fascinating demonstration of the power of numbers is found in the autobiography of George Ball, the Undersecretary of State in the Kennedy and Johnson administration. He writes about his experience in the White House meetings as follows:

> The personalities who played key roles in my own sphere of interest varied depending on the nature of particular problem. I would sort out economic or financial problems with the Secretary of the Treasury, Douglas Dillon—though the Secretary of Commerce and the Secretary of Labor were sometimes involved. But, in any group where Robert McNamara was present, he soon emerged as a dominant voice. I was impressed by his extraordinary self-confidence—based not on bluster but on detailed knowledge of objective facts. He gave the impression of knowing every detail of the Defense Department's vast operations and had concise and impressive views on any subject that arose, reinforcing his opinions with huge verbal footnotes of statistics. Since I am quite incapable of thinking in quantitative terms, I found McNamara's performances formidable and scintillating. He quoted precise figures, not mere orders of magnitudes. During the Vietnam War, if asked to appraise the chances of success for different optional projects, he would answer with apparent precision: one operation would have a 65 percent chance, another a 30 percent chance. Once I tried to tease him, suggesting that perhaps the chances were 64 percent and 29 percent, but the joke was not well taken.[46]

---

[45] For a more detailed discussion of the role of an analyst within an organization, see Martha Feldman, *Order Without Design: Information Production and Policy Making* (Stanford, CA: Stanford University Press, 1989).

[46] George Ball, *The Past Has Another Pattern: Memoirs* (New York: W. W. Norton, 1982), pp. 173–74.

Laconically, George Ball adds:[47]

> [McNamara's] mastery of that capricious behemoth, the defense establishment, was not achieved merely by a virtuosity with statistics; it required force of character. McNamara, moreover, is a man of humanity and imagination, capable of strong commitments to cause. . . .

The profile of Robert McNamara, as drawn by George Ball, opens our eyes to the power of numbers as well as the capacity of their being misused. Without belaboring the point, it may be worthwhile to consider another example of the power of numbers. A *Wall Street Journal* story reports on the tricky act of "risk analysis," or the process of assigning numbers to the probability of health and safety risks associated with many public policies and regulations.[48] For instance, using risk analysis, the Environmental Protection Agency (EPA) calculates the risk to life from environmental pollution to be as minimal as one in 100,000. Astronomers claim the odds that the earth would be hit by a killer asteroid are 2 million to one. At the time of building the space shuttles, the National Aeronautics and Space Administration (NASA) proudly predicted that the probability of an accident was so infinitesimally small, that one could fly one of the shuttles every day for 300 years without an accident. The space shuttle Challenger tragically proved the precariousness of such predictions. The report correctly comments that

> This is the bizarre world of risk analysis, the studies federal agencies prepare to show their regulations are worth adopting. Risk analysis is so inexact and malleable that even its practitioners concede it hasn't the rigor of science. But it is so broadly applied that it guides the spending of $150 billion a year on health, safety and environmental rules. Regulations based on risk analysis touch nearly every industry and worker in the U.S., but the methods are so loose that both the White House and the National Academy of Sciences are devising plans to change them.

Indeed, like the predictions of the *Star Trek* character Mr. Spock, scientists and researchers in every field of public policy are spewing out numbers of incredulous precision through computer programs of bewildering complexity. Billions of dollars of public expenditure depend on the outcomes of analyses based on numbers.

These examples underscore the basic dilemma around which the discussion of this book has been based. On the one hand, we can see how powerful analyses based on numbers can be. On the other hand, we have also examined in great detail the vulnerability and subjective nature of these highly complex quantitative techniques. Despite a reassuring examination of the methods of analysis, it is indeed

---

[47] George Ball, Ibid, p. 174.

[48] *The Wall Street Journal*, "What Price Safety? Risk Analysis Measures Need for Regulation, But It's No Science," August 6, 1992, p. 1.

doubtful that either the White House or the mighty Academy of Sciences will be able to solve this fundamental dilemma of policy analysis. Therefore, the question is, What is the proper role of a quantitative analyst? It is clear to me that knowing the power and the vulnerability of quantitative analysis, we cannot but approach our job with appropriate humility and responsible circumspection.

When Time Is of the Essence: Researched Analysis Versus Quick Decision Making

In the course of this book, we have discussed a number of important quantitative techniques for the analysis of public policy. These techniques frequently require the investment of a great deal of time and money. It is, of course, a matter of common wisdom that for mundane, everyday decisions we do not use elaborate analysis, but save it for the important decisions. This is often not true. In our private lives, and even in public policy making, important decisions are often snappy, based on quick analysis. For instance, as individuals, the most important economic decisions that we make involve the choice of employment or the purchase of a home. These are primarily economic decisions and should be undertaken with a great deal of care and cool calculation. Yet think of how often we embark upon such important decisions on the basis of intuition alone. In choosing between two homes, we may do all the calculations involving costs of purchase, maintenance, commuting, and the prospect of future price increases, only to scuttle this information for something that appeals to us at an intuitive level. Similarly, the memoirs of important political personages are replete with examples of going against the best analytical advice on some of the most momentous decisions, and basing these decisions on intuition alone.

Paradoxes and dilemmas are never fun. They violate some of the basic principles of decision theory: They both seem attractive or fraught with danger. In fact, dilemmas never come with all the necessary data or clear-cut methods of choosing between competing alternatives.

In an important study, Behn and Vaupel dealt with this very aspect of decision making: a quick analysis.[49] If you do not have the necessary time or the data to conduct what they call a "researched analysis," you are apt to make decisions based on some "rules of thumb," such as the mini-max strategy of minimizing the option with the least regret (least amount of potential loss).

Professors Behn and Vaupel suggest five steps for quick analysis:

1. Think
2. Decompose

---

[49] Robert D. Behn and James W. Vaupel, *Quick Analysis for Busy Decision Makers*, (New York: Basic Books, 1982).

3. Simplify
4. Specify
5. Rethink.

Think. The process of quick decision making starts with thinking. The thinking part essentially involves framing the problem. A problem is almost never unidimensional. Clichés abound about focusing on the essentials by ignoring the trivial. "You should not miss the forest for a tree!" "You must not be like those blind men trying to describe an elephant," etc. However, they all essentially underscore the need to look squarely at the heart of a complex, multidimensional problem. This reduction of a large problem into a manageable form often requires the use of simple numbers—numbers that can convey the essence of a problem. If there is nothing that you retain from this book, it will be worth more than your effort if you can simply train your mind to think in terms of the simple arithmetic calculations of adding, subtracting, multiplying, and dividing.

Decompose. As Behn and Vaupel point out, the essence of analysis is decomposition: the ability to see the problem as an amalgam of various elements. Our brains only offer us limited space for processing complex information. Therefore, if we can see a problem in its various parts, some complemetary and some inconsistent, we have made significant progress in the right direction. Bewildered students who cannot decide where to start their research projects often seek my help. I ask them to write down the title of the paper. Once that is done, I insist that they prepare a detailed table of contents. The very process of naming the project compels them to frame the issue in its bare minimum. Then the preparation of the table of contents forces them to decompose the problem.

Simplify. If we had unlimited time, we could be exhaustive in our analyses. However, we work within the limits of time. Therefore, when time is of the essence, we do not have the opportunity to go through all the possible alternatives, all the possible outcomes to achieve the best (global) solution. In such cases, we may have to simplify the process by drastically eliminating all but the most important components of the problem. The process of structured simplification is so effective in problem-solving situations because (1) without simplification a problem can push us well beyond our cognitive capabilities; (2) a simplied problem takes it out of the realm of intuition or simple "gut reaction" to conscious manipulation and informed judgment; and (3) once a problem has been simplified and broken into its essential components, the decision makers' intuitions can be used to their fullest advantage. In our lives we often come across people who are obsessed with perfection. There is, of course, nothing wrong in being a perfectionist unless it prevents you from making a decision on time when you absolutely must. After all, a perfect decision past its time cannot be an ideal choice.

Specify. Decision making, in its final analysis, is intuitive. No matter how cogent the analysis is, at the ultimate stage it calls for the subjective judgments of the decision maker. Yet subjective judgment is aided by the specificity of the posed problem and is harmed by the lack of it. Therefore, try to be specific in your description of the process. It may help if you do a quick decision tree analysis with the bare minimum branches of action (which Behn and Vaupel call "saplings") and a "do-nothing" option. While so doing, you may force yourself to specify what you mean by "uncertainty" or calling something "risky" or "iffy." Put down your subjective assessment of the situation in numbers. If you think that your favorite team is going to win, put it in terms of numbers. After all, both 55% and 95% chances can be described as having "a great probability of winning." But by imputing a number you are specifying the extent of your confidence, which can then be compared with another person's assessment of the situation.

Rethink.   Based on the quick decision rule, you have arrived at a solution. Should you stick to it once you have made up your mind? Perhaps not. If there is time, rethink! Since all analysis is ultimately incomplete and is dependent on subjective judgments, you should not waste the opportunity to rethink your position if you have the time. If there is enough time, and you are still uncertain about your decision, start from the beginning once again, and make a *second cut*. Given enough time and the importance of the decision, do not hesitate to go back and start from the beginning again and again. Go on rethinking until you have come to the conclusion that, given the constraint of time, you have done your best.

In this section I have described the essence of quick analysis, based on the work of professors Behn and Vaupel. If you are not convinced that this process merits your serious consideration, take this challange: Consider either a complex problem troubling the world, the nation, or you. If you are confounded by its complexity and cannot seem to solve it "in your head," sit down with a pencil and a sheet of paper. First, write down what you think is the bare essence of the problem. Then systematically decompose it into its essential aspects. If you follow these simple mental steps, you may not find a unique solution, but in most cases you will feel more comfortable about your decision, which is perhaps at the heart of rational analysis.

Using Quantitative Techniques: Some Parting Suggestions

Quantitative models and numerical analyses are simply tools, aids to your natural analytical capabilities. Like all other tools, by themselves they are neither good nor bad—their ultimate value to you, your organization, and society at large depends on the way they have been used. However, I would argue that the primary strengths of the techniques lie in two areas.

In the process of a scientific inquiry into a complex problem, along with knowing what you know, it is imperative to know what you don't know. The first contribution of the proper use of quantitative analysis is its identification of the zone of ignorance. By using an objective analysis, we can proceed up to a certain point, beyond which we require judgments based on personal, political, or social values.

Quantitative techniques will take you to this boundary, well marked by objective reasoning. To proceed further, you will have to call for help beyond the scope of these techniques. Thus, recalling our discussion of choosing among alternatives, we can identify the dominant alternatives following the logic of objective analysis. But where there are questions of trade-off, as analysts we are helpless. This is the area of the decision makers and the goal setters. Once these goals are properly identified, we can settle on a unique optimal choice for society.

The other important contribution of quantitative techniques is the fullest possible disclosure of biases, hidden values, prejudices, and presuppositions. The glare of the process of quantification significantly reduces the dark, hidden crevasses of objective analysis. When a problem has been fully specified, we can agree or disagree on its formulation on a much more level ground, without hyperbolic rhetoric masking our value judgments. When a policy based on an objective analysis fails, we can learn from its failure and recalibrate through the appropriate process of feedback. Since at the very core of human rationality lies learning through experience (which, incidentally, separates a free-thinking human from a mechanical mind), these techniques chalk out the paths of a decidedly more reasoned analysis.

Therefore, the function of an objective analysis goes far beyond its substantive contribution and enters into the process of procedural justice in a public policy debate; an objective analysis provides not only clearly defined evidence and a set of corresponding arguments, but also an intellectual structure for an open discussion. Even when its conclusions are deemed unacceptable or infeasible, these analyses shape the structure, language, and issues of a policy debate.[50] The debate, concentrating on the methodology of deriving the conclusion rather than the conclusion itself, sets the stage for a broader understanding and consequent acceptance of the policy process. Thus, the wisdom of King Solomon is made evident not when we accept his decision to give the disputed custody of a child to his natural mother, but when we understand the logical process that elicited the judgment.[51] Once a policy has been adopted through public debate, the successful adoption of the analytical solution of a particular course of action depends on its economic viability, administrative feasibility, and, above all, political acceptability filtered through the legitimacy of the policy makers, a discussion of which falls well outside the scope of this book.[52]

---

[50] See Giandomenico Majone, *Evidence, Argument and Persuasion in the Policy Process* (New Haven: Yale University Press, 1989). Also see E. S. Quade, *Analysis for Public Decisions*, 3rd ed. (New York: North-Holland, 1989).

[51] For an excellent discussion of the analogy between objective analysis and legal procedure, see Harvey Brooks, "Environmental Decision Making: Analysis and Values," in L. H. Tribe, C. S. Schilling, and J. Voss (eds.), *When Values Conflict* (Cambridge, MA: Ballinger, 1976).

[52] See, for example, Stephen Brooks and Alain-G. Gagnon (eds.), *Social Scientists, Policy, and the State* (New York: Praeger, 1990).

Framing an Objective Analysis: A Few Suggestions

- **Do not start with an agenda.** Everybody has points of view—but do not start with an agenda, which obscures your objective vision. Activists on any side are often the worst analysts, since they start with hidden or explicit goals of their own, either conclusively to prove or disprove something. If you start with such a frame of reference, it is likely that you will be led astray by your zeal.

- **Know the subjective nature of analysis.** It is extremely important to know the limits of proof when it comes to an uncontrolled society. We might as well accept that it is a subjective world with few absolutes. So let us not expect these models to give us incontrovertible truths. They will simply outline the range within which a reasonable analysis can expect the answers to lie. Consider your conclusions to be starting point of a larger policy debate rather than a resolution of a controversy.

- **Objectivity simply applies to the process.** Make clear the assumptions you made about the world during the analysis and let the readers know how their amendments may change your conclusions.

- **Be exhaustive in your analysis.** Include everything important, and don't be afraid to exclude what you consider to be irrelevant. But always be prepared to defend not your conclusion but your methodology of analysis.

- **The models are no more clever than their user.** Do not expect them to provide any special insight over and beyond what lies within the analytical capabilities of these techniques. Do not be obsessed with the mathematical sophistication of the analytical tools. Mathematical intricacy by itself does not imply good analysis. In fact, it may stand in the way of its ready understanding and, hence, its implementation by political decision-makers.

- **Know the limits of your assumptions.** Know what you know, and know what you have left out.

- **Be openminded about criticisms.** Nobody has a lock on the truth. In the final analysis, the most important accolade you can get as an analyst is that, given all the limitations, you have done the most reasonable analysis.

- **Don't overquantify.** Do not quantify to the point of absurdity. Leave out those data that are not amenable to quantification. Let others make subjective judgments about them.

- **Know your role as an analyst.** Everybody has a role to play in a complex organizational setup. There is a division of labor. It is not your job to adopt a policy, only to analyze its possible impacts. So do not be emotionally involved with the conclusions or the cause.

Exercises

1. Explain some of the sources of the serious errors in judgment in the following scenarios. From the descriptions given, you will quickly understand the context. It is not my intention to suggest that the outcomes of these scenarios were necessarily flawed. As part of a class exercise, think about and discuss some of the possible sources of organizational biases in analyzing these events. Imagine that you, in your present capacity, have been chosen to be a member of these groups. Explain the sources of some of the personal biases you might have in analyzing these cases. Without getting into specifics, suggest some ways which might have improved the decision-making process in each of these cases.

   i) A young President of the United States has been assassinated. A committee, composed of a Supreme Court justice and, a few prominent members of the Congress and the military, has been formed to inquire into the causes of this incident.

   ii) The federal Food and Drug Agency (FDA) is considering the approval of pills that induce abortion. The studies conducted by two major manufacturers of the product show the products to be safe and effective.

   iii) There is a swamp area at the edge of your town which has been declared a wetland and a sanctuary for migratory birds. A developer has drawn up a plan to build a golf course around the swamp. The developer is claiming that the plan is environmentally safe. The town's planning commission is considering its approval.

2. Write a short essay on the process of quick decision-making, using the example of an actual problem. Set a definite time limit on your decision (say, 15 minutes, or an hour). Analyze your experience.

Areas of the Standard Normal Distribution (the Z table)

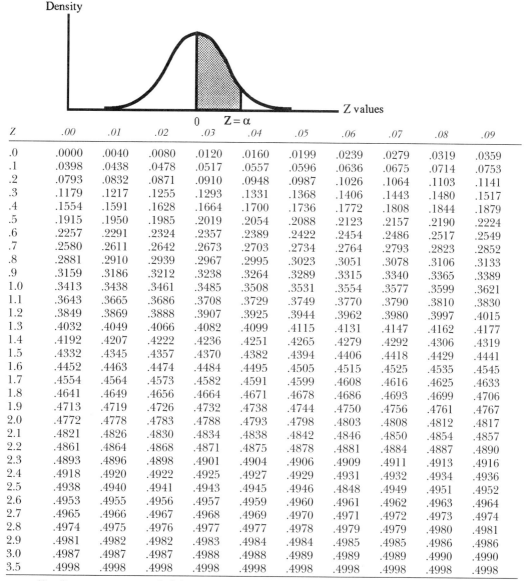

Z	.00	.01	.02	.03	.04	.05	.06	.07	.08	.09
.0	.0000	.0040	.0080	.0120	.0160	.0199	.0239	.0279	.0319	.0359
.1	.0398	.0438	.0478	.0517	.0557	.0596	.0636	.0675	.0714	.0753
.2	.0793	.0832	.0871	.0910	.0948	.0987	.1026	.1064	.1103	.1141
.3	.1179	.1217	.1255	.1293	.1331	.1368	.1406	.1443	.1480	.1517
.4	.1554	.1591	.1628	.1664	.1700	.1736	.1772	.1808	.1844	.1879
.5	.1915	.1950	.1985	.2019	.2054	.2088	.2123	.2157	.2190	.2224
.6	.2257	.2291	.2324	.2357	.2389	.2422	.2454	.2486	.2517	.2549
.7	.2580	.2611	.2642	.2673	.2703	.2734	.2764	.2793	.2823	.2852
.8	.2881	.2910	.2939	.2967	.2995	.3023	.3051	.3078	.3106	.3133
.9	.3159	.3186	.3212	.3238	.3264	.3289	.3315	.3340	.3365	.3389
1.0	.3413	.3438	.3461	.3485	.3508	.3531	.3554	.3577	.3599	.3621
1.1	.3643	.3665	.3686	.3708	.3729	.3749	.3770	.3790	.3810	.3830
1.2	.3849	.3869	.3888	.3907	.3925	.3944	.3962	.3980	.3997	.4015
1.3	.4032	.4049	.4066	.4082	.4099	.4115	.4131	.4147	.4162	.4177
1.4	.4192	.4207	.4222	.4236	.4251	.4265	.4279	.4292	.4306	.4319
1.5	.4332	.4345	.4357	.4370	.4382	.4394	.4406	.4418	.4429	.4441
1.6	.4452	.4463	.4474	.4484	.4495	.4505	.4515	.4525	.4535	.4545
1.7	.4554	.4564	.4573	.4582	.4591	.4599	.4608	.4616	.4625	.4633
1.8	.4641	.4649	.4656	.4664	.4671	.4678	.4686	.4693	.4699	.4706
1.9	.4713	.4719	.4726	.4732	.4738	.4744	.4750	.4756	.4761	.4767
2.0	.4772	.4778	.4783	.4788	.4793	.4798	.4803	.4808	.4812	.4817
2.1	.4821	.4826	.4830	.4834	.4838	.4842	.4846	.4850	.4854	.4857
2.2	.4861	.4864	.4868	.4871	.4875	.4878	.4881	.4884	.4887	.4890
2.3	.4893	.4896	.4898	.4901	.4904	.4906	.4909	.4911	.4913	.4916
2.4	.4918	.4920	.4922	.4925	.4927	.4929	.4931	.4932	.4934	.4936
2.5	.4938	.4940	.4941	.4943	.4945	.4946	.4848	.4949	.4951	.4952
2.6	.4953	.4955	.4956	.4957	.4959	.4960	.4961	.4962	.4963	.4964
2.7	.4965	.4966	.4967	.4968	.4969	.4970	.4971	.4972	.4973	.4974
2.8	.4974	.4975	.4976	.4977	.4977	.4978	.4979	.4979	.4980	.4981
2.9	.4981	.4982	.4982	.4983	.4984	.4984	.4985	.4985	.4986	.4986
3.0	.4987	.4987	.4987	.4988	.4988	.4989	.4989	.4989	.4990	.4990
3.5	.4998	.4998	.4998	.4998	.4998	.4998	.4998	.4998	.4998	.4998

Note: Suppose you want to find the area under the standard normal curve between the values $Z = 0$ and $Z_\alpha = 1.77$. In that case, come down the first column of Z values and locate the row for $Z = 1.7$. Then move along this row and find the number corresponding to the colum .07 (in effect, you just added 1.70 + .07 to get the value for 1.77). This number is .4616.

Critical Values of the *t* Distribution

Density

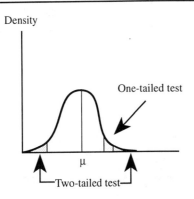

One-tailed test

μ

└─Two-tailed test─┘

	Levels of Significance				
	One-Tailed Test				
Degrees	*10%*	*5%*	*2.5%*	*1%*	*0.5%*
of Freedom	*Two-Tailed Test*				
	20%	*10%*	*5%*	*2%*	*1%*
1	3.078	6.314	12.706	31.821	63.657
2	1.886	2.920	4.303	6.965	9.925
3	1.638	2.353	3.182	4.541	5.841
4	1.533	2.132	2.776	3.747	4.604
5	1.476	2.015	2.571	3.365	4.032
6	1.440	1.943	2.447	3.143	3.707
7	1.415	1.895	2.365	2.998	3.499
8	1.397	1.860	2.306	2.898	3.355
9	1.383	1.833	2.262	2.821	3.250
10	1.372	1.812	2.228	2.764	3.169
11	1.363	1.796	2.201	2.718	3.106
12	1.356	1.782	2.179	2.681	3.055
13	1.350	1.771	2.160	2.650	3.012
14	1.345	1.761	2.145	2.624	2.977
15	1.341	1.753	2.131	2.602	2.947
16	1.337	1.746	2.120	2.583	2.921
17	1.333	1.740	2.110	2.567	2.898
18	1.330	1.734	2.101	2.552	2.878
20	1.325	1.725	2.086	2.528	2.845
21	1.323	1.721	2.080	2.518	2.831
22	1.321	1.717	2.074	2.508	2.819
23	1.319	1.714	2.069	2.500	2.807

Degrees of Freedom	Levels of Significance				
	One-Tailed Test				
	10%	5%	2.5%	1%	0.5%
	Two-Tailed Test				
	20%	10%	5%	2%	1%
24	1.318	1.711	2.064	2.492	2.797
25	1.316	1.708	2.060	2.485	2.787
26	1.315	1.706	2.056	2.479	2.779
28	1.313	1.701	2.048	2.467	2.763
30	1.310	1.697	2.042	2.457	2.750
60	1.296	1.671	2.000	2.390	2.660
120	1.289	1.658	1.980	2.358	2.617
Infinity (normal distribution)	1.282	1.645	1.960	2.326	2.576

Critical Values of the *F* Statistic:
5 Percent Level of Significance

v_1 = Degrees of Freedom for Numerator

	1	2	3	4	5	6	7	8	10	20
1	161	200	216	225	230	234	237	239	242	248
2	18.5	19.0	19.2	19.2	19.2	19.3	19.4	19.4	19.4	19.4
3	10.1	9.55	9.28	9.12	9.01	8.94	8.89	8.85	8.79	8.66
4	7.71	6.94	6.59	6.39	6.26	6.16	6.09	6.04	5.96	5.80
5	6.61	5.79	5.41	5.19	5.05	4.95	4.88	4.82	4.74	4.56
6	5.99	5.14	4.76	4.53	4.39	4.28	4.21	4.15	4.06	3.87
7	5.59	4.74	4.35	4.12	3.97	3.87	3.79	3.73	3.64	3.44
8	5.32	4.46	4.07	3.84	3.69	3.58	3.50	3.44	3.35	3.15
9	5.12	4.26	3.86	3.63	3.48	3.37	3.29	3.23	3.14	2.94
10	4.96	4.10	3.71	3.48	3.33	3.22	3.14	3.07	2.98	2.77
11	4.84	3.98	3.59	3.36	3.20	3.09	3.01	2.95	2.85	2.65
12	4.75	3.89	3.49	3.26	3.11	3.00	2.91	2.85	2.75	2.54
13	4.67	3.81	3.41	3.18	3.03	2.92	2.83	2.77	2.67	2.46
14	4.60	3.74	3.34	3.11	2.96	2.85	2.76	2.70	2.60	2.39
15	4.54	3.68	3.29	3.06	2.90	2.79	2.71	2.64	2.54	2.33
16	4.49	3.63	3.24	3.01	2.85	2.74	2.66	2.59	2.49	2.28
17	4.45	3.59	3.20	2.96	2.81	2.70	2.61	2.55	2.45	2.23
18	4.41	3.55	3.16	2.93	2.77	2.66	2.58	2.51	2.41	2.19
19	4.38	3.52	3.13	2.90	2.74	2.63	2.54	2.48	2.38	2.16
20	4.35	3.49	3.10	2.87	2.71	2.60	2.51	2.45	2.35	2.12
21	4.32	3.47	3.07	2.84	2.68	2.57	2.49	2.42	2.32	2.10
22	4.30	3.44	3.05	2.82	2.66	2.55	2.46	2.40	2.30	2.07
23	4.28	3.42	3.03	2.80	2.64	2.53	2.44	2.37	2.27	2.05
24	4.26	3.40	3.01	2.78	2.62	2.51	2.42	2.36	2.25	2.03
25	4.24	3.39	2.99	2.76	2.60	2.49	2.40	2.34	2.24	2.10
30	4.17	3.32	2.92	2.69	2.53	2.42	2.33	2.27	2.16	1.93
60	4.00	3.23	2.84	2.61	2.45	2.34	2.25	2.18	2.08	1.84
120	3.92	3.07	2.68	2.45	2.29	2.18	2.09	2.02	1.91	1.66
infinity	3.84	3.00	2.60	2.37	2.21	2.10	2.01	1.94	1.83	1.57

v_2 = Degrees of Freedom for Denominator

Note: *F*-statistic is a joint probability distribution and measures statistical significance on the basis of two-sided hypotheses about more than one regression coefficient at a time. Unlike the *t* statistic, the *F* statistic is measured by two sets of degrees of freedom. v_1, the degrees of freedom for the numerator (the column values), is calculated by *K*, the number of restrictions (coefficients for the independent variables plus the intercept term) and the denominator (the row values) $v_2 = n - K - 1$, where *n* is the number of observations. Thus, if in an estimated equation there are 50 observations and 5 independent variables, then the numerator value (v_1) for the *F* statistic is 5 + 1 = 6, and the denominator value (v_2) is 50 - 5 - 1 = 44. Since we do not have the exact value corresponding to these degrees of freedom, approximate it with the closest number, which is $F(6,30) = 2.42$.

Critical Values of the *F* Statistic: 1 Percent Level of Significance

					$v_1 = $ *Degrees of Freedom for Numerator*					
	1	*2*	*3*	*4*	*5*	*6*	*7*	*8*	*10*	*20*
1	4052	5000	5403	5625	5764	5859	5928	5982	6056	6209
2	98.5	99.0	99.2	99.2	99.3	99.3	99.4	99.4	99.4	99.4
3	34.1	30.8	29.5	28.7	28.2	27.9	27.7	27.5	27.2	26.7
4	21.2	18.0	16.7	16.0	15.5	15.2	15.0	14.8	14.5	14.0
5	16.3	13.3	12.1	11.4	11.0	10.7	10.5	10.3	10.1	9.55
6	13.7	10.9	9.78	9.15	8.75	8.47	8.26	8.10	7.87	7.40
7	12.2	9.55	8.45	7.85	7.46	7.19	6.99	6.84	6.62	6.16
8	11.3	8.65	7.59	7.01	6.63	6.37	6.28	6.03	5.81	5.36
9	10.6	8.02	6.99	6.42	6.06	5.80	5.61	5.47	5.26	4.81
10	10.0	7.56	6.55	5.99	5.64	5.39	5.20	5.06	4.85	4.41
11	9.65	7.21	6.22	5.67	5.32	5.07	4.89	4.74	4.30	4.10
12	9.33	6.93	5.95	5.41	5.06	4.82	4.64	4.50	4.10	3.86
13	9.07	6.70	5.74	5.21	4.86	4.62	4.44	4.30	3.94	3.66
14	8.86	6.51	5.56	5.04	4.70	4.46	4.28	4.14	3.80	3.51
15	8.68	6.36	5.42	4.89	4.56	4.32	4.14	4.00	3.69	3.37
16	8.53	6.23	5.29	4.77	4.44	4.20	4.03	3.89	3.59	3.26
17	8.40	6.11	5.19	4.67	4.34	4.10	3.93	3.79	3.51	3.16
18	8.29	6.01	5.09	4.58	4.25	4.01	3.84	3.71	3.43	3.08
19	8.19	5.93	5.01	4.50	4.17	3.94	3.77	3.63	3.37	3.00
20	8.10	5.85	4.94	4.43	4.10	3.87	3.70	3.56	3.31	2.94
21	8.02	5.78	4.87	4.37	4.04	3.81	3.64	3.25	3.51	2.88
22	7.95	5.72	4.82	4.31	3.99	3.76	3.59	3.45	3.26	2.83
23	7.88	5.66	4.76	4.26	3.94	3.71	3.54	3.41	3.21	2.78
24	7.82	5.61	4.72	4.22	3.90	3.67	3.50	3.36	3.17	2.74
25	7.77	5.57	4.68	4.18	3.86	3.63	3.46	3.32	3.13	2.70
30	7.56	5.39	4.51	4.02	3.70	3.47	3.30	3.17	2.98	2.55
40	7.31	5.18	4.31	3.83	3.51	3.29	3.12	2.99	2.80	2.37
60	7.08	4.98	4.13	3.65	3.34	3.12	2.95	2.82	2.63	2.20
120	6.85	4.79	3.95	3.48	3.17	2.96	2.79	2.66	2.47	2.03
infinity	6.63	4.61	3.78	3.32	3.02	2.80	2.64	2.51	2.32	1.88

$v_2 = $ *Degrees of Freedom for Denominator*

471

The Chi-Square Distribution

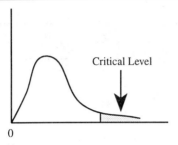

Critical Level

0

	Level of Significance (Probability of a Value of at Least as Large as the Table Entry)			
Degrees of Freedom	10%	5%	2.5%	1%
1	2.71	3.84	5.20	6.63
2	4.61	5.99	7.38	9.21
3	6.25	7.81	9.35	11.34
4	7.78	9.49	11.14	13.28
5	9.24	11.07	12.83	15.09
6	10.64	12.59	14.45	16.81
7	12.02	14.07	16.01	18.48
8	13.36	15.51	17.53	20.1
9	14.68	16.92	19.02	21.7
10	15.99	18.31	20.5	23.2
11	17.28	19.68	21.9	24.7
12	18.55	21.0	23.3	26.2
13	19.81	22.4	24.7	27.7
14	21.1	23.7	26.1	29.1
15	22.3	25.0	27.5	30.6
16	23.5	26.3	28.8	32.0
17	24.8	27.6	30.2	33.4
18	26.0	28.9	31.5	34.8
19	27.2	30.1	32.9	36.2
20	28.4	31.4	34.2	37.6

Business

MYSTAT ®

**An instructional business version of SYSTAT
for the Macintosh**

An instructional business version of SYSTAT

SYSTAT, Inc.
1800 Sherman Avenue
Evanston, IL 60201
Tel. 708.**864.5670**
FAX 708.**492.3567**

Introduction

This is a real statistics program—it is not just a demonstration. You can use MYSTAT to enter, transform, and save data, and to perform a wide range of statistical evaluations. Please use MYSTAT to solve *real* problems.

Business MYSTAT is a fully operational subset of SYSTAT, our premier statistics package. We've geared Business MYSTAT especially for teaching business statistics, with special forecasting and time series routines all in a single, easy-to-use machine.

Also available is our original MYSTAT program, geared for teaching non-business statistics. MYSTAT offers nonparametric tests in place of forecasting routines, and shares most of Business MYSTAT's other features.

Both versions of MYSTAT are available in Macintosh, IBM-PC/compatible, and VAX/VMS versions. Copies are available at a nominal cost.

For more information about SYSTAT, SYGRAPH, and our other top-rated professional statistics and graphics packages, please call or write.

Contents

Business	Installation	2
MYSTAT	Windows	2
	Menus	3
	Help	4
	Data Editor	4
	Entering data	4
	Editing data	7
	Saving data	8
	Editor menu	8
	Math...	8
	Recode...	9
	Find case...	9
	Fill worksheet	10
	Delete	11
	Formats...	11
	Data menu	11
	Sort...	11
	Rank...	11
	Weight...	11
	Formats...	11
	Results to...	11
	Analyze menu	12
	Stats	12
	Tables	13
	Ttest	13
	Corr	13
	Regress	14
	ANOVA	14
	Graph menu	15
	Plot	17
	Box	18
	Hist	19
	Stem	19
	Forecast menu	20
	Transform	20
	Smooth	20
	Series	20
	Redirecting output	21
	Optional command interface	22
	Why use commands?	22
	Using commands	22
	General commands	23
	Data Editor commands	24
	Statistical commands	25
	Regression and ANOVA	25
	Graphing commands	26
	Forecasting commands	27
	Index	28

Installation   MYSTAT requires one megabyte of memory and either a hard disk drive or two 800K floppy disk drives. It can handle up to 50 variables and as many cases as you can fit onto your disk.

On the MYSTAT disk, you should find four files. MYSTAT is the actual application, MYSTATA.HLP and MYSTATB.HLP are help files, and USSTATS.SYS is a sample data file.

Floppy disk system
- Insert the MYSTAT disk in a disk drive
- Double-click the MYSTAT disk icon
- Start MYSTAT: double-click the MYSTAT application icon

Hard disk system
- Use **File/New Folder** to create a MYSTAT folder
- Insert the MYSTAT disk in the floppy disk drive
- Double-click the MYSTAT disk icon
- Drag all the MYSTAT files to the MYSTAT folder
- Start MYSTAT: double-click the MYSTAT application icon.

Once you have created MYSTAT data files, you can double-click them to enter MYSTAT.

We urge you to use a copy of the MYSTAT disk store the original disk as a backup.

Windows   MYSTAT uses four different windows: the Data Editor window, the View window, the Analysis (text output) window and the Command window. All of the windows are resizable.

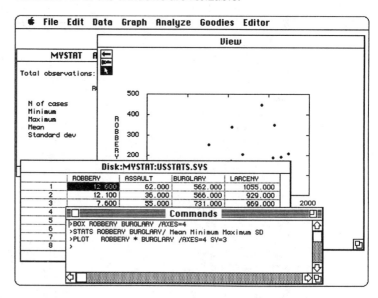

© 1990, SYSTAT, Inc.

Data are displayed in the *Data Editor.* You enter, edit, and view data with the Data Editor. You can cut, copy, and paste data to and from the Data Editor. MYSTAT executes transformations on columns of the Data Editor.

Graphs are displayed in the *View window.* You can open and close it with **Show/Hide view window** from the **Goodies** menu.

Statistical output is displayed in the *Analysis window.* The Analysis window is a text editor. You may type comments, cut and paste, and reformat output to write reports. You may also use the window as a text editor for writing batch files of commands (see the last section, "Optional Command Interface.")

You can use the optional command interface in the Commands window. Because MYSTAT operates entirely with menus and dialog boxes, the Command window is only open if you select **Show command window** from the **Goodies** menu. The Command window is also a text editor. You may find it useful to use **Cut**, **Copy**, and **Paste** to fix mistakes and re-enter commands.

Menus

The menu bar at the top of the screen shows MYSTAT's seven menus:

 File   Edit   Data   Graph   Analyze   Goodies   Editor

You open, close, and save data files with the **File** menu. You can print and save selected text and graphs, submit commands from a file or the Clipboard, and quit MYSTAT.

The **Edit** menu contains items for copying, cutting, pasting, and displaying the Clipboard.

The **Data** menu allows you to sort, rank, and standardize variables; redirect analysis output to the printer or a file; and control the format settings of the Analysis window.

Use the **Graph** menu to plot graphs. For each item, MYSTAT presents a dialog box where you select variables and plotting options.

Use the **Analyze** menu to compute statistics. For each item, MYSTAT presents a dialog box where you select variables and options.

The **Goodies** menu provides an introduction to MYSTAT and information about SYSTAT. Other items let you open the view and command windows and transfer to another application.

The **Editor** menu offers items for working with the Data Editor: for creating, changing, and deleting variables, finding cases, and generating random data.

Help   You can obtain on-screen help for MYSTAT in three ways:

- Click the question mark (?) icon in the upper left corner of any of MYSTAT's dialog boxes for help regarding that procedure

- Select **Help** from the **Editor** menu for help with the Data Editor.

- Use the HELP command in the Commands window for help using the command interface. "HELP <command>" displays information about the command you specify.

Introduction from the **Goodies** menu introduces MYSTAT. Also in the **Goodies** menu, **Information about SYSTAT...** provides information about our premier package.

The help files, MYSTATA.TXT, MYSTATB.TXT, and MYSTAT.TXT, are text files you can edit and customize—see **Goodies/Introduction**.

Data Editor   The MYSTAT Data Editor lets you enter and edit data, view data, and transform variables algebraically.

When you start MYSTAT, an empty Editor window appears. MYSTAT stores data in a rectangular format. Variables fill vertical columns and contain cases—each horizontal row represents a case. The top row holds variable names, and the first column automatically numbers the cases.

Entering data   You can enter data three ways:

- Type data from the keyboard, using the mouse or cursor arrow keys to move around and make corrections.

- Copy or cut data from another application into the Clipboard, start MYSTAT, and paste the data from the Clipboard into the Editor.

- Import data by reading plain text (ASCII) files.

Entering data from the keyboard
To type data from the keyboard, first enter variable names in the top row and then enter values in the cells underneath. Variable names must begin with a letter and can be no longer than 8 characters.

Character variables (those whose values are words and letters) must have names ending with a dollar sign ($). The dollar sign does not count toward the eight character limit.

Numeric variables (those whose values are numbers) can be named with subscripts; e.g. ITEM(3). Subscripts are sometimes useful because they allow you to specify a range of variables when using the Command window. For example, STATS ITEM(1–3) does descriptive statistics on the first three ITEM(n) variables.

The cursor is already positioned on the first cell in the top row. To name your first variable, CITY$, just type "city$" and press Return.

```
┌─────────────────────────────────────────────────┐
│ ▤□▤▤▤▤▤▤ MYSTAT Data Editor ▤▤▤▤ ▣▤ │
│         │  CITY$  │███████████│          │    ⇧ │
│    1    │         │           │          │      │
│    2    │         │           │          │      │
│    3    │         │           │          │      │
│    4    │         │           │          │      │
│    5    │         │           │          │      │
│    6    │         │           │          │      │
│    7    │         │           │          │      │
│    8    │         │           │          │      │
│    9    │         │           │          │      │
│   10    │         │           │          │    ⇩ │
│ ◁▤▤▤▤▤▤▤▤▤▤▤▤▤▤▤▤▤▤▤▤▤▤▤▤▤▤▤▤▤▤▤▤▤ ⇨▣ │
└─────────────────────────────────────────────────┘
```

Notice that MYSTAT enters the name in upper-case regardless of
whether you used lower- or upper-case. The cursor moves to the second column. You're now ready to name the rest of the variables,
STATE$, POP, and RAINFALL, pressing Return to enter them into the
worksheet.

```
┌─────────────────────────────────────────────────┐
│ ▤□▤▤▤▤▤▤ MYSTAT Data Editor ▤▤▤▤ ▣▤ │
│      │ STATE$  │   POP   │RAINFALL│████████│  ⇧ │
│   1  │         │         │        │        │    │
│   2  │         │         │        │        │    │
│   3  │         │         │        │        │    │
│   4  │         │         │        │        │    │
│   5  │         │         │        │        │    │
│   6  │         │         │        │        │    │
│   7  │         │         │        │        │    │
│   8  │         │         │        │        │    │
│   9  │         │         │        │        │    │
│  10  │         │         │        │        │  ⇩ │
│ ◁▤▤▤▤▤▤▤▤▤▤▤▤█▤▤▤▤▤▤▤▤▤▤▤▤▤▤▤▤▤▤ ⇨▣ │
└─────────────────────────────────────────────────┘
```

Now you can enter values. Move the cursor to the first blank cell under CITY$ and click the mouse button. The cell is selected, and you
can type the first data point, New York, and press Return to enter it.

```
┌─────────────────────────────────────────────────┐
│ ▤□▤▤▤▤▤▤ MYSTAT Data Editor ▤▤▤▤ ▣▤ │
│      │  CITY$  │ STATE$  │   POP   │RAINFALL│ ⇧ │
│   1  │New York │█████████│         │        │   │
│   2  │         │         │         │        │   │
│   3  │         │         │         │        │   │
│   4  │         │         │         │        │   │
│   5  │         │         │         │        │   │
│   6  │         │         │         │        │   │
│   7  │         │         │         │        │   │
│   8  │         │         │         │        │   │
│   9  │         │         │         │        │   │
│  10  │         │         │         │        │ ⇩ │
│ ◁▤▤▤▤▤▤▤▤▤▤▤▤▤▤▤▤▤▤▤▤▤▤▤▤▤▤▤▤▤▤▤ ⇨▣ │
└─────────────────────────────────────────────────┘
```

MYSTAT accepts the value and moves the cursor one cell to the right.
If you choose [Enter down] from **Editor/Formats...**, the cursor will
move down rather than to the right when you press Return. You
could also move the cursor down with the Down-arrow key.

Character values can be up to twelve characters long and must begin
with a letter be surrounded by single or double quotation marks. (If
you need to use single or double quotation marks as part of a value,
surround the whole value with the opposite marks.) Unlike variable
names, character values are case sensitive—use whichever
combination of upper- and lower-case you desire. To represent missing character values, enter a blank space surrounded by quotation
marks.

Numeric values can be up to 1035 in absolute magnitude. Scientific notation is used for long numbers; e.g., .000000000015 is equivalent to 1.5E–11. For missing numeric values, enter a decimal (.).

Now enter the data values: type a value, press Return, and then type the next value. The cursor automatically moves to the beginning of the next case when a row is filled.

	CITY$	STATE$	POP	RAINFALL
1	New York	NY	7164742.000	57.000
2	Los Angeles	CA	3096721.000	7.000
3	Chicago	IL	2992472.000	34.000
4	Dallas	TX	974234.000	33.900
5	Phoenix	AZ	853266.000	14.900
6	Miami	FL	346865.000	60.000
7	Washington	DC	638432.000	37.700
8	Kansas City	MO	448159.000	38.800
9				
10				

Pasting data from the Clipboard

You can enter data by pasting it in from the Clipboard. Your data must be in the correct row and column format and values must be separated by either commas, tabs, or spaces. Any character values containing a space must be surrounded by double or single quotation marks, e.g. "New York".

To copy or cut data from the Editor, position the cursor in one corner of the range you want to cut or copy. Press the mouse button, drag the pointer to the diagonally opposite corner of the range, and release the button. (If you want to add more cells to the selected range, hold the Shift key and drag the pointer.) To select large ranges, click the cell in one corner of the range, hold the Shift key, and click the diagonally opposite cell.

Once you have selected a range of data, you can use **Copy** or **Cut** from the **Edit** menu to move the data (or a copy) to the Clipboard. If you use **Cut**, MYSTAT fills the vacated cells with missing values.

For example, if you cut the range selected below:

	CITY$	STATE$	POP	RAINFALL
1	New York	NY	7164742.000	57.000
2	Los Angeles	CA	3096721.000	7.000
3	Chicago	IL	2992472.000	34.000
4	Dallas	TX	974234.000	33.900
5	Phoenix	AZ	853266.000	14.900
6	Miami	FL	346865.000	60.000
7	Washington	DC	638432.000	37.700
8	Kansas City	MO	448159.000	38.800
9				
10				

the worksheet would look like this:

	CITY$	STATE$	POP	RAINFALL
1	New York	NY	7164742.000	57.000
2	Los Angeles	CA	3096721.000	7.000
3	Chicago	IL	2992472.000	34.000
4	Dallas	TX	974234.000	33.900
5	Phoenix			14.900
6	Miami			60.000
7	Washington			37.700
8	Kansas City	MO	448159.000	38.800
9				
10				

To paste data from the Clipboard, position the cursor in the upper left corner of the area you want to fill with data. Then, select **Paste** from the **Edit** menu.

You can use **Cut**, **Copy**, and **Paste** to move data from one place in the Editor to another, or to copy data from another application. **Clear** works like the Delete key—MYSTAT replaces the selected range with missing values without involving the Clipboard.

You can select the entire data file with **Select all** from the **Edit** menu.

Importing text files
You can read raw data from a text file into MYSTAT. The file you are reading must be text only (plain text, ASCII) and must contain only raw data—*no variable labels*. Values in the file must be separated by either commas, spaces, or tabs. Any character values containing a space must be surrounded by double or single quotation marks. Before reading a text file, you must start with a new worksheet (use **File/New**).

Select **Open** from the **File** menu and click the [Text] option of the dialog box. Select the text file containing your data and click [Open]. MYSTAT names the columns in the MYSTAT data file COL01, COL02, COL03, …, COL*n*. MYSTAT adds a dollar sign ($) for character variables. You may edit the variable names.

Editing data

You can select individual cells by moving the cursor with the mouse or the cursor arrow keys. You can move around with the scroll bars at the bottom and right edges of the window. If you pass the end of the screen, the worksheet scrolls to the next row or column. To change a value or variable name, select the cell, type the new value, and press Return.

Deleting an entire row or column
You can delete an entire row or column from the Editor. First, select the row or column you want to delete by double-clicking the cell containing its case number or variable name. Then select **Delete** from the **Editor** menu. *Be careful: once a row or column is deleted, it is gone forever.*

Saving data   You can save the data currently in the Editor into either a MYSTAT data file or a text file with **Save as...** from the **File** menu. You must specify a filename and choose which folder to put it in.

The buttons at the bottom of the **Save as...** dialog box allow you to choose the type of file you want saved. To save a MYSTAT data file, click the [Mystat] button. To save a text (ASCII) file with values separated by comma delimiters and character values surrounded by quotation marks, click [Text]. To save a text file with tab delimiters, click [Tab delimited]. Start the save by clicking Save.

Editor menu   The Editor menu contains items that allow you to define new variables algebraically or to redefine (recode) existing variables.

Math...   **Math...** allows you to transform existing variables and define new ones algebraically.

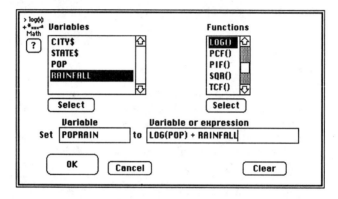

- Select **Math...** from the **Editor** menu
- Use any combination of selecting and typing to fill in the Set statement
- Click OK

Select a variable or function by double-clicking on it or by clicking it and then clicking [Select]. To create a new variable, type a valid variable name in the [Variable] box. New variables are added to the end of the file.

To move between boxes, press Tab or use the mouse. Choose any valid combination of variables, functions, and operators to define the new or transformed variable. Character values must be specified in double or single quotation marks.

Be sure to place the arguments of functions inside the parentheses. If you fill the [Variable or expression] box by using the selection lists, MYSTAT will generally interpret your selections correctly.

The following are examples of valid statements.

```
Set ALPHA$ to 'abcdef'
Set LPOP to LOG(POP)
Set LOGIT1 to 1/(1+EXP(A+B*X))
```

You may edit in the window by moving the cursor with the mouse and typing. Click [OK] to start the transformation.

Recode...

Recode... does conditional transformations. MYSTAT transforms the variable as specified for every case that the If-clause evaluates true.

```
If SEX$ = 'male' then set GROUP to 1
If group > 2 then set NEWGROUP to 2
```

If you click [Complex recode], a new dialog box lets you use logical AND and OR. With these you can create a complex test condition. Examples of complex recodings are:

```
If SEX$='male' AND AGE>20 then set GROUP to 1
If TEMP>100 OR TEMP<0 then set TEMP$ to 'EXTREME'
```

Find case...

Find case... searches through the Data Editor and highlights the first value that meets the condition you specify, starting from the current cursor position. For the data we entered earlier, the following Find statement moves the cursor to case 4.

```
Find POP < 1000000
```

Subsequently you may use **Find next** to repeat a search and find the next case that meets the search condition. The [Complex find] button opens a dialog box that allows you to use logical AND and OR in the test condition to build statements like the following:

```
Find INCOME<10000 AND STATE$<>'NY'
```

Functions, relations, and operators for Math, Recode, and Find

+	addition	**CASE**	current case number
-	subtraction	**URN**	uniform random number (0,1)
*	multiplication	**ZRN**	normal random number (0,1)
/	division		
^	exponentiation	**AND**	logical and
> ·	greater than	**OR**	logical or
<	less than	**INT**	integer truncation
>=	greater than or equal to	**SQR**	square root
<=	less than or equal to	**LOG**	natural logarithm (base *e*)
=	equal to	**EXP**	exponential function
<>	not equal to	**ABS**	absolute value

Distribution functions

MYSTAT offers the following cumulative and inverse distribution functions:

Distribution	Cumulative	Inverse
Normal	ZCF(z)	ZIF(alpha)
Exponential	ECF(x)	EIF(alpha)
Chi-square	XCF(chisq,df)	XIF(alpha,df)
T	TCF(t,df)	TIF(alpha,df)
F	FCF(F,df1,df2)	FIF(alpha,df1,df2)
Poisson	PCF(k,lambda)	PIF(alpha,k)
Binomial	NCF(p,k,n)	NIF(alpha,k,n)
Logistic	LCF(x)	LIF(alpha)
Studentized range	SCF(x,k,df)	SIF(alpha,k,df)
Weibull	WCF(x,p,q)	WIF(alpha,p,q)

Cumulative distribution functions compute the probability that a random value from the specified distribution falls below a given value; that is, it shows the proportion of the distribution below that value. Inverse distribution functions do the same thing backwards: you specify an alpha value (a probability or proportion) between zero and one, and MYSTAT shows the critical value below which lies that proportion.

The uniform distribution is uniformly distributed from zero to one. The normal distribution is a standard normal distribution with mean zero and standard deviation one. The exponential distribution has parameter one. The cumulative Poisson function calculates the probability of the number of random events between zero and k when the expected value is *lambda*. The binomial cumulative function provides the probability of k or more occurrences in n trials with the binomial probability p.

Use the cumulative distribution functions to obtain probabilities associated with observed sample statistics. Use the inverse distribution to determine critical values and to construct confidence intervals. Finally, to generate pseudo-random data for the functions, apply the appropriate inverse cumulative distribution function to uniform random data.

Fill
worksheet...

Fill worksheet... fills a specified number of cases with missing values which may then be replaced with random data.

• Name the variables you want to fill

• Select **Fill worksheet...** from the **Editor** menu
• Specify the number of rows (cases) to be filled with missing values
• Click OK

• Select **Math...** from the **Editor** menu
• Fill in the Set statement; e.g., Set A to URN, or Set B to ZRN
• Click OK

Delete	**Delete** removes an entire case or variable from the dataset currently in the Editor. Select the row or column by double-clicking the variable name or case number cell, and then select **Delete**. *Be careful: you cannot undo a deletion.*
Formats...	**Editor/Formats...** lets you choose the number of digits displayed after the decimal in the Editor. Note that the **Data** menu has a similar **Formats** item for controlling analysis output.
	You can also choose [Enter down] or [Enter right] to control whether the cursor moves down or right when you are entering values.
Data menu	The **Data** menu has items for sorting, ranking, weighting, redirecting output, and controlling the Analysis output.
Sort...	**Sort...** sorts cases according to the variables you specify. Values are sorted in ascending order. You may select up to ten numeric and/or character variables for a nested sort.
	The sorted data are saved in a new file, which you must then **Open...** Note that you *must* sort a variable by its group to get grouped statistics with **Stats** from the **Analyze** menu.
Rank...	**Rank...** replaces the values of a variable with their rank order for that variable. Tied ranks are averaged.
	The ranked data are saved in a new file. You must **Open...** the ranked file to use the ranked data.
Weight...	**Weight...** replicates cases according to the integer portions of the values of the weighting variable you select. The weighted data are used until you select the [Weighting off] option in the **Weight** dialog box.
Formats...	The results of statistical analyses appear in the Analysis window. Usually, the window is cleared before each analysis. You can instead have output scroll up and accumulate by checking [Scroll analyses] in **Data/Formats...**
	You can select fonts for text and graphic output. Choose [Text] or [Graphics] and select a font and size. You cannot change text and graph fonts at the same time. To change both, first change one, click OK, and then change the other.
	You should use a non-proportional font such as Monaco or Courier for statistical output; proportional fonts destroy the tidy columns.
Results to...	The three **Results to...** items let you save and print statistical and graphic output. See the later section "Redirecting output" for instructions.

Analyze menu

Once your data are in a MYSTAT data file, you can use MYSTAT's statistical and graphics routines to examine them. You must have the file open in the Editor.

Analysis results appear in the Analysis window; recall that this is a text editor. You can edit your output and add comments right in the window, and then save or print your report.

Stats

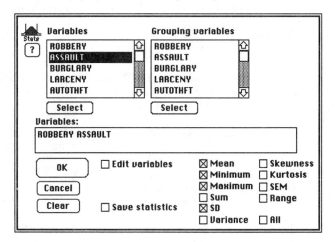

Stats provides basic descriptive statistics for numerical variables. MYSTAT displays the following dialog box.

```
Total Observations:    48

                    ROBBERY       ASSAULT

  N of cases               48            48
  Minimum               6.500        21.000
  Maximum             443.300       293.000
  Mean                102.925       136.667
  Standard dev         92.834        68.110
```

You can get statistics on as many variables as you want. If you do not specify a variable, you get statistics on every numeric variable in the file. You can ask for any combination of the statistics provided.

If you select a grouping variable, MYSTAT does a separate analysis for each group. The file must be sorted according to the grouping variable(s).

The [Save statistics] option allows you to save one—and only one—statistic into a MYSTAT data file. Or, you can Copy the statistical output from the Analysis window and paste it into the Editor.

12

Tables

Tables

Tables provides frequency and multi-way tables. For two-way tables, MYSTAT provides chi-square test statistics, association coefficients and proportional reduction of error (PRE) statistics with their asymptotic standard errors. You can produce a table containing frequencies, cell percents, row percents, or column percents. You can tell MYSTAT to ignore missing data.

One-way tables show the number of times a distinct value appears in a variable. Two-way and multi-way tables count the appearances of each unique combination of values. Multi-way tables count the appearances of a value in each subgroup. Percent tables convert the frequencies to percentages of the total count: row percent tables show percentages of the total for each row, and column percent tables show percentages of the total for each column.

Ttest

Ttest

Ttest does dependent and independent *t*-tests. A dependent (paired samples) *t*-test tests whether the means of two continuous variables differ. An independent *t*-test tests whether the means of two groups of a single variable differ.

To request a dependent (paired) *t*-test, select two or more continuous variables from the left selection list. MYSTAT tests each possible pairing of the variables you select.

To request an independent *t*-test, select one or more continuous variables from the left selection list and one grouping variable from the right list. The grouping variable must have exactly two values. MYSTAT tests each continuous variable you select against the grouping variable.

You can also do a one-sample *t*-test by adding a variable to your data file that has a constant value corresponding to the population mean of your null hypothesis. Then do a dependent *t*-test on this variable and your data variable.

Corr

Corr

Corr computes a matrix of Pearson correlation coefficients for the variables you select. MYSTAT uses all numerical variables by default. You can select pairwise or listwise deletion of missing data. Rank the variables before correlating to compute Spearman rank-order correlations.

Correlation measures the strength of linear association between two variables. A value of 1 or –1 indicates a perfect linear relationship; a value of 0 indicates that neither variable can be linearly predicted from the other.

Regress

Regress computes simple and multiple regression models and balanced or unbalanced ANOVA designs. For unbalanced designs, MYSTAT uses the method of weighted squares of means. You can calculate non-factorial designs and models with factor-by-covariate interactions. For fully factorial designs use **ANOVA**.

First, select the dependent variable. Then select your independent variable(s). MYSTAT adds a CONSTANT (intercept) term to the equation unless you click off the [Constant] box. You should almost always include a constant term in your model.

If the independent variable is categorical, click the [Categorical] button before you select the variable. MYSTAT asks you to specify the number of factor levels (grouping values) the variable has. All categorical variable must have integer values 1 to k, where k is the number of categories.

For complex models, click [Edit equation] and type your equation.

Here are some examples of valid models:

```
Y=X                        simple regression—no constant
Y=CONSTANT + X             simple regression with constant
Y=CONSTANT + X + Z         multiple regression
Y=CONSTANT + X + A + B +   ANOCOVA with categorical factors
   A*B + A*X + B*X + A*B*X    A and B and covariate X
```

The last example tests the homogeneity of regression slopes assumption by including interactions with the covariate.

Saving residuals

If you click [Save residuals], MYSTAT saves a data file containing the variables in your equation, estimated values, residuals, standard error of prediction, leverage, Cook's D, and externally studentized residuals. MYSTAT names these variables ESTIMATE, RESIDUAL, SEPRED, LEVERAGE, COOK, and STUDENT. For linear models, MYSTAT lists cases with extreme studentized residuals or leverage values and displays the Durbin-Watson statistic and first order autocorrelation coefficient.

ANOVA

ANOVA produces fully-factorial ANOVAs and ANCOVAs. Select the dependent variable, and then select the categorical variables and enter the number of levels for each variable. To include a covariate, click the [Covariate(s)] box and type the name of the covariate(s).

For example, if you select Y as a dependent variable with A and B as factors, MYSTAT estimates the equation Y=CONSTANT + A + B + A*B. If you add X as a covariate, MYSTAT estimates Y=CONSTANT + X + A + B + A*B.

Graph menu   Graphical analyses are provided in the **Graph** menu. Formatting items useful in graphing are found in the **Goodies** and **Data** menus. Graphs appear in the View window.

Resizing graphs

To resize *subsequent* graphs, trace a marquee in the View window. Press the mouse button, drag a marquee, and release the button. The bottom of the window shows the size of the box. (If you have not displayed a graph, you can open the View window with **Show view window** from the **Goodies** menu.)

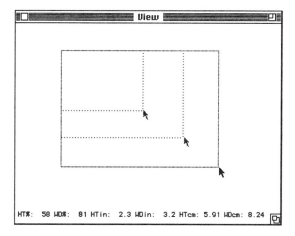

You cannot plot or print a graph larger than the View window. You can, however, resize the View window to accommodate larger plots.

Moving graphs in the View window

You can move subsequent graphs to a new position in the View window by clicking inside the marquee. The bottom of the screen shows the coordinates of the bottom left corner of the marquee.

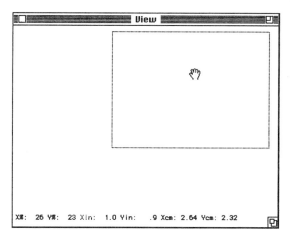

MYSTAT prints your next plot in the new area with the new size.

Setting axis scales

Graph dialog boxes allow you to set axis scales with the options labeled MIN, MAX, XMIN, XMAX, YMIN, or YMAX. You can also select the axes and grids you want. To use no axes or grids, click off the highlighted options.

Overlaying graphs

You can overlay several graphs in one View window. For each plot after the first, MYSTAT asks whether to overlay the next plot on top of the previous or to clear the View window before drawing the next plot.

You can use the sizing and relocating facility described above to place consecutive graphs at various locations in the window before clicking [Overlay plot].

For example, here is a scatterplot with a box plot overlaid above it. The scatterplot has already been plotted, and the box plot will go in the marquee. Note that we omit the axis from the box plot.

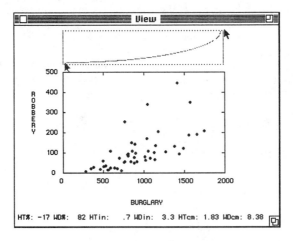

After tracing the new position, click [Overlay plot].

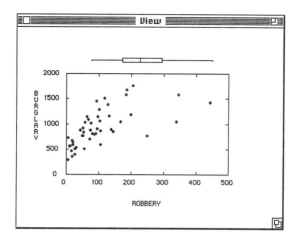

Plot

Plot provides scatterplots, influence plots, bubble plots, and line plots.

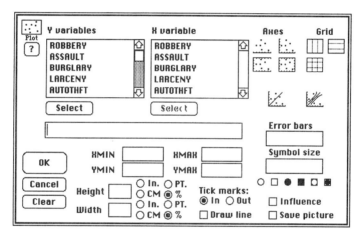

First, select variables. You can plot more than one Y variable against a single X variable. Then select options for the plot. If you specify a symbol size, plotting symbols are scaled by that factor.

Error bars

You can add error bars by specifying the error variable in the [Error bars] box. MYSTAT draws tick marks above and below each point according to the value of the error variable.

Bubble plots

You can draw bubble plots by specifying an appropriately-scaled numeric variable for [Symbol size].

Influence plots

[Influence] scales the size of each plotting symbol according to that case's influence on the correlation coefficient. [Draw line] draws lines connecting all the points, beginning with the first case in the file and ending with the last.

Regression lines and confidence bands

You can also request a regression line or a regression line with confidence bands. If you request confidence intervals, MYSTAT asks you to specify a percentage.

Box

Box plots simple, grouped, and notched box plots. Select the variable(s) you want to plot. A grouping variable is optional.

Here is a simple box plot of POP from the USSTATS dataset.

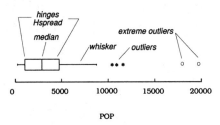

POP

The center line of the box marks the *median*. The edges of the box show the upper and lower *hinges*. The median splits the ordered batch of numbers in half, and the hinges split these halves in half again. The distance between the hinges is called the *Hspread*. The *whiskers* show the range of points within 1.5 Hspreads of the hinges. Points outside this range are marked with asterisks, and points more than 3 Hspreads from the hinges are marked with circles.

[Notched]

The [Notched] option produces notched grouped box plots. Notches give simultaneous confidence intervals for group medians. The median of each box is notched and the box returns to full width at the lower and upper confidence interval values. If the intervals around two medians do not overlap, you can be confident at about the 95% level that the two population medians are different.

[Transpose] and [Groups]

[Transpose] rotates the plot 90 degrees clockwise. You can enter a number in the [Groups] box to limit the number of boxes in a grouped box plot.

Hist

Hist

Hist provides histograms for one or more variables. A histogram shows the distribution of a variable. The data are divided into equal-sized intervals along the horizontal axis. The number of values in each interval is represented by a vertical bar. The height of each bar can be measured in two ways: the axis on the right side shows the actual number of cases that have that value, and the left axis shows the same information in proportion per standard unit.

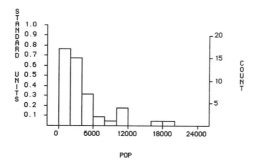

Stem

Stem

Stem plots a stem-and-leaf diagram for one or more variables and the median and quartiles of the variable(s). The numbers on the left side are *stems* (the most significant digit that varies). The *leaves* on the right are the subsequent digits.

Here is a stem-and-leaf plot of the variable POP from USSTATS. The stems are 1000's digits and the leaves are 100's. You can see that POP had eight cases in the 2000's.

```
        Stem and leaf plot of variable:     POP    , N =    48
Minimum is:        328.000
Lower hinge is:        1029.000
Median is:        2888.000
Upper hinge is:        4798.500
Maximum is:      19715.000

        0    344566667999
        1 H  04778
        2 M  01124579
        3    1335788
        4 H  34569
        5    16
        6    6
        7    0
        8    7
    ***Outside values***
       10    599
       11    6
       17    9
       19    7
```

Forecast menu

MYSTAT's time series routines operate within the computer's working memory. That is, the results of transformations and smoothings are not saved to your disk data file (unless you check the [Save file] box in the appropriate dialog box). To see your results, you must do a time series, autocorrelation, or partial autocorrelation plot. MYSTAT uses the smoothed and/or transformed values. Select **Clear** from the **Forecast** menu when you want to restore the variable's original values.

Note: items in the **Forecast** menu require that your series data have *no missing values.*

Transform
$t=t_2-t_1$
$\log(t)$
$\Sigma \ x=x^2$
Transform

Forecast/Transform replaces the values of the series according to the option you choose:

[Mean]	Subtracts the variable's mean from each value.
[Log]	Replaces each value with its natural logarithm.
[Square]	Squares each value.
[Trend]	Removes linear trend.
[Percent change]	Replaces each value with its percentage difference from the immediately preceding value.
[Difference]	Replaces each value with its differences from the immediately preceding value (unless you specify a different [Lag]).
[Index]	Divides each value by the first value of the series, or by the [Base] value you specify.

Smooth

Smooth

Forecast/Smooth removes the local variations from a series and makes it easier to see the series' general shape.

Running smoothers replace each value with the mean or median of that value and its neighbors. The "window" is the number of values considered at a time. You can optionally specify weights for each value, separated by commas.

Seasonal decomposition removes additive or multiplicative seasonal effects according to the periodicity you specify.

Exponential smoothing forecasts future observations as a weighted average (running smooth) of previous observations. You can optionally specify a linear or percentage growth component and an additive or multiplicative seasonal effects component. Specify the number or range of cases to be forecast.

Series
CASE
ACF
Series

Series produces time series plots, or case plots, which show the variable you select plotted against Case (time). Click [Standardize] to standardize the variable (subtract the mean from each value and divide by the standard deviation) before plotting. MYSTAT plots the first fifteen cases unless you specify otherwise.

ACF plots show how closely each value is related to the value immediately preceding. An autocorrelation is like an ordinary correlation of a series with itself shifted once, twice, etc. If each point is related to the previous point's value, then the correlation is high. The second autocorrelation reveals dependencies that go back two points, etc.

PACF plots show how closely each point in a series is related to preceding values after partialing out the influence of intervening points. Examine partial autocorrelations for effects that do not depend linearly on previous (smaller lag) autocorrelations.

ACF and PACF plots show correlation coefficients for each lag and also plot the coefficients in a sideways bar chart.

Redirecting output

Ordinarily, MYSTAT sends its results to the screen. You can use the **Results to...** items in the **Data** menu to route output to the printer or a text file.

Results to window	Sends all subsequent stats and graphs to the Analysis and View windows only.
Results to printer	Sends all subsequent stats and graphs to the printer.
Results to file as...	Sends all subsequent stats to a text file. You cannot redirect graphs to a text file.

Saving graphs in files

You cannot save graphs in text files with **Results to file as...**; however, you *can* save graphs in PICT files, one graph per file. Either check [Save picture] in the dialog box before clicking OK *or* select **Save graph as...** from the **File** menu.

Printing graphs

You can print a single graph by selecting **Print graph** from the **File** menu when the View window is active.

Printing and saving selected analysis results

To save a specific piece of Analysis output in a text file, use the mouse to select the range of text you want, and then select **Save selected text as...** from the **File** menu.

Optional command interface

You can operate MYSTAT interactively with menus and dialog boxes or by typing commands in the Command window. You can also operate in batch mode by submitting commands from the Clipboard or a file.

Why use commands?

If you're doing a lot of repetitive analyses, generating many variables algebraically, or using ranges of variables frequently, command lines are more efficient.

If all you want is a record of your work, you don't even need to use commands. Just open the Command window before you start working, do your usual point-and-click routine, and then save or print the contents of the Commands window, which automatically generates commands while you work. If you publish your results and a reader disputes your analyses, you can recreate your work from start to finish with MYSTAT's commands. Otherwise, you *cannot defend your work*. In the private sector, auditors often require lists of command statements.

Using commands

To open the Command window, select **Show command window** from the **Goodies** menu. The prompt (>) indicates that MYSTAT is ready to accept a command. Press Return at the end of each line.

If you are ever unsure about how to use a particular command, just select **Show command window**, use menus, and study the commands that are generated.

Notation used in the command reference

Any item in *italic typeface* is representative—insert an actual value or variable in its place. Replace *var* with a variable name, *varlist* with one or more variable names, *gvar* with a grouping variable, *yvar* with a *y* variable, *n* with a number, and so on.

A straight vertical line (|) means *or*. Any item in brackets ([ ]) is optional. Underlining indicates default options—those that are selected unless you specify otherwise. For example, "TICK=IN | OUT" indicates that ticks are automatically used for graphs, and the default is for ticks to be placed inside the axes.

You *must* place a comma at the end of any line where the command continues on a subsequent line. File names and character values are case sensitive and must be surrounded by single or double quotation marks. You can abbreviate command words to the first three letters, but variable names, filenames, and character values must be typed in full.

Options, indented in the reference, are separated from the main part of the command with a slash (/). Use only one slash, even if including several options.

Submitting batches

You can submit batches of commands from the Clipboard or a text file. Commands in batches must appear exactly as in the command window, but without the prompts (>). You can type a list of commands in either text window, select them, Cut or Copy them to the Clipboard, or save them in a file. You can then submit the batch with **Submit command file** or **Submit Clipboard** from the **File** menu.

General commands

EDIT "*filename*"	Opens *filename* in Data Editor.
USE "*filename*"	Opens *filename* without Editor.
WRITE "*filename*"	Saves worksheet into data file *filename*.

SAVE saves statistics from the next procedure in a data file, as if you had checked [Save] in a dialog box. You must use SAVE before sorting or ranking data to save the transformed file.

SAVE "*filename*"	Saves subsequent statistics.
PICT "*filename*"	Saves current graph in PICT file.
MAC "*filename*"	Saves worksheet in tab-delimited text file for exporting to other Mac applications.
GET "*filename*"	Imports text file and displays it in Data Editor.
PUT "*filename*"	Saves worksheet in comma delimited text file for exporting to other applications.
NEW	Clears windows and opens Editor.
SUBMIT "*filename*"	Executes batch file *filename*.
FORMAT=*n*	Shows *n* digits after decimal point. For *n*=–1, shows no decimal point.

OUTPUT
  *
  @
  "*filename*"
	Controls output according to argument:
	Sends subsequent output to the screen only.
	Sends all subsequent output to the printer.
	Sends subsequent *text* output to *filename*.

NOTE="*comment*"	Displays *comment* in output.
ORIGIN=(*n, m*)	Sets origin of graph display area to (*n, m*).
QUIT	Ends MYSTAT session.
HELP *command*	Help for *command* or list of valid commands.
INTRO	Introduction to MYSTAT.
SYSTAT	Provides information about SYSTAT.

Data Editor commands	`SORT varlist`	Sorts by *varlist*. Use SAVE first.
	`RANK varlist`	Transforms all variables in *varlist* to their ranked value. Use SAVE first.
	`WEIGHT var`	Replicates cases in worksheet according to *var*.
	`LET var = exprn`	Assigns value given by *exprn* to *var*.
	`IF exprn1 THEN LET var = exprn2`	Assigns value given by *exprn2* to *var* when the test condition (IF *exprn1*) is true.
	`REPEAT n`	Fills first *n* cases with missing values.
	`FIND exprn`	Finds first case that meets the condition given by *exprn*. Without an argument, FIND repeats the last search.

Statistical commands	`STATS varlist`	Descriptive statistics for each variable.

	`/BY gvarlist`
	`MEAN MINIMUM MAXIMUM`
	`  SD SUM VARIANCE`
	`  SKEWNESS KURTOSIS`
	`  SEM RANGE ALL`
		Statistics for each group given by g*varlist.*
		Specify which statistics are calculated.

	`ALL`	Specifies that all ten statistics be calculated.
	`TABULATE varlist` `  [*gvar1*gvar2*…]`	Frequency tables for each variable in *varlist,* or all numeric variables. Multi-way tables are produced from grouping variables.
	`/COLPCT FREQUENCY` `  PERCENT ROWPCT`	Specify the type/s of table/s to be computed.
	`LIST`	Produces list format tables.
	`MISS`	Excludes missing values.
	`PEARSON varlist`	Pearson correlation matrix for all variables in *varlist,* or all numeric variables.
	`/LISTWISE	PAIRWISE`	Choose type of deletion of missing values.
	`TTEST varlist [*var]`	Performs a *t*-test on the numeric variables given in *varlist.* For an independent *t*-test, include **var.* For a dependent *t*-test, *varlist* must be two or more numeric variables.

Regression and ANOVA

The MODEL and ESTIMATE commands provide linear regression. MODEL specifies the regression equation and ESTIMATE tells MYSTAT to start working. Your MODEL should almost always include a CONSTANT.

`>MODEL Y=CONSTANT+X` `>ESTIMATE`	Simple linear regression.
`>MODEL Y=CONSTANT+X+Z` `>ESTIMATE`	Multiple linear regression.

Use CATEGORY and ANOVA for fully factorial ANOVA. CATEGORY specifies the number of categories (levels) for one or more variables used as categorical predictors (factors). ANOVA specifies the dependent variable and produces a fully-factorial design from the factors given by CATEGORY.

`>CATEGORY SEX=2`
`>ANOVA SALARY`
`>ESTIMATE`
	One-way design where factor SEX has two levels

`>CATEGORY A=2,B=3`
`>ANOVA Y`
`>ESTIMATE`
	Two-by-three ANOVA

Use COVARIATE to specify covariates in a fully factorial design.

`>CATEGORY A=2 B=3`
`>COVARIATE X`
`>ANOVA Y`
`>ESTIMATE`
	This ANOCOVA includes factor (A,B) by covariate (X) interactions, which test the assumption of homogeneity of regression slopes.

Use a SAVE command before MODEL or ANOVA to save residuals in a file.

The following options are available for many graph commands. We summarize them once here and merely list them after the commands for which they are available.

MIN=*n*, MAX=*m* YMIN=*n*, YMAX=*m* XMIN=*n*, XMAX=*m* ZMIN=*n*, ZMAX=*m*	Specifies scale (*n, m*) for the corresponding axis.
HEIGHT=*n* | *n*IN | *n*CM | *n*PT	Specifies the height of the graph.
WIDTH=*n* | *n*IN | *n*CM | *n*PT	Specifies the width of the graph.
AXES=*n*	Draws *n* axes, 1≤*n*≤4. The default is 4.
GRIDS=*n*	Draws vertical grid for *n*=1, horizontal for *n*=2, both for *n*=3.
TICK=IN | OUT	Places tick marks inside or outside the axes.
PLOT *yvarlist * xvar*	Graphs a single scatterplot with *yvarlist* as dependent variable(s) and *xvar* as the independent variable.
/SMOOTH	Draws linear smooth (regression).
CONF=*n*	Includes confidence bands, 0≤*n*≤1. For example, CONF=.95 specifies 95% confidence bands.
INFLUENCE	The plotting symbols are scaled to represent the influence of each point on the Pearson correlation of the two variables.
LINE	Draws a line connecting points.
ERROR=*var*	Draws error bars according to the estimates given by *var*.
SYMBOL=*n* | *var$* | '*charlist* ' XMIN XMAX YMIN YMAX HEIGHT WIDTH AXES GRIDS TICK	Labels data points on the graph.
BOX *varlist* [**gvar*]	Draws box and whisker plots of the numerical variable(s) given by *varlist*. If you omit *varlist*, all numeric variables are used. The optional numeric grouping variable *gvar* specifies that a unique box be plotted for each level.
/NOTCH	Draws notched boxes showing 95% confidence intervals.
GROUPS=*n*	Plots for only the first *n* groups in *gvar*.
TRANSPOSE	Rotates plot 90°.
MIN MAX HEIGHT WIDTH AXES TICK	
HISTOGRAM *varlist*	Produces separate histogram(s) for variable(s) in *varlist*. If you omit *varlist*, all numeric variables are used.
/BARS=*n*	Forces histogram to have *n* bars.
SCALE	Changes the scale so that its minima and maxima are the nearest round numbers outside the data extrema.
MIN MAX HEIGHT WIDTH AXES TICK	

STEM *varlist*	Produces stem-and-leaf diagrams for each variable in *varlist*. Variables must be numeric. If you omit *varlist*, all numeric variables are used.
/LINES=*n*	Forces diagram to use *n* lines.

Forecasting commands

The forecasting commands all use the first numeric variable in the file if you do not specify a variable yourself.

LOG *var*	Logs the variable specified.
MEAN *var*	Demeans the variable specified.
SQUARE *var*	Squares the values of the variable specified.
TREND *var*	Removes linear trend.
PCNTCHNG *var*	Replaces each value with its percentage difference from the preceding value.
DIFFERENCE *var*	Replaces each value with difference between value and preceding value.
/LAG=*n*	Compute difference from value *n* cases previous.
INDEX *var*	Divides each value by first value of series.
/BASE=*n*	Divides each value by *n*.
SMOOTH *var*	Smooths the variable specified.
/MEAN=*n* | MEDIAN=*n*	Mean or median smoothing with window size *n*.
ADJSEAS *var*	Seasonal decomposition of the variable.
/SEASON=*n*	Seasonal periodicity of *n* cases per period.
ADDI=*n* | MULTI=*n*	Additive or multiplicative seasonal effects with weight *n*.
EXP *var*	Exponential smoothing of specified variable.
/LINEAR=*n* | PERCENT=*n*	Remove linear or percentage growth trend with weight *n*.
SEASON=*n*	Specify seasonal periodicity.
ADDI=*n* | MULTI=*n*	Remove additive or multiplicative seasonal effects with weight *n*.
FORECAST=*n*|*n-m*	Forecast *n* cases or from case *n* to *m*.
SMOOTH=*n*	Specify weight for level component.
EXP	
TPLOT *var*	Produces time series plot of *var*. The first numeric variable is the default.
/LAG=*n*	Plots the first *n* cases. 15 is the default.
STANDARDIZE	Standardizes values before plotting.
MIN MAX HEIGHT WIDTH AXES GRID TICK	

Index

[Scroll analyses], 11
[Text] option, 7
ACF plots, 21
Analysis (text output) window, 2, 3
Analyze menu, 3
ANOVA, ANCOVA, 14
association coefficients, 13
axes, 16
batch files of commands, 3, 22
box plots, 18
bubble plots, 17
case plots, 20
character values, 5
character variables, 4
chi-square test statistics, 13
command interface, 2, 22
comments, 12
conditional transformations, 9
confidence intervals, 18
Copy, 6, 7
correlation, 13
Cut, 6, 7
Data Editor, 2, 3, 4
Data menu, 3, 11
decimal places, 11
deleting a row or column, 7, 11
dependent (paired) t-test, 13
descriptive statistics, 12
distribution functions, 10
Edit menu, 3, 6
editing data, 7
Editor menu, 3, 8
entering data, 4
error bars, 17
exponential smoothing, 20
File menu, 3
Fill worksheet..., 10
Find case..., 9
fonts, 11
Formats..., 11
functions, relations, & operators, 9
Goodies menu, 3
Graph menu, 3, 15
grids, 16
grouping variables, 12, 13, 18
help, 4
help files, 2
histograms, 19
importing text files, 7
independent t-test, 13
influence plots, 17, 18
Information about SYSTAT..., 4
installing, 2
Introduction, 4

line plots, 10
logical AND and OR, 9
Math..., 8, 10
menus, 3
missing values, 10
moving graphs, 15
numeric values, 6
numeric variables, 4
one-sample t-test, 13
Open, 7
overlaying graphs, 16
PACF plots, 21
Paste, 6, 7
Pearson correlation, 13
Plot, 17
Print graph, 21
printing and saving, 21
proportional reduction of error, 13
quotation marks, 5, 7, 8
random data, 10
Rank..., 11, 13
Recode..., 9
redirecting output, 21
regression, 14
resizing graphs, 15
Results to..., 21
Save as..., 8
Save selected text as..., 21
saving data, 8
saving graphs in files, 21
saving residuals, 14
scatterplots, 17
searches, 9
seasonal decomposition, 20
Select all, 7
Series, 20
Show command window, 22
smoothing, 20
Sort, 11
Spearman correlations, 13
standardize, 20
Stats, 12
stem-and-leaf diagram, 19
Submit Clipboard, 23
Submit command file, 23
Tables, 13
text editor, 3, 12
text file, 8
time series, 20
transform, 8, 20
Ttest, 13
View window, 2, 3
Weight..., 113

Business

MYSTAT ®

An instructional business version of SYSTAT for IBM-PC/compatibles

Business MYSTAT Version 1.2

An instructional version of SYSTAT

SYSTAT, Inc.
1800 Sherman Avenue
Evanston, IL 60201
Tel. 708.**864.5670**
FAX 708.**492.3567**

Contents

Business	Introduction	1
MYSTAT	Installation	2
	Hard disk	2
	Floppy disk	3
	Getting Started	4
	Command menu	4
	Data Editor	4
	Demo	5
	Help	5
	Data Editor	6
	Entering data	6
	Moving around	8
	Editing data	8
	Data Editor commands	8
	DELETE and DROP	9
	Saving files	9
	Reading files	9
	Starting new data files	9
	Importing data from other programs	10
	Finding a case	10
	Decimal places in the Editor	10
	Transforming variables	10
	Leaving the Data Editor	12
	General MYSTAT commands	13
	Sorting and ranking data	14
	Weighting data	14
	Quitting	14
	Statistics	15
	Descriptive statistics	15
	Tabulation	15
	T-tests	16
	Correlation	16
	Regression and ANOVA	17
	Graphics	18
	Scatterplots	18
	Box-and-whisker plots	19
	Histograms	19
	Stem-and-leaf diagrams	20
	Forecasting	21
	Transforming	21
	Smoothing	22
	Plotting	23
	Clearing the series	23
	Submitting files of commands	24
	Redirecting output	24
	Putting comments in output	25
	Saving data in text files	25
	Index of commands	25

Introduction   **This is a real statistics program—it is not just a demonstration.** You can use Business MYSTAT to enter, transform, and save data, and to perform a wide range of statistical evaluations. Please use Business MYSTAT to solve *real* problems.

Business MYSTAT is a subset of SYSTAT, our premier statistics package. We've geared Business MYSTAT especially for teaching business statistics, with special forecasting and time series routines all in a single, easy-to-use package.

Business MYSTAT provides descriptive statistics, cross-tabulation, Pearson and Spearman correlation coefficients, multiple regression, time series forecasting, and much more.

Business MYSTAT is available in Macintosh, IBM-PC/compatible, and VAX/VMS versions. Copies are available at a nominal cost.

For more information about SYSTAT, FASTAT, and our other top-rated professional statistics and graphics packages, please call or write.

1

Installation   Business MYSTAT requires 512K of RAM and a floppy or hard disk
drive. It can handle up to 50 variables and up to 32,000 cases.

Your Business MYSTAT disk contains three files: MYSTAT.EXE (the
program), MYSTATB.HLP (a file with information for on-line help),
and DEMO.CMD (a demonstration that creates a data file and
demonstrates some of Business MYSTAT's features).

Hard disk   ### Set up the CONFIG.SYS file
The CONFIG.SYS file in your root directory must have a line that says
FILES=20. If you don't have a CONFIG.SYS file, you can create one
with the COPY CON command:

```
>CD \
>COPY CON CONFIG.SYS
FILES=20
[F6]
```

Press the Enter key after each line to tell the computer to start working. Nothing happens until you press Enter. (On some keyboards, the
key is marked Return or with a ⏎ symbol.)

After typing "FILES=20" and pressing Enter, press the F6 key and then
press Enter. F6 signals the computer that you are done writing to
CONFIG.SYS, so you get another DOS prompt (>).

Set up the AUTOEXEC.BAT file
The AUTOEXEC.BAT file in the root directory must have the following PATH line. You can create an AUTOEXEC.BAT file with the following commands. Remember to press Enter at the end of each line.

```
>COPY CON AUTOEXEC.BAT
PATH=C:\;C:\SYSTAT
[F6]
```

Reboot your machine

Copy the files on the MYSTAT disk into a \SYSTAT directory
Now, make a \SYSTAT directory, insert the MYSTAT disk in drive A,
and copy the Business MYSTAT files into the directory. (You must
have the help file in the same directory as MYSTAT.EXE. If you put
MYSTAT.EXE in a directory other than \SYSTAT, the help file
MYSTATB.HLP must be either in that directory or the \SYSTAT directory.)

```
>MD \SYSTAT
>CD \SYSTAT
>COPY A:*.*
```

You are now ready to begin using Business MYSTAT. From now on,
all you need to do to get ready to use Business MYSTAT is boot and
move (CD) into the \SYSTAT directory. Save your MYSTAT master
disk as a back up copy.

Floppy disk   ***Boot your machine***

Insert a "boot disk" into drive A. Close the door of the disk drive and turn on the machine.

Set up a CONFIG.SYS file on your boot disk

The boot disk must contain a file named CONFIG.SYS with a line FILES=20. If you don't have such a file, type the following lines when you get a DOS prompt (>).

```
>COPY CON CONFIG.SYS
FILES=20
[F6]
```

Press the Enter key at the end of every line to tell the computer to start working. Nothing happens until you press Enter. (On some keyboards this key is marked Return or with a ↵ symbol.)

After typing "FILES=20" and pressing Enter, press the F6 key and then press Enter. F6 signals the computer that you are done writing to CONFIG.SYS, so you get another DOS prompt (>).

Set up an AUTOEXEC.BAT file on your boot disk

The boot disk must also contain a file named AUTOEXEC.BAT with a line PATH=A:\;B:\. You can create one as follows:

```
>COPY CON AUTOEXEC.BAT
PATH=A:\;B:\
[F6]
```

Reboot your machine

Make a copy of the Business MYSTAT disk

When you get a DOS prompt (>), remove the boot disk. Put the Business MYSTAT disk in drive A and a blank, formatted disk in drive B and type the COPY command at the prompt:

```
>COPY A:*.* B:
```

Remove the master disk from drive A and store it. If anything happens to your working copy, use the master to make a new copy.

Use Business MYSTAT

Now, switch your working copy into drive A. If necessary, make drive A the "logged" drive (the drive your machine reads from) by issuing the command A: at the DOS prompt (>).

Business MYSTAT reads and writes its temporary work files to the currently logged drive. Since there is limited room on the Business MYSTAT disk, you should read and write all your data, output, and command files from a data disk in drive B.

From now on, all you need to do to use Business MYSTAT is boot, insert your working copy, and log the A drive.

Getting started

To start, type MYSTAT and press Enter.

```
>MYSTAT
```

When you see the MYSTAT logo, press Enter. You'll see a command menu listing all the commands you can use in MYSTAT.

Command menu

The command menu shows a list of all the commands that are available for Business MYSTAT. The menu divides the commands into six groups: information, file handling, miscellaneous, graphics, statistics, and forecasting.

DEMO	EDIT	MENU	PLOT	STATS	LOG
HELP		NAMES	BOX	TABULATE	MEAN
SYSTAT	USE	LIST	HISTOGRAM	TTEST	SQUARE
	SAVE	FORMAT	STEM	CORRELATE	TREND
	PUT	NOTE			PCNTCHNG
	SUBMIT				DIFFRNCE
					INDEX
QUIT	OUTPUT	SORT	CHARSET	MODEL	SMOOTH
		RANK		CATEGORY	ADJSEAS
		WEIGHT		ANOVA	EXP
				ESTIMATE	TPLOT
					ACF, PACF
					CLEAR

As you become more experienced with MYSTAT, you might want to turn the menu off. Turn it on and off with the MENU command.

```
>MENU
```

Data Editor

MYSTAT has a built-in Data Editor with its own set of commands. To enter the Editor, use the EDIT command.

```
>EDIT
```

Inside the Editor, you can enter, view, edit, and transform data. When you are done with the Editor, type QUIT to get out of the Editor and back to MYSTAT, where you can do statistical and graphical analyses. To quit MYSTAT itself, type QUIT again.

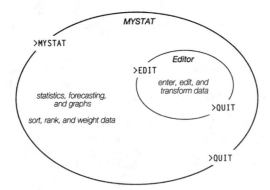

The Data Editor is an independent program inside MYSTAT and has its own commands. Five commands—USE, SAVE, HELP, QUIT, and FORMAT—appear both inside *and* outside the Editor.

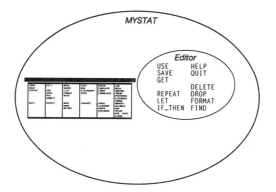

Demo

To see an on-line demonstration of MYSTAT, use the DEMO command. (Remember to press Enter after you type the command.)

```
>DEMO
```

When the demonstration is finished, Business MYSTAT returns you to the command menu. After you've seen the demo, you might want to remove the DEMO.CMD file and the CITIES.SYS data file that it creates to save disk space.

Help

The HELP command provides instructions for any command—inside *or* outside the Editor. HELP lists and describes all the commands.

```
>HELP
```

You can get help for any specific command . For example:

```
>HELP EDIT
EDIT starts the MYSTAT full screen editor.

EDIT [filename]

EDIT  (edit a new file)
EDIT CITIES  (edit CITIES.SYS)

For further information, type EDIT [Enter], [ESC], and then type
HELP [Enter] inside the data editor.
```

The second line shows *a* summary of the command. You see that any EDIT command must begin with the command word EDIT. The brackets indicate that specifying a file is optional. Anything in lowercase, like "filename," is just a placeholder—you should type a real file name (or a real variable name, or whatever).

Customizing DEMO and HELP

All help information is stored in the text file MYSTATB.HLP. You can use a text editor to customize your help information. Teachers can design special demonstrations by editing the file DEMO.CMD.

Information about SYSTAT

For information about SYSTAT and how to order it, use the SYSTAT command.

Data Editor   The Business MYSTAT Data Editor lets you enter and edit data, view data, and transform variables. First, we enter data; later, we show you how to use commands.

To use the Editor to create a new file, type EDIT and press Enter. If you already have a MYSTAT data file that you want to edit, specify a filename with the EDIT command.

```
>EDIT [<filename>]
```

If you do not specify a filename, you get an empty Editor like the one above. MYSTAT stores data in a rectangular worksheet. *Variables* fill vertical columns and each horizontal row represents a *case*.

Entering data   First enter variable names in the top row. Variable names *must* be surrounded by single or double quotation marks, must begin with a letter, and can be no longer than 8 characters.

Character variables (those whose values are words and letters) must have names ending with a dollar sign ($). The quotation marks and dollar sign do not count toward the eight character limit.

Numeric variables (those whose values are numbers) can be named with subscripts; e.g., ITEM(3). Subscripts allow you to specify a range of variables for analyses. For example, STATS ITEM(1-3) does descriptive statistics on the first three ITEM(*i*) variables.

The cursor is already positioned in the first cell in the top row of the worksheet. Type 'CITY$' or "CITY$" and then press Enter.

Business MYSTAT enters variable names in upper-case whether you enter them in lower- or upper-case.

6   © 1990, SYSTAT, Inc.

The cursor automatically moves to the second column. You are now ready to name the rest of the variables, pressing Enter to store each name in the worksheet.

```
'STATE$'
"POP"
'RAINFALL'
```

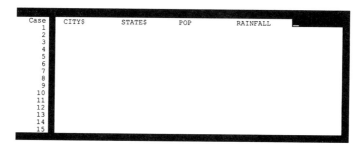

Now you can enter values. Move the cursor to the first blank cell under CITY$ by pressing Home. (On most machines, Home is the 7 key on the numeric keypad. If pressing the 7 key types a 7 rather than moving the cursor, press the NumLock key and try again.)

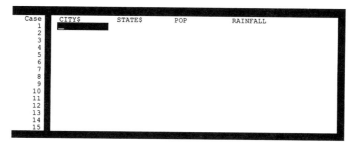

When the cell under CITY$ is selected, enter the first data value:

```
'New York'
```

When you press Enter, Business MYSTAT accepts the value and moves the cursor to the right. You can also use the cursor arrow keys to move the cursor.

Character values can be no longer than twelve characters. Like variable names, character values must be surrounded by single or double quotation marks. Unlike variable names, character values are case sensitive—upper-case is not the same as lower-case (for example, 'TREE' is not the same as 'tree' or 'Tree'). Enter a blank space surrounded by quotation marks for missing character values. To use single or double quotation marks as part of a value, surround the whole value with the opposite marks.

Numeric values can be up to 10^{35} in absolute magnitude. Scientific notation is used for long numbers; e.g., .000000000015 is equivalent to 1.5E–11. Enter a decimal (.) for missing numeric values.

Enter the first few cases: type a value, press Enter, and type the next value. The cursor automatically moves to the beginning of the next case when a row is filled.

"New York"	"NY"	7164742	57.03
"Los Angeles"	"CA"	3096721	7.81
"Chicago"	"IL"	2992472	34

(etc.)

Case	CITY$	STATE$	POP	RAINFALL
1	New York	NY	7164742.000	57.030
2	Los Angeles	CA	3096721.000	7.810
3	Chicago	IL	2992472.000	34.000
4	Dallas	TX	974234.000	33.890
5	Phoenix	AZ	853266.000	14.910
6	Miami	FL	346865.000	60.020
7	Washington	DC	638432.000	37.730
8	Kansas City	MO	448159.000	38.770
9				
10				
11				
12				
13				
14				
15				

Moving around

Use the cursor keys on the numeric keypad to move around in the Editor.

Esc		toggle between Editor and command prompt (>)
Home	7	move to first cell in worksheet
↑	8	move upward one cell
PgUp	9	scroll screen up
←	4	move left one cell
→	6	move right one cell
End	1	move to last case in worksheet
↓	2	move down one cell
PgDn	3	scroll screen down

If these keys type numbers rather than move the cursor, press the NumLock key which toggles the keypad back and forth between typing numbers and performing the special functions. (If your computer does not have a NumLock key or something similar, consult the manual that came with your machine.)

Editing data

To change a value or variable name move to the cell you want, type the new value, and press Enter. Remember to enclose character values and variable names in quotation marks.

Data Editor commands

When you have entered your data, press the Esc key to move the cursor to the prompt (>) below the worksheet. You can enter editor commands at this prompt. Commands can be typed in upper- or lower-case. Items in <angle brackets> are placeholders; for instance, you should type a specific filename in place of <filename>.

DELETE and DROP	DELETE lets you remove an entire case (row) from the dataset in the Editor. You can specify a range or list of cases to be deleted. The following are valid DELETE commands.

```
DELETE 3              Deletes third case from dataset.
DELETE 3-10           Deletes cases 3 through 10.
DELETE 3, 5-8, 10     Deletes cases 3, 5, 6, 7, 8, and 10.
```

DROP removes variables from the dataset in the Editor. You can specify several variables or a range of subscripted variables.

```
DROP RAINFALL         Drops RAINFALL from dataset.
DROP X(1-3)           Drops subscripted variables X(1-3).
DROP X(1-3), GROUP$   Drops X(1-3) and GROUP$.
```

Saving files

The SAVE command saves the data in the Editor to a Business MYSTAT data file. You must save data in a data file before you can analyze them with statistical and graphic commands.

```
SAVE <filename>       Saves data in a MYSTAT file.
  /DOUBLE | SINGLE    Choose single or double precision.
```

Business MYSTAT filenames can be up to 8 characters long and must begin with a letter. Business MYSTAT adds a ".SYS" extension that labels the file as a Business MYSTAT data file. To specify a path name for a file, enclose the entire file name, including the file extension, in single or double quotation marks.

Business MYSTAT stores data in double-precision by default. You can choose single precision if you prefer: add /SINGLE to the end of the command. Always type a slash before command options.

```
SAVE CITIES/SINGLE    Saves CITIES.SYS in single precision
```

Single precision requires approximately half as much disk space as double precision and is accurate to about 9 decimal places. The storage option (single or double precision) does not affect computations, which always use double precision arithmetic (accurate to about 15 places).

```
SAVE CITIES           Creates data file CITIES.SYS.
SAVE b:new            Creates file NEW.SYS on B drive.
SAVE 'C:\DATA\FIL.SYS'  Creates FIL.SYS in \DATA directory of C.
```

You can save data in text files for exporting to other programs with the PUT command. PUT is not an Editor command, though. First QUIT the Editor, USE the data file, and PUT the data to a text file.

Reading files

USE reads a MYSTAT data file into the Editor.

```
USE [<filename>]      Reads data from MYSTAT data file.
```

Starting new data files

Use the NEW command to clear the worksheet and start editing a new data file.

9

Importing data from other programs	You can import data from other programs through plain text (ASCII) file. ASCII files contain only plain text and numbers—they have no special characters or formatting commands.

Start the program and save your data in a plain ASCII file according to the instructions given by that program's manual. The ASCII file must have a ".DAT" extension, data values must be separated by blanks or commas, and each case must begin on a new line.

Then, start Business MYSTAT. Use EDIT to get an empty worksheet, and enter variable names in the worksheet for each variable in the ASCII file. Next, use GET to read the text file. Finally, SAVE the data.

```
GET [<filename>]          Reads data from ASCII text file.
```

Finding a case	FIND searches through the Editor starting from the current cursor position, and moves the cursor to the first value that meets the condition you specify. Try this:

```
>FIND POP<1000000
```

This moves the cursor to case 4. After Business MYSTAT finds a value, use the FIND command without an argument (that is, "FIND" is the entire command) to find the next case meeting the same condition. All functions, relations, and operators listed above are available.

Some valid FIND commands:

```
>FIND AGE>45 AND SEX$='MALE'
>FIND INCOME<10000 AND STATE$='NY'
>FIND (TEST1+TEST2+TEST3)>90
```

Decimal places in the Editor	The FORMAT command specifies the number (0–9) of decimal places to be shown in the Editor. The default is 3. Numbers are stored the way you enter them regardless of the FORMAT setting; FORMAT affects the Editor display only.

```
FORMAT=<#>               Sets number of decimal places to <#>.
  /UNDERFLOW             Displays tiny numbers in scientific notation.
```

For example, to set a two-place display with scientific notation for tiny numbers use the command:

```
>FORMAT=2/UNDERFLOW
```

Transforming variables	Use LET and IF...THEN to transform variables or create new ones.

```
LET <var>=<exprn>           Transforms <var> according to <exprn>.
IF <exprn> THEN LET         Transforms <var> conditionally according to
  <var>=<exprn>                <exprn>.
```

For example, we can use LET to create LOGPOP from POP:

```
>LET LOGPOP=LOG(POP)
```

10   © 1990, SYSTAT, Inc.

```
Case   CITY$        STATE$    POP          RAINFALL    LOGPOP
  1      New York      NY    7164742.000     57.030     15.785
  2    Los Angeles     CA    3096721.000      7.810     14.946
  3      Chicago       IL    2992472.000     34.000     14.912
  4       Dallas       TX     974234.000     33.890     13.789
  5      Phoenix       AZ     853266.000     14.910     13.657
  6       Miami        FL     346865.000     60.020     12.757
  7     Washington     DC     638432.000     37.730     13.367
  8    Kansas City     MO     448159.000     38.770     13.013
  9
 10
 11
 12
 13
 14
 15
```

LET labels the last column of the worksheet LOGPOP and sets the values to the natural logs of the POP values. (If LOGPOP had already existed, its values would have been replaced.)

Use IF...THEN for *conditional* transformations. For example:

```
>IF POP>1000000 THEN LET SIZE$='BIG'
```

creates a new character variable, SIZE$, and assigns the value BIG for every city that has population greater than one million.

For both LET and IF...THEN, character values must be enclosed in quotation marks and are case sensitive (i.e., "MALE" is not the same as "male"). Use a period to indicate missing values.

Some valid LET and IF-THEN commands:

```
>LET ALPHA$='abcdef'
>LET LOGIT1=1/(1+EXP(A+B*X))
>LET TRENDY=INCOME>40000 AND CAR$='BMW'
>IF SEX$='Male' THEN LET GROUP=1
>IF group>2 THEN LET NEWGROUP=2
>IF A=-9 AND B<10 OR B>20 THEN LET C=LOG(D)*SQR(E)
```

Functions, relations, and operators for LET and IF...THEN

+	addition	CASE	current case number
-	subtraction	INT	integer truncation
*	multiplication	URN	uniform random number
/	division	ZRN	normal random number
^	exponentiation		
<	less than	AND	logical and
<=	less than or equal to	OR	logical or
=	equal to	SQR	square root
<>	not equal to	LOG	natural log
>=	greater than or equal	EXP	exponential function
>	greater than	ABS	absolute value

Logical expressions

Logical expressions evaluate to one if true and to zero if false. For example, for LET CHILD=AGE<12, a variable AGE would be filled with ones for those cases where AGE is less than 12 and zeros whenever AGE is 12 or greater.

Random data

You can generate random numbers using the REPEAT, LET, and SAVE commands in the Editor. First, enter variable names. Press Esc to move the cursor to the command line. Then, use REPEAT to fill cases with missing values and LET to redefine the values.

REPEAT 20	Fills 20 cases with missing values.
LET A=URN	Fills A with uniform random data.
LET B=ZRN	Fills B with normal random data.
SAVE RANDOM	Saves data in file RANDOM.SYS.

Distribution functions

MYSTAT can compute the following distribution functions.

Cumulative distribution functions compute the probability that a random value from the specified distribution falls below a given value; that is, it shows the proportion of the distribution below that value. Inverse distribution functions do the same thing backwards: you specify an alpha value (a probability or proportion) between zero and one, and MYSTAT shows the critical value below which lies that proportion.

Distribution	Cumulative	Inverse
Normal	ZCF(z)	ZIF(alpha)
Exponential	ECF(x)	EIF(alpha)
Chi-square	XCF(chisq,df)	XIF(alpha,df)
T	TCF(t,df)	TIF(alpha,df)
F	FCF(F,df1,df2)	FIF(alpha,df1,df2)
Poisson	PCF(k,lambda)	PIF(alpha,k)
Binomial	NCF(p,k,n)	NIF(alpha,k,n)
Logistic	LCF(x)	LIF(alpha)
Studentized range	SCF(x,k,df)	SIF(alpha,k,df)
Weibull	WCF(x,p,q)	WIF(alpha,p,q)

The uniform distribution is uniformly distributed from zero to one. The normal distribution is a standard normal distribution with mean zero and standard deviation one. The exponential distribution has parameter one. The cumulative Poisson function calculates the probability of the number of random events between zero and k when the expected value is *lambda*. The binomial cumulative function provides the probability of k or more occurrences in n trials with the binomial probability p.

Use the cumulative distribution functions to obtain probabilities associated with observed sample statistics. Use the inverse distributions to determine critical values and to construct confidence intervals. Finally, to generate pseudo-random data for the functions, apply the appropriate inverse cumulative distribution function to uniform random data.

Leaving the Data Editor

Use the QUIT command to leave the Editor and return to the main Business MYSTAT menu.

```
>QUIT
```

12

General MYSTAT commands

Once your data are in a Business MYSTAT data file, you can use Business MYSTAT's statistical and graphics routines to examine them.

Open a data file

First, you must open the file containing the data you want to analyze:

```
USE <filename>                reads the data in <filename>
```

To analyze the data we entered earlier, type:

```
>USE CITIES
```

MYSTAT responds by listing the variables in the file.

```
VARIABLES IN MYSTAT FILE ARE:
     CITY$       STATE$      POP      RAINFALL    LOGPOP
```

See variable names and data values

The NAMES command shows the variable names in the current file.

```
>NAMES
VARIABLES IN MYSTAT FILE ARE:
     CITY$       STATE$.     POP      RAINFALL    LOGPOP
```

The LIST command displays the values of variables you specify. If you specify no variables, all variables are shown.

```
>LIST CITY$
                          CITY$

CASE      1          New York
CASE      2       Los Angeles
CASE      3           Chicago
CASE      4            Dallas
CASE      5           Phoenix
CASE      6             Miami
CASE      7        Washington
CASE      8       Kansas City

   8 CASES AND    5 VARIABLES PROCESSED
```

Decimal places

Use the FORMAT command to specify the number of digits to be displayed after the decimal in statistical output. This FORMAT command has the same syntax and works the same as in the Editor:

```
FORMAT=<#>                Sets number of decimal places to <#>.
   /UNDERFLOW             Uses scientific notation for tiny numbers.
```

Sorting and ranking data	SORT reorders the cases in a file in ascending order according to the variables you specify. You can specify up to ten numeric or character variables for nested sorts. Use a SAVE command after the USE command to save the sorted data into a MYSTAT file. Then, open the sorted file to do analysis.

```
>USE MYDATA
>SAVE SORTED
>SORT CITY$ POP
>USE SORTED
```

RANK replaces each value of a variable with its rank order within that variable. Specify an output file before ranking.

```
>USE MYDATA
>SAVE RANKED
>RANK RAINFALL
>USE RANKED
```

Weighting data	WEIGHT replicates cases according to the integer parts of the values of the weighting variable you specify.

```
WEIGHT <variable>
```
Weights according to variable specified.

To turn weighting off, use WEIGHT without an argument.

```
>WEIGHT
```

Quitting	When you are done with your analyses, you can end your session with the QUIT command. Remember that the Data Editor also has a QUIT. To quit MYSTAT from the Editor, enter QUIT twice.

```
>QUIT
```

Notation used in command summaries

Any item in angled brackets (< >) is representative—insert an actual value or variable in its place. Replace <var> with a variable name, replace <#> with a number, <var$> with a character variable, and <gvar> with a numeric or character grouping variable.

Some commands have *options* you can use to change the type of output you get. Place a slash / before listing any options for your command. You only need one slash, no matter how many options.

A vertical line (|) means "or." Items in brackets ([ ]) are optional. Commas and spaces are interchangeable, except that *you must use a comma at the end of the line when a command continues to a second line.* You can abbreviate commands and options to the first two characters and use upper- and lower-case interchangeably. I

Most commands allow you to specify particular variables. If you don't specify variables, MYSTAT uses its defaults (usually the first numeric variable or all numeric variables, depending on the command).

Statistics
Descriptive
statistics

STATS produces basic descriptive statistics.

```
>STATS
TOTAL OBSERVATIONS:  8

                        POP      RAINFALL  LOGPOP

N OF CASES              8          8         8
MINIMUM          346865.000      7.810    12.757
MAXIMUM         7164742.000     60.020    15.785
MEAN            2064361.375     35.520    14.028
STANDARD DEV    2335788.226     18.032     1.068
```

Here is a summary of the STATS command. The box on the facing page describes the notation we use for command summaries in this manual.

```
STATS <var1> <var2>…          Statistics for the variables specified.
    MEAN SD SKEWNESS,         Choose which statistics you want.
      KURTOSIS MINIMUM,
      MAXIMUM RANGE SUM,
      SEM
    /BY <gvar>                Statistics for each group defined by the
                                grouping variable <gvar>. The data must
                                first be SORTed on the grouping variable.
```

For example, you can get the mean, standard deviation, and range for RAINFALL with the following command.

```
>STATS RAINFALL / MEAN SD RANGE
TOTAL OBSERVATIONS:  8

                RAINFALL

N OF CASES          8
MEAN            35.520
STANDARD DEV    18.032
RANGE           52.210
```

Tabulation

TABULATE provides one-way and multi-way frequency tables. For two-way tables, MYSTAT provides the Pearson chi-square statistic. You can produce a table of frequencies, percents, row percents, or column percents. You can tell MYSTAT to ignore missing data with the MISS option and suppress the chi-square statistic with NOSTAT.

```
TAB <var1>*<var2>…            Tabulates the variables you specify
    /LIST                    Special list format table.
    FREQUENCY PERCENT        Different types of tables
      ROWPCT COLPCT MISS
      NOSTAT
TABULATE                     Frequency tables of all numeric variables.
TABULATE AGE/LIST            Frequency table of AGE in list format.
TAB AGE*SEX                  Two-way table with chi-square.
TAB AGE*SEX$*STATE$,         Three-way row percent table.
    /ROWPCT
TAB A,AGE*SEX/FREQ,          Two two-way frequency and cell percent ta-
    PERC                       bles (A*SEX and AGE*SEX).
TAB AGE*SEX/MISS             Two-way table excluding missing values.
TAB AGE*SEX/NOSTAT           Two-way table excluding chi-square.
```

One-way frequency tables show the number of times a distinct value appears in a variable. Two-way and multi-way tables count the appearances of each unique combination of values. Multi-way tables count the appearances of a value in each subgroup. Percent tables convert the frequencies to percentages of the total count; row percent tables show percentages of the total for each row; and column percent tables show percentages of the total for each column.

T-tests

TTEST does dependent and independent t-tests. A dependent (paired samples) t-test tests whether the means of two continuous variables differ. An independent test tests whether the means of two groups of a single variable differ.

To request an independent (two-sample) t-test, specify one or more continuous variables and one grouping variable. Separate the continuous variable(s) from the grouping variable with an asterisk. The grouping variable must have only two values.

To request a dependent (paired) t-test, specify two or more continuous variables. MYSTAT does separate dependent t-tests for each possible pairing of the variables.

TTEST <var1>...[*<gvar>]	Does t-tests of the variables you specify.
TTEST A B	Dependent (paired) t-test of A and B.
TTEST A B C	Paired tests of A and B, A and C, B and C.
TTEST A*SEX$	Independent test.
TTEST A B C*SEX	Three independent tests.

You can also do a one-sample test by adding a variable to your data file that has a constant value corresponding to the population mean of your null hypothesis. Then do a dependent t-test on this variable and your data variable.

Correlation

PEARSON computes Pearson product moment correlation coefficients for the variables you specify (or all numerical variables). You can select pairwise or listwise deletion of missing data; pairwise is the default. RANK the variables before correlating to compute Spearman rank-order correlations. CORRELATE is a synonym for PEARSON.

PEARSON <var1> ...	Pearson correlation matrix.
/PAIRWISE | LISTWISE	Pairwise or listwise deletion of missing values.
PEARSON	Correlation matrix of all numeric variables.
CORR HEIGHT IQ AGE	Matrix of three variables.
PEARSON /LISTWISE	Listwise deletion rather than pairwise.

Correlation measures the strength of linear association between two variables. A value of 1 or –1 indicates a perfect linear relationship; a value of 0 indicates that neither variable can be linearly predicted from the other.

Regression and ANOVA

Business MYSTAT computes simple and multiple regression and balanced or unbalanced ANOVA designs. For unbalanced designs, MYSTAT uses the method of weighted squares of means.

The MODEL and ESTIMATE commands provide linear regression. MODEL specifies the regression equation and ESTIMATE tells MYSTAT to start working. Your MODEL should almost always include a CONSTANT term.

```
>MODEL Y=CONSTANT+X
>ESTIMATE
```
Simple linear regression.

```
>MODEL Y=CONSTANT+X+Z
>ESTIMATE
```
Multiple linear regression.

Use CATEGORY and ANOVA commands for fully factorial ANOVA. CATEGORY specifies the number of categories (levels) for one or more variables used as categorical predictors (factors). ANOVA specifies the dependent variable and produces a fully-factorial design from the factors given by CATEGORY.

All CATEGORY variables must have integer values from 1 to k, where k is the number of categories.

```
>CATEGORY SEX=2
>ANOVA SALARY
>ESTIMATE
```
One-way design with independent variable SALARY and one factor (SEX) with 2 levels

```
>CATEGORY A=2,B=3
>ANOVA Y
>ESTIMATE
```
Two-by-three ANOVA

Saving residuals

Use a SAVE command before MODEL or ANOVA to save residuals in a file. MYSTAT saves model variables, estimated values, residuals, and standard error of prediction as the variables ESTIMATE, RESIDUAL, and SEPRED. When you use SAVE with a linear model, MYSTAT lists cases with extreme studentized residuals or leverage values and prints the Durbin-Watson and autocorrelation statistics.

```
>SAVE RESIDS                  >SAVE RESID2
>MODEL Y=CONSTANT+X+Z         >CATEGORY SEX=2
>ESTIMATE                     >ANOVA SALARY
                             >ESTIMATE
```

You can USE the residuals file to analyze your residuals with MYSTAT's statistical and graphic routines.

| **Graphics** | Use the CHARSET command to choose the type of graphic characters to be used for printing and screen display. If you have IBM screen or printer graphic characters, use GRAPHICS; if not, use GENERIC. The GENERIC setting uses characters like +, –, and l. |

```
CHARSET GRAPHICS        For IBM graphic characters.
CHARSET GENERIC         For any screen or printer.
```

| Scatterplots | PLOT draws a two-way scatterplot of one or more Y variables on a vertical scale against an X variable on a horizontal scale. Use different plotting symbols to distinguish Y variables. |

```
PLOT <yvar1>…*<xvar>      Plots <yvar(s)> against <xvar>.
  /SYMBOL=<var$> |         Use character variable values or character
    '<char>'                 string as plotting symbol.
  YMAX=<#>  YMIN=<#>       Specify range of X and Y values.
    XMAX=<#>  XMIN=<#>
  LINES=<#>               Specify number of screen lines for graph.
PLOT A*B/SYMBOL='*'       Uses asterisk as plotting symbol.
PLOT A*B/SYMBOL=SEX$      Uses SEX$ values for plotting symbol.
PL Y1 Y2*X/SY='1','2'     Plot Y1 points as 1 and Y2 points as 2.
PLOT A*B/LINES=40         Limits graph size to 40 lines on screen.
```

For example, we can plot LOGPOP against RAINFALL using the first letter of the values of CITY$ for plotting symbols.

```
>PLOT LOGPOP*RAINFALL/SYMBOL=CITY$
```

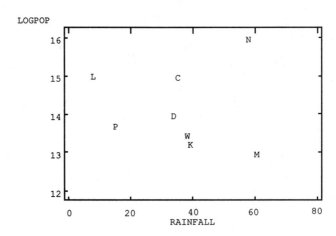

The SYMBOL option is powerful. If you are plotting several Y variables, you can label each variable by specifying its own plotting symbol.

```
>PLOT Y1 Y2*X/SYMBOL='1','2'
```

Or, you can name a character variable to plot each point with the first letter of the variable's value for the corresponding case:

```
>PLOT WEIGHT*AGE/SYMBOL=SEX$
```

Box-and-whisker plots	BOX produces box-and-whisker plots. Include an asterisk and a grouping variable for grouped box plots.

BOX <var1>...[*<gvar>]	[Grouped] box plots of the variables.
/GROUPS=<#>,	Show only the first <#> groups.
MIN=<#> MAX=<#>	Specify scale limits.
BOX	Box plots of every numeric variable.
BOX SALARY	Box plot of SALARY only.
BOX SALARY*RANK	Grouped box plots of SALARY by RANK
BOX INCOME*STATE$/GR=10	Box plots of first 10 groups only

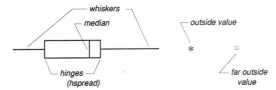

The center line of the box marks the *median*. The edges of the box show the upper and lower *hinges*. The median splits the ordered batch of numbers in half and the hinges split these halves in half again. The distance between the hinges is called the *Hspread*. The *whiskers* show the range of points within 1.5 Hspreads of the hinges. Points outside this range are marked by asterisks and those more than 3 Hspreads from the hinges are marked with circles.

Histograms	HISTOGRAM displays histograms for one or more variables.

HISTOGRAM <var1> ...	Histograms of variables specified
/BARS=<#>	Limits the number of bars used.
SCALE,	Forces round cutpoints between bars.
MIN=<#> MAX=<#>	Specifies scale limits.
HISTOGRAM	Histograms of every numeric variable.
HISTOGRAM A B/BARS=18	Forces 18 bars for histograms of A and B.
HIST A/MIN=0 MAX=10	Histogram of A with scale from 0 to 20.

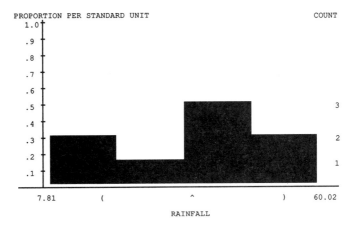

A histogram shows the *distribution* of a variable. The data are divided into equal-sized intervals along the horizontal axis. The number of values in each interval is represented by a vertical bar. The height of each bar can be measured in two ways: the axis on the right side shows the actual number of cases that have that value, and the left axis shows the same information in proportion per standard unit.

Stem-and-leaf diagrams

STEM plots a stem-and-leaf diagram.

```
STEM <var1>..                    Diagrams of variables specified.
  /LINES=<#>                     Specify number of lines in diagram.
STEM                             Stem-and-leaf of every numeric variable.
STEM TAX                         Stem-and-leaf of TAX.
STEM TAX/LINES=20                Stem-and-leaf with 20 lines.
```

The numbers on the left side are *stems* (the most significant digits in which variation occurs) . The *leaves* (the subsequent digits) are printed on the right. For example, in the following plot, the stems are 10's digits and the leaves are 1's digits.

```
        STEM AND LEAF PLOT OF VARIABLE: RAINFALL, N =    48

MINIMUM IS:          7.000
LOWER HINGE IS:         26.500
MEDIAN IS:          36.000
UPPER HINGE IS:         43.000
MAXIMUM IS:         60.000

            0   78
            1   0114
            1   55556
            2
            2 H 588
            3   00113333
            3 M 5557999
            4 H 001123333
            4   55567999
            5   0
            5   9
            6   0
```

(We added 40 more cases to the dataset for this plot. You will get a different plot if you try this example with the CITIES.SYS data file.)

Hinges are defined under "Box-and-whisker plots," above.

© 1990, SYSTAT, Inc.

Forecasting   MYSTAT's forecasting routines let you transform, smooth, and plot time series data. All of the forecasting routines operate in the computer's memory; that is, the results are saved in the working memory rather than being saved to a data file. When you execute a transformation or a smooth, the only results you see are messages like "Series is smoothed" or "Series is transformed."

Your usual strategy will be to plot the series with TPLOT, ACF, or PACF; do a transformation or smoothing operation; and then replot the data to see your progress. You can save a modified series in a new data file by preceding the transformation or smoothing command with a SAVE command. You can use the CLEAR command at any time to restore the variable's original values.

Usually, you will do your work in memory, and when you find some satisfactory results, CLEAR the series, and then repeat the successful transformation using the SAVE command. Suppose, for example, that you wanted to save a demeaned and then smoothed series:

```
>MEAN MYSERIES
>SAVE A:NEWSERIES
>SMOOTH MYSERIES
```

This saves the smoothed, demeaned series in the file NEWSERIES.SYS. If you also want to save the intermediate (demeaned but not smoothed) series, use two SAVE commands:

```
>SAVE A:MEANSERIES
>MEAN MYSERIES
>SAVE A:FINALSERIES
>SMOOTH MYSERIES
```

Transforming   LOG replaces each value in a series with its natural logarithm. Logging removes nonstationary variability, such as increasing variances across time.

```
LOG <var>          Logs the variable specified.
LOG                Logs first numerical variable in file.
LOG SPEED          Logs SPEED.
```

MEAN subtracts the variable's mean from each value. Demeaning centers a series vertically on zero.

```
MEAN <var>         Demeans the variable specified
MEAN               Demeans the first numeric variable.
MEAN SUNSPOTS      Demeans SPEED.
```

SQUARE squares each value. Squaring can help normalize variance in a series.

```
SQUARE <var>
SQUARE
SQUARE MAGNITUD
```

TREND removes linear trend to make a series "level."

```
TREND <var>
TREND
TREND WEATHER
```

PCNTCHNG replaces each value with its percentage difference from the immediately preceding value.

```
PCNTCHNG <var>
PCNTCHNG
PCNTCHNG SERIES
```

DIFFRNCE replaces each value with its difference from the immediately preceding value; you can specify a different lag to show differences from a greater number of positions previous. Differencing helps make some series "stationary" by removing the dependence of one point on the previous point.

```
DIFFRNCE
  /LAG=<#>]              Compute differences between values <#>
                          cases apart.
DIFFRNCE                Difference interval of 3 values.
DIFFRNCE TROKES/LAG=3
```

INDEX divides each value by the first value of the series, or by the base you specify.

```
INDEX <var>              Indexes series to its 12th value.
INDEX SERIES/BASE=12
```

Smoothing

Smoothing removes local variations from a series and makes it easier to see the general shape of the series. Running smoothers replace each value with the mean or median of that value and its neighbors. The "window" is the number of values considered at a time; 3 is the default. You can optionally specify weights for each value, separated by commas.

```
SMOOTH <var1>...         Smooths the variables specified.
  /MEAN=<#>|MEDIAN=<#>   Mean or median smoothing with window
                          size of <#>
  WT=<#,#,...>           Specifies smoothing weights for each value.
SMOOTH SERIES            Running mean smoother, window of 3.
SMOOTH SERIES/MEAN=5     Running mean smoother with window 5.
SMOOTH SERIES/MEDIAN=4   Running median smoother, window 4
SMOOTH SERIES,           Weighted mean smoother, window 3
  /WT=.1,.2,.1
```

Seasonal decomposition removes additive or multiplicative seasonal effects according to the period you specify; the default is 12.

```
ADJSEAS <var>            Smooths specified variable.
  /SEASON=<#>,           Number of observations per period.
  ADDI=<#>|MULT=<#>      Removes additive or multiplicative seasonal
                          effects with weight <#>.
ADJSEAS                  Adjusts first variable with period 12.
ADJSEAS SALES/SEASON=4   Adjusts SALES with period 4.
```

Exponential smoothing forecasts future observations as a weighted average (running smooth) of previous observations. You can optionally specify a linear or percentage growth component and an additive or multiplicative seasonal effects component. Specify the weights for each component and the number or range of cases to be forecast.

`EXP <var>`	Smooths specified variable.
`/LINEAR=<#>|PERCENT=<#>,`	Remove linear or percentage growth trend.
`SEASON=<#>,`	Number of observations per period.
`ADDI=<#>|MULT=<#>,`	Removes additive or multiplicative seasonal effects with weight <#>.
`FORECAST=<#>|<#>-<#>,`	Forecasts number or range of cases.
`SMOOTH=<#>`	Specifies weight for level component.
`EXP/FORE=4`	Default model with 4 forecasted cases.
`EXP SALES/LINEAR ADD`	Holt-Winter's model: linear trend, additive seasonals with period 12.
`EXP SERIES/MULT SEAS=4`	Multiplicative seasonality with period 4.

Plotting

TPLOT produces time series plots, which plot the variable against Case (time). TPLOT's STANDARDIZE option removes the series mean from each value and divides each by the standard deviation. MYSTAT uses the first fifteen cases unless you specify otherwise with LAG.

By default, TPLOT fills the area from the left axis to the plotted point. Include the NOFILL option to specify that the plot not be filled. Use the CENTER option to fill the plot from the observed value to the mean of the series.

`TPLOT <var>`	Case plot of variable specified.
`/LAG=<#>`	Plots first <#> cases.
`STANDARDIZE,`	Standardizes before plotting.
`CENTER|NOFILL,`	Changes the way the plot is filled.
`MIN=<#>,MAX=<#>`	Sets scale limits.
`TPLOT`	Case plot of first numeric variable.
`TPLOT PRICE/LAG=10`	First 10 cases of PRICE.
`TPLOT PRICE/STAN`	Standardizes before plotting.

ACF plots show how closely the points in a series relate to the values immediately preceding them.

`ACF <var>`	Autocorrelation plot of specified variable.
`/LAG=<#>`	Plots first <#> cases.
`ACF`	Autocorrelation plot of first variable.
`ACF PRICE/LAG=10`	First 10 cases of PRICE.

PACF plots show the relationship of values in a series to preceding points after partialing out the influence of intervening points.

`PACF <var>`	Partial autocorrelation plot of variable.
`/LAG=<#>`	Plots first <#> cases.
`PACF`	Partial autocorrelation plot of first variable.
`PACF PRICE/LAG=10`	First 10 cases of PRICE.

Clearing the series

CLEAR restores the initial values of the series, removing the effects of smoothings and transformations.

Submitting files of commands

You can operate MYSTAT in batch mode, where MYSTAT executes a series of commands from a file and you sit back and watch. (You've already seen a command file in action: the DEMO demonstration uses a file of commands, DEMO.CMD.)

The SUBMIT command reads commands from a file and executes the commands as though they were typed from the keyboard. Command files must have a ".CMD" file extension.

Use a word processor to create a file of commands—one command per line, with no extraneous characters. Save the file as a text (ASCII) file. (Use the command "COPY CON BATCH.CMD" and [F6] to type commands into a file if you have no word processor.)

```
SUBMIT <filename>       Submits file of commands.
SUBMIT COMMANDS         Reads commands from COMMANDS.CMD.
SUBMIT B:NEWJOB         Reads commands from file on drive B.
```

Redirecting output

Ordinarily, Business MYSTAT sends its results to the screen. OUTPUT routes *subsequent* output to an ASCII file or a printer.

```
OUTPUT *                Sends output to the screen only
OUTPUT @                Sends output to the screen and the printer.
OUTPUT <filename>       Sends output to the screen and a text file.
```

MYSTAT adds a .DAT suffix to ASCII files produced by OUTPUT. You must use OUTPUT *or QUIT the program to stop redirecting.

Printing and saving analysis results

To print analysis results, use OUTPUT @ before doing the analysis or analyses. Use OUTPUT <filename> to save analysis results in a file. Use OUTPUT * to turn saving or printing off when you are finished.

Printing data or variable names

You can print your data by using OUTPUT @ and then using the LIST command. Use LIST <var1>... to print only certain variables. Don't forget to turn printing off when you are done.

You can print your variable names by using OUTPUT @ and then NAMES. Don't forget to turn printing off when you are done.

Putting comments in output

NOTE allows you to write comments in your output. Surround each line with quotation marks, and issue another NOTE command for additional lines:

```
>NOTE 'Following are descriptive statistics for the POP'
>NOTE "and RAINFALL variables of the CITIES dataset."
>STATS POP RAINFALL
TOTAL OBSERVATIONS:  8

                        POP     RAINFALL

N OF CASES               8          8
MINIMUM           346865.000     7.810
MAXIMUM          7164742.000    60.020
MEAN             2064361.375    35.520
STANDARD DEV     2335788.226    18.032
>NOTE "Note that the average annual rainfall for these"
>NOTE 'cities is 35.52 inches.'
```

Saving data in text files

You can save datasets to ASCII text files with the PUT command. PUT saves the current dataset in a plain text file suitable for use with most other programs. Text files have a .DAT extension.

```
USE <filename>              Opens the dataset to be exported
PUT <filename>              Saves the dataset as a text file
```

Note that the PUT command is *not* an Editor command. To save a newly created dataset in a plain text file, you must QUIT from the Editor, USE the datafile, and finally PUT the data in an ASCII file.

```
>EDIT
[editing session here]
 >SAVE A:NEWSTUFF
 >QUIT
>USE A:NEWSTUFF
>PUT A:NEWTEXT
```

The above commands would create a plain ASCII file called NEWTEXT.DAT on the A disk.

Index of commands

This index lists all of MYSTAT's commands and the Editor commands, describes each briefly, and shows where to look for a description in this booklet.

Editor commands			
	DELETE	9	delete a row (case)
	DROP	9	drop a column (variable)
	Esc key	8	toggle between command line and worksheet
	FIND	10	find a particular data value
	FORMAT	10	set number of decimal places in Editor
	GET	10	read data from an ASCII file
	HELP	5	get help for Editor commands
	IF...THEN	10–12	conditionally transform or create a variable
	LET	10–12	transform or create a variable
	NEW	9	create a new data file
	QUIT	12	quit the Editor and return to MYSTAT
	REPEAT	12	fill cases with missing values
	SAVE	9	save data in a data file
	USE	9	read a data file into Editor

MYSTAT commands	ACF	23	autocorrelation plot
	ADJSEAS	22	seasonal decomposition
	ANOVA	17	analysis of variance
	BOX	19	box-and-whisker plot
	CATEGORY	17	specify factors for ANOVA
	CHARSET	18	choose type of characters for graphs
	CLEAR	23	restore original values of series
	CORRELATE	16	Pearson correlation matrix
	DEMO	5	demonstration of Business MYSTAT
	DIFFRNCE	22	difference transformation
	EDIT	4,6	edit a new or existing data file
	ESTIMATE	17	start computations for regression
	EXP	23	exponential smoothing
	FORMAT	13	set number of decimal places in output
	HELP	5	get help for MYSTAT commands
	HISTOGRAM	19	draw histogram
	INDEX	22	index transformation
	LIST	13	display data values
	LOG	21	log transformation
	MEAN	21	demean a series
	MENU	4	turn the command menu on/off
	MODEL	17	specify a regression model
	NAMES	13	display variable names
	NOTE	25	put comment in output
	OUTPUT	24	redirect output to printer or text file
	PACF	23	partial autocorrelation plot
	PCNTCHNG	22	percent transformation
	PEARSON	16	Pearson correlation matrix
	PLOT	18	scatterplot (X-Y plot)
	PUT	25	save data in text file
	QUIT	14	quit the MYSTAT program
	RANK	14	rank data
	SAVE	17, 21	save results in a file
	SMOOTH	22	smooth a series
	SORT	14	sort data
	SQUARE	21	square transformation
	STATS	15	descriptive statistics
	STEM	20	stem-and-leaf diagram
	SUBMIT	24	submit a batch file of commands
	SYSTAT	5	get information about SYSTAT
	TABULATE	15	one-way or multi-way tables
	TPLOT	23	case plot
	TREND	22	remove trend from a series
	TTEST	16	independent and dependent t-tests
	USE	13	read a data file for analysis
	WEIGHT	14	weight data

Subject Index

A

Assumption of continuity, 127
Autoregressive model, *See* Lagged dependent variable

B

Benefit-cost analysis, 326-56
  benefit-cost ratio, 354-55
  choosing the best alternative, 343
  defining goals, 334
  estimating and valuating benefits and costs, 336-43
  identifying alternatives, 334-35
  listing costs and benefits, 335-36
  redistribution of income, 354
  steps toward conducting, 333-34
  uncertainty, 354
Biases,
  collection, 78
  confirmation bias, 452
  errors due to observation, 78
  halo effect, 453
  inappropriate sample, 77
  individual biases, 446
  in survey instruments, 79
  organizational biases, 446-56
  random, 76
  self selection, 77
  self-serving biases, 453
  systematic, 76

C

Cash management, 299-309
  investments and withdrawals, 304-5
  miller-Orr method, 306-07
  optimal number of withdrawals, 302-4
  practical steps, 307-9
Causal connection, 127
Central limits theorem, 41-43, 270
Central tendency, 20-26
  mean, 21-22
  median, 22
  mode, 23
  weighted mean, 25
Cognitive dissonance, 452
Cognitive miser, 451
Consumer surplus, 326, 328

D

Correlation coefficient, *See* Pearson's R
Cost-effectiveness analysis, 355
Critical path method (CPM), 261

Data,
  interval scale, 73-74
  nominal scale, 72-73
  primary, 72, 75-97
  ratio scale, 74
  secondary, 72, 97-100
Data series,
  cross-section, 103
  time series/longitudinal, 103
Decision tree, 390-95
  action, 391
  dominant and dominated strategy, 394-95
  outcome, 391
Defensive avoidance, 450
Delphi, technique, 133
  policy delphi technique, 135
Dependent variable, 93, 127, 182
Descriptive statistics, 20
Design, survey, 80-91
Dispersion, measures of, 20
  coefficient of variation, 30-31
  hinge, 27-28
  mean absolute deviation, 27-28
  midspread, 27
  range, 27-33
  skewness, 31-33
  standard deviation, 27, 29-30
  variance, 27, 29

E

Effect, rashoman, 114
Elasticity of demand, 330
Error, random sampling, 79-80
Errors of estimation, 180-82
  heteroskedasticity, 248-53
  imperfect data, 253-54
  of interval forecasting, 218-20
  multicollinearity, 240-46
  serial correlation, 246-48
Explicit, function, 227
Externalities, 331-33

F

Feasibility assessment technique, *see*
    Projection
Fiscal impact analysis, *see* Projection
Forecasting, 214
    conditional and unconditional, 217
    ex post and ex ante, 217
    interval forecast, 217-20
    point forecast, 216-17
Free-rider problem, 436
F-twist theory, 432

G

Gantt chart, 261-62
Groupthink, 132

H

Halo effect, *see* Biases
Heteroskedasticity, *see* Errors of estimation
Hypothesis, null, 191
Hypothesis testing, 43-60
    critical value,
    chi-squared test, 54-57
    confidence interval, 43, 47–48
    correlation, 57-58
    critical value, 44
    difference between means, 50-54
    F-test, 194
    level of significance, 44
    one-tailed test, 44
    t test, 48-54
    type I and type II errors, 58-59
    z test, 44-48

I J K

Illegal immigration in San Diego County, 132
Implicit, function, 226
Independent variable, 93, 127, 182
Indifference curves, 315
Intangible costs and benefits, 336
Integer programming, 380-81
    steps toward, 382-83
Internal rate of return, 352-53
Interval scale, *See* Data
Inventory management, 283-99
    economic ordering quantity model (EOQ), 289-93
    inventory classification, 298-99
    quantity discount, 294-95
    reordering, 285-87
    safety stock model, 287-89
    uncertain usage and supply, 295-98
    variable ordering cost, 293-94
Judgmental method of prediction, 133-46
Kaldor-Hicks criterion, 441-443

L

Least square, method of, 178
    adjusted R-squared, 188
    best linear unbiased estimator (BLUE), 204-5
    errors of omitted variables, 231-32
    intercept coefficient, 182
    irrelevant independent variables, 233
    lagged dependent variable, 220-21
    R-squared (coefficient of determination), 187
    trend coefficients, 182
Lens model, 457
Library search, 98
Likert scale, 92
Limits, theorem central, 41-43
Linear programming, 361-79
    change in social preference, 369-70
    constraints, 361
    dual solution, 374
    feasibility zone, 363, 372
    minimization problem, 374
    nonbinding constraint, 373
    objective function, 365
    policy consideration, 369
    primal solution, 374
    simplex method, 371
    steps toward, 382-83
Loss, dead weight, *see* Producer surplus

M

Markov's chain, 164-72, 432
    absorbing state, 170-71
Mean, 21-22
Median, 22
Methods, judgmental, 133-46
Miller-Orr method, *see* Cash management
Mini-max strategy, 400
Mode, 23
Multicollinearity, *see* Errors of estimation

N O P

Nash equilibrium, 397
Numbers, law of large, *see* Central limits theorem
Objectivism, 1
Opportunity cost, 350, 372-74
Paradigm, 451
Pareto principle, 434, 438
Pearson's R, 57-58
Pecuniary effect, 329
Planning programming budgeting system (PPBS), 425
Policy delphi technique, *see* Delphi technique
Prediction, 9, 127, 225-55
Present value analysis, 344-49
    choice of discount rate, 350-52
    social time preference, 351
    time horizon, 349-50
    time preference, 346
Primary data, 72, 75-97
Prisoner's dilemma, 399-403
Probability distribution, 39-57

F-distribution, 194
negative exponential, 412-13
normal distribution, 40-43
poisson distribution, 411-12
T distribution, 49, 192
Procedural justice, 444-45
Producer surplus, 330
Program evaluation review technique (PERT), 261, 262-79
    activity, 262
    crashing time, 275-77
    critical path, 268
    dummy activity, 264
    event, 262
    expected time of duration, 265
    optimistic time of duration, 265
    pessimistic time of duration, 265
    project time, 267
    slack time, 268
    use of variance, 269-71
Projection, 127-222
    by the mean, 161-62
    delphi technique, 133-46
    expected utility model, 142-46
    feasibility assessment technique, 138-41
    fiscal impact analysis, 130
    judgmental method, 133-46
    Markov's chain, 164-72
    moving average, 162-63
    naive projection, 161
    single-factor projection, 128-32

Q R

Queuing Theory, 406-16
    arrival, 407, 410-13
    arriving unit, 407
    deterministic solution, 408-10
    exit, 407
    multiple phase, 408
    queuing system, 407
    service, 407, 414
    single-phase, 407-08
    structure and discipline, 413
    uncertainty, 410
    waiting, 407
Random error, regression, 150, 179
Random error, sampling, 79-80
Random numbers/series, 419-20
Rashoman effect, 114
Required compensation principle, 341
Research design, 427-31
    experimental design, 427-28
    quasi-experimental design, 427, 429-31

S

Sampling,
    cluster, 82-83

    error, 84-86
    random, 81
    size, 83
    stratified, 81-82
Sampling theory, 75
Sensitivity analysis, 379
Serial correlation, *see* Errors of estimation
Series, data, 136
Simplex method, *see* Linear programming
Simulation, 416-20
    game simulation, 418
    heuristic simulation, 418
    Monte Carlo simulation, 418-20
    system simulation, 417
Single-factor projection, *see* Projection
Social welfare, 314
    attributes, 314
    dominant alternative, 320
    inconsistency in choice, 316-18
    multiple-attributes, problems of, 322-23
    objective function, 314, 365
    optimum choice, 315
    social preference, rules of, 318-22

T

Table, contingency, 93
Trend, 149
    abrupt changes in, 196-205
    catastrophic, 154
    cyclical, 149, 151
    exponential, 153
    gradual changes in, 205-15
    horizontal (no trend), 151
    inverse form, 214-15
    linear, 150
    logistic, 154
    log transformed forms, 212-14
    negative, 149
    positive trend, 149
    quadratic, 152, 207-10
    seasonal, 149, 151
    seasonal adjustment, 156-57
    smoothing, 159-61
    stationary, 151
    straight line, estimation of, 182-96
    trend adjustment, 158-59

U V W

Unanimity law, 435
Uncertainty, 389
    expected payoff, 390
Utilitarians, 433
Variable, dependent, 93, 127
Variable, independent, 93, 127
Whistle blowing, 456

Author Index

Adelman, I., 73
Akutogawa, R., 114
Allais, M., 64
Ames, E., 189
Anderson, C., 452
Aronson, J. R., 286
Arrow, K., 7, 434, 440, 444
Auditor General of California, 132
Axelrod, R., 401

Ball, G., 459, 460
Beck, D., 143
Becker, G., 313
Behn, R., 461
Bentham, J., 433
Binmore, K., 396
Blackwell, K., 456
Bradford, D. F., 352
Brooks, H., 464
Brooks, S., 464
Brunwick, E., 457
Buchanan, J., 455
Bueno de Mesquita, B., 142, 143, 396
Bush, G., 396-397n.
Butts, R. E., 399

Camus, A. L., 446
Carson, R., 425
Corrigan, T., 119

Diesing, P. 458
Dixit, A., 396, 398, 399
Dunn, W., 3, 134, 136

Erikson, C., 424

Feldman, M., 459
Feldstein, M., 426
Festinger, L., 452
Fireman, B., 448
Fisher, R., 396, 402
Ford, G., 389n.
Frank, R. H., 455
Friedman, M., 431-432

Gagnon, A., 464
Gamson, W., 448
Gleick, J., 74
Glovich, T., 396
Gramlich, E., 341, 352
Grossbard-Sechtman, A., 313
Gupta, D., 73, 74, 313
Gurr, T., 73

Harsanyi, J. C., 399
Haveman, R. H., 352

Hibbs, D., 73
Hicks, J. R., 438
Hintikka, J., 399
Hirschleifer, J., 313
Hoffman, F., 119, 120
House, P. W., 458
Huff, D., 113, 118
Hussein, S., 396-397n.

Janis, I., 132, 447, 450

Kahneman, D., 452, 454
Kaldor, N., 438, 441-443
Karmarkar, N., 371
Kemperer, P., 396
Kennedy, P., 178
Krep, D., 396
Kuhn, T., 3, 451
Kuran, T., 132

Lane, R., 444, 445
Lekachman, R., 424
Lenin, V. I., 434
Lewin, K., 448, 451
Lindblom, C., 425

Majone, G., 464
Makridakis, S., 150
Mann, L., 450
Margolis, J., 352
Marx, K., 434
Mayo, E., 78n.
McGee, V., 150
Mesquita, B. Bueno de, 140
Mikesell, J. L., 341
Milgram, S., 448
Morris, C., 73
Mosher, F. C., 425
Mullen, J. D., 446, 454
Murrey, C., 5
Musgrave, A., 432
Musgrave, P., 104
Musgrave, R., 104

Nachmias, C., 91, 428
Nachmias, D., 91, 428
Nader, R., 456
Nagel, T., 5
Nalebuff, B., 396, 398, 399
Niskanen, W., 455

Olson, M., 437

Pareto, V., 435n.
Parker, R., 75
Patton, C. V., 428

Petkas, P., 456
Pill, J., 134
Popper, K., 3, 120, 433

Quade, E. S., 464

Rawls, J., 438
Rea, L., 74, 75
Reiter, S., 189
Retina, S., 448
Ridely, J., 424
Roelithsberger, F., 78n.
Rosenthal, A., 96
Ross, L., 452
Roth, B. M., 454
Rousseau, J. J., 433n.

Sabine, G. H., 433
Sackman, H., 132
Sapolsky, H., 444
Sawicki, D. S., 428
Schick, A., 444
Schilling, C. S., 464
Schwartz, E., 286
Sen, A. K., 7
Shull, R. D., 458
Simon, H., 335, 453

Singh, H., 457
Slovic, P., 452
Stockey, E., 353, 439, 440
Stockman, D., 119
Stone, L., 19, 20

Thierauf, R., 286
Thomas, P., 96
Tribe, L. H., 464
Tversky, A., 60-61, 63, 396, 452, 454

Uri, W., 396, 402

Vallone, R., 396
Vaupel, J. W., 461
Voss, J., 464

Weber, M., 448
Wheelwright, S., 150
Wicksell, K., 435
Wildavsky, A., 8, 425, 453, 458
Williamson, J., 120

Zagare, F. C., 399
Zeckhauser, R., 353, 439, 440